Automating Junos Administration

Doing More with Less

Jonathan Looney & Stacy Smith

Beijing • Boston • Farnham • Sebastopol • Tokyo

Automating Junos Administration

by Jonathan Looney and Stacy Smith

Printed in the United States of America.

Published by O'Reilly Media, Inc., 1005 Gravenstein Highway North, Sebastopol, CA 95472.

O'Reilly books may be purchased for educational, business, or sales promotional use. Online editions are also available for most titles (*http://safaribooksonline.com*). For more information, contact our corporate/institutional sales department: 800-998-9938 or *corporate@oreilly.com*.

Editors: Brian Anderson and Courtney Allen
Production Editor: Colleen Cole
Copyeditor: Rachel Head
Proofreader: Jasmine Kwityn
Indexer: Lucie Haskins
Interior Designer: David Futato
Cover Designer: Karen Montgomery
Illustrator: Rebecca Demarest

April 2016: First Edition

Revision History for the First Edition

2016-04-12: First Release

See *http://oreilly.com/catalog/errata.csp?isbn=9781491928882* for release details.

978-1-491-92888-2

[LSI]

Jonathan Looney:

To him that is able to do exceeding abundantly above all that we ask or think, according to the power that worketh in us.

Stacy Smith:

To my Lord and Savior, Jesus Christ. See Colossians 3:23.

Table of Contents

Foreword

As someone reading a book on network automation, you're clearly aware of the benefits of automation, the cost of human mistakes, and the ability of software to perform routine tasks with accuracy, diligence, caution, and reliability. Automation can add robustness and fluidity to your network, prevent outages, and decrease the impact of networking issues and the mean time to resolution.

In my work as the architect and coder of the JUNOS user interface, I've preached automation since the early days. We knew automation would be a key differentiator for our customers and wanted to allow application programmers to escape the world of "screen scraping," where command-line interface (CLI) output designed for readability and human digestion is filtered using regular expressions to extract useful information, a process that is error prone, fragile, and difficult to maintain. If a change is made to the CLI to add a new data item to the output or the format of the output is changed, a regular expression may fail to match correctly, leading to errors that cannot be easily detected.

We built into JUNOS an XML-based API that would allow immediate access to data items in a robust, simple, and future-proof way. XPath expressions can extract specific data values while ignoring new content or changes in the way values are organized. Complex expressions can find precise values such as the remote address of every point-to-point link that has a large MTU and high error rates.

We also knew that automation depended on complete access to the device's capabilities. If an API allows you to do 80% of what's needed, but you have to resort to "screen scraping" for the other 20%, the value of the API is greatly diminished. By layering the CLI directly over the API infrastructure, we fully expose all JUNOS configuration and operational output, guarantee each release of JUNOS ships with feature parity between the API and CLI, and reduce our internal cost in maintaining the API.

As customers have deployed our devices in the real world, we've seen a great variety in terms of network automation. Every network operator sits somewhere along an automation spectrum, somewhere between a network of hand-maintained devices and a fully automated network. Some have completely committed to automation, using external databases as the "database of record," enacting policies stating that changing configuration on network devices is a firing offense. But many networks are still maintained by hand, using expensive human resources to make configuration changes and debug networking problems.

Automation efforts are often focused where the benefits matter, principally in situations where the cost of failure is high, the rate of change is high, the complexity is high, or the number of affected devices is large. Such projects are typically key to demonstrating the value of automation, and lead to further automation projects. The "devops" and "netdevops" movements take this approach, starting with the biggest current problems, solving them, and building an identify-solve-test cycle.

Data centers have done a great deal to push automation, using server deployment tools such as Puppet, Chef, Ansible, and Salt. These tools make cookie-cutter servers deployment trivial while allowing customization in uniform, predictable ways. The days where a missing software patch can lead to unique, obscure failures are gone. When changes to your servers are simple and immediate, while changes to your network infrastructure are done by hand, with the associated higher error rates and delays, the value of automation becomes clear.

More recently, the YANG data modeling language (based heavily on the data modeling language we built for JUNOS) has fostered the creation of data models for networking. The IETF is developing YANG data models for many areas, over 160 at last count. In addition, the OpenConfig group is building models focused on the needs of the service provider community. Support for the OpenConfig models is already shipping on networking devices.

It's clearly not reasonable to expect every network operator to start programming, but by understanding what can be done using automation, people can start to "think like a programmer," allowing identification of scenarios where automation can be successfully applied. In particular, programmers have a disdain for doing the same thing over and over. We write code instead, allowing the computer to do the work for us. "Lazy like a fox," I call it.

In this book, you'll find the concepts and tools needed to help you advance your skill set in automation. Jonathan and Stacy are automation veterans with deep knowledge of this area, and have done a fantastic job of translating their experience onto these pages, helping you build robust automation into your network.

— Phil Shafer
Distinguished Engineer,
Juniper Networks
March 2016

Preface

More and more, network administration and software development are converging. On the one hand, there is a push to develop new services that can be provisioned and managed at very high speeds and at a scale that would not be possible without software. This is typically known as *software-defined networking* (SDN). On the other hand, there is also a push for network administrators to deploy and manage existing services more efficiently by using automation to assist with day-to-day tasks. This book focuses on the latter problem.

While day-to-day network administration may not be the "hot" topic of the day, it is essential. Even very complex SDN solutions are built upon the foundation laid by a well-managed, reliable network. And, while the latest SDN technologies may come and go, it does not appear likely that the need for sound network management practices will disappear anytime soon.

Just as new technologies have presented some interesting and powerful solutions to certain network design problems, Junos supports a number of automation tools that present interesting and powerful solutions to common network automation tasks. Consider some of these possibilities:

- Representing your devices as Python objects and using Python to manage your devices
- Managing your devices from a central provisioning/administration system such as Ansible or Puppet
- Customizing the Junos software to detect and block commits that violate your network standards
- Developing custom CLI commands that present the information you need in the way you want to see it
- Programming the Junos software with the intelligence to automatically react to network events

- Provisioning customers and services using a dynamically applied template
- Deploying new devices into your network rapidly

This book covers these items, and more. Our aim is to teach you about some of the automation technologies that the Junos software includes or supports. You should also gain new ideas about ways you can apply automation to problems or repetitive tasks in your network—perhaps even things you had not realized were handled so easily through automation.

The goal of this book is to make you successful at deploying automation tools to manage Junos devices in your network. We have attempted to thoroughly cover the things you need to know in order to use a variety of network automation tools. Some information about these tools is available elsewhere; however, the information is not consolidated into one place. Also, the other information that is currently available may be missing important details that are important to understand in order to successfully use the tools to solve real-world problems. Finally, having information about multiple tools in one place lets you compare features and functionality to determine which tool is most suitable to solve any given automation task.

Depending on your background, you may be approaching this as a network engineer who is trying to create automation tools to make your job easier, or as a software developer who is tasked with writing tools to automate network management tasks. Whichever of these two backgrounds most closely matches yours, this book should provide you with information to help you achieve your goal.

We have personally seen the benefits of automation in our careers. Even 15 years ago, network automation was a key competitive advantage in large service provider networks. We have also seen the tools and techniques change and improve over the years. Through the exciting improvements in automation tools, the benefits of automation have only increased. As we share this knowledge with you, we hope you will likewise find it useful. We hope you will come to understand—if you don't already—why we chose the subtitle "Doing More with Less."

Assumptions

In this book, we assume that you have access to a device running the Junos software that you can use to follow the examples in this book, as well as to practice your newly acquired skills. Except where otherwise noted, the book covers the features available in Junos release 15.1 and generally assumes the feature set of an MX series product line.

We also assume that you have access to a Unix/Linux host that you can use to install and run some of the tools discussed in the book. If you don't have access to a physical machine, there are free virtualization products that should enable you to quickly create a virtual machine to meet this need.

In this book, we assume a moderate knowledge of working with the Junos software. In Chapter 1, we cover some basic information about this software. Depending on your background, you may need to supplement this with additional outside education. In addition to some hands-on experience, you might consider reading Aviva Garrett's *Junos Cookbook* (O'Reilly) or *Day One: Junos Tips, Techniques, and Templates 2011* (*http://www.juniper.net/books*), edited by Jonathan Looney et al. (Juniper Networks Books).

We also assume a basic knowledge of IP routing, Layer 2 switching, and routing protocols. While not critical to understanding the automation tools themselves, this knowledge will help you understand some of the examples used in the book.

Finally, we assume a basic knowledge of Python programming. We use Python 2.7 for a number of examples in the book. While we explain some of the more advanced Python code, it will be helpful to understand the basics of Python programming before you start. If you want to learn more about Python, you may find it helpful to consult another O'Reilly book, such as *Learning Python* by Mark Lutz.

How to Read This Book

We recommend that everyone read Chapters 1 and 2, which provide important foundational material about the way the Junos software works and the way you can manage it programmatically. Even if you already have deep familiarity with the Junos software, we think these chapters contain important information that may prove helpful to you. Later chapters will assume the knowledge found in these two chapters.

From there, you can explore the remaining chapters. We recommend you read the whole book and explore the tools that are available to you. If you don't already know about all of these tools, you may find it helpful to learn the situations in which each tool excels. This knowledge will help you choose the best tool for each automation task.

If you do choose to skip around, be aware that some chapters build on others. For example, some of the information in Chapter 5 is prerequisite information for Chapters 6 and 7. Similarly, some of the information in Chapters 4 and 8 is useful background information for understanding Chapter 10.

Finally, everyone should read Chapter 11, which contains examples of the ways you can use the tools in this book to help automate real-world network administration tasks. That chapter also contains important suggestions for best practices you should follow while writing automation for your network.

What's in This Book?

Chapter 1, Introduction
: This chapter provides important foundational material about the operation of the Junos software's management system.

Chapter 2, RPC Mechanisms
: This chapter describes the way you use remote procedure calls (RPCs) to manage the Junos software.

Chapter 3, The RESTful API Service
: This chapter describes the Junos RESTful API and provides examples of using the RESTful API to manage the Junos software.

Chapter 4, Junos PyEZ
: This chapter describes the way you can use the PyEZ Python package to manage the Junos software. The chapter also describes the way you can use YAML and Jinja2 to extend the functionality of PyEZ.

Chapter 5, Commit Scripts
: This chapter describes the way you can use commit scripts to customize the commit process. The chapter also introduces SLAX, a language you can use to write op, commit, and event scripts.

Chapter 6, Op Scripts
: This chapter describes the way you can use op scripts to add custom command-line interface (CLI) commands or customize the output from existing commands.

Chapter 7, Event Scripts and Event Policies
: This chapter describes the way you can use event scripts and event policies to program the Junos software to automatically respond to events it observes.

Chapter 8, Initial Provisioning
: This chapter introduces the ZTP and Netconify tools you can use to automate the initial configuration of new Junos devices.

Chapter 9, Puppet
: This chapter describes the way you can add a Puppet agent to the Junos software and manage the Junos software using the Puppet system.

Chapter 10, Ansible
: This chapter introduces the way you can manage the Junos software using the Ansible automation engine.

Chapter 11, Putting Automation into Practice
: This chapter begins by describing various scenarios where you might use automation and the way you can use the tools described in the book to meet the needs presented by these scenarios. The chapter and book conclude by discussing some best practices to consider as you write your own automation programs.

Conventions Used in This Book

The following typographical conventions are used in this book:

Italic
: Indicates new terms, URLs, email addresses, file and directory names, file extensions, and RPCs.

`Constant width`
: Used for program listings, as well as within paragraphs to refer to program elements such as variable or function names, databases, data types, environment variables, statements, and keywords. Also used for commands and command-line options.

`Constant width bold`
: Shows commands or other text that should be typed literally by the user.

`Constant width italic`
: Shows text that should be replaced with user-supplied values or by values determined by context.

This element signifies a tip or suggestion.

This element signifies a general note.

This element indicates a warning or caution.

Using Code Examples

Supplemental material (code examples, exercises, etc.) is available for download at *https://github.com/AutomatingJunosAdministration*.

This book is here to help you get your job done. In general, if example code is offered with this book, you may use it in your programs and documentation. You do not need to contact us for permission unless you're reproducing a significant portion of the code. For example, writing a program that uses several chunks of code from this book does not require permission. Selling or distributing a CD-ROM of examples from O'Reilly books does require permission. Answering a question by citing this book and quoting example code does not require permission. Incorporating a significant amount of example code from this book into your product's documentation does require permission.

We appreciate, but do not require, attribution. An attribution usually includes the title, author, publisher, and ISBN. For example: "*Automating Junos Administration* by Jonathan Looney and Stacy Smith (O'Reilly). Copyright 2016 Jonathan Looney and Stacy Smith, 978-1-491-92888-2."

If you feel your use of code examples falls outside fair use or the permission given above, feel free to contact us at *permissions@oreilly.com*.

Safari® Books Online

Safari Books Online (*www.safaribooksonline.com*) is an on-demand digital library that delivers expert content in both book and video form from the world's leading authors in technology and business.

Technology professionals, software developers, web designers, and business and creative professionals use Safari Books Online as their primary resource for research, problem solving, learning, and certification training.

Safari Books Online offers a range of plans and pricing for enterprise, government, and education, and individuals.

Members have access to thousands of books, training videos, and prepublication manuscripts in one fully searchable database from publishers like O'Reilly Media, Prentice Hall Professional, Addison-Wesley Professional, Microsoft Press, Sams, Que, Peachpit Press, Focal Press, Cisco Press, John Wiley & Sons, Syngress, Morgan Kaufmann, IBM Redbooks, Packt, Adobe Press, FT Press, Apress, Manning, New Riders, McGraw-Hill, Jones & Bartlett, Course Technology, and hundreds more. For more information about Safari Books Online, please visit us online.

How to Contact Us

Please address comments and questions concerning this book to the publisher:

O'Reilly Media, Inc.
1005 Gravenstein Highway North
Sebastopol, CA 95472
800-998-9938 (in the United States or Canada)
707-829-0515 (international or local)
707-829-0104 (fax)

We have a web page for this book, where we list errata, examples, and any additional information. You can access this page at *http://bit.ly/automating-junos*.

To comment or ask technical questions about this book, send email to *bookquestions@oreilly.com*.

For more information about our books, courses, conferences, and news, see our website at *http://www.oreilly.com*.

Find us on Facebook: *http://facebook.com/oreilly*

Follow us on Twitter: *http://twitter.com/oreillymedia*

Watch us on YouTube: *http://www.youtube.com/oreillymedia*

Acknowledgments

We would like to acknowledge and express our gratitude to our management team, who not only had the vision for this book, but gave us the time and resources needed to turn that vision into reality. If it weren't for Pallavi Mahajan, Piyush Rai, and Ken Sacca, this book would not have been possible. They each embody the Juniper Way.

Patrick Ames has been a constant champion of this book and a helpful guide to its authors. We appreciate his continual encouragement and support, as well as his practical advice in writing this book.

It has truly been a pleasure to work with everyone at O'Reilly, including Courtney Allen and Brian Anderson, Colleen Cole, Rebecca Demarest, and Rachel Head.

We would like to thank our lead technical reviewers, Phil Shafer and Diogo Montagner. Phil is the "father" of the Junos user interface and probably knows more about the Junos management system than anyone else. Diogo supports a major Australian ISP and brought a real-world perspective to his review. We appreciate their insights and helpful suggestions.

In addition to our lead technical reviewers, several professionals at Juniper Networks took time from their busy schedules to help us better understand the material in this book and to provide technical review of the finished product. We appreciate Sri Ram Sankar, Raymond Cheh, and Edward Arcuri taking time to meet with us in the early stages of the project. They provided feedback on early outlines and helped us understand some of the subtleties of the features in the book. In addition, David Gethings, Maruf Yunus, Deepak Jadhav, Guy Davies, Damien Garros, Nitin Kumar, Rick Sherman, Lalit Shinde, Nilesh Simaria, and Ajay Kumar Chintala provided assistance in answering questions, reviewing drafts, or discussing ideas. We also appreciate the automation work that Jeremy Schulman did during his time at Juniper Networks, which resulted in a legacy of automation tools and information that forms an important foundation for much of the automation work related to Junos. Many of these folks are also directly responsible for *creating* the rich set of automation tools presented in this book. We appreciate their help in keeping us honest, and also their work creating great software.

In addition to the people we've named, many other unnamed contributors to internal and external network automation discussion groups have unwittingly contributed to this book. We thank them for sharing their real-world network automation problems and solutions. Their questions and insights have been useful input into understanding the challenges faced by our readers.

We have attempted to thank all of those who assisted us, but if we have accidentally missed you, we apologize and we appreciate your help!

From Jonathan Looney

I would like to thank my wife, Elisabeth, and my children, Isabel and David, for selflessly supporting me as I worked on this book in addition to my already busy schedule. I appreciate their encouragement even as they sacrificed date nights, meals together, and evenings of "chase" as I devoted time to this project. I look forward to making up for those missed activities soon.

I would also like to thank Stacy for putting up with me over the past year as we worked on the book. Writing a book is never easy and could easily strain a friendship. I appreciate his helpful suggestions on improving my chapters and his patience with me even through our disagreements. I have enjoyed working with him, and look forward to continuing our friendship.

Finally, I would like to thank the many people who have spent time teaching and mentoring me over the years. I would like to thank the managers in my career who gave me freedom to explore new ideas and try new things. And I would like to thank the people who have believed in me and encouraged me to try things I wasn't sure I could accomplish. In a sense, they are all responsible for this book.

From Stacy Smith

I would like to acknowledge my wife, Wanda, and my sons, Ezra and Eli, for extending patience and grace as I spent many evenings and weekends working on this project. Your willingness to support me in this endeavor were key to its success. Thank you for your sacrifice.

I would also like to thank Jonathan for inviting me to write with him. It's always a pleasure to work with someone so talented, yet so humble. I'm grateful to have had that opportunity many times in the last 13 years, and I hope it continues for many years to come. Thanks for your friendship.

CHAPTER 1

Introduction

Welcome to the world of automating Junos management! Since its introduction in the late 1990s, the user interface (UI) of the Junos software has set it apart from its competitors by making it easy for network operators to manage their devices using the command-line interface (CLI). In addition, Juniper has been a leader in network automation, shipping an API in the first Junos release and delivering the first external API in Junos 4.1.

However, times have changed. More and more, as operators look to automate their networks, other management interfaces are growing in importance. Juniper has kept up with this trend and is striving to be an industry leader by enabling automation to work with its devices.

This chapter sets the stage for the rest of the book by discussing the benefits of automation, reviewing some background information about the way the Junos management system works, and giving some basic information about the book.

Benefits of Automation

Network automation has grown to be a hot topic in recent years, and for good reason: the benefits of automation are quite large, both for a company and for the individuals who run its network.

Because you are reading this book, you probably already know at least some of the benefits of automation. However, we find that whenever you review the possibilities of automation, you may find a new way to use it beyond the ones you were planning. Let's review some common benefits.

What Is Automation?

This is probably a good point to address a basic question: just what is network automation? If you ask 10 different people, you may get 11 different answers. Is it software-defined networking (SDN)? Is it a complete CLI replacement, or CLI customization (like YANG, defined in RFC 6020 (*https://tools.ietf.org/html/rfc6020*))? Or is it merely customizing the behavior of the existing UI tools?

The answer is, basically, "yes." Automation can encompass all of these things, and many things in between. You can use automation to configure and monitor every aspect of your devices such that no one needs to use the on-box CLI unless there is an emergency. You can use automation to do very complex, high-speed activities, such as programming all the routes your network needs. Or you can use automation to customize the commit process, simplify repetitive tasks, and customize the UI.

It may be helpful to compare network automation to computer programming. You can write a computer program in C or C++ to conduct complex, high-speed operations. Or you can write a simple shell script to simplify the process of running a common sequence of commands. Or you can use Python to write a fairly lightweight menu program as a frontend for some common operations. Likewise, with network automation, there are different tools that are available that allow you to do different things. Just as we call it programming whether we use C, C++, Python, or shell scripting, we also call it network automation regardless of the complexity of the operation we are trying to undertake.

And, coincidentally, many of those same programming tools are available to you when you do network automation. You can do simple things using simple tools you may already know, or you can do more powerful things using appropriate tools.

Automation Saves Time

One of the most basic benefits of automation is that it saves time. Many of us have repetitive tasks that we need to conduct. One method of simplifying these repetitive tasks is to use automation.

For example, assume that you have a standard methodology for troubleshooting failed Border Gateway Protocol (BGP) sessions. First, you check the `show interfaces` output for the interface connected to the peer. After that, you ping the peer. Then, you look at the `show bgp neighbor` output for the peer. Finally, you look for log errors related to the peer or its interface.

It is completely acceptable to maintain a list of the appropriate commands and run them each time you need to troubleshoot a failed BGP session. However, you may be able to save time by reducing these to an automation script that runs the appropriate commands.

In fact, you may be able to save even more time by having the script actually interpret the command output for you. For example, what do you really want to know from the `show interfaces` output? You probably want to see whether the interface is up or down. You probably also want to look for unusual statistics (such as a very high data rate or a high error rate). Depending on what you see here, you may already know the reason for the session failure. (If the link is down, it isn't necessary to look any further: no traffic will reach the peer.) By having the script look for obvious clues like this, you may be able to write a script that simply *tells you* why the BGP session is down when it is obvious. (That automated analysis can be a big help when you get a 4 a.m. call to troubleshoot a network problem.)

But why stop there? Why should you even need to run the script? Why not have your device automatically run the script for you whenever a peering session goes down and stays down for more than five minutes? Junos has the automation hooks to enable this sort of event-driven script execution.

And, of course, one of the big ways automation can save time is by simplifying the repetitive provisioning process, which often amounts to the use of standard fill-in-the-blanks templates. We'll talk more about that in "Automation Prevents Copy/Paste Errors" on page 4.

Automation Prevents Human Error

The alternate title for this section should be: "Automation Prevents 4 A.M. Phone Calls." How many emergencies have been caused by someone making a typo or making a simple omission during a change?

For example, let's say that your network core uses Multiprotocol Label Switching (MPLS) to forward traffic. Further, let's assume MPLS is required because you have a large number of applications (such as virtual private networks [VPNs]) that require MPLS in order to operate correctly. Now imagine that someone provisions new network interconnects between core and edge routers, but forgets to enable MPLS processing for those interfaces on the core router. That scenario is a network outage waiting to happen! Once the other paths between the core and edge routers go down, MPLS traffic will be unable to flow over these new links.

Wouldn't it be great if you could prevent someone from doing this by programming the network to know the expected configurations and catch omissions like this? Again, Junos has the automation hooks to enable this protection.

Automation Saves Memory

We all probably have complicated tasks that we only need to perform once in a while. It is not uncommon for me to answer a colleague's question by scratching my head and saying, "I remember looking up the command to do that. Now, just give me a minute to find it."

It is certainly the case that not every command should be reduced to automation. But things that are particularly critical and are typically needed in time-sensitive situations are good candidates for automation. Likewise, things that are particularly complicated are also candidates for automation.

Automation Prevents Copy/Paste Errors

A number of common network management tasks can be reduced to following a template with variables that need to be completed. Perhaps the paradigmatic example of this is network provisioning (although the same concept can apply in other contexts, such as troubleshooting).

Network provisioning often involves templates: a template for the base device configuration, a template for internal connections, a template for transit or peer connections, and multiple templates for different types of customer connections. These templates usually have very few variables that an operator needs to change in order to use them. However, it is easy for someone to accidentally omit an important line, forget to change one of the variables, or change one of the variables to an invalid value. And even if the user makes no mistakes while creating the configuration from the template, sometimes an error is introduced during the process of copying and pasting a large configuration block or a large set of commands.

We'll talk more about provisioning templates when we talk about commit scripts in Chapter 5. Commit scripts are one way to easily apply a template. Commit scripts even provide an optional way to reduce the size of the Junos configuration file by having Junos display the template parameters (rather than their full expansion) by default.

In this instance, automation can both save time and reduce the number of unintended errors. If the provisioning process is reduced to a simple script that asks for values for the few variables that are in a template, the script can make sure that the entire configuration is applied. The script can even ask the questions necessary to choose the correct template. In addition, the script can perform checks to validate that the values provided by the user make sense.

In fact, it is possible to even further reduce the information that a user needs to supply by having the script gather the information in the first place. Let's assume that the customer data is all maintained in a SQL database. When prompted by the user, the script can query the database to gather the correct values for all the variables and present them to the user for validation. This further reduces the possibility of inadvertent errors.

From there, it is only a small step to fully automating the process. When a new customer is added to the database, an automated process can automatically activate the changes in the network.

It will probably not be possible to *completely* eliminate the possibility of someone entering incorrect information at some point in the process. However, using automation can reduce the number of places where incorrect information can be introduced. And it can promote consistency among the different systems that maintain information about the network by ensuring that the *same* information is used everywhere (whether that information is correct or incorrect).

Automation Enables New Services

Automation can enable new services that could not be conducted by humans in an efficient manner. In this context, a "service" can either be external or internal.

SDN can be a good example of an external service enabled by automation. Imagine that a network operator wants to optimize their traffic flow every five minutes based on a complex set of algorithms, but they want to conduct the recalculation faster than that if certain events occur. This is the kind of complex network service that requires automation to effectively implement it.

An example of an internal service enabled by automation is an automated troubleshooting service. Imagine that a network operator implements an automated troubleshooting service that monitors for network events that may indicate a network error. The automation tool then responds to those events according to a set troubleshooting template. If it finds a problem that it can automatically correct, it does so. Otherwise, it sends the output of its findings to the network operator's trouble ticket system. That output should have all the information necessary to continue troubleshooting the problem. This has the potential to reduce the amount of time that network engineers spend gathering basic information and trying "simple" fixes. It also has the potential to suppress false errors, reducing the amount of time that network engineers spend responding to false alerts and allowing them to start working on the real problems more quickly. Finally, it has the potential to reduce the time to resolution for network problems.

Management System Internals

It is helpful to have a good understanding of the way "management data" usually flows through the Junos system. Some examples of the types of management data that may flow through a system include configuration information, operational commands, and statistics. Having a good understanding of this management data flow will help you understand the distinctions between various methods of accessing this data.

As we look at the flow of management data, you will see that the management daemon (MGD) is a central hub of activity. Most management data flows through MGD. The Junos software accepts management connections through a variety of mechanisms; however, most eventually turn into Junoscript or NETCONF sessions that connect to MGD. MGD has three primary mechanisms for interacting with daemons: a management socket (which it uses to pass along operational command requests and responses), the shared configuration database, and Unix signals.

Accessing the Management System

Let's start with ways of accessing the management system. Here, all roads lead to MGD.

All CLI sessions invoke a binary (coincidentally, named *cli*) that is a Junoscript client. The CLI binary opens a Junoscript session with MGD and exchanges information with MGD in an XML format.

It is also possible for a user to interact with the Junos software using a NETCONF or Junoscript session. These sessions also connect to MGD.

Additionally, a user can interact with the Junos software using the REST API. As described in "Internal Design" on page 159, these sessions are piped through some extra plumbing, but eventually reach MGD.

Finally, it is possible for a user to interact with the Junos software using PyEZ, or to have op, commit, or event scripts launch remote procedure calls (RPCs). In all of these cases, a Junoscript or NETCONF session is used to connect to the software. Again, these Junoscript or NETCONF sessions all terminate with MGD.

Figure 1-1 illustrates how these various connection mechanisms all eventually wind up as sessions connected to MGD.

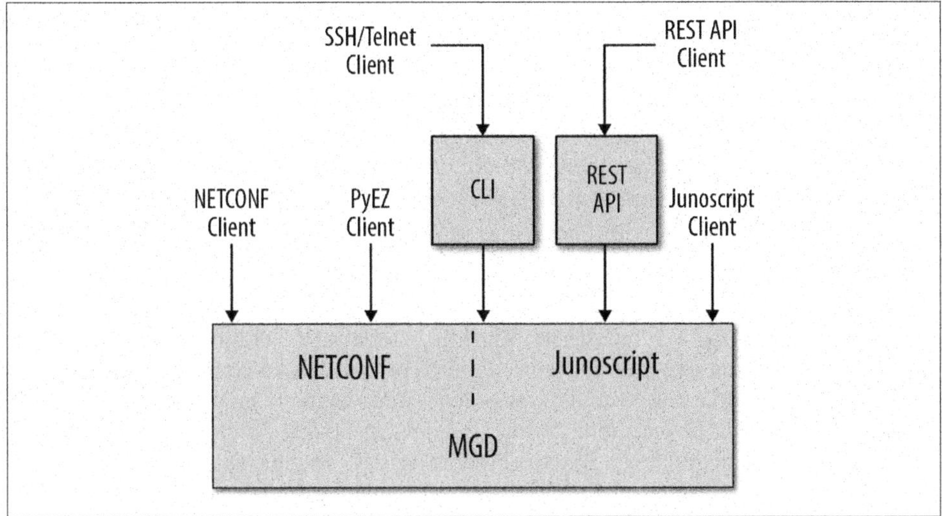

Figure 1-1. Various management connections that connect to MGD

Operational Command Flow

Operational commands arrive at MGD over one of the connection methods just described. When MGD receives the operational commands, it can either satisfy them itself, pass them along to other daemons to satisfy the requests, or invoke other tools to satisfy the requests.

For example, the *get-authorization-information* RPC (which is equivalent to the `show cli authorization` CLI command) is a prototypical example of the kind of request MGD fulfills itself. With this command, the user is asking for information about her authorization level. This is information that MGD maintains for each session, and it is easy for MGD to satisfy this request itself. (Another prototypical example in this category is the *get-configuration* RPC, or the `show configuration` CLI command. Again, this request is asking for information that MGD maintains internally.)

Two classic examples of the kinds of operational commands that are passed on to a daemon are the *get-route-information* RPC (equivalent to the `show route` CLI command) and the *clear-bgp-neighbor* RPC (equivalent to the `clear bgp neighbor` CLI command). In both cases, the routing protocol daemon (RPD) is the daemon that satisfies this request. It is the daemon that maintains information on the routing table (also known as the routing information base, or RIB); therefore, it is the daemon that can authoritatively answer a request for route information. Likewise, RPD is the daemon that maintains BGP neighbor relationships; therefore, it is the daemon that handles a request to reset one of those relationships. In these cases, MGD serves as a two-way pipe, passing the request from the user to RPD and passing the response from RPD to the user. Figure 1-2 illustrates this data flow. To support this communication,

MGD maintains a management socket with most daemons. Operational requests and responses flow over this management socket.

In a few cases, MGD invokes tools to satisfy requests. One example is the Junos upgrade process, which requires more complex handling than a normal CLI command. MGD invokes an external tool to conduct part of the upgrade. Another example is op and commit scripts, which are actually run by the CSCRIPT utility. This process is all transparent to the user, and is just included here for the sake of completeness.

As Figure 1-2 illustrates, some requests must go all the way to the packet forwarding engine (PFE) to be satisfied. Interface statistics are an example of this type of request. To gather interface statistics, MGD invokes *ifinfo*, which queries the kernel. The kernel often needs to query a PFE to obtain these statistics. In this way, operational commands sometimes have important impacts on the system.

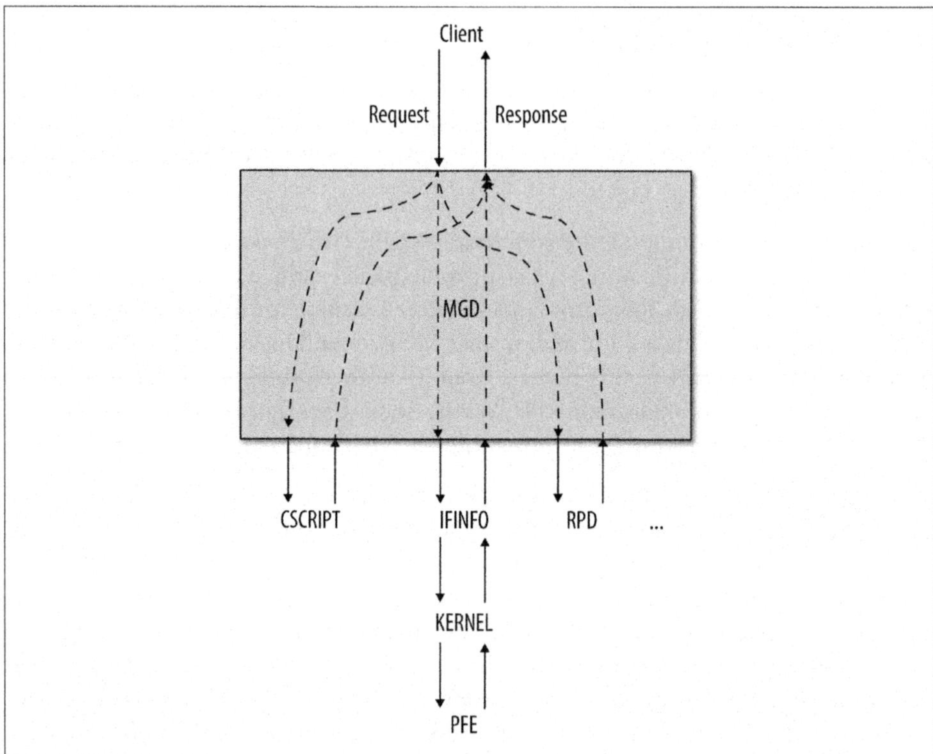

Figure 1-2. Data flow between a user and a daemon

Configuration Data Flow

When you commit configuration changes, the new configuration data is placed into a shared database that all the daemons can access. When this configuration database changes, MGD uses Unix signals to signal the appropriate daemons to reread the new configuration. After reading the configuration, the daemons activate its contents. If the new configuration requires changes in the forwarding plane, this data will be propagated to the PFEs. This process is illustrated in Figure 1-3.

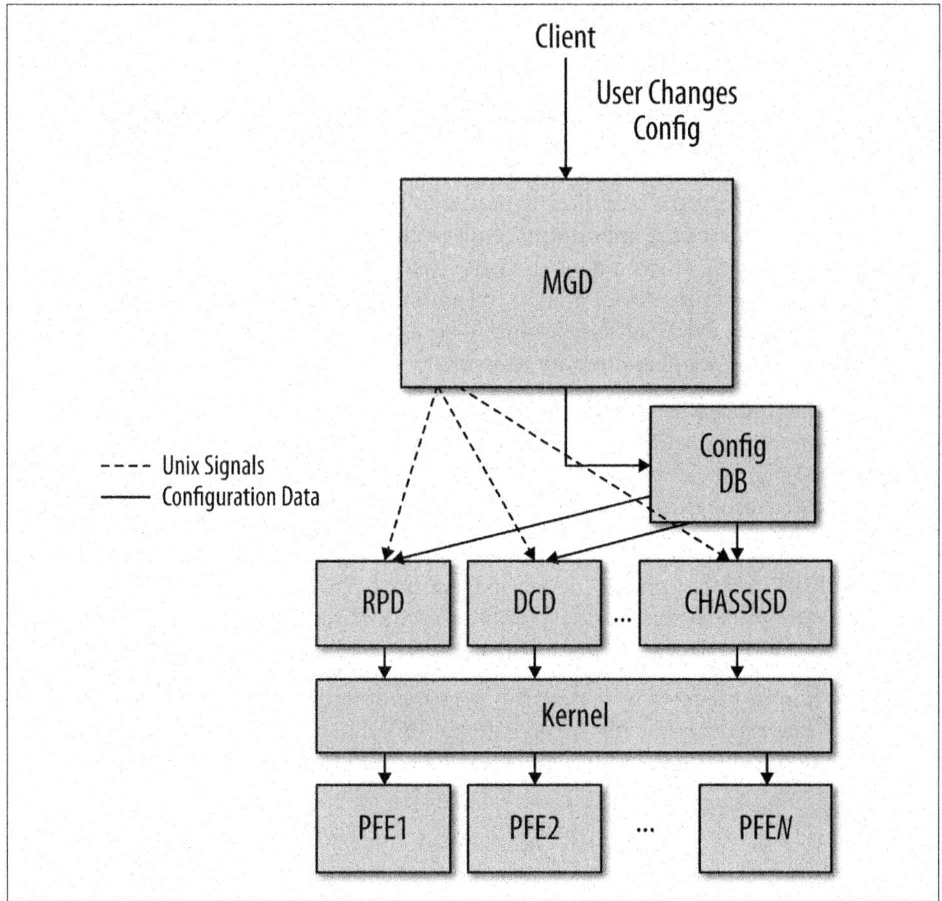

Figure 1-3. Configuration data flow

A Word About Op, Commit, and Event Scripts

Op, commit, and event scripts are interesting animals. Op and commit scripts are invoked by MGD in response to user activity. MGD acts as a conduit for them. It receives information from the user and passes it to the script, and it receives information from the script and passes it to the user.

However, op and commit scripts can also invoke operational RPCs. When they do this, they create a new Junoscript or NETCONF session to MGD. At this point, they act like any other Junoscript or NETCONF client. This presents the interesting picture where they are both in the lower part of our diagrams, as something that responds to user input, and also in the upper part of our diagrams, as something that connects to MGD.

The output from op scripts is directly passed to the user as raw XML. This behavior provides some interesting opportunities for creating a structured data format appropriate for the user's environment. Imagine the possibility of an automation script (whether run on a Junos device or a central automation host) invoking an op script as an RPC call over a NETCONF session. The automation script can use the XML returned by the op script as input for its work.

On the other hand, when a user invokes an op script from the Junos CLI, the Junos CLI will attempt to display the XML it recognizes using its normal display rules. This lets you program op scripts to return XML, which the Junos CLI will display in a format that users recognize.

Unlike op scripts, the XML output from commit scripts is consumed by MGD and the CSCRIPT utility. Commit scripts may instruct MGD to modify the candidate configuration prior to committing it, or the commit scripts may instruct MGD to display one or more warnings and/or errors to the user.

Event scripts are executed by the event-processing daemon (EVENTD) in response to events. When event scripts invoke operational RPCs, they create a new Junoscript or NETCONF session to MGD and act like any other Junoscript or NETCONF client.

All of this is illustrated in Figure 1-4.

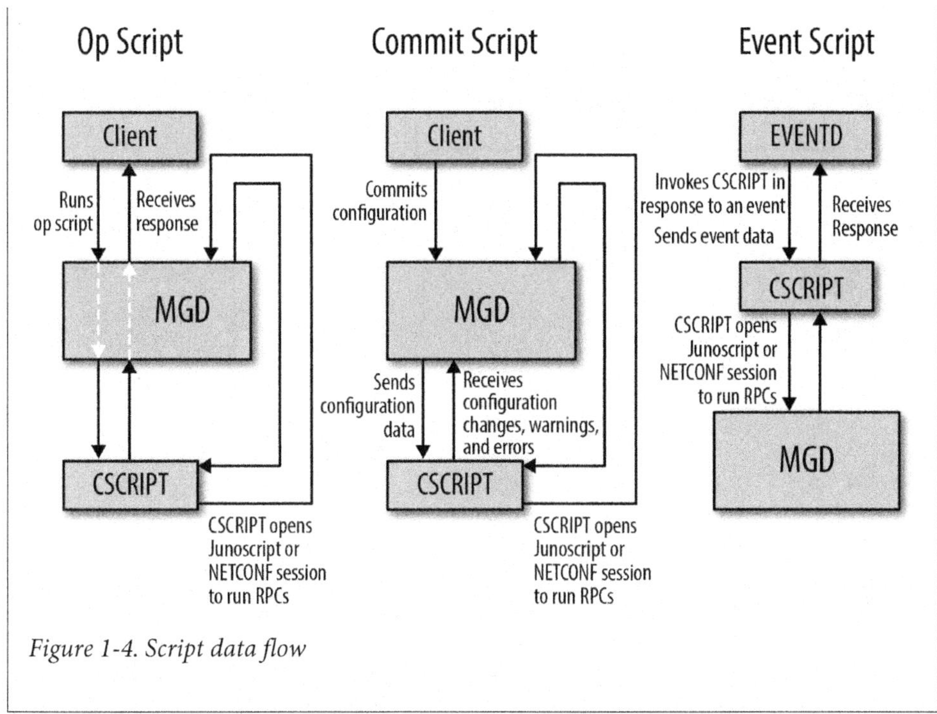

Figure 1-4. Script data flow

Configuration Databases and the Commit Model

The rest of this book assumes some knowledge of the configuration databases and the commit model. Although this is basic information, it is important that you review these concepts to understand portions of the book where it is referenced.

Configuration Databases

Every Junos system has at least two configuration databases: the *committed configuration* and the *candidate configuration*. As the names imply, the committed configuration is the configuration that is currently active, while the candidate configuration is the copy of the configuration a user is in the process of editing. As illustrated in Figure 1-5, when a user commits the configuration, the candidate configuration becomes the committed configuration and a copy of the new committed configuration becomes the candidate configuration. The Junos software saves a copy of each previous committed configuration in case you need to reference these in the future. (You can reference these saved configurations as the `rollback` configurations.)

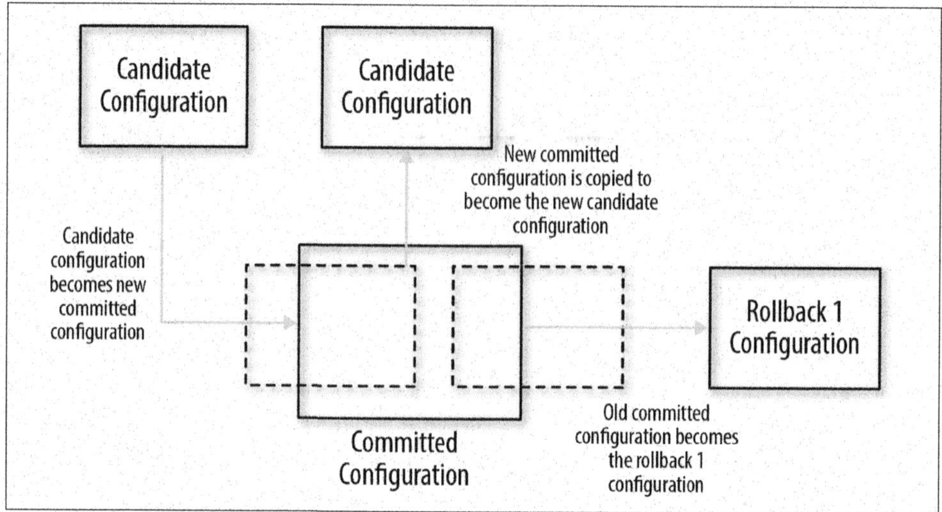

Figure 1-5. A candidate configuration becoming the committed configuration

Note the specific language here: the new candidate configuration is a copy of the new committed configuration. In some cases (notably, when a commit script modifies the configuration as part of a commit), the new committed configuration may not match the candidate configuration at the time the user triggers the commit.

The shared candidate configuration database

When a user enters the `configure` command, by default he will begin editing the shared candidate configuration database. As illustrated in Figure 1-6, all users will edit the same candidate configuration database. This behavior leaves open the possibility that multiple users can have unintended interactions with each other if they are editing the configuration at the same time. Any changes made in one session will impact any other configuration session using the shared database. And anytime a user commits the shared database, she will commit all changes made in the shared database, regardless of who made the changes.

It can be very dangerous to commit changes in the shared database while multiple users are editing the database. Suppose `user1` is configuring a BGP session while `user2` is changing the IP address assigned to a customer interface. Imagine that `user1` creates a new BGP session, but has not yet assigned an import policy when `user2` completes his work and commits the configuration. Figure 1-7 illustrates what happens.

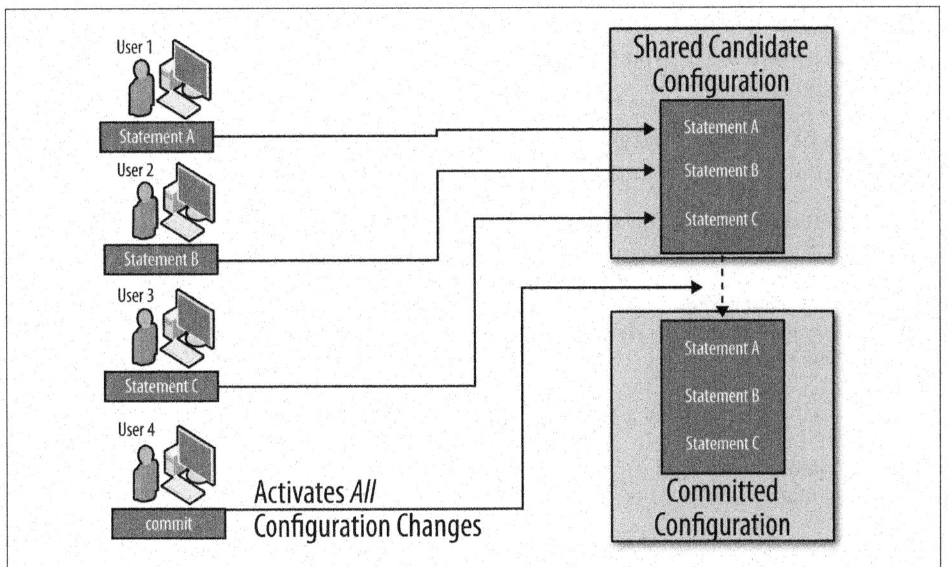

Figure 1-6. Multiple users editing the shared candidate configuration database

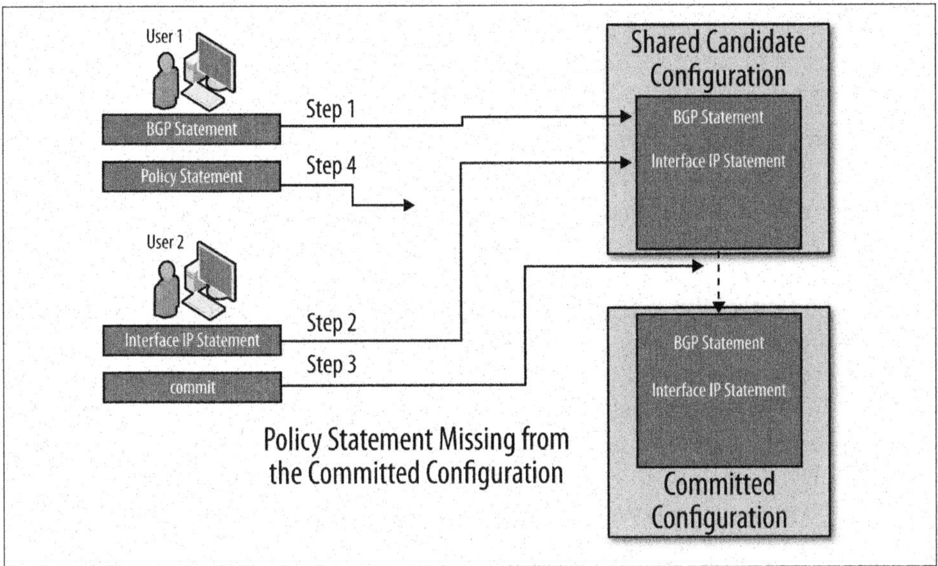

Figure 1-7. Commit of an incomplete shared candidate configuration database

The committed configuration now contains a BGP session with no import policy. Given the potential for problems that can cause, many service providers would consider this an error.

And it can be even worse. It is easy to imagine a scenario where a user causes an outage by committing a partial configuration added by another user.

To help detect these situations, Junos will warn you if you enter a configuration session using the shared database while other users are editing that database:

```
user1@r0> configure
Entering configuration mode
Users currently editing the configuration:
  user2 terminal p0 (pid 38905) on since 2015-04-25 07:27:27 PDT ❶
      [edit protocols bgp] ❷
  user1 terminal p1 (pid 38903) on since 2015-04-25 07:28:18 PDT, idle 00:28:09
      [edit interfaces ge-0/0/0]
The configuration has been changed but not committed ❸

[edit]
user1@r0#
```

❶ This line shows a user session that is editing the configuration. It includes information about the user session, such as the terminal the user session is using, the time when the user started editing the configuration, and the amount of time the session has been idle.

In this case, there are two other user sessions editing the configuration; therefore, there are two entries, one for each session. As you can see, the second entry shows that `user1` is already editing the configuration. This may remind `user1` about a configuration session she'd forgotten!

❷ This line shows the configuration hierarchy that a user is editing. This information provides *some* clue about the area of configuration the user is changing. However, the Junos CLI is flexible enough that a user really could be editing any portion of the configuration at any time. (If nothing else, he may use the `edit` command to move to a new portion of the configuration right after this message is displayed.) So, it is wise to be a bit skeptical of this information, understanding that it is only displaying a snapshot of the information at a given point in time.

❸ This text is displayed whenever the shared candidate configuration database contains changes that have not been committed. It may be displayed even if no other users are currently editing the shared database. This text warns the user that there may be other changes she will activate if she commits the candidate configuration. A user can enter `show | compare` to display the changes that have been made to the candidate configuration.

If you make changes to the shared candidate configuration database and try to exit without committing them, the software will warn you about this and ask you to confirm your intentions:

```
[edit]
user@r0# exit
The configuration has been changed but not committed
Exit with uncommitted changes? [yes,no] (yes)
```

There are times when it is desirable to exit with changes in the shared database, but there are also potential dangers to this action. Any user may accidentally commit these changes before you intended, or another user may modify or delete your changes. These dangers are part of the reason for the warning in the CLI.

What Changes?

There are times when you will see something like this:

```
user@r0> configure
Entering configuration mode
The configuration has been changed but not committed

[edit]
user@r0# show | compare

[edit]
user@r0#
```

This output seems contradictory because it says that there are changes, but the comparison shows no changes. This can be caused by several situations. One sequence of events that can lead to this is when a user makes a change and then manually reverts it. For example:

```
user@r0> configure
Entering configuration mode

[edit]
user@r0# set interfaces ge-0/0/0 unit 0

[edit]
user@r0# delete interfaces ge-0/0/0

[edit]
user@r0# show | compare

[edit]
user@r0# exit
The configuration has been changed but not committed
Exit with uncommitted changes? [yes,no] (yes) yes

Exiting configuration mode
```

```
user@r0> configure
Entering configuration mode
The configuration has been changed but not committed

[edit]
user@r0# show | compare

[edit]
user@r0#
```

In this case, the software knows that a change has been made. (And, indeed, two changes *have* been made: an interface has been added and an interface has been deleted.) This is the reason the software shows that a change has been made. Now, it happens that in this case, these changes cancel each other out, resulting in no net change to the configuration. That is why the `show | compare` output shows no changes.

The solution to this situation is simple: just rollback the configuration. This action will cause the software to delete the current shared candidate configuration database and make a new one from a copy of the current committed configuration. This lets the software know that no changes have been made:

```
user@r0> configure
Entering configuration mode
The configuration has been changed but not committed

[edit]
user@r0# rollback
load complete

[edit]
user@r0# exit
Exiting configuration mode

user@r0> configure
Entering configuration mode

[edit]
user@r0#
```

Note that the CLI no longer warns that the configuration has been changed.

Other configuration editing modes

In addition to editing the shared candidate configuration database, there are at least two other ways of editing the configuration: you can edit the shared candidate configuration database in exclusive mode, or you can edit a private candidate configuration.

Exclusive configuration mode. When you enter `configure exclusive`, the software ensures that you will be the only one making changes to the shared candidate configuration database. In addition, it ensures that no one else has previously made uncommitted changes to the shared database. Finally, it will not let you save changes to the shared candidate configuration database unless you commit them.

This behavior makes the exclusive configuration mode quite useful for automated scripts. It ensures they will not interact with other configuration sessions in an unexpected way. Configuration sessions that use NETCONF can obtain equivalent behavior using the *lock-configuration* remote procedure call. NETCONF is covered in "Management System Internals" on page 6 and RPCs are discussed in Chapter 2.

If you attempt to enter the exclusive configuration mode while someone else is editing the shared candidate configuration database, you will see an error:

```
user1@r0> configure exclusive
error: configuration database locked by:
  user2 terminal p0 (pid 38905) on since 2015-04-25 08:34:03 PDT, idle 00:04:20
      exclusive [edit]

user1@r0>
```

Likewise, you will see an error if you attempt to enter the exclusive configuration mode while there are uncommitted changes in the shared configuration database:

```
user@r0> configure exclusive
error: configuration database modified

user@r0>
```

Finally, when you enter the exclusive configuration mode, the software will warn you that you cannot save uncommitted changes in the shared candidate configuration database when you exit. And if you do attempt to exit with uncommitted changes, it will ask you to confirm that you want to discard these changes:

```
user@r0> configure exclusive
warning: uncommitted changes will be discarded on exit
Entering configuration mode

[edit]
user@r0# set system host-name r1

[edit]
user@r0# exit
The configuration has been changed but not committed
warning: Auto rollback on exiting 'configure exclusive'
Discard uncommitted changes? [yes,no] (yes)
```

Private configuration mode. Another option for controlling unintended interactions between configuration sessions is to work on private copies of the candidate configuration database (Figure 1-8). This option has some of the same restrictions as working on an exclusive copy of the candidate configuration, except it allows simultaneous editing of the configuration. Once you commit your changes, the changes will be applied to the committed configuration. Similar to the way revision control systems (like SVN or CVS) work, the Junos software can merge nonconflicting changes from multiple simultaneous sessions; however, the software cannot merge conflicting changes.

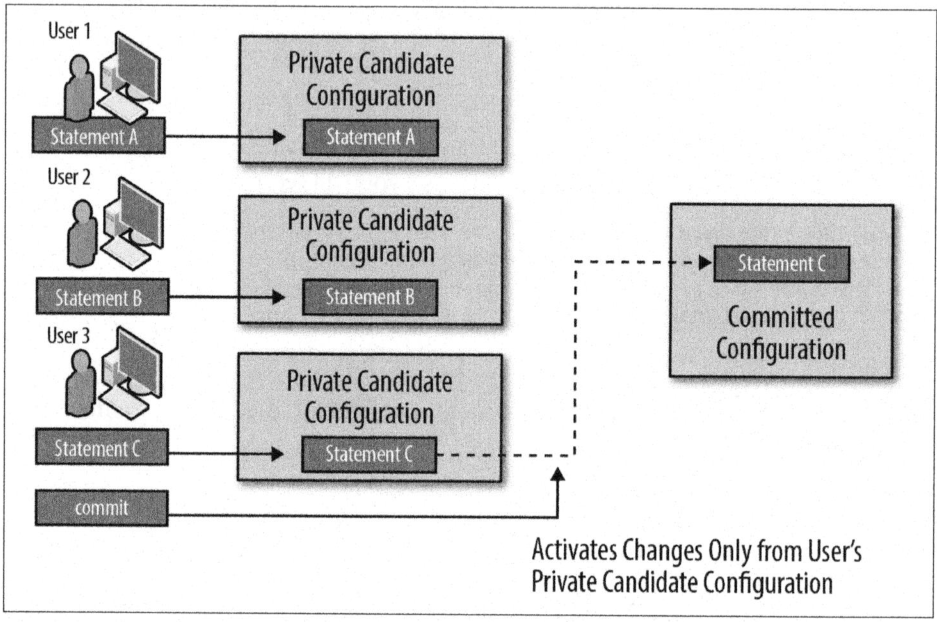

Figure 1-8. Multiple users editing private configuration databases

When you enter `configure private`, the Junos software creates a new, private copy of the committed device configuration. Your changes go into this private copy of the configuration. The Junos software will ensure that no one else has previously made uncommitted changes to the shared candidate configuration database. (It is fine for others to be making changes to other private databases.) Finally, it will not let you save changes to the private candidate configuration database unless you commit them.

This behavior makes the private configuration mode useful for automation scripts. It ensures that an automated session will not commit changes from another configuration session. And, unlike with the exclusive configuration mode, multiple scripts can simultaneously work on making nonoverlapping changes using the private configuration mode.

As compared to the exclusive configuration mode, there are some different failure modes to consider. For example, the script will probably not be able to automatically resolve conflicts with its changes. And, even though multiple scripts can work on applying changes to their own configuration databases simultaneously, it requires a separate commit to activate the changes from each private configuration database, and the actual commits still happen serially.

Configuration sessions that use NETCONF can obtain equivalent behavior using the `private` option to the *open-configuration* RPC:

```
<open-configuration>
    <private/>
</open-configuration>
```

This example provides a preview of the XML syntax Junos uses for RPCs. Additional information on RPCs and this XML syntax is provided in Chapter 2.

If another user commits a conflicting change before you commit your changes, you may get a warning when you commit your changes. Here, two users try to configure the same interfaces. The second user gets this output:

```
[edit]
user2@r0# set interfaces ge-0/0/0 description "description #2"

[edit]
user2@r0# set interfaces ge-0/0/1.0 family inet address 192.168.1.1/24

[edit]
user2@r0# commit
[edit interfaces ge-0/0/0 description]
  'description "description #1"'
    warning: statement exists (discarding old value, replacing with 'description
#2') ❶
[edit interfaces ge-0/0/1]
  'unit 0'
    warning: statement already exists ❷
[edit interfaces ge-0/0/1 unit 0 family]
  'inet'
    warning: statement already exists
```

```
[edit]
user2@r0#
```

❶ This warning shows that there is a conflict for an item that can only have one value. An interface can only have one description. Here, the current description is `description #1`. The warning indicates that the Junos software will replace that description with the new description (`description #2`) if `user2` continues with the commit operation.

❷ This warning shows that there is a conflict for part of the configuration hierarchy that may be mergeable. This warning indicates that the Junos software will try to merge `user2`'s changes to this configuration hierarchy with other changes that another user has already made to the same configuration hierarchy.

When you get a warning like this, the Junos software does *not* continue with the commit operation. (This is indicated by the lack of a `commit complete` message in the CLI, the `<commit-success/>` element in Junoscript output, or the `<ok/>` element in NETCONF output.) When you encounter this situation, you have two options to proceed further with the commit.

First, you can use the `update` command to merge the changes from the current committed configuration into your private database. The software does not, generally, overwrite your changes; rather, it computes the configuration that results from merging your changes into the current committed configuration and then installs this into your private database. (Perhaps it would be helpful to think of this as being analogous to a `git rebase`.) You can view the results of this merge by examining your private configuration database.

Once you have updated your private database, you can commit the changes without getting another warning (unless, of course, another user makes more conflicting changes between the time you update your database and the time you commit the changes).

The other thing you can do when you get a warning like this is to simply execute the `commit` command again. This action causes the Junos software to attempt to merge your changes into the committed configuration. In general, a second `commit` command is not recommended, as you may not accurately predict the final configuration that will result from these changes. However, if you fully consider the consequences, you may choose to use this functionality.

You can choose to mix the exclusive and private configuration modes. If you do this, you will be able to open a private configuration database while another user holds an exclusive lock on the configuration database. However, you will be unable to commit changes made to your private database while another user holds an exclusive lock on the configuration database. Instead, you will receive an error. You will need to wait until the user releases the exclusive lock, at which point you can proceed with your commit operation.

The Commit Process

When you execute the `commit` command, the Junos software follows a carefully orchestrated process to ensure that the device ends up with a usable configuration.

In this process, we describe a system with redundant routing engines (REs). In fact, we describe a system with more than two REs, as that system follows the most complicated commit process. To simplify this process for a system with fewer REs (even a single-RE system), simply omit the steps that apply to the other REs.

The steps are as follows:

1. The master RE runs its commit checks. This may include:
    - Checking for consistency in the data. (For example, if a BGP group refers to a policy, that policy should be defined.)
    - Running commit scripts. (Commit scripts can return warnings or errors that are caught at this stage.)
    - Running daemons in a special mode that conducts more in-depth analysis of the candidate configuration.
2. The master RE pushes the configuration to the other REs and asks those REs to conduct their commit checks.
3. The other REs activate the new configuration.
4. The master RE activates the new configuration.

If an error is detected at any step in the process, the commit process is aborted and the software returns to using the previous active configuration.

This process enforces a contract with the user: Junos will take the time it needs to thoroughly validate that the configuration is acceptable, and in return it will ensure that the Junos software components will be able to parse the configuration at the end of the process. In essence, you are sacrificing time in return for reliability.

Validating the configuration

Configuration validation occurs in several stages.

As you enter configuration statements, the management daemon validates that each statement is *syntactically* correct. (Here, "syntactic correctness" refers to each command being properly formed and constructing a valid configuration block.) If it notices a problem, it typically rejects the configuration statement.

Additionally, MGD conducts some *semantic* checks as you modify the configuration. (Here, "semantic correctness" refers to the state where the entire configuration is coherent and understandable.) If it notices a problem, it typically adds a comment to the configuration to warn you of the problem. In this example, the BGP configuration references an export policy, but the policy it references is not in the configuration:

```
[edit]
user@r0# show protocols bgp export
export does_not_exist; ## 'does_not_exist' is not defined
```

Once you commit the configuration, MGD will again conduct its semantic checks; however, these checks will either result in an error or warning, as appropriate. For example, if you attempt to commit the configuration with the BGP export policy still undefined, you will see this output:

```
[edit]
user@r0# commit
error: Policy error: Policy does_not_exist referenced but not defined
[edit protocols bgp]
  'export'
    BGP: export list not applied
error: configuration check-out failed
```

If the MGD semantic checks pass, MGD applies any commit scripts that are listed in the candidate configuration. The commit scripts can return warnings or errors. Warnings are displayed to the user but do not impact the commit process. Errors are displayed to the user and abort the commit process. (There is more information about commit scripts in Chapter 5.)

If the commit scripts return no errors, MGD calls the various daemons interested in the changes and asks them to verify that the configuration is semantically correct. These daemons can return warnings or errors. Again, both are displayed to the user, but only errors abort the commit process.

Use the command `commit check` to view the results of these commit checks without actually committing the configuration.

Activating the configuration

When the RE activates the new configuration, the configuration is merged with other data (such as the platform defaults and transient changes from commit scripts). The new configuration then atomically becomes the new "active" configuration.

You can see the platform defaults for a particular platform by running the following command:

```
show configuration groups junos-defaults
```

These configuration statements are applied like any other configuration group. That means that they can be overridden by user configuration. (Put differently, configuration groups are applied "behind" the user-supplied configuration, which means that user-supplied configuration can obscure conflicting portions of the default configuration.) This is a fancy and long-winded way of saying that the default configuration statements behave exactly the way you would expect default configuration statements to behave.

Signaling daemons

Once the configuration is committed, MGD makes any changes it needs to make (such as adding or deleting user accounts, or other changes that MGD is responsible for making) and signals other daemons to read the new configuration and activate the configuration changes each is responsible for. Because the Junos software tracks the changes a user has made, it only needs to signal the daemons that are interested in the parts of the configuration that have changed. Therefore, depending on the exact change, MGD may signal more or fewer daemons to reread the configuration. This means the device may do more or less work for each configuration change, depending on the content of the change.

This behavior becomes more relevant as the size of the configuration grows. For example, it takes much less time for the routing protocol daemon (RPD) to read a configuration with only a single routing instance and 10 static routes than it does for RPD to read a configuration with 1,000 routing instances and 400,000 static routes. Knowing the nature of your commit performance can help you develop smart strategies for handling configuration commits.

You can see this behavior by adding the `| display detail` directive to the end of the `commit` command. This causes the CLI to display the details about the activities MGD undertakes in order to activate the configuration. Among other details, you should see which daemons MGD signals to reread the configuration.

In rare circumstances you may encounter a bug in the logic that may cause MGD to miss signaling a daemon. (Juniper doesn't like to see those bugs, but they can occur occasionally.) In those cases, you can use the command `commit full` to cause MGD to take all the actions to commit the entire configuration without regard to what has changed. If you do this, MGD acts as if the entire configuration has changed and all daemons are signaled to reread their configuration.

Creating the merged configuration view

Figure 1-9 gives a fuller expansion of the way configuration data, including transient commit script changes and platform defaults, is combined into a "merged view" that the daemons can use to activate the new configuration.

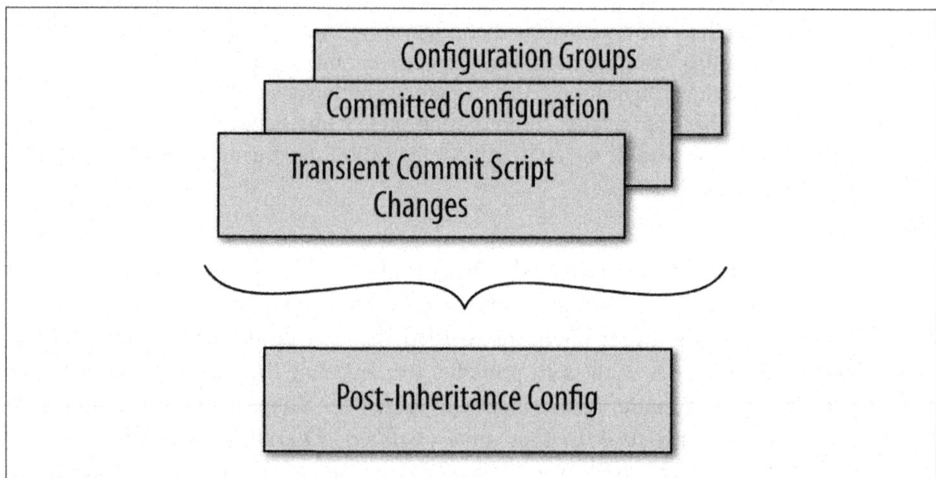

Figure 1-9. The combination of configuration information from multiple sources

In general, configuration data is applied with this precedence:

1. Transient changes from commit scripts
2. The committed configuration (note that this includes any permanent changes made by a commit script)
3. Configuration applied from configuration groups (which includes platform defaults)

Chapter 5 contains more information on commit scripts, including the difference between transient and permanent configuration changes. For now, it is sufficient to understand that commit scripts can produce different kinds of changes, which will be applied with different precedence.

Actually, to be a little more precise, transient changes from commit scripts, the committed configuration, and configuration groups in the static configuration are merged together. After the data from these various sources is merged together, this "merged" view of the configuration (you can call it the "post-inheritance" configuration) is what the various daemons read when they activate a new configuration.

Configuration groups are only applied to configuration in the static configuration database. They are not applied to transient changes from commit scripts.

Information About the Book

Network automation occurs at the interesting intersection of programming and network engineering. There certainly are good programmers who are also excellent engineers (or vice versa), but we need to be honest with ourselves and realize that those few people can probably fit in a fairly small room.

What is much more common is that a network engineer decides to do some programming, or a programmer is tasked with applying his skills to network automation. This happens for various reasons. Perhaps a company asks a network engineer to deploy new services that require automation, such as SDN. Or perhaps a network engineer simply decides that she wants to automate her tasks to save time. Or a company may hire a programmer to implement network automation. However it happens, it is easy to get stuck outside of your comfort zone if you are asked to combine skills you already have with new skills to do something that seems really complicated, like network automation.

Our goal is to help make learning these new skills simpler for you. If you are very familiar with operating Junos devices, we will give you the information you need to use those skills in network automation. Network automation does not *need* to be complicated. In fact, using the REST API (which we describe in Chapter 3), you can be doing basic network automation in no time. For other topics that are more advanced, you may need to consult outside references to understand the programming languages in use. In this book, we'll use Python a lot. If you are not comfortable with Python, you might want to consult another book that covers Python, such as *Learning Python* by Mark Lutz (O'Reilly).

If you are very familiar with programming, we will help you apply your skills to Junos. We describe the methods that you can use to automate with Junos, as well as some of the tools, libraries, and protocols that support these methods. However, we will not be covering Junos fundamentals in detail. To make sure you have some required background information, we covered some of the fundamentals in this chapter. For additional information about Junos, you might want to consult one of the other references available to you. For example, *Day One: Junos Tips, Techniques, and Templates 2011* (*http://www.juniper.net/books*), edited by Jonathan Looney et al. (Juniper Networks Books), has information that may be helpful to you as you seek to become familiar with the Junos software.

One piece of advice is to not sacrifice the good for the perfect. There are many choices for automation, and there are many ways that a network can benefit from automation. We encourage you to pick something and start using it to make things easier for you. If you are new to programming, you may find that the REST API provides an easy way to begin automation using not much more than a shell script. If you are familiar with programming but new to the Junos software, you may find that the PyEZ library is the easiest entry point.

Another piece of advice is to keep an open mind. There are a number of tools. This provides you with the flexibility you need to choose the right tool for the right task. It is easy to get tunnel vision and try to solve everything the same way. However, there usually are no "one size fits all" answers when it comes to automation. A commit script might be the right answer for one problem, while a PyEZ script might be the correct solution for a different problem. Therefore, it is best to learn about all the tools and apply them where they are best suited.

Along the same lines, it is worth remembering that tools can be combined. For example, you might use PyEZ to deploy some configuration and use a commit script to expand that configuration. In this way, the two tools can work together to produce the configuration you want.

As you read the rest of the book, we hope you will find it useful to learn about the ways you can save time, improve efficiency, increase accuracy, and make your life easier by automating your network using the Junos software.

CHAPTER 2

RPC Mechanisms

The building block of Junos management automation is the remote procedure call (RPC). Just as the drivers of the CLI are the commands a user enters, the drivers of Junos management automation are RPCs.

RPCs are equivalent to commands in many ways, but there are some differences. The main difference is that RPCs take structured input. (They also return structured output by default; however, that is orthogonal to the input format, as both the CLI and some automation mechanisms can return various output formats.) A secondary difference is that MGD assumes that CLI commands are being run from the *cli* process on the router, while it makes no such assumption with RPCs. While the CLI commands and RPCs often access the same code, there are times when they follow slightly different code paths. One example of slightly different code paths is discussed in "The file Commands: The Exceptions That Prove the Rule" on page 70.

For automation purposes, it is helpful to be able to use structured data for both input and output. Using structured data allows the automation script and the Junos software to clearly communicate information to each other. The next section begins by talking about the structured data model, then applies the structured data model to RPC input and output.

Structured Data Model

Structured data has many benefits for the purposes of automation. I remember writing automation scripts years ago that used the Expect language. These scripts sent input to a router and expected to see a response in a certain format. Any change in the CLI output format could break the scripts.

For example, consider the following output change. With no families configured for a BGP neighbor, you will see this output for the `show bgp summary` command:

```
user@r0> show bgp summary
Groups: 1 Peers: 1 Down peers: 0
Table          Tot Paths  Act Paths Suppressed    History Damp State    Pending
inet.0                 0          0          0          0          0          0
inet6.0                0          0          0          0          0          0
Peer                     AS      InPkt     OutPkt    OutQ   Flaps  Last Up/Dwn
State|#Active/Received/Accepted/Damped...
10.2.3.4              65530          3          3       0       0           1
0/0/0/0              0/0/0/0
```

However, with families configured for a BGP neighbor, you see this output for the same command:

```
user@r0> show bgp summary
Groups: 1 Peers: 1 Down peers: 0
Table          Tot Paths  Act Paths Suppressed    History Damp State    Pending
inet.0                 0          0          0          0          0          0
inet6.0                0          0          0          0          0          0
Peer                     AS      InPkt     OutPkt    OutQ   Flaps  Last Up/Dwn
State|#Active/Received/Accepted/Damped...
10.2.3.4              65530       1053       1045       0       0     7:50:41
Establ
  inet.0: 0/0/0/0
```

Note the subtle differences between these outputs. The first output has an implied state of "Established," while the second output has an explicit state (abbreviated to `Establ`). The first output has an implied table of `inet.0`, while the second output explicitly includes the table name. While these differences seem subtle, they are important when you are parsing CLI output to gather information.

Perhaps more importantly, this is a *known and expected* difference for which you can plan—imagine what kinds of problems you could encounter when Juniper makes a subtle change to the CLI! Further, this is a single CLI command.

By contrast, a structured data format passes along the information in a structured format that can usually be parsed by standard libraries. You then can access the data you want using a particular string. Depending on the language, library, and data format, retrieving the value of a field may seem very similar to retrieving the value of a variable.

Here is the same BGP peer information in XML format. (To save a tree, we are only showing the portion relevant to the BGP peer.) With no families configured for a BGP neighbor, this is the XML output for the `show bgp summary` command:

```
<bgp-peer junos:style="terse" heading="Peer                     AS  ...">
  <peer-address>10.2.3.4</peer-address>
  <peer-as>65530</peer-as>
  <input-messages>36</input-messages>
```

```
    <output-messages>35</output-messages>
    <route-queue-count>0</route-queue-count>
    <flap-count>0</flap-count>
    <elapsed-time junos:seconds="897">14:57</elapsed-time>
    <peer-state junos:format="0/0/0/0             0/0/0/0">Established</peer-state>
    <bgp-rib>
      <name>inet.0</name>
      <active-prefix-count>0</active-prefix-count>
      <received-prefix-count>0</received-prefix-count>
      <accepted-prefix-count>0</accepted-prefix-count>
      <suppressed-prefix-count>0</suppressed-prefix-count>
    </bgp-rib>
  </bgp-peer>
```

And, with address families configured for a BGP neighbor, this is the XML output for the same command:

```
  <bgp-peer junos:style="terse" heading="Peer                      AS  ...">
    <peer-address>10.2.3.4</peer-address>
    <peer-as>65530</peer-as>
    <input-messages>3</input-messages>
    <output-messages>3</output-messages>
    <route-queue-count>0</route-queue-count>
    <flap-count>0</flap-count>
    <elapsed-time junos:seconds="17">17</elapsed-time>
    <peer-state junos:format="Establ">Established</peer-state>
    <bgp-rib junos:style="terse">
      <name>inet.0</name>
      <active-prefix-count>0</active-prefix-count>
      <received-prefix-count>0</received-prefix-count>
      <accepted-prefix-count>0</accepted-prefix-count>
      <suppressed-prefix-count>0</suppressed-prefix-count>
    </bgp-rib>
  </bgp-peer>
```

As you can see, the preceding data structures are equivalent in all important respects: they contain the same fields, which represent the data in the same way. The only major difference is in the XML metadata (the `junos:format` attribute on the `<peer-state>` tag). (For more on XML, see "XML data" on page 32.)

This example illustrates one of the advantages of structured data formats. Even though the CLI outputs differ in a way that makes Expect scripts difficult, it is trivial to consistently retrieve the information you need from the structured data.

For the input side, a structured data format lets us ensure both sides of the conversation are speaking about the same things. Want to have some fun with your router? Put a host on your network named `verbose` and try pinging it:

```
user@r0> ping verbose
                     ^
missing argument.
```

```
user@r0> ping "verbose"
missing mandatory argument: host.

user@r0>
```

When you try to use these commands to ping the hostname `verbose` through the CLI, the CLI has no way to distinguish between the hostname and the `verbose` option to the `ping` command. The CLI resolves the ambiguity by assuming that you intended to provide the `verbose` option. By contrast, look what happens when you use a structured data format to communicate this information:

```
<rpc>
  <ping>
    <host>verbose</host>
    <count>1</count>
  </ping>
</rpc>

<rpc-reply xmlns="urn:ietf:params:xml:ns:netconf:base:1.0"
           xmlns:junos="http://xml.juniper.net/junos/15.1R1/junos">
  <ping-results xmlns="http://xml.juniper.net/junos/15.1R1/junos-probe-tests">
    <target-host>verbose</target-host>
    <target-ip>10.92.250.10</target-ip>
    <packet-size>56</packet-size>
    <probe-result date-determined="1430770335">
      <probe-index>1</probe-index>
      <probe-success/>
      <sequence-number>0</sequence-number>
      <ip-address>10.92.250.10</ip-address>
      <time-to-live>53</time-to-live>
      <response-size>64</response-size>
      <rtt>69383</rtt>
    </probe-result>
    <probe-results-summary>
      <probes-sent>1</probes-sent>
      <responses-received>1</responses-received>
      <packet-loss>0</packet-loss>
      <rtt-minimum>69383</rtt-minimum>
      <rtt-maximum>69383</rtt-maximum>
      <rtt-average>69383</rtt-average>
      <rtt-stddev>0</rtt-stddev>
    </probe-results-summary>
    <ping-success/>
  </ping-results>
</rpc-reply>
```

In this output, the RPC request is enclosed in `<rpc>` XML tags, while the reply from the Junos software is enclosed in `<rpc-reply>` XML tags. This matches the way the RPCs are actually passed on the wire. Depending on the exact method you use to access the RPCs, some of this may be hidden from you. But, for now, it is a handy way to distinguish between the input and output XML documents. (XML tags and documents are discussed in "XML data" on page 32.)

Structured Data Formats

The Junos software currently supports two structured data formats: XML and JSON. Both have their adherents and both have their benefits. However, our concern here is the way you can use these data formats in *this particular application*: managing the Junos software.

The Junos management API is fundamentally an XML API. The Junos software receives requests in XML format and produces its responses in XML format. It does not accept requests in JSON format, nor does it natively produce JSON responses to non-configuration RPCs. Rather, it first produces the XML output and mechanically repackages the XML output as JSON output.

Therefore, even if you prefer the JSON data format, it is important that you understand the basics of the XML interactions with the Junos software. You will need to produce your requests in the XML format, and the JSON-formatted responses will be based on the XML-formatted output the software produces.

When programming against the Junos API, it is fully expected that you will use some sort of library to ease your interactions with the API. Thus, you may rarely have to create or parse raw XML or JSON data yourself. However, because these libraries will present request options and response data that are abstracted from the API, it is important that you understand the API itself. And, because the Junos API is fundamentally an XML API, it is important that you understand the XML format of these API requests and responses.

For that reason, this chapter contains a lot of XML. The details of the XML API and the XML samples are here to help you understand the underlying API, even though some (or many) of the finer details should be hidden by the library or libraries you use to enable your communication with the Junos API.

XML data

There is no way to cover XML in its entirety in this book; instead, a brief overview is provided of XML and XPath, and the way Juniper uses these standards. For a more complete description of XML, you should consult another resource that covers the language, such as *Learning XML* by Erik T. Ray (O'Reilly).

XML is a structured data format used to communicate data, together with metadata. XML allows multiple levels of hierarchy. The structure of an XML document (its "schema") can be communicated using a document type definition (DTD). Juniper publishes its schema in both DTD and YANG formats.

There are several important concepts in understanding an XML document:

Documents
: An XML document consists of a single root element.

Tags
: Tags define the start and end of an element. There are three kinds of tags: opening tags, closing tags, and empty tags. All of the tags appear in angle brackets, like this opening tag for the element named "sample":

```
<sample>
```

Closing tags differ from opening tags in that they have a forward slash (/) before the element name:

```
</sample>
```

The element begins with an opening tag and ends with a closing tag, like this:

```
<sample>...</sample>
```

If an element is empty (i.e., if it contains no content), you can combine the opening and closing tags into a single empty tag. An empty tag differs from an opening tag in that it has a forward slash after the element name. Therefore, the following two sets of tags are equivalent:

```
<sample></sample>
<sample/>
```

Although tags define the opening and ending of elements, we often refer to an element's name as its "tag."

Elements
: An element can contain data or other elements. An element can also be empty. (In these cases, its mere presence may have a meaning, similar to a Boolean argument to a command-line tool.) The element's name (together with the DTD) defines the nature of the element.

While elements can contain any number of other elements, an XML document must contain a single root element. The remaining elements that make up an XML document must be nested within this root element.

Technically, an element can contain a mixture of data and other elements; however, the Junos software does not mix data and elements at the same level. In the Junos software's XML usage, an element will either contain data, contain one or more elements, or be empty.

Therefore, while the following is technically valid XML data, the Junos software will not produce it:

```
<rpc-reply>
  <bgp-peer>
    Peer <name>1</name> is <state>established</state>.
  </bgp-peer>
</rpc-reply>
```

CDATA

CDATA is just a fancy XML term for character data. In essence, whatever text is not part of a tag is CDATA. Even the whitespace between tags is considered to be part of the enclosing element's CDATA.

CDATA can contain escaped characters. These escaped characters can represent any sort of data that is not readily representable in the chosen character set. (For example, binary data may be encoded in escapes.) Also, certain characters (such as `&`, `>`, and `<`) must be escaped.

Attributes

Attributes are metadata items that help describe the element. Attributes are listed in key/value pairs (e.g., `color="black"`) and appear inside the starting tag of an element (or inside an empty tag for an empty element).

For example, Junos often provides a `junos:seconds` attribute for elements containing times or timestamps. This additional information provides an alternate way to describe the data the element contains. In this sample output from the *get-system-uptime-information* RPC (equivalent to the `show system uptime` CLI command), you see that the contents of the `<date-time>` element show the current timestamp, while the `junos:seconds` attribute provides the number of seconds in Unix time format (seconds since the Unix "epoch"):

```
<system-uptime-information>
  <current-time>
    <date-time junos:seconds="1453131467">
      2016-01-18 07:37:47 PST
    </date-time>
  </current-time>
```

```
    ...output trimmed...
</system-uptime-information>
```

In another example, when you load an XML configuration, you can include attributes on a configuration element to indicate additional steps you would like the Junos software to take with that configuration element (such as replacing it, deleting it, or moving it). These are detailed further in "Changing the Configuration" on page 81.

Attributes contain useful metadata, but they shouldn't be used to distinguish between different elements with the same name. Instead, you need to use a child element to do that.

For example, this XML syntax is not the correct way to distinguish between two interfaces:

```
<interface-state>
  <interface name="ge-0/0/0">
    <state>Up</state>
  </interface>
  <interface name="ge-0/0/1">
    <state>Up</state>
  </interface>
</interface-state>
```

However, this XML syntax does show a correct method for distinguishing between two elements with the same tag:

```
<interface-state>
  <interface>
    <name>ge-0/0/0</name>
    <state>Up</state>
  </interface>
  <interface>
    <name>ge-0/0/1</name>
    <state>Up</state>
  </interface>
</interface-state>
```

Nodes

You can think of an XML document as a tree, containing a hierarchical set of elements. When we think of an XML document as a tree, we refer to an element as a particular node on that tree.

Elements are related to each other in parent/child relationships. Elements that contain other elements are said to be the *parent* nodes of the elements they contain. Likewise, the elements within a parent node are said to be *child* nodes of the parent.

Namespaces

Each element name and attribute name in an XML document can have a namespace. A namespace helps disambiguate multiple element or attribute names that are the same, but have different meanings. This can occur when the same name is defined to mean different things in different schemas. For example, the `<name>` element may mean different things in different schemas. By associating this element with a particular namespace, the author of the XML document can make the meaning of the element clear.

An element can inherit a default namespace from its parent, or it can have its own default namespace. A default namespace is defined with the `xmlns` attribute.

For example, in this document, the `<is>` element is assigned a default namespace identified by the `http://www.example.org/secrets` URI. The `<is>` and `<hidden>` elements are in this XML namespace:

```
<the-secret>
  <is xmlns="http://www.example.org/secrets">
    <hidden/>
  </is>
</the-secret>
```

You can also associate a namespace with a prefix. When an element name or attribute name contains that prefix, the name is interpreted as being part of the namespace associated with that prefix.

For example, in this document, the `<is>` element and the `special` attribute are in the XML namespace identified by the `http://www.example.org/secrets` URI; however, the `<hidden>` element itself is not in that namespace:

```
<the-secret xmlns:secrets="http://www.example.org/secrets">
  <secrets:is>
    <hidden secrets:special="very"/>
  </secrets:is>
</the-secret>
```

Technically, there is no special meaning given to any namespace prefix. Rather, to fully understand the meaning of an XML namespace prefix, you must refer back to the URI associated with the namespace. In the preceding example, we could just as easily have used the namespace prefix `foo` and the document would have had the same meaning.

In practice, Junos uses few namespace prefixes, and the ones it uses are predictable. Therefore, if you know XML and want to use the full namespace information, you may. In fact, you can use the schema and the namespace information to do some advanced things, such as offline configuration validation. On the other hand, for many automation purposes, it is acceptable to either strip off the namespace information or treat it like part of the element name.

Accessing XML data with XPath

A common way to access XML data is via XPath. XPath expressions describe the path to the element that you want to examine.

A basic XPath expression simply lists the path to a value, using slashes between each level of the XML hierarchy. For example, consider this XML hierarchy:

```
<interface-state>
  <interface>
    <name>ge-0/0/1</name>
    <state>Up</state>
  </interface>
</interface-state>
```

To access the `<state>` element, you would use the XPath expression `interface-state/interface/state`. In this simple expression, each level of the hierarchy appears in the XPath expression separated by a slash.

However, what do you do when there are multiple elements that match the same XPath expression? For example, consider this XML hierarchy:

```
<interface-state>
  <interface>
    <name>ge-0/0/0</name>
    <state>Up</state>
  </interface>
  <interface>
    <name>ge-0/0/1</name>
    <state>Up</state>
  </interface>
</interface-state>
```

The XPath expression `interface-state/interface/state` would match both interfaces. What if you only want to match one of the interfaces? In this case, you can use conditional expressions to limit the query to elements that match particular criteria. You can include multiple sets of conditions in a single XPath query.

You include the conditions within square brackets that follow the element to which you want to apply the condition. XPath expressions within the square brackets are relative to the element to which they are attached. For example, the XPath expression `interface-state/interface[name="ge-0/0/0"]/state` says that we want to find `<interface>` elements that themselves contain a `<name>` element equal to `"ge-0/0/0"` and then select the `<state>` elements from the matching `<interface>` elements.

If the condition is a "simple" XPath expression, it is true if any elements match that XPath expression. For example, the XPath statement `interface-state/interface[state]` selects all `<interface>` elements that contain a `<state>` child element.

XPath expressions are quite powerful. Of course, that also means there are a large number of options. This section is not intended to be a thorough overview of XPath expressions. Rather, it is merely intended to give you a basic grounding so you can understand XPath expressions used in this book and also write some simple XPath expressions of your own. Later chapters will cover XPath expressions further. For example, "Using XPath with lxml" on page 185 contains information on XPath expressions supported by the `lxml` Python module. Chapters 5, 6, and 7 also make use of XPath expressions.

For a more complete overview of XPath expressions, see the W3Schools XPath Tutorial (*http://www.w3schools.com/xsl/xpath_intro.asp*).

JSON data

The Junos software also supports the JavaScript Object Notation (JSON) format for transmitting structured data. At the time of this writing, the Junos software only supports the output of JSON data. It does not currently accept JSON input.

Certain languages include good support for trivially converting JSON-formatted data to the language's native data formats. For example, Python has the `json` module, which converts JSON input to dictionaries, lists, and appropriate primitive types.

The JSON format supports objects, arrays, and various data types. However, JSON does not support metadata (which XML supports through its attributes). This means that any effort to transform XML to JSON format requires some sort of effort to make both the data and the metadata available. As one expert in the field recently said, "There are a number of ways to do this, and they all have problems."

The Junos software produces JSON output by mechanically transforming the XML into JSON. It uses one of the available methods to do this translation, and it isn't perfect.

The conversion generally follows these rules:

- The top level of the JSON document is an object (much like a Python dictionary). The XML elements that are children of the `<rpc-reply>` node are added to this top-level object.
- Each XML element's name is a key in its parent's object. The value associated with this key is an array. If there is only one XML element with a given tag, then the array will only contain a single member. If there is more than one XML element with the same tag, then the array for that element name will contain one member for each element with that tag.

- Each array member that represents an XML element contains an object. If the XML element is an empty element with no attributes, then the object will be empty. Otherwise, it will contain one or more of the following keys:
  — The tags of child elements will appear as keys.
  — The `data` key will exist if there is CDATA left after stripping leading and trailing whitespace. The value associated with the `data` key is the value of the CDATA after stripping leading and trailing whitespace.
  — The `attributes` key will exist if the XML element has attributes. The value associated with the `attributes` key is an object containing the XML attribute names and values.
- This processing continues recursively until the entire tree has been processed.

As an example, let's look at some sample output from the *get-system-users-information* RPC (equivalent to the `show system users` CLI command). First, let's examine the XML output (Example 2-1).

Example 2-1. Sample XML response to the get-system-users-information RPC

```
<rpc-reply xmlns:junos="http://xml.juniper.net/junos/15.1R2/junos">
  <system-users-information xmlns="http://xml.juniper.net/junos/15.1R2/junos">
    <uptime-information>
      <date-time junos:seconds="1452906616">5:10PM</date-time>
      <up-time junos:seconds="60060">16:41</up-time>
      <active-user-count junos:format="2 users">2</active-user-count>
      <load-average-1>0.07</load-average-1>
      <load-average-5>0.15</load-average-5>
      <load-average-15>0.15</load-average-15>
      <user-table>
        <user-entry>
          <user>user</user>
          <tty>pts/0</tty>
          <from>h0.example.com</from>
          <login-time junos:seconds="1452904660">4:37PM</login-time>
          <idle-time junos:seconds="0">-</idle-time>
          <command>cli</command>
          </user-entry>
        <user-entry>
          <user>user</user>
          <tty>pts/1</tty>
          <from>h0.example.com</from>
          <login-time junos:seconds="1452906400">5:06PM</login-time>
          <idle-time junos:seconds="0">-</idle-time>
          <command>cli</command>
          </user-entry>
      </user-table>
    </uptime-information>
```

```
  </system-users-information>
</rpc-reply>
```

Now, let's look at the JSON representation of this same data (Example 2-2).

Example 2-2. Sample JSON response to the get-system-users-information RPC


```
{
 "system-users-information" : [
 {
    "attributes" : {"xmlns" : "http://xml.juniper.net/junos/15.1R2/junos"},
    "uptime-information" : [
    {
        "date-time" : [
        {
            "data" : "5:10PM",
            "attributes" : {"junos:seconds" : "1452906616"}
        }
        ],
        "up-time" : [
        {
            "data" : "16:41",
            "attributes" : {"junos:seconds" : "60060"}
        }
        ],
        "active-user-count" : [
        {
            "data" : "2",
            "attributes" : {"junos:format" : "2 users"}
        }
        ],
        "load-average-1" : [
        {
            "data" : "0.07"
        }
        ],
        "load-average-5" : [
        {
            "data" : "0.15"
        }
        ],
        "load-average-15" : [
        {
            "data" : "0.15"
        }
        ],
        "user-table" : [
        {
            "user-entry" : [
            {
                "user" : [
                {
```

```
            "data" : "user"
        }
        ],
        "tty" : [
        {
            "data" : "pts/0"
        }
        ],
        "from" : [
        {
            "data" : "h0.example.com"
        }
        ],
        "login-time" : [
        {
            "data" : "4:37PM",
            "attributes" : {"junos:seconds" : "1452904660"}
        }
        ],
        "idle-time" : [
        {
            "data" : "-",
            "attributes" : {"junos:seconds" : "0"}
        }
        ],
        "command" : [
        {
            "data" : "cli"
        }
        ]
    },
    {
        "user" : [
        {
            "data" : "user"
        }
        ],
        "tty" : [
        {
            "data" : "pts/1"
        }
        ],
        "from" : [
        {
            "data" : "h0.example.com"
        }
        ],
        "login-time" : [
        {
            "data" : "5:06PM",
            "attributes" : {"junos:seconds" : "1452906400"}
        }
```

```
                ],
                "idle-time" : [
                {
                    "data" : "-",
                    "attributes" : {"junos:seconds" : "0"}
                }
                ],
                "command" : [
                {
                    "data" : "cli"
                }
                ]
            }
            ]
        }
        ]
    }
    ]
}
]
}
```

As you can see, all the original XML data is present, but it has been mechanically converted into JSON format according to the described algorithm. Consider the `<system-users-information>` element. It is a child of the `<rpc-reply>` node, so it appears as a key in the top-level object. Its value is an array. Because there is only a single `<system-users-information>` element, the array only has a single member. That single member has an object that represents the corresponding `<system-users-information>` element. The `<system-users-information>` element has a single child node, which appears as a key in this object. The `<system-users-information>` element also has an attribute (the `xmlns` attribute), so the object contains an `attributes` key, which points to an object with the attribute information.

Looking farther down, we see the `<load-average-1>` node, which contains the CDATA `0.07`. In the JSON format, the `load-average-1` key points to an array with a single member. The array's single member contains an object. The object contains the `data` key with a value of `0.07`.

If you look farther down in the output, you see that there are two `<user-entry>` nodes in the XML output. Accordingly, the `user-entry` key in the JSON output points to an array with two members, one for each `<user-entry>` node.

As you can see, one of the key features of this translation format is arrays. This format produces consistency because every element name contains an array. However, it also produces quite a few levels of arrays.

If you load the JSON from the previous example in Python and store the result in a variable named user_info, you can access the uptime value using this command:

```
>>> user_info['system-users-information'][0]['uptime-information'][0]
...           ['up-time'][0]['data']
'16:41'
```

Given the verbosity of the JSON format, it may be better to look for a high-quality, easy-to-use library or module that enables you to easily use the XML data. After all, the JSON format is just a mechanical repackaging of the XML data. If you can find an XML library that proves easier to use than the JSON data format, you would probably be best served by using that library. On the other hand, if you find the JSON format easy enough to use, feel free to do so.

Using Structured Data in Python

As we indicated in "Information About the Book" on page 25, we are planning to use Python for the examples in this book. This is not because it is particularly easier to use XML in Python than other languages. Rather, it is simply because Python is a scripting language that is used by many people who are attempting to automate Junos. For that reason, we want to give you some more information about the way we recommend using structured data in Python.

First, let's explain why we are recommending XML. In our opinion, it makes sense to have your scripts use XML for communicating with Junos when you are able to do so. XML supports both data and metadata, and the Junos XML API uses both. While there is a format to represent metadata in JSON, the data format is imperfect. Also, because of the mechanical way in which the translation is performed, the JSON output creates arrays at just about every level of the hierarchy, even if they aren't needed. That makes data selectors longer and more complex. Finally, there is a processing cost for the router to do the translation from XML to JSON. For that reason, it doesn't make sense to use the JSON format unless there are clear benefits to it. In our opinion, the benefits just aren't there. On top of this, support for the JSON format is a relatively new addition to the Junos software and may not be available on all platforms.

In the end, the Junos API is an XML API. Other representations (such as the JSON representation, or even most CLI output) are simply alternative representations of the data in the XML API. Unless you have a particular need to use one of the alternate formats, we recommend that you use the XML API (and the XML-formatted data) in your communication with the Junos software.

However, we understand why there has been hesitancy to use XML. The XML format is more robust, which makes it more complex to parse, and the libraries that parse it generally do a better job at being robust than simple. But the lack of a good client library doesn't mean that XML is the wrong tool; rather, it just means that we need to find a good client library. And for those who want a simple XML client library, we think we have a good choice for Python.

We've created an open source project called `jxmlease`. You can use the `jxmlease` Python module to convert XML data to a Python data structure that maintains the XML metadata, but also uses data structures more familiar to a Python user. The module provides an option to convert the XML data to Python dictionaries, lists, and "string-like" objects. It stores the metadata as attributes of these objects and provides a consistent set of methods to access it.

Like all attempts to balance simplicity and robustness, `jxmlease` makes many things simple by making a few things harder. If you already are comfortable with using a more robust library, such as `lxml`, you should by all means continue to do so. We created the `jxmlease` project to make it easier to do many of the common tasks associated with the Junos XML API. However, `jxmlease` does not support advanced `lxml` functionality such as XPath expressions.

Installing jxmlease

You can view the current installation instructions for `jxmlease` at its GitHub repository (*https://github.com/Juniper/jxmlease*). As of this writing, it is believed that `jxmlease` supports both Python 2 and 3. Further, it has very few dependencies. On most (if not all) Python installations, the dependencies are all included in the base system.

The GitHub site also has documentation on `jxmlease`. However, we will introduce some of the basic uses here.

Parsing XML with jxmlease

You parse XML text using the `Parser` class. When you call the `Parser` class, it returns a callable object to do the parsing. In this example, you parse the given XML string and store a reference to the resulting `jxmlease` object in the `xmlroot` variable:

```
>>> xmlparser = jxmlease.Parser()
>>> xmlroot = xmlparser("<a>foo</a>")
```

Alternatively, you can call the `parse()` method directly. This method creates an instance of the `Parser` class and then calls it with the given arguments. This example produces the same results as the preceding example:

```
>>> xmlroot = jxmlease.parse("<a>foo</a>")
```

You can pass various arguments to either the `Parser` class or the `parse()` method to modify their behavior. When you pass arguments to the `Parser` class when creating a callable parser object, those values become default arguments used for invocations of the resulting object. Therefore, if you will be calling the parser many times with the same arguments, you may find it useful to create a `Parser` object with these defaults. Alternatively, if you are satisified with the default behavior of the `Parser` class (or will be providing different arguments each time you use the parser), you will probably be satisfied with just using the `parse()` method.

For example, the following two calls are equivalent. In both cases, the parser will leave leading and trailing whitespace in each XML node's CDATA (instead of stripping leading and trailing whitespace from CDATA, which is the default behavior):

```
# Create a Parser object with a default argument of strip_whitespace=False.
xmlparser = jxmlease.Parser(strip_whitespace=False)

# Parse the string stored in the xmldoc variable.
# The parser will use the default we defined when creating the xmlparser object.
xmlroot1 = xmlparser(xmldoc)

# Now, parse the string using the jxmlease parser. We need to provide the
# nondefault value for the strip_whitespace argument.
xmlroot2 = jxmlease.parse(xmldoc, strip_whitespace=False)

# xmlroot1 is now equivalent to xmlroot2.
```

There are several arguments you can provide to the `Parser` class or the `parse()` method to modify their behavior. These are documented in the `jxmlease` documentation. Generally, you should not need to modify the default behavior of `jxmlease` in order to understand the examples in this book (or to use the package for most uses with the Junos XML API), so we will not cover many of the options here. One option you may find particularly useful is the `generator` argument. That is discussed in "Iterating over jxmlease objects" on page 50.

There is also an `EtreeParser` class, which is equivalent to the `Parser` class but parses an `ElementTree` or `lxml.etree` object rather than an XML text document. Correspondingly, there is a `parse_etree()` method, which creates an instance of the `EtreeParser` class and then calls it with the given arguments.

jxmlease objects

The XML data is converted to appropriate Python objects, while the metadata (the XML attributes) is stored as metadata (Python attributes) in the Python object.

For instance, consider the conversion shown in Example 2-3.

Example 2-3. Basic jxmlease parsing

```
>>> animal_xml = """\
... <animals>
...   <animal type="fierce">
...     <name>lion</name>
...     <sound>roar</sound>
...   </animal>
...   <animal type="cute">
...     <name>cat</name>
...     <sound>meow</sound>
...   </animal>
... </animals>
... """
>>> result = jxmlease.parse(animal_xml)
>>> result.prettyprint()
{u'animals': {u'animal': [{u'name': u'lion', u'sound': u'roar'},
                          {u'name': u'cat', u'sound': u'meow'}]}}
>>> for animal in result['animals']['animal']:
...   print "\"a %s is %s\"" % (animal['name'], animal.get_xml_attr("type"))
...
"a lion is fierce"
"a cat is cute"
```

As you can see, the XML data is available as "normal" data within the object, while the XML attributes are stored with the object and available through object methods.

There are three classes of objects that `jxmlease` uses to represent XML data. All three classes are meant to be usable as common Python data types, while also having extra functionality to handle the extra XML-specific tasks. All three of these classes are subclasses of the `jxmlease.XMLNodeBase` class:

`jxmlease.XMLDictNode`
: The `jxmlease.XMLDictNode` class produces objects that look like `OrderedDict` objects (if available in the system) or normal Pyhon dictionaries. XML nodes that have child XML nodes are represented by `jxmlease.XMLDictNode` objects. The tag of each child node appears as a key in the dictionary, and the value associated with the key is the data for the child node(s) with that tag.

  The return value of the `parse()` method is always an instance of the `jxmlease.XMLDictNode` class. The root element's tag appears as a key in this dictionary.

`jxmlease.XMLListNode`
: The `jxmlease.XMLListNode` class produces objects that look like Python list objects. When multiple XML nodes have the same name, `jxmlease` creates a list (a `jxmlease.XMLListNode` object) to hold the list of objects representing the

XML nodes with the same tag. The entry for this tag in the parent object's dictionary will point to this list.

For instance, in the previous example there are two `<animal>` elements. Therefore, the `animal` key in the parent dictionary points to a `jxmlease.XMLListNode` object with a list of `jxmlease` objects. Each member of the list represents a single `<animal>` element.

`jxmlease.XMLCDATANode`
: The `jxmlease.XMLCDATANode` class produces objects that look like Python Unicode strings. You can use them in string comparisons. In fact, they should act like strings in just about every way except for the addition of the extra `jxmlease` methods.

  XML nodes that contain only CDATA are represented by `jxmlease.XMLCDATANode` objects. Empty XML nodes are represented by a `jxmlease.XMLCDATANode` object with an empty string.

  Like the Python string objects that these build upon, the strings in `jxmlease.XMLCDATANode` objects are immutable. That creates some complications when trying to modify XML trees that use these objects, but creates no problems for simply viewing the data.

The `jxmlease` objects have the same methods as the types on which they are based (dict or `OrderedDict`, list, and string). In addition, they have other methods you can use to view, process, or modify the data they contain. Some of the methods you can use include:

`prettyprint([...])`
: This attempts to use Python's `pprint` library to produce formatted output for the underlying data. (If you attempt to use Python's `pprint` library directly, it will not print out a pretty representation of these nodes. It does not know how to do that, as it recognizes that they are not actually dict, list, and string objects.)

  This method takes the same arguments as the Python `pprint()` function, except that you do not need to provide the name of the object to be displayed. The `prettyprint()` method will pass the arguments you provide to the `pprint()` function.

`has_xml_attrs()`
: This method returns `True` if the node has XML attributes, or `False` otherwise.

`get_xml_attr(*attr*[, *defval*])`
: This method returns the value of the XML attribute named *`attr`*. If no attribute of that name exists, it will return *`defval`*. If *`defval`* is not provided, it will raise a `KeyError`.

`get_xml_attrs()`
: This method returns a dictionary of XML attributes associated with the node. If a node has no XML attributes, it returns an empty dictionary.

`set_xml_attr(`*`attr`*`, `*`val`*`)`
: This method sets the XML attribute named *`attr`* to have the value *`val`*. If the XML attribute does not already exist for this node, it will add the XML attribute to the node.

`delete_xml_attr(`*`attr`*`)`
: This method deletes the XML attribute named *`attr`*. If the XML attribute does not exist, it will raise a `KeyError`.

You might be wondering why you would want to add, change, or delete XML attributes. These methods are useful in cases where you are using these objects to build your own XML hierarchy. We demonstrate building an XML hierarchy in "Build a Candidate Configuration" on page 151 and "Apply and Commit the Candidate Configuration" on page 152.

`list()`
: When run against a `jxmlease.XMLListNode` object, this method returns the list object itself. When run against another `jxmlease` object, it returns a single-member list containing that object.

This method allows you to produce predictable behavior when your XML document may contain one or more elements with the same name. If the document contains multiple elements with the same name, the entry in the dictionary will point to a list of multiple nodes, such as the list of `<animal>` elements in our previous example. However, if the document only contains a single element with that name, the entry in the dictionary will point to a single element. Attempting to iterate over that element will not produce the desired results:

```
>>> single_animal_xml = """\
... <animals>
...   <animal type="fierce">
...     <name>lion</name>
...     <sound>roar</sound>
...   </animal>
... </animals>
... """
>>> singleresult = jxmlease.parse(single_animal_xml)
>>> singleresult.prettyprint()
{u'animals': {u'animal': {u'name': u'lion', u'sound': u'roar'}}}
>>> for animal in singleresult['animals']['animal']:
...   print "\"a %s is %s\"" % (animal['name'],
```

```
...                                     animal.get_xml_attr("type"))
...
Traceback (most recent call last):
  File "<stdin>", line 2, in <module>
TypeError: string indices must be integers
```

You can ease your logic by using the `list()` method. If the object is already a list, this will produce no change. If the object is not already a list, it will create a single-member list containing the object. This lets you use the same logic whether there is a single element or multiple elements with the same name:

```
>>> for animal in singleresult['animals']['animal'].list():
...     print "\"a %s is %s\"" % (animal['name'],
...                                     animal.get_xml_attr("type"))
...
"a lion is fierce"
>>> for animal in multiresult['animals']['animal'].list():
...     print "\"a %s is %s\"" % (animal['name'],
...                                     animal.get_xml_attr("type"))
...
"a lion is fierce"
"a cat is cute"
```

`dict()`, `jdict()`
: The `dict()` method takes several optional arguments. It allows you to process a list of `jxmlease.XMLDictNode` objects and create a dictionary to contain these objects, with the dictionary keyed appropriately based on the contents of the `jxmlease.XMLDictNode` objects or their children. The `jdict()` method performs an equivalent function, but the details of finding the correct key should be preset in a way that is appropriate for use on Junos configuration data, as well as the data produced by some operational-mode RPCs.

For example, consider this partial XML configuration:

```
>>> xml_config = """\
... <configuration>
...   <interfaces>
...     <interface>
...       <name>ge-1/0/0</name>
...       <description>Port #1</description>
...     </interface>
...     <interface>
...       <name>ge-1/0/1</name>
...       <description>Port #2</description>
...     </interface>
...   </interfaces>
... </configuration>
... """
>>> parsed_xml = jxmlease.parse(xml_config)
```

```
>>> parsed_config = parsed_xml['configuration']
{u'interfaces': {u'interface': [{u'description': u'Port #1',
                                 u'name': u'ge-1/0/0'},
                                {u'description': u'Port #2',
                                 u'name': u'ge-1/0/1'}]}}
```

Using the `jdict()` method, you are able to process the list of `<interface>` elements and create a dictionary keyed off the `<name>` elements they contain:

```
>>> int_dict = parsed_config['interfaces']['interface'].jdict()
>>> int_dict.prettyprint()
{u'ge-1/0/0': {u'description': u'Port #1', u'name': u'ge-1/0/0'},
 u'ge-1/0/1': {u'description': u'Port #2', u'name': u'ge-1/0/1'}}
```

The `dict()` method allows you to specify the criteria used to select a key. The simplest criterion is a list of tags which it should use as a key. For example, you can use the `dict()` method to process the list of `<interface>` elements and create a dictionary keyed off the `<description>` elements they contain:

```
>>> int_dict = parsed_config['interfaces']['interface'].dict(
...     tags=['description'])
>>> int_dict.prettyprint()
{u'Port #1': {u'description': u'Port #1', u'name': u'ge-1/0/0'},
 u'Port #2': {u'description': u'Port #2', u'name': u'ge-1/0/1'}}
```

The `dict()` method has a number of options to allow you to select keys. Also, both the `dict()` and `jdict()` methods take other arguments that are not detailed here. The official `jxmlease` documentation includes further information on using these options.

`find_nodes_with_tag(`*`tag`*`[, `*`recursive`*`])`, `has_node_with_tag(`*`tag`*`[, `*`recursive`*`])`

The `find_nodes_with_tag()` method searches for nodes with a matching tag in the XML hierarchy rooted at the current node. The method returns a generator that allows you to iterate over these nodes. By default, the method searches the current node (the node on which the method was executed) as well as all descendants of the current node. However, if you specify a `False` value for the optional `recursive` argument, the method will only search the current node and its direct children.

The `has_node_with_tag()` method takes the same arguments and operates the same way as the `find_nodes_with_tag()` method; however, it immediately returns `True` once it finds the first matching node. If it does not find a matching node, it returns `False`.

For an example use of the `find_nodes_with_tag()` method, see "Check for XML Warnings and Errors" on page 147.

`emit_xml()`
: This method produces an XML representation of the hierarchy. By default, it will often include an opening XML declaration in the output. For most uses with the Junos API, you will want to include the `full_document` argument and set it to `False`, which will suppress the opening XML declaration.

Iterating over jxmlease objects

Because `jxmlease` objects behave like dictionaries, lists, or strings, you can use the normal Python operations to iterate over these objects. However, you can also iterate over the objects at parse time. This may be beneficial when you only want to match a small set of XML objects and you can extract all of your data in a loop.

When calling the `Parser` class or `parse()` method, you can supply the `generator` argument with a list of one or more XML paths that the parser should match in the XML. You can specify the paths as either relative or absolute paths. If you supply a list of XML paths in the `generator` argument, the parser will return a Python generator that you can use to iterate over the matching nodes.

For example, let's assume that the XML response shown in Example 2-1 is stored in the variable `xmldoc`. You can iterate over the users as shown in Example 2-4.

Example 2-4. Using a jxmlease generator to parse XML data

```
>>> from jxmlease import parse
>>> for (_, _, userentry) in parse(xmldoc, generator=['user-table/user-entry']):
...     print "Found %s on %s" % (user_entry['user'], user_entry['tty'])
...
Found user on pts/0
Found user on pts/1
```

For each matching node, the generator returns a tuple of (*path*, *match*, *jxmlease_object*). These are described in more detail here:

path
: A textual representation of the XML path to the matching node, similar to the XPath representation of the path to a node. In the case of the XML response shown in Example 2-1, the path to each `<user-entry>` node is `/rpc-reply/system-users-information/uptime-information/user-table/user-entry`.

match
: The match string which triggered the match. In Example 2-4, the match string will always be `user-table/user-entry`.

jxmlease_object
: A jxmlease object representing the matching node. jxmlease objects were described in detail in the previous section.

If you only need a few pieces of information, you can even use the generator feature to extract those few bits of information from the output. For example, this code extends the previous example by extracting the current uptime and user count in addition to the user information it already extracted:

```
>>> from jxmlease import Parser
>>> xmlparser = Parser(generator=['up-time', 'active-user-count', 'user-entry'])
>>> for (_, match, value) in xmlparser(xmldoc):
...     if match == 'up-time':
...         print "Up time: " + value
...     elif match == 'active-user-count':
...         print "User count: " + value
...     elif match == 'user-entry':
...         print "Found %s on %s" % (value['user'], value['tty'])
...     else:
...         print "Error: Unexpected match condition"
...
Up time: 16:41
User count: 2
Found user on pts/0
Found user on pts/1
```

Producing XML output

It is easy to produce XML output from jxmlease objects, using the emit_xml() method. If you have an existing hierarchy of jxmlease objects, you can simply call this method to produce the output. However, if you want to use jxmlease to create XML output from your own data, you will need to create jxmlease objects to hold your data.

You can create your own jxmlease objects in two ways: you can create empty jxmlease objects (or reuse existing ones) and use those objects' methods to modify the XML hierarchy, or you can convert Python data structures into jxmlease objects. You can consult the jxmlease documentation in its GitHub repository for information on the first method. Here, we'll examine the second method: converting Python data structures into jxmlease objects.

The easiest way to create a jxmlease object is to convert your own data, by providing it as an initializer to the appropriate jxmlease class. Normally, you will simply provide a dictionary of XML nodes as an initializer to the jxmlease.XMLDictNode class. As part of the initialization process, the code will recursively descend through the dictionary's data, converting it to appropriate jxmlease objects.

For example, here we create a jxmlease structure from a simple dictionary and emit it as XML:

```
>>> root
{'a': {'c': 'bar', 'b': 'foo'}}
>>> xml_root = jxmlease.XMLDictNode(root)
>>> print xml_root.emit_xml()
<?xml version="1.0" encoding="utf-8"?>
<a>
    <c>bar</c>
    <b>foo</b>
</a>
```

If you don't need to add any XML attributes or make other modifications, you can create the jxmlease object and produce the XML output at the same time:

```
>>> root
{'a': {'c': 'bar', 'b': 'foo'}}
>>> print jxmlease.XMLDictNode(root).emit_xml()
<?xml version="1.0" encoding="utf-8"?>
<a>
    <c>bar</c>
    <b>foo</b>
</a>
```

By default, the jxmlease.XMLDictNode initializer creates a tagless jxmlease.XMLDictNode object to serve as the root node (a "tagless root node"). That top-level object's dictionary contains a key for the actual root XML element. However, by including the tag parameter at initialization time, you can override this default behavior and have the jxmlease.XMLDictNode initializer create a jxmlease.XMLDictNode object with a tag that will function as the root XML element (a "hidden root node"). The members of that top-level object's dictionary will be children of the root XML element. This lets you add one additional layer of hierarchy, if necessary, without modifying the data structure you use as an initializer.

In this example, we call the jxmlease.XMLDictNode initializer with a tag parameter of "newroot". We can see the tag exists by viewing the object's tag attribute. When we view the contents of the dictionary, the tag does not appear in the data structure (hence, a "hidden root node"), but it does appear when we emit the XML:

```
>>> root
{'a': {'c': 'bar', 'b': 'foo'}}
>>> xml_root = jxmlease.XMLDictNode(root, tag="newroot")
>>> print xml_root.tag
newroot
>>> xml_root.prettyprint()
{'a': {'b': u'foo', 'c': u'bar'}}
>>> print xml_root.emit_xml()
<?xml version="1.0" encoding="utf-8"?>
<newroot>
```

```
    <a>
        <c>bar</c>
        <b>foo</b>
    </a>
</newroot>
```

We can combine these behaviors to take a current Python data structure, wrap it in a new tag, and emit XML all in a single command:

```
>>> record = {'firstname': 'Sally', 'lastname': 'Jones'}
>>> print jxmlease.XMLDictNode(record, tag="person").emit_xml()
<?xml version="1.0" encoding="utf-8"?>
<person>
    <lastname>Jones</lastname>
    <firstname>Sally</firstname>
</person>
```

As mentioned in "jxmlease objects" on page 44, you will often want to use the `full_document=False` argument when using the `emit_xml()` method with Junos. Specifying this argument will eliminate the opening XML declaration, as illustrated in the following example:

```
>>> print xml_root.emit_xml(full_document=False)
<a>
    <c>bar</c>
    <b>foo</b>
</a>
```

We can also use the methods described in "jxmlease objects" on page 44 to modify XML attributes prior to emitting the output. For example, here we create `jxmlease` objects from a Python dictionary, add attributes, and emit the resulting XML:

```
>>> xml_root = jxmlease.XMLDictNode(conf_change)
>>> xml_root.prettyprint()
{'configuration': {'interfaces': {'interface': {'description': u'port #1',
                                                'name': u'ge-1/0/0'}}}}
>>> xml_root['configuration']['interfaces']['interface'].set_xml_attr("replace",
...                                                                  "replace")
>>> print xml_root.emit_xml(full_document=False)
<configuration>
    <interfaces>
        <interface replace="replace">
            <name>ge-1/0/0</name>
            <description>port #1</description>
        </interface>
    </interfaces>
</configuration>
```

Running RPCs on a Junos Device

The Junos software provides a standardized interface for conducting operations on the router using the RPC mechanism. These RPCs are documented and publicly available, they run over a standards-based communication channel (NETCONF), and they use a standard format for transferring structured data (XML). In addition, Juniper provides several other mechanisms for executing RPCs, ranging from a RESTful mechanism to Junoscript execution within automation scripts. As described in "JSON data" on page 37, Juniper also supports the JSON data format. For the purposes of this chapter, we will generally focus on XML over NETCONF.

Except where otherwise noted, we will be using NETCONF for the examples in this chapter that involve running RPCs. Although you will probably use a library (or libraries) to ease your interaction with the Junos API, RPCs are such a critical element of automation on a Junos router that you may want to open a NETCONF session on a Junos device and execute some of these RPCs as you read the book. This will give you a feel for the way the RPCs look in practice.

Also, when you encounter difficulties executing RPCs through a client library, it can be helpful to be able to directly execute an RPC on the Junos software. This will eliminate any potential bugs introduced by the library and allow you to directly observe the interaction with the router.

The easiest way to start an interactive NETCONF session is to log in to the CLI and type **netconf**:

```
user@r0> netconf
<!-- No zombies were killed during the creation of this user interface -->
<!-- user user, class j-superuser -->
<hello xmlns="urn:ietf:params:xml:ns:netconf:base:1.0">
  <capabilities>
    <capability>urn:ietf:params:netconf:base:1.0</capability>
    <capability>urn:ietf:params:netconf:capability:candidate:1.0</capability>
    ...output trimmed...
  </capabilities>
  <session-id>3280</session-id>
</hello>
]]>]]>
```

This will change your CLI session into a NETCONF session. Note that it literally transforms the session, so when you end the NETCONF session, you are disconnected from the Junos device. (To end your session, you can use the *request-end-session* RPC.)

Another way to start NETCONF sessions remotely is to enable the NETCONF-over-SSH service. When this service is enabled (using the `set system services netconf ssh` configuration command), you can launch a NETCONF session by making an SSH connection and invoking the `netconf` subsystem. On a Linux machine running OpenSSH, this is accomplished with this syntax:

```
user@h0$ ssh -s user@r0 netconf
Password:
<!-- No zombies were killed during the creation of this user interface -->
<!-- user user, class j-superuser -->
<hello xmlns="urn:ietf:params:xml:ns:netconf:base:1.0">
  <capabilities>
    <capability>urn:ietf:params:netconf:base:1.0</capability>
    <capability>urn:ietf:params:netconf:capability:candidate:1.0</capability>
    ...output trimmed...
  </capabilities>
  <session-id>3504</session-id>
</hello>
]]>]]>
```

The Python `ssh` and `paramiko` libraries have an `invoke_subsystem()` method that serves a similar purpose.

If you are trying to use Python to run NETCONF, you can also try the `ncclient` library. That library should automatically handle some of these details for you. Or, better yet, you can use the PyEZ library, which we describe in more detail in Chapter 4.

What Happened to Junoscript?

Some long-time Junos users may wonder what happened to Junoscript. Junoscript was the pre-NETCONF communication channel for RPCs. Junos contained (and, in fact, still contains) mechanisms for remotely connecting to the router via Junoscript and executing RPCs. However, now that NETCONF has been standardized, Juniper recommends switching to the NETCONF standards-based communication channel.

There are still a few places where you might run into Junoscript, though. Most notably, op, commit, and event scripts written in SLAX or XSLT still use Junoscript when you use `jcs:invoke()` or the default parameters to the `jcs:open()` function. Normally, the functional difference between the two mechanisms is negligible, as both mechanisms will return the same data. Therefore, if you are using a library or tool that will automatically establish and stop the connection for you, you can ignore most of the differences between the two.

One major difference that might impact the way you write scripts is the error handling. While the NETCONF mechanism will typically return an `<rpc-error>` element, the Junoscript mechanism will typically return an `<xnm:error>` element instead. Another major difference occurs in the commit process. When the commit process succeeds, the NETCONF mechanism will typically return an `<ok/>` element, while Junoscript will return a `<commit-success/>` element. Because these small differences change the way you look for indications of errors or success in the RPC responses, you should consider them when writing scripts that will interact with Junoscript.

While preparing an op, commit, or event script, you might find it useful to launch a Junoscript session on a router. If you want to launch an interactive Junoscript session on the router, the easiest way to do that is with the `junoscript interactive` command:

```
user@r0> junoscript interactive version 1.0
<!-- No zombies were killed during the creation of this user interface -->
<!-- user user, class j-superuser -->
```

RPC Authorization

MGD has a schema that tracks all possible CLI commands and RPCs. For each command, the schema lists all possible arguments, the actions that MGD should take to fulfill the command, and the permissions required to execute the command.

When a user attempts to execute an RPC, it generally resolves to the same node in the input schema as the equivalent CLI command. Therefore, if a user has permission to run the CLI command, he should have permission to run the equivalent RPC (and vice versa). This even works when the permissions for individual commands are overridden through RADIUS/TACACS+ attributes or the login class configuration.

For example, suppose the user named `user2` is a member of the `view-clear` class, which has `view` permissions. The class also has an `allow-commands` configuration that gives users permission to run commands that start with `clear bgp`:

```
[edit system login]
user1@r0# show
class view-clear {
    permissions view;
    allow-commands "^clear bgp .*";
}
user user2 {
    uid 2001;
    class view-clear;
    authentication {
        encrypted-password "$5$xGKjch14$W1.bdVB.b9WVs6mX6CobXMMXqUMvq8hTzgDJPD";
    }
}
...output trimmed...
```

When that user attempts to run the *clear-bgp-neighbor* RPC (the equivalent to the `clear bgp neighbor` CLI command), the Junos software correctly authorizes the user to execute the RPC:

```
user2@r0> netconf
...output trimmed...
<rpc>
  <clear-bgp-neighbor>
    <all/>
  </clear-bgp-neighbor>
</rpc>

<rpc-reply xmlns="urn:ietf:params:xml:ns:netconf:base:1.0" xmlns:junos="...">
  <output>Cleared 2 connections</output>
</rpc-reply>
```

There are a few occasions where the command authorization may not exactly match the RPC authorization. This can occur when the same operation is implemented differently when run as an RPC than it is when run as a CLI command. ("The file Commands: The Exceptions That Prove the Rule" on page 70 provides an example where this occurs.) In those cases, the CLI command and RPC point to different entries in MGD's schema, and it is possible that the authorization may differ slightly between those entries. In general, Junos *should* have the same default authorization requirements for the two different entries; however, the RPC's authorization may not change to reflect per-command overrides you made using RADIUS/TACACS+ attributes or the login class configuration.

On the other hand, MGD has a single configuration schema, so there are no differences whether the configuration is loaded through the CLI or using an RPC. A user has the same permissions to view or change portions of the configuration using an RPC as she does using the CLI.

Operational RPCs

The building block of most Junos automation is the RPC. RPCs (sent over NETCONF or a few other channels) tell the router to execute some operation and return results.

There is generally a one-to-one correspondence between CLI commands and RPCs; however, there are some small variations. For example, some CLI commands may use different RPCs depending on the arguments you provide, and other RPCs may not exactly correspond to CLI commands. Still other RPCs may not have CLI command equivalents, just as CLI commands may not have RPC equivalents. (This primarily occurs when the operation does not make sense in a different context. For example, the command `set cli prompt` does not make sense over a NETCONF session.)

When you send an RPC, you enclose it in <rpc> tags. The RPC itself is an XML element, which may have children.

For example, this RPC call gets software information from the router (equivalent to the show version command):

```
<rpc>
  <get-software-information/>
</rpc>
```

And this RPC call gets a briefer version of the software information from the router (equivalent to the show version brief command):

```
<rpc>
  <get-software-information>
    <brief/>
  </get-software-information>
</rpc>
```

The router places its responses in <rpc-reply> tags. By reading the contents of the <rpc-reply> element, you can determine the results of the operation. The response follows a published standard (YANG or DTD); therefore, you are able to reliably parse it and discover the data you seek.

For example, here is a session showing the brief software information for a particular device:

```
<rpc>
  <get-software-information>
    <brief/>
  </get-software-information>
</rpc>
<rpc-reply xmlns:junos="http://xml.juniper.net/junos/12.3R8/junos">
  <software-information>
    <host-name>r0</host-name>
    <product-model>mx80</product-model>
    <product-name>mx80</product-name>
    <package-information>
      <name>junos</name>
      <comment>JUNOS Base OS boot [12.3R8.7]</comment>
    </package-information>
    <package-information>
      <name>jbase</name>
      <comment>JUNOS Base OS Software Suite [12.3R8.7]</comment>
    </package-information>
    <package-information>
      <name>jkernel</name>
      <comment>JUNOS Kernel Software Suite [12.3R8.7]</comment>
    </package-information>
    <package-information>
      <name>jcrypto</name>
      <comment>JUNOS Crypto Software Suite [12.3R8.7]</comment>
```

```
    </package-information>
    <package-information>
      <name>jpfe</name>
      <comment>JUNOS Packet Forwarding Engine Support (MX80) [12.3R8.7]</comment>
    </package-information>
    <package-information>
      <name>jdocs</name>
      <comment>JUNOS Online Documentation [12.3R8.7]</comment>
    </package-information>
    <package-information>
      <name>jroute</name>
      <comment>JUNOS Routing Software Suite [12.3R8.7]</comment>
    </package-information>
  </software-information>
</rpc-reply>
```

If there is an error, the router will place that output in `<rpc-error>` or `<xnm:error>` tags, depending on the access mechanism. For example, here is the response to an invalid command issued over NETCONF:

```
<rpc>
  <get-software-information>
    <summary/>
  </get-software-information>
</rpc>
<rpc-reply xmlns:junos="http://xml.juniper.net/junos/12.3R8/junos">
  <rpc-error>
    <error-type>protocol</error-type>
    <error-tag>operation-failed</error-tag>
    <error-severity>error</error-severity>
    <error-message>syntax error, expecting &lt;invoke-on&gt;</error-message>
    <error-info>
      <bad-element>summary</bad-element>
    </error-info>
  </rpc-error>
</rpc-reply>
```

RPC Output Formats

You can request that the router output the data in various formats, including XML (the default), JSON, or even the text format that the CLI would display. You do this by including the `format` attribute on the RPC request.

For example, let's compare the terse interface information about the `fxp0` interface in XML, JSON, and text formats. Here is the XML output:

```
<rpc>
  <get-interface-information format="xml">
    <terse/>
    <interface-name>fxp0</interface-name>
  </get-interface-information>
</rpc>
```

```
<rpc-reply xmlns="urn:ietf:params:xml:ns:netconf:base:1.0"
           xmlns:junos="http://xml.juniper.net/junos/15.1R2/junos">
  <interface-information xmlns="http://xml.juniper.net/junos/15.1R2/..."
                         junos:style="terse">
    <physical-interface>
      <name>
        fxp0
      </name>
      <admin-status>
        up
      </admin-status>
      <oper-status>
        up
      </oper-status>
      <logical-interface>
        <name>
          fxp0.0
        </name>
        <admin-status>
          up
        </admin-status>
        <oper-status>
          up
        </oper-status>
        <filter-information>
        </filter-information>
        <address-family>
          <address-family-name>
            inet
          </address-family-name>
          <interface-address>
            <ifa-local junos:emit="emit">
              10.92.250.9/23
            </ifa-local>
          </interface-address>
        </address-family>
      </logical-interface>
    </physical-interface>
  </interface-information>
</rpc-reply>
```

Here is the JSON format of the same output:

```
<rpc>
  <get-interface-information format="json">
    <terse/>
    <interface-name>fxp0</interface-name>
  </get-interface-information>
</rpc>
<rpc-reply xmlns="urn:ietf:params:xml:ns:netconf:base:1.0"
           xmlns:junos="http://xml.juniper.net/junos/15.1R2/junos">
{
 "interface-information" : [
```

```
{
    "attributes" : {"xmlns" : "http://xml.juniper.net/junos/15.1R2/...",
                    "junos:style" : "terse"
                   },
    "physical-interface" : [
    {
        "name" : [
        {
            "data" : "fxp0"
        }
        ],
        "admin-status" : [
        {
            "data" : "up"
        }
        ],
        "oper-status" : [
        {
            "data" : "up"
        }
        ],
        "logical-interface" : [
        {
            "name" : [
            {
                "data" : "fxp0.0"
            }
            ],
            "admin-status" : [
            {
                "data" : "up"
            }
            ],
            "oper-status" : [
            {
                "data" : "up"
            }
            ],
            "filter-information" : [
            {
            }
            ],
            "address-family" : [
            {
                "address-family-name" : [
                {
                    "data" : "inet"
                }
                ],
                "interface-address" : [
                {
                    "ifa-local" : [
```

```
                    {
                        "data" : "10.92.250.9/23",
                        "attributes" : {"junos:emit" : "emit"}
                    }
                    ]
                }
                ]
            }
            ]
        }
        ]
    }
    ]
  }
  ]
}
</rpc-reply>
```

And here is the text format of the same output:

```
<rpc>
  <get-interface-information format="text">
    <terse/>
    <interface-name>fxp0</interface-name>
  </get-interface-information>
</rpc>
<rpc-reply xmlns="urn:ietf:params:xml:ns:netconf:base:1.0"
           xmlns:junos="http://xml.juniper.net/junos/15.1R2/junos">
  <output>
Interface               Admin Link Proto    Local                 Remote
fxp0                    up    up
fxp0.0                  up    up   inet     10.92.250.9/23
  </output>
</rpc-reply>
```

The process of converting data from its native XML representation to one of the alternate formats can be processor-intensive. It often involves the router creating the XML data and then mechanically converting it to the alternate format prior to returning it to the user. This can lead to increased latency in returning the data, as well as higher CPU utilization during the data processing.

For most CLI commands with small output documents, this difference should be negligible. However, it is worth noting that you may observe these changes with large output documents or a large number of RPCs being executed in a small time frame.

Discovering Operational RPC Syntax

One of the obvious questions is: how do I discover which RPCs to use to get a set of information? There are several methods. First, you can use the "Junos XML API Operations Developer Reference," (*http://www.juniper.net/techpubs/en_US/junos15.1/information-products/topic-collections/junos-xml-ref-oper/index.html?junos-xml-ref-oper.html*) which documents these RPCs. Second, you can look at example scripts that exist on the Internet. But perhaps the easiest method is to simply ask the CLI to help you.

When You Just Need Your CLI Command...

The special *command* RPC will let you execute CLI commands over an XML session (such as NETCONF or Junoscript) and return XML output. In many cases, this is equivalent to executing a properly formed unique RPC.

For example, here we execute the `show system uptime` command using the *command* RPC:

```
<rpc>
  <command>show system uptime</command>
</rpc>
<rpc-reply xmlns="urn:ietf:params:xml:ns:netconf:base:1.0"
           xmlns:junos="http://xml.juniper.net/junos/15.1R2/junos">
  <system-uptime-information xmlns="http://xml.juniper.net/junos/15.1R2/...">
    <current-time>
      <date-time junos:seconds="1446843691">
        2015-11-06 13:01:31 PST
      </date-time>
    </current-time>
    <time-source>
      LOCAL CLOCK
    </time-source>
    ...output trimmed...
  </system-uptime-information>
</rpc-reply>
```

While the *command* RPC can be useful, it can have some unintended consequences when it causes the system to run a different set of code than the equivalent RPC. As described in "The file Commands: The Exceptions That Prove the Rule" on page 70, some of the `file` commands are particularly susceptible to unintended consequences.

The `display xml rpc` pipe command will show the XML RPC equivalent for most CLI command strings, including a command's arguments. For example, to see the equivalent RPCs for the `show version` and `show version brief` commands, enter these commands:

```
user@r0> show version | display xml rpc
<rpc-reply xmlns:junos="http://xml.juniper.net/junos/12.3R8/junos">
    <rpc>
        <get-software-information>
        </get-software-information>
    </rpc>
    <cli>
        <banner></banner>
    </cli>
</rpc-reply>

user@r0> show version brief | display xml rpc
<rpc-reply xmlns:junos="http://xml.juniper.net/junos/12.3R8/junos">
    <rpc>
        <get-software-information>
            <brief/> </get-software-information>
    </rpc>
    <cli>
        <banner></banner>
    </cli>
</rpc-reply>
```

This output shows that `<get-software-information></get-software-information>` is the equivalent RPC for the `show version` command and that `<get-software-information><brief/></get-software-information>` is the equivalent RPC for the `show version brief` command.

Data Modeling Differences: The Exceptions That Prove the Rule

Due to slight differences in data modeling, some commands don't return correct RPCs when issued through the CLI. A good example is the `op` command (covered in more detail in Chapter 6).

Here is what the CLI returns:

```
user@r0> op url /var/tmp/test.xslt argument1 value1 | display xml rpc
<rpc-reply xmlns:junos="http://xml.juniper.net/junos/12.3R8/junos">
    <rpc>
        <op-url>
            <url-name>/var/tmp/test.xslt</url-name>
            <argument>
                <name>argument1</name>
                <value>value1</value>
            </argument>
        </op-url>
```

```
    </rpc>
    <cli>
        <banner></banner>
    </cli>
</rpc-reply>
```

However, if you try to use this RPC, you get an error:

```
<rpc>
  <op-url>
    <url-name>/var/tmp/test.xslt</url-name>
    <argument>
      <name>argument1</name>
      <value>value1</value>
    </argument>
  </op-url>
</rpc>
<rpc-reply xmlns="urn:ietf:params:xml:ns:netconf:base:1.0"
           xmlns:junos="http://xml.juniper.net/junos/12.3R8/junos">
  <rpc-error>
    <error-type>protocol</error-type>
    <error-tag>operation-failed</error-tag>
    <error-severity>error</error-severity>
    <error-message>syntax error</error-message>
    <error-info>
      <bad-element>name</bad-element>
    </error-info>
  </rpc-error>
  <rpc-error>
    <error-type>protocol</error-type>
    <error-tag>operation-failed</error-tag>
    <error-severity>error</error-severity>
    <error-message>syntax error</error-message>
    <error-info>
      <bad-element>name</bad-element>
    </error-info>
  </rpc-error>
</rpc-reply>
```

This error is caused by a data modeling difference between the XML and MGD's internal data representation. MGD's internal data representation maintains separate `argument` elements for each argument, with `name` and `value` children. However, when processing the XML, MGD expects to see the argument name be used as the tag for an element and to see the value be given as the value for the element. Therefore, this RPC works much better:

```
<rpc>
  <op-url>
    <url-name>/var/tmp/test.xslt</url-name>
    <argument1>value1</argument1>
  </op-url>
</rpc>
<rpc-reply xmlns="urn:ietf:params:xml:ns:netconf:base:1.0"
```

```
            xmlns:junos="http://xml.juniper.net/junos/12.3R8/junos">
  <pipe>
    <no-custom-handlers/>
  </pipe>
  <output>
    Success
  </output>
</rpc-reply>
```

Another example of a data modeling difference is the XML RPC equivalent for `show route receive-protocol bgp` *`peer`*. Here is the XML RPC you get from the CLI:

```
user@r0> show route receive-protocol bgp 10.0.0.1 | display xml rpc
<rpc-reply xmlns:junos="http://xml.juniper.net/junos/12.3R8/junos">
    <rpc>
        <get-route-information>
            <bgp/>
            <peer>10.0.0.1</peer>
        </get-route-information>
    </rpc>
    <cli>
        <banner></banner>
    </cli>
</rpc-reply>
```

However, if you try to use this RPC, you get an error:

```
<rpc>
  <get-route-information>
    <bgp/>
    <peer>10.0.0.1</peer>
  </get-route-information>
</rpc>
<rpc-reply xmlns="urn:ietf:params:xml:ns:netconf:base:1.0"
           xmlns:junos="http://xml.juniper.net/junos/12.3R8/junos">
  <rpc-error>
    <error-type>protocol</error-type>
    <error-tag>operation-failed</error-tag>
    <error-severity>error</error-severity>
    <error-message>syntax error, expecting &lt;invoke-on&gt;</error-message>
    <error-info>
      <bad-element>bgp</bad-element>
    </error-info>
  </rpc-error>
</rpc-reply>
```

This error is caused by another data modeling discrepancy. This time, instead of the CLI displaying a level of hierarchy that the system does not expect from the XML, it fails to display a level of hierarchy that the system expects to be present. This is caused by a difference between the data structure required of CLI commands and the data structure required of XML RPCs. The CLI command schema actually contains an element that encloses the `bgp` protocol name, but it is marked in the schema as an element that the user is not required to enter when running the command via the CLI. However, the XML formatting does require this element (the `<receive-protocol-name>` tag):

```
<rpc>
  <get-route-information>
    <receive-protocol-name>bgp</receive-protocol-name>
    <peer>10.0.0.1</peer>
  </get-route-information>
</rpc>
<rpc-reply xmlns="urn:ietf:params:xml:ns:netconf:base:1.0"
           xmlns:junos="http://xml.juniper.net/junos/12.3R8/junos">
  <route-information xmlns="http://xml.juniper.net/junos/12.3R8/...">
    <!-- keepalive -->
    <route-table>
      <table-name>inet.0</table-name>
      <destination-count>43</destination-count>
      <total-route-count>43</total-route-count>
      <active-route-count>42</active-route-count>
      <holddown-route-count>0</holddown-route-count>
      <hidden-route-count>1</hidden-route-count>
    </route-table>
    <route-table>
      <table-name>iso.0</table-name>
      <destination-count>1</destination-count>
      <total-route-count>1</total-route-count>
      <active-route-count>1</active-route-count>
      <holddown-route-count>0</holddown-route-count>
      <hidden-route-count>0</hidden-route-count>
    </route-table>
    <route-table>
      <table-name>mpls.0</table-name>
      <destination-count>4</destination-count>
      <total-route-count>4</total-route-count>
      <active-route-count>4</active-route-count>
      <holddown-route-count>0</holddown-route-count>
      <hidden-route-count>0</hidden-route-count>
    </route-table>
    <route-table>
      <table-name>inet6.0</table-name>
      <destination-count>6</destination-count>
      <total-route-count>6</total-route-count>
      <active-route-count>6</active-route-count>
      <holddown-route-count>0</holddown-route-count>
      <hidden-route-count>0</hidden-route-count>
    </route-table>
  </route-information>
</rpc-reply>
```

Juniper does know about these two discrepancies (in fact, they may even be fixed by the time this book is published!). However, if you run into strange things like this, you can always fall back to one of the two methods mentioned earlier: consulting the

"Junos XML API Operations Developer Reference" (*http://www.juniper.net/techpubs/en_US/junos15.1/information-products/topic-collections/junos-xml-ref-oper/index.html?junos-xml-ref-oper.html*) or searching the Internet. It is quite probable that someone else has already encountered the same problem and found the correct syntax.

Discovering RPC Reply Syntax

In addition to determining the syntax for issuing RPCs, you also need to be able to determine the syntax you can expect in reply. Again, you can determine the RPC reply syntax through multiple methods. One method is to consult Juniper's official API reference material (including the YANG and/or DTD models). Another method is to simply look to the router for help.

You can certainly just run RPCs over NETCONF and view the responses. However, you can also use the `display xml` pipe command to view the XML output of a particular CLI command. For example, here we see the XML output in response to the `show route protocol bgp table inet.0` CLI command:

```
user@r0> show route protocol bgp table inet.0 | display xml
<rpc-reply xmlns:junos="http://xml.juniper.net/junos/15.1R2/junos">
    <route-information xmlns="http://xml.juniper.net/junos/15.1R2/junos-routing">
        <!-- keepalive -->
        <route-table>
            <table-name>inet.0</table-name>
            <destination-count>44</destination-count>
            <total-route-count>44</total-route-count>
            <active-route-count>43</active-route-count>
            <holddown-route-count>0</holddown-route-count>
            <hidden-route-count>1</hidden-route-count>
        </route-table>
    </route-information>
    <cli>
        <banner></banner>
    </cli>
</rpc-reply>
```

If you are using Expect scripts to parse CLI output, you can gain an immediate advantage by changing your scripts to parse the XML output. This should provide you with a more stable interface from which to gather information. And, because you can use more robust tools to parse the XML output, it should make the scripts less susceptible to breaking when there are minor changes in the CLI output.

To change your scripts to use XML output, simply append the `display xml` pipe command. (However, do be careful of using certain commands. See "The file Commands: The Exceptions That Prove the Rule" on page 70.)

By using the combination of the `display xml rpc` and `display xml` pipe commands, you can see the RPC syntax equivalent to a CLI command string and the RPC reply syntax. This information is very useful when building automation scripts that use RPCs.

The syntax discovery mechanisms provided in this chapter can be quite useful. However, it is important that you thoroughly test your scripts on any platform on which they will run. There are sometimes slight differences between platforms. It could even be the case that the RPC or RPC reply syntax varies slightly between Junos platforms.

There are certain cases where you would expect this to occur, such as with platform-specific Class of Service (CoS) features. However, these differences sometimes impact features that you might expect to be the same across platforms (such as LLDP).

Additionally, the same RPCs can produce different output syntax on multichassis systems (such as virtual chassis or SRX cluster configurations) when compared to standalone systems of the same model. On multichassis systems, the output may include an additional level of hierarchy that identifies the chassis that produced the output.

By thoroughly testing your scripts on any platform on which they will run, you can attempt to ensure you have accounted for any variations that may occur.

The file Commands: The Exceptions That Prove the Rule

Just as there are some commands that don't quite behave as expected with the `display xml rpc` pipe command, there are some commands that don't quite behave as expected with the `display xml` pipe command.

As described in "Operational Command Flow" on page 7, the CLI has a special relationship with the router's daemons. Part of this special relationship is that the router can send directives back to the CLI for the CLI to execute. One area where MGD does this is with some of the `file` commands.

For example, observe the results of this simple `file copy` command:

```
user@r0> file copy /dev/null /tmp/test | display xml
<rpc-reply xmlns:junos="http://xml.juniper.net/junos/15.1R2/junos">
    <rpc>
        <file>
            <file-fetch>
                <source-filename>/dev/null</source-filename>
            </file-fetch>
        </file>
    </rpc>
```

The CLI hangs at that point, and the command never returns. This is one of those cases where MGD is providing a directive to the CLI. Normally, when you run the `file copy` command from the CLI, MGD sends a request to the CLI for it to fetch the source file. (You see that request in the preceding output.) Once the CLI has completed fetching the source file, it will send an XML response to MGD telling MGD where it has temporarily stored the file. Then, MGD will send another request to the CLI to transfer the file from that location to its final destination.

Here, the process hangs because the CLI displays the XML request, rather than executing it. Therefore, the CLI never responds to MGD with the location of the temporary file. In the meantime, MGD continues to wait for a response.

Of course, you have ample warning that something a little different is at work in these commands. If you use the `display xml rpc` pipe command to determine the RPC string to use for this command string, it will tell you that no equivalent is available:

```
user@r0> file copy /dev/null /tmp/test | display xml rpc
<rpc-reply xmlns:junos="http://xml.juniper.net/junos/15.1R2/junos">
    <message>
        xml rpc equivalent of this command is not available.
    </message>
    <cli>
        <banner></banner>
    </cli>
</rpc-reply>
```

This message may seem a little misleading, as there actually *is* an equivalent RPC. However, the CLI command and the equivalent RPC access different functions within the management system, and the management system is not able to associate the two automatically.

If you use the *file-copy* RPC, you will see that the router copies files correctly:

```
<rpc>
  <file-copy>
    <source>/dev/null</source>
    <destination>/tmp/test</destination>
  </file-copy>
</rpc>
<rpc-reply xmlns="urn:ietf:params:xml:ns:netconf:base:1.0"
           xmlns:junos="http://xml.juniper.net/junos/15.1R2/junos">
</rpc-reply>
```

You can use the *file-list* RPC to confirm that the router performed the file copy operation:

```
<rpc>
  <file-list>
    <path>/tmp/test</path>
  </file-list>
</rpc>
<rpc-reply xmlns="urn:ietf:params:xml:ns:netconf:base:1.0"
           xmlns:junos="http://xml.juniper.net/junos/15.1R2/junos">
  <directory-list root-path="/tmp/test" junos:seconds="1437072676"
                  junos:style="brief">
    <directory name="">
      <file-information>
        <file-name>
          /tmp/test
        </file-name>
      </file-information>
      <total-files>
        1
      </total-files>
    </directory>
  </directory-list>
</rpc-reply>
```

Configuration with RPCs

To configure a Junos device, you simply run the correct set of RPCs in the correct order. However, there are some special considerations that may seem specific to the configuration RPCs.

In this section, we start by describing the XML representation of the configuration. That XML representation serves as an argument to one or more RPCs. Once we've discussed the way the configuration is represented, we'll move on to discuss the RPCs you can use to configure a device or view the device's configuration.

Configuration Representation in XML

Even in text format, the Junos configuration is represented in a highly structured way. Consider this example of a typical interface configuration:

```
interfaces {
    ge-1/0/0 {
        vlan-tagging;
        unit 0 {
            vlan-id 60;
            family inet {
                address 192.168.2.1/24;
            }
        }
    }
}
```

Here, the information is maintained in a clear hierarchy. The `interfaces` hierarchy, contains the configuration of the interfaces in the system. In this case, there is an interface named `ge-1/0/0` that has data within it. There is a leaf node called `vlan-tagging`, which is a directive without data (an "empty element," if you will), and a unit named `0` that has configuration data. Within that unit's configuration, there is a leaf node called `vlan-id`, which has a value of `60`. There is also configuration for an address family named `inet`, which contains an `address` element with a value of `192.168.2.1/24`. Here, the structured data format is fairly obvious.

Likewise, the conversion to XML is fairly straightforward. If you simply guessed at the conversion, you would probably come pretty close to being correct. However, let's explore some of the details of the official Juniper representation of the preceding configuration:

```
<configuration> ❶
  <interfaces>
    <interface>
      <name>ge-1/0/0</name> ❷
      <vlan-tagging/>
      <unit>
        <name>0</name> ❸
        <vlan-id>60</vlan-id>
        <family>
          <inet> ❹
            <address>
              <name>192.168.2.1/24</name> ❺
            </address>
          </inet>
        </family>
      </unit>
```

```
    </interface>
  </interfaces>
</configuration>
```

❶ When used as an argument to an RPC, a Junos configuration snippet is always enclosed in the `<configuration>` tag and contains the intermediate hierarchy between the root `<configuration>` tag and the elements that are specified in the configuration snippet.

Likewise, when the Junos software returns a portion of the configuration to a user, it will always enclose the configuration in the `<configuration>` tag and provide the intermediate hierarchy between the root `<configuration>` tag and the elements it is trying to return. (You can demonstrate this behavior for yourself using the CLI command `show configuration interfaces` *`interface`* `| display xml`.)

❷ Here, you see the interface configuration is actually within an `<interface>` element. Each `<interface>` element is identified by a `<name>` element. This differs slightly from the text representation of the configuration (where the `interface` identifier is not used). However, this additional hierarchy produces XML that is easier to parse.

The published DTD or YANG schema for the `<interface>` element contains all the configuration a user is allowed to place there. The user can use as many of those configuration statements as are required to correctly configure each interface. Each interface is then distinguished using the unique identifier in the `<name>` element.

❸ Like the `<interface>` element, each unit is in a separate `<unit>` element that is uniquely identified by the value of the `<name>` element. Unlike with the `<interface>` element, the word `unit` does appear in the text representation of the configuration.

❹ This element may seem to break the rule we just discussed for the `<interface>` and `<unit>` elements. Following that rule, it seems like this element should be: `<family><name>inet</name></family>`.

However, the XML structure Juniper uses here really does make sense when considered from a data modeling point of view. All `<interface>` elements can contain (mostly) the same configuration. Likewise, all `<unit>` elements can contain (mostly) the same configuration. However, different families have different configuration requirements. Therefore, while it makes sense to use a common schema for all interfaces and a common schema for all units, it also makes sense to have different XML schemas for the different address families. And having different schemas means that the different address families should use different tags.

❺ At first glance, this syntax may appear somewhat awkward. After all, couldn't this element just be `<address>192.168.2.1/24</address>`?

However, the address actually can have configuration associated with it. Therefore, the `<address>` element needs to be an element that can contain other elements. The `<name>` element uniquely identifies this `<address>` element.

The preceding example introduces several important concepts in the XML representation of the Junos configuration:

- Junos configurations—even configuration snippets—start from the root `<configuration>` element.
- Elements that can appear multiple times with the same schema use a common tag name. Each element is distinguished by a unique key. (In these examples, the value of the `<name>` element was the unique key. However, that is not always the case. There may even be instances where a key is derived from more than one element.)
- Configuration elements with different schemas are generally contained in different tags.

Discovering the Unique Key Used to Identify Configuration Elements

It is important to determine the unique key, or keys, used to differentiate different elements of the same tag. For example, as shown previously, the `<name>` child element distinguishes different `<interface>` elements. You must include the `<name>` child element to uniquely identify the parent element (e.g., when using the *get-configuration* RPC). Also, subsequent configuration elements that use the same key are merged into a single configuration element. In short, to understand *which* `<interface>` element you are modifying, you must look for the `<name>` child element.

You can determine which child element is the unique key for a configuration element by consulting the Junos configuration YANG module (*http://juni.pr/1TDPV9o*). (Look for the `key` item.)

Alternatively, you can include the `junos:key="key"` attribute on the *get-configuration* RPC. This causes Junos to include the `junos:key="key"` attribute on configuration elements that serve as a key for their parent element.

The following example illustrates two important concepts. First, it shows that you must include the key within an element in order to uniquely identify the configuration element. We do this by specifying the `<name>` element within the `<interface>`

hierarchy. This lets us specify exactly *which* `<interface>` element we want to retrieve. Second, this example shows how including the `junos:key="key"` attribute on the *get-configuration* RPC causes Junos to tell you which elements are keys. Here, the presence of the `junos:key="key"` attribute on some elements of the reply tells us that the `<name>` element is the key for the `<interface>`, `<unit>`, and `<address>` elements.

Suppose you issue this XML request:

```
<rpc>
  <get-configuration junos:key="key">
    <configuration>
      <interfaces>
        <interface>
          <name>ge-1/0/0</name>
        </interface>
      </interfaces>
    </configuration>
  </get-configuration>
</rpc>
```

After issuing the XML request, you will receive this response:

```
<rpc-reply xmlns="urn:ietf:params:xml:ns:netconf:base:1.0"
           xmlns:junos="http://xml.juniper.net/junos/15.1R2/junos">
  <configuration xmlns="http://xml.juniper.net/xnm/1.1/xnm"
                 junos:changed-seconds="1437219681"
                 junos:changed-localtime="2015-07-18 04:41:21 PDT">
    <interfaces>
      <interface>
        <name junos:key="key">ge-1/0/0</name>
        <vlan-tagging/>
        <unit>
          <name junos:key="key">0</name>
          <vlan-id>60</vlan-id>
          <family>
            <inet>
              <address>
                <name junos:key="key">192.168.2.1/24</name>
              </address>
            </inet>
          </family>
        </unit>
      </interface>
    </interfaces>
  </configuration>
</rpc-reply>
```

Discovering XML Configuration Syntax

Discovering the XML configuration syntax is similar to discovering the XML RPC syntax. Your three choices are to look at the official API documentation (the "Junos

XML API Configuration Developer Reference" (*https://www.juniper.net/techpubs*)), look for samples on the Internet, or ask the router for help.

Juniper publishes a DTD and a YANG module for the configuration. Using the DTD, it is possible to use a tool such as *xmllint* to do offline validation of your configuration stanza, verifying that it is well-formed, valid configuration syntax. (Note that even well-formed configuration syntax may still fail various runtime validation checks once it is entered on the router.) The YANG module provides additional data (such as data typing and the keys used to uniquely identify elements) that may be helpful in understanding the nuances of the data model. For these reasons, it may be wise to explore these formal documents as you do more Junos automation.

However, in many cases, the easiest way to discover XML configuration syntax is to ask the device to tell you the syntax. Often, automation is meant to configure a small set of configuration parameters. In those cases, you can just ask the device to describe the syntax for those parameters.

For example, let's assume that you want to configure interfaces with a set of parameters that may include descriptions, VLAN IDs, IPv4 addresses, MPLS, and IPv4 firewall filters. In that case, you can configure such an interface and then ask the CLI to show you the equivalent XML:

```
user@r0> configure
Entering configuration mode

[edit]
user@r0# edit interfaces ge-1/1/1

[edit interfaces ge-1/1/1]
user@r0# set description "sample IFD description"

[edit interfaces ge-1/1/1]
user@r0# set vlan-tagging

[edit interfaces ge-1/1/1]
user@r0# set unit 0 description "sample IFL description"

[edit interfaces ge-1/1/1]
user@r0# set unit 0 vlan-id 10

[edit interfaces ge-1/1/1]
user@r0# set unit 0 family inet address 10.1.1.1/30

[edit interfaces ge-1/1/1]
user@r0# set unit 0 family inet filter input my-input-filter

[edit interfaces ge-1/1/1]
user@r0# set unit 0 family inet filter output my-output-filter

[edit interfaces ge-1/1/1]
```

```
user@r0# set unit 0 family mpls

[edit interfaces ge-1/1/1]
user@r0# show | display xml | no-more
<rpc-reply xmlns:junos="http://xml.juniper.net/junos/15.1R2/junos">
    <configuration junos:changed-seconds="1437219681"
                   junos:changed-localtime="2015-07-18 04:41:21 PDT">
        <interfaces>
            <interface>
                <name>ge-1/1/1</name>
                    <description>sample IFD description</description>
                    <vlan-tagging/>
                    <unit>
                        <name>0</name>
                        <description>sample IFL description</description>
                        <vlan-id>10</vlan-id>
                        <family>
                            <inet>
                                <filter>
                                <input>
                                    <filter-name>my-input-filter</filter-name>
                                </input>
                                <output>
                                    <filter-name>my-output-filter</filter-name>
                                </output>
                            </filter>
                            <address>
                                <name>10.1.1.1/30</name>
                            </address>
                        </inet>
                        <mpls>
                        </mpls>
                    </family>
                </unit>
            </interface>
        </interfaces>
    </configuration>
    <cli>
        <banner>[edit interfaces ge-1/1/1]</banner>
    </cli>
</rpc-reply>
```

Note that the router only showed us the configuration for the ge-1/1/1 interface because we were editing the configuration at that level of the configuration hierarchy. However, as mentioned earlier, the router returns a document rooted at the <configuration> element, and includes the intermediate XML hierarchy between the <configuration> element and the specific <interface> element in question.

You can now use this XML configuration document as a template for your script to use when making configuration changes.

Most automation scripts work on a constrained set of configuration parameters. In such cases, this is probably the easiest method to use to discover the appropriate XML configuration syntax.

The YANG module and DTD remain available for you to use to determine the full configuration syntax. However, their full value probably becomes more apparent as the complexity of the automation script rises. For example, in the extreme, an automation product that must handle *all* router configuration should probably make extensive use of the YANG module and/or DTD.

However, for many common uses, where the script only needs to handle a constrained set of configuration parameters, discovering the syntax using the `display xml` pipe command is probably sufficient.

Operational RPCs to View and Change the Configuration

The Junos software contains a set of operational RPCs that allow you to view and set the configuration. In order to understand these RPCs, it is important to understand the different configuration databases available on the router, and the different configuration modes (such as "private" and "exclusive"). These concepts are covered in detail in "Configuration Databases and the Commit Model" on page 11.

In brief, here are the RPCs covered in this section:

get-configuration
: This RPC retrieves a configuration. By default, it retrieves the candidate configuration for the current configuration database. However, by providing different XML attributes, a user can modify which configuration database is displayed.

lock-configuration
: This RPC locks the candidate configuration. (This is roughly equivalent to typing `configure exclusive` in the CLI.)

unlock-configuration
: This RPC unlocks a candidate configuration that the user previously locked with the *lock-configuration* RPC. If the candidate configuration contains uncommitted changes, those changes are discarded.

open-configuration
: This RPC allows you to "open" a configuration database. As described in "Configuration Databases and the Commit Model" on page 11, this allows a user to access a private configuration database.

close-configuration
: This RPC "closes" a private configuration database that the user opened with the *open-configuration* RPC. If the private candidate configuration contains uncommitted changes, those changes are discarded.

load-configuration
: This RPC allows you to change the candidate configuration database. You can use this RPC to make a variety of changes, including the equivalents of the `load`, `set`, `rollback`, and `delete` configuration-mode CLI commands.

commit-configuration
: This RPC allows you to commit configuration changes. It does not unlock or close configuration databases; you must perform those actions separately.

Viewing the Configuration

You can view the configuration using the *get-configuration* RPC. Just as you can limit the portions of the configuration you see by adding the configuration hierarchy to the `show configuration` CLI command, you can likewise limit the portions of the configuration you view with the *get-configuration* RPC. You do this by placing the configuration hierarchy within the `<get-configuration>` XML element.

For example, this RPC will show you the configuration of interface `ge-1/0/1.0`. This is equivalent to typing `show configuration interfaces ge-1/0/1 unit 0` at the Junos CLI:

```
<rpc>
  <get-configuration>
    <configuration>
      <interfaces>
        <interface>
          <name>ge-1/0/1</name>
          <unit>
            <name>0</name>
          </unit>
        </interface>
      </interfaces>
    </configuration>
  </get-configuration>
</rpc>
```

After issuing the XML request, you will receive this reply:

```
<rpc-reply xmlns="urn:ietf:params:xml:ns:netconf:base:1.0"
           xmlns:junos="http://xml.juniper.net/junos/15.1R2/junos">
  <configuration xmlns="http://xml.juniper.net/xnm/1.1/xnm"
                 junos:changed-seconds="1437230164"
                 junos:changed-localtime="2015-07-18 07:36:04 PDT">
    <interfaces>
```

```
      <interface>
        <name>ge-1/0/1</name>
        <unit>
          <name>0</name>
          <family>
            <inet>
              <address>
                <name>2.2.3.4/24</name>
              </address>
            </inet>
          </family>
        </unit>
      </interface>
    </interfaces>
  </configuration>
</rpc-reply>
```

Note how you must specify the `<name>` child element for both the `<interface>` and `<unit>` parent elements. As explained in "Discovering the Unique Key Used to Identify Configuration Elements" on page 74, you must include the keys to differentiate between multiple elements that use the same tag. Here, because we only wanted to see a particular unit of a particular interface, we needed to include the keys at both those levels.

In addition to limiting the results to a particular section of the configuration hierarchy, you can include several attributes to the *get-configuration* RPC that modify its behavior. We will summarize some of the important ones here:

`changed="changed"`

Including this attribute will cause the Junos software to indicate which portions of the candidate configuration have changed by including the `changed="changed"` XML attribute with any element that has changed. The attribute will also be applied to the parents of those elements. (Therefore, the `<configuration>` tag will always have the `changed="changed"` attribute anytime the configuration has been modified.

If you are instead viewing the committed configuration, the `changed="changed"` attribute will tell you which portions of the configuration were changed in the last commit. (Because automation scripts may not be able to determine which other entities may have committed the configuration since the script last committed the configuration, or even how many commits may have occurred in the intervening time, this functionality may not often be useful to automation scripts. But this description at least explains the expected behavior.) This is the same information the Junos software uses during the commit process to determine which daemons it needs to signal and which portions of the configuration they need to process. (That process is described in more detail in "Signaling daemons" on page 23.)

`database="database"`
: Here, you can specify whether you want to see the `candidate` or `committed` configuration. The default is to view the `candidate` configuration.

`format="format"`
: Here, you can specify the format in which you want to see the configuration. The options are the same as the options for other RPCs: `xml`, `json`, or `text`. (See "RPC Output Formats" on page 59.)

`inherit="what"`
: By default, the returned configuration document does not include any configuration elements inherited from configuration groups, `apply-path` statements, or the default configuration. If you include the `inherit="inherit"` attribute, the returned configuration document will include configuration elements inherited from configuration groups and `apply-path` statements. If you instead include the `inherit="defaults"` attribute, the returned configuration document will include configuration elements inherited from configuration groups, `apply-path` statements, and the default configuration.

`junos:key="key"`
: As described in "Discovering the Unique Key Used to Identify Configuration Elements" on page 74, this attribute will cause the Junos software to include the `junos:key="key"` attribute on child configuration elements that serve as keys for their parents.

Changing the Configuration

When you change the configuration, you typically follow the same flow:

1. You choose the database you will modify. Your choices include using the normal shared configuration database (which is the default), gaining an exclusive lock on the shared configuration database, or using a private configuration database.
2. You load the configuration changes. While doing this, you can choose various loading styles (or "actions"), such as merging the configuration changes, replacing the current configuration with the loaded configuration, or replacing just portions of the configuration.
3. You commit the configuration change. Again, you can use several commit styles or actions to control the way the commit operation works.
4. If necessary, you close or unlock the configuration database.

In this section, we cover the most common options used in automation scripts. We do *not* try to exhaustively cover all possible options for changing the configuration. For more comprehensive coverage of options that are less common in automation scripts, see Juniper's "NETCONF XML Management Protocol Developer Guide" (*http://www.juniper.net/techpubs*).

This section is rather XML-heavy. If you have an ingrained negative feeling about XML, don't let that stop you from reading it. You can use these same RPCs to apply text configuration statements, and understanding the way these RPCs work should still be helpful when using other methods (such as PyEZ) that hide the details of the NETCONF interaction from you.

Choosing a database

When configuring a device, you need to choose the database you will modify. By default, the Junos software will work on the shared configuration database without a lock. However, you can instead choose to gain an exclusive lock on the shared configuration database or use a private configuration database. (These options are described in more detail in "Configuration Databases and the Commit Model" on page 11.)

Typically, you want an automation script to use one of the nondefault methods. Put differently, you typically *do not* want an automation script to modify the shared candidate configuration database without a lock. With the default method, multiple scripts or users that are trying to modify the configuration at the same time may interact with each other in unpredictable ways. One user or script may commit partial changes that another user or script is in the process of loading. Worse still, a script may be making changes that are predicated on the current state of the configuration. If another user or script changes that predicate configuration, the changes that the script wants to make may then be incorrect.

For these reasons, it is best to use one of the configuration methods that limit the unintended interactions between scripts and users (or other scripts). If a script relies on predicate configuration (this includes the case where a script reads the current configuration to determine which changes should be made), it should probably make changes with an exclusive lock on the shared configuration database. The exclusive lock ensures the predicate configuration exists prior to making changes.

If a script does not interact with existing configuration, it can make its changes either with an exclusive lock on the shared configuration database or in a private database. Both provide protection from unintended interactions between multiple sessions that attempt to change the configuration at the same time. However, the actual behavior differs between these mechanisms. Modifying a private configuration database provides the possibility of multiple independent configuration changes occurring in parallel; however, the commits are still serialized, and any conflict between two commits causes the second commit to fail (until the conflict is resolved).

Another consideration is the way scripts interact with users who are manually editing the configuration. When a user is editing the configuration, scripts are not able to either gain an exclusive lock on the configuration or open a private database. This means that by simply leaving a configuration session open, a user could potentially block automation scripts that try to gain an exclusive configuration lock or edit a private database. If the user doesn't realize this interaction exists, he might leave the session open for hours, blocking automation scripts from committing changes during that entire time. Therefore, if it is common to have time-sensitive configuration changes from automation scripts intermingled with manual changes by users, it may be best to have scripts make their changes in a private configuration database and force all users to use `configure private` to edit the configuration.

As described in "Operational RPCs to View and Change the Configuration" on page 78, you gain an exclusive lock on the shared configuration database using the *lock-configuration* RPC, or open a private configuration database using the *open-configuration* RPC.

For the reasons described in this section and in "Configuration Databases" on page 11, automation scripts should typically use an exclusive lock or a private database to commit their changes. However, as described in "Other configuration editing modes" on page 16, there are various errors your script may encounter while acquiring an exclusive lock or using a private configuration database. Your automation scripts must handle these occurrences.

An error that is typically easy to handle is a failure to acquire an exclusive lock. In that case, the script can simply wait several seconds and try again to acquire the lock. However, the script should only retry a limited number of times, lest it become stuck in an infinite loop. If the script is unable to acquire the lock after retrying several times, the problem becomes more difficult to handle: should the script attempt to detect the reason it is unable to acquire the lock and resolve it (by forcibly logging out a user, or by rolling back configuration changes in the shared database)? Perhaps, but you must carefully consider the implications of this decision.

Other error conditions may require different considerations. See "Other configuration editing modes" on page 16 for further information.

Loading configuration changes

There are two main decisions you need to make when loading configuration changes: the source of the configuration data, and the way it is applied. You communicate this information to the Junos software using attributes or child elements of the *load-configuration* RPC.

You can load configuration data from several sources. You can load from a file using the `url` attribute. The URL can be any file specifier you would use at the Junos CLI. For local files, you can simply specify the file. For files on a particular RE, you can use the `reN:/path/to/file` syntax. For remote files, you can use a normal URL.

Alternatively, you can load a rollback configuration using the `rollback="N"` attribute.

Be careful loading rollback configurations other than the current committed configuration (`rollback="0"`) in an automation script. Unless you hold an exclusive lock on the configuration database, you cannot accurately predict how many commits will occur between the time you choose which rollback configuration to load and the time you actually load the rollback configuration.

Finally, you can supply the configuration as a child element of the *load-configuration* RPC. The configuration data can be in XML or text format. If the data is in XML format, you enclose it in a `<configuration>` element (as described in "Configuration Representation in XML" on page 72). If the data is in text format, you enclose it in a `<configuration-text>` element if it is in the normal Junos configuration (curly brace) format, or in a `<configuration-set>` element if it is a list of CLI configuration commands (such as `set`, `delete`, `deactivate`, etc.). If using a format other than XML, you must specify the format using the `format` attribute.

Once you have supplied the configuration, you also need to specify the way Junos should merge the new configuration statements with the existing statements. You do this by including an `action` attribute on the *load-configuration* RPC. The value of the `action` attribute can be one of the values from the following list:

`merge`
: This action is the default. Junos simply adds the new configuration to the existing configuration. Statements in the new configuration that can only have a single value (such as an interface description) override the previous value in the existing configuration. Otherwise, the new configuration will simply be added to the existing configuration.

`replace`
: This action behaves the same as the `merge` action, with one very important exception. If any portion of the configuration hierarchy is marked with the `replace="replace"` attribute, that portion of the configuration hierarchy is deleted before the new configuration data is merged into the configuration.

`override` *or* `update`
: These actions effectively delete the *entire* shared configuration database before merging in the changes. In effect, the entire shared configuration database is replaced with the configuration you are loading.

  These two actions work in slightly different ways. The `override` action uses less CPU while loading the configuration, but causes all daemons to reread the entire configuration at commit time. On the other hand, the `update` action uses more CPU while loading the configuration, but allows daemons to determine the configuration differences, which may reduce the CPU used at commit time and reduce the time needed to activate the new configuration.

`set`
: This action causes the Junos software to apply a list of CLI configuration commands (such as `set`, `delete`, `deactivate`, etc.) that you supply. If you specify this action, you must obviously provide the input data in "text" format and enclose the configuration statements in a `<configuration-set>` element.

Some examples may be helpful. To load the currently committed configuration (the `rollback 0` configuration), effectively undoing any changes to the candidate configuration, use this syntax:

```
<rpc>
  <load-configuration rollback="0"/>
</rpc>
```

To replace the existing `ge-1/0/0` configuration, use syntax like the following. Note the `replace="replace"` attribute on the `<interface>` element means the matching element in the existing configuration will be deleted prior to merging in the new configuration. However, as we have seen earlier, the `<interface>` element is identified by the `<name>` child element. Therefore, only the `ge-1/0/0` interface will be replaced in this example:

```
<rpc>
  <load-configuration action="replace">
    <configuration>
      <interfaces>
        <interface replace="replace">
          <name>ge=1/0/0</name>
          <unit>
            <name>0</name>
            <family>
              <inet>
                <address>
                  <name>172.16.1.1/24</name>
                </address>
              </inet>
            </family>
```

```
            </unit>
          </interface>
        </interfaces>
      </configuration>
    </load-configuration>
  </rpc>
```

To add the `ge-1/0/0` interface using Junos text configuration format, use this syntax:

```
<rpc>
  <load-configuration format="text">
    <configuration-text>
      interfaces {
          ge-1/0/0 {
              unit 0 {
                  family inet {
                      address 172.16.1.1/24;
                  }
              }
          }
      }
    </configuration-text>
  </load-configuration>
</rpc>
```

Finally, to load a text-formatted configuration from a file stored on the RE named */var/tmp/newconf.conf*, use this syntax:

```
<rpc>
  <load-configuration url="/var/tmp/newconf.conf"
                      format="text"/>
</rpc>
```

Reordering configuration elements

Certain configuration elements, such as firewall filters and routing policies, contain ordered elements where the order is important. You can use the XML API to reorder elements, or place new elements at the correct location.

The Junos software defaults to adding all new elements to the end of an ordered set. You can then move them after you have added them, but before you commit the configuration. You can move existing elements at any time.

To change the order of an element, you add the `insert` attribute to the element. The `insert` attribute takes three values: `before`, `after`, or `first`. The `first` value moves the element to the top of the ordered set. The `before` and `after` values cause the element to be placed before or after the element indicated by the `name` attribute.

The operation takes this general form:

```
<element-name insert="before|after|first" name="reference-element-id">
    <name>moving-element-id</name>
</element-name>
```

Here is an example of a firewall filter that we want to modify. The firewall filter is named `example` and has two terms, `reject-one` and `default-accept`, in that order:

```
<configuration>
  <firewall>
    <family>
      <inet>
        <filter>
          <name>example</name>
          <term>
            <name>reject-one</name>
            <from>
              <prefix-list>
                <name>abc</name>
              </prefix-list>
            </from>
            <then>
              <reject>
              </reject>
            </then>
          </term>
          <term>
            <name>default-accept</name>
            <then>
              <accept/>
            </then>
          </term>
        </filter>
      </inet>
    </family>
  </firewall>
</configuration>
```

This XML will add a new term named `reject-two` and insert it before the `default-accept` term:

```
<rpc>
  <load-configuration>
    <configuration>
      <firewall>
        <family>
          <inet>
            <filter>
              <name>example</name>
              <term> ❶
                <name>reject-two</name>
                <from>
```

```
                        <prefix-list>
                          <name>reject-prefixes-two</name>
                        </prefix-list>
                      </from>
                      <then>
                        <reject/>
                      </then>
                    </term>
                    <term insert="before" name="default-accept"> ❷
                      <name>reject-two</name>
                    </term>
                  </filter>
                </inet>
              </family>
            </firewall>
          </configuration>
        </load-configuration>
      </rpc>
```

❶ This <term> element adds the new reject-two term.

❷ This <term> element moves the new reject-two term (identified by the <name> element) before the default-accept element (identified by the name XML attribute).

Deleting configuration elements

You can delete configuration elements by including the delete="delete" attribute on the element. If the element requires a key to identify it, you will need to include the key to identify the specific element you wish to delete.

For example, this XML will delete the term named reject-two from the example firewall filter:

```
<rpc>
  <load-configuration>
    <configuration>
      <firewall>
        <family>
          <inet>
            <filter>
              <name>example</name>
              <term delete="delete">
                <name>reject-two</name>
              </term>
            </filter>
          </inet>
        </family>
      </firewall>
    </configuration>
```

```
    </load-configuration>
  </rpc>
```

Choosing a commit style

You have several options available to modify the way the commit operation is completed. You specify the way you want the commit to be completed by adding child elements to the `<commit-configuration>` element. Here are some of the common elements:

`<log>`*`A text log message`*`</log>`
: This option allows you to specify a log message that describes the commit. This message is available in the Junos event that records the commit. It is also available via the `show system commit` CLI command.

`<confirmed/>`
: This option specifies that you want to use the confirmed commit functionality. If the commit is not followed by another commit prior to the confirmation timeout, the Junos software will automatically rollback to the previous configuration. Once you (or your script) are sure that the configuration is "safe," you execute a second (nonconfirmed) commit operation to cancel the confirmation timer. In this way, you can detect (and attempt to automatically undo) a configuration change that renders your Junos device unreachable.

  Of course, this only works with a low rate of commits. With a high commit rate, it is difficult to use the confirmed commit functionality.

`<confirm-timeout>`*`N`*`</confirm-timeout>`
: If the `<confirmed>` element is also present, this element specifies the confirmation timeout, in minutes, used for the confirmed commit. (If this element is omitted, the default confirmation timeout is 10 minutes.)

`<synchronize/>`
: This option specifies the configuration should be synchronized to all routing engines. Note you can make this action the default for all commit operations on a Junos device by setting the `synchronize` configuration element in the `[edit system commit]` hierarchy. For Junos devices with multiple routing engines, we highly recommend you use this configuration statement to avoid the situation where some commits are synchronized and others are not.

`<force-synchronize/>`
: This option specifies the device should attempt to make the synchronized commit operation succeed in the face of certain errors. Certain situations, such as a user having an open configuration session on the backup RE, can make a synchronized commit fail where a nonsynchronized (single-RE) commit would succeed. Including the `<force-synchronize>` element tells the Junos software to

attempt to make the commit succeed in spite of these errors. As a side effect of this behavior, all users with open configuration sessions on the backup RE will have their CLI sessions disconnected.

As you can imagine, it requires wisdom to determine when an automation script should use this option. Is it better to have the automation script try to make the commit succeed, even if that may impact a user trying to legitimately make a change on the backup RE? Or is it better to have the automation script fail? The best answer to this question varies based on the script, the environment in which it is executed, the operational policies of the organization that manages the device, and the function the script is performing.

`<full/>`
: This option specifies the device should conduct a "full" commit, acting as if every piece of the configuration had been changed. Normally, the device only takes the minimum actions necessary to activate the portions of the configuration that have changed. This option tells the device to bypass this important Junos optimization. You should only use this option in the rare circumstances where Juniper has suggested you use the `commit full` command (e.g., to work around a bug in the optimization process).

`<check/>`
: This option specifies that the device should conduct its normal commit checks, but not actually activate the new configuration.

For example, this RPC produces a normal commit operation:

```
<rpc>
  <commit-configuration/>
</rpc>
```

This RPC produces a synchronized commit operation that also tells the Junos software to try to make the commit operation succeed in spite of certain errors on the backup RE:

```
<rpc>
  <commit-configuration>
    <synchronize/>
    <force-synchronize/>
  </commit-configuration>
</rpc>
```

This RPC conducts a synchronized commit operation with a log message:

```
<rpc>
  <commit-configuration>
    <synchronize/>
    <log>This is a sample log message for a commit.</log>
  </commit-configuration>
</rpc>
```

Example configuration session

In this example, we get an exclusive lock on the shared configuration database, replace the `ge-1/0/0` configuration, and conduct a synchronized commit.

First, lock the configuration database:

```
<rpc>
  <lock-configuration/>
</rpc>
```

Next, replace the `ge-1/0/0` configuration:

```
<rpc>
  <load-configuration action="replace">
    <configuration>
      <interfaces>
        <interface replace="replace">
          <name>ge=1/0/0</name>
          <unit>
            <name>0</name>
            <family>
              <inet>
                <address>
                  <name>172.16.1.1/24</name>
                </address>
              </inet>
            </family>
          </unit>
        </interface>
      </interfaces>
    </configuration>
  </load-configuration>
</rpc>
```

Finally, commit the configuration:

```
<rpc>
  <commit-configuration/>
</rpc>
```

Chapter Summary

This chapter covered some foundational information about interacting with the Junos software's management system. The chapter described structured data formats, RPCs, and RPC responses. You should now be able to discover the correct RPC syntax to execute many common Junos commands, as well as the expected RPC responses for many common Junos commands. You should also understand the steps necessary to change the Junos configuration, and the different options that are available to you during the process of changing the configuration.

Because the XML API forms the basis on which automation tools build, the remainder of the book builds upon this information. In the next chapter, you will see how you can use the REST API to execute these RPCs on the Junos software.

CHAPTER 3

The RESTful API Service

Chapter 2 introduced the structured data models Junos software uses to represent both its configuration and operational output. Chapter 2 also explored the Junoscript and NETCONF methods for making remote procedure calls (RPCs) to modify the configuration or retrieve operational output. While it is important to understand the underlying mechanism the Junos software uses to handle RPCs, access to the Junoscript and NETCONF interfaces is much more efficient when it is mediated by a frontend mechanism that abstracts the lower-level Junoscript or NETCONF interaction. This chapter explores one such mechanism, the Junos RESTful API service. The Junos RESTful API service enables RPCs to be invoked and structured data responses to be returned without directly entering Junoscript or NETCONF syntax.

Beginning with release 14.2R1, the Junos software provides an application programming interface (API) based on the Representational State Transfer (REST) software architecture style. REST is not a protocol, but a set of architectural constraints for building scalable web services. Web services that provide APIs based on the REST architecture style are referred to as RESTful APIs.

Details of the REST architecture[1] and RESTful web services could be, and in fact are, the topic of entire books. In this section, we're going to primarily focus on using the Junos RESTful API rather than describing the REST architecture. RESTful APIs typically utilize the Web's Hypertext Transfer Protocol (HTTP) as their transport and define lightweight mechanisms for invoking requests via HTTP's various methods (such as GET, PUT, POST, and DELETE). Responses are typically returned in structured data formats, such as XML and JSON, that are easily parsed by programs. The

1 The original description of the REST architecture style can be found in Chapter 5 of Roy Fielding's PhD dissertation, "Architecture Styles and the Design of Network-based Software Architectures." (*https://www.ics.uci.edu/~fielding/pubs/dissertation/top.htm*)

Junos RESTful API service follows this model and uses HTTP GET and POST requests to invoke NETCONF RPCs. In turn, each request generates a response that contains the output of the RPC.

Because RESTful web services have become ubiquitous, most programming languages include libraries and frameworks for making RESTful API queries and processing the resulting responses. In addition, RESTful web services allow client and server to be developed independently. The client and server can each be written in any language that supports HTTP/HTTPS communication. Maybe you already have experience developing web services clients that interact with popular services on the Internet. If so, those same tools and skills can now be applied to network automation. This chapter provides the RESTful API specifics you need to get started. Don't worry, if you don't already have experience developing web services clients, though; this chapter walks you through the details and also provides an example of developing a small web services client using Python.

Enabling the RESTful API Service

The Junos RESTful API service can operate over unencrypted HTTP or over SSL/TLS-encrypted HTTPS. The service is included in the standard Junos software installation package, but is not enabled by default. The minimal configuration necessary to enable the RESTful API service over HTTP is:

```
set system services rest http
```

When operating over HTTP, the RESTful API service listens on TCP port 3000 by default.[2] The following Junos CLI output demonstrates configuring the RESTful API service over HTTP and verifying that the service is indeed listening on TCP port 3000:

```
user@r0> configure
Entering configuration mode

[edit]
user@r0# set system services rest http

[edit]
user@r0# commit and-quit
commit complete
```

2 On Junos devices with multiple routing engines, the RESTful API service runs only on the master RE. If each RE is configured with a unique IP address on its management interface, the RESTful API service will be reachable only on the IP address of the current master RE. In this case, we recommend adding an additional management interface shared IP address that includes the `master-only` configuration statement. This configuration ensures the RESTful API service is always accessible via this master-only IP address, regardless of which RE is currently the master.

```
Exiting configuration mode

user@r0> show system connections | match 3000
tcp4       0      0  *.3000                    *.*                    LISTEN
```

This minimal configuration is sufficient to develop and test automation scripts that use the Junos RESTful API service over the unencrypted HTTP transport. However, a production environment should always be configured to use only the encrypted HTTPS transport. The Junos software also offers additional configuration parameters to protect the RESTful API service from potential attackers. These optional (but highly recommended) configuration parameters are covered in "Additional RESTful API Service Configuration" on page 157. For now, let's concentrate on making queries of and processing responses from the RESTful API service—but make sure you enable HTTPS (and disable HTTP) before deploying the RESTful API service in a production network!

HTTP GET Requests

Each remote procedure call to the RESTful API service can be invoked using the HTTP request message's GET method.[3] The uniform resource locater (URL) of an HTTP GET request uniquely identifies the remote procedure to be executed. The general format of the URL is:

```
protocol://device:port/rpc/procedure
```

Table 3-1 details the meaning of each value in this URL format.

Table 3-1. URL components for RESTful API HTTP GET requests

Component	Description
protocol	The protocol of the request. Must be `http` or `https`.
device	A hostname, domain name, or IPv4 address on which the Junos device is running the RESTful API service. If a hostname or domain name is used, it must resolve to an IPv4 address.
port	The TCP port number on which the Junos RESTful API service is listening. By default, this is port 3000 when the service is operating over HTTP and port 3443 when the service is operating over HTTPS. However, it is possible to configure the Junos RESTful API service to listen on any nonreserved port number (between 1024 and 65535).
procedure	The method name of a Junos RPC. For example, the method name to get information about the version of Junos software running on the device is *get-software-information*.

3 The rest of this section will refer to HTTP methods, headers, responses, etc. Unless otherwise stated, these operations apply equally to both the unencrypted HTTP and encrypted HTTPS transports.

At this time, the Junos RESTful API service does not operate over IPv6. Therefore, you cannot use an IPv6 address, or a hostname that resolves to an IPv6 address, in the *device* portion of the URL.

As an example, the URL `http://r0.example.com:3000/rpc/get-software-information` can be used to execute the *get-software-information* RPC over HTTP on port 3000, the default port, of the device `r0.example.com`. Because a standard web browser makes an HTTP GET request when we type a URL in the location bar, we can execute this RPC and see its result by simply typing the URL in a standard web browser, as shown in Figure 3-1.

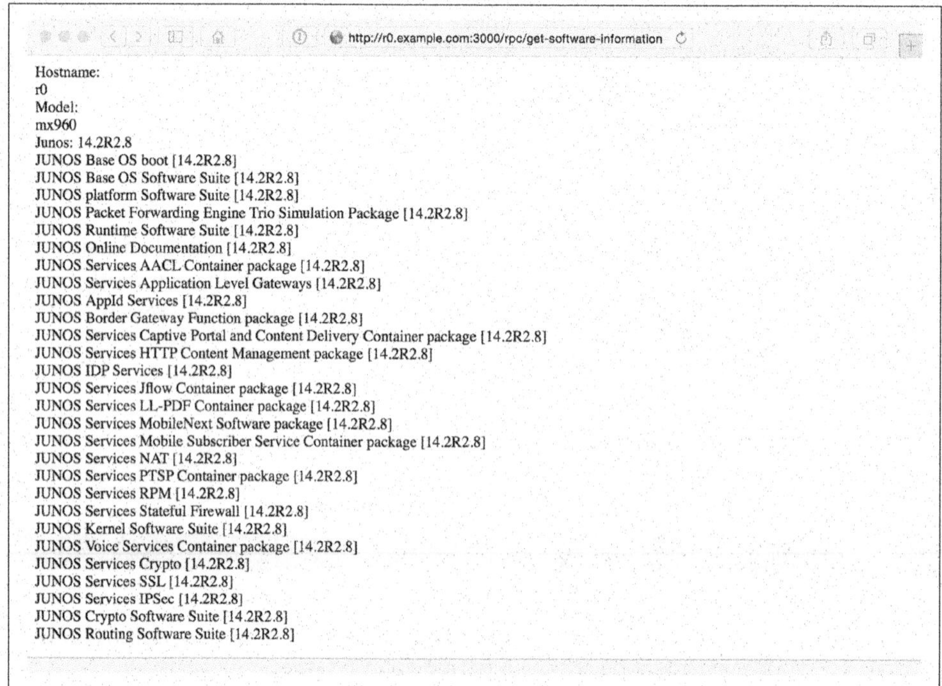

Figure 3-1. Invoking the get-software-information RPC from a web browser

Before seeing the result shown in Figure 3-1, you will be prompted to enter username and password authentication credentials. Every RESTful API query must include authentication information in the HTTP request. "Authentication and Authorization" on page 99 discusses authentication in more detail. For now, simply enter the username and password of a user who can log in to the Junos device via the CLI.

While viewing the output of a RESTful API query in your web browser's GUI can be interesting, it does not help in developing software to automate network operation. For that task, a programmatic interface to make queries and parse the resulting data is needed. That's the general idea behind web services. Web services leverage the same protocols and architecture as a human-visible website, but they add protocols such as XML and JSON to allow data to be represented in a way more easily parsed by computers.

Most modern programming languages abstract the HTTP interaction needed to communicate with a RESTful API. This abstraction may be supported natively by the language or provided through libraries or utilities. However, it is still important to understand the basics of HTTP communication in order to provide the necessary parameters to invoke RESTful APIs that have the intended effect.

Each HTTP request includes a *request line* and *header fields*. The request line contains the HTTP verb (such as GET or POST) along with the URL being queried. Header fields include additional information about the query, such as authentication information (covered in "Authentication and Authorization" on page 99) or the desired response format (covered in "Formatting HTTP Responses" on page 103). Making a RESTful API query is a matter of setting the correct library or utility parameters so that an HTTP request includes the correct HTTP verb, URL, and headers. This chapter demonstrates making RESTful API queries with both the open source cURL command-line utility and the Python Requests library; however, other languages and libraries offer similar mechanisms for setting the correct query parameters.

The corresponding HTTP response includes a status line, header fields, and the response body. The status line includes a status code, which provides information on whether or not the query was successfully processed by the RESTful API service. The header fields provide metadata about the response, and the body provides the actual response data. For RESTful API queries, the body usually contains XML or JSON data. This chapter demonstrates checking the status code and response headers with the Python Requests library. Again, similar mechanisms are available in other languages and libraries.

When querying the Junos RESTful API service, a `200 OK` status code means that the query was processed by the RESTful API service, but does not necessarily mean that the RPC was successfully executed. There may be times, as described in "Authentication and Authorization" on page 99, where the `200 OK` status code is returned, but the body of the response contains a warning or error message rather than the output of a successfully executed RPC.

One helpful utility for interacting with the Junos RESTful API service is the open source command-line utility cURL (*http://curl.haxx.se*). The cURL utility transfers data via many protocols that support URL syntax. This includes the HTTP and HTTPS protocols used by the Junos RESTful API service. Even if your programming language of choice provides a library for abstracting HTTP interaction, cURL can be helpful to quickly check the syntax of RESTful API queries and responses. If you are already comfortable writing Unix shell scripts, the cURL utility also provides a quick and simple method for invoking RESTful API queries and redirecting the responses to your script for further processing. Some operating systems, such as Mac OS X and many Linux distributions, include the `curl` command in their standard installations. If your OS of choice does not already include cURL, you can download the source code or pre-compiled packages for your system at the cURL download page (*http://curl.haxx.se/download.html*).

Because cURL lets us make RESTful API queries in a language-independent way, and without entering low-level HTTP on the TCP socket, it is useful to demonstrate the API syntax and behavior. Let's begin by using the `curl` command to make an RPC equivalent to the query we previously made with a web browser.

In the following example, and several other places in this chapter, we use the Unix shell's line continuation character, \, to avoid long commands being truncated in the printed versions of this book. If you see a line that ends with \, and the following line begins with >, the second line is the continuation of a single long command. When entering these commands, you may choose to omit the \ and carriage return. In this case, you will not see the shell's > line continuation prompt.

Enter the command as shown here, substituting in the appropriate values for your environment:

```
user@h0$ curl http://r0.example.com:3000/rpc/get-software-information ❶ \
> -u "user:user123" ❷ -H "Accept: text/html" ❸
<div class="top"> ❹
... output trimmed ... ❺
</div> ❻
user@h0$ ❼
```

❶ The URL follows the format specified at the beginning of this section, and is exactly the same URL entered in the web browser in Figure 3-1.

❷ The username and password are specified with the `-u` command-line option. The username and password are separated by a colon. They should be placed in quotes to avoid shell interpolation of any special characters.

While specifying the username and password with a command-line option is convenient for demonstration and prototyping, it is not secure for production use. The clear-text password is clearly visible by any user in the `ps` command output.

❸ The `-H` command-line option tells cURL to include an HTTP header field with the specified string. HTTP header fields are composed of a field name followed by a colon, a space, and a field value. The `curl` command allows multiple `-H` command-line options to be specified: one for each HTTP header field to be included in the request. "Formatting HTTP Responses" on page 103 explains how the `Accept` header controls the format of HTTP responses. While the `text/html` format is rarely used by programs that query the Junos RESTful API, it is the default queried by a web browser. Specifying `text/html` format in this example makes this `curl` query equivalent to Figure 3-1.

❹ The body of the HTTP response is returned on the shell's standard output. In this case, the HTTP body begins with an HTML `<div>` tag. The HTTP status line and response headers can also be viewed by adding cURL's `-i` command-line option.

❺ The bulk of the HTML response has been omitted for brevity.

❻ The body of the response ends with the closing HTML `</div>` tag.

❼ Once the HTTP response is received, the connection is closed and cURL exits, returning execution to the calling program (the Unix shell, in this case).

Currently, the Junos RESTful API service does not support HTTP persistent connections. Only one HTTP request message can be sent per connection. The server closes the connection after transferring the response.

Authentication and Authorization

As mentioned in the previous section, the Junos software requires that every RESTful API query include a username and password for authentication. Junos software currently supports only the HTTP basic authentication mechanism.[4] HTTP basic

4 The HTTP basic authentication mechanism is defined in RFC 2617 (*http://tools.ietf.org/html/rfc2617*) and updated by RFC 7235 (*http://tools.ietf.org/html/rfc7235*).

authentication sends a username and password string in an HTTP `Authorization` header field.

While HTTP basic authentication does Base64 encode the username and password for transport over the TCP connection, it does *not* encrypt this authentication information. Therefore, it is essential to configure the encrypted HTTPS transport in order to prevent capture of sensitive authentication information.

The RESTful API service passes the username and password from the HTTP basic authentication mechanism to the standard Junos authentication and authorization system specified at the `[edit system]` hierarchy level of the Junos configuration. The same authentication and authorization that is applied to the Junos CLI is also applied to RESTful API queries. This allows the username and password to be specified locally in the Junos configuration, or on a remote RADIUS or TACACS+ server. Authorization to execute a specific RPC is determined by mapping a user, or potentially a template user in the case of RADIUS/TACACS+ authentication, to a login class. In turn, the login class specifies a set of permissions that determine if an RPC call is permitted or denied.

Specifying incorrect authentication parameters will result in an HTTP `401 Unauthorized` status code being returned. To see this in action, use `curl` to enter an HTTP GET request that invokes the *get-system-alarm-information* [5] RPC.

The `-u` command-line option takes the format *`username:password`* and causes `curl` to automatically include an HTTP `Authorization` header field in the format required by the HTTP basic authentication mechanism.

First, purposely provide an authentication string with an incorrect password (the `-i` command-line option includes HTTP response headers in the cURL output):

```
user@h0$ curl http://r0:3000/rpc/get-system-alarm-information -i -u "user:bad"
HTTP/1.1 401 Unauthorized
Status: 401
Transfer-Encoding: chunked
Date: Wed, 13 Jan 2016 16:19:20 GMT
Server: lighttpd/1.4.32

Failed to open session to execute RPC
```

5 *get-system-alarm-information* is equivalent to the `show system alarms` CLI command.

As expected, a `401 Unauthorized` status code is returned. Now, what happens when the same RPC is invoked with the user `foo`? In this case, the user `foo` is not authorized to execute the *get-system-alarm-information* RPC. The Junos configuration for user `foo` is:

```
user@r0> show configuration system login user foo
uid 2002;
class unauthorized;
authentication {
    encrypted-password "$1$H//finuG$SX4T7wgZBzgzkjzOSbTcF1"; ## SECRET-DATA
}
```

Notice user `foo` is a member of the predefined login class `unauthorized`. This login class prevents this user from executing any CLI commands. Again, use `curl` to enter an HTTP GET request to invoke the *get-system-alarm-information* RPC. This time include the username `foo` and the correct password, `bar123`:

```
user@h0$ curl http://r0:3000/rpc/get-system-alarm-information -i -u "foo:bar123"
HTTP/1.1 200 OK
Content-Type: application/xml; charset=utf-8
Transfer-Encoding: chunked
Date: Wed, 13 Jan 2016 17:16:32 GMT
Server: lighttpd/1.4.32

<xnm:warning xmlns="http://xml.juniper.net/xnm/1.1/xnm" xmlns:xnm="...">
<message>
user "foo" does not have access privileges.
</message>
</xnm:warning>
```

This authorization failure results in different behaviors: rather than returning the HTTP `401 Unauthorized` error code seen for authentication failures, an HTTP `200 OK` status is returned. However, the body of the response contains an XML warning or error message. In this case, an XML warning message with the content `user "foo" does not have access privileges` is returned.

In addition to using predefined login classes to control the authorization of RPCs, a custom login class that uses the `allow-commands` and `deny-commands` configuration statements can be defined. When using these configuration statements to control authorization, specify the corresponding CLI command, *not the name of the RPC*. Because the *get-system-alarm-information* RPC corresponds to the `show system alarms` CLI command, use this configuration to deny execution of the *get-system-alarm-information* RPC (which would have otherwise been allowed by the `view` permission of the login class):

```
user@r0> show configuration system login user foo
uid 2002;
class no-alarms;
authentication {
```

```
        encrypted-password "$1$H//finuG$SX4T7wgZBzgzkjzOSbTcF1"; ## SECRET-DATA
    }

user@r0> show configuration system login class no-alarms
permissions view;
deny-commands "show system alarms|show chassis alarms";

user@r0>
```

Now log in to the CLI as user `foo`. As this output confirms, the `show system uptime` CLI command can be executed by this user, but the `show system alarms` CLI command cannot be executed:

```
foo@r0> show system uptime
Current time: 2016-01-13 09:32:15 PST
System booted: 2016-01-11 11:41:57 PST (1d 21:50 ago)
Protocols started: 2016-01-11 11:42:50 PST (1d 21:49 ago)
Last configured: 2016-01-13 09:31:04 PST (00:01:11 ago) by user
 9:32AM  up 1 day, 21:50, 1 user, load averages: 0.01, 0.02, 0.00

foo@r0> show system al?
No valid completions
foo@r0> show system al
```

Repeating the execution of the *get-system-alarm-information* RPC again returns an HTTP `200 OK` status code, but with an XML error message of `permission denied`:

```
user@h0$ curl http://r0:3000/rpc/get-system-alarm-information -u "foo:bar123" -v
* Hostname was NOT found in DNS cache
*   Trying 10.102.163.237...
* Connected to r0 (10.102.163.237) port 3000 (#0)
* Server auth using Basic with user 'foo'
> GET /rpc/get-system-alarm-information HTTP/1.1
> Authorization: Basic Zm9vOmJhcjEyMw==
> User-Agent: curl/7.38.0
> Host: r0:3000
> Accept: */*
>
< HTTP/1.1 200 OK
< Content-Type: application/xml; charset=utf-8
< Transfer-Encoding: chunked
< Date: Wed, 13 Jan 2016 17:33:48 GMT
* Server lighttpd/1.4.32 is not blacklisted
< Server: lighttpd/1.4.32
<
<xnm:error xmlns="http://xml.juniper.net/xnm/1.1/xnm" xmlns:xnm="...">
<token>get-system-alarm-information</token>
<message>permission denied</message>
</xnm:error>
* Connection #0 to host r0 left intact
user@h0$
```

In this example, the cURL `-v` command-line option produces verbose output that shows the request line and header fields of the HTTP request *plus* the HTTP response headers produced by the `-i` option. The `-v` option allows us to see the `Authorization: Basic Zm9vOmJhcjEyMw==` header, which is automatically created from the `-u` command-line option.

When developing scripts that use the RESTful API, it is important that the scripts handle HTTP `401 Unauthorized` responses as well as HTTP `200 OK` responses that contain an XML error or warning message in the HTTP body.

Formatting HTTP Responses

"HTTP GET Requests" on page 95 described how to invoke RPCs using HTTP GET requests, and the previous section showed how to properly authenticate and authorize those RPCs. This section focuses on the format of the response received from the RPCs. The Junos RESTful API service currently supports four different ways of formatting the response data:

Plain text
: The format displayed when executing a command at the Junos CLI. The output is optimized for viewing by humans.

HTML
: Designed to be displayed using a web browser. The web browser's output is optimized for viewing by humans.

Junos software currently only supports displaying operational output in HTML. Configuration data cannot be viewed in HTML.

XML
: A structured data format suitable for parsing by computers. As "Discovering Operational RPC Syntax" on page 63 explained, XML output can be viewed in the Junos CLI using `| display xml`.

JSON
: Another structured data format suitable for parsing by computers. Many people consider JSON easier to understand than XML, so it is often the preferred format for web services. As described in "Discovering Operational RPC Syntax" on page 63, JSON output can be viewed in the Junos CLI using `| display json`.

The real benefit of Junos automation APIs comes from the data being formatted in the structured XML or JSON formats that can be easily parsed by programs. You should always use the XML or JSON format when writing a program that parses a RESTful API response. The plain text and HTML formats should only be used when exploring and troubleshooting the RESTful API service. These formats are unstructured and subject to change in future releases. If you have ever tried to develop network automation using screen scraping techniques, you've probably experienced the pain of parsing unstructured data that was really only intended for human consumption.

There are two ways a RESTful API query can specify the format of the response. The first way is to append `@format=`*`value`* to the end of the HTTP GET request's URL. When using the `@format=` method, the *`value`* should be one of:

```
xml
json
text
html
```

The second way of specifying the format of the response is by including an `Accept` header field in the HTTP GET request. This is the method that's been used in a few of the examples in this chapter, although the purpose of this header field has not been emphasized until now. When using this method, the full header field should be one of:

```
Accept: application/xml
Accept: application/json
Accept: text/html
Accept: text/plain
```

Each response includes a `Content-Type` header, which specifies the format of the HTTP response body. By default, the Junos RESTful API service produces output in XML format. If a query does not specify a format for the response, the HTTP response includes a `Content-Type: application/xml; charset=utf-8` header field, and the HTTP body is an XML document. However, best practice dictates not depending on this default format. Instead, explicitly request the data to be formatted in the XML or JSON format that the calling program expects.

The cURL utility, with the `-v` command-line option, can be used to see each of these output formats in action. First, make an HTTP GET request for the *get-system-alarm-information* RPC without specifying a specific output format:

```
user@h0$ curl http://r0:3000/rpc/get-system-alarm-information \
> -u "user:user123" -v
*   Trying 10.102.180.178...
* Connected to r0 (10.102.180.178) port 3000 (#0)
* Server auth using Basic with user 'user'
> GET /rpc/get-system-alarm-information HTTP/1.1
> Authorization: Basic dXNlcjp1c2VyMTIz
> User-Agent: curl/7.37.1
> Host: r0:3000
> Accept: */* ❶
>
< HTTP/1.1 200 OK
< Content-Type: application/xml; charset=utf-8 ❷
< Transfer-Encoding: chunked
< Date: Tue, 28 Apr 2015 15:43:28 GMT
* Server lighttpd/1.4.32 is not blacklisted
< Server: lighttpd/1.4.32
<
<alarm-information xmlns="http://xml.juniper.net/junos/14.2R2/junos-alarm">
<alarm-summary>
<no-active-alarms/>
</alarm-summary>
</alarm-information>
* Connection #0 to host r0 left intact
```

❶ cURL adds an `Accept: */*` header field indicating to the Junos RESTful API service that any output format will be accepted.

❷ The `Content-Type` header field indicates the HTTP body is in XML format. XML is the default format returned when no format is explicitly requested.

Explicitly requesting the XML format using either the `@format=` URL syntax or the `Accept: application/xml` header field produces the same result:

```
user@h0$ curl http://r0:3000/rpc/get-system-alarm-information@format=xml ❶ \
> -u "user:user123" -v
* Hostname was NOT found in DNS cache
*   Trying 10.102.180.178...
* Connected to r0 (10.102.180.178) port 3000 (#0)
* Server auth using Basic with user 'user'
> GET /rpc/get-system-alarm-information@format=xml HTTP/1.1
> Authorization: Basic dXNlcjp1c2VyMTIz
> User-Agent: curl/7.37.1
> Host: r0:3000
> Accept: */* ❷
>
< HTTP/1.1 200 OK
< Content-Type: application/xml; charset=utf-8 ❸
< Transfer-Encoding: chunked
< Date: Tue, 28 Apr 2015 16:03:03 GMT
* Server lighttpd/1.4.32 is not blacklisted
```

```
< Server: lighttpd/1.4.32
<
<alarm-information xmlns="http://xml.juniper.net/junos/14.2R2/junos-alarm">
<alarm-summary>
<no-active-alarms/>
</alarm-summary>
</alarm-information>
* Connection #0 to host r0 left intact

user@h0$ curl http://r0:3000/rpc/get-system-alarm-information \
> -u "user:user123" -H "Accept: application/xml" ❹ -v
* Hostname was NOT found in DNS cache
*   Trying 10.102.180.178...
* Connected to r0 (10.102.180.178) port 3000 (#0)
* Server auth using Basic with user 'user'
> GET /rpc/get-system-alarm-information HTTP/1.1
> Authorization: Basic dXNlcjp1c2VyMTIz
> User-Agent: curl/7.37.1
> Host: r0:3000
> Accept: application/xml ❺
>
< HTTP/1.1 200 OK
< Content-Type: application/xml; charset=utf-8 ❻
< Transfer-Encoding: chunked
< Date: Tue, 28 Apr 2015 16:03:56 GMT
* Server lighttpd/1.4.32 is not blacklisted
< Server: lighttpd/1.4.32
<
<alarm-information xmlns="http://xml.juniper.net/junos/14.2R2/junos-alarm">
<alarm-summary>
<no-active-alarms/>
</alarm-summary>
</alarm-information>
* Connection #0 to host r0 left intact
```

❶ XML format is explicitly requested in the URL with `@format=xml`.

❷ The cURL utility still adds an `Accept: */*` header field, but the Junos RESTful API service prefers the format requested in the `@format=xml` attribute of the URL.

❸ A `Content-Type` header field indicates that the HTTP body is in XML format.

❹ XML format is explicitly requested using an `Accept: application/xml` header field.

❺ The cURL utility includes the `Accept: application/xml` header field that was specified with the `-H` command-line option. The `Accept: */*` header field is no longer included in this request.

❻ Again, the `Content-Type` header field indicates that the HTTP body is in XML format.

Now repeat both queries requesting the nondefault JSON format. Again, try both the `@format=json` URL attribute and the `Accept: application/json` header field. Observe that both methods produce the same JSON-formatted result:

```
user@h0$ curl http://r0:3000/rpc/get-system-alarm-information@format=json ❶ \
> -u "user:user123" -v
* Hostname was NOT found in DNS cache
*   Trying 10.102.180.178...
* Connected to r0 (10.102.180.178) port 3000 (#0)
* Server auth using Basic with user 'user'
> GET /rpc/get-system-alarm-information@format=json HTTP/1.1
> Authorization: Basic dXNlcjp1c2VyMTIz
> User-Agent: curl/7.37.1
> Host: r0:3000
> Accept: */* ❷
>
< HTTP/1.1 200 OK
< Content-Type: application/json; charset=utf-8 ❸
< Transfer-Encoding: chunked
< Date: Tue, 28 Apr 2015 16:35:30 GMT
* Server lighttpd/1.4.32 is not blacklisted
< Server: lighttpd/1.4.32
<
{
 "alarm-information" : [
 {
    "attributes" : {"xmlns" : "http://xml.juniper.net/junos/14.2R2/junos-alarm"},
    "alarm-summary" : [
    {
        "no-active-alarms" : [
        {
            "data" : null
        }
        ]
    }
    ]
 }
 ]
}
* Connection #0 to host r0 left intact

user@h0$ curl http://r0:3000/rpc/get-system-alarm-information \
> -u "user:user123" -H "Accept: application/json" ❹ -v
* Hostname was NOT found in DNS cache
*   Trying 10.102.180.178...
* Connected to r0 (10.102.180.178) port 3000 (#0)
* Server auth using Basic with user 'user'
> GET /rpc/get-system-alarm-information HTTP/1.1
```

```
> Authorization: Basic dXNlcjp1c2VyMTIz
> User-Agent: curl/7.37.1
> Host: r0:3000
> Accept: application/json ❺
>
< HTTP/1.1 200 OK
< Content-Type: application/json; charset=utf-8 ❻
< Transfer-Encoding: chunked
< Date: Tue, 28 Apr 2015 16:35:39 GMT
* Server lighttpd/1.4.32 is not blacklisted
< Server: lighttpd/1.4.32
<
{
 "alarm-information" : [
 {
    "attributes" : {"xmlns" : "http://xml.juniper.net/junos/14.2R2/junos-alarm"},
    "alarm-summary" : [
    {
        "no-active-alarms" : [
        {
            "data" : null
        }
        ]
    }
    ]
 }
 ]
}
* Connection #0 to host r0 left intact
```

❶ JSON format is explicitly requested in the URL with `@format=json`.

❷ The cURL utility still adds an `Accept: */*` header field, but the Junos RESTful API service prefers the format requested in the `@format=json` attribute of the URL.

❸ A `Content-Type` header field indicates that the HTTP body is in JSON format.

❹ JSON format is explicitly requested using an `Accept: application/json` header field.

❺ The cURL utility includes the `Accept: application/json` header field that was specified with the `-H` command-line option. The `Accept: */*` header field is no longer included in this request.

❻ The `Content-Type` header field indicates that the HTTP body is in JSON format.

Examples of requesting the HTML or plain text formats have not been included because those formats, while available, are not typically used in web services programs.

If multiple Accept header fields are specified, the first format will be used. In the following example, the output is rendered in JSON format:

```
user@h0$ curl http://r0:3000/rpc/get-system-alarm-information \
> -u "user:user123" -H "Accept: application/json" -H "Accept: text/plain" -v
* Hostname was NOT found in DNS cache
*   Trying 10.102.180.178...
* Connected to r0 (10.102.180.178) port 3000 (#0)
* Server auth using Basic with user 'user'
> GET /rpc/get-system-alarm-information HTTP/1.1
> Authorization: Basic dXNlcjp1c2VyMTIz
> User-Agent: curl/7.37.1
> Host: r0:3000
> Accept: application/json
> Accept: text/plain
>
< HTTP/1.1 200 OK
< Content-Type: application/json; charset=utf-8
< Transfer-Encoding: chunked
< Date: Tue, 28 Apr 2015 17:16:54 GMT
* Server lighttpd/1.4.32 is not blacklisted
< Server: lighttpd/1.4.32
<
{
 "alarm-information" : [
 {
    "attributes" : {"xmlns" : "http://xml.juniper.net/junos/14.2R2/junos-alarm"},
    "alarm-summary" : [
    {
        "no-active-alarms" : [
        {
            "data" : null
        }
        ]
    }
    ]
 }
 ]
}
* Connection #0 to host r0 left intact
```

Because the `Accept: application/json` header field appeared first, the `Accept: text/plain` header field was ignored. If both an `@format=` URL attribute and an `Accept` header field are specified, as shown in the next example, the `@format=` URL attribute is preferred:

```
user@h0$ curl http://r0:3000/rpc/get-system-alarm-information@format=text \
> -u "user:user123" -H "Accept: application/json" -v
* Hostname was NOT found in DNS cache
*   Trying 10.102.180.178...
* Connected to r0 (10.102.180.178) port 3000 (#0)
* Server auth using Basic with user 'user'
> GET /rpc/get-system-alarm-information@format=text HTTP/1.1
> Authorization: Basic dXNlcjp1c2VyMTIz
> User-Agent: curl/7.37.1
> Host: r0:3000
> Accept: application/json
>
< HTTP/1.1 200 OK
< Content-Type: text/plain; charset=utf-8
< Transfer-Encoding: chunked
< Date: Tue, 28 Apr 2015 17:25:12 GMT
* Server lighttpd/1.4.32 is not blacklisted
< Server: lighttpd/1.4.32
<
No alarms currently active
* Connection #0 to host r0 left intact
```

The preceding output was rendered in plain text format because the `@format=text` attribute takes precedence over the `Accept: application/json` header field.

One final caution on the output format of RESTful API queries. If the requested output format is not understood, the Junos RESTful API service returns the default XML format: if a response is received in XML format when JSON format was expected, double-check to make sure there's no typo in the value of the `@format=` URL attribute or the `Accept` header field.

HTTP POST Requests

The Junos RESTful API service offers an alternative syntax for executing a single RPC using the HTTP POST method. Depending on the capabilities of the web services library you are using to communicate with the Junos RESTful API service, you may find it easier to use this HTTP POST method than the HTTP GET method discussed in "HTTP GET Requests" on page 95. When executing a single RPC, the HTTP POST syntax is very similar to that of the HTTP GET method. The URL format remains exactly the same as specified in "HTTP GET Requests" on page 95. The key differences are that the HTTP request line uses the POST verb in place of the GET verb, and a message body is added to the request.[6]

6 The length of the message body is indicated by the `Content-Length` header field. Most web services libraries will automatically add an appropriate `Content-Length` header field to an HTTP POST request.

When invoking a single RPC using an HTTP POST request, this message body is typically empty. However, the message body may be used to pass parameters to the RPC. This method of parameter passing is discussed in the next section.

Let's look at an HTTP POST request using the `curl` command. Specifying the `-d` command-line option causes the cURL utility to send an HTTP POST request. The value of the `-d` command-line argument specifies the data to be sent in the message body. In this example, we specify an empty message body using `-d ""`. The `-v` command-line option has also been included to display the full HTTP request and HTTP response header fields:

```
user@h0$ curl http://r0:3000/rpc/get-system-alarm-information ❶ \
> -u "user:user123" -H "Accept: application/json" -d "" ❷ -v
* Hostname was NOT found in DNS cache
*   Trying 10.102.180.178...
* Connected to r0 (10.102.180.178) port 3000 (#0)
* Server auth using Basic with user 'user'
> POST ❸ /rpc/get-system-alarm-information HTTP/1.1
> Authorization: Basic dXNlcjp1c2VyMTIz
> User-Agent: curl/7.37.1
> Host: r0:3000
> Accept: application/json
> Content-Length: 0 ❹
> Content-Type: application/x-www-form-urlencoded ❺
>
< HTTP/1.1 200 OK
< Content-Type: application/json; charset=utf-8
< Transfer-Encoding: chunked
< Date: Wed, 29 Apr 2015 17:59:29 GMT
* Server lighttpd/1.4.32 is not blacklisted
< Server: lighttpd/1.4.32
<
{
 "alarm-information" : [
 {
    "attributes" : {"xmlns" : "http://xml.juniper.net/junos/14.2R2/junos-alarm"},
    "alarm-summary" : [
    {
        "no-active-alarms" : [
        {
            "data" : null
        }
        ]
    }
    ]
 }
 ]
}
* Connection #0 to host r0 left intact
```

❶ The URL to invoke the *get-system-alarm-information* RPC remains exactly the same as with an HTTP GET request.

❷ The `-d ""` command-line argument instructs cURL to send an HTTP POST request with an empty message body.

❸ The POST verb is specified in place of the GET verb that was used in "HTTP GET Requests" on page 95.

❹ The `Content-Length: 0` header field specifies that the message body of the request is empty.

❺ The `Content-Type` header field specifies the format of the message body. In this case, the `curl` command added this header field by default. The `Content-Type` header field is ignored when the `Content-Length: 0` header field is present. In fact, the `Content-Type` header field can even be omitted in this case.

Adding Parameters to RPCs

Some Junos RPCs take optional parameters. When describing the RPC in XML format, these parameters appear as nested XML tags. As an example, the XML RPC for the Junos CLI command `show interfaces descriptions lo0.0` is:

```
<rpc>
    <get-interface-information>
            <descriptions/>
            <interface-name>lo0.0</interface-name>
    </get-interface-information>
</rpc>
```

The `<descriptions>` and `<interface-name>` tags represent optional parameters to the *get-interface-information* RPC. These parameters filter the output of the `show interfaces` command to display only the description of a single interface named `lo0.0`. How can the Junos RESTful API be used to make an RPC equivalent to the `show interfaces descriptions lo0.0` CLI command? One option is to invoke the *get-interface-information* RPC and programmatically search the resulting JSON or XML data structure for the subset of information that contains the description of the `lo0.0` interface. This tactic works, but may not be the most efficient method because it requires the Junos device to transmit the entire RPC response to the client. On the other hand, adding parameters to an RPC causes the Junos device to filter the output and only deliver a subset of the RPC information to the client. As a general rule, it is best to filter needed information as close to the source as possible.

While some parameters simply filter the RPC's output, other parameters actually cause the RPC to produce different, or additional, information than would be produced without the parameter. One example is the optional `media` parameter to the *get-interface-information* RPC. The `media` parameter produces media-specific output for an interface that is not included in the standard *get-interface-information* RPC output. The auto-negotiation status of Ethernet interfaces is one example of information that is only present when the `media` parameter is specified. For the cases where a parameter causes an RPC to produce different or additional output, there must be a way of specifying RPC parameters using the RESTful API.

The RESTful API service does provide a way to specify RPC parameters in these cases. In fact, it provides multiple ways to specify RPC parameters. The first method is to specify the parameters as a CGI query string at the end of the requested URL. The query string begins with a question mark (`?`) and then contains a set of key/value pairs in the format *`key=value`*. If multiple key/value pairs are present, they are separated with an ampersand (`&`). The `@format=` URL attribute was discussed in "Formatting HTTP Responses" on page 103. If this `@format=` attribute is present, the query string appears after it. The query string format leads to an expansion of the general request URL format introduced in "HTTP GET Requests" on page 95. The URL request format, including parameters in the CGI query string, is:

```
protocol://device:port/rpc/procedure[@format=output-specifier]
[[[?param1=value1]&param2=value2]...]
```

The following examples apply this format to create RESTful API queries equivalent to the `show interfaces descriptions lo0.0` and `show interfaces media ge-0/0/0` CLI commands:

```
user@h0$ curl "http://r0:3000/rpc/\
> get-interface-information@format=json?descriptions=&interface-name=lo0.0" \
> -u "user:user123"
{
 "interface-information" : [
 {
    "attributes" : {"xmlns" : "...",
                    "junos:style" : "description"
                   },
    "logical-interface" : [
    {
        "name" : [
        {
            "data" : "lo0.0"
        }
        ],
        "admin-status" : [
        {
            "data" : "up"
        }
        ],
        "oper-status" : [
        {
```

```
            "data" : "up"
        }
        ],
        "description" : [
        {
            "data" : "R0 (10.102.180.178) Loopback"
        }
        ]
    }
    ]
 }
 ]
}
user@h0$ curl "http://r0:3000/rpc/\
> get-interface-information?media=&interface-name=ge-0/0/0" \
> -u "user:user123" -H "Accept: application/xml"
<interface-information xmlns="..." xmlns:junos="..." junos:style="normal">
<physical-interface>
<name>ge-0/0/0</name>
<admin-status junos:format="Enabled">up</admin-status>
...output trimmed...
<ethernet-autonegotiation>
<autonegotiation-status>incomplete</autonegotiation-status>
</ethernet-autonegotiation>
<interface-transmit-statistics>Disabled</interface-transmit-statistics>
</physical-interface>
</interface-information>
```

Some important points of these examples include:

- The URLs for requests can become quite long when parameters are included. In these examples, the URL is longer than the maximum line length for this book. Therefore, the Unix shell's \ line continuation character is used in the middle of each URL. The backslash is not part of the URL. It is interpreted by the Unix shell and has only been added to allow the long URL to continue on the next line.
- The first query uses the `@format=` URL attribute to specify that the output should be in JSON format. This attribute appears before the query string.
- The `descriptions` and `media` parameters do not take a value; however, the `=` for these parameters must still be specified in the query string. The value is empty.
- When using the `curl` command from a Unix shell, the URL must be enclosed in quotes to prevent the shell from interpolating special characters, such as the `&`, in the URL's content.
- The second query uses the `Accept` header field to specify the output should be in XML format. In this case, the query string appears directly after the RPC name.

The second format for specifying RPC parameters also uses the *key=value* format. However, each key/value pair is separated from the procedure, and other key/value pairs, using the slash (/) character. The URL request format becomes:

```
protocol://device:port/rpc/procedure[@format=output-specifier]
[[[/param1=value1]/param2=value2]...]
```

The following examples apply this format to the `show interfaces descriptions lo0.0` and `show interfaces media ge-0/0/0` CLI commands:

```
user@h0$ curl http://r0:3000/rpc/\
> get-interface-information@format=json/descriptions=/interface-name=lo0.0 \
> -u "user:user123"
{
 "interface-information" : [
 {
    "attributes" : {"xmlns" : "...",
                    "junos:style" : "description"
                   },
    "logical-interface" : [
    {
        "name" : [
        {
            "data" : "lo0.0"
        }
        ],
        "admin-status" : [
        {
            "data" : "up"
        }
        ],
        "oper-status" : [
        {
            "data" : "up"
        }
        ],
        "description" : [
        {
            "data" : "R0 (10.102.180.178) Loopback"
        }
        ]
    }
    ]
 }
 ]
}

user@h0$ curl http://r0:3000/rpc/\
> get-interface-information/media=/interface-name=ge-0%2F0%2F0 \
> -u "user:user123" -H "Accept: application/xml"
<interface-information xmlns="..." xmlns:junos="..." junos:style="normal">
<physical-interface>
<name>ge-0/0/0</name>
```

```
<admin-status junos:format="Enabled">up</admin-status>
...output trimmed...
<ethernet-autonegotiation>
<autonegotiation-status>incomplete</autonegotiation-status>
</ethernet-autonegotiation>
<interface-transmit-statistics>Disabled</interface-transmit-statistics>
</physical-interface>
</interface-information>
```

Some important points of these examples include:

- Again, the URLs have been split between lines using the Unix shell's line continuation character, \.
- The first query uses the `@format=` URL attribute to specify the output should be in JSON format. Again, the format attribute appears before the parameters.
- Parameters that do not take a value, such as `descriptions` and `media`, still require the equals sign (=). The value is empty.
- The URLs do not include special characters that will be interpolated by the Unix shell, so they don't have to be enclosed in quotes (although they still could be).
- The value for the `interface-name` parameter is `ge-0/0/0`. Because this format uses slashes to separate *key*=*`value`* pairs, the slashes in this value must be escaped as `%2F`. Otherwise, the `interface-name=ge-0/0/0` key/value pair would be interpreted as three separate parameters.

Most HTTP libraries provide a method that can perform this URL encoding for you.

The final option for encoding RPC parameters applies only to single RPCs using the HTTP POST request method, as discussed in "HTTP POST Requests" on page 110. When making an HTTP POST request for a single RPC, the RPC's parameters can be specified as *key*=*`value`* pairs in the message body. Multiple key/value pairs are separated with an ampersand (`&`). If this option is used, a `Content-Type: text/plain` header field must be included for the parameters to be properly interpreted. Here's an example of this option using the `curl` command:

```
user@h0$ curl http://r0:3000/rpc/get-interface-information@format=json
    \-u "user:user123"
> -H "Content-Type: text/plain"
> /-d "descriptions=&interface-name=lo0.0"
{
 "interface-information" : [
 {
```

```
"attributes" : {"xmlns" : "...",
                "junos:style" : "description"
               },
"logical-interface" : [
{
    "name" : [
    {
        "data" : "lo0.0"
    }
    ],
    "admin-status" : [
    {
        "data" : "up"
    }
    ],
    "oper-status" : [
    {
        "data" : "up"
    }
    ],
    "description" : [
    {
        "data" : "R0 (10.102.180.178) Loopback"
    }
    ]
}
]
}
]
}
```

Multiple RPCs in One Request

While the Junos RESTful API service does not currently support multiple HTTP requests over a single TCP session, it does offer the ability to execute multiple RPCs in one request. This ability is implemented using HTTP POST requests. "HTTP POST Requests" on page 110 already showed how to invoke a single RPC using an HTTP POST request. Invoking multiple RPCs in a single HTTP POST request is similar, but the URL does not include the specific RPCs to invoke. Instead, the RPCs are encoded in XML format and delivered as the message body of the HTTP POST request. When invoking multiple RPCs, the URL format is simply:

```
protocol://device:port/rpc
```

In this case, the output format must be specified with an `Accept` header field rather than an `@format=` URL attribute, and the `Content-Type: application/xml` header field must be included to specify the message body is in XML format. Here's an example that uses the `curl` command to invoke the *get-isis-adjacency-information*

RPC followed by the *get-system-alarm-information* RPC (the `-v` command-line option displays request and response header fields):

```
user@h0$ curl http://r0:3000/rpc -u "user:user123" \
> -H "Accept: application/xml" \
> -H "Content-Type: application/xml" \
> -d "<get-isis-adjacency-information/><get-system-alarm-information/>" -v
* Hostname was NOT found in DNS cache
*   Trying 10.102.180.178...
* Connected to r0 (10.102.180.178) port 3000 (#0)
* Server auth using Basic with user 'user'
> POST /rpc HTTP/1.1
> Authorization: Basic dXNlcjp1c2VyMTIz
> User-Agent: curl/7.37.1
> Host: r0:3000
> Accept: application/xml
> Content-Type: application/xml
> Content-Length: 64
>
* upload completely sent off: 64 out of 64 bytes
< HTTP/1.1 200 OK
< Content-Type: multipart/mixed; boundary=nwlrbbmqbhcdarz
< Transfer-Encoding: chunked
< Date: Thu, 30 Apr 2015 20:43:33 GMT
* Server lighttpd/1.4.32 is not blacklisted
< Server: lighttpd/1.4.32
<
--nwlrbbmqbhcdarz
Content-Type: application/xml; charset=utf-8

<isis-adjacency-information xmlns="..." xmlns:junos="..." junos:style="brief">
<isis-adjacency>
<interface-name>ge-0/0/0.0</interface-name>
<system-name>r1</system-name>
<level>2</level>
<adjacency-state>Up</adjacency-state>
<holdtime>20</holdtime>
</isis-adjacency>
</isis-adjacency-information>
--nwlrbbmqbhcdarz
Content-Type: application/xml; charset=utf-8

<alarm-information xmlns="http://xml.juniper.net/junos/14.2R2/junos-alarm">
<alarm-summary>
<no-active-alarms/>
</alarm-summary>
</alarm-information>
--nwlrbbmqbhcdarz--
* Connection #0 to host r0 left intact
```

When multiple RPCs are executed, the output is in multipart format, as indicated by the `Content-Type: multipart/mixed; boundary=nwlrbbmqbhcdarz` header field.

The individual responses are separated by boundary lines that include `--` followed by the boundary string specified in the header (`nwlrbbmqbhcdarz`, in this case). Each individual response also begins with its own `Content-Type` header field.

There is one case where the `Content-Type` header field is not included in the multipart output, though. If the RPC simply returns a NETCONF response with an empty `<rpc-reply>` node, the response does not contain a `Content-Type` header. The example `parse_multipart_messages()` function in "Parse Multi-RPC Responses" on page 155 provides an example of decoding multiple RPC responses in Python and handles this special case.

Because these two RPCs did not require parameters, they can be specified with a single XML tag using the closing `/>` characters. Alternatively, the RPCs could have been specified with the more verbose string `<get-isis-adjacency-information></get-isis-adjacency-information><get-system-alarm-information></get-system-alarm-information>`. This more verbose format must be used to enclose XML tags that represent RPC parameters. Because parameters are unique to each RPC, when making a multi-RPC request, parameters cannot be specified using the formats described in the previous section. Instead, the parameters' XML tags are enclosed within the RPC's XML tags. Here is an example:

```
user@h0$ curl http://r0:3000/rpc -u "user:user123" \
> -H "Accept: application/xml" -H "Content-Type: application/xml" -d '
> <get-interface-information>
>   <descriptions/>
>   <interface-name>lo0.0</interface-name>
> </get-interface-information>
> <get-interface-information>
>   <media/>
> <interface-name>ge-0/0/0</interface-name>
> </get-interface-information>'
--nwlrbbmqbhcdarz
Content-Type: application/xml; charset=utf-8

<interface-information xmlns="..." xmlns:junos="..." junos:style="description">
<logical-interface>
<name>lo0.0</name>
<admin-status>up</admin-status>
<oper-status>up</oper-status>
<description>R0 (10.102.180.178) Loopback</description>
</logical-interface>
</interface-information>
--nwlrbbmqbhcdarz
Content-Type: application/xml; charset=utf-8

<interface-information xmlns="..." xmlns:junos="..." junos:style="normal">
```

```
<physical-interface>
<name>ge-0/0/0</name>

<ethernet-autonegotiation>
<autonegotiation-status>incomplete</autonegotiation-status>
</ethernet-autonegotiation>
<interface-transmit-statistics>Disabled</interface-transmit-statistics>
</physical-interface>
</interface-information>
--nwlrbbmqbhcdarz--
```

In this example, the value of the `-d` command-line option is a multiline single-quoted string. The shell allows carriage returns within a single-quoted string, making it easier to input the XML without requiring a backslash at the end of each line. The single quote after the last `</get-interface-information>` tag terminates the string.

This HTTP POST request first invokes the *get-interface-information* RPC with the `descriptions` and `interface-name` parameters. The `descriptions` parameter does not take a value. It is specified with the single XML tag `<descriptions/>`. The `interface-name` parameter does require a value, and that value is specified between the parameter's XML tags as `<interface-name>lo0.0</interface-name>`. The HTTP POST request then invokes a second instance of the *get-interface-information* RPC with the `media` and `interface-name` parameters.

When a RESTful API query includes multiple RPCs, the RPCs are invoked sequentially in the order they are listed in the query. Likewise, the response output is also in the same order as the corresponding RPCs in the query. If an RPC returns an error, the default behavior is to continue executing the remaining RPCs in the query. This behavior can be modified by appending the `?stop-on-error=1` query string to the end of the request's URL. The following example attempts to invoke two RPCs. The first RPC, *get-foo-information*, does not exist, while the second RPC, *get-system-alarm-information*, is valid. The example shows the behavior with and without the `?stop-on-error=1` query string:

```
user@h0$ curl http://r0:3000/rpc -u "user:user123" \
> -H "Accept: application/xml" -H "Content-Type: application/xml" -d '
> <get-foo-information/>
> <get-system-alarm-information/>'
--nwlrbbmqbhcdarz
Content-Type: application/xml; charset=utf-8

<xnm:error xmlns="http://xml.juniper.net/xnm/1.1/xnm"
           xmlns:xnm="http://xml.juniper.net/xnm/1.1/xnm">
<token>get-foo-information</token>
<message>syntax error</message>
</xnm:error>
```

```
--nwlrbbmqbhcdarz
Content-Type: application/xml; charset=utf-8

<alarm-information xmlns="http://xml.juniper.net/junos/14.2R2/junos-alarm">
<alarm-summary>
<no-active-alarms/>
</alarm-summary>
</alarm-information>
--nwlrbbmqbhcdarz--

user@h0$ curl http://r0:3000/rpc?stop-on-error=1 -u "user:user123" \
> -H "Accept: application/xml" -H "Content-Type: application/xml" -d '
> <get-foo-information/>
> <get-system-alarm-information/>'
--nwlrbbmqbhcdarz
Content-Type: application/xml; charset=utf-8

<xnm:error xmlns="http://xml.juniper.net/xnm/1.1/xnm"
           xmlns:xnm="http://xml.juniper.net/xnm/1.1/xnm">
<token>get-foo-information</token>
<message>syntax error</message>
</xnm:error>
--nwlrbbmqbhcdarz--
```

In the first query, the *get-foo-information* RPC returns a syntax error, but the *get-system-alarm-information* RPC is still executed. In the second query, the `?stop-on-error=1` query string is appended to the URL. In this case, the *get-system-alarm-information* RPC is not executed. Execution stops when the *get-foo-information* RPC returns an error.

Configuration

Up until this point, the examples have demonstrated using the RESTful API service to invoke only operational RPCs. That omission has been intentional because making configuration changes to a Junos device requires invoking multiple RPCs. Now that you know how to invoke multiple RPCs using the RESTful API, it is time for a more complex example that both modifies the configuration and invokes operational RPCs. The example query:

1. Gets the description of the `lo0.0` logical interface using the *get-interface-information* RPC with appropriate arguments.
2. Gets a summary of the routing information using the *get-route-summary-information* RPC. This RPC is equivalent to the `show route summary` CLI command. The output will include the device's autonomous system (AS) if one is configured.
3. Opens a private candidate configuration.

4. Adds configuration to place the device in autonomous system `64512`.
5. Adds configuration to replace the description of the `lo0.0` logical interface. The new description includes the AS number.
6. Commits the newly modified private candidate configuration.
7. Closes the private candidate configuration.
8. Gets the description of the `lo0.0` logical interface using the *get-interface-information* RPC with appropriate arguments. The output should now include the newly configured description.
9. Gets a summary of the routing information using the *get-route-summary-information* RPC. The output should now include the newly configured AS.

The query looks like this:

```
user@h0$ curl http://r0:3000/rpc?stop-on-error=1 ❶ -u "user:user123" \
> -H "Accept: application/xml" -H "Content-Type: application/xml" ❷ \
> -d ' ❸
> <get-interface-information> ❹
>   <descriptions/>
>   <interface-name>lo0.0</interface-name>
> </get-interface-information>
> <get-route-summary-information/> ❺
> <open-configuration> ❻
>   <private/>
> </open-configuration>
> <load-configuration action="merge" format="xml"> ❼
>   <configuration>
>     <routing-options>
>       <autonomous-system>
>         <as-number>64512</as-number> ❽
>       </autonomous-system>
>     </routing-options>
>     <interfaces>
>       <interface>
>         <name>lo0</name>
>         <unit>
>           <name>0</name>
>           <description>R0 (AS 64512) Loopback</description> ❾
>         </unit>
>       </interface>
>     </interfaces>
>   </configuration>
> </load-configuration>
> <commit-configuration/> ❿
> <close-configuration/> ⓫
> <get-interface-information> ⓬
>   <descriptions/>
>   <interface-name>lo0.0</interface-name>
> </get-interface-information>
```

```
> <get-route-summary-information/> ⓭
> '
```

❶ The URL includes the `?stop-on-error=1` query string. If any RPC produces an error, the execution will stop and further RPCs will not be executed. This avoids attempting to commit a partial or invalid configuration.

❷ Multiple RPCs can only be entered in XML format. The query must include a `Content-Type: application/xml` header to correctly specify the HTTP POST body is in XML.

❸ The value of the `-d` command-line option contains the HTTP POST body. Enclosing the value in single quotes allows it to extend across multiple lines without requiring the line continuation character at the end of each line.

❹ The *get-interface-information* RPC is executed with the `descriptions` and `interface-name` arguments. The value of the `interface-name` argument is set to `lo0.0`.

❺ The *get-route-summary-information* RPC is executed next. This RPC has no arguments.

❻ The *open-configuration* RPC causes a candidate configuration to be created. The `private` argument makes this RPC equivalent to the `configure private` CLI command.

❼ The *load-configuration* RPC encloses the configuration snippet used to modify the private candidate configuration. The `action="merge"` attribute indicates the configuration snippet should be merged with the private candidate configuration. The `format="xml"` attribute indicates the configuration snippet will be in XML format.

❽ The configuration snippet sets the autonomous system to `64512`. This is equivalent to entering `set routing-options autonomous-system 64512` in the CLI's configuration mode.

❾ The configuration snippet sets the `lo0.0` interface description to include the AS number. This is equivalent to entering `set interfaces interface lo0 unit 0 description "R0 (AS 64512) Loopback"` in the CLI's configuration mode.

❿ The *commit-configuration* RPC commits the private candidate configuration that was modified by the previous RPC.

⓫ The *close-configuration* RPC closes the private candidate configuration database.

⓬ The *get-interface-information* RPC is executed again to confirm the change in interface description.

⓭ The *get-route-summary-information* RPC is executed again to confirm the autonomous system number.

The response is as follows:

```
--nwlrbbmqbhcdarz ❶
Content-Type: application/xml; charset=utf-8 ❷

<interface-information xmlns="..." xmlns:junos="..." junos:style="description">
<logical-interface>
<name>lo0.0</name>
<admin-status>up</admin-status>
<oper-status>up</oper-status>
<description>R0 (10.102.180.178) Loopback</description> ❸
</logical-interface>
</interface-information>
--nwlrbbmqbhcdarz
Content-Type: application/xml; charset=utf-8

<route-summary-information xmlns="...">
<router-id>10.210.255.200</router-id> ❹
... output trimmed ...
</route-summary-information>
--nwlrbbmqbhcdarz
Content-Type: application/xml; charset=utf-8

<xnm:warning xmlns="http://xml.juniper.net/xnm/1.1/xnm" xmlns:xnm="...">
<message>
uncommitted changes will be discarded on exit ❺
</message>
</xnm:warning>
--nwlrbbmqbhcdarz
Content-Type: application/xml; charset=utf-8

<load-configuration-results>
<load-success/> ❻
</load-configuration-results>
--nwlrbbmqbhcdarz
Content-Type: application/xml; charset=utf-8

<commit-results xmlns:junos="http://xml.juniper.net/junos/*/junos">
<load-success/>
<load-success/>
<routing-engine junos:style="normal">
<name>re0</name>
<commit-success/> ❼
```

```
</routing-engine>
</commit-results>
--nwlrbbmqbhcdarz
❽
--nwlrbbmqbhcdarz
Content-Type: application/xml; charset=utf-8

<interface-information xmlns="..." xmlns:junos="..." junos:style="description">
<logical-interface>
<name>lo0.0</name>
<admin-status>up</admin-status>
<oper-status>up</oper-status>
<description>R0 (AS 64512) Loopback</description> ❾
</logical-interface>
</interface-information>
--nwlrbbmqbhcdarz
Content-Type: application/xml; charset=utf-8

<route-summary-information xmlns="...">
<as-number>64512</as-number> ❿
<router-id>10.210.255.200</router-id>
... output trimmed ...
</route-summary-information>
--nwlrbbmqbhcdarz--
```

❶ While the HTTP response headers have not been included in this output, a `Content-Type: multipart/mixed; boundary=nwlrbbmqbhcdarz` response header field is present. This header indicates the string that separates the output for each RPC.

❷ Each individual response has its own `Content-Type` header field indicating the output is in XML format.

❸ The current interface description includes the loopback IP address `10.102.180.178`.

❹ The `<router-id>` tag is present in this response, but no `<autonomous-system>` tag is present.

❺ Adding the `private` argument to the *open-configuration* RPC causes this warning to be emitted. This is the desired behavior, so the warning message can be ignored.

❻ The *load-configuration* RPC successfully loaded the configuration snippet.

❼ The *commit-configuration* RPC successfully committed the modified configuration.

❽ The *close-configuration* RPC successfully closed the private candidate configuration. Notice there is no output from this RPC and the `Content-Type` header is missing from this message.

❾ The modified interface description now includes the AS number.

❿ The route summary information now includes the AS number.

RESTful API Explorer

"Discovering Operational RPC Syntax" on page 63 explored the CLI's `| display xml rpc` capability. This capability allows the Junoscript/NETCONF RPC for a specific CLI command to be discovered. The same capability can be used to discover the name of an RPC to be used with the Junos RESTful API service. The procedure's name is simply the XML tag name discovered with `| display xml rpc`. Let's look at a few examples:

```
user@r0> show isis adjacency | display xml rpc
<rpc-reply xmlns:junos="http://xml.juniper.net/junos/14.2R2/junos">
    <rpc>
        <get-isis-adjacency-information>
        </get-isis-adjacency-information>
    </rpc>
    <cli>
        <banner></banner>
    </cli>
</rpc-reply>

user@r0> show chassis hardware | display xml rpc
<rpc-reply xmlns:junos="http://xml.juniper.net/junos/14.2R2/junos">
    <rpc>
        <get-chassis-inventory>
        </get-chassis-inventory>
    </rpc>
    <cli>
        <banner></banner>
    </cli>
</rpc-reply>
```

These examples demonstrate that the *get-isis-adjacency-information* procedure corresponds to the `show isis adjacency` CLI command, and the *get-chassis-inventory* procedure corresponds to the `show chassis hardware` CLI command. The corresponding URLs to query the Junos RESTful API service with an HTTP GET request would be `http://r0:3000/rpc/get-isis-adjacency-information` and `http://r0:3000/rpc/get-chassis-inventory`, respectively.

Once the procedure to be executed is known, the Junos RESTful API service offers an additional tool to help format the query and inspect the resulting output. The tool is the *REST-API explorer*, and it offers a quick way of testing RPCs before adding them to a program. The REST-API explorer is an optional component that can be enabled with the Junos RESTful API service. Enabling the REST-API explorer requires adding the `enable-explorer` configuration statement at the `[edit system services rest]` configuration hierarchy level:

```
set system services rest enable-explorer
```

After adding this configuration, you can point a web browser at a URL of the form *protocol://device:port/*, where *protocol*, *device*, and *port* identify the protocol, device, and port already running the Junos RESTful API service. Here is an example that adds the `enable-explorer` configuration to our existing minimal RESTful API service configuration. The RESTful API service is enabled for HTTP on port 3000 of `r0`:

```
user@r0> configure
Entering configuration mode

[edit]
user@r0# show system services rest
http;

[edit]
user@r0# set system services rest enable-explorer

[edit]
user@r0# commit and-quit
commit complete
Exiting configuration mode

user@r0> show configuration system services rest
http;
enable-explorer;

user@r0>
```

It is recommended that you only enable the REST-API explorer on a test device in your lab or as a temporary tool while developing automation using the Junos RESTful API service. Once your program has been written and debugged, there is no longer a need for the REST-API explorer to be enabled.

Now that the REST-API explorer has been enabled, it can be used to test the behavior of specific RPC queries on the device. Open a web browser and navigate to *http://r0:3000/*, as shown in Figure 3-2.

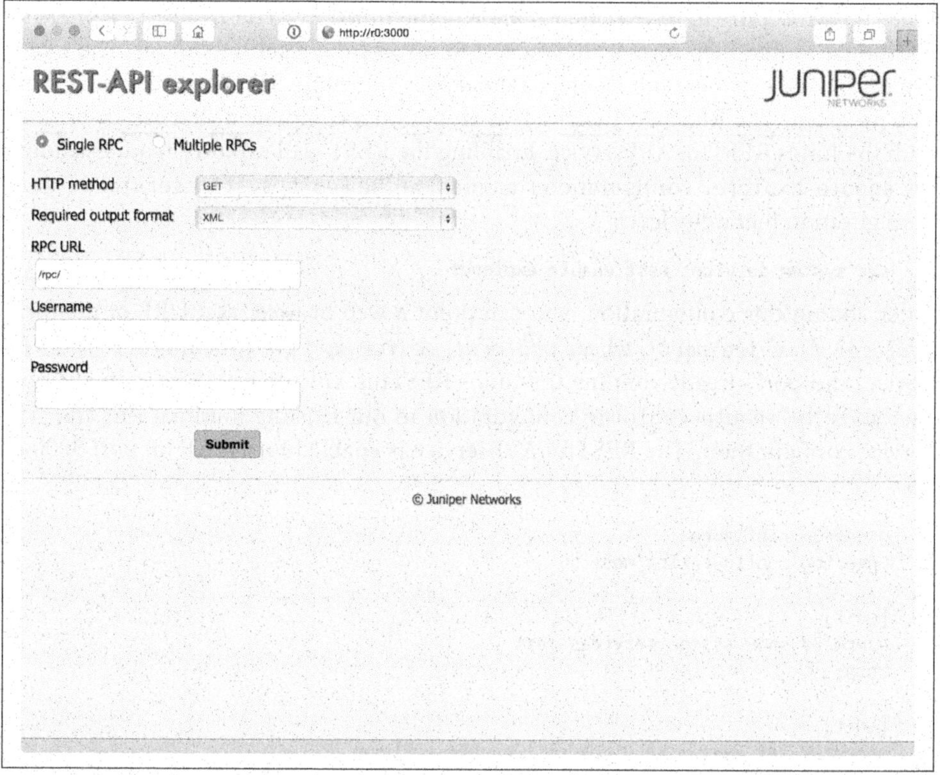

Figure 3-2. The REST-API explorer

The user interface of the REST-API explorer consists of the following fields:

- A radial selection to choose between a single-RPC query, which can be either a GET or a POST request, and a multiple-RPC query, which can only be a POST request.
- If "Single RPC" is selected, the "HTTP method" drop-down allows a GET request or a POST request to be selected.
- The "Required output format" drop-down specifies the output format that will be requested using an `Accept` header field, as discussed in "Formatting HTTP Responses" on page 103. If you prefer to specify the output with an `@format=` URL attribute, enter the desired attribute in the "RPC URL" field.
- The "RPC URL" field is populated with the hierarchical path and optional query component of the RPC call's URL. That is the portion of the URL that appears after the TCP port number.

- The "Username" and "Password" fields are used for authentication and authorization, as described in "Authentication and Authorization" on page 99.

If you choose the "Multiple RPCs" radial, two additional fields are added to the form:

"Stop on Error" checkbox
: Defines whether or not the `stop-on-error=1` parameter is added to the RPC URL. As discussed in "Multiple RPCs in One Request" on page 117, this parameter specifies the behavior when multiple RPCs are specified and one of the RPCs returns an error.

"Request body" field
: Specifies the RPCs to be used in the HTTP body of the POST request, as discussed in "Multiple RPCs in One Request" on page 117.

After filling in the appropriate fields in the REST-API explorer UI, click the Submit button to see the results of the specified RPC(s). The result of a single-RPC query using a GET request for the *get-isis-adjacency-information* procedure is shown in Figure 3-3. In this example, the JSON output format was specified in the "Required output format" field of the submission.

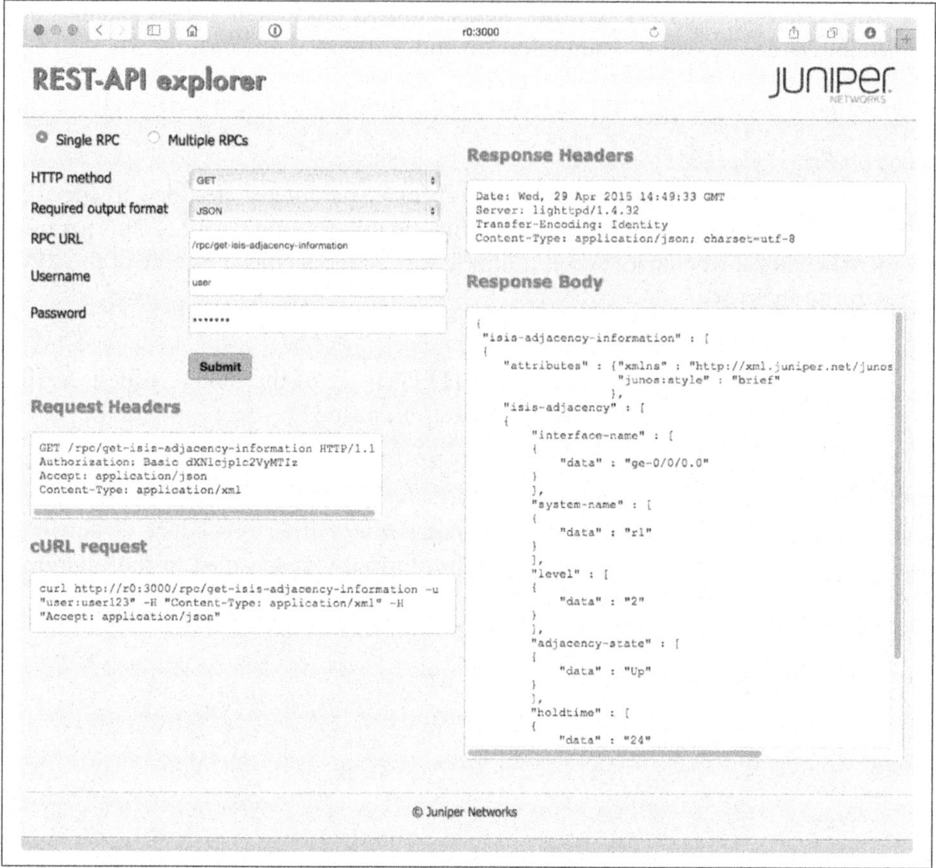


```
{
"isis-adjacency-information" : [
{
   "attributes" : {"xmlns" : "http://xml.juniper.net/junos
                   "junos:style" : "brief"
                  },
   "isis-adjacency" : [
   {
      "interface-name" : [
      {
         "data" : "ge-0/0/0.0"
      }
      ],
      "system-name" : [
      {
         "data" : "r1"
      }
      ],
      "level" : [
      {
         "data" : "2"
      }
      ],
      "adjacency-state" : [
      {
         "data" : "Up"
      }
      ],
      "holdtime" : [
      {
         "data" : "24"
```


Figure 3-3. Resulting output of a REST-API explorer submission

The result of the REST-API explorer submission consists of the following fields:

- The "Response Headers" field displays the HTTP header fields that were returned in response to the submitted query. This field confirms whether the expected output format was returned. In this case, the output is in the expected JSON format, as indicated by the `Content-Type: application/json; charset=utf-8` header field.
- The "Response Body" field shows the actual data returned in response to the submitted query. In this case, the data is in JSON format and describes a single ISIS (Intermediate System–to–Intermediate System) adjacency to `r1` that is in an `Up` state. This output is helpful in determining the exact format of the JSON or XML data structure returned for a given RPC.

- The "Request Headers" field shows the exact HTTP data—request line and header fields—corresponding to the submitted query. As discussed in "Formatting HTTP Responses" on page 103, if the output format was specified with an `@format=` URL attribute, the `Accept` header field is redundant and may be omitted from the query.
- The "cURL request" field shows the exact `curl` command-line corresponding to the submitted query. It can be copied and pasted at a shell prompt to invoke the RPC using the cURL utility.

Using the RESTful APIs in Python

The previous sections in this chapter have covered the intricacies of making queries of the Junos RESTful API service; now it is time to put this knowledge into practice with a small Python script. The example script makes single-RPC queries and receives responses in both JSON and XML formats. In addition, it demonstrates configuring the device using a multi-RPC query.

Two libraries that are not part of Python's standard library are used in the example script. The first library, Requests (*http://www.python-requests.org/*), is an HTTP library that is simpler to use than Python's standard `urllib2` (*https://docs.python.org/2/library/urllib2.html*). Requests provides a higher-level HTTP client interface that simplifies HTTP basic authentication and eases the handling of HTTP errors. The second library, jxmlease (*https://github.com/Juniper/jxmlease*), parses XML documents into Python data structures. It was discussed in detail in "Using Structured Data in Python" on page 42. It also provides the reverse operation to easily "unparse" a Python data structure into an XML document.

Before diving into the example code, it's helpful to understand the purpose and overall architecture of the script. The script discovers and monitors the network topology of one or more Junos devices running the Link Layer Discovery Protocol (LLDP) and the RESTful API service. Information discovered from LLDP is stored in the interface description fields of the device's configuration. The current LLDP-discovered information is compared against the previous information that may be stored in the interface description field, and the user is notified of any changes in LLDP state (up, change, and down) since the previous snapshot.

The script is invoked by a user at the command line and takes one or more device names, or IP addresses, as command-line arguments. The syntax is:

```
user@h0$ python lldp_interface_descriptions_rest.py r0 r1 r2 r3 r4 r5
```

In order to execute successfully, the following prerequisite configuration should be present on each device:

- The RESTful API service should be configured and reachable on the device:

  ```
  user@r0> show configuration system services
  rest {
      http;
  }
  ```

- A user account with the necessary authorization should be configured on the device:

  ```
  user@r0> show configuration system login
  user user {
      uid 2001;
      class super-user;
      authentication {
          encrypted-password "$1$jCvocDbA$KeOycEvIDtSV/VOdPRHo5.";
      }
  }
  ```

- LLDP should be configured on all nonmanagement interfaces of the device. It is recommended that the `port-id-subtype interface-name` statement also be configured at the `[edit protocols lldp]` hierarchy level:

  ```
  user@r0> show configuration protocols lldp
  port-id-subtype interface-name;
  interface all;
  interface fxp0 {
      disable;
  }
  ```

  The `port-id-subtype interface-name` configuration statement ensures that the remote port of an LLDP neighbor is reported as an interface name (i.e., `ge-0/0/0`) rather than an SNMP interface index.

The script's output is printed to the user's terminal. It prints a notification for each device checked. If the script detects any changes in LLDP state since the last snapshot, those changes are printed to the terminal. The new interface descriptions are configured and a message indicates whether or not the device's configuration was successfully updated. The following example shows a sample output from the script:

```
user@h0$ python lldp_interface_descriptions_rest.py r0 r1 r2 r3 r4 r5
Device Username: user
Device Password:
Getting LLDP information from r0...
Getting interface descriptions from r0...
    ge-0/0/4 LLDP Up. Was: r1 ge-0/0/0 Now: r1 ge-0/0/0
    ge-0/0/3 LLDP Change. Was: r7 ge-0/0/4 Now: r5 ge-0/0/0
    ge-0/0/2 LLDP Change. Was: r3 ge-0/0/0 Now: r3 ge-0/0/2
    ge-0/0/1 LLDP Up. Now: r2 ge-0/0/2
    ge-0/0/0 LLDP Up. Now: r4 ge-0/0/2
    ge-0/0/5 LLDP Down. Was: r6 ge-0/0/8
```

```
    Successfully committed configuration changes on r0.
Getting LLDP information from r1...
Getting interface descriptions from r1...
    ge-0/0/2 LLDP Up. Now: r2 ge-0/0/0
    ge-0/0/1 LLDP Up. Now: r5 ge-0/0/1
    ge-0/0/0 LLDP Up. Now: r0 ge-0/0/4
    Successfully committed configuration changes on r1.
Getting LLDP information from r2...
Getting interface descriptions from r2...
    ge-0/0/2 LLDP Up. Now: r0 ge-0/0/1
    ge-0/0/1 LLDP Up. Now: r3 ge-0/0/0
    ge-0/0/0 LLDP Up. Now: r1 ge-0/0/2
    Successfully committed configuration changes on r2.
Getting LLDP information from r3...
Getting interface descriptions from r3...
    No LLDP changes to configure on r3.
Getting LLDP information from r4...
Getting interface descriptions from r4...
    ge-0/0/2 LLDP Up. Now: r0 ge-0/0/0
    ge-0/0/1 LLDP Up. Now: r3 ge-0/0/1
    ge-0/0/0 LLDP Change. Was: r6 ge-0/0/5 Now: r5 ge-0/0/2
    ge-0/0/3 LLDP Down. Was: r7 ge-0/0/3
    Successfully committed configuration changes on r4.
Getting LLDP information from r5...
Getting interface descriptions from r5...
    No LLDP changes to configure on r5.
```

As the script sequentially loops through each device specified on the command line, it performs the following steps:

1. Gather LLDP neighbor information.
2. Gather interface descriptions; parse the LLDP neighbor information that was previously stored in the interface descriptions.
3. Compare current and previous LLDP neighbor information; print LLDP up, change, and down messages; calculate new interface descriptions.
4. Build a candidate configuration with updated interface descriptions.
5. Apply and commit the candidate configuration.

The example tries to provide a useful and realistic function while also concentrating on code that demonstrates the Junos RESTful API service. The example script is invoked by the user at the command line, but a more complex program using the RESTful API service might be invoked by an event or on a schedule. In addition, the output might integrate with an existing network monitoring or alerting system rather than simply being printed to the terminal. A more realistic implementation would provide additional exception handling. It would also store the LLDP information gathered from the device in an off-device database or in on-device `apply-macro` configuration statements rather than the interface `description` configuration statements. Finally, each device could be queried and configured in parallel to speed the program's execution.

Let's analyze the Python code used to perform each of these steps. The best way to understand the code is by following along and typing each line of the program listing into your own script file named *lldp_interface_descriptions_rest.py*. After completing "Putting It All Together" on page 157, you will have a working example to execute against your own network.

The Preamble

The first step in our example script is to import the required libraries and perform some one-time initialization. The callouts give more information on each line of the program listing:

```
#!/usr/bin/env python ❶
"""Use interface descriptions to track the topology reported by LLDP. ❷

This includes the following steps:
1) Gather LLDP neighbor information.
2) Gather interface descriptions.
3) Parse LLDP neighbor information previously stored in the descriptions.
4) Compare LLDP neighbor info to previous LLDP info from the descriptions.
5) Print LLDP Up / Change / Down events.
6) Store the updated LLDP neighbor info in the interface descriptions.

Interface descriptions are in the format:
[user-configured description ]LLDP: <remote system> <remote port>[(DOWN)]

The '(DOWN)' string indicates an LLDP neighbor which was previously
present, but is now not present.
"""

import sys ❸
import email
import getpass
```

```
import requests ❹
import jxmlease

# Should be set appropriately for the network environment.
SCHEME = 'http' ❺
PORT = 3000

SINGLE_RPC_URL_FORMAT = SCHEME + '://%s:' + str(PORT) + '/rpc/%s@format=%s' ❻
MULTIPLE_RPC_URL_FORMAT = SCHEME + '://%s:' + str(PORT) + '/rpc'

# Create a jxmlease parser with desired defaults.
parser = jxmlease.Parser() ❼
```

❶ The `#!` line (sometimes called the hashbang or shebang line) allows the option of running the script without specifying the `python` command. (This mechanism works on Unix-like platforms and on Windows platforms using the Python Launcher for Windows.) In other words, you could execute the script with *`path`*`/lldp_interface_descriptions_rest.py` *`r0 r1 r2 r3 r4 r5`* instead of `python` *`path`*`/lldp_interface_descriptions_rest.py` *`r0 r1 r2 r3 r4 r5`*. Executing the script directly does require executable permissions to be set on the *lldp_interface_descriptions_rest.py* file. Using the */usr/bin/env* shell command to invoke Python means the script is not dependent on the location of the `python` command.

❷ This triple-quoted multiline block string is a documentation string, or docstring, which provides a high-level overview of the script's purpose and operation. The example also begins each function with a docstring.

❸ Three standard Python modules, `sys`, `email`, and `getpass`, are imported. The `sys` module provides access to objects maintained by the Python interpreter. The `email` module provides tools for parsing multipart MIME messages into their individual message components, and the `getpass` module allows the script to interactively prompt for the required password without echoing the input to the user's terminal.

❹ Two additional libraries are imported. As we just mentioned, the `requests` module provides an HTTP client library used to make HTTP GET and POST requests and receive HTTP responses. The `jxmlease` library parses XML into native Python data structures. You must ensure both of these modules are installed on your system.

❺ The `SCHEME` and `PORT` variables are used as constants that define the URL scheme and TCP port number used to reach the Junos RESTful API service, respectively. These variables centralize environment-specific settings. You should change the value of each variable to match your network environment.

❻ The `SINGLE_RPC_URL_FORMAT` and `MULTIPLE_RPC_URL_FORMAT` variables are also used as constants. Later, these variables are used as string format specifiers to create the URL for single- and multiple-RPC RESTful API queries.

❼ A `jxmlease` parser instance is created for parsing XML documents into Python data structures. The `jxmlease.Parser()` method creates an instance of the `jxml.Parser` class with a set of default parameters. While the `jxmlease.Parser()` method supports several parameters, the defaults are reasonable for parsing the XML that is returned from a Junos device.

Each of the script's major steps has been encapsulated into a Python function which will be executed from the `main()` function of the *lldp_interface_descriptions_rest.py* file.

Loop Through Each Device

Let's begin by analyzing the `main()` function, which prompts for a username and password and then loops over each device specified on the command line. The `main()` function calls several functions, which are each analyzed in later sections:

```
def main():
    """The main loop.

    Prompt for a username and password.
    Loop over each device specified on the command line.
    Perform the following steps on each device:
    1) Get LLDP information from the current device state.
    2) Get interface descriptions from the device configuration.
    3) Compare the LLDP information against the previous snapshot of LLDP
       information stored in the interface descriptions. Print changes.
    4) Build a configuration snippet with new interface descriptions.
    5) Commit the configuration changes.

    Return an integer suitable for passing to sys.exit().
    """

    if len(sys.argv) == 1: ❶
        print("\nUsage: %s device1 [device2 [...]]\n\n" % sys.argv[0])
        return 1

    rc = 0 ❷

    # Get username and password as user input.
    user = raw_input('Device Username: ') ❸
    password = getpass.getpass('Device Password: ')

    for hostname in sys.argv[1:]: ❹
        print("Getting LLDP information from %s..." % hostname)
        lldp_info = get_lldp_neighbors(device=hostname,
```

```
                                    user=user,
                                    pw=password) ❺
        if not lldp_info:
            if lldp_info == None:
                print("    Error retrieving LLDP info on " + hostname +
                      ". Make sure LLDP is enabled.")
            else:
                print("    No LLDP neighbors on " + hostname +
                      ". Make sure LLDP is enabled.")
            rc = 1
            continue

        print("Getting interface descriptions from %s..." % hostname)
        desc_info = get_description_info_for_interfaces(device=hostname, ❻
                                                         user=user,
                                                         pw=password)
        if desc_info == None:
            print("    Error retrieving interface descriptions on %s." %
                  hostname)
            rc = 1
            continue

        desc_changes = check_lldp_changes(lldp_info, desc_info) ❼
        if not desc_changes:
            print("    No LLDP changes to configure on %s." % hostname)
            continue

        config = build_config_changes(desc_changes) ❽
        if config == None:
            print("    Error generating configuration changes for %s." %
                  hostname)
            rc = 1
            continue

        if load_merge_xml_config(device=hostname, ❾
                                 user=user,
                                 pw=password,
                                 config=config):
            print("    Successfully committed configuration changes on %s." %
                  hostname)
        else:
            print("    Error committing description changes on %s." % hostname)
            rc = 1
    return rc ❿
```

❶ The script requires that at least one device be specified as a command-line argument. The `sys.argv` list will contain the name of the script at index 0. User-specified arguments begin at index 1. If no user-specified arguments are present (`len(sys.argv) == 1`), the usage message is printed and the script exits with a status code of `1` to indicate an error.

❷ The `rc` variable holds the status code to be returned at the end of the script. The value is initialized to `0` which indicates success. Later, if an error is encountered, `rc` will be set to `1` and processing will continue with the next device specified on the command-line.

❸ The `raw_input()` and `getpass.getpass()` functions are used to prompt for the username and password, respectively. Both functions take a prompt string as an argument. The `raw_input()` function echoes the user's input, while `getpass.getpass()` does not. The script assumes all devices listed on the command-line have the same username and password configured.

❹ This loop iterates over each device the user specified on the command-line. The hostname of the current device is stored in the `hostname` variable. Again, the `sys.argv` list will contain the name of the script at index 0, and user-specified arguments begin at index 1.

❺ The `get_lldp_neighbors()` function is invoked and the result is stored in `lldp_info`. The `lldp_info` variable is normally a dictionary containing the device's LLDP-discovered neighbors. The variable will have a value of `None` if there is an error retrieving LLDP neighbor information. An empty `lldp_info` dictionary indicates that no LLDP neighbors were discovered, but no error was encountered. This might mean that LLDP is not configured on the device, or simply that no LLDP neighbors are currently present. No further processing of `hostname` occurs if there is an error or no LLDP neighbors are present.

❻ The `get_description_info_for_interfaces()` function is invoked and the result is stored in the `desc_info` variable. The `desc_info` variable is normally a dictionary containing user-configured descriptions and a snapshot of the device's LLDP neighbor state from the previous script execution. The variable will have a value of `None` if there is an error retrieving the interface description information. In this case, no further processing of `hostname` occurs.

❼ The `check_lldp_changes()` function takes the `lldp_info` and `desc_info` dictionaries as input. It returns a dictionary assigned to the `desc_changes` variable. This dictionary contains the information needed to create new interface descriptions. If no new interface descriptions need to be configured, the loop continues with the next user-specified device.

❽ The `build_config_changes()` function takes the `desc_changes` information and returns the configuration snippet needed to configure the interface descriptions that have changed. If the `config` variable is empty, there was a problem generating the configuration. In this case, a message is printed, the `rc` variable is set to `1` to indicate the error, and the loop continues with the next `hostname`.

❾ The `load_merge_xml_config()` function attempts to apply the `config` configuration to the device. If the function returns `True`, the device has been successfully configured with new interface descriptions. A message is printed, and processing continues with the next `hostname` in the `for` loop. If the function returns `False`, there was an error applying the configuration. In this case, a message is printed, the `rc` variable is set to indicate the error, and processing continues with the next device in the `for` loop.

❿ Once all devices in the `for` loop have been processed, the script exits, returning the value of the `rc` variable as the status code.

Now, let's look at each of the functions that are called from the `for` loop in more detail.

Gather LLDP Neighbor Information

The first function, `get_lldp_neighbors()`, uses the RESTful API to query the *get-lldp-neighbors-information* RPC. The `@format=json` attribute is added to the URL to specify the response should be in JSON format. Before we look at the function itself, it's helpful to see the structure of the data that is returned by the *get-lldp-neighbors-information* RPC. Here's a small sample of that JSON information:


```
{
    "lldp-neighbors-information" : [
    {
        "attributes" : {"junos:style" : "brief"},
        "lldp-neighbor-information" : [
        {
            "lldp-local-port-id" : [
            {
                "data" : "ge-0/0/1"
            }
            ],
            "lldp-local-parent-interface-name" : [
            {
                "data" : "-"
            }
            ],
            "lldp-remote-chassis-id-subtype" : [
            {
                "data" : "Mac address"
            }
            ],
            "lldp-remote-chassis-id" : [
            {
```

```
                "data" : "00:05:86:08:d4:c0"
            }
            ],
            "lldp-remote-port-id-subtype" : [
            {
                "data" : "Interface name"
            }
            ],
            "lldp-remote-port-id" : [
            {
                "data" : "ge-0/0/1"
            }
            ],
            "lldp-remote-system-name" : [
            {
                "data" : "r5"
            }
            ]
        },
        {
            "lldp-local-port-id" : [
            {
                "data" : "ge-0/0/0"
            }
            ],
            "lldp-local-parent-interface-name" : [
            {
                "data" : "-"
            }
            ],
            "lldp-remote-chassis-id-subtype" : [
            {
                "data" : "Mac address"
            }
            ],
            "lldp-remote-chassis-id" : [
            {
                "data" : "00:05:86:58:6f:c0"
            }
            ],
            "lldp-remote-port-id-subtype" : [
            {
                "data" : "Interface name"
            }
            ],
            "lldp-remote-port-id" : [
            {
                "data" : "ge-0/0/4"
            }
            ],
            "lldp-remote-system-name" : [
            {
```

```
                    "data" : "r0"
                }
                ]
            },
            ... output trimmed ...
            ]
        }
        ]
    }
```


The `get_lldp_neighbors()` function gathers the LLDP neighbor's system and port information for each local interface from this JSON data structure. The information is returned to the caller in a dictionary:

```
def get_lldp_neighbors(device, user, pw):
    """Get current LLDP neighbor information.

    Return a two-level dictionary with the LLDP neighbor information.
    The first-level key is the local port (aka interface) name.
    The second-level keys are 'system' for the remote system name
    and 'port' for the remote port ID. On error, return None.

    For example:
    {'ge-0/0/1': {'system': 'r1', 'port', 'ge-0/0/10'}}
    """

    url = SINGLE_RPC_URL_FORMAT % (device, ❶
                                   'get-lldp-neighbors-information',
                                   'json')

    http_resp = requests.get(url, auth=(user,pw)) ❷
    http_resp.raise_for_status() ❸

    # Check for an XML error message. ❹
    if http_resp.headers['Content-Type'].startswith('application/xml'):
        _ = check_for_warnings_and_errors(parser(http_resp.text))
        return None

    resp = http_resp.json() ❺

    lldp_info = {} ❻
    try: ❼
        ni = resp['lldp-neighbors-information'][0]['lldp-neighbor-information']
    except KeyError:
        return None

    for nbr in ni: ❽
        try:
            local_port = nbr['lldp-local-port-id'][0]['data'] ❾
            remote_system = nbr['lldp-remote-system-name'][0]['data']
            remote_port = nbr['lldp-remote-port-id'][0]['data']
            lldp_info[local_port] = {'system': remote_system, ❿
```

```
                                  'port': remote_port}
        except KeyError: ⓫
            return None

    return lldp_info
```

❶ The `url` variable is constructed using the `SINGLE_RPC_URL_FORMAT` string format specifier defined earlier. The device name (the value of the `device` variable), the RPC (`get-lldp-neighbors-information`), and the desired format (`json`) are combined to produce the complete URL. Assuming the value of the `device` variable is `r0`, the resulting value of `url` would be: `http://r0:3000/rpc/get-lldp-neighbors-information@format=json`.

❷ The `requests.get()` function performs an HTTP GET of `url`. The `auth` parameter adds an HTTP basic authentication header field using the values from the `user` and `pw` variables that were passed to the function. A Requests `Response` object is returned and assigned to the `http_resp` variable.

❸ The `raise_for_status()` method causes an exception to be raised if any HTTP status code other than `200 OK` is returned. The example script does not handle this exception, so any RESTful API queries that receive an HTTP status code other than `200 OK` will cause the script to exit. A more robust implementation might choose to handle these exceptions in a more graceful manner.

❹ As described in the waning at the end of "Formatting HTTP Responses" on page 103, there are situations where an XML error is returned in response to a JSON query. This block handles that situation by checking the `Content-Type` header of the response. If an XML response is received, the `check_for_warnings_and_errors()` function is called to print the content of the XML error message. The return value of `None` indicates an error was encountered.

❺ The Requests library includes a built-in JSON decoder that is accessed with the `json()` method. The `resp` variable is assigned a dictionary that represents the decoded JSON response as a native Python data structure.

❻ The `lldp_info` dictionary will be populated with information gathered from the RESTful API query. Here, it is initialized with an empty dictionary. Initializing `lldp_info` before the `try` block ensures the variable is assigned before it is referenced in the `return` statement at the end of the function. It also ensures an empty dictionary is returned if LLDP is configured, but no neighbors are currently present.

(7) The variable `ni` is assigned to the subset of the parsed JSON response found at `resp['lldp-neighbors-information'][0]['lldp-neighbor-information']`. If there is LLDP neighbor information present in `resp`, then `ni` will point to a list of dictionaries. Each dictionary will contain information about a particular LLDP neighbor. It is very important to note that the parsed response may *not* contain LLDP neighbor information. *Any time a dictionary key or list index is accessed in the parsed Python response, you must consider the possibility that the key or index does not exist.* This assignment statement will raise a `KeyError` exception if no LLDP neighbor information is present in `resp`. Enclosing this statement in a `try` block ensures that the `KeyError` condition is handled gracefully and the function simply returns `None`.

(8) The `for` loop iterates over each dictionary of LLDP neighbor information that is present in the `ni` variable. The `nbr` variable is assigned the current LLDP neighbor information dictionary for each iteration through the loop.

(9) The local device's port (aka interface) is accessed in `nbr` and assigned to the `local_port` variable. A similar assignment is repeated for the LLDP neighbor's remote system and port information. It is possible that one of the referenced indexes or keys may not be present in the `nbr` variable. In that case, a `KeyError` exception is raised.

(10) A new `local_port` key is added to the `lldp_info` dictionary. The value contains both `'system'` and `'port'` keys with values of the remote system name and remote port name, respectively.

(11) The `except` statement catches `KeyError` exceptions. A `KeyError` exception returns a value of `None`, which indicates an error has occurred.

Gather and Parse Interface Descriptions

The next function, `get_description_info_for_interfaces()`, makes a RESTful API query using the *get-interface-information* RPC. The `descriptions` parameter is added to the RPC in order to retrieve only the interface descriptions. This time, the output is requested in XML format. Here's a small sample of the XML structure returned by the RPC:

```
<interface-information xmlns="..." junos:style="description">
    <physical-interface>
        <name>ge-0/0/0</name>
        <admin-status>up</admin-status>
        <oper-status>up</oper-status>
        <description>LLDP: r0 ge-0/0/4</description>
    </physical-interface>
```

```
    <physical-interface>
        <name>ge-0/0/1</name>
        <admin-status>up</admin-status>
        <oper-status>up</oper-status>
        <description>LLDP: r5 ge-0/0/1</description>
    </physical-interface>
    <physical-interface>
        <name>ge-0/0/2</name>
        <admin-status>up</admin-status>
        <oper-status>up</oper-status>
        <description>LLDP: r2 ge-0/0/0</description>
    </physical-interface>
</interface-information>
```

The content of the interface's `<description>` tag is parsed based on a simple convention that has been chosen for this example script. The convention is:

```
[user-defined description ]LLDP: remote_system remote_port[(DOWN)]
```

The first portion of the interface description may optionally contain a user-defined description. If present, the description can contain any content other than the string `'LLDP: '`. The string `'LLDP: '` is used to delimit the user-defined portion of the description from the portion of the description where LLDP information is stored. The portion after this delimiter stores the interface's remote system name and remote port name, which that were learned from LLDP and configured during a previous execution of the script. The remote system and remote port are separated by a single space. If LLDP information was previously learned on an interface but is no longer present, the string `'(DOWN)'` will be appended to the previous remote system and remote port information. The information gathered is parsed and returned to the caller in a dictionary:

```
def get_description_info_for_interfaces(device, user, pw):
    """Get current interface description for each interface.

    Parse the description into the user-configured description, remote
    system, and remote port components.

    Return a two-level dictionary. The first-level key is the
    local port (aka interface) name. The second-level keys are
    'user_desc' for the user-configured description, 'system' for the
    remote system name, 'port' for the remote port, and 'down', which is
    a Boolean indicating if LLDP was previously down. On error, return None.

    For example:
    {'ge-0/0/1': {'user_desc': 'test description', 'system': 'r1',
                  'port': 'ge-0/0/10', 'down': True}}
    """

    url = SINGLE_RPC_URL_FORMAT % (device, 'get-interface-information', 'xml') ❶

    http_resp = requests.get(url, ❷
```

```
                                auth=(user, pw),
                                params={'descriptions': ''},
                                stream=True)
    http_resp.raise_for_status()
    resp = parser(http_resp.raw) ❸

    (error_count, warning_count) = check_for_warnings_and_errors(resp) ❹
    if error_count > 0:
        return None

    desc_info = {}
    try:
        pi = resp['interface-information']['physical-interface'].jdict() ❺
    except KeyError:
        return desc_info

    for (local_port, port_info) in pi.items(): ❻
        try:
            (udesc, _, ldesc) = port_info['description'].partition('LLDP: ') ❼
            udesc = udesc.rstrip() ❽
            (remote_system, _, remote_port) = ldesc.partition(' ') ❾
            (remote_port, down_string, _) = remote_port.partition('(DOWN)') ❿
            desc_info[local_port] = {'user_desc': udesc, ⓫
                                     'system': remote_system,
                                     'port': remote_port,
                                     'down': True if down_string else False}
        except (KeyError, TypeError): ⓬
            pass
    return desc_info
```

❶ A `url` variable is again constructed from the `SINGLE_RPC_URL_FORMAT` string format specifier defined earlier. The device name (the value of the `device` variable), the RPC (`get-interface-information`), and the desired format (`xml`) are combined to produce the complete URL. Assuming the value of the `device` variable is `r0`, the resulting value of `url` would be: `http://r0:3000/rpc/get-interface-information@format=xml`.

❷ The `requests.get()` function performs an HTTP GET of `url`. As before, the `auth` parameter adds authentication information. The `params` parameter defines a set of key/value pairs, which are treated as a CGI query string. The `params={'descriptions': ''}` argument to the `requests.get()` function results in `?descriptions=` being appended to the end of the URL. The `stream=True` argument allows the response to be read iteratively in streaming mode rather than downloading it all at once. While not necessary in this small example, streaming mode improves performance and efficiency for very large XML responses. A Requests `Response` object is returned and assigned to the `http_resp` variable.

❸ The `parser` object was previously created as an instance of the `jxmlease.Parser` class. It parses the stream-level `http_resp.raw` output containing the XML response returned from the HTTP GET request. The parsed output is a `jxmlease.XMLDictNode` that is assigned to the `resp` variable.

❹ The `resp` variable is passed to the `check_for_warnings_and_errors()` function. If any errors are found, the function returns `None`. The next section explores the `check_for_warnings_and_errors()` function in more detail.

❺ The `pi` variable is assigned to a subset of the parsed response contained in the variable `resp`. Just like when the response is returned in JSON format, it is possible that an expected key may not be present in the data structure. If the `'interface-information'` or `'physical-interface'` key is not present, this line will raise a `KeyError` exception and return the empty `desc_info` dictionary indicating no descriptions are present. The `jdict()` method from the `jxmlease` library returns a dictionary keyed on the value of the `<name>` tags that were present at this level of the XML response.

❻ This `for` loop iterates over the items in the `pi` dictionary. The `items()` method returns a tuple containing the key and value for each item in the `pi` dictionary. The `local_port` and `port_info` variables are assigned the key and value of the current item.

❼ The string `partition()` method is used to separate the description value into the portions before and after the string `'LLDP: '`. An optional user-configured description may appear before this string. The user-configured description is assigned to the variable `udesc`. If no user -configured description is present, `udesc` will be assigned an empty string. The LLDP remote system name and port name configured by a previous execution of the script are assigned to the `ldesc` variable. The `partition()` method also returns the separator string `'LLDP: '` into the variable `_`. As you might guess by the variable name, this variable is not used later in the function.

❽ The string `rstrip()` method is used to strip any trailing whitespace from the right side of the user-defined description stored in `udesc`. Because Python strings are immutable, the result of the `rstrip()` method must be assigned back to the variable `udesc`. The argument to the `rstrip()` method can be used to strip any trailing set of characters from a string. When the argument is omitted, as it was in this line, trailing whitespace is removed from the string.

❾ The string `partition()` method is used again, this time to separate the `ldesc` variable into the components before and after a space. The component before a space is assigned to the `remote_system` variable and the component after the space is assigned to the `remote_port` variable. Again, the separator string `' '` is assigned to the variable _ and is not accessed later in the function.

❿ The string `partition()` method is used for a third time. This time, the separator string being searched for is `'(DOWN)'`. The separator string, if present, will be stored in the variable `down_string`. If the string is not present in `remote_port`, then `down_string` will be assigned an empty string. In this case, it's the portion after the separator string that is not needed and is assigned to the variable _.

⓫ The `udesc`, `remote_system`, and `remote_port` variables that have been parsed from the interface description are stored in a dictionary. The resulting dictionary is then assigned to the `local_port` key in the `desc_info` dictionary. A `down` key is also added to the dictionary. The `down` key's value is a Boolean indicating if the LLDP neighbor was previously down, as indicated by `down_string`.

⓬ The `except` statement catches `KeyError` and `TypeError` exceptions. These exceptions are ignored, which simply results in no information with the key `local_port` being saved into `desc_info`.

Check for XML Warnings and Errors

The two preceding functions, `get_lldp_neighbors()` and `get_description_info_for_interfaces()`, both called the `check_for_warnings_and_errors()` function to check for XML warnings and errors in the RESTful API response. Let's look at `check_for_warnings_and_errors()` in more detail:

```
def check_for_warnings_and_errors(root):
    """Check a jxmlease.XMLDictNode for warnings and errors.

    Prints the warning or error message.
    (Note: Ignores the warning:
           'uncommitted changes will be discarded on exit'
           This warning is an expected output of the open-configuration RPC.)

    Returns a tuple of (error_count, warning_count).
    """

    error_count = 0 ❶
    warning_count = 0
    for node in root.find_nodes_with_tag(('xnm:warning','xnm:error')): ❷
        msg = node.get('message','(empty message)') ❸
        if node.tag == 'xnm:warning': ❹
            if msg == 'uncommitted changes will be discarded on exit':
```

```
            continue
        level = 'Warning'
        warning_count += 1
    elif node.tag == 'xnm:error': ❺
        level = 'Error'
        error_count += 1
    else:
        level = 'Unknown'
    print "    %s: %s" % (level,msg) ❻
return (error_count, warning_count) ❼
```

❶ The error_count and warning_count variables track the number of errors and warnings that are present. Both variables are initialized with a value of 0.

❷ The jxmlease method find_nodes_with_tag() is used to return all nodes with the XML tags of either <xnm:warning> or <xnm:error>.

❸ If the node contains a <message> tag, the variable msg is set to the message. Otherwise, msg is set to the string '(empty message)'.

❹ If the node was a warning (XML tag of <xnm:warning>), this block is executed. The message 'uncommitted changes will be discarded on exit' is an expected output from the *open-configuration* RPC. Therefore, this message is ignored. For any other message, level is set to Warning and warning_count is incremented.

❺ If the node was an error (XML tag of <xnm:warning>), level is set to Error and error_count is incremented.

❻ A string containing both the level and msg is printed to the user's terminal.

❼ A tuple containing the number of errors and the number of warnings is returned to the calling function.

Compare Current and Previous LLDP Neighbor Information

The next function does not query the RESTful API. Instead, it compares the dictionaries produced by the two previous functions. That is, check_lldp_changes() function compares the previous LLDP information found in the interface description fields (and now stored in the desc_info dictionary) to the current LLDP information (now stored in lldp_info dictionary). A message is printed for LLDP up, change, and down events. In addition, the new interface description is computed and returned in the desc_changes dictionary:

```
def check_lldp_changes(lldp_info, desc_info): ❶
    """Compare current LLDP info with previous snapshot from descriptions.
```

```
Given the dictionaries produced by get_lldp_neighbors() and
get_description_info_for_interfaces(), print LLDP up, change,
and down messages.

Return a dictionary containing information for the new descriptions
to configure.
"""

desc_changes = {}

# Iterate through the current LLDP neighbor state. Compare this
# to the saved state as retrieved from the interface descriptions.
for local_port in lldp_info: ❷
    lldp_system = lldp_info[local_port]['system']
    lldp_port = lldp_info[local_port]['port']
    has_lldp_desc = desc_info.has_key(local_port) ❸
    if has_lldp_desc: ❹
        desc_system = desc_info[local_port]['system']
        desc_port = desc_info[local_port]['port']
        down = desc_info[local_port]['down']
        if not desc_system or not desc_port:
            has_lldp_desc = False
    if not has_lldp_desc: ❺
        print("    %s LLDP Up. Now: %s %s" %
              (local_port,lldp_system,lldp_port))
    elif down:
        print("    %s LLDP Up. Was: %s %s Now: %s %s" %
              (local_port,desc_system,desc_port,lldp_system,lldp_port))
    elif lldp_system != desc_system or lldp_port != desc_port:
        print("    %s LLDP Change. Was: %s %s Now: %s %s" %
              (local_port,desc_system,desc_port,lldp_system,lldp_port))
    else:
        # No change. LLDP was not down. Same system and port.
        continue
    desc_changes[local_port] = "LLDP: %s %s" % (lldp_system,lldp_port) ❻

# Iterate through the saved state as retrieved from the interface
# descriptions. Look for any neighbors that are present in the
# saved state, but are not present in the current LLDP neighbor
# state.
for local_port in desc_info: ❼
    desc_system = desc_info[local_port]['system']
    desc_port = desc_info[local_port]['port']
    down = desc_info[local_port]['down']
    if (desc_system and desc_port and not down and
        not lldp_info.has_key(local_port)):
        print("    %s LLDP Down. Was: %s %s" %
              (local_port,desc_system,desc_port))
        desc_changes[local_port] = "LLDP: %s %s(DOWN)" % (desc_system,
                                                           desc_port)
```

```
    # Iterate through the list of interface descriptions we are going
    # to change. Prepend the user description, if any.
    for local_port in desc_changes: ❽
        try:
            udesc = desc_info[local_port]['user_desc']
        except KeyError:
            continue
        if udesc:
            desc_changes[local_port] = udesc + " " + desc_changes[local_port]

    return desc_changes
```

❶ This function takes two arguments. The `lldp_info` dictionary contains information returned from `get_lldp_neighbors()` and the `desc_info` dictionary contains information returned from `get_description_info_for_interfaces()`.

❷ This line contains the first of three `for` loops in the function. This loop iterates over every `local_port` in the `lldp_info` dictionary. The LLDP-learned system and port values are assigned to the convenience variables `lldp_system` and `lldp_port` on the following two lines.

❸ The Boolean variable `has_lldp_desc` is set to `True` if an interface description exists for `local_port` (`desc_info` has a `local_port` key).

❹ If a description exists for `local_port` (`has_lldp_des` is `True`) the `desc_system`, `desc_port`, and `down` variables are set based on the interface description information in `desc_info`. If either the `desc_system` or `desc_port` is empty, the `has_lldp_desc` variable is reset to a value of `False`.

❺ This `if/else` block checks for four different conditions that correspond to the events: a new LLDP neighbor is up on the interface, an LLDP neighbor is up on an interface where the interface previously had a neighbor but was most recently down, an LLDP neighbor changed on the interface, or there has been no change in the LLDP neighbor state for the interface. Unless there has been no LLDP neighbor state change for the interface, a message is printed.

❻ This line is reached when there has been a change in `local_port`'s LLDP neighbor state. The new state is saved in the `desc_changes` dictionary under the `local_port` key.

❼ The second `for` loop in the function iterates over each `local_port` in `desc_info`. The purpose of this loop is to find potential LLDP down events. The details of the `for` loop are very similar to the previous loop.

❽ The final for loop of the function prepends any new description in the desc_changes dictionary with the user-defined portion of the description. If the udesc variable is empty, or there is no 'user_desc' key in desc_info[local_port], then no changes to the desc_changes dictionary are required.

Build a Candidate Configuration

The next function takes the desc_changes dictionary returned by get_lldp_description_changes() as its input. The build_config_changes() function creates a jxmlease.XMLDictNode object, which can later be "unparsed" into a Junos XML configuration snippet. When "unparsed" into its XML format, the return value of this function contains a Junos configuration snippet similar to this example:

```
<configuration>
    <interfaces>
        <interface>
            <name>ge-0/0/2</name>
            <description>LLDP: r2 ge-0/0/0</description>
        </interface>
        <interface>
            <name>ge-0/0/1</name>
            <description>LLDP: r5 ge-0/0/1</description>
        </interface>
        <interface>
            <name>ge-0/0/0</name>
            <description>LLDP: r0 ge-0/0/4</description>
        </interface>
    </interfaces>
</configuration>
```

Now, let's analyze how this configuration snippet is produced by the build_config_changes() function:

```
def build_config_changes(desc_changes):
    """Generate a configuration snippet with new interface descriptions.

    Given a dictionary of new description values to be configured, build
    a configuration snippet as a jxmlease.XMLDictNode. The configuration
    snippet will configure the new description for each interface.

    Return the configuration snippet as a jxmlease.XMLDictNode.
    """

    interface_list = [] ❶
    for local_port in desc_changes: ❷
        interface_list.append({'name': local_port,
                               'description': desc_changes[local_port]})
    config = {'configuration': {'interfaces': {'interface':interface_list}}} ❸
    return jxmlease.XMLDictNode(config) ❹
```

❶ The `interface_list` variable is initialized with an empty list.

❷ For each `local_port` in the `desc_changes` dictionary, a new entry is appended to `interface_list`. The entry is a dictionary with the keys `'name'` and `'description'`. The value of the `'name'` key is the name of the interface. The value of the `'description'` key is the new interface description being configured.

❸ A `config` variable is created. The value is a dictionary with multiple levels of keys. The value of the lowest-level `'interface'` key is the previously created `interface_list`.

❹ The data structure in the `config` variable is used to initialize a `jxmlease.XMLDictNode` instance. This Python data structure is equivalent to the desired XML configuration snippet. The `jxmlease.XMLDictNode()` instance is returned to the calling function.

Apply and Commit the Candidate Configuration

The `load_merge_xml_config()` function takes a configuration snippet as a `jxmlease.XMLDictNode`. The data structure is converted to an XML document, which is then loaded and committed using a multi-RPC RESTful API query. The *open-configuration*, *load-configuration*, *commit-configuration*, and *close-configuration* RPCs are used to perform the equivalent of the CLI commands `configure private`, `load merge`, `commit`, and `exit`:

```
def load_merge_xml_config(device, user, pw, config): ❶
    """Load a configuration using "configure private" and "load merge".

    Given a configuration snippet as a jxmlease.XMLDictNode, do:
        configure private,
        load merge of the config snippet,
        commit (and close the configuration),
        and check the results.

    Return True if the config was committed successfully, False otherwise.
    """

    load_config_node = jxmlease.XMLDictNode(config, tag='load-configuration') ❷
    load_config_node.set_xml_attr('action', 'merge')
    load_config_node.set_xml_attr('format', 'xml')

    rpcs = [] ❸
    rpcs.append({'open-configuration':{'private':''}})
    rpcs.append(load_config_node)
    rpcs.append({'commit-configuration':''})
```

```
rpcs.append({'close-configuration':''})
payload_string = jxmlease.XMLListNode(rpcs).emit_xml(full_document=False) ❹

args = {'stop-on-error':'1'} ❺
headers = {'Accept': 'application/xml', ❻
           'Content-Type': 'application/xml'}
url = MULTIPLE_RPC_URL_FORMAT % (device)
http_resp = requests.post(url, auth=(user,pw), params=args, ❼
                          headers=headers, data=payload_string)
http_resp.raise_for_status()

responses = parse_multipart_messages(type=http_resp.headers['Content-Type'],
                                     response=http_resp.text)❽

rc = True

if len(responses) != len(rpcs): ❾
    print "    Error: Fewer responses than expected!"
    rc = False

for xml_response in responses: ❿
    if xml_response == None:
        print "    Error: Unable to parse an RPC response!"
        rc = False
    else:
        (error_count, warning_count) = check_for_warnings_and_errors(
            parser(xml_response)
        )
        if error_count > 0:
            rc = False

return rc
```

❶ The `config` produced by the `build_config_changes()` function is passed as an argument to `load_merge_xml_config()`.

❷ A `load_config_node` instance of `jxmlease.XMLDictNode` is created with a `load-configuration` tag and with the content of the `config` configuration snippet. The `set_xml_attr()` method is then used to add `action=merge` and `format=xml` attributes to `load_config_node`. When "unparsed," the `load_config_node` variable results in an XML document similar to this sample:

```
<load-configuration action="merge" format="xml">
    <configuration>
        <interfaces>
            <interface>
                <name>ge-0/0/2</name>
                <description>LLDP: r2 ge-0/0/0</description>
            </interface>
            <interface>
```

```
                <name>ge-0/0/1</name>
                <description>LLDP: r5 ge-0/0/1</description>
            </interface>
            <interface>
                <name>ge-0/0/0</name>
                <description>LLDP: r0 ge-0/0/4</description>
            </interface>
        </interfaces>
    </configuration>
</load-configuration>
```

❸ The `rpcs` list variable is set to the list of RPCs. This order is essential to ensure the RPCs are invoked in the correct order. The `private` argument is specified for the *open-configuration* RPC. The *load-configuration* RPC is created from the `load_config_node` variable rather than a simple string.

❹ A `jxmlease.XMLListNode` instance is created from the `rpcs` list. The `emit_xml()` method then converts this object into an XML fragment. The resulting string, containing an XML fragment, is assigned to `payload_string`. The `full_document=False` argument prevents `emit_xml()` from including an `<?xml ?>` declaration in its output.[7] The resulting `payload_string` value is similar to this example:

```
<open-configuration>
    <private></private>
</open-configuration>
<load-configuration action="merge" format="xml">
    <configuration>
        <interfaces>
            <interface>
                <name>ge-0/0/2</name>
                <description>LLDP: r2 ge-0/0/0</description>
            </interface>
            <interface>
                <name>ge-0/0/1</name>
                <description>LLDP: r5 ge-0/0/1</description>
            </interface>
            <interface>
                <name>ge-0/0/0</name>
                <description>LLDP: r0 ge-0/0/4</description>
            </interface>
```

7 In this particular case, the `full_document=False` argument is technically not necessary. Because the XML fragment contains multiple top-level tags, it is not a valid XML document. The `emit_xml()` method recognizes this condition and does not include the `<?xml ?>` declaration. Because the `<?xml ?>` declaration would result in invalid NETCONF, it's best practice to include the `full_document=False` argument so an `<?xml ?>` declaration is never included.

```
            </interfaces>
        </configuration>
    </load-configuration>
    <commit-configuration></commit-configuration>
    <close-configuration></close-configuration>
```

❺ The args dictionary contains a single key of stop-on-error with a value of 1. This dictionary will be used later to append the ?stop-on-error=1 CGI query string to the URL used in the RESTful API query.

❻ The headers dictionary will be used to include request headers in the RESTful API query. The Accept and Content-Type headers are both set to the value application/xml to indicate that the POST body of the request is in XML format, and the response should also be in XML format.

❼ The requests.post() method is used to initiate an HTTP POST request. The data=payload_string argument sets the POST body of the request to be the XML fragment stored in payload_string.

❽ The get_multipart_messages() function is invoked. The type argument is set to http_resp.headers['Content-Type'], which contains the value of the Content-Type header from the HTTP response, and the response argument is set to http_resp.text, which contains the HTTP body of the response. The resulting list of messages is stored in msgs. The get_multipart_messages() function is analyzed in the next section.

❾ This if block ensures there is one response for each RPC.

❿ This for loop checks each xml_response for errors. The parser instance parses each xml_response into a jxmlease.XMLDictNode, which is then passed to the check_for_warnings_and_errors() function.

Parse Multi-RPC Responses

The load_merge_xml_config() function called the get_multipart_messages() function to parse the multi-RPC RESTful API response. The get_multipart_messages() function takes a type argument and a response argument. The response argument is a multi-part MIME message that is parsed into a list of sub messages and returned to the caller:

```
def parse_multipart_messages(type, response): ❶
    """Parse the response from a multi-RPC API call.

    Parse the response from a multi-RPC API call into a list of the
    individual messages.
```

```
    Note: Some RPCs return an empty response. In this case, there is no
          content type or payload, and the email package returns the
          default content type of text/plain. This case is expected, and
          not an error.

    Return a list of messages on success. If there is a problem parsing a
    message, the value of the message is None.
    """

    # Add a MIME header to allow the email package to correctly parse
    # the remainder of the message.
    msg = email.message_from_string('Content-Type: %s\n\n%s' % (type,response)) ❷

    if not msg.is_multipart(): ❸
        return [msg.get_payload(decode=True)]

    # Iterate over the message parts and add them to the list.
    msg_list = []
    for sub_msg in msg.get_payload(): ❹
        payload = sub_msg.get_payload(decode=True) ❺
        sub_type = sub_msg.get_content_type() ❻
        if (sub_type == 'application/xml' or
            sub_type == 'application/json' or
            (sub_type == 'text/plain' and payload == "")):
            msg_list.append(payload)
        else:
            print("    Error: Unknown submessage.\n" +
                  "           Type: %s\n" +
                  "           Content: %s" % (sub_type,payload))
            msg_list.append(None)
    return msg_list
```

❶ The type argument is the value of the Content-Type header from a multi-RPC RESTful API response. The response argument is the HTTP body of the response.

❷ The email library provides classes for parsing multipart MIME messages. The email.message_from_string() method instantiates an email object from the string contents. A complete MIME message begins with a Content-Type header followed by a blank line and then the remaining message contents. The type and response variables are combined into a string that matches this format, and the resulting string is passed to the email.message_from_string() method.

❸ If msg is not a multipart message, the get_payload(decode=True) method is invoked to decode the message content. The message content is returned as a list with a single item.

❹ The `get_payload()` method is used in a `for` loop to iterate over each submessage inside the multipart MIME message.

❺ The `payload` variable is set to the text of the `sub_msg` using the `get_payload(decode=True)` method.

❻ The content type of the `sub_msg` is retrieved using the `get_content_type()` method. If the `sub_type` is `application/xml` or `application/json`, then `payload` is added to `msg_list`. If the `sub_type` is `text/plain`, the default, and the `payload` is empty, the empty `payload` is also appended to `msg_list`. This condition occurs when an RPC returns an empty `<rpc-reply>` node, as described in the warning in "Multiple RPCs in One Request" on page 117. If the `sub_type` is anything else, an error is printed and the error is indicated by appending the value `None` to `msg_list`.

Putting It All Together

The final block of code in the example script calls the `main()` function when the script is executed. After entering this code block, the example script is functional:

```
if __name__ == "__main__":
  sys.exit(main())
```

At this point, the script is complete and ready to test on a set of Junos devices running the LLDP protocol and RESTful API service. If you encounter errors running the script, review and carefully compare your code with the example. The full working *lldp_interface_descriptions_rest.py* file is also available on GitHub (*https://github.com/AutomatingJunosAdministration/examples*).

Additional RESTful API Service Configuration

"Enabling the RESTful API Service" on page 94 gave the minimal configuration to enable the Junos RESTful API service. That configuration was sufficient for understanding the API and developing the simple example in the previous section. However, simply enabling the service over HTTP is *not* recommended for production employment.

As explained in "Authentication and Authorization" on page 99, the HTTP basic authentication mechanism, required by the Junos RESTful API service, sends the username and password as a Base64-encoded clear-text string. Enabling the RESTful API service over HTTPS instead of HTTP protects the authentication credentials from eavesdropping. HTTPS is enabled with:

```
set system services rest https server-certificate certificate-name
```

The value *certificate-name* is a reference to an X.509 certificate installed on the router. Junos software provides several options to the `request security pki` operational-mode command for requesting, loading, enrolling, and generating X.509 certificates. You should refer to Juniper's technical documentation (*https://www.juniper.net/techpubs/*) for details on public key infrastructure (PKI) and X.509 certificates. If you want a quick recipe to disable HTTP, disable the REST API explorer, and enable HTTPS with a locally generated self-signed certificated, you can follow this example:

```
user@r0> request security pki generate-key-pair certificate-id my-self-cert
Generated key pair my-self-cert, key size 1024 bits

user@r0> request security pki local-certificate generate-self-signed
 certificate-id my-self-cert subject CN=Example domain-name r0.example.com
 email user@example.com
Self-signed certificate generated and loaded successfully

user@r0> configure
Entering configuration mode

[edit]
user@r0# edit system services rest

[edit system services rest]
user@r0# show
http;
enable-explorer;

[edit system services rest]
user@r0# delete http

[edit system services rest]
user@r0# delete enable-explorer

[edit system services rest]
user@r0# set https server-certificate my-self-cert

[edit system services rest]
user@r0# top commit and-quit
commit complete
Exiting configuration mode
```

By default, the Junos RESTful API services listens for HTTPS connections on TCP port 3443. You can alter this behavior with the following configuration:

```
set system services rest https port port-number
```

There are also configuration parameters to control which clients can connect to the RESTful API service and the number of concurrent client connections allowed. By default, any client can connect, and 64 concurrent client connections are supported.

Here's an example of limiting the concurrent connections to 32 and specifying two specific client IP addresses that are allowed to connect:

```
[edit system services rest]
user@r0# set control connection-limit 32

[edit system services rest]
user@r0# set control allowed-sources [ 10.1.1.1 192.168.1.1 ]
```

The `set system services rest control allowed-sources` command is enforced by the Junos RESTful API service, not by the device's packet forwarding engine (PFE). It is best practice to protect a Junos device from potential denial-of-service (DoS) attacks by applying to the loopback interface a firewall filter that only permits needed services and protocols. A loopback firewall filter is implemented by the device's PFE and helps prevent malicious traffic from overloading the control plane.

Internal Design

While not strictly necessary to use the RESTful API, it can be helpful to understand the components that the Junos software uses to deliver the RESTful API service. Understanding how these components fit into the architecture described in Chapter 1 (see "Accessing the Management System" on page 6) can assist in troubleshooting. Understanding the design can also help identify the proper automation tool to apply to a particular task. This design is illustrated in Figure 3-4.

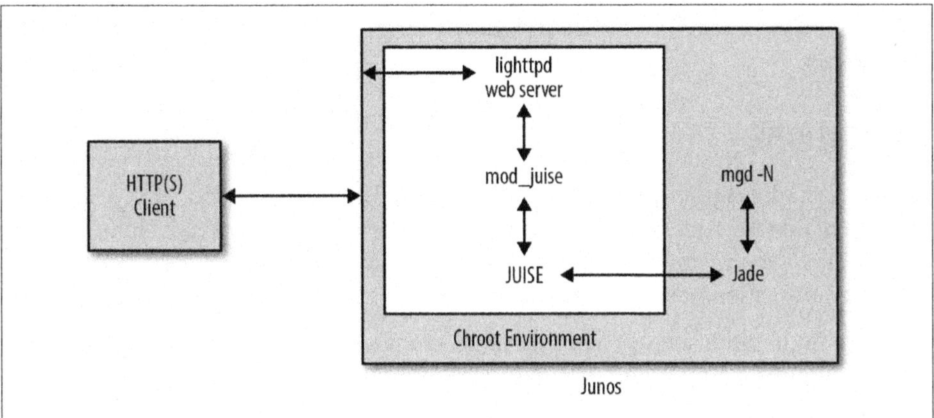

Figure 3-4. Junos RESTful API service internal design

As you might have noticed in the `Server` response header field in previous outputs, the Junos RESTful API service uses the open source lighttpd (*http://www.lighttpd.net*) daemon to implement the HTTP and HTTPS web server. When an HTTP client makes a connection to the Junos RESTful API service, that connection is initially handled by lighttpd. The lighttpd web server implements the HTTP or HTTPS protocol and runs inside a restricted chroot environment within the Junos software.

The lighttpd daemon then uses the `mod_juise` plugin to invoke the Junos User Interface Scripting Environment (JUISE)[8] for each HTTP request. JUISE receives the requested URL, HTTP headers, and HTTP request body from lighttpd. In turn, JUISE makes a Junoscript connection to another internal component, called Jade, over an internal Unix socket. Authentication information is extracted from the `Authentication` header and passed to the Jade component. The Jade component uses the provided username and password to authenticate the connection. Once authenticated, JUISE passes one or more Junoscript RPCs to Jade. Jade then interacts with the Junos management daemon, MGD, to execute the Junoscript RPCs and pass the results back to JUISE. The response is then propagated back to the client by `mod_juise` and lighttpd.

If you need to troubleshoot the operation of the Junos RESTful API service, you can enable traceoptions. There are currently two traceoptions flags, `lighttpd` and `juise`:[9]

```
[edit system services rest]
user@r0# set traceoptions flag ?
Possible completions:
  all                    Enable all traces
  juise                  Enable tracing for JUISE
  lighttpd               Enable tracing for lighttpd
```

As you might guess, the flags correspond to the components of the same name. If you enable the `lighttpd` or `juise` flags, the corresponding traceoptions will be found in the files */var/chroot/rest-api/var/log/lighttpd* and */var/chroot/rest-api/var/log/juise*, respectively.

Limitations

No tool accomplishes every task, and the Junos RESTful API service is no exception. Understanding the RESTful API service can help you use this tool to its full potential, and also help you realize when a different tool might be better for meeting a specific network automation goal.

The first limitation has to do with the stateless nature of REST. Each client request is fulfilled independent of other requests. Therefore, the Junos RESTful API service

8 JUISE is open source software that can also be used as a standalone tool for automating Junos devices using SLAX. It essentially allows the development and debugging of "off-box" op and commit scripts. See the JUISE wiki (*https://github.com/Juniper/juise/wiki*) for more information on JUISE.

9 The `all` flag enables both the `lighttpd` and `juise` traceoptions.

does not support operations that depend on state from previous operations. As an example, the `get-interface-information` RPC can be used to get information about all of the interfaces on the device. Further, the `interface-name` parameter can be added to get information about a specific interface. However, there is no ability to request information on one interface and then make a second request to get information on the "next" interface. In fact, there's really no concept of "next" when it comes to the RESTful API service.

The second limitation is a byproduct of the current implementation of the RESTful API service. Each request invokes a new instance of JUISE to generate and process the NETCONF RPC. This means each API request incurs the latency of invoking a new binary and, more importantly, the latency of authenticating the username and password of the request. This authentication latency can be significantly greater if a remote authentication server must be queried. Provisioning a local user account to be used for RESTful API queries is best practice. Even if a network uses RADIUS or TACACS+ to authenticate human users, a local user account, with restricted permissions, can be configured specifically for use with the RESTful API service. And even with local authentication, the RESTful API service may not be your best tool if you need to make frequent requests of the Junos device during a short time interval.

The third limitation affects long-running RPCs or RPCs that return very large responses. The Junos RESTful API service currently has a hardcoded timeout of approximately 5 seconds. If an RPC takes longer than 5 seconds to execute, the request fails and the Junos RESTful API service returns a `500 Internal Server Error` status code. Therefore, you should use another tool (such as PyEZ) to execute any RPC that might take more than 5 seconds to return a response.

Finally, while the RESTful API service allows you to receive responses in JSON format, it does not allow you to specify RPCs or RPC parameters in JSON format. As described, single RPCs are specified in the request URL, and multiple RPCs must be specified in the body of an HTTP POST request. Currently, multiple RPCs can only be specified in XML format. "Multiple RPCs in One Request" on page 117 explained how configuring a Junos device requires multiple RPCs, and described the corresponding multi-RPC request format. While it is possible to retrieve the device configuration in JSON format, these limitations currently prevent configuring the device with JSON.

Chapter Summary

In summary, the RESTful API service provides a familiar interface if you are already familiar with programming web services. It allows you to invoke operational RPCs using the ubiquitous HTTP/HTTPS protocols and retrieve structured responses in either XML or JSON format. In addition, the RESTful API service can be used to apply new configurations in XML format.

CHAPTER 4
Junos PyEZ

This chapter looks at Junos PyEZ, another automation tool that allows remote procedure calls to be invoked on Junos devices. PyEZ is a Python library that enables administration and automation of Junos devices. It is an open source project maintained and supported by Juniper Networks with contributions from the user community. The Junos PyEZ project is hosted on GitHub at *https://github.com/Juniper/py-junos-eznc*.

The PyEZ APIs provide a "mini-framework" that can be used to solve both simple and complex automation tasks. PyEZ can be used from the interactive Python shell to quickly perform simple tasks on one or more Junos devices, or incorporated in full-blown Python scripts of varying complexity to automate the management and administration of an entire network of Junos devices. The first several sections of this chapter demonstrate entering commands at the interactive Python shell indicated by the >>> prompt. "A PyEZ Example" on page 231 will demonstrate a full Python script utilizing the PyEZ library.

PyEZ provides an abstraction layer built on top of the NETCONF protocol covered in Chapter 2. It does not require direct NETCONF interaction, but utilizes the vendor-agnostic `ncclient`[1] library for its NETCONF transport. Because the PyEZ library utilizes NETCONF for its remote procedure calls, it can be used with all currently supported Junos software versions and Junos platforms.

Like the Junos RESTful API covered in Chapter 3, the PyEZ library supports invoking individual Junos RPCs and retrieving the resulting responses. However, unlike the Junos RESTful API service, PyEZ also offers optional features for further simpli-

1 `ncclient` is a community-led and community-supported open source project hosted on GitHub (*https://github.com/leopoul/ncclient*).

fying common automation tasks. One example of these features happens automatically upon initial connection to a Junos device with the PyEZ library. By default, the PyEZ library gathers basic information about the device and stores this information in a Python dictionary. This dictionary can be easily accessed with the `facts` attribute, covered in "Facts Gathering" on page 173.

Other abstraction features of the PyEZ library involve dealing with RPC responses. Rather than returning RPC responses as XML or JSON strings, PyEZ utilizes the `lxml` library to directly return XML-specific Python data structures. It may also be combined with the jxmlease library, introduced in "Using Structured Data in Python" on page 42, to simplify parsing these XML-specific data structures into a native Python data structure. Tables and views are another tool for mapping RPC responses into native Python data structures. PyEZ provides several predefined tables and views for common RPCs and also allows users to define their own to extract information from any Junos RPC.

For configuration, PyEZ supports changes in text, XML, or set formats. In addition, it includes an engine for combining user-supplied values with templates to dynamically produce device, customer, or feature-specific configuration changes.

Installation

Running a Python script that utilizes the Junos PyEZ library requires that Junos PyEZ be installed on the automation host executing the script. Junos PyEZ is dependent upon Python and several system libraries whose installation is operating system–specific. These dependencies are also subject to change with new PyEZ releases. Therefore, this book does not attempt to cover the procedure for installing the prerequisite system software. Instead, refer to the "Installing PyEZ" section of the release-specific "Junos PyEZ Developer Guide" found on Juniper's Junos PyEZ landing page (*http://www.juniper.net/techpubs/en_US/release-independent/junos-pyez/information-products/pathway-pages/index.html*) for information on installing the required system software on common operating systems.

At the time of this writing, PyEZ does not support Python 3.x. Ensure Python 2.7 (or a later 2.x release) is installed on your system, and the system is properly configured to use Python 2.x for any scripts that utilize the Junos PyEZ library.

Once the appropriate system libraries are installed on the host system, PyPI, the Python Package Index (*https://pypi.python.org/pypi*), can be used to install Junos PyEZ and its dependent Python libraries. Simply execute the command `pip install junos-eznc` at a root shell prompt to install the latest stable release of Junos PyEZ. You can also use the command `pip install git+https://github.com/Juniper/`

py-junos-eznc.git[2] to install the latest development version of Junos PyEZ directly from the GitHub repository.

PyPI automatically installs prerequisite Python modules when you install Junos PyEZ with the `pip install` command. One of those prerequisite Python modules is lxml. As part of its installation, the lxml module insists on downloading and compiling the `libxml2` C library from source code, even if your system already has a functional `libxml2` library installed. This requirement means that your host must have all of the necessary tools installed to compile `libxml2`. These include a C compiler, a *make* program, and a `zlib` compression library including header files (usually found in a `zlib-dev` package). If the host is missing any of these required tools, the Junos PyEZ installation may fail.

Device Connectivity

As explained in the chapter introduction, PyEZ uses NETCONF to communicate with a remote Junos device. Therefore, PyEZ requires NETCONF to be enabled on the target device. All currently supported releases of the Junos software support the NETCONF protocol over an SSH transport, but this NETCONF-over-SSH service is not enabled by default. The minimal configuration necessary to enable the NETCONF-over-SSH service is:

```
set system services netconf ssh
```

The NETCONF-over-SSH service listens on TCP port 830, by default, and can operate over both IPv4 and IPv6. The following Junos CLI output demonstrates configuring the NETCONF-over-SSH service and verifying that the service is indeed listening on TCP port 830:

```
user@r0> configure
Entering configuration mode

[edit]
user@r0# set system services netconf ssh

[edit]
user@r0# commit and-quit
commit complete
Exiting configuration mode

user@r0> show system connections inet | match 830
```

2 In addition to the Junos PyEZ software requirements, installing from the GitHub repository requires *git* to be installed.

```
tcp4       0      0  *.830                         *.*                     LISTEN

user@r0> show system connections inet6 | match 830
tcp6       0      0  *.830                         *.*                     LISTEN
```

When the SSH service is enabled with the `set system services ssh` configuration, it is also possible to reach the NETCONF-over-SSH service on TCP port 22. However, the `set system services netconf ssh` configuration is preferred because the PyEZ library attempts to connect to the NETCONF-over-SSH port (TCP port 830) by default.

Once the NETCONF-over-SSH service has been configured, the device is ready to use with Junos PyEZ.

Creating a Device Instance

The PyEZ library provides a `jnpr.junos.Device` class to represent a Junos device being accessed by the PyEZ library. The first step in using the library is to instantiate an instance of this class with the parameters specific to the Junos device:

```
user@h0$ python ❶
Python 2.7.9 (default, Mar  1 2015, 12:57:24)
[GCC 4.9.2] on linux2
Type "help", "copyright", "credits" or "license" for more information.
>>> from jnpr.junos import Device ❷
>>> r0 = Device(host='r0',user='user',password='user123') ❸
```

❶ First invoke the Python interactive shell with the `python` command.

The exact command to invoke the Python interactive shell is specific to the operating system and Python installation of the automation host. Use the command appropriate for your specific environment.

❷ Before the `jnpr.junos.Device` class can be used, it must first be imported. This line imports the `jnpr.junos` Python package and copies the `Device` name into the local namespace, allowing you to simply reference `Device()`. An alternative syntax is `import jnpr.junos`. Again, this imports the `jnpr.junos` Python package, but it does not copy the `Device` name into the local namespace. Using this syntax requires you to reference the class as an attribute of `jnpr.junos` using the syntax `jnpr.junos.Device()`.

❸ Calling the `Device` class object with the `Device()` syntax creates a new instance object. This instance represents a specific NETCONF-over-SSH session to a specific Junos device. In this case, the instance object is assigned to the variable named `r0`. There's nothing special about the name `r0`, and any valid Python variable name could be used in its place. The parameters to the `Device()` call set the initial values of the instance's attributes. In this example, the `host`, `user`, and `password` parameters have been set to appropriate values for the Junos device with a hostname of `r0`.

While it is typical to specify the `host`, `user`, and `password` parameters, the only mandatory argument to the `Device()` call is the `host` parameter. The host information can also be specified as the first (unnamed) argument to the `Device()` call. Table 4-1 details the `Device()` parameters and their default values.

Table 4-1. Parameters to the jnpr.junos.Device class

Parameter	Description	Default value
`host`	A hostname, domain name, or IPv4 or IPv6 address on which the Junos device is running the NETCONF-over-SSH service. If a hostname or domain name is used, it must resolve to an IPv4 or IPv6 address. This parameter can alternatively be specified as the first unnamed argument to the `Device()` call.	None (Must be specified by the caller.)
`port`	The TCP port on which the NETCONF-over-SSH service is reachable. If `set system services ssh` is configured on the Junos device, you can reach the NETCONF service by specifying the argument `port = 22` to the `Device()` call.	`830`

`user`	The username used to log in to the Junos device. As discussed in "Authentication and Authorization" on page 170, RPC execution is controlled by the authorization configuration of this user account on the Junos device.	The value of the `$USER` environment variable for the account running the Python script on the automation host. This is usually set to the username of the user executing the Python script. The default behavior can be useful if the username on the automation host and the Junos device are the same. At the Python interactive shell, you can confirm the value of the `$USER` environment variable with:
		`>>> import os`
		`>>> print(os.environ['USER'])`
		`user`

Parameter	Description	Default value
`password`	The password used to authenticate the user on the Junos device. If SSH keys are being used, this value is used as the passphrase to unlock the SSH private key. Otherwise, this value is used for password authentication.	None (A password is not needed for an SSH key with an empty passphrase.)
`gather_facts`	A Boolean that indicates whether or not basic information is gathered from the device upon initial connection with the `open()` instance method. See "Facts Gathering" on page 173 for details.	`True` (Facts are gathered.)
`auto_probe`	This setting attempts to check if the TCP port specified by `port` is reachable by first attempting a simple TCP connection to that port. Only after this test connection succeeds is the real NETCONF-over-SSH connection attempted. The `auto_probe` value is an integer defining the number of seconds to attempt to make this test TCP connection to `port` before timing out. If the value is `0`, auto probing is disabled and no test TCP connection is attempted. (In this case, the real NETCONF-over-SSH connection is attempted immediately.)	`0` (Autoprobing is disabled. This value is inherited from the `Device` class's `auto_probe` attribute upon instantiation. The `auto_probe` value can be changed for all device instances by setting `Device.auto_probe = value` before instantiating any device instances.)
`ssh_config`	The path, on the automation host, to an SSH client configuration file used for the SSH connection. The SSH client configuration file can be used to control many aspects of the SSH connection. For Unix-like automation hosts, use `man ssh_config` for details on the available settings.	`~/.ssh/config` (The ~ is expanded to the user's home directory. If no SSH configuration file is found, the system-wide defaults are used.)
`ssh_private_key_file`	The path, on the automation host, to an SSH private key file used with SSH key authentication.	None (If specified, the SSH key files configured in the `ssh_config` file are used.)
`normalize`	A Boolean to indicate whether or not the XML responses from this device should have whitespace normalized. See "Response Normalization" on page 190 for more information.	`False` (Whitespace is not normalized.)

Parallel Execution

The `ncclient` library used by PyEZ is synchronous and blocking. This behavior means when an RPC function is invoked on a `Device` instance, execution of your script is paused until the resulting RPC response, or an exception, is received from the device and returned in the function's response. It is possible to execute RPCs on multiple Junos devices in parallel by having your script create multiple threads or fork multiple processes. Each process can instantiate a `Device` instance to a different Junos device and execute RPCs on that Junos device. In fact, it is even possible to have parallel processes, each with different `Device` instances to the same Junos device. Each `Device` instance would have its own NETCONF connection to the Junos device and each connection would handle RPC execution independently.

Making the Connection

Creating an instance of the `Device` class does *not* initiate a NETCONF connection to the instance. While the instance has been initialized with all the necessary information to make a NETCONF connection, the actual connection is only made when the `open()` instance method is invoked. A NETCONF connection to the `r0` device instance created in the previous example is initiated with:

```
>>> r0.open()
Device(r0)
```

The `open()` method returns the device instance, as shown by the `Device(r0)` output[3] in our example. This return value is unneeded in this example, because it points to the same object as the variable `r0`. However, returning the device instance has a purpose—this enables an alternative syntax that chains the `Device()` and `open()` invocations on a single line. Here's that alternative syntax:

```
>>> r0 = Device(host='r0',user='user',password='user123').open()
>>>
```

Regardless of whether the `open()` call is invoked on an existing instance variable or chained with the `Device()` instantiation, the NETCONF connection is opened using the information stored in the device instance attributes. These attributes include the `auto_probe`, `host`, `port`, `user`, and `password` parameters, as well as the SSH configuration information. All of these attributes are set when the instance is instantiated by passing arguments to the `Device()` call, or using the default values detailed in Table 4-1. However, it is possible to override the `auto_probe`, `gather_facts`, and

3 The string representation of a `jnpr.junos.Device` class instance is simply `Device(`*`host`*`)`.

normalize settings by specifying parameters to the open() call. If any of these parameters are supplied as arguments to the open() call, they override the device instance's attributes.

Authentication and Authorization

Unlike the RESTful API service, PyEZ does not require each API call to be authenticated. Instead, authentication happens only when the NETCONF-over-SSH session is initiated by the open() call. The authentication of the NETCONF-over-SSH service can use either SSH public key or password authentication methods.

The SSH authentication methods used, and the order in which they are tried, is dependent upon the client's SSH configuration. A typical client SSH configuration attempts to use public key authentication first, and then tries password authentication. In either case, the Junos device uses the standard Junos authentication system specified at the [edit system] hierarchy level of the Junos configuration to permit or deny the authentication. In other words, NETCONF-over-SSH sessions are authenticated exactly the same as standard SSH connections to the CLI.

When the public key authentication method is used, the SSH public key must be configured on the Junos device at the [edit system login user *username* authentication] level of the configuration hierarchy. Depending on the type of the SSH public key, the key is specified using the ssh-dsa, ssh-ecdsa, ssh-ed25519, or ssh-rsa configuration statement. In addition to having the public key configured on the Junos device, the corresponding SSH private key must exist on the automation host. In order to be used by PyEZ, this SSH private key must be in the default location, or in the path specified by the ssh_private_key_file device instance attribute. If the private SSH key requires a passphrase, the open() method attempts to use the instance's password attribute as the passphrase. If the private SSH key's passphrase is empty, then the instance's password attribute does not need to be set.

Here's an example Junos configuration snippet with a public key configured for the user user:

```
user@r0> show configuration system login user user
uid 2001;
class super-user;
authentication {
    ssh-dsa "ssh-dss AAAAB3Nza ...output trimmed... SJCS9boQ== user@h0";
}
```

The corresponding private SSH key is in the default location, *~/.ssh/id_dsa*, on the automation host:

```
user@h0$ cat ~/.ssh/id_dsa
-----BEGIN DSA PRIVATE KEY-----
MIIBugIBAAKBgQCqBuyGycDhwXmEDb3hXcEfSpD5gaomT91ojlcsSPVtoj773KqZ
```

```
...ouput trimmed...
PO+bL6L74rIKIi3cfFk=
-----END DSA PRIVATE KEY-----
```

This private key has an empty passphrase,[4] allowing a NETCONF connection to `r0` without specifying a password:

```
user@h0$ python
Python 2.7.9 (default, Mar  1 2015, 12:57:24)
[GCC 4.9.2] on linux2
Type "help", "copyright", "credits" or "license" for more information.
>>> from jnpr.junos import Device
>>> r0 = Device('r0')
>>> r0.open()
Device(r0)
>>>
```

In this example, the `user` parameter was also omitted from the `Device()` call. This works because the `$USER` environment variable is `user`, which matches the remote username on `r0`.

When password authentication is used, the Junos device can use RADIUS, TACACS+, or a local password database to verify the password. The exact authentication order is determined by the `[edit system authentication-order]` configuration hierarchy. Again, this is exactly the same as authenticating an SSH connection to the CLI. The configured `authentication-order` may try multiple password databases before ultimately permitting or denying the authentication attempt.

Authentication occurs when the NETCONF-over-SSH session is established, but authorization occurs for each remote procedure call. NETCONF authorization uses the exact same mechanism and configuration as CLI authorization. Authorization to execute a specific RPC is determined by mapping a user, or potentially a template user in the case of RADIUS/TACACS+ authentication, to a login class. In turn, the login class specifies a set of permissions that determine if an RPC call is permitted or denied. If needed, you can refer back to "Authentication and Authorization" on page 99 for a refresher on the relationship between the Junos configuration and RPC authorization.

Connection Exceptions

The Junos PyEZ library defines several exceptions that may be raised when the `open()` call fails. These exceptions are subclasses of the more general `jnpr.junos.exception.ConnectError` class, although a generic

4 It is more secure to protect the private key with a passphrase. In fact, a passphrase should be considered best practice for production network environments.

jnpr.junos.exception.ConnectError exception may also be raised for other unrecognized connection errors. Table 4-2 provides a list and descriptions of these exceptions and of the situation in which each exception is raised.

Table 4-2. Possible exceptions raised by the open() method

Exception	Description
jnpr.junos.exception.ProbeError	Raised if auto_probe is nonzero and the probe action fails. This generally indicates the host device is not reachable on TCP port port. This could indicate a name resolution issue, an IP reachability issue, or device misconfiguration. While this exception does not provide a very specific indication of the problem, it is an indication that the NETCONF connection cannot succeed.
jnpr.junos.exception.ConnectUnknownHostError	Raised if the hostname specified in the host attribute cannot be resolved to an IP address. This generally indicates a problem with the Domain Name System (DNS) resolution process.
jnpr.junos.exception.ConnectTimeoutError	Raised if there is an IP reachability problem connecting to port on host. This indicates no response was received from the Junos device. Possible causes include an incorrect IP address, firewall filtering, or general routing issues between the automation host and the Junos device.
jnpr.junos.exception.ConnectRefusedError	Raised if the Junos device rejects the TCP connection to port. This might indicate the NETCONF-over-SSH service is not configured on port, or it might indicate the maximum number of simultaneous connections has been reached.
jnpr.junos.exception.ConnectAuthError	Raised if the user or password is incorrect and the Junos device rejects the authentication attempt.
jnpr.junos.exception.ConnectNotMasterError	Raised if the connection is made to a non-master routing engine on a multi-RE device.
jnpr.junos.exception.ConnectError	A generic exception raised if the ncclient library raises an unrecognized exception during the connection process.

In order to catch and handle these exceptions gracefully, wrap the open() method in a try/except block. Here's a simple example that prints a message when one of these exceptions is encountered. In the output, a jnpr.junos.exception.ConnectAuthError is intentionally raised by specifying an incorrect password:

```
>>> from jnpr.junos import Device
>>> import jnpr.junos.exception
```

```
>>> r0 = Device(host='r0',user='user',password='badpass')
>>> try:
...     r0.open()
... except jnpr.junos.exception.ConnectError as err:
...     print('Error: ' + repr(err))
...
Error: ConnectAuthError(r0)
>>>
```

The `jnpr.junos.exception` module must be imported by the `import` statement before the specific `jnpr.junos.exception.ConnectError` exception is referenced in the `except` statement.

Because all of these exceptions are subclasses of the `jnpr.junos.exception.ConnectError` class, specifying the single exception catches all of the possible exceptions raised by `open()`.

Facts Gathering

By default, the PyEZ library gathers basic information about the Junos device during the `open()` call. PyEZ refers to this basic information as *facts*, and the information is accessible via the device instance's `facts` dictionary attribute. This example uses the `pprint` module to "pretty print" the `facts` dictionary gathered during the `r0.open()` call:

```
>>> r0.open()
Device(r0)
>>> from pprint import pprint
>>> pprint(r0.facts)
{'2RE': False,
 'HOME': '/var/home/user',
 'RE0': {'last_reboot_reason': 'Router rebooted after a normal shutdown.',
         'mastership_state': 'master',
         'model': 'RE-VMX',
         'status': 'OK',
         'up_time': '6 days, 7 hours, 36 minutes, 44 seconds'},
 'domain': 'example.com',
 'fqdn': 'r0.example.com',
 'hostname': 'r0',
 'ifd_style': 'CLASSIC',
 'master': 'RE0',
 'model': 'MX960',
 'personality': 'MX',
 'serialnumber': 'VMX5868',
 'switch_style': 'BRIDGE_DOMAIN',
 'vc_capable': False,
 'version': '15.1R1.9',
 'version_RE0': '15.1R1.9',
```

```
 'version_info': junos.version_info(major=(15, 1), type=R, minor=1, build=9)}
>>>
```

These facts can be easily tested in a script to implement logic based on the facts. This code shows a simple example based on the `model` key in the `facts` dictionary. The `model` key indicates the model of the Junos device:

```
if r0.facts['model'] == 'MX480':
    # Handle the MX480 case
    ... MX480 code ...
else:
    # Handle the case of other models
    ... Other models code ...
```

The example follows one code path if the Junos device is an MX480 and another code path for all other models of Junos device.

While facts gathering is enabled by default, it can be disabled by setting the optional `gather_facts` parameter to `False` in the `Device()` or `open()` calls. You might want to disable facts gathering to speed the initial connection or if there is an unexpected problem gathering facts on a device.

If facts gathering is disabled during the initial NETCONF connection, it can still be initiated later by invoking the `facts_refresh()` instance method. As the name implies, the `facts_refresh()` method can also be used to refresh an existing `facts` dictionary with the latest information from the Junos device.

Closing the Connection

The `close()` method cleanly shuts down the NETCONF session that was initiated by the successful execution of the `open()` method. The `close()` method should be invoked when you have finished making RPC calls to the device instance:

```
>>> r0.close()
```

Calling the `close()` method does not destroy the device instance; it just closes its NETCONF session. Calling an RPC after an instance has been closed causes a `jnpr.junos.exception.ConnectClosedError` exception to be raised, as shown in this example:

```
>>> r0.close()
>>> version_info = r0.rpc.get_software_information()
Traceback (most recent call last):
...ouput trimmed...
jnpr.junos.exception.ConnectClosedError: ConnectClosedError(r0)
>>> r0.open()
Device(r0)
>>> version_info = r0.rpc.get_software_information()
>>> r0.close()
```

The example also shows how an instance that has previously been closed can be reopened by invoking the `open()` instance method again. The RPC is executed, and the instance is again closed.

RPC Execution

This section begins with one of PyEZ's *low-level* capabilities. PyEZ allows the user to invoke Junos XML RPCs using simple Python statements. While PyEZ offers higher-level abstractions, like tables and views (covered in "Operational Tables and Views" on page 194), it still simplifies the process of invoking Junos XML RPCs and parsing the corresponding XML responses. PyEZ does not require formatting the RPC as XML, and it does not require directly interacting with NETCONF.

RPC on Demand

Once a device instance has been created and the `open()` method has been invoked to initiate the NETCONF session, the device instance's `rpc` property can be used to execute an RPC. Each Junos XML RPC can be invoked as a method of the `rpc` property. The general format of these method calls is:

```
device_instance_variable.rpc.rpc_method_name()
```

For example, the *get-route-summary-information* RPC is invoked on the already opened `r0` device instance with:

```
>>> route_summary_info = r0.rpc.get_route_summary_information()
```

The XML RPC name is *get-route-summary-information*, while the method name is `get_route_summary_information`. The method name is derived from the XML RPC name by simply substituting underscores for hyphens. This substitution is required because Python's naming rules don't allow method names to include dashes.

The response from the *get-route-summary-information* RPC is returned by the `r0.rpc.get_route_summary_information()` method and stored in the `route_summary_info` variable. For now, don't worry about the content of the response. RPC response content will be covered in detail in "RPC Responses" on page 183.

PyEZ refers to this concept as "RPC on Demand" because the PyEZ library does *not* contain a method for each Junos XML RPC. Having an actual method for each Junos XML RPC would require thousands of methods. In addition, to avoid these methods being perpetually out of sync with the device's capabilities, PyEZ would have to be tightly coupled to the Junos platform and version. With RPC on Demand, there is no tight coupling; new features are added to each platform with each Junos release and the existing version of PyEZ can instantly access those RPCs.

Instead, RPC on Demand is implemented using the concept of *metaprogramming*. Each RPC method is generated, and executed, dynamically at the time it is invoked. PyEZ users aren't required to understand the details of how this metaprogramming is implemented, but it is helpful to understand the general concept.

Because these RPC methods are generated "on demand," an RPC method can be invoked for *every* Junos XML RPC on *any* Junos platform. If a Junos device supports a particular XML RPC, that XML RPC can *always* be invoked from PyEZ using RPC on Demand.

The corresponding aspect of this design paradigm is that the PyEZ library cannot know in advance if an XML RPC is valid. Any RPC method name will be first converted to its corresponding XML RPC name by substituting hyphens for underscores, then wrapped in proper XML elements and sent over the NETCONF session to the device. Only after the NETCONF response is received from the device can an error be discovered and an exception raised. "RPC Exceptions" on page 180 details this case and other possible exceptions.

PyEZ also provides a `cli()` device instance method, but this method is primarily intended for debugging and should be avoided in PyEZ scripts. By default, this method returns a text string containing the normal CLI output:

```
>>> response = r0.cli('show system uptime')
/usr/local/lib/python2.7/dist-packages/jnpr/junos/devi...
  warnings.warn("CLI command is for debug use only!", ...)
>>> print response

Current time: 2015-07-13 14:02:00 PDT
Time Source:  NTP CLOCK
System booted: 2015-07-13 07:42:46 PDT (06:19:14 ago)
Protocols started: 2015-07-13 07:42:46 PDT (06:19:14 ago)
Last configured: 2015-07-13 08:07:26 PDT (05:54:34 ago) by root
 2:02PM  up 6:19, 1 users, load averages: 0.59, 0.41, 0.33

>>>
```

The `cli()` method is prone to all of the "gotchas" of traditional "screen scraping" network automation. Neither the command nor the response is in a structured data format. Both are subject to errors in parsing or even changes between Junos versions. For this reason, you should avoid using this method in any production automation effort.

RPC Discovery with PyEZ

"Discovering Operational RPC Syntax" on page 63 explained how to discover the RPC for a given CLI command by using the `| display xml rpc` pipe command. This technique can easily be used while developing a PyEZ script by opening a separate terminal window to the device's CLI. However, PyEZ also offers an RPC discovery method that can be used from within Python itself: the `display_xml_rpc()` instance method. You can fetch the RPC for the `show system users` CLI command with:

```
>>> r0.display_xml_rpc('show system users')
<Element get-system-users-information at 0x7fa22b1294d0>
```

Notice this command returned an object, not a string. By default, all PyEZ RPC responses are returned as an `lxml.etree.Element` object. "RPC Responses" on page 183 provides much more detail on using these responses. For now, it's sufficient to know that an `lxml.etree.Element` object represents an XML element. In this case, it's the first XML element inside the response's `<rpc-reply>` tag. You can view the actual RPC name by invoking the `tag` property on this response object. This example imports the `etree` module from the lxml library and fetches the XML tag by appending the `tag` property to the previous example:

```
>>> from lxml import etree
>>> r0.display_xml_rpc('show system users').tag
'get-system-users-information'
```

You can take this one step further by using the built in `replace()` string method to substitute hyphens with underscores:

```
>>> r0.display_xml_rpc('show system users').tag.replace('-','_')
'get_system_users_information'
```

This recipe can be used to discover the RPC name for any Junos CLI command, but does not provide details on an RPC's parameters. Passing the response from the `display_xml_rpc()` method to the `etree.dump()` function displays the full XML response (including RPC parameters):

```
>>> from lxml import etree
>>> etree.dump(
...       r0.display_xml_rpc(
...         'show route protocol isis 10.0.15.0/24 active-path'
...       )
... )
<get-route-information>
    <destination>10.0.15.0/24</destination>
    <active-path/>
    <protocol>isis</protocol>
</get-route-information>
```

RPC Parameters

As you saw with the Junos RESTful API service in "Adding Parameters to RPCs" on page 112, some Junos XML RPCs support optional parameters that limit or alter the XML response. When describing the RPC in XML format, these parameters appear as nested XML tags within the RPC name's XML tag. As an example, here's the equivalent XML RPC for the `show route protocol isis 10.0.15.0/24 active-path` CLI command:

```
user@r0> show route protocol isis 10.0.15.0/24 active-path | display xml rpc
<rpc-reply xmlns:junos="http://xml.juniper.net/junos/15.1R1/junos">
    <rpc>
        <get-route-information>
                <destination>10.0.15.0/24</destination>
                <active-path/>
                <protocol>isis</protocol>
        </get-route-information>
    </rpc>
    <cli>
        <banner></banner>
    </cli>
</rpc-reply>
```

In the preceding output, you can see three XML elements are nested within the RPC's `<get-route-information>` XML element. The `<destination>` and `<protocol>` tags have values in their content, while the `<active-path/>` tag is an empty XML element. The PyEZ RPC mechanism allows the user to specify these parameters without having to format them in XML. The parameters are simply specified as keyword arguments to the RPC methods introduced in "RPC on Demand" on page 175. An equivalent PyEZ method invocation for the `show route protocol isis 10.0.15.0/24 active-path` CLI command is:

```
>>> isis_route = r0.rpc.get_route_information(protocol='isis',
...                                           destination='10.0.15.0/24',
...                                           active_path=True)
```

The XML tags become keyword arguments, and any XML content becomes the value of the keyword. Just like in the RPC method names, underscores are substituted for any hyphens in the XML tags. So, the `<active-path/>` tag becomes the `active_path` keyword. If the RPC parameter does not require a value, as is the case with `<active-path/>`, the keyword's value should be set to `True`.

RPC Timeout

By default, an RPC method call will time out if the complete response is not received from the Junos device within 30 seconds. While this default is reasonable for most RPC calls, there are times when you may need to override the default. One example of an RPC that might take longer than 30 seconds to execute is *get-flow-session-*

information on an SRX-Series firewall that has many thousands of active security flows. Another example is *get-route-information* on a router carrying the full Internet routing table (500K+ routes and growing).

When you encounter one of these situations, your first question should always be: "Do I really need all of this information?" Maybe you only need the routes from a particular peer AS, or the security flows with a TCP destination port of 443. In those cases, have the RPC filter the output directly on the device by passing appropriate parameters to the RPC as discussed in the previous section.

There are, however, other times where the situation is unavoidable. The best example may be installing a Junos software package with the *request-package-add* RPC. In this case, you need to override the 30-second timeout with a longer timeout. In other situations, you might want to shorten the default timeout to have your script more quickly detect an unresponsive device. Regardless of whether you need to increase or decrease the 30-second timeout, there are two ways of achieving this objective.

The first method for changing the RPC timeout is to simply set the device instance's `timeout` property. Setting the `timeout` property affects *all* RPCs invoked on this device handle. Here is an example using the existing `r0` instance variable:

```
>>> r0.timeout
30
>>> r0.timeout = 10
>>> r0.timeout
10
```

The preceding example confirms the default 30-second timeout by displaying the value of the `r0.timeout` attribute. The timeout is then set to 10 seconds, and the final line confirms the value is now 10 seconds.

The second method for modifying the RPC timeout only changes the timeout value for a single RPC. Future RPCs will continue to use the default value, or the value set by assigning the device instance's `timeout` attribute. This second method is accomplished by passing a `dev_timeout` keyword parameter to the RPC's method. Here's an example of this method:

```
>>> summary_info = r0.rpc.get_route_summary_information()
>>> bgp_routes = r0.rpc.get_route_information(dev_timeout = 180,
...                                           protocol='bgp')
>>> isis_routes = r0.rpc.get_route_information(protocol='isis')
```

In this example, the *get-route-summary-information* RPC is executed with the default 30-second timeout. BGP routes are then gathered with a specific 180-second timeout. Finally, ISIS routes are gathered with the default 30-second timeout.

RPC Exceptions

In addition to the connection-related exceptions discussed in "Connection Exceptions" on page 171, the Junos PyEZ library defines several exceptions that may be raised when an RPC on Demand method fails. Table 4-3 provides a list and descriptions of these exceptions and of the situation in which each exception is raised.

Table 4-3. Possible exceptions raised by RPC on Demand methods

Exception	Description
`jnpr.junos.exception.ConnectClosedError`	Raised if the underlying NETCONF session closed unexpectedly before the RPC method was invoked. This might happen because of an RE switchover on the target device, a network reachability problem between the automation host and the target device, or a failure of the target device itself, or because you forgot to call the `open()` method.
`jnpr.junos.exception.RpcTimeoutError`	Raised if the underlying NETCONF session is connected, and the RPC was successfully sent to the device, but a response is not received from the device within the RPC timeout period (as discussed in the previous section).
`jnpr.junos.exception.PermissionError`	Raised if authorization, as discussed in "Authentication and Authorization" on page 170, does not permit the RPC being executed.
`jnpr.junos.exception.RpcError`	Raised if there are `<xnm:error>` or `<xnm:warning>` elements present in the RPC response. This exception is also raised if there are NETCONF `<rpc-error>` elements present in the response or if the `ncclient` library raises an unrecognized exception.

Exactly how each of these exceptions should be handled can be very specific to your particular automation requirements. For example, if the response from a particular RPC is required for further processing, a `jnpr.junos.exception.PermissionError` exception would indicate an error that prevents further processing (at least for that specific device instance). In this case, printing the error and exiting the script (or continuing to the next device instance in the loop) might be appropriate. However, there might be other cases where the user provides input that selects the RPC to be executed. In this case, you might want to gracefully handle the `jnpr.junos.exception.PermissionError` exception by printing the error and asking the user to specify a different RPC.

A common exception handling requirement is attempting to reopen the NETCONF connection when a `jnpr.junos.exception.ConnectClosedError` exception is received. Because this exception may indicate a transient condition, it may be possible to gracefully recover from the condition. However, this exception may also indicate a more persistent problem. Attempting to reopen the NETCONF connection with no constraints could lead to an infinite loop.

The following Python code snippet illustrates an algorithm for attempting to reopen the NETCONF connection, and reexecute the failed RPC, a limited number of times. Not only does it illustrate a common requirement, but it provides a framework for additional more specific exception handling. By simply adding another `except` block, additional graceful error handling could be added for other exceptions:

```
import jnpr.junos.exception ❶
from time import sleep

MAX_ATTEMPTS = 3 ❷
WAIT_BEFORE_RECONNECT = 10

# Assumes r0 already exists and is a connected device instance

for attempt in range(MAX_ATTEMPTS): ❸
    try: ❹
        routes = r0.rpc.get_route_information()
    except jnpr.junos.exception.ConnectClosedError: ❺
        sleep(WAIT_BEFORE_RECONNECT) ❻
        try: r0.open()
        except jnpr.junos.exception.ConnectError: pass
    else: ❼
        # Success. No exception was raised.
        # break will skip the for loop's else.
        break
else: ❽
    # Max attempts exceeded. All attempts have failed.
    # Re-raise most recent exception from last attempt.
    raise

# ... continue with the rest of script if RPC succeeded ...
```

❶ Importing the PyEZ exception module is required before specific PyEZ exceptions can be caught by an `except` statement. Import the `sleep()` function from the `time` module into the local namespace.

❷ `MAX_ATTEMPTS` is used as a constant to indicate the maximum number of times an RPC should be retried. For this example, an RPC will be retried a maximum of three times. `WAIT_BEFORE_RECONNECT` is used as a constant to indicate the number of seconds to wait after an RPC failure before attempting to reopen the NETCONF connection. This allows up to 30 seconds (`WAIT_BEFORE_RECONNECT * MAX_ATTEMPTS`) for a transient condition to be resolved.

❸ The `for` loop will attempt to execute the RPC up to `MAX_ATTEMPTS` times.

❹ The `try` statement marks a block of statements that will be executed until an exception occurs. The RPC on Demand feature executes the *get-route-*

information RPC inside this `try` block. The result of the RPC is stored in the `routes` variable. This RPC may succeed without an exception, or it may raise any of the exceptions listed in Table 4-3.

❺ If an exception is raised by the statement in the `try` block, the exception is checked to see if it matches a `jnpr.junos.exception.ConnectClosedError` exception. If the exception matches, the statements in this `except` block are run. If the exception doesn't match this `except` block, Python's default exception handler will stop the program execution and print the error. Additional exception statements could be added to handle other possible exceptions. Each `except` block will be tested in order until a match is found, or the list of exceptions is exhausted.

❻ Immediately attempting to reconnect a closed NETCONF connection is likely to fail. Instead, waiting some period of time provides an opportunity for a transient condition (RE switchover, network reconvergence, etc.) to pass. The `sleep` statement suspends execution of the script for `WAIT_BEFORE_RECONNECT` seconds. Execution then proceeds to the next line. The `open()` method is wrapped in a `try` block to catch any exceptions that will occur if the call fails because the underlying network condition still exists. The `except: pass` statement will catch and ignore all `jnpr.junos.exception.ConnectError` exceptions raised by `r0.open()`.

All exceptions raised by `r0.open()` are listed in Table 4-2. These exceptions are all subclasses of `jnpr.junos.exception.ConnectError`. Therefore, catching this one exception class catches all exceptions raised by `r0.open()`.

If the NETCONF connection is still not open, this condition will be caught as another `jnpr.junos.exception.ConnectClosedError` exception during the next attempt to execute the RPC.

❼ The `else` block of a `try/except/else` compound statement is executed only if no exceptions were raised by the `try` block. In other words, the `else` block is executed only if `r0.rpc.get_route_information()` executed successfully. The `break` statement will exit the `for` loop when the RPC succeeds. Exiting a `for` loop with a `break` statement skips the `else` clause of the loop.

❽ The `else` clause of a Python `for` loop is executed only if the loop exits normally. In this code, "exiting normally" means all attempts have been exhausted (`attempt > MAX_ATTEMPTS`) and the RPC execution has failed (raised an exception) on each attempt. If all attempts have failed, the most recent exception is raised.

This example assumes the `r0` variable has already been assigned a device instance, as described in "Creating a Device Instance" on page 166, and already has a NETCONF connection opened, as described in "Making the Connection" on page 169. The example also purposely treats any exception raised by the RPC other than `jnpr.junos.exception.ConnectClosedError` as a fatal error. Finally, if the `jnpr.junos.exception.ConnectClosedError` exception persists for more than `MAX_ATTEMPTS`, the most recent exception will be propagated to Python's default error handling mechanism. The most recent exception will likely be one of the exceptions from Table 4-2, raised by the final attempt to reopen the connection.

RPC Responses

Now that you've seen how to invoke Junos XML RPCs using simple Python statements, this section covers what to do with the resulting responses. PyEZ offers multiple ways to parse a response into Python data structures, and also offers an optional mechanism for removing extraneous whitespace from the response. This section covers each of the features for controlling RPC responses.

lxml Elements

The default response to a NETCONF XML RPC is a string representing an XML document. As you've seen, this RPC response is the same as the output displayed by the CLI when the `| display xml` modifier is appended to the equivalent CLI command. For example:

```
user@r0> show system users | display xml
<rpc-reply xmlns:junos="http://xml.juniper.net/junos/15.1R1/junos">
    <system-users-information xmlns="http://xml.juniper.net/junos/15.1R1/junos">
        <uptime-information>
            <date-time junos:seconds="1436915514">4:11PM</date-time>
            <up-time junos:seconds="116940">1 day,  8:29</up-time>
            <active-user-count junos:format="4 users">4</active-user-count>
            <load-average-1>0.56</load-average-1>
            <load-average-5>0.43</load-average-5>
            <load-average-15>0.36</load-average-15>
            <user-table>
                <user-entry>
                    <user>root</user>
                    <tty>u0</tty>
                    <from>-</from>
                    <login-time junos:seconds="1436897214">11:06AM</login-time>
                    <idle-time junos:seconds="60">1</idle-time>
                    <command>cli</command>
                </user-entry>
```

```
                <user-entry>
                    <user>foo</user>
                    <tty>pts/0</tty>
                    <from>172.29.104.149</from>
                    <login-time junos:seconds="1436884614">7:36AM</login-time>
                    <idle-time junos:seconds="30900">8:35</idle-time>
                    <command>-cli (cli)</command>
                </user-entry>
                <user-entry>
                    <user>bar</user>
                    <tty>pts/1</tty>
                    <from>172.29.104.149</from>
                    <login-time junos:seconds="1436884614">7:36AM</login-time>
                    <idle-time junos:seconds="30900">8:35</idle-time>
                    <command>-cli (cli)</command>
                </user-entry>
                <user-entry>
                    <user>user</user>
                    <tty>pts/2</tty>
                    <from>172.29.104.149</from>
                    <login-time junos:seconds="1436884614">7:36AM</login-time>
                    <idle-time junos:seconds="0">-</idle-time>
                    <command>-cli (cli)</command>
                </user-entry>
            </user-table>
        </uptime-information>
    </system-users-information>
    <cli>
        <banner></banner>
    </cli>
</rpc-reply>
```

Rather than returning this XML document string directly to the user, as you saw with the RESTful API service in "Formatting HTTP Responses" on page 103, the PyEZ library uses the lxml library (*http://lxml.de*) to parse the XML document and return the already parsed response. The response is an `lxml.etree.Element` object rooted at the first child element of the `<rpc-reply>` element. In the case of the `show system users` command, or the equivalent *get-system-users-information* RPC, the first child element of the `<rpc-reply>` element is the `<system-users-information>` element. This is demonstrated by displaying the `tag` attribute of the *get-system-users-information* RPC response:

```
>>> response = r0.rpc.get_system_users_information(normalize=True)
>>> response.tag
'system-users-information'
```

This example passed the argument `normalize=True` to the `r0.rpc.get_system_users_information()` method. Response normalization is covered in detail in "Response Normalization" on page 190. For the purposes of these examples, simply make sure you also include the `normalize` argument. Failing to do so will cause some of the following examples to return different results or fail completely.

Each `lxml.etree.Element` object has links to parent, child, and sibling `lxml.etree.Element` objects, which form a tree representing the parsed XML response. For debugging purposes, the `lxml.etree.dump()` function can be used to dump the XML text of the response (albeit without the pretty formatting of the Junos CLI):

```
>>> from lxml import etree
>>> etree.dump(response)
<system-users-information>
<uptime-information>
...ouput trimmed...
</uptime-information>
</system-users-information>

>>>
```

While `lxml.etree.Element` objects may seem more complicated than a data structure composed of native Python lists and dicts, `lxml.etree.Element` objects do offer a robust set of APIs for selecting and extracting portions of the RPC response. Many of these APIs use an XPath expression to match a subtree, or subtrees, from the response. You were introduced to XPath expressions in "Accessing XML data with XPath" on page 36. The following sidebar augments the previous introduction with specific information on the subset of XPath expressions available within lxml. For a more detailed study of XPath in general, check out the W3Schools XPath Tutorial (*http://www.w3schools.com/xsl/xpath_intro.asp/*).

Using XPath with lxml

Several lxml methods support a subset of the full XPath expression syntax. Table 4-4 details the most common XPath syntax supported by the lxml `find()`, `findall()`, and `findtext()` methods. In addition, lxml offers an `xpath()` method, which supports the full XPath syntax. The `xpath()` method is outside the scope of this book. Refer to the lxml library (*http://lxml.de*) documentation for details on `xpath()` and other more advanced XPath usage with lxml.

Table 4-4. XPath syntax supported by the lxml library

Syntax	Description
`.`	Selects the current node. While XPath expressions are relative by default, prefixing a path with `./` gives a more explicit indication that the XPath is relative to the current node.
`..`	Selects the parent node. Allows traversing up a subtree to select a sibling subtree.
`//`	Selects all subtree elements. Allows finding an element regardless of its position in the XML.
`tag`	Selects all child elements with tag *`tag`*.
`*`	Selects all child elements.
`[`*`tag`*`]`	Selects all elements that have an immediate child with tag *`tag`*.
`[`*`tag`*`='`*`value`*`']`	Selects all elements that have an immediate child with tag *`tag`* and value *`value`*.
`[@`*`attribute`*`]`	Selects all elements that have an attribute named *`attribute`*.
`[@`*`attribute`*`='`*`value`*`']`	Selects all elements that have an attribute named *`attribute`* and value *`value`*.
`[`*`position`*`]`	Selects the element in *`position`*. This is essentially an index into a list of elements, but unlike with a Python list, the first element is at position 1, not position 0. The expression `last()` can be used to select the element in the last position. Positions can also be expressed relative to the last position. For example, the expression `last()-1` selects the element in the penultimate position.

Now that you're armed with a basic understanding of XPath, let's look at some examples of how the lxml APIs can be used to select information from an RPC response. These examples use the same *get-system-users-information* RPC `response` variable from previous examples. It may help to analyze each of these statements and their results using the `show system users | display xml` output at the beginning of this section.[5]

5 Be aware that PyEZ strips XML namespaces from the response. So, while the CLI output includes XML elements with attributes in the `junos` namespace, such as `<up-time junos:seconds="102120">1 day, 4:22</up-time>`, the attribute in the response object is `seconds` rather than `junos:seconds`.

The text content of the first XML element matching an XPath expression can be retrieved with the `findtext()` method:

```
>>> response.findtext("uptime-information/up-time")
'1 day, 8:29'
```

The argument to the `findtext()` method is an XPath relative to the `response` element. Because `response` represents the `<system-users-information>` element, the `uptime-information/up-time` XPath matches the `<up-time>` tag in the response.

The `<up-time>` element also contains a `seconds` attribute that provides the system's uptime in an easier to parse number of seconds since the system booted. The value of this attribute can be accessed by chaining the `find()` method and the `attrib` attribute:

```
>>> response.find("uptime-information/up-time").attrib['seconds']
'116940'
```

While the `findtext()` method returns a string, the `find()` method returns an `lxml.etree.Element` object. The XML attributes of that `lxml.etree.Element` object can then be accessed using the `attrib` dictionary. The `attrib` dictionary is keyed using the XML attribute name.

In the `response` variable, there is one `<user-entry>` XML element for each user currently logged into the device. Each `<user-entry>` element contains a `<user>` element with the user's username. The `findall()` method returns a list of `lxml.etree.Element` objects matching an XPath. In this example, `findall()` is used to select the `<user>` element within every `<user-entry>` element:

```
>>> users = response.findall("uptime-information/user-table/user-entry/user")
>>> for user in users:
...     print user.text
...
root
foo
bar
user
>>>
```

The result of this example is a list of usernames for all users currently logged into the Junos device.

The next example combines the `findtext()` method with an XPath expression that selects the first matching XML element that has a specific matching child element:

```
>>> response.findtext("uptime-information/user-table/user-entry[tty='u0']/user")
'root'
```

The result of this example is the username of the user currently logged into the Junos device's console. (On this device, the console has a tty name of `u0`.) The XPath selects the <user> element from the first <user-entry> element that also has a <tty> child element with the value u0.

The next example retrieves the number of seconds that the user bar's session has been idle. This is done by combining the find() method, an XPath with the [*tag*='text'] predicate, and the attrib attribute dictionary:

```
>>> XPATH = "uptime-information/user-table/user-entry[user='bar']/idle-time"
>>> response.find(XPATH).attrib['seconds']
'30900'
```

In the preceding example, the XPATH variable is used as a constant simply to avoid line wrap in the printed book.

Because the preceding example used the find() method, it will only return information for the bar user's *first* CLI session. If the bar user has multiple CLI sessions open, you could retrieve a list of the idle times by replacing find() with findall().

One significant difference between lxml.etree.Element objects, with their corresponding methods, and native Python data structures is how nonexistent data is handled. In order to demonstrate this, we'll create an equivalent multilevel Python dictionary to store the uptime information:

```
>>> from pprint import pprint
>>> example_dict = { 'uptime-information' : { 'up-time' : '1 day, 8:29' }}
>>> pprint(example_dict)
{'uptime-information': {'up-time': '1 day, 8:29'}}
```

Accessing the information in this dictionary is arguably easier than using the findtext() method:

```
>>> example_dict['uptime-information']['up-time']
'1 day, 8:29'
```

However, consider what happens when you try to access data that doesn't exist in the response. The native Python dictionary raises a KeyError exception:

```
>>> example_dict['foo']['bar']
Traceback (most recent call last):
  File "<stdin>", line 1, in <module>
KeyError: 'foo'
```

If there's a possibility that a piece of information may be missing from the response, then the dictionary access needs to be wrapped in a try/except block that gracefully handles the resulting KeyError exception. Conversely, if the requested information is missing from an lxml.etree.Element object, the find() and findtext() methods simply return None rather than raising an exception:

```
>>> print response.find("foo/bar")
None
>>> print response.findtext("foo/bar")
None
```

The findall() method exhibits a similar behavior. It returns an empty list when the XPath expression fails to match any XML elements:

```
>>> print response.findall("foo/bar")
[]
```

It's also important to remember the findall() method always returns a list of lxml.etree.Element objects. It does not return an lxml.etree.Element object directly. This behavior remains true even when there's only one object in the list:

```
>>> user_entries = response.findall("uptime-information/user-table/user-entry")
>>> type(user_entries)
<type 'list'>
>>> len(user_entries)
4
```

When multiple users are logged in, this list contains one object for each user. However, the next example demonstrates the response when only one user is logged in:

```
>>> new_response = r0.rpc.get_system_users_information(normalize=True)
>>> new_users = new_response.findall("uptime-information/user-table/user-entry")
>>> type(new_users)
<type 'list'>
>>> len(new_users)
1
```

In this single-user case, notice that the response is still a list; it's just a list with a single item. This behavior allows the program to loop over the list of user entries without having to create different code paths for the no users, one user, and multiple users cases.

There is one final situation that is important to understand. Attempting to access a nonexistent XML attribute still raises a KeyError. That's because an lxml.etree.Element object's attrib attribute is a Python dictionary keyed on the XML attribute name:

```
>>> response.find("uptime-information/up-time").attrib['foo']
Traceback (most recent call last):
  File "<stdin>", line 1, in <module>
  File "lxml.etree.pyx", line 2366, in lxml.etree._Attrib.__getitem__ (src/lx...
KeyError: 'foo'
```

A related but slightly different situation is attempting to access an XML attribute on a nonexistent element. In this example, the `find()` method returns `None` because there is no XML element that matches the XPath expression.

One way of handling access to the `attrib` dictionary is wrapping the access in a `try/except` block that catches both the `AttributeError` and the `KeyError`:

```
>>> try: foo_attrib = response.find("uptime-information/bar").attrib['foo']
... except (AttributeError, KeyError): foo_attrib = None
...
>>> print foo_attrib
None
>>> try: foo_attrib = response.find("uptime-information/up-time").attrib['foo']
... except (AttributeError, KeyError): foo_attrib = None
...
>>> print foo_attrib
None
```

While this hasn't been an exhaustive set of examples, you've now seen the basics of accessing PyEZ RPC responses in the default `lxml.etree.Element` object format. These examples have demonstrated some of the most common ways to access the response information, but the lxml library does offer many more tools. Full documentation on `lxml`'s API is available at the `lxml` website (*http://lxml.de*). The lxml API is also mostly compatible with the well-known `ElementTree` API. Documentation on the `ElementTree` API is part of the Python Standard Library documentation (*https://docs.python.org/2/library/xml.etree.elementtree.html*) at the ElementTree XML API.

The next section begins to explore the other optional formats that PyEZ can use to return RPC responses.

Response Normalization

Response normalization is a PyEZ feature that actually alters the XML content returned from an RPC method. There are some Junos RPCs that return XML data where the values of certain XML elements are wrapped in newline or other whitespace characters. An example of this extra whitespace can be seen with the *get-system-users-information* RPC we used in the previous section:

```
>>> response = r0.rpc.get_system_users_information()
>>> response.findtext("uptime-information/up-time")
'\n4 days, 17 mins\n'
```

Notice the text for the `<up-time>` element has a newline character before and after the value string. Response normalization is designed to address this situation. When response normalization is enabled, all whitespace characters at the beginning and end of each XML element's value are removed. Response normalization is disabled by default (except when using tables and views, as discussed in "Operational Tables and

Views" on page 194). It can be enabled by adding the `normalize=True` argument to an RPC method:

```
>>> response = r0.rpc.get_system_users_information(normalize=True)
>>> response.findtext("uptime-information/up-time")
'4 days, 17 mins'
```

Notice the newline characters at the beginning and end of the value have been removed, but the whitespace within the value is maintained.

You may have noticed the `normalize=True` argument was added to the `r0.rpc.get_system_users_information()` method invocation in the previous section. Why was the argument used in those examples? The additional whitespace characters present with some RPC responses make some XPath expressions more difficult and less intuitive. As an example, consider the XPath expression used to find the user logged into the Junos device's console (on this device the console has a tty name of `u0`). Without response normalization, the previous XPath example fails to return a matching XML element:

```
>>> response = r0.rpc.get_system_users_information()
>>> response.findtext("uptime-information/user-table/user-entry[tty='u0']/user")
>>>
```

The empty response is because the value in the `[`*tag*`='`*value*`']` portion of the XPath expression must match exactly. Explicitly displaying the value of the `<tty>` tag for the desired user entry (which just happens to be in position 7 in this specific example) reveals that the value has leading and trailing newline characters:

```
>>> response.findtext("uptime-information/user-table/user-entry[7]/tty")
'\nu0\n'
>>>
```

You could modify the XPath expression to look for this specific value, as shown in this example:

```
>>> response.findtext(
        ...     "uptime-information/user-table/user-entry[tty='\nu0\n']/user"
        ... )
'\nroot\n'
>>>
```

However, it can be somewhat unpredictable if additional whitespace is present for the value of any given XML element in any given RPC response. Instead, it's easier to simply use response normalization to allow the expected value to be matched without having to worry about leading or trailing whitespace:

```
>>> response = r0.rpc.get_system_users_information(normalize=True)
>>> response.findtext("uptime-information/user-table/user-entry[tty='u0']/user")
'root'
>>>
```

Response normalization removes leading and trailing whitespace from the values of *all* XML elements in the response. So, not only does this simplify the XPath expression, but it avoids the need to do additional processing to remove whitespace from the username value being accessed.

One final note on response normalization: it can be enabled on a per-RPC basis, as shown so far, or it can be enabled for all RPCs on a device instance or in a NETCONF session by specifying the `normalize=True` argument to the `Device()` or `open()` calls, respectively. Here's an example of enabling it for the device instance:

```
>>> r0 = Device(host='r0',user='user',password='user123',normalize=True)
>>> r0.open()
Device(r0)
>>> response = r0.rpc.get_system_users_information()
>>> response.findtext("uptime-information/up-time")
'4 days, 2:03'
```

If response normalization is enabled for the device instance, as just shown, it's still possible to override the behavior on a per-RPC basis by specifying a `normalize=False` argument when invoking the RPC method.

jxmlease

In addition to parsing XML documents into `lxml.etree.Element` objects, you can also use the jxmlease library to parse RPC responses into jxmlease objects. You may find you prefer jxmlease, described in "Using Structured Data in Python" on page 42, over using XPath and the lxml library. This format offers an excellent balance between functionality and ease of use. The values of XML elements can be accessed using the same tools as native Python dictionaries and lists. You saw an example of using jxmlease in the example script in Chapter 3. In that example, jxmlease was used to parse the XML string returned from the Junos RESTful API service. However, jxmlease can also be used to directly parse an `lxml.etree.Element` object. This parsing is done by passing an `lxml.etree.Element` object to an instance of the `jxmlease.EtreeParser` class. Here's an example of using this technique to return the output of the *get-system-users-information* RPC as an `jxmlease.XMLDictNode` object:

```
>>> import jxmlease
>>> parser = jxmlease.EtreeParser()
>>> response = parser(r0.rpc.get_system_users_information())
>>> response.prettyprint(depth=3)
{'system-users-information': {'uptime-information': {'active-user-count': u'6',
                                                     'date-time': u'12:39PM',
                                                     'load-average-1': u'0.29',
                                                     'load-average-15': u'0.41',
                                                     'load-average-5': u'0.43',
                                                     'up-time': u'3 days, 4:57',
                                                     'user-table': {...}}}}
```

```
>>> type(response)
<class 'jxmlease.XMLDictNode'>
```

The response is actually a `jxmlease.XMLDictNode` object, but behaves much like an ordered dictionary.

You can access any level of the `jxmlease.XMLDictNode` object by specifying a chain of dictionary keys. The tag of each XML element is used as a dictionary key, and begins with the tag of the RPC response's root element. As an example, this statement accesses the system uptime:

```
>>> print response['system-users-information']['uptime-information']['up-time']
3 days, 4:19
```

Notice that the keys begin with `['system-users-information']` and the equivalent of response normalization is applied to `jxmlease.XMLDictNode` objects by default.

For XML elements that have attributes, you can use the object's `get_xml_attr()` method to retrieve the attribute's value:

```
>>> ut = response['system-users-information']['uptime-information']['up-time']
>>> ut.get_xml_attr('seconds')
'274740'
```

`get_xml_attr()` also allows a default value to be returned if the XML attribute name does not exist:

```
>>> ut.get_xml_attr('foo',0)
0
```

The PyEZ example script in "A PyEZ Example" on page 231 further demonstrates using jxmlease with PyEZ RPC responses.

JSON

Junos began supporting the JSON output format in release 14.2 or later. When using PyEZ to invoke an RPC on a Junos device running release 14.2 and later, PyEZ can request this JSON output. You request JSON output from an RPC by passing an argument that is a *dictionary* with a single `'format'` key with a value of `'json'`. This argument causes the Junos device to return the RPC response as a JSON string. However, the JSON string is not returned directly to the user. Instead, PyEZ invokes `json.loads()` to parse the JSON string into a native Python data structure composed of dictionaries and lists. Here's an example:

```
>>> response = r0.rpc.get_system_users_information({'format': 'json'})
>>> type(response)
<type 'dict'>
>>> from pprint import pprint
>>> pprint(response, depth=3)
{u'system-users-information': [{u'attributes': {...},
                                u'uptime-information': [...]}]}
```

This behavior of automatically parsing the JSON response into a Python data structure is analogous to the behavior with the default XML format. When using the default XML format, the device returns a string containing an XML document and PyEZ parses the XML document into a Python data structure. The resulting response can be accessed with all of Python's normal tools for handling dictionaries and lists. See "JSON data" on page 37 for more details on the JSON format, including its limitations.

Operational Tables and Views

In addition to the "RPC on Demand" feature, PyEZ offers another method for invoking an operational RPC and mapping the response into a Python data structure. This "tables and views" feature provides precise control for mapping portions of the RPC response into a Python data structure. In addition, it allows this mapping to be stored for e asy reuse. In fact, PyEZ comes prepackaged with a set of example tables and views that you can use or modify to suit your particular needs.

The operational data of a Junos device is the set of state representing the current running conditions of the device. Operational data is read-only information that is separate from the device's configuration data. You typically view operational data using CLI `show` commands or using operational XML RPCs. You can think of this operational data as similar to a database. Databases are organized into a collection of tables, and in a similar way, PyEZ conceptually organizes a Junos device's operational data into a collection of tables.

In PyEZ, a "table" represents the information that is returned by a particular XML RPC. A PyEZ table is further divided into a list of "items." These items are all of the XML nodes in the RPC output that match a specific XPath expression.

Similar to how a database view selects and presents a subset of fields from a database table, a PyEZ "view" selects and maps a set of fields (XML nodes) from each PyEZ table item into a native Python data structure. Each PyEZ table has at least one view, the default view, for mapping an item's fields into a native Python data structure. Additional views may be defined, but only the default view is required.

Multiple views are used to select different information from the table items. Multiple views are similar in concept to the `terse`, `brief`, `detail`, and `extensive` flags to various CLI commands. Just like each of these CLI flags outputs different information from the same CLI command, different views present different information from the same table.

Prepackaged Operational Tables and Views

Let's begin by using some of the existing tables and views included with PyEZ. Tables and views are defined in YAML files, which have a *.yml* filename extension. The contents of these YAML files will be covered in detail in the next session when explaining how to create your own tables and views.

The prepackaged tables and views included with PyEZ are located in the *op* sub directory of the `jnpr.junos` module's installation directory, as shown by this directory listing:

```
user@h0$ pwd
/usr/local/lib/python2.7/dist-packages/jnpr/junos
user@h0$ ls op/*.yml
op/arp.yml                     op/fpc.yml            op/lacp.yml  op/phyport.yml
op/bfd.yml                     op/idpattacks.yml     op/ldp.yml   op/routes.yml
op/ccc.yml                     op/intopticdiag.yml   op/lldp.yml  op/teddb.yml
op/ethernetswitchingtable.yml  op/isis.yml           op/nd.yml    op/vlan.yml
op/ethport.yml                 op/l2circuit.yml      op/ospf.yml  op/xcvr.yml
```

The *op* sub directory is relative to the location where the `jnpr.junos` module of the PyEZ library is installed. On the example automation host this directory is */usr/local/lib/python2.7/dist-packages/jnpr/junos*, but the location is installation-specific and may be different on your machine. Determine the directory location on your machine by displaying the directory of the `jnpr.junos.__file__` attribute. Use this recipe:

```
>>> import jnpr.junos
>>> import os.path
>>> os.path.dirname(jnpr.junos.__file__)
'/usr/local/lib/python2.7/dist-packages/jnpr/junos'
```

In order to use the prepackaged tables and views, you will need to know the names of the available tables. You can determine the table names by searching the *.yml* files for the string `Table:`, as shown in this example:

```
user@h0$ pwd
/usr/local/lib/python2.7/dist-packages/jnpr/junos
user@h0$ grep Table: op/*.yml
op/arp.yml:ArpTable:
op/bfd.yml:BfdSessionTable:
op/bfd.yml:_BfdSessionClientTable:
op/ccc.yml:CCCTable:
op/ethernetswitchingtable.yml:EthernetSwitchingTable:
op/ethernetswitchingtable.yml:_MacTableEntriesTable:
op/ethernetswitchingtable.yml:_MacTableInterfacesTable:
op/ethport.yml:EthPortTable:
op/fpc.yml:FpcHwTable:
op/fpc.yml:FpcMiReHwTable:
op/fpc.yml:FpcInfoTable:
op/fpc.yml:FpcMiReInfoTable:
op/idpattacks.yml:IDPAttackTable:
op/intopticdiag.yml:PhyPortDiagTable:
op/isis.yml:IsisAdjacencyTable:
op/isis.yml:_IsisAdjacencyLogTable:
```

```
op/l2circuit.yml:L2CircuitConnectionTable:
op/lacp.yml:LacpPortTable:
op/lacp.yml:_LacpPortStateTable:
op/lacp.yml:_LacpPortProtoTable:
op/ldp.yml:LdpNeighborTable:
op/ldp.yml:_LdpNeighborHelloFlagsTable:
op/ldp.yml:_LdpNeighborTypesTable:
op/lldp.yml:LLDPNeighborTable:
op/nd.yml:NdTable:
op/ospf.yml:OspfNeighborTable:
op/phyport.yml:PhyPortTable:
op/phyport.yml:PhyPortStatsTable:
op/phyport.yml:PhyPortErrorTable:
op/routes.yml:RouteTable:
op/routes.yml:RouteSummaryTable:
op/routes.yml:_rspTable:
op/teddb.yml:TedTable:
op/teddb.yml:_linkTable:
op/teddb.yml:TedSummaryTable:
op/vlan.yml:VlanTable:
op/xcvr.yml:XcvrTable:
```

The first step in using one of these tables is to import the appropriate Python class. (The Python class name is the same as the table name defined in the YAML file.) Let's use `ArpTable` from the first line of the preceding output as an example. In order to import the `ArpTable` class, enter the following `from` statement:

```
>>> from jnpr.junos.op.arp import ArpTable
```

Just like RPC on Demand methods, tables and views operate on a PyEZ device instance with an open NETCONF session. As before, we use the `Device()` and `open()` calls to create and open the `r0` device instance variable:

```
>>> from jnpr.junos import Device
>>> r0 = Device(host='r0',user='user',password='user123')
>>> r0.open()
Device(r0)
>>>
```

Create an empty table instance by passing the device instance variable (`r0`) as an argument to the class constructor (`ArpTable()`):

```
>>> arp_table = ArpTable(r0)
```

The `arp_table` instance variable can now be populated with all table items by invoking the `get()` instance method:

```
>>> arp_table.get()
ArpTable:r0: 9 items
```

In the preceding output, the `get()` method executes an RPC and uses the results to populate the `arp_table` instance with nine items.

In the case of ArpTable, each item represents an <arp-table-entry> node from the *get-arp-table-information* RPC's XML output.

An alternative way of creating and populating the table is to bind the table as an attribute of the device instance variable. The get() method is then invoked on this bound attribute:

```
>>> from jnpr.junos.op.arp import ArpTable
>>> r0.bind(arp_table=ArpTable)
>>> r0.arp_table.get()
ArpTable:r0: 9 items
```

In the preceding output, we again see the get() method executes an RPC and populates the r0.arp_table attribute with nine items. Storing the arp_table as an attribute of the device instance variable is a convenient notation when you're maintaining a table for multiple devices. For example, you can easily store and access separate ArpTable tables for the devices r0, r1, and r2. You can then access each table as an attribute of the respective device instance variable.

It is also possible to retrieve specific table items by passing arguments to the get() method. When the get() method is invoked, it executes a corresponding XML RPC defined in the table's YAML file. The get() method can be passed the same parameters as if you were invoking the RPC using RPC on Demand. In the case of ArpTable, the *get-arp-table-information* RPC is executed. The *get-arp-table-information* RPC supports an <interface> argument to limit the response to ARP entries on a specific interface. Here's an example of retrieving only the ARP entries on the ge-0/0/0.0 logical interface:

```
>>> arp_table.get(interface='ge-0/0/0.0')
ArpTable:r0: 1 items
>>> pprint(arp_table.items())
[('00:05:86:18:ec:02',
  [('interface_name', 'ge-0/0/0.0'),
   ('ip_address', '10.0.4.2'),
   ('mac_address', '00:05:86:18:ec:02')])]
```

Invoking a table's get() method always updates the table's items by executing an XML RPC against the Junos device and receiving the RPC's response. When you invoke the get() method, the new response overwrites all previous data in the table. Remember to invoke the get() method, with the appropriate arguments, any time you need to refresh the data stored in the table.

Normalization of table and view data is enabled by default. Refer back to "Response Normalization" on page 190 for more information on normalization. If you need to disable normalization, pass the `normalize=False` argument to the `get()` method:

```
>>> arp_table.get(normalize=False)
ArpTable:r0: 9 items
```

When you create an instance of a table, it returns a `jnpr.junos.factory.OpTable` object. Each `jnpr.junos.factory.OpTable` object operates similarly to a Python `OrderedDict` of view objects. The following example refreshes the `arp_table` instance with all ARP table entries and then shows `arp_table`'s type is `jnpr.junos.factory.OpTable.ArpTable`, which is a subclass of `jnpr.junos.factory.OpTable`. Like with a dictionary, the keys and values of `arp_table` are accessed using the `items()` method:

```
>>> arp_table.get()
ArpTable:r0: 9 items
>>> type(arp_table)
<class 'jnpr.junos.factory.OpTable.ArpTable'>
>>> from pprint import pprint
>>> pprint(arp_table.items())
[('00:05:86:48:49:00',
  [('interface_name', 'ge-0/0/4.0'),
   ('ip_address', '10.0.1.2'),
   ('mac_address', '00:05:86:48:49:00')]),
 ('00:05:86:78:2a:02',
  [('interface_name', 'ge-0/0/1.0'),
   ('ip_address', '10.0.2.2'),
   ('mac_address', '00:05:86:78:2a:02')]),
 ('00:05:86:68:0b:02',
  [('interface_name', 'ge-0/0/2.0'),
   ('ip_address', '10.0.3.2'),
   ('mac_address', '00:05:86:68:0b:02')]),
 ('00:05:86:18:ec:02',
  [('interface_name', 'ge-0/0/0.0'),
   ('ip_address', '10.0.4.2'),
   ('mac_address', '00:05:86:18:ec:02')]),
 ('00:05:86:08:cd:00',
  [('interface_name', 'ge-0/0/3.0'),
   ('ip_address', '10.0.5.2'),
   ('mac_address', '00:05:86:08:cd:00')]),
 ('10:0e:7e:b1:f4:00',
  [('interface_name', 'fxp0.0'),
   ('ip_address', '10.102.191.252'),
   ('mac_address', '10:0e:7e:b1:f4:00')]),
 ('10:0e:7e:b1:b0:80',
  [('interface_name', 'fxp0.0'),
   ('ip_address', '10.102.191.253'),
   ('mac_address', '10:0e:7e:b1:b0:80')]),
```

```
 ('00:00:5e:00:01:c9',
  [('interface_name', 'fxp0.0'),
   ('ip_address', '10.102.191.254'),
   ('mac_address', '00:00:5e:00:01:c9')]),
 ('56:68:a6:6a:47:b2',
  [('interface_name', 'em1.0'),
   ('ip_address', '128.0.0.16'),
   ('mac_address', '56:68:a6:6a:47:b2')])]
>>>
```

The previous example used the first method of creating and populating the table, the `arp_table` instance variable. If the table has been bound to the device instance variable, using the second method, you would access it with `r0.arp_table` rather than `arp_table`:

```
>>> type(r0.arp_table)
<class 'jnpr.junos.factory.OpTable.ArpTable'>
```

Because the table operates similarly to an `OrderedDict`, the individual items (which are `jnpr.junos.factory.View.ArpView` objects) can be accessed by either position or key:

```
>>> type(arp_table[0])
<class 'jnpr.junos.factory.View.ArpView'>
>>> pprint(arp_table[0].items())
[('interface_name', 'ge-0/0/4.0'),
 ('ip_address', '10.0.1.2'),
 ('mac_address', '00:05:86:48:49:00')]
>>> pprint(arp_table['00:05:86:48:49:00'].items())
[('interface_name', 'ge-0/0/4.0'),
 ('ip_address', '10.0.1.2'),
 ('mac_address', '00:05:86:48:49:00')]
>>>
```

Individual values within a view item can be accessed with two-level references using either an index or a key value for the outer reference:

```
>>> arp_table['00:05:86:48:49:00']['ip_address']
'10.0.1.2'
>>> arp_table[0]['ip_address']
'10.0.1.2'
>>> arp_table['00:05:86:48:49:00']['interface_name']
'ge-0/0/4.0'
>>> arp_table[0]['interface_name']
'ge-0/0/4.0'
```

If you assign a view object (a subclass of `jnpr.junos.factory.View`) to a variable, you can also access each of the view object's fields as Python properties, or as a dictionary:

```
>>> arp_item = arp_table[0]
>>> arp_item.ip_address
'10.0.4.2'
>>> arp_item.interface_name
'ge-0/0/0.0'
>>> arp_item.mac_address
'00:05:86:18:ec:02'
>>>
>>> arp_item.keys()
['interface_name', 'ip_address', 'mac_address']
>>> arp_item.items()
[('interface_name', 'ge-0/0/0.0'),
 ('ip_address', '10.0.4.2'),
 ('mac_address', '00:05:86:18:ec:02')]
```

In addition, every view object has two special properties, `name` and `T`. The `name` property provides the view's unique name, or key, within the table. The `T` property is a reference back to the associated table containing the view:

```
>>> arp_item.name
'00:05:86:18:ec:02'
>>> arp_item.T
ArpTable:r0: 9 items
```

In this section, you've seen how to instantiate, populate, and access prepackaged tables and views. Now, let's take a look at how to define a custom table and view rather than being restricted to the prepackaged tables and views that are included with PyEZ.

Creating New Operational Tables and Views

PyEZ tables and views are defined in *.yml* files using the YAML format. YAML uses a simple and intuitive human-readable syntax to define hierarchical data structures formed from scalars, lists, and associative arrays (similar to Python dictionaries). For more information on YAML, refer to the following sidebar, "YAML at a Glance", and for comprehensive information on YAML refer to the YAML specification (*http://www.yaml.org/spec/1.2/spec.html*).

YAML at a Glance

YAML is a recursive acronym for "YAML Ain't Markup Language." YAML is a language-independent data serialization format that is easily parsed by humans. It is designed for data structures or configuration files that are often hand-edited. This is the case for the YAML files that define tables and views, and for the Ansible IT automation framework you will see in Chapter 10. Ansible also uses the YAML format for its configuration files.

YAML supports scalar, list, and associative array (similar to a Python dictionary) data types. It also supports the ability to combine these basic types into more complex hierarchical data structures. Similar to Python, YAML uses indentation to signal hierarchical relationships rather than using quotation marks, braces, brackets, or other balanced enclosure markers that some people may find hard to read. The amount of indentation is unimportant as long as elements at the same level of the hierarchy share the same left indentation. *YAML does not allow tab characters to be used for indentation.*

A file contains one or more YAML "documents." Each document begins with three hyphens (---). Comments begin with # and continue to the end of the line. Blank lines may be added for readability.

YAML autodetects the data type of scalar values based on context. The core data types include integers, floating-point numbers, strings, and Booleans. Some examples of each data type:

```
--- # Example data types
answer: 42            # Integer
pi:     3.14159265    # Float
status: Foo Bar       # String - Internal whitespace is maintained
state:    Foobar      # String -  Leading and trailing whitespace is removed
response: Yes         # Boolean - True
countdown: "54321"    # String - Quotes used to disambiguate
```

A list is defined by placing each list item on a separate line at the same hierarchy level (same left indentation). Each list item begins with a hyphen followed by a space:

```
--- # List of most populated countries per continent
- China
- United States of America
- Brazil
- Nigeria
- Germany
- Australia
```

Alternatively, a list can be defined by enclosing the list in brackets and separating each item with a comma and space:

```
--- # List of most populated countries per continent
[China, United States of America, Brazil, Nigeria, Germany, Australia]
```

An associative array is specified as a set of key/value pairs. Each key/value pair is specified on a separate line at the same hierarchy level (same left indentation). The key is separated from the value using a colon and one or more spaces:

```
--- # Associative array of most populated countries per continent
Asia:          China
North_America: United States of America
South_America: Brazil
Africa:        Nigeria
Europe:        Germany
Australia:     Australia
```

Again, an alternative syntax exists for specifying an associative array. The associative array is surrounded by braces and each key/value pair is separated by a comma and a space. Key/value pairs continue to be separated by a colon and space:

```
--- # Associative array of most populated countries per continent
{Asia: China, North_America: United States of America, South_America: Brazil}
```

Associative arrays and lists can be combined into hierarchical data structures of arbitrary complexity, and both the indented and inline syntaxes can be can be combined:

```
--- # Country info
Asia:
    - Name: China
      Capital: Beijing
      Population: 1357000000
      Area:
          sq_km:    9597000
          sq_miles: 3705000
    - Name: India
      Capital: New Delhi
      Population: 1252000000
      Area:
          sq_km:    3288000
          sq_miles: 1269000
Africa:
    - Name: Nigeria
      Capital: Abuja
      Population: 173600000
      Area: {sq_km: 923768, sq_miles: 356669}
    - Name: Ethiopia
      Capital: Addis Ababa
      Population: 94100000
      Area: {sq_km: 1127000, sq_miles: 435200}
```

Notice that both the `Asia` and `Africa` keys have values that are two-item lists. Each list item is an associative array with `Name`, `Capital`, `Population`, and `Area` keys. The value of the `Area` key is an associative array with the keys `sq_km` and `sq_miles`. For `China` and `India`, the `Area` associative array is specified using the normal (indented) syntax, but for `Nigeria` and `Ethiopia` the `Area` associative array is specified using the alternative syntax.

PyEZ table and view definitions use a subset of the full YAML syntax. They primarily use associative arrays with multiple levels of hierarchy. Values are typically string data types. Here's an example using the *arp.yml* file, which defines the `ArpTable` and `ArpView` classes used in the previous section:

```
---
ArpTable: ❶
  rpc: get-arp-table-information ❷
  item: arp-table-entry ❸
  key: mac-address ❹
  view: ArpView ❺

ArpView: ❻
  fields: ❼
    mac_address: mac-address ❽
    ip_address: ip-address ❾
    interface_name: interface-name ❿
```

❶ The PyEZ YAML loader assumes that anything in the first column is a table or view definition. View definitions are distinguished from table definitions based on their keys. This line begins a table definition. The table name becomes the name of the corresponding Python class. The only restriction on the table name is that it must be a valid name for a Python class.

❷ The Junos XML RPC (*get-arp-table-information*) which is invoked to retrieve the table's item data.

❸ An XPath expression used to select each table item from the RPC response.

❹ The name of an XML element within each table item. The value of this XML element becomes the key used to access each item within the native Python data structure.

❺ The name of the default view used to map a table item into a native Python data structure. This value must exactly match a view name defined in the same YAML document. In this document, the only view is `ArpView`, defined by the top-level associate array key.

❻ The PyEZ YAML loader assumes that anything in the first column is a table or view definition. View definitions are distinguished from table definitions based on their keys. This line begins a view definition.

7. The value of the `fields` key is an associative array that maps XPath expressions to names. The names are used as the keys in the native Python data structure (the view object). The XPath expressions are used to fetch values from each item's XML object.

8. The `mac-address` XPath expression is used to set the value of the `mac_address` key in the native Python view object. Because `mac_address` is used as a key in a Python data structure, it must conform to Python variable naming requirements (it should use underscores, not hyphens).

9. Again, `ip-address` is an XPath expression and `ip_address` is the name of the key in the Python view object.

10. The final key in each Python view object is `interface_name`. The value of the `interface_name` key is determined by the `interface-name` XPath expression.

While the *arp.yml* file demonstrates the required structure and content of PyEZ table and view definitions, it does not include every possible key/value pair. Table 4-5 provides a description of every available key/value pair that may be used in a table definition.

Table 4-5. Keys for defining a PyEZ table

Key name	Required or optional	Description
`rpc`	Required	The name of the Junos XML RPC that is invoked to retrieve the table's item data. This value should use the actual RPC XML tag name (with hyphens) rather than the PyEZ RPC on Demand method name (with underscores).
`args`	Optional	An associative array whose items are passed as default arguments to `rpc`. The `args` parameter should only be specified if `rpc` should always be called with `args` arguments. The keys of the associative array are the arguments passed to the PyEZ RPC on Demand method (with underscores, not hyphens). If an RPC argument is a flag, set the value of the associative array to `True`.

`args_key`	Optional	The name of one optional unnamed first argument to the `get()` method. For example, the prepackaged `RouteTable` definition includes:
		`RouteTable:`
		`  rpc: get-route-information`
		`  args_key: destination`
		This definition allows the user to call:
		`>>> route_table.get('10.0.0.0/8')`
		Which causes the following RPC to be sent to the Junos device:
		`<get-route-information>`
		`    <destination>10.0.0.0/8</destination>`
		`</get-route-information>`

Key name	Required or optional	Description
item	Required	An XML XPath expression that selects each table item (record of data) from the RPC response. Each XML element in the RPC response which matches the XPath expression becomes a table item. The XPath expression is relative to the first element in the response after the <rpc-reply> tag. This is the same behavior we observed in "lxml Elements" on page 183 when using lxml methods with RPC responses.
key	Optional, but recommended	An XPath to select an XML element within each table item. The value of the XML element becomes the key used to access each item within the native Python data structure. If key is not specified, the XPath name is used as the key. If multiple XML elements are required to uniquely identify a table item, the value of this key is a YAML list containing an XPath for each XML element that forms the key. It is recommended to explicitly specify key even if its value is set to the default of name.
view	Required[a]	The name of the default view used to map a table item into a native Python data structure. This value must exactly match the name of a view defined in the same YAML document.

[a] If a view key is not present, then each table item is returned as an lxml.etree.Element object. This negates much of the benefit of tables and views, so the view key is effectively required.

Let's put the information from Table 4-5 into practice by creating a new table definition for the show system users CLI command we used earlier in this chapter. First, the show system users CLI command maps to the *get-system-users-information* XML RPC. Our table definition will include the no-resolve RPC argument to avoid DNS lookups on the <from> elements in the RPC response:

```
user@r0> show system users no-resolve | display xml rpc
<rpc-reply xmlns:junos="http://xml.juniper.net/junos/15.1R2/junos">
    <rpc>
        <get-system-users-information>
                <no-resolve/>
        </get-system-users-information>
    </rpc>
    <cli>
        <banner></banner>
    </cli>
</rpc-reply>
```

It is helpful to reference the structure of the expected RPC response when creating the new table and view definition. An abbreviated version of the *get-system-users-information* response is included here for your reference. This RPC response includes both system-wide information (<up-time>, <active-user-count>, <load-average-1>, etc.) and per-login-specific information (the <user-entry> elements):

```
user@r0> show system users no-resolve | display xml
<rpc-reply xmlns:junos="http://xml.juniper.net/junos/15.1R2/junos">
    <system-users-information xmlns="http://xml.juniper.net/junos/15.1R2/junos">
        <uptime-information>
            <date-time junos:seconds="1437696318">5:05PM</date-time>
```

```
            <up-time junos:seconds="192060">2 days,  5:21</up-time>
            <active-user-count junos:format="8 users">8</active-user-count>
            <load-average-1>0.46</load-average-1>
            <load-average-5>0.50</load-average-5>
            <load-average-15>0.44</load-average-15>
            <user-table>
                <user-entry>
                    <user>root</user>
                    <tty>u0</tty>
                    <from>-</from>
                    <login-time junos:seconds="0">Wed08PM</login-time>
                    <idle-time junos:seconds="16860">4:41</idle-time>
                    <command>cli</command>
                </user-entry>
                <user-entry>
                    <user>user</user>
                    <tty>pts/2</tty>
                    <from>172.29.98.24</from>
                    <login-time junos:seconds="1437694518">4:35PM</login-time>
                    <idle-time junos:seconds="0">-</idle-time>
                    <command>-cli (cli)</command>
                </user-entry>
                <user-entry>
                    <user>user</user>
                    <tty>pts/3</tty>
                    <from>172.29.104.116</from>
                    <login-time junos:seconds="1437667698">9:08AM</login-time>
                    <idle-time junos:seconds="6420">1:47</idle-time>
                    <command>-cli (cli)</command>
                </user-entry>
                ... additional user-entry elements omitted ...
            </user-table>
        </uptime-information>
    </system-users-information>
    <cli>
        <banner></banner>
    </cli>
</rpc-reply>
```

The table definition will focus on the login-specific information by extracting the <user-entry> elements into table items. Here is the table definition and explanations for each field. Follow along by typing this content into a *users.yml* file. Remember to use spaces, *not tabs*, for indentation:

```
---
### ------------------------------------------------------
### show system users no-resolve
### ------------------------------------------------------

UserTable:
    rpc: get-system-users-information
    args:
```

```
        no_resolve: True
    item: uptime-information/user-table/user-entry
    key:
        - user
        - tty
    view: UserView
```

This YAML file defines a table named `UserTable`. The table is populated by running the *get-system-users-information* RPC with the `<no-resolve/>` argument. The table will contain one item for each XML entry that matches the XPath expression `uptime-information/user-table/user-entry`. And, by default, the `UserView` view will be applied to each table item. This example shows an example of a multielement key. Each part of the key (`tty` and `user`) is an XPath expression relative to a table item (a `<user-entry>` element). The key for each table item will be a tuple formed from the `user` and `tty` values.

In most cases, there is a single XML element that uniquely identifies each item. In this case, the `<tty>` element uniquely identifies each `<user-entry>` and could have been used as a simple key. However, for demonstration purposes, we've chosen to demonstrate a multielement key using the combination of both the `<user>` and `<tty>` elements.

The `item` key in the previous table definition is a relatively simply XPath that specifies a three-level hierarchy, `uptime-information/user-table/user-entry`, to select all `<user-entry>` elements. While advanced XPath expressions are outside the scope of this book, it can be helpful to see how a more complicated XPath expression is used to control table item selection. For example, substituting this XPath expression will select only the user logins that have been idle for more than 1 hour (3600 seconds):

```
item: "uptime-information/user-table/user-entry[idle-time[@seconds>3600]]"
```

Each table item still represents a `<user-entry>` element, but only certain `<user-entry>` elements are selected. Specifically, the `<user-entry>` elements that have an `<idle-time>` child element, and where the `<idle-time>` element has a `seconds` attribute with a value greater than `3600`, are selected.

The preceding XPath expression must be enclosed in double quotes. It contains brackets, which YAML would otherwise interpret as an inline list.

Now that we've seen how to define a more complex table, let's focus our attention on the corresponding view definition. The sole purpose of a view definition is to map values to keys in a Python view object. The value for a given key comes from a corresponding XPath expression. The XPath expression is relative to each table item, and typically selects a single element from the table item. The selected element's text node becomes the key's value in the Python view object.

Append this view definition to the same *users.yml* file that contains the `UserTable` definition:

```
UserView:
    fields:
        from: from
        login_time: login-time
        idle_time: idle-time
        command: command
```

Do *not* put a YAML document separator (`---`) between the table and view definitions. They are both part of the same YAML document.

Each view definition begins with the name of the view in the first column. Again, view definitions are distinguished from table definitions based on their keys. If an `rpc` key is present, PyEZ assumes it's a table definition. If no `rpc` is present, PyEZ assumes it's a view definition.

In the example, the name of the view is `UserView`. The view name becomes the name of a corresponding Python class, so the name should follow Python's conventions for class names. There also must be a view name that exactly matches the table definition's `view` property. This is the default view for the table. Additional views may be defined, but only the default view is required.

Notice the colon after `UserView`. This colon indicates `UserView` is a key in an associative array. The value of the `UserView` key is another associative array, which can have four kinds of keys: `fields`, `extends`, `groups`, and `fields_`*`groupname`*. The example uses the simplest of these keys, `fields`. The value of the `fields` key is another associative array.

The `fields` associative array defines a set of names and corresponding XPath expressions (which are relative to the table item). Because the names become attributes of the corresponding Python view object, they must conform to Python naming conventions for variables. In the example, `from`, `login_time`, `idle_time`, and `command` are the field names.

View instance attributes (property or method names) *cannot* be used as the names of fields. Currently, view instance attributes include: asview, items, key, keys, name, refresh, to_json, updater, values, xml, D, FIELDS, GROUPS, ITEM_NAME_XPATH, and T. *Do not use these names as field names.* You should also avoid field names that begin with an underscore.

The XPath expressions are from, login-time, idle-time, and command. Each of these XPath expressions selects a single matching child element from a table item. Refer back to the XML output and note how each <user-entry> element contains <from>, <login-time>, <idle-time>, and <command> child elements.

It is also possible to use more complicated XPath expressions for field selection. Take this example field definition from the prepackaged RouteTableView in the *routes.yml* file:

```
via: "nh/via | nh/nh-local-interface"
```

The field name is via. The XPath expression is nh/via | nh/nh-local-interface. This XPath expression selects all <via> *and* <nh-local-interface> elements under the item's <nh> child elements. If only one matching element is present, then the via field will be the string value of the matching element. However, if the XPath expression selects more than one element, the value of the via field will be a list of string values. The string values are taken from each matching element.

By default, field values are Python strings. However, there are times when the XML response elements contain numeric values. In these cases, the field's value can be defined as a Python int or float. As an example, consider the <login-time> and <idle-time> elements of each <user-entry>:

```
<login-time junos:seconds="0">Wed08PM</login-time>
<idle-time junos:seconds="16860">4:41</idle-time>
```

The value of each element is a date/time string, not a numeric value. These strings are the values of the login_time and idle_time fields in the previous UserView definition. However, these XML elements also contain a seconds attribute[6] with a numeric value. Let's define a new UserExtView that includes integer values for the login time and idle time. Append this new view definition to the same *users.yml* file:

```
UserExtView:
    extends: UserView
    fields:
```

6 Remember that PyEZ strips namespaces from XML responses. So, the junos:seconds attribute in the raw XML response is specified simply as seconds within PyEZ.

```
        login_seconds: {"login-time/@seconds": int}
        idle_seconds: {"idle-time/@seconds": int}
```

The YAML specification reserves the `@` character for future use. Currently, YAML will accept an `@` that appears internal to an unquoted string. However, it will produce an error if the string begins with an `@` character, such as `@seconds`. Enclosing these strings in quotes avoids any potential errors with future versions of YAML.

The new `UserExtView` view definition demonstrates several points. First, look at the values of the `login_seconds` and `idle_seconds` fields. Instead of specifying an XPath expression, an inline associative array is used. This associative array includes an XPath expression *and* the Python data type to be used for the resulting value (`int`, in this case). The field definitions also use more complex XPath expressions that select the value of the `seconds` attribute within each element.

The type of a view field can be defined as `int`, `float`, or `flag`. The `flag` type sets a Boolean value that is `True` if the element is present and `False` if the element is not present. Here is an example from the prepackaged `EthPortView` in the *ethport.yml* file:

```
running: { ifdf-running: flag }
present: { ifdf-present: flag }
```

Now, notice the `extends` key in the `UserExtView` definition. The `extends` key is simply a way to create a new view that's a superset of another view. The `extends: UserView` line causes all fields from the `UserView` definition to be included in `UserExtView`. In addition to the fields from `UserView`, `UserExtView` will also include the new `login_seconds` and `idle_seconds` fields defined under the `fields` key.

In addition to containing `<user-entry>` elements for each login, the *get-system-users-information* RPC response includes system-wide information such as the `<active-user-count>` and `<load-average-1>` elements. While a bit unusual, it is possible to include this system-wide information in each `UserExtView` object. This is done by appending two additional fields to the `UserExtView` definition. The full `UserExtView` definition is now:

```
UserExtView:
    extends: UserView
    fields:
        login_seconds: {"login-time/@seconds": int}
        idle_seconds: {"idle-time/@seconds": int}
        num_users: {../../active-user-count: int}
        load_avg:  {../../load-average-1: float}
```

Like all field definitions, the new `num_users` and `load_avg` fields each specify an XPath expression that is relative to each table item. These XPath expressions just happen to use the parent element notation (`..`) to traverse *up* the XML hierarchy of the response to select nodes that are not contained within the `<user-entry>` element. Because each `<user-entry>` element shares a common `<user-table>` parent element, the result is that each `UserExtView` object will contain `num_users` and `load_avg` fields with the exact same values. The other fields—`from`, `login_time`, `idle_time`, `commands`, `login_seconds`, and `idle_seconds`—continue to have login-specific values because those fields are selected from the per-item `<user-entry>` element. Notice how the `load_avg` field is defined to be a Python `float`.

There is one final tool available when defining views. That tool is `groups`. Groups are completely optional. They are simply a way of grouping together a set of fields that share XPath expressions with a common prefix. In the `UserExtView` definition, the `num_users` and `load_avg` fields share the `../..` prefix. Here is an alternate definition of `UserExtView` using the `groups` tool:

```
UserExtView:
    groups:
        common: ../..
    fields_common:
        num_users: {active-user-count: int}
        load_avg:  {load-average-1: float}
    fields:
        from: from
        login_time: login-time
        idle_time: idle-time
        command: command
        login_seconds: {"login-time/@seconds": int}
        idle_seconds: {"idle-time/@seconds": int}
```

Each group has a name and an XPath prefix. In this example, the name is `common` and `../..` is the XPath prefix. A corresponding `fields_`*`groupname`* key is then used to define the fields that share the XPath prefix. In this case, the `fields_common` key defines the `num_users` and `load_avg` fields. The full XPath expressions for these fields will be `../../active-user-count` and `../../load-average-1`, respectively.

You may have noticed the preceding `UserExtView` did not include the `extends` key. Instead, each of the fields from `UserView` are copied into the `UserExtView` fields. At this time, the `groups` and `extends` keywords are mutually exclusive. You cannot use both keys in a view definition.

Before moving on, let's combine the table and view definitions into the complete *users.yml* file. This file does *not* use `groups` in the `UserExtView` definition:

```
---
### ---------------------------------------------------
### show system users no-resolve
### ---------------------------------------------------

UserTable:
    rpc: get-system-users-information
    args:
        no_resolve: True
    item: uptime-information/user-table/user-entry
    key:
        - user
        - tty
    view: UserView

UserView:
    fields:
        from: from
        login_time: login-time
        idle_time: idle-time
        command: command

UserExtView:
    extends: UserView
    fields:
        login_seconds: {"login-time/@seconds": int}
        idle_seconds: {"idle-time/@seconds": int}
        num_users: {../../active-user-count: int}
        load_avg:  {../../load-average-1: float}
```

Using the New Operational Table and View

Now that we've created the complete *users.yml* file, let's use those table and view definitions. Begin by creating and opening a device instance:

```
>>> from jnpr.junos import Device
>>> r0 = Device(host='r0',user='user',password='user123')
>>> r0.open()
Device(r0)
```

Table and view definitions are loaded using the `loadyaml()` function from the `jnpr.junos.factory` module. This function creates the Python classes and returns a dictionary that maps table and view names to their corresponding class functions:

```
>>> from jnpr.junos.factory import loadyaml
>>> user_defs = loadyaml('users.yml')
>>> from pprint import pprint
>>> pprint(user_defs)
{'UserExtView': <class 'jnpr.junos.factory.View.UserExtView'>,
 'UserTable': <class 'jnpr.junos.factory.OpTable.UserTable'>,
 'UserView': <class 'jnpr.junos.factory.View.UserView'>}
```

The `loadyaml()` function takes a path to the YAML file containing the table and view definitions. This can be an absolute or relative file path. Relative paths are relative to the current working directory.

Once the table and view definitions have been created, an instance of the table class is created. The class function is accessed by indexing the `users_def` dictionary with the table name. The class function takes a device instance as its sole argument:

```
>>> user_table = user_defs['UserTable'](r0)
```

Alternatively, copy the class names into the global namespace, and invoke the class function using the table name:

```
>>> globals().update(user_defs)
>>> user_table = UserTable(r0)
```

Either of these methods results in an empty `UserTable` instance. The instance is assigned to the `user_table` variable. Just like with a prepackaged table, the `get()` method populates the table by invoking the specified RPC:

```
>>> user_table.get()
UserTable:r0: 8 items
>>> pprint(user_table.items())
[(('root', 'u0'),
  [('command', 'cli'),
   ('idle_time', '4:41'),
   ('from', '-'),
   ('login_time', 'Wed08PM')]),
 (('foo', 'pts/0'),
  [('command', '-cli (cli)'),
   ('idle_time', '7:56'),
   ('from', '172.29.104.116'),
   ('login_time', '9:08AM')]),
 (('bar', 'pts/1'),
  [('command', '-cli (cli)'),
   ('idle_time', '7:56'),
   ('from', '172.29.104.116'),
   ('login_time', '9:08AM')]),
 (('user', 'pts/2'),
  [('command', '-cli (cli)'),
   ('idle_time', '-'),
   ('from', '172.29.98.24'),
   ('login_time', '4:35PM')]),
 (('user', 'pts/3'),
  [('command', '-cli (cli)'),
   ('idle_time', '1:47'),
   ('from', '172.29.104.116'),
   ('login_time', '9:08AM')]),
 (('user', 'pts/4'),
  [('command', '-cli (cli)'),
   ('idle_time', '29'),
   ('from', '172.29.98.24'),
```

```
  ('login_time', '4:35PM')]),
 (('foo', 'pts/5'),
  [('command', '-cli (cli)'),
   ('idle_time', '29'),
   ('from', '172.29.98.24'),
   ('login_time', '4:35PM')]),
 (('bar', 'pts/6'),
  [('command', '-cli (cli)'),
   ('idle_time', '29'),
   ('from', '172.29.98.24'),
   ('login_time', '4:35PM')])]
>>>
```

Take time to compare the output of `pprint(user_table.items())` to the `UserTable` and `UserView` definitions in the *users.yml* file. Pay attention to the view fields and values. Also, notice the key for each table item. It's a tuple formed from the `user` and `tty` values. You can access a property in a specific view by specifying the tuple as the table key:

```
>>> user_table[('foo','pts/5')]['from']
'172.29.98.24'
```

Another method for loading a user-defined operational table and view is to create a corresponding *.py* file that executes the `loadyaml()` function and updates the global namespace. Save the following content to a *users.py* file in the same directory as *users.yml*:

```
"""
Pythonifier for UserTable and UserView
"""
from jnpr.junos.factory import loadyaml
from os.path import splitext
_YAML_ = splitext(__file__)[0] + '.yml'
globals().update(loadyaml(_YAML_))
```

This code determines the YAML file to load by replacing the *.py* extension with *.yml*. It then uses the same `loadyaml()` and `globals().update()` functions demonstrated earlier. Here's an example of using the *users.py* file to create and populate a `UserTable` instance:

```
>>> from users import UserTable
>>> user_table = UserTable(r0)
>>> user_table.get()
UserTable:r0: 8 items
>>>
```

With the addition of the *<name>.py* file, the procedure for creating a new table instance is the same regardless of whether the YAML definition file is prepackaged with PyEZ or user-defined.

PyEZ users are encouraged to submit their own table and view definitions to the PyEZ project via a GitHub pull request. As the library of tables and views grows, you become more likely to find an existing table and view to reuse or modify to suit your needs.

Applying a Different View

Remember the `UserExtView` defined in the *users.yml* file? The `UserExtView` defines additional fields for each table item. How do you apply that view to the `user_table` table instance? Simply import the view class and set the `user_table`'s `view` property to the new `UserExtView` class:

```
>>> from users import UserExtView
>>> user_table.view = UserExtView
>>> pprint(user_table.items())
[(('root', 'u0'),
  [('idle_seconds', 16860),
   ('from', '-'),
   ('idle_time', '4:41'),
   ('login_seconds', 0),
   ('num_users', 8),
   ('command', 'cli'),
   ('load_avg', 0.51),
   ('login_time', 'Wed08PM')]),
 (('foo', 'pts/0'),
  [('idle_seconds', 28560),
   ('from', '172.29.104.116'),
   ('idle_time', '7:56'),
   ('login_seconds', 1437667701),
   ('num_users', 8),
   ('command', '-cli (cli)'),
   ('load_avg', 0.51),
   ('login_time', '9:08AM')]),
 (('bar', 'pts/1'),
  [('idle_seconds', 28560),
   ('from', '172.29.104.116'),
   ('idle_time', '7:56'),
   ('login_seconds', 1437667701),
   ('num_users', 8),
   ('command', '-cli (cli)'),
   ('load_avg', 0.51),
   ('login_time', '9:08AM')]),
 (('user', 'pts/2'),
  [('idle_seconds', 0),
   ('from', '172.29.98.24'),
   ('idle_time', '-'),
   ('login_seconds', 1437694521),
   ('num_users', 8),
   ('command', '-cli (cli)'),
   ('load_avg', 0.51),
```

```
       ('login_time', '4:35PM')]),
     (('user', 'pts/3'),
      [('idle_seconds', 6420),
       ('from', '172.29.104.116'),
       ('idle_time', '1:47'),
       ('login_seconds', 1437667701),
       ('num_users', 8),
       ('command', '-cli (cli)'),
       ('load_avg', 0.51),
       ('login_time', '9:08AM')]),
     (('user', 'pts/4'),
      [('idle_seconds', 1740),
       ('from', '172.29.98.24'),
       ('idle_time', '29'),
       ('login_seconds', 1437694521),
       ('num_users', 8),
       ('command', '-cli (cli)'),
       ('load_avg', 0.51),
       ('login_time', '4:35PM')]),
     (('foo', 'pts/5'),
      [('idle_seconds', 1740),
       ('from', '172.29.98.24'),
       ('idle_time', '29'),
       ('login_seconds', 1437694521),
       ('num_users', 8),
       ('command', '-cli (cli)'),
       ('load_avg', 0.51),
       ('login_time', '4:35PM')]),
     (('bar', 'pts/6'),
      [('idle_seconds', 1740),
       ('from', '172.29.98.24'),
       ('idle_time', '29'),
       ('login_seconds', 1437694521),
       ('num_users', 8),
       ('command', '-cli (cli)'),
       ('load_avg', 0.51),
       ('login_time', '4:35PM')])]
>>>
```

Alternatively, you can apply the `asview()` method to a single view instance (which represents a single table item), as shown in the following example. First, the table's view is reset to `UserView`:

```
>>> from users import UserView
>>> user_table.view = UserView
```

Next, the first table item is assigned to `one_view`:

```
>>> one_view = user_table[0]
```

The items within one_view are printed using the default UserView, and then printed again using the UserExtView:

```
>>> pprint(one_view.items())
[('command', 'cli'),
 ('idle_time', '4:41'),
 ('from', '-'),
 ('login_time', 'Wed08PM')]
>>> pprint(one_view.asview(UserExtView).items())
[('idle_seconds', 16860),
 ('from', '-'),
 ('idle_time', '4:41'),
 ('login_seconds', 0),
 ('num_users', 8),
 ('command', 'cli'),
 ('load_avg', 0.51),
 ('login_time', 'Wed08PM')]
>>>
```

Saving and Loading XML Files from Tables

One final note on tables and views before moving on to configuring Junos devices with PyEZ is that PyEZ tables are normally populated by executing an XML RPC over an open NETCONF connection. However, it is also possible to save, and later reuse, the XML RPC response. Saving the XML RPC response is accomplished by invoking the savexml() method on the table instance. The path argument is required and specifies where (an absolute or relative file path) to store the XML output. The optional hostname and timestamp flags can be used to save multiple tables into unique XML files:

```
>>> user_table.savexml(path='/tmp/user_table.xml',hostname=True,timestamp=True)
>>> quit()
user@h0$ ls /tmp/*.xml
/tmp/user_table_r0_20150723151807.xml
```

Later, an XML file can be used to populate a table. Loading a table from an XML file does not require a NETCONF connection to the device that originally produced the RPC response. To load the table from an XML file, provide the path argument to the table's class function:

```
>>> user_table = UserTable(path='/tmp/user_table_r0_20150723151807.xml')
>>> user_table.get()
UserTable:/tmp/user_table_r0_20150723151807.xml: 8 items
>>>
```

The get() method must still be called to populate the table.

Now that we've seen multiple ways to invoke operational RPCs and parse the resulting responses, let's turn our attention to device configuration.

Configuration

PyEZ provides a `Config` class which simplifies the process of loading and committing configuration changes to a Junos device. In addition, PyEZ integrates with the Jinja2 templating engine to simplify the process of creating the actual configuration snippet. Finally, PyEZ offers utilities for comparing configurations, rolling back configuration changes, and locking or unlocking the configuration database.

The first step in using the `Config` class is creating an instance variable. Here's an example of creating a configuration instance variable using the already-opened `r0` device instance variable:

```
>>> from jnpr.junos.utils.config import Config
>>> r0_cu = Config(r0)
>>> r0_cu
jnpr.junos.utils.Config(r0)
```

Alternatively, the configuration instance can be bound as a property of the device instance:

```
>>> from jnpr.junos.utils.config import Config
>>> r0.bind(cu=Config)
>>> r0.cu
jnpr.junos.utils.Config(r0)
```

For the rest of this section, we will use this `r0.cu` device property syntax. However, there's nothing special about the name of the device property. In our examples, we have chosen the name `cu`, but any valid Python variable name (that isn't already a property of the device instance) could be used in its place. Let's begin by loading configuration snippets into the device's candidate configuration.

Loading Configuration Changes

The `load()` method can be used to load a configuration snippet, or full configuration, into the device's candidate configuration. The configuration can be specified in text (aka "curly brace"), set, or XML syntax. Alternatively, the configuration may be specified as an `lxml.etree.Element` object.

Configuration snippets in text, set, or XML syntax can be loaded from a file on the automation host or a Python string object. Files are specified using the `path` argument to the `load()` method. Strings are passed as the first unnamed argument to the `load()` method. The `load()` method attempts to determine the format of the configuration content automatically. The format of a configuration string is determined by the string's content. The format of a configuration file is determined by the path's filename extension, per Table 4-6. In either case, the automatic format can be overridden by setting the `format` argument to `text`, `set`, or `xml`.

Table 4-6. Mapping path filename extensions to configuration format

Path filename extension	Configuration format
.conf, *.text*, or *.txt*	Text in "curly brace" configuration format
.set	Text in set configuration format
.xml	Text in XML configuration format

The `load()` method's `overwrite` and `merge` Boolean flags control how the new configuration affects the current configuration. The default behavior is equivalent to the `load replace` CLI configuration mode command. If the `overwrite` flag is set, the behavior is equivalent to `load override`, and if the `merge` flag is set the behavior is equivalent to the `load merge` command. The `overwrite` and `merge` flags are mutually exclusive. You cannot set both at the same time. In addition, you cannot set the `overwrite` flag when the configuration is in set format.

Here's a simple example of changing the device's hostname by passing a configuration string in set format:

```
>>> from lxml import etree
>>> new_hostname = "set system host-name r0.new"
>>> result = r0.cu.load(new_hostname)
>>> etree.dump(result)
<load-configuration-results>
<ok/>
</load-configuration-results>

>>>
```

The `load()` method returns an `lxml.etree.Element` object indicating the result.

Here are several additional examples of using the `load()` method:

```
# load merge set
result = r0.cu.load(path='hostname.set', merge=True)

# load override
result = r0.cu.load(path='new_config.txt', overwrite=True)

# load merge
result = r0.cu.load(path='hostname.conf', merge=True)

# load replace xml
result = r0.cu.load(path='hostname.xml')
```

If an error occurs, a `jnpr.junos.exception.ConfigLoadError` exception is raised:

```
>>> r0.cu.load('bad config syntax', format='set')
Traceback (most recent call last):
  File "<stdin>", line 1, in <module>
  File "/usr/local/lib/python2.7/dist-packages/jnpr/junos/utils/config.py", l...
    return try_load(rpc_contents, rpc_xattrs)
  File "/usr/local/lib/python2.7/dist-packages/jnpr/junos/utils/config.py", l...
    raise ConfigLoadError(cmd=err.cmd, rsp=err.rsp, errs=err.errs)
jnpr.junos.exception.ConfigLoadError: ConfigLoadError(severity: error, bad_el...
>>>
```

By default, the `load()` method modifies the shared configuration database. The equivalent of the `configure exclusive` CLI command can be achieved by first calling the `lock()` method. The `lock()` method returns `True` if the configuration is successfully locked, and raises a `jnpr.junos.exception.LockError` exception if the configuration database lock fails because the configuration is already locked:

```
>>> r0.cu.lock()
True
>>> result = r0.cu.load(path='hostname.xml')
>>> r0.cu.pdiff()

[edit system]
-  host-name r0;
+  host-name r0.new;

>>> r0.cu.unlock()
True
>>> r0.cu.pdiff()
None
>>>
```

Notice the `unlock()` method can be used to unlock the configuration database and discard the candidate configuration changes. The `pdiff()` method displays configuration difference and is used for debugging. It is explained further in "Viewing Configuration Differences" on page 226.

The equivalent of the `configure private` CLI command can be achieved by calling the *open-configuration* and *close-configuration* RPCs. An example is shown in "Build, Apply, and Commit the Candidate Configuration" on page 243.

Configuration Templates

Templates allow large blocks of configuration to be generated with minimal effort. PyEZ utilizes the Jinja2 templating engine to generate configuration files from templates. Jinja2 is a popular, open source Python library from the Pocoo team. For more detailed documentation on Jinja2, you can visit the Jinja2 website (*http://jinja.pocoo.org*).

Jinja2 templates combine a reusable text form with a set of data used to fill in the form and render a result. Jinja2 offers variable substitution, conditionals, and simple loop constructs. In effect, Jinja2 is its own "mini programming language." Jinja2 templates are not unique to Junos; they allow any text file to be built from a "template" or "form" and set of data. Any text-based configuration file, including Junos configuration files in curly brace, set, or even XML syntax, can be generated from a Jinja2 template.

Let's look at a very simple template example that configures a hostname on the router based on a template. In this example, the configuration is expressed using a `set` statement. It could just as easily have been expressed in text or XML format. Here is the configuration `set` statement to configure a hostname of `r0.new`:

```
set system host-name r0.new
```

Save this statement in a file named *hostname.set* in the current working directory.

As you saw in the previous section, a configuration file is loaded into the device's candidate configuration with the `load()` method:

```
>>> result = r0.cu.load(path='hostname.set')
>>>
```

Jinja2 uses double braces to indicate an expression, and the simplest Jinja2 expression is just the name of the variable:

```
{{ variable_name }}
```

A Jinja2 variable expression evaluates to the variable's value. Jinja2 variable names follow the same syntax rules as Python variable names.

Apply this syntax to the one-line *hostname.set* file. Replace the hardcoded `r0.new` hostname with a reference to the `host_name` variable. The updated *hostname.set* file is now:

```
set system host-name {{ host_name }}
```

As you just saw, a configuration file is loaded into the device's candidate configuration by passing the `path` argument to the `load()` method. In a similar fashion, a templated configuration is loaded into the device's candidate configuration by passing the `template_path` argument to the `load()` method. However, templates also require an additional argument to the `load()` method. The `template_vars` argument takes a dictionary as its value. Each variable in the Jinja2 template must be a key in this dictionary. Here's an example that uses the *hostname.set* template to configure the hostname `foo`:

```
>>> result = r0.cu.load(template_path='hostname.set',
...                     template_vars= {'host_name' : 'foo'})
>>> r0.cu.pdiff()

[edit system]
-  host-name r0;
+  host-name foo;

>>>
```

The `template_path` argument may specify an absolute or relative filename. Relative filenames are searched against the current working directory, and a *templates* subdirectory of the module path.[7] Just like with the `path` argument, the filename extension of the `template_path` argument determines the expected format of the template. The same filename extension–to–configuration format mapping specified in Table 4-6 also applies to the `template_path`.

Now that you've seen the basics of creating and loading a template, let's look at some additional Jinja2 syntax. First, an expression can contain zero or more filters separated by the | character. Similar to a Unix pipeline or Junos pipe (`|`) display filters, Jinja2 filters are sets of functions that can be chained to modify an expression. Jinja2 filters modify the variable at the beginning of an expression.

For example, you can use a Jinja2 filter to provide a default value for a variable. Observe what happens with the previous template when no `host_name` key is present in the `template_vars` argument to the `load()` method:

```
>>> result = r0.cu.load(template_path='hostname.set',tempate_vars={})
Traceback (most recent call last):
  File "<stdin>", line 1, in <module>
  File "/usr/local/lib/python2.7/dist-packages/jnpr/junos/utils/config.py", l...
    return try_load(rpc_contents, rpc_xattrs)
  File "/usr/local/lib/python2.7/dist-packages/jnpr/junos/utils/config.py", l...
    raise ConfigLoadError(cmd=err.cmd, rsp=err.rsp, errs=err.errs)
jnpr.junos.exception.ConfigLoadError: ConfigLoadError(severity: error, bad_el...
```

The missing `host_name` variable results in the generation of an incomplete configuration `set` statement, which causes a `jnpr.junos.exception.ConfigLoadError` exception to be raised. In this case, an error might be an appropriate response to indicate to the template's user that `host_name` is a mandatory variable. However, in other cases, it's better to provide a default value when a variable is missing. The Jinja2 provided `default()` filter can be used for this purpose.

---

7 On the example automation host, the module path is */usr/local/lib/python2.7/dist-packages/jnpr/junos*, but the location is installation-specific and may be different on your machine. You can discover the correct location for your machine using the instructions at the beginning of "Prepackaged Operational Tables and Views" on page 194.

Here the `default()` filter is used to provide a default value of `Missing.Hostname`. The Jinja2 `lower` filter is also used to lowercase the hostname:

```
set system host-name {{ host_name | default('Missing.Hostname') | lower }}
```

Now look at the result of omitting the `host_name` key from the `template_vars` argument:[8]

```
>>> result = r0.cu.load(template_path='hostname.set')
>>> r0.cu.pdiff()

[edit system]
-  host-name r0;
+  host-name missing.hostname;

>>>
```

The hostname `missing.hostname` is configured as a result of chaining the `default()` and `lower` filters.

Specifying a hostname of `Foo` in `template_vars` results in a hostname of `foo` being configured:

```
>>> result = r0.cu.load(template_path='hostname.set',
...                     template_vars= {'host_name' : 'Foo'})
>>> r0.cu.pdiff()

[edit system]
-  host-name r0;
+  host-name foo;

>>>
```

Consult the Jinja2 template documentation (*http://jinja.pocoo.org/docs/dev/templates/*) for a list of the built-in filters available. It is also possible to write your own Python function that operates as a custom filter. Reference the Jinja2 API documentation (*http://jinja.pocoo.org/docs/dev/*) for more details on custom filters.

In addition to variable substitution and filters, Jinja2 offers tags that control the logic of template rendering. Tags are enclosed in `{% tag %}` delimiters. One such tag is the conditional `if` statement. An `if` statement allows different content to be included in the rendered file depending on whether an expression evaluates to true or false.

The following example demonstrates configuring the device's hostname depending on whether or not the device has dual routing engines. If two routing engines are present, the hostname is configured within the special `re0` and `re1` configuration

---

8 If the `template_vars` argument is omitted completely, as in this example, it defaults to `{}`, an empty Python dictionary.

groups and has `re0.` or `re1.` prepended. If the device has a single routing engine, the hostname is configured at the `[edit system]` configuration hierarchy level as before. This time, the configuration is specified in text (aka curly brace) syntax and saved into the file *hostname.conf* in the current working directory. Here is the content of *hostname.conf*:

```
{% if dual_re %}
groups {
    re0 {
        system {
            host-name {{ "re0." + host_name }};
        }
    }
    re1 {
        system {
            host-name {{ "re1." + host_name }};
        }
    }
}
{% else %}
system {
    host-name {{ host_name }};
}
{% endif %}
```

Notice the template begins with an `{% if *expression* %}` statement, which is dependent on the value of the `dual_re` variable. The `{% else %}` statement marks the end of the text that will be rendered if `dual_re` is true; it also marks the beginning of the text that will be rendered if `dual_re` is false. The `{% endif %}` statement closes the conditional block.

Also notice the expression used to render the hostname in the dual-RE case. It uses a static string and Python's + string concatenation character to prepend the appropriate value to the `host_name` variable.

Here's an example of rendering this template on a device with dual REs. Notice the value of the `dual_re` key is set from the value of `r1.facts['2RE']` supplied by PyEZ's default facts gathering:

```
>>> r1.facts['2RE']
True
>>> result = r1.cu.load(template_path='hostname.conf',
...                     template_vars= { 'dual_re' : r1.facts['2RE'],
...                                      'host_name' : 'r1' })
>>> r1.cu.pdiff()

[edit groups re0 system]
+   host-name re0.r1;
[edit groups re1 system]
+   host-name re1.r1;
```

```
>>>
```

The same template applied to a device with a single RE sets the hostname at the `[edit system]` configuration hierarchy level:

```
>>> r0.facts['2RE']
False
>>> result = r0.cu.load(template_path='hostname.conf',
...                     template_vars= { 'dual_re' : r0.facts['2RE'],
...                                      'host_name' : 'r0' })
>>> r0.cu.pdiff()

[edit system]
+  host-name r0;

>>>
```

Notice the `dual_re` key is again supplied from the facts information. Using a template with a conditional block generates the correct configuration for the device, automatically generated based on whether or not dual routing engines are present.

While Jinja2 templates offer a plethora of additional capabilities, let's wrap up this section by looking at the `{% for` *`scalar_var`* `in` *`list_var`* `%}` looping construct. In this example, the loop actually iterates over the items in a dictionary and uses the dictionary key and values to configure a set of IPv4 addresses on a set of interfaces. This time, the configuration is specified in XML syntax and saved into the file *interface_ip.xml* in the current working directory. Here is the content of *interface_ip.xml*:

```
<interfaces>
{% for key, value in interface_ips.iteritems() %}
    <interface>
        <name>{{ key }}</name>
        <unit>
            <name>0</name>
            <family>
                <inet>
                    <address>{{ value }}</address>
                </inet>
            </family>
        </unit>
    </interface>
{% endfor %}
</interfaces>
```

The content of the `for` loop is very similar to a Python `for` statement. In fact, this example uses the `iteritems()` dictionary method to iterate over each key/value pair in the dictionary. In Jinja2 syntax, the loop ends with a `{% endfor %}` statement.

Now create an `interface_ips` dictionary with a set of interface names as the keys and a set of IPv4 addresses and prefix lengths as the values:

```
>>> interface_ips = {
...       'ge-0/0/0' : '10.0.4.1/30',
...       'ge-0/0/1' : '10.0.2.1/30',
...       'ge-0/0/2' : '10.0.3.1/30',
...       'ge-0/0/3' : '10.0.5.1/30' }
```

Let's use this dictionary and template to configure IP addresses on `r0`. The `interface_ips` dictionary becomes the value of the `interface_ips` key in the template_`vars` argument:

```
>>> result = r0.cu.load(template_path='interface_ip.xml',
...                     template_vars= { 'interface_ips' : interface_ips })
>>> r0.cu.pdiff()

[edit interfaces ge-0/0/0 unit 0 family inet]
+       address 10.0.4.1/30;
[edit interfaces ge-0/0/1 unit 0 family inet]
+       address 10.0.2.1/30;
[edit interfaces ge-0/0/2 unit 0 family inet]
+       address 10.0.3.1/30;
[edit interfaces ge-0/0/3 unit 0 family inet]
+       address 10.0.5.1/30;

>>>
```

As expected, the resulting configuration adds the correct addresses on multiple interfaces using the `for` loop.

Jinja2 templates offer many additional features that we are unable to cover directly in this book. Take a look at the Jinja2 documentation (*http://jinja.pocoo.org/docs/dev/*) and experiment with the features that might be applicable in your particular environment.

Viewing Configuration Differences

You've seen the `pdiff()` method used in previous examples to display the differences that have been configured in the candidate configuration. The `pdiff()` method is intended for debugging purposes, which is how we've been using it in those examples. It simply prints the differences between the candidate configuration and a rollback configuration. By default, the `pdiff()` method compares the candidate configuration to the `rollback 0` configuration. The `rollback 0` configuration is the same as the currently committed configuration:

```
>>> r0.cu.pdiff()

[edit system]
-  host-name r0;
+  host-name r0.new;

>>>
```

Rather than printing the differences, the `diff()` method returns a string containing the differences between the candidate and rollback configurations:

```
>>> r0.cu.diff()
'\n[edit system]\n-  host-name r0;\n+  host-name r0.new;\n'
```

Both the `diff()` and `pdiff()` methods take an unnamed optional argument. The argument is an integer representing the rollback ID:

```
>>> r0.cu.pdiff(1)

[edit system]
-  host-name r0;
+  host-name r0.new;
[edit system login]
+    user bar {
+        uid 2002;
+        class super-user;
+        authentication {
+            encrypted-password "$5$0jDrGxJT$PXj0TWwtu5LPJ4Nvlc1YpmCKy7yAwOUH...
+        }
+    }
+    user foo {
+        uid 2003;
+        class super-user;
+        authentication {
+            encrypted-password "$5$WfsXdd11$4LXuWOIwQA5HsWvF8oxMZGyzodIHsnZP...
+        }
+    }

>>>
```

Now that we've seen how to view configuration differences, let's look at how to commit the modified candidate configuration.

Committing Configuration Changes

The PyEZ `Config` class provides a `commit_check()` method to validate the candidate configuration and a `commit()` method to commit the changes. The `commit_check()` method returns `True` if the candidate configuration passes all commit checks, and raises a `jnpr.junos.exception.CommitError` exception if the candidate configuration fails any commit checks, including warnings:

```
>>> r0.cu.load("set system host-name r0")
<Element load-configuration-results at 0x7f6503180ea8>
>>> r0.cu.commit_check()
True
>>> r0.cu.load("set protocols bgp export FooBar")
<Element load-configuration-results at 0x7f650317d488>
>>> r0.cu.commit_check()
Traceback (most recent call last):
```

```
  File "<stdin>", line 1, in <module>
  File "/usr/local/lib/python2.7/dist-packages/jnpr/junos/utils/config.py", l...
    raise CommitError(cmd=err.cmd, rsp=err.rsp)
jnpr.junos.exception.CommitError: CommitError(edit_path: [edit groups junos-d...
>>>
```

The `commit()` method takes several optional arguments, which are detailed in Table 4-7. It returns `True` if the candidate configuration is successfully committed and raises a `jnpr.junos.exception.CommitError` exception if there is an error or warning when committing the configuration.

Table 4-7. Arguments to the commit() method

Argument	Description
`comment`	The value is a comment string describing the commit.
`confirm`	The value is an integer specifying the number of minutes to wait for a confirmation of the commit. The commit is confirmed by invoking `commit()` again before the `confirm` timer expires.
`sync`	A Boolean flag. If `True`, performs a `commit synchronize`, which commits the new configuration on both routing engines of a dual-RE system. It is possible that a `commit synchronize` will happen anyway if the user has configured the `synchronize` statement at the `[edit system commit]` configuration hierarchy level.
`detail`	A Boolean flag. If `True`, the `commit()` method returns an `lxml.etree.Element` object with additional details about the commit process. This argument should only be used for debugging purposes.
`force_sync`	A Boolean flag. If `True`, performs a `commit synchronize force`. This argument should only be used for debugging purposes.
`full`	A Boolean flag. If `True`, all Junos daemons are notified and reparse their full configuration, even if no configuration changes have been made that affect the daemons. This argument should only be used for debugging purposes.

Here is an example of both a successful and a failed commit:

```
>>> r0.cu.load("set system host-name r0")
<Element load-configuration-results at 0x7f650317b5a8>
>>> r0.cu.commit(comment='New hostname',sync=True)
True
>>> r0.cu.load("set protocols bgp export FooBar")
<Element load-configuration-results at 0x7f65031765f0>
>>> r0.cu.commit()
Traceback (most recent call last):
  File "<stdin>", line 1, in <module>
  File "/usr/local/lib/python2.7/dist-packages/jnpr/junos/utils/config.py", l...
    raise CommitError(cmd=err.cmd, rsp=err.rsp)
jnpr.junos.exception.CommitError: CommitError(edit_path: [edit groups junos-d...
>>>
```

If the configuration database has been locked with the `lock()` method, it is *not* unlocked by calling `commit()`. You must still invoke the `unlock()` method to release the configuration lock.

Using the Rescue Configuration

The `Config` class also provides a `rescue()` method for performing actions on the Junos device's rescue configuration. The rescue configuration is intended to aid device recovery in the event of an erroneous configuration change. The idea is that the user defines a minimal configuration needed to restore the device to a known good state and saves that minimal configuration as the "rescue" configuration. The `rescue()` method takes an unnamed argument that indicates the action to be taken on the rescue configuration. The valid values of this argument are `get`, `save`, `delete`, and `reload`. If the action is `get`, a second optional named argument, `format`, may be specified. The default format is `text,` which indicates the configuration is in the text (aka curly brace) syntax. The `format` argument may also be set to `xml`, which retrieves the configuration as an `lxml.etree.Element` object.

The following example demonstrates deleting, saving, getting, and then reloading the rescue configuration using the existing `r0.cu` device configuration attribute:

```
>>> r0.cu.rescue('delete')
True
>>> r0.cu.rescue('save')
True
>>> r0.cu.rescue('get',format='xml')
<Element rescue-information at 0x7f885ac76128>
>>> resp = r0.cu.rescue('reload')
>>> from lxml import etree
>>> etree.dump(resp)
<load-configuration-results>
<ok/>
</load-configuration-results>

>>>
```

Notice the `save` and `delete` actions return a Boolean value indicating success or failure. The `save` action saves the current committed configuration as the rescue configuration, while the `delete` action deletes the current rescue configuration. The `get` action returns the current rescue configuration. In the preceding example this configuration is returned as an `lxml.etree.Element` object because `format='xml'` was specified. If the `format` argument had not been specified, a string containing the rescue configuration would have been returned instead. The `reload` action loads the rescue configuration into the candidate configuration. It returns the same response as the `load()` method. Like the `load ()` method, `rescue('reload')` only modifies the candidate configuration. A `commit()` must be issued to activate the rescue configuration.

Utilities

PyEZ also supplies a set of utility methods that can be used to perform common tasks on the Junos operating system. These tasks provide filesystem access or access to the Junos Unix-level shell, perform secure copies, and execute Junos software upgrades. The filesystem utilities defined in the `FS` class of the `jnpr.junos.utils.fs` module provide common commands that access the filesystem on the Junos device. The `jnpr.junos.utils.scp` module defines an `SCP` class for performing secure copies to or from the Junos device. The `jnpr.junos.utils.start_shell` module provides a `StartShell` class that allows an SSH connection to be initiated to a Junos device. Additional `StartShell` methods are provided to execute commands over the SSH connection and wait for an expected response. Finally, the `SW` class in the `jnpr.junos.utils.sw` module provides a set of methods for upgrading the Junos software on a device as well as rebooting or powering off the device.

Because these utilities are outside the base functionality of PyEZ, and because they are being expanded with each new PyEZ release, this book does not attempt to cover each utility in detail. Instead, you are encouraged to use Python's built-in `help()` function to display the documentation strings for these classes. Here's an example of displaying the documentation strings for the `FS` class:

```
>>> from jnpr.junos.utils.fs import FS
>>> help(FS)
Help on class FS in module jnpr.junos.utils.fs:

class FS(jnpr.junos.utils.util.Util)
 |  Filesystem (FS) utilities:
 |
 |  * :meth:`cat`: show the contents of a file
 |  * :meth:`checksum`: calculate file checksum (md5,sha256,sha1)
 |  * :meth:`cp`: local file copy (not scp)
 |  * :meth:`cwd`: change working directory
 |  * :meth:`ls`: return file/dir listing
 |  * :meth:`mkdir`: create a directory
 |  * :meth:`pwd`: get working directory
 |  * :meth:`mv`: local file rename
 |  * :meth:`rm`: local file delete
 |  * :meth:`rmdir`: remove a directory
 |  * :meth:`stat`: return file/dir information
 |  * :meth:`storage_usage`: return storage usage
 |  * :meth:`storage_cleanup`: perform storage storage_cleanup
...
```

The same recipe can be followed to display the documentation strings for the other PyEZ utility classes.

A PyEZ Example

Now that you've seen the capabilities of PyEZ, it is time to put this knowledge into practice by rewriting the *lldp_interface_descriptions_rest.py* example covered in "Using the RESTful APIs in Python" on page 131. This example uses PyEZ's RPC on Demand feature to query the current LLDP neighbors and interface descriptions. It handles responses using both the lxml and jxmlease libraries. The new configuration is applied using a Jinja2 template.

The purpose and overall architecture of the script closely follows those of the previous *lldp_interface_descriptions_rest.py* example. The new script is named *lldp_interface_descriptions_pyez.py* and uses PyEZ to discover and monitor the network topology of one or more Junos devices running the Link Layer Discovery Protocol (LLDP). Information discovered from LLDP is stored in the interface description fields of the device's configuration. The current LLDP-discovered information is compared against the previous information that is stored in the interface description field, and the user is notified of any changes in LLDP state (up, change, or down) since the previous snapshot.

The script is invoked by a user at the command line and takes one or more device names or IP addresses as command-line arguments. The syntax is:

```
user@h0$ python lldp_interface_descriptions_pyez.py r0 r1 r2 r3 r4 r5
```

In order to execute successfully, the NETCONF-over-SSH service should be configured on each device, and a common username and password with appropriate authorization should be configured on each device:

```
user@r0> show configuration system services
netconf {
    ssh;
}

user@r0> show configuration system login
user user {
    uid 2001;
    class super-user;
    authentication {
        encrypted-password "$1$jCvocDbA$KeOycEvIDtSV/VOdPRHo5."; ## SECRET-DATA
    }
}
```

The script prompts for the username and password to use to connect to the devices and then prints its output to the user's terminal. It prints a notification for each device being checked. If the script detects any changes in LLDP state since the last snapshot, those changes are printed to the terminal. The new interface descriptions are configured and a message indicates whether or not the device's configuration was successfully updated. The following example shows a sample output from the script:

```
user@h0$ ./lldp_interface_descriptions_pyez.py r0 r1 r2 r3 r4 r5
Device Username: user
Device Password:
Connecting to r0...
Getting LLDP information from r0...
Getting interface descriptions from r0...
    ge-0/0/4 LLDP Change. Was: r7 ge-0/0/6 Now: r1 ge-0/0/0
    ge-0/0/3 LLDP Up. Now: r5 ge-0/0/0
    ge-0/0/2 LLDP Up. Now: r3 ge-0/0/2
    ge-0/0/0 LLDP Up. Now: r4 ge-0/0/2
    ge-0/0/5 LLDP Down. Was: r6 ge-0/0/8
    Successfully committed configuration changes on r0.
    Closing connection to r0.
Connecting to r1...
Getting LLDP information from r1...
Getting interface descriptions from r1...
    ge-0/0/2 LLDP Down. Was: r2 ge-0/0/0
    Successfully committed configuration changes on r1.
    Closing connection to r1.
Connecting to r2...
Getting LLDP information from r2...
Getting interface descriptions from r2...
    ge-0/0/2 LLDP Down. Was: r0 ge-0/0/1
    ge-0/0/1 LLDP Down. Was: r3 ge-0/0/0
    ge-0/0/0 LLDP Down. Was: r1 ge-0/0/2
    Successfully committed configuration changes on r2.
    Closing connection to r2.
Connecting to r3...
Getting LLDP information from r3...
Getting interface descriptions from r3...
    ge-0/0/0 LLDP Down. Was: r2 ge-0/0/1
    Successfully committed configuration changes on r3.
    Closing connection to r3.
Connecting to r4...
Getting LLDP information from r4...
Getting interface descriptions from r4...
    No LLDP changes to configure on r4.
    Closing connection to r4.
Connecting to r5...
Getting LLDP information from r5...
Getting interface descriptions from r5...
    ge-0/0/2 LLDP Up. Now: r4 ge-0/0/0
    ge-0/0/0 LLDP Up. Now: r0 ge-0/0/3
    Successfully committed configuration changes on r5.
    Closing connection to r5.
user@h0$
```

As the script sequentially loops through each device specified on the command line, it performs the following steps:

1. Gather LLDP neighbor information.
2. Gather interface descriptions; parse the LLDP neighbor information that was previously stored in the interface descriptions.
3. Compare current and previous LLDP neighbor information; print LLDP up, change, and down messages; calculate new interface descriptions.
4. Build, load, and commit a candidate configuration with updated interface descriptions.

Like the RESTful API example script, this example tries to provide a useful and realistic function while also concentrating on code that demonstrates PyEZ. The same caveats apply. Specifically, the example script is invoked by the user at the command line, but a more complex program might be invoked by an event or on a schedule. In addition, the output might integrate with an existing network monitoring or alerting system rather than simply being printed to the terminal. A more realistic implementation would store the LLDP information gathered from the device in an off-device database or in on-device `apply-macro` configuration statements rather than in the interface `description` configuration statements. Finally, each device could be queried and configured in parallel to speed the program's execution.

Let's analyze the Python code used to perform each of these steps. Again, we recommend following along and typing each line of the program listings into your own script file named *lldp_interface_descriptions_pyez.py*. After completing "Putting It All Together" on page 247, you will have a working example to execute against your own network.

The Preamble

The first step in our example script is to import required libraries and perform some one-time initialization. The callouts give more information on each line of the program listing:

```
#!/usr/bin/env python ❶
"""Use interface descriptions to track the topology reported by LLDP.

This includes the following steps:
1) Gather LLDP neighbor information.
2) Gather interface descriptions.
3) Parse LLDP neighbor information previously stored in the descriptions.
```

```
4) Compare LLDP neighbor info to previous LLDP info from the descriptions.
5) Print LLDP Up / Change / Down events.
6) Store the updated LLDP neighbor info in the interface descriptions.

Interface descriptions are in the format:
[user-configured description ]LLDP: <remote system> <remote port>[(DOWN)]

The '(DOWN)' string indicates an LLDP neighbor which was previously
present, but is now not present.
"""

import sys ❷
import getpass

import jxmlease ❸

from jnpr.junos import Device ❹
from jnpr.junos.utils.config import Config
import jnpr.junos.exception

TEMPLATE_PATH = 'interface_descriptions_template.xml' ❺

# Create a jxmlease parser with desired defaults.
parser = jxmlease.EtreeParser() ❻

class DoneWithDevice(Exception): pass ❼
```

❶ The `#!` line (sometimes called the hashbang or shebang line) allows the option of running the script without specifying the `python` command. (This mechanism works on Unix-like platforms and on Windows platforms using the Python Launcher for Windows.) In other words, you could execute the script with `*path*/lldp_interface_descriptions_pyez.py *r0 r1 r2 r3 r4 r5*` instead of `python *path*/lldp_interface_descriptions_pyez.py *r0 r1 r2 r3 r4 r5*`. Executing the script directly does require executable permissions to be set on the *lldp_interface_descriptions_pyez.py* file. Using the */usr/bin/env* shell command to invoke Python means the script is not dependent on the location of the `python` command.

❷ Two standard Python modules, `sys` and `getpass`, are imported. The `sys` module provides access to objects maintained by the Python interpreter, and the `getpass` module allows the script to interactively prompt for the required password without echoing the input to the user's terminal.

❸ The `jxmlease` library parses XML into native Python data structures. You must ensure this module is installed on your system.

❹ Three PyEZ modules are imported. The PyEZ `Device` class is used to create a device instance. This is the basic PyEZ class for interacting with a Junos device. The PyEZ `Config` class offers methods for dealing with the Junos device configuration. The `exception` module defines several PyEZ-specific exceptions that may be raised to indicate a potential problem.

❺ The `TEMPLATE_PATH` variable is used as a constant to identify the name of the Jinja2 configuration template used to generate the configuration of new interface descriptions.

❻ A `jxmlease` parser instance is created for parsing `lxml.etree.Element` objects into Python data structures. The `jxmlease.EtreeParser()` method creates an instance of the `jxmlease.EtreeParser` class with a set of default parameters. Whereas a parser created with the `jxmlease.Parser()` method expects an XML input document as a string, an instance of the `jxmlease.EtreeParser` class expects an XML input document as an `lxml.etree.Element` object.

❼ A custom `DoneWithDevice` class is created for indicating when processing on each device in the main device loop has been completed. This new class is a subclass of `Exception`.

Each of the script's major steps has been encapsulated into a Python function which will be executed from the `main()` function of the *lldp_interface_descriptions_pyez.py* file.

Loop Through Each Device

Let's begin by analyzing the `main()` function, which prompts for a username and password and then loops over each device specified on the command line. The `main()` function calls several functions, which are each analyzed in later sections:

```
def main():
    """The main loop.

    Prompt for a username and password.
    Loop over each device specified on the command line.
    Perform the following steps on each device:
    1) Get LLDP information from the current device state.
    2) Get interface descriptions from the device configuration.
    3) Compare the LLDP information against the previous snapshot of LLDP
       information stored in the interface descriptions. Print changes.
    4) Build a configuration snippet with new interface descriptions.
    5) Commit the configuration changes.

    Return an integer suitable for passing to sys.exit().
    """
```

```
if len(sys.argv) == 1: ❶
    print("\nUsage: %s device1 [device2 [...]]\n\n" % sys.argv[0])
    return 1

rc = 0 ❷

# Get username and password as user input.
user = raw_input('Device Username: ')
password = getpass.getpass('Device Password: ') ❸

for hostname in sys.argv[1:]: ❹
    try:
        print("Connecting to %s..." % hostname)
        dev = Device(host=hostname, ❺
                     user=user,
                     password=password,
                     normalize=True)
        dev.open() ❻

        print("Getting LLDP information from %s..." % hostname)
        lldp_info = get_lldp_neighbors(device=dev) ❼
        if lldp_info == None: ❽
            print("    Error retrieving LLDP info on " + hostname +
                  ". Make sure LLDP is enabled.")
            rc = 1
            raise DoneWithDevice

        print("Getting interface descriptions from %s..." % hostname)
        desc_info = get_description_info_for_interfaces(device=dev) ❾
        if desc_info == None:
            print("    Error retrieving interface descriptions on %s." %
                  hostname)
            rc = 1
            raise DoneWithDevice

        desc_changes = check_lldp_changes(lldp_info, desc_info) ❿
        if not desc_changes:
            print("    No LLDP changes to configure on %s." % hostname)
            raise DoneWithDevice

        if load_merge_template_config( ⓫
            device=dev,
            template_path=TEMPLATE_PATH,
            template_vars={'descriptions': desc_changes}):
            print("    Successfully committed configuration changes on %s." %
                  hostname)
        else:
            print("    Error committing description changes on %s." %
                  hostname)
            rc = 1
            raise DoneWithDevice
```

```
        except jnpr.junos.exception.ConnectError as err: ⓬
            print("    Error connecting: " + repr(err))
            rc = 1
        except DoneWithDevice:
            pass
        finally: ⓭
            print("    Closing connection to %s." % hostname)
            try:
                dev.close()
            except:
                pass
    return rc
```

❶ The script requires that at least one device be specified as a command-line argument. The `sys.argv` list will contain the name of the script at index 0. User-specified arguments begin at index 1. If no user-specified arguments are present (`len(sys.argv) == 1`), the usage message is printed and the script exits with a status code of `1` to indicate an error.

❷ The `rc` variable holds the status code to be returned at the end of the script. The value is initialized to `0` which indicates success. Later, if an error is encountered, `rc` will be set to `1` and processing will continue with the next device specified on the command line.

❸ This statement and the previous statement prompt the user for the username and password used to establish the NETCONF session to the Junos devices. It is assumed each device is configured with the same user authentication credentials. The `getpass()` function from the Python standard library prompts the user for a password and disables echoing the response to the screen.

❹ This `for` loop iterates over every device name (or IP address) specified in the command-line arguments. Because `sys.argv[0]` is the name of the script, the slice `sys.argv[1:]` is used to return the list of devices.

❺ A device instance is created and assigned to the variable `dev`. The username and password entered by the user are passed as the `user` and `password` arguments. The `normalize=True` argument ensures that response normalization is applied to every RPC on Demand call using the `dev` device instance.

❻ The `open()` method is invoked on the `dev` device instance. This establishes a NETCONF session to the device and invokes PyEZ's default facts gathering. If the `open()` call fails, a `jnpr.junos.exception.ConnectError` (or one of its subclasses) is raised. This potential exception is handled later, in the `main()` function.

❼ The `get_lldp_neighbors()` function is invoked on the current device instance, `dev`. The result is stored in the `lldp_info` dictionary.

❽ If `get_lldp_neighbors()` reports an error (by returning the value `None`), an error message is printed, `rc` is set to `1` to indicate the error, and the `DoneWithDevice` exception is raised. This exception causes execution to jump to the `except DoneWithDevice` line toward the end of the `main()` function.

❾ The `get_description_info_for_interfaces()` function is executed on the current device, `dev`. The result is stored in the `desc_info` dictionary. Similar to the `get_lldp_neighbors()` function, if the `get_description_info_for_interfaces()` function reports an error (by returning the value `None`), an error message is printed, `rc` is set to `1` to indicate the error, and the `DoneWithDevice` exception is raised. This exception causes execution to jump to the `except DoneWithDevice` line toward the end of the `main()` function.

❿ The `get_lldp_description_changes()` function parses the `lldp_info` and `desc_info` dictionaries and returns the new interface descriptions in the `desc_changes` dictionary. If no descriptions have changed, the `DoneWithDevice` exception is raised. In this case, the exception does not indicate an error. It simply skips the section of code that loads and commits the configuration change if there is no new configuration to be applied.

⓫ The `load_merge_template_config()` function is called. The `template_path` argument is set to the value of `TEMPLATE_PATH` and the `descriptions` key of the `template_vars` argument is set to the `desc_changes` dictionary. The return value of the function indicates whether the new configuration was successfully committed. If an error occurs, an error message is printed, `rc` is set to `1` to indicate the error, and `DoneWithDevice` is raised.

⓬ A `jnpr.junos.exception.ConnectError` (or any subclass) exception indicates the NETCONF session to the device was not opened. In this case, the error is printed, `rc` is set to `1` to indicate the error, and the script continues on to the `finally` block.

⓭ Placing the `dev.close()` method invocation inside a `finally` block ensures the NETCONF session is gracefully closed regardless of whether there was an exception raised in gathering information or committing the new configuration. Because `dev.close()` might raise an exception itself, the statement is placed inside a `try` block. The corresponding `except` block simply ignores any exceptions that were raised by `dev.close()`.

Now, let's look at each of the functions that are called from the `for` loop in more detail.

Gather LLDP Neighbor Information

The first function, `get_lldp_neighbors()`, uses the PyEZ RPC on Demand feature to query the *get-lldp-neighbors-information* RPC. The RPC response is the default format of lxml `Element` objects. The function gathers the LLDP neighbor's system and port information for each local interface using lxml methods, and returns the information to the caller in a dictionary:

```
def get_lldp_neighbors(device): ❶
    """Get current LLDP neighbor information.

    Return a two-level dictionary with the LLDP neighbor information.
    The first-level key is the local port (aka interface) name.
    The second-level keys are 'system' for the remote system name
    and 'port' for the remote port ID. On error, return None.

    For example:
    {'ge-0/0/1': {'system': 'r1', 'port', 'ge-0/0/10'}}
    """

    lldp_info = {}
    try: ❷
        resp = device.rpc.get_lldp_neighbors_information()
    except (jnpr.junos.exception.RpcError,
            jnpr.junos.exception.ConnectError)as err:
        print "    " + repr(err)
        return None

    for nbr in resp.findall('lldp-neighbor-information'): ❸
        local_port = nbr.findtext('lldp-local-port-id') ❹
        remote_system = nbr.findtext('lldp-remote-system-name')
        remote_port = nbr.findtext('lldp-remote-port-id')
        if local_port and (remote_system or remote_port):
            lldp_info[local_port] = {'system': remote_system, ❺
                                     'port': remote_port}

    return lldp_info
```

❶ The `get_lldp_neighbors()` function requires a `device` argument. This argument is a PyEZ device instance that has an active NETCONF session open.

❷ The RPC on Demand call and the processing of the RPC response are surrounded by a `try` block to avoid unexpected script termination. If an exception is raised, an error message is printed and the value `None` is returned to the caller to indicate the error. The PyEZ RPC on Demand feature invokes the *get-lldp-neighbors-information* XML RPC.

❸ The lxml `findall()` method will return a list of all `lxml.etree.Element` objects that match the XPath expression `lldp-neighbor-information`. This results in looping through each LLDP neighbor. The `nbr` variable is assigned the `lxml.etree.Element` object representing the current LLDP neighbor.

❹ The lxml `findtext()` method selects the first XML element matching an XPath expression. It is used to select the values of the `local_port`, `remote_system`, and `remote_port` variables.

❺ The `remote_system` and `remote_port` values are stored in the `lldp_info` dictionary. This dictionary is keyed on the `local_port` value extracted from the current LLDP neighbor.

Gather and Parse Interface Descriptions

The next function, `get_description_info_for_interfaces()`, makes another PyEZ RPC on Demand query using the *get-interface-information* RPC. The `descriptions` parameter is added to the RPC in order to retrieve only the interface descriptions. This time, the output is parsed by the jxmlease library to produce a `jxmlease.XMLDictNode` object. The content of the interface description field is then parsed from this response based on a simple convention that has been chosen for this example script. Refer back to "Gather and Parse Interface Descriptions" on page 143 if you need a refresher on the convention used. The function is defined as follows:

```
def get_description_info_for_interfaces(device): ❶
    """Get current interface description for each interface.

    Parse the description into the user-configured description, remote
    system, and remote port components.

    Return a two-level dictionary. The first-level key is the
    local port (aka interface) name. The second-level keys are
    'user_desc' for the user-configured description, 'system' for the
    remote system name, 'port' for the remote port, and 'down', which is
    a Boolean indicating if LLDP was previously down. On error, return None.

    For example:
    {'ge-0/0/1': {'user_desc': 'test description', 'system': 'r1',
                  'port': 'ge-0/0/10', 'down': True}}
    """

    desc_info = {}
    try: ❷
        resp = parser(device.rpc.get_interface_information(descriptions=True))
    except (jnpr.junos.exception.RpcError,
            jnpr.junos.exception.ConnectError) as err:
        print "    " + repr(err)
```

```
        return None

    try:
        pi = resp['interface-information']['physical-interface'].jdict() ❸
    except KeyError:
        return desc_info

    for (local_port, port_info) in pi.items(): ❹
        try:
            (udesc, _, ldesc) = port_info['description'].partition('LLDP: ') ❺
            udesc = udesc.rstrip()
            (remote_system, _, remote_port) = ldesc.partition(' ')
            (remote_port, down_string, _) = remote_port.partition('(DOWN)')
            desc_info[local_port] = {'user_desc': udesc,
                                     'system': remote_system,
                                     'port': remote_port,
                                     'down': True if down_string else False}
        except (KeyError, TypeError): ❻
            pass
    return desc_info
```

❶ `get_description_info_for_interfaces()` requires a `device` argument. This argument is a PyEZ device instance that has an active NETCONF session open.

❷ Again, the RPC on Demand call is surrounded by a `try` block to handle exception conditions. The RPC on Demand feature is used to execute the *get-interface-information* XML RPC. The `descriptions` argument is passed to the RPC and specifies that only interface descriptions should be returned. The `lxml.etree.Element` object is then passed to the `jxmlease.EtreeParser()` instance, `parser()`.

❸ The `pi` variable is assigned a dictionary based on the physical interface information in the RPC response. The `jdict()` method (discussed in "jxmlease objects" on page 44) is used to return a dictionary from the physical interface information. The `jdict()` method automatically produces a dictionary keyed on the value of the `<name>` elements in each `<pyhsical-interface>` element of the response. A `KeyError` exception indicates that either the `<interface-information>` or the `<physical-interface>` element is missing from the response. This simply indicates that no interface descriptions are currently configured.

❹ The `for` loop iterates over the `local_port`, the key to the `pi` dictionary, and the `port_info`, the value of the `pi` dictionary.

❺ The existing interface description is parsed into components by the next several lines. The descriptions are stored in the `desc_info` dictionary, which is keyed on the `local_port` value. Reference "Gather and Parse Interface Descriptions" on page 143 in the RESTful API example script if this code is unclear.

❻ When accessing the data, a `KeyError` exception is raised when the specified key does not exist. A `TypeError` exception is raised when the type being accessed doesn't match the data structure. If either of these conditions occurs, the exception is ignored. Processing continues with the next `local_port` in the `pi` dictionary.

Compare Current and Previous LLDP Neighbor Information

The `check_lldp_changes()` function compares the previous LLDP information found in the description fields and now stored in the `desc_info` dictionary to the LLDP information now stored in the `lldp_info` dictionary. Because this function operates solely on the `desc_info` and `lldp_info` dictionaries returned by the previous functions, its content is exactly the same as the RESTful API version. The function is included here without repeating the explanations of each line. If you're unsure of the purpose or behavior of any line, refer back to the explanations in "Compare Current and Previous LLDP Neighbor Information" on page 148. The function definition is as follows:

```
def check_lldp_changes(lldp_info, desc_info):
    """Compare current LLDP info with previous snapshot from descriptions.

    Given the dictionaries produced by get_lldp_neighbors() and
    get_description_info_for_interfaces(), print LLDP up, change,
    and down messages.

    Return a dictionary containing information for the new descriptions
    to configure.
    """

    desc_changes = {}

    # Iterate through the current LLDP neighbor state. Compare this
    # to the saved state as retrieved from the interface descriptions.
    for local_port in lldp_info:
        lldp_system = lldp_info[local_port]['system']
        lldp_port = lldp_info[local_port]['port']
        has_lldp_desc = desc_info.has_key(local_port)
        if has_lldp_desc:
            desc_system = desc_info[local_port]['system']
            desc_port = desc_info[local_port]['port']
            down = desc_info[local_port]['down']
            if not desc_system or not desc_port:
                has_lldp_desc = False
        if not has_lldp_desc:
            print("    %s LLDP Up. Now: %s %s" %
```

```
                (local_port,lldp_system,lldp_port))
    elif down:
        print("    %s LLDP Up. Was: %s %s Now: %s %s" %
                (local_port,desc_system,desc_port,lldp_system,lldp_port))
    elif lldp_system != desc_system or lldp_port != desc_port:
        print("    %s LLDP Change. Was: %s %s Now: %s %s" %
                (local_port,desc_system,desc_port,lldp_system,lldp_port))
    else:
        # No change. LLDP was not down. Same system and port.
        continue
    desc_changes[local_port] = "LLDP: %s %s" % (lldp_system,lldp_port)

# Iterate through the saved state as retrieved from the interface
# descriptions. Look for any neighbors that are present in the
# saved state, but are not present in the current LLDP neighbor
# state.
for local_port in desc_info:
    desc_system = desc_info[local_port]['system']
    desc_port = desc_info[local_port]['port']
    down = desc_info[local_port]['down']
    if (desc_system and desc_port and not down and
        not lldp_info.has_key(local_port)):
        print("    %s LLDP Down. Was: %s %s" %
                (local_port,desc_system,desc_port))
        desc_changes[local_port] = "LLDP: %s %s(DOWN)" % (desc_system,
                                                          desc_port)

# Iterate through the list of interface descriptions we are going
# to change. Prepend the user description, if any.
for local_port in desc_changes:
    try:
        udesc = desc_info[local_port]['user_desc']
    except KeyError:
        continue
    if udesc:
        desc_changes[local_port] = udesc + " " + desc_changes[local_port]

return desc_changes
```

Build, Apply, and Commit the Candidate Configuration

The `load_merge_template_config()` function takes a device instance, a Jinja2 template, and template variables as its arguments. It uses RPC on Demand as well as the PyEZ configuration `load()` and `commit()` methods to perform the equivalent of the CLI commands `configure private`, `load merge`, and `commit`. It also checks the results for potential errors:

```
def load_merge_template_config(device,
                               template_path,
                               template_vars): ❶
    """Load templated config with "configure private" and "load merge".
```

```
    Given a template_path and template_vars, do:
        configure private,
        load merge of the templated config,
        commit,
        and check the results.

    Return True if the config was committed successfully, False otherwise.
    """

    class LoadNotOKError(Exception): pass ❷

    device.bind(cu=Config) ❸

    rc = False

    try:
        try:
            resp = device.rpc.open_configuration(private=True) ❹
        except jnpr.junos.exception.RpcError as err: ❺
            if not (err.rpc_error['severity'] == 'warning' and
                    'uncommitted changes will be discarded on exit' in
                    err.rpc_error['message']):
                raise

        resp = device.cu.load(template_path=template_path,
                              template_vars=template_vars,
                              merge=True) ❻
        if resp.find("ok") is None: ❼
            raise LoadNotOKError
        device.cu.commit(comment="made by %s" % sys.argv[0]) ❽
    except (jnpr.junos.exception.RpcError, ❾
            jnpr.junos.exception.ConnectError,
            LoadNotOKError) as err:
        print "    " + repr(err)
    except:
        print "    Unknown error occurred loading or committing configuration."
    else: ❿
        rc = True
    try: ⓫
        device.rpc.close_configuration()
    except jnpr.junos.exception.RpcError as err:
        print "    " + repr(err)
        rc = False
    return rc
```

❶ The `device`, `template_path`, and `template_vars` arguments are required parameters of the `load_merge_template_config()` function.

❷ A new `Exception` subclass is defined. This class is raised, and handled, when there is a problem loading the new configuration.

❸ A new PyEZ configuration instance is created and bound to the device's `cu` attribute.

❹ The *open-configuration* XML RPC is called by the RPC on Demand method. The `private` argument makes this RPC equivalent to the `configure private` CLI command.

❺ `jnpr.junos.exception.RpcError` exceptions are caught and handled by this `except` block. It is normal for the *open-configuration* XML RPC to return an `uncommitted changes will be discarded on exit` warning when the `private` argument is specified. This expected warning is ignored. All other `jnpr.junos.exception.RpcError` exceptions are raised and handled by the enclosing `try`/`except` block.

❻ This statement passes the `template_path` and `template_vars` arguments to the configuration instance's `load()` method. The configuration is generated from the template and user-supplied values. The `merge=True` argument causes the new configuration to be merged with the existing candidate configuration.

❼ An `<ok>` XML element in the `load()` method's XML response indicates the new configuration was loaded successfully. A `LoadNotOKError` exception, defined earlier in this function, is raised when the `<ok>` XML element is not found in the response. In most situations, an error loading the new candidate configuration will raise some subclass of the PyEZ `RpcError` exception. This block simply handles the possible situation where the `load()` method does not raise an exception and returns an unexpected RPC response.

❽ The configuration's `commit()` method is used to commit the new candidate configuration. A comment that includes the script's name is added to the commit with the `comment` argument.

❾ `jnpr.junos.exception.RpcError`, `jnpr.junos.exception.ConnectError`, and `LoadNotOKError` exceptions and subclasses are caught and handled by this `except` block. The contents of these exceptions are simply printed. A different message is printed for all other exceptions that may have been raised during the `try` block.

❿ This `else` block is executed only if no exception has been raised. This indicates the configuration has been successfully loaded and committed. In this case, `rc` is assigned the value of `True` to indicate the success. (Earlier, `rc` was initialized to `False`.)

⓫ Regardless of whether a previous exception was raised, this `try` block is executed and the private candidate configuration is closed by the *close-configuration* RPC. If there is an error closing the configuration, the exception is printed and `rc` is assigned `False` to indicate the error.

The `load_merge_template_config()` function is written to be independent of the configuration being applied. By passing the device instance, Jinja2 template file, and template variables, you can use it to apply any configuration to the device. The real work of producing the configuration is done in the Jinja2 template. In this example, the template lives in the *interface_descriptions_template.xml* file in the current working directory. As the *.xml* filename extension implies, this template generates a configuration in XML format. The callouts explain each line of the template:

```
<configuration>
    <interfaces> ❶
    {% for key, value in descriptions.iteritems() %} ❷
        <interface> ❸
            <name>{{ key }}</name> ❹
            <description>{{ value }}</description> ❺
        </interface>
    {% endfor %} ❻
    </interfaces>
</configuration>
```

❶ This template generates a configuration in XML syntax. Only the configuration-related XML tags need to be included. The `<interfaces>` XML tag corresponds to the `[edit interfaces]` level of the Junos configuration hierarchy.

❷ This line is a Jinja2 `for` loop that iterates over the items in the `descriptions` dictionary. The key to the `descriptions` dictionary is the interface's name, and the value is the new description to be configured.

❸ The opening XML tag for each interface. This tag will be repeated for each interface in the `descriptions` dictionary.

❹ The name of the interface. The `{{ key }}` expression evaluates to each key in the `descriptions` dictionary.

❺ The description of the interfaces. The `{{ value }}` expression evaluates to each value in the `descriptions` dictionary.

❻ The `{% endfor %}` tag identifies the end of the `for` loop that iterates over each interface in the `descriptions` dictionary.

Putting It All Together

The final block of code in the example script calls the `main()` function when the script is executed. After entering this code block, the example script is functional:

```
if __name__ == "__main__":
  sys.exit(main())
```

At this point, the script is complete and ready to test on a set of Junos devices running the NETCONF-over-SSH service and the LLDP protocol. If you encounter errors running the script, review and carefully compare your code with the example. The full working *lldp_interface_descriptions_pyez.py* file is also available on GitHub (*https://github.com/AutomatingJunosAdministration/examples*).

Limitations

Like all of the automation tools discussed in this book, PyEZ fills a very useful role in automating Junos networks, but it is not the solution to every network automation problem. The first, and most obvious, limitation is that PyEZ is Python-specific. If you're fluent in Python or augmenting a current system written in Python, you may see this as an asset. However, if your project requires another language, there may be other options. Refer to the next section for more information on ways to access Junos devices using NETCONF in the language of your choice.

Another (almost as obvious) limitation is that PyEZ requires NETCONF. Because all currently supported Junos devices support NETCONF, this requirement isn't a big limitation. However, it does require that the NETCONF-over-SSH service, or the standalone SSH service, be configured and reachable from your automation host. When using NETCONF over SSH, ensure that TCP destination port 830 is not being filtered along the network path between your automation host and the target Junos device.

NETCONF Libraries for Other Languages

While this book doesn't discuss them in detail, there are various libraries for several languages that implement the NETCONF protocol and provide some level of abstraction that avoids you having to send direct NETCONF RPCs. Most of these libraries do not support the higher-level abstractions, like tables and views, that Junos PyEZ supports, but they can still be extremely useful.

Table 4-8 provides a current survey of some of these libraries. Refer to the corresponding link for more information on each library.

Table 4-8. Available NETCONF libraries

Language	Description	Link
Ruby	Popular open source NETCONF library for Ruby. Easy to install, limited dependencies, and active support.	*http://rubygems.org/gems/netconf*
Java	Open source NETCONF library for Java. Already in use by enterprise customers. Easy installation with zero dependencies.	*http://www.juniper.net/support/downloads/?p=netconf*
Perl	Supported by Juniper Networks JTAC. Oldest of the NETCONF libraries. Installation can be difficult, with multiple dependencies.	*http://www.juniper.net/support/downloads/?p=netconf#sw*
PHP	Open source NETCONF library for PHP. Undergoing active development and may not be ready for production use.	*https://github.com/Juniper/netconf-php*
Python	Vendor-agnostic open source NETCONF library for Python. Utilized by PyEZ.	*https://github.com/leopoul/ncclient*

These libraries can be helpful if your project requires direct NETCONF support or a specific development language; however, PyEZ is highly recommended for new Junos automation development.

Chapter Summary

In summary, Junos PyEZ provides a friendly balance between simplicity and power. This balance makes it the obvious choice for users already familiar with Python. PyEZ offers fact gathering and utility functions that simplify many common tasks, and it simplifies RPC execution by providing an abstraction layer built on top of the NETCONF protocol.

Much of PyEZ's power involves dealing with the resulting RPC responses. For the most power and flexibility, use XPath expressions with the lxml library. For a quick and easy mapping between XML and native Python data structures, use the jxmlease library to parse the lxml response. For a reusable mapping between complex XML elements and simple Python data structures, choose the table and view mechanism.

In addition to operational RPCs, PyEZ offers tools for making configuration changes. These tools include a powerful "template building" feature that allows large and complex configurations to be generated with minimal effort.

CHAPTER 5

Commit Scripts

Commit scripts are a powerful way to modify the commit process. They let you transform the configuration between the time the user types `commit` and the time the configuration is read by the daemons. You can enforce custom configuration checks, automatically fix common configuration mistakes, and dynamically expand the configuration. In short, you can customize the configuration process to make it work for *your* environment.

Use Cases

Before diving into the details, let's take a look at some of the target use cases for commit scripts.

Custom Configuration Checks

The Junos software enforces a set of configuration checks that ensure basic configuration sanity. For example, the Junos software may prevent you from committing a BGP configuration that references a policy that is undefined, or it may prevent you from configuring the same IP address for two different BGP peers. However, these configuration checks do not ensure the configuration is correct for *your* environment. Rather, they merely check that the configuration may be suitable for *some* environment. Put differently, they check that the configuration is syntactically correct, not contextually correct. And this behavior makes sense. After all, how is the Junos software to know what makes sense in any given network?

However, *you* may know a certain configuration is appropriate, or inappropriate, for your environment. Some organizations distill this knowledge into standards or configuration templates. Using commit scripts, you can add configuration checks to enforce these standards.

For example, assume that you know that all BGP neighbors should be in one of three BGP groups: `internal`, `peers`, or `customers`. You can add a commit check that ensures no additional BGP groups are configured.

Next, let's assume your configuration standard requires all BGP neighbors in the `peers` and `customers` groups to have both import and export policies applied to them, and that the last policy in each policy chain must be the `deny-all` policy. You can add commit checks to enforce these constraints.

If you find the configuration changes do not meet your standards, you can have the commit script issue a warning to the user (but allow the commit process to continue), issue an error to the user (and stop the commit process), or take other actions (such as logging an error message through syslog).

This gives you a small idea of the kinds of commit checks you can do. However, there are many (almost limitless!) possibilities for commit checks.

Automatically Fixing Mistakes

Just as you can find places where the configuration does not meet your standards, you can also attempt to automatically correct the configuration.

Perhaps the best examples of this use case are in the area of MPLS or ISIS configuration. For both protocols, something must often be configured at both the `[edit interfaces]` and `[edit protocols]` hierarchy levels in order to achieve the desired results.

For MPLS, it is often the case that any interface listed in the `[edit protocols mpls]` hierarchy should also have `family mpls` configured on the interface. For ISIS, any non-passive interface listed in the `[edit protocols isis]` hierarchy should also have `family iso` configured on the interface.

If this is not the case, using a commit script, you can detect this error and attempt to correct it by adding the missing configuration. You can also include your configuration corrections in the static configuration database.

Dynamically Expanding Configuration

Often, configuration elements are formed from a template. For example, all customer BGP sessions may use the same configuration, except for the IP address, AS number, import policy, and export policy. This network standard allows customer BGP configurations to be simplified to a template with variables that are replaced as appropriate. For example, the template in a particular network might look like Example 5-1.

Example 5-1. A sample BGP configuration template

```
protocols {
    bgp {
        group customers {
            neighbor $ip_addr {
                import [ filter-customer-generic prefix-size
                         handle-communities as-$peer_as deny-all ];
                family inet {
                    unicast {
                        accepted-prefix-limit {
                            maximum $limit;
                            teardown 80 idle-timeout 10;
                        }
                    }
                }
                family inet6 {
                    unicast {
                        accepted-prefix-limit {
                            maximum $limit;
                            teardown 80 idle-timeout 10;
                        }
                    }
                }
                export [ $route_type deny-all ];
                peer-as $peer_as;
            }
        }
    }
}
```

Here, the critical pieces of information are the neighbor IP, peer AS, prefix limit, and type of routes the user wants to receive. You can write a commit script that takes those options as input parameters and outputs the correct neighbor configuration. You can even choose to have the commit script dynamically modify the configuration every time there is a commit. This functionality has the impact of reducing the size of the candidate configuration, while also ensuring that any changes to the template are reflected in the existing BGP sessions. (In other words, the configuration can be dynamically updated to reflect the new template when the configuration template is updated.)

A commit script's input values can be stored in `apply-macro` configuration statements or derived from other configuration elements, or you can simply use default values. For example, the configuration for a customer BGP session could look like Example 5-2.

Example 5-2. A sample configuration snippet that provides values for a commit script

```
interfaces {
    ge-1/0/0 {
        unit 0 {
            family inet {
                address 192.168.1.1/30 {
                    apply-macro bgp {
                        peer_as 65534;
                        route_type full_routes;
                    }
                }
            }
        }
    }
}
```

The commit script can read this configuration snippet and infer the remote IP address, apply a default prefix limit of 10,000 prefixes, and use the supplied values from the `apply-macro bgp` configuration hierarchy. It can expand this configuration to that shown in Example 5-3.

Example 5-3. A sample configuration after a commit script has applied a template

```
interfaces {
    ge-1/0/0 {
        unit 0 {
            family inet {
                address 192.168.1.1/30;
            }
        }
    }
}
protocols {
    bgp {
        group customers {
            neighbor 192.168.1.2 {
                import [ filter-customer-generic prefix-size
                         handle-communities as-65534 deny-all ];
                family inet {
                    unicast {
                        accepted-prefix-limit {
                            maximum 10000;
                            teardown 80 idle-timeout 10;
                        }
                    }
                }
                family inet6 {
                    unicast {
                        accepted-prefix-limit {
                            maximum 10000;
```

```
                            teardown 80 idle-timeout 10;
                        }
                    }
                }
                export [ full_routes deny-all ];
                peer-as 65534;
            }
        }
    }
}
```

There are, of course, many options for expanding the configuration. Some users may prefer to configure the customer's BGP information, stored in the `apply-macro bgp` statement, under the `[edit protocols bgp]` hierarchy, while others may prefer to group all customer information together in the `[edit interfaces]` hierarchy. Likewise, some users may prefer to keep the simple template values (shown in Example 5-2) in their static configuration, while others may prefer to have the commit script expand the template one time and store the expanded configuration (shown in Example 5-3) in their static configuration. Whichever way you choose to use commit scripts, they can help you apply templates to your network.

Basic Execution Flow

You configure commit scripts at the `[edit system scripts commit]` configuration hierarchy level. When a user initiates a commit operation, MGD launches a utility (called CSCRIPT) to process each commit script. After the results of each commit script have been incorporated into the commit process, the commit process continues and the final configuration is committed.

This flow is one of the only places where something in your configuration takes effect before the commit process has completed. But it makes sense, if you really think about it.

When a user initiates a commit operation, MGD processes the configuration through the commit scripts listed in the *candidate* configuration. If a user makes changes to the set of commit scripts listed in the candidate configuration, the new set of commit scripts will be used to process any commit operations for that candidate configuration, even a `commit check`.

This makes sense if you consider commit scripts to be an indispensable part of the configuration. (Indeed, they may be indispensable, as the actual committed configuration is the candidate configuration *as modified by* the commit scripts.) Therefore, don't be surprised when Junos uses your newly configured commit scripts before they are even completely committed the first time.

Commit scripts are applied whenever a commit operation occurs. In this context, the `commit check` command counts as a commit operation. Therefore, even running `commit check` can cause a change in the candidate configuration:

```
[edit]
user@r0# show | compare

[edit]
user@r0# commit check
[edit interfaces interface ge-1/0/0 unit 0]
  warning: Adding 'family mpls' to ge-1/0/0.0
configuration check succeeds

[edit]
user@r0# show | compare
[edit interfaces ge-1/0/0 unit 0]
+      family mpls;
```

XML Transformations

When you execute a SLAX or XSLT script, the script undertakes an *XML transformation*. As illustrated in Figure 5-1, the script works on an input document and transforms it into an output document.

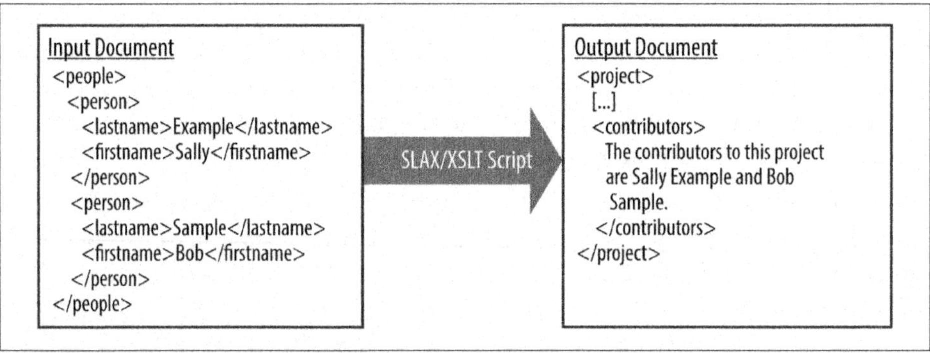

Figure 5-1. A sample XML transformation

With Junos SLAX or XSLT scripts, the input document contains information for the script's execution and the output document contains information for the Junos software. In the case of op or event scripts, the output document contains XML data that the CLI can render for the user. In the case of commit scripts, the output document contains instructions for how the Junos software should proceed with the commit operation.

Commit Script XML Input and Output Documents

MGD (through CSCRIPT) sends each commit script a copy of the candidate configuration (in XML format) as its input document. The candidate configuration includes the expansion of configuration data from configuration groups. (Essentially, commit scripts work on the output of `show | display inheritance`.)

Each commit script gets the same candidate configuration. Commit scripts do not see each other's changes. Therefore, you should ensure that each commit script does not take actions that rely on another script's changes, or which may interact in unpredictable ways with the changes your other scripts make.

Likewise, MGD (through CSCRIPT) expects to receive an XML output document (which may include zero or more directives) from the commit script. This XML response document's root tag must be the `<commit-script-results>` tag; however, the Junos infrastructure should produce this tag for you automatically. Within the response document, you can include directives specified by the following XML tags:

`<xnm:error>`
: Contains an error message that is displayed to the user, and directs MGD to stop the configuration process.

`<xnm:warning>`
: Contains a warning that is displayed to the user.

`<syslog>`
: Directs CSCRIPT to send a message to the syslog system.

`<change>`
: Directs MGD to make the indicated configuration change in the candidate database prior to completing the commit process.

`<transient-change>`
: Directs MGD to make the indicated configuration change to the committed configuration as part of the commit process, but not to include the change in the configuration that is shown to users. (The difference between `<change>` and `<transient-change>` is explained further in "Changing the Configuration" on page 258.)

In practice, you don't always need to use these XML tags directly. Instead, you can sometimes call predefined templates that insert these tags for you. However, they are listed here so you can better understand the communication mechanism that occurs behind the scenes.

Figure 5-2 illustrates commit script input and output documents. The figure shows a sample XML input document containing a Junos configuration. The SLAX or XSLT script processes the input and produces an XML output document. The output document contains an error indicating that the configuration for interface `ge-0/0/0` used an unauthorized VLAN value.

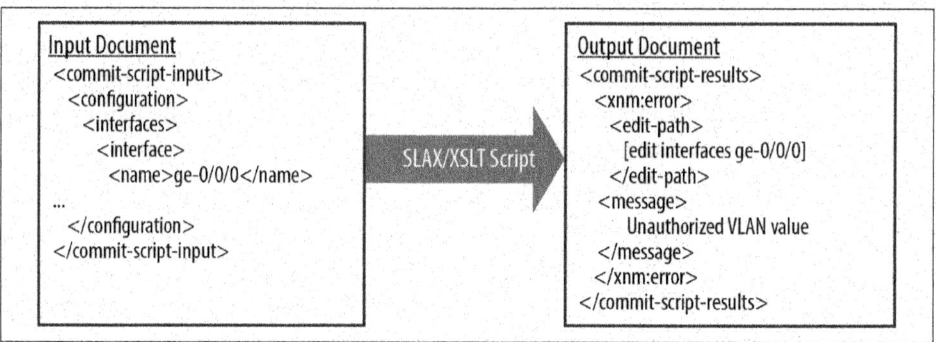

Figure 5-2. Sample commit script XML documents

Optimization for large configurations

With large configurations, the process of generating the configuration, passing it to CSCRIPT, and parsing it within CSCRIPT can take a large amount of time and memory. To overcome this limitation, you can configure `[edit system scripts commit direct-access]`. When you configure this setting, CSCRIPT directly reads the shared configuration database instead of expecting to receive a copy from MGD. This should reduce processing time and memory consumption for large configurations.

Passing information to commit scripts

One of the useful ways you can pass information to commit scripts is using the hidden `apply-macro` configuration statement. As demonstrated in Example 5-2, the `apply-macro` statement takes a name and a list of attribute/value pairs. The `apply-macro` statement is meaningless to any Junos daemon. Its *raison d'être* is to provide a way to pass information to commit scripts.

When you write a commit script, you can program it to read data from `apply-macro` statements that appear at various places in the configuration. Your commit script then processes this information according to the logic you provide.

In addition to users manually configuring `apply-macro` statements, you can also use this statement as a communication mechanism between the current invocation of a commit script and a commit script invoked during a future commit. For example, a commit script might add an `apply-macro` statement to tell itself which template version was used to expand a piece of the configuration. By reading this data, it can then ensure it uses the same template version during future invocations.

Using `apply-macro` statements, you can do better than passing a single set of global arguments to the commit script. In fact, you can pass a different set of arguments for each configuration stanza, if necessary. This can be a powerful tool that you can use to customize the way commit scripts work.

The `apply-macro` statement is useful to pass information to future commit operations (future invocations of a commit script), but it cannot be used to pass information between commit scripts during the same commit operation. As explained at the beginning of "Changing the Configuration" on page 258, each commit script receives its own copy of the candidate configuration. A commit script cannot see the changes another commit script may make to the candidate configuration during the commit process.

Performing Other Operations

While processing the configuration, a commit script can execute operational RPCs against the local system, or even against remote systems. "Interacting with Operational State" on page 338 contains a description of the way to execute these RPCs.

While these operations are allowed, care must be taken to use the information appropriately. The general Junos philosophy is to allow configuration that is valid even if it is not meaningful in the current operational state. A good example of this is the ability to preconfigure interfaces. Even though an interface may not be present at the time the configuration is committed, Junos still accepts valid configuration statements for that interface. Once the interface becomes available, Junos begins using that portion of the configuration.

Likewise, there may be cases where a user attempts to configure statements that are not currently meaningful in your environment. Perhaps the user is trying to preconfigure a customer BGP session, or preconfigure a new internal route reflector. If you add commit checks that, for example, condition acceptance of a BGP configuration on whether the router can currently ping the BGP neighbor, you may prevent the user from including valid configuration. Even worse, when he tries to commit an unrelated configuration change later, the commit may fail if *any* BGP neighbors are unreachable.

While there are times that operational state can help inform commit checks, you must take care to ensure your checks are not so stringent that they prevent users from making valid changes, or cause unrelated commits to fail inappropriately.

Changing the Configuration

Commit scripts can make two kinds of changes to the configuration: *permanent changes* and *transient changes*. Both have value in different circumstances. Thankfully, you can choose which to use. A commit script can use either kind or even both kinds of changes.

Let's give an example of the two kinds of changes, referring back to "Dynamically Expanding Configuration" on page 250. (At this point, you might also find it useful to refer to the information in "Creating the merged configuration view" on page 24, including Figure 1-9.)

Prior to committing the candidate configuration, it contains the statements shown in Example 5-2. A commit script expands the candidate configuration to the statements shown in Example 5-3. This expanded configuration becomes part of the "post-inheritance" static configuration, which is combined with other data sources and passed to the Junos daemons to activate.

If the commit script makes this change as a permanent change, the committed configuration looks like Example 5-3. Running `show configuration` displays the configuration from Example 5-3, and the commit script does not expand the configuration again during future commit operations.

On the other hand, if the commit script makes this change as a transient change, the committed configuration looks like Example 5-2. Running `show configuration` displays the configuration from Example 5-2, and the commit script does expand the configuration again during each future commit operation.

As you can imagine, there are cases where each of these options may be desirable. You should be able to integrate either approach with proper operational policies and procedures to produce a solution that meets your users' needs.

Handling Transient Changes

Using transient changes provides several important benefits. First, it lets you group configuration in ways that you find useful. (Referring again to Example 5-2, you can see how an organization that likes to configure all customer information at the interface level may find this sort of configuration useful.) Second, it reduces the size of the committed configuration by only showing the pieces that are unique to a particular customer. The defaults are not shown. Third, because the commit script performs the expansion for each commit operation, using transient changes allows a company to easily update a template and apply that update to all customer configurations. (This can be especially handy when it is necessary to fix an error in the template!) Fourth, it makes it easy to *remove* the configuration. When you remove the `apply-macro` statement, the software will not expand the (now-deleted) configuration in the next commit operation.

On the other hand, because the expanded configuration is not included in the configuration database users see, some users may feel that transient changes obscure the full configuration. Additionally, there may be legitimate concern about applying updated templates to the existing configuration. Also, because the expanded configuration is not stored in the committed configuration, there may be concerns about the traceability of configuration changes. Finally, because the expanded configuration does not appear in the committed configuration, you cannot easily make changes to just one aspect of it.

To address these concerns, we suggest the following methodology:

1. Train users to use the `display commit-scripts` pipe command to see the expanded configuration.
2. Write scripts to support template versioning. When a new configuration snippet is added, the scripts can automatically use the latest template version and store that version identifier with the configuration snippet. Then, as you update the configuration templates, you can choose whether to have the scripts apply updates to various template versions. This process lets you quickly deploy changes to existing customer configurations, while also still allowing you to deploy template changes that will only apply to new customer configurations.
3. Treat commit script changes like configuration changes. (In fact, commit script changes essentially *are* configuration changes.) Always deploy new commit script versions with a new name, and leave the old files available for some time. This recommendation has a few benefits:

    - The new commit script is only used once you modify the configuration to use the new commit script. When you commit the configuration change to use the new commit script, the router will immediately return any errors caused by the way the commit script expanded the present router configuration. If this initial commit detects errors, you can easily rollback the configuration to resume using the previous commit script.
    - If you encounter unexpected operational results after you commit the new commit script, you can easily rollback the configuration to a point that uses the old commit script. (In fact, you can even use `commit confirmed` if you follow this recommendation.)
    - This practice provides traceability to determine the configuration that was deployed at any given point. A previously active configuration can be expanded from the rollback configuration and the commit scripts referenced in that rollback configuration.

- There is no question of whether you actually activated the configuration produced by the new commit script. If you merely update the contents of the existing commit script file, without changing its filename, the new commit script will not alter the active configuration until the next time you perform a commit.

4. If you think users may need to customize the configurations expanded from templates, you should either use permanent changes (instead of transient changes), or provide a user-configurable option to expand a particular configuration stanza using permanent changes.

The `display commit-scripts` pipe command dynamically applies the commit scripts listed in the configuration. If you change the contents of a commit script file on the disk, without changing its name, the output from the `display commit-scripts` pipe command reflects the contents of the new commit script, even if you have not yet committed the configuration using the new commit script.

Therefore, if you modify the contents of a commit script file on the disk without changing its name, the output from the `display commit-scripts` pipe command may not accurately reflect the active configuration.

This is yet another reason to follow the practice we recommend in this section when making changes to your commit scripts.

Handling Permanent Changes

After reading about transient changes, you might think that using permanent changes will be a piece of cake. In reality, they have their own considerations.

First, because permanent changes modify the committed configuration, the size of the committed configuration can grow very quickly. This behavior may prove to be unwieldy in some situations. Second, because permanent changes are expanded and applied only once, you cannot easily correct errors in your templates. Third, if you need to remove the configuration, you will need to manually delete all the configuration elements the commit script created.

To effectively use permanent changes, we suggest the following methodology:

1. Delete the appropriate `apply-macro` statements as part of your configuration change. This action ensures the commit script does not attempt to reapply the same configuration changes the next time you commit the configuration.

2. Use the hidden `apply-flags omit` configuration statement to hide pieces of the configuration hierarchy that are cumbersome for users to view directly on a regular basis. If you do this, you should educate users that they can use the `display omit` pipe command to view the hidden portions of the configuration.
3. Use good version control on your commit scripts, including the practices we suggest in "Handling Transient Changes" on page 258. Here, the reasoning is slightly different; however, it is still good practice to ensure you can track which commit scripts were in use at a given time, and be sure that commit operations with the new commit script will succeed.

Writing Commit Scripts in SLAX/XSLT

You have two language choices for commit scripts: SLAX and XSLT. Phil Shafer, the creator of SLAX, has said that SLAX is just "syntactic eye candy" on top of XSLT. In other words, its primary function is to make it easier to read and write XSLT. For this reason, we will essentially treat them as having equivalent functionality for the purposes of the book.

In this section, we give an overview of the SLAX language. This is not intended to be a comprehensive language reference. Rather, it is meant to give an overview of some of the important concepts in the language, with particular attention to the concepts that arise in the context of Junos automation scripts. For a more complete language reference, refer to the SLAX language documentation (*http://www.libslax.org/the-slax-language*).

If you are new to "XML transformations" (which is the term used to describe XSLT's work), you may find SLAX and XSLT to be a little awkward to use. However, while SLAX and XSLT have a limited set of capabilities, they are very good at what they do: find XML, parse XML, and produce XML. And that really is a core part of a commit script's activities: parse an input XML document (the candidate configuration) and produce an output XML document (the directives giving the management system actions to take).

SLAX Versus XSLT

Because SLAX *does* make it much easier to read and write XSLT, we generally just discuss SLAX (and, in particular, SLAX 1.1). However, if you already know XSLT, you are free to use it. And, if you already know how to use XSLT, a quick skim of this section should help you discover the Juniper-specific things you need to know.

When calling the templates Juniper provides, you use the same names and arguments in both SLAX and XSLT. Also, many (but not all) of the extension functions that are available in the `http://xml.libslax.org/slax` (`slax`) namespace are also available in the `http://xml.juniper.net/junos/commit-scripts/1.0` (`jcs`) namespace. The Juniper documentation (*http://www.juniper.net/techpubs*) contains a list of extension functions in these namespaces.

Armed with these bits of Juniper-specific information, combined with the information in this section about how to use the input document and create the output document, you should be able to use your preexisting XSLT knowledge to successfully write commit scripts.

On the other hand, if you are new to both XSLT and SLAX, we recommend you use SLAX. If you are familiar with procedural programming languages, but new to XML transformations, you will probably find it much easier to use SLAX than XSLT.

Overview of a SLAX Script

A SLAX script parses XML input and produces XML output. It uses one or more match templates (see "Templates" on page 275) to match portions of the XML input document and begin processing them. Once a match template is executing, the SLAX script begins producing XML output.

A SLAX script consists of a series of statements. Statements can span multiple lines, and the SLAX processor generally ignores extra whitespace. Each statement ends with a semicolon or a code block enclosed in curly braces.

Because the whole point of a SLAX script is to produce an XML output document, the language has a unique property: any XML element enclosed in angle brackets becomes a statement. As shown in "XML output" on page 265, you can use this property of the language to produce an XML hierarchy.

As the script is executed, each code block produces results, which can be text or XML node sets. The results of these code blocks are used appropriately, depending on the context. The results of the match templates' code blocks become the script's output document.

Some common SLAX statements include:

`match`, `template`
: These statements introduce template definitions. Templates contain SLAX code. The processor runs match templates when it encounters XML nodes in the input document that match the given pattern. The processor runs named templates when the user includes a `call` statement. Templates are described in more detail in "Templates" on page 275.

  Templates can return data. The data is either included in the output XML document or included in the results of the code block that called the template.

`call`
: This statement tells the SLAX processor to run a named template. The SLAX processor runs the indicated template. The output of the template forms part of the results of the code block containing the `call` statement. The `call` statement is described in more detail in "Templates" on page 275.

`var`
: This statement introduces a variable declaration. The value of the variable can be provided in an XPath expression, in text, or in a code block. Variables are scoped and are also immutable. Variables are described in more detail in "SLAX variables" on page 272.

`copy-of`
: This statement takes an XPath expression argument and outputs a complete copy of the XML hierarchy indicated by the XPath expression. The result of the `copy-of` statement forms part of the results of the enclosing code block.

`expr`
: This statement takes an XPath expression argument and returns the "value of" the XPath expression. Normally, you should use the `copy-of` statement to make copies of XML hierarchies; however, you can use the `expr` statement to return the value of a particular XML leaf node.

  The `expr` statement is useful when you want to include raw text or the value of a variable in the results of a code block. The `expr` statement is also useful when you want to execute a function and include the function's return value in the results of a code block.

Basic SLAX template

You can start writing a SLAX commit script using the basic template shown in Example 5-4.

Example 5-4. Template for a SLAX commit script

```
version 1.1;

ns junos = "http://xml.juniper.net/junos/*/junos";
ns xnm = "http://xml.juniper.net/xnm/1.1/xnm";
ns jcs = "http://xml.juniper.net/junos/commit-scripts/1.0";

import "../import/junos.xsl";

match configuration {
    /* Insert code here */
}
```

The `ns` statement defines namespaces. As described in "XML data" on page 32, namespaces help disambiguate multiple elements with the same name. In the case of SLAX or XSLT scripts, they are very important. Certain extension functions and templates appear in alternate namespaces (most commonly, the `jcs` and `slax` namespaces). You must use the appropriate namespace prefix when using one of the functions or templates in these namespaces.

The next thing the template does is import a standard XSLT file. This XSLT file includes some Juniper templates that can help you perform certain tasks. The XSLT file also contains code that automatically extracts some information from the input document and encloses the output document in the correct XML tags. (Again, if you don't understand XML translations in detail, suffice it to say that you always want to include this.)

Finally, the template script has a match template. In XSLT and SLAX, templates serve a role similar to subroutines or functions in other languages. (Actually, XSLT and SLAX also have functions, which are distinct from templates, so it is important to maintain the terminology distinction. However, it may be helpful if you think about templates serving a similar role as subroutines or functions in other languages.)

A match template tells SLAX to execute the template once for each piece of the input document hierarchy with a matching XML tag. In the context of a commit script, the `<configuration>` tag only appears once and is the root tag for the input document, the candidate configuration. Therefore, a template that matches the `<configuration>` tag (as this one does) can serve the same role as a `main()` function in a C program.

Inside a template, you put code that examines the XML data, obtains external data using function calls, and outputs appropriate data for the script's XML output document.

Building an Output Document

As described in "Commit Script XML Input and Output Documents" on page 255, the main goal of a commit script is to produce an output document telling the Junos software what actions it should take. However, in some cases, there may be no action to take. In those cases, you simply return an empty document, which is perfectly acceptable. However, the overall goal of a SLAX commit script is to return an XML document that tells the Junos system what actions to take.

In fact, one of the important things to understand about SLAX is that the SLAX script is building an output document. You can place XML output directly in that document. You can also call functions or templates and place the results of those calls directly in the output document.

SLAX also supports various forms of logic (such as loops and conditional statements). However, these loops can contain direct XML output that will form part of the output document, or populate a variable. Once you understand the way these items can be combined seamlessly, it opens up opportunities to write powerful and compact scripts.

XML output

Returning XML is as easy as putting it right in your SLAX script. XML that appears in an executed code path that is not assigned to a variable or used as an argument to a template or function will form part of the return document. In SLAX, you can use a shorthand syntax to express XML tags in a format that looks similar to the Junos configuration syntax. Here are some examples of the way you would represent sample XML hierarchies in a SLAX script:

XML syntax	SLAX syntax
`<tag>example</tag>`	`<tag> "example";`
`<tag/>`	`<tag>;`

`<tag>`
`    <tag2>example</tag2>`
`</tag>`
	`<tag> {`
	`    <tag2> "example";`
	`}`

`<tag>`
`    <tag2>`
`        <name>example</name>`
`        <function>explaining</function>`
`        <important/>`
`    </tag2>`
`</tag>`
	`<tag> {`
	`    <tag2>`
	`        <name> "example";`
	`        <function> "explaining";`
	`        <important>;`
	`    }`
	`}`

Here, the SLAX commit script uses the `<xnm:warning>` tag to return a simple warning message when it sees the `<configuration>` hierarchy of the candidate configuration:

```
[edit]
user@r0# show system scripts commit
file basic.slax {
    optional;
}

[edit]
user@r0# run file show /var/db/scripts/commit/basic.slax
version 1.1;

ns junos = "http://xml.juniper.net/junos/*/junos";
ns xnm = "http://xml.juniper.net/xnm/1.1/xnm";
```

```
ns jcs = "http://xml.juniper.net/junos/commit-scripts/1.0";

import "../import/junos.xsl";

match configuration {
    <xnm:warning> {
        <edit-path> "[edit]";
        <message> "Saw 'configuration' hierarchy.";
    }
}

[edit]
user@r0# commit check
[edit]
  warning: Saw 'configuration' hierarchy.
configuration check succeeds
```

Formatting text

There are times when you need to do something more advanced. In those instances, SLAX has a few features you can use to help you format your text correctly.

Accessing variables and XML data. You can output variables and data from the XML input document as text (as long as they are representable as text). To do this, you simply place the appropriate expression in the output document (outside quotes).

In summary, to access a variable, you use `$varname`. To access XML data, you use an XPath expression. "Working with Variables and XML Data" on page 270 contains much more information about variables and using data from the XML input document.

For example, the XPath expression to get the name of the current XML node in the input document is `name(.)`. Therefore, you could modify the preceding example to print the name of the current XML node, `configuration`:

```
[edit]
user@r0# show system scripts commit
file basic.slax {
    optional;
}

[edit]
user@r0# run file show /var/db/scripts/commit/basic.slax
version 1.1;

ns junos = "http://xml.juniper.net/junos/*/junos";
ns xnm = "http://xml.juniper.net/xnm/1.1/xnm";
ns jcs = "http://xml.juniper.net/junos/commit-scripts/1.0";

import "../import/junos.xsl";
```

```
match configuration {
    <xnm:warning> {
        <edit-path> "[edit]";
        <message> name(.);
    }
}

[edit]
user@r0# commit check
[edit]
  warning: configuration
configuration check succeeds
```

Text splicing. SLAX offers Perl-style text splicing using the underscore (_) character. For example, the SLAX syntax `"Yes, " _ "I " _ "can!"` would produce a single string rendered as `"Yes, I can!"`.

Text splicing is useful for concatenating static strings together with values obtained dynamically from XML data or variables.

For example, we can refine our preceding examples like this:

```
[edit]
user@r0# show system scripts commit
file basic.slax {
    optional;
}

[edit]
user@r0# run file show /var/db/scripts/commit/basic.slax
version 1.1;

ns junos = "http://xml.juniper.net/junos/*/junos";
ns xnm = "http://xml.juniper.net/xnm/1.1/xnm";
ns jcs = "http://xml.juniper.net/junos/commit-scripts/1.0";

import "../import/junos.xsl";

match configuration {
    <xnm:warning> {
        <edit-path> "[edit]";
        <message> "Saw '" _ name(.) _ "' hierarchy.";
    }
}

[edit]
user@r0# commit check
[edit]
  warning: Saw 'configuration' hierarchy.
configuration check succeeds
```

printf()-like formatting. Sometimes you just need `printf()`-like formatting. When this occurs, you can use the `jcs:printf()` function. This function works very similarly to the standard Unix `printf()` call; however, Juniper provides a few extensions that you may find useful. (You can read about the extensions in Juniper's documentation (*http://www.juniper.net/techpubs*).)

Here is an example of using the `jcs:printf()` function to obtain the same results as from the preceding example:

```
[edit]
user@r0# show system scripts commit
file basic.slax {
    optional;
}

[edit]
user@r0# run file show /var/db/scripts/commit/basic.slax
version 1.1;

ns junos = "http://xml.juniper.net/junos/*/junos";
ns xnm = "http://xml.juniper.net/xnm/1.1/xnm";
ns jcs = "http://xml.juniper.net/junos/commit-scripts/1.0";

import "../import/junos.xsl";

match configuration {
    <xnm:warning> {
        <edit-path> "[edit]";
        <message> jcs:printf("Saw '%s' hierarchy.", name(.));
    }
}

[edit]
user@r0# commit check
[edit]
  warning: Saw 'configuration' hierarchy.
configuration check succeeds
```

Concatenation. You can use code to create XML node content or the values used for variable assignments. You use curly braces to enclose the code that the parser runs to create the value. If the code produces text, any text will be automatically concatenated to produce the final output. For example, consider the following two `<message>` elements:

```
<message> {
    expr "t";
    expr "e";
    expr "s";
    expr "t";
```

```
}
<message> "test";
```

Both of the preceding `<message>` elements will produce this XML node:

```
<message>test</message>
```

Logical statements

One interesting thing about SLAX is that you can intermix XML output and logical statements. For example, using the `call` statement (which we will discuss in "Defining and calling named templates" on page 277), you can call other templates to produce XML that is inserted at the point of the `call` statement.

Here is a common example used when generating errors or warnings. In this example, the `call jcs:edit-path()` statement is replaced by the results of the `jcs:edit-path()` template. The `jcs:edit-path()` template emits an XML hierarchy that represents the current XML node in the input document in the normal Junos `[edit]` format:

```
match configuration {
    <xnm:warning> {
        call jcs:edit-path();
        <message> "Saw 'configuration' hierarchy.";
    }
}
```

You can even include `for` loops, `if` statements, and other logical constructs. This example lists all interfaces in the configuration using a `for-each` operator (which we will discuss in "for-each loops over XML nodes" on page 282):

```
match configuration {
    <xnm:warning> {
        call jcs:edit-path();
        <message> {
            expr "Saw these interfaces: ";
            for-each (interfaces/interface) {
                expr " " _ name;
            }
        }
    }
}
```

If you run this script, you'll see output like the following. For each interface, the `expr` statement prints a space and the interface name, resulting in a space-separated list of interfaces:

```
[edit]
user@r0# commit check
[edit]
```

```
  warning: Saw these interfaces: ge-1/0/0 ge-1/0/1 lo0 fxp0
configuration check succeeds
```

Working with Variables and XML Data

Obviously, static script elements (such as those we've used up to this point) are useful. However, most scripts need to access some piece of dynamic information. SLAX has two mechanisms for working with dynamic information: XML data and variables.

XML data

It is fairly easy to access XML data in the candidate configuration (the commit script's XML input document). Simply reference the XPath expression. (See "Accessing XML data with XPath" on page 36 for more information on XPath expressions.) For example, consider this input document:

```
<configuration>
    <interfaces>
        <interface>
            <name>ge-1/0/0</name>
            <description>interface 1</description>
        </interface>
        <interface>
            <name>ge-1/0/1</name>
            <description>interface 2</description>
        </interface>
    </interfaces>
</configuration>
```

To access the description of interface `ge-1/0/0`, use the XPath expression `interfaces/interface[name="ge-1/0/0"]/description`. This code prints the interface description for `ge-1/0/0`:

```
match configuration {
    <xnm:warning> {
        <edit-path> "[edit]";
        <message> "ge-1/0/0 description is: " _
                  interfaces/interface[name="ge-1/0/0"]/description;
    }
}
```

Note that XPath expressions are relative to the current position in the input document's hierarchy. Like in a Unix filesystem, you can use `/` to refer to the root of the document, `.` to refer to the current node, `..` to refer to the parent node, and the tag name of a child node to refer to that child node.

The root node of the input document is a `<commit-script-input>` element. To access the root of the Junos configuration, you can use the XPath expression `/commit-script-input/configuration`.

The current node can change in a few circumstances (which we will cover in more detail elsewhere), including `for` loops and match templates. When a node matches a match template, the SLAX parser executes the match template and sets the current node to the node that matched the template's expression.

As an example, imagine we want to print the descriptions for all interfaces. We could rewrite our SLAX script like this:

```
match configuration/interfaces/interface {
    <xnm:warning> {
        <edit-path> "[edit]";
        <message> name _ " description is: " _ description;
    }
}
```

Note we've used the XPath expressions `name` and `description` to access the `<name>` and `<description>` nodes within the interface. When the match template matches a node, SLAX moves the current node (the "dot" location, if you will) to each matching node as it executes the template. Therefore, our XPath expressions are stated relative to the matching node. Note how easy it is to retrieve information about the matching node!

When we run this script, we see it produces this output:

```
[edit]
user@r0# commit check
[edit]
  warning: ge-1/0/0 description is: interface 1
[edit]
  warning: ge-1/0/1 description is: interface 2
[edit]
  warning: lo0 description is:
[edit]
  warning: fxp0 description is:
configuration check succeeds
```

Note the `lo0` and `fxp0` interfaces show up with blank descriptions. Those two interfaces exist in the configuration, but don't have descriptions configured; therefore, there is no `<description>` element for those interfaces. A nonexistent XML node is rendered as an empty string, which is perfectly fine in this case.

SLAX variables

Variables in XSLT have a seemingly simple quirk that can produce trouble at times: they are usually immutable. Once you set an XSLT variable, you cannot change it or unset it. Like in XSLT, SLAX variables are usually immutable; however, SLAX does have an extension that relaxes these rules. (We discuss this extension in the next section.)

In addition to being immutable, variables in XSLT and SLAX are scoped. You can define variables at various levels of the hierarchy, and use the variables at the same or lower levels. However, variables disappear once the script exits the code block in which they were defined.

Once you have set a variable using the `var` statement, you access the value of the variable using the `$varname` syntax.

Here, we rewrite the preceding example to use variables:

```
[edit]
user@r0# run file show /var/db/scripts/commit/basic.slax | find "^m"
match configuration/interfaces/interface {
    var $intname = name;
    var $intdescr = description;
    <xnm:warning> {
        <edit-path> "[edit]";
        <message> $intname _ " description is: " _ $intdescr;
    }
}

[edit]
user@r0# commit check
[edit]
  warning: ge-1/0/0 description is: interface 1
[edit]
  warning: ge-1/0/1 description is: interface 2
[edit]
  warning: lo0 description is:
[edit]
  warning: fxp0 description is:
configuration check succeeds
```

Note that variables can hold various data types, including XML hierarchies. Here, we modify the script from the preceding example. Instead of directly accessing XML nodes, we first assign the current XML node to a variable and then use an XPath expression to reference data in XML nodes within that variable's value:

```
[edit]
user@r0# run file show /var/db/scripts/commit/basic.slax | find "^m"
match configuration/interfaces/interface {
    var $current = .;
    <xnm:warning> {
```

```
            <edit-path> "[edit]";
            <message> $current/name _ " description is: " _
                      $current/description;
        }
    }

[edit]
user@r0# commit check
[edit]
  warning: ge-1/0/0 description is: interface 1
[edit]
  warning: ge-1/0/1 description is: interface 2
[edit]
  warning: lo0 description is:
[edit]
  warning: fxp0 description is:
configuration check succeeds
```

You wouldn't normally use this method to access XML nodes in the current hierarchy. Instead, you would just reference the node directly. In the preceding example, `$current/name` is equivalent to `name`. Normally, you would just use the simpler `name` expression. However, assigning the current node to the variable `$current` served as a good (albeit contrived) example of assigning an XML hierarchy to a variable.

Also, note that variable assignments can use a code block to assign the variable value. For example, this code block assigns the value `test` to the `$test` variable:

```
var $test = {
    expr "t";
    expr "e";
    expr "s";
    expr "t";
}
```

XML Result Tree Fragments

This is probably as good a place as any to talk about XML result tree fragments and node sets. In short, result tree fragments: bad; node sets: good.

When you work with XML data in XSLT and SLAX, you are usually working with node sets. You can use XPath expressions to select data from these node sets.

However, when you create XML nodes in XSLT and SLAX, but don't immediately emit them as output, they become "result tree fragments." Typically, this occurs when you assign an XML fragment to a variable, or pass it as a parameter to a template or function. It is fine for something to be a result tree fragment if you don't need to process the XML in the result tree fragment.

However, result tree fragments are bad when you actually do need to process the XML data they contain. This can be challenging because you can't use XPath expressions on a fragment.

Consider this simple example. Imagine that a template called `current-time()` returns the current Unix timestamp in this simple XML format:

```
<time>
    <seconds>12345689</seconds>
</time>
```

To use this result tree fragment, you must access the value of the `<seconds>` node. So, you try this SLAX code:

```
var $time-raw = {
    call current-time();
}
var $time = $time-raw/time/seconds;
```

However, when you run a script with this code, you see an error pointing to the second line. Why? The error occurs because `$time-raw` is a result tree fragment, and you can't use the / selector on a result tree fragment.

Thankfully, there is an easy way to convert result tree fragments to the more familiar XML node sets, where you can use the full range of XPath selectors. In SLAX, you can use the := operator to perform the node set conversion.

Using the := operator, our example works much better:

```
var $time-raw := {
    call current-time();
}
var $time = $time-raw/time/seconds;
```

You also regularly hit this problem with XML that your script produces while initializing variables. This example creates a result tree fragment:

```
var $example = {
    <foo> {
        <bar> "baz";
    }
}
```

Of course, a result tree fragment is good enough as long as you don't need to process the data within the variable. However, if you do need to process the data, this example creates a node set instead of a result tree fragment:

```
var $example := {
    <foo> {
        <bar> "baz";
    }
}
```

Mutable variables. SLAX has an extension over XSLT variables: mutable variables. If you declare a variable with `mvar` instead of `var`, the SLAX processing engine allows you to change the variable's value using the `set` statement.

Additionally, you can append XML node sets using the special `append` statement, such as in this example:

```
mvar $rv = <output> "foo";
append $rv += <output> "bar";
set $rv = <output> "foo";
append $rv += <output> "baz";
```

At the end of all of this, `$rv` is set to:

```
<output>foo</output>
<output>baz</output>
```

Templates

There are two kinds of templates in XSLT and SLAX: *named templates* and *match templates*. The boilerplate template shown in Example 5-4 contains a match template that will be executed when the parser encounters an element with the `<configuration>` tag.

Named templates have names, they can accept arguments, and they are only executed when you call them using the `call` SLAX statement. By contrast, match templates take an XPath expression, and they are automatically executed for each matching XML element in the input document. Match templates do not have names and they do not accept arguments. However, when SLAX executes a match template, it automatically moves the current XML node (the "dot" location) to the matching node. (Recall the significance of the "dot" location from our discussion of XPath expressions in "XML data" on page 270. In XPath expressions, you specify XML nodes relative to the "dot" location.) Named templates leave the current XML node unchanged.

In this sense, the `match configuration` template in the boilerplate template is really only an *example* template. You can have many different templates that only match the specific pieces of the input document in which you are interested. Depending on your mindset, this may be an easier way to write your code. On the other hand, you may prefer the concept of a single `main()` function. In that case, you can stick with the `match configuration` template. As explained in "Overview of a SLAX Script" on page 262, this template only matches the root of the configuration; therefore, it is always executed once, and only once.

Defining match templates

Match templates are one of the fundamental control-flow constructs within SLAX. They operate similarly to a `for-each` loop, but with different syntax (and slightly different behavior). By the end of this section, you should understand why match templates are powerful.

You define match templates by specifying an XPath expression. When the SLAX processor finds a matching XML hierarchy in the input document, it executes the match template against that XML hierarchy. For example, `match configuration` matches any XML `<configuration>` node.

As the SLAX parser processes the XML hierarchy, beginning at the root and descending to all the leaf nodes, it looks for matching templates. Once it finds a matching template, it executes the matching template for that node and ceases further processing on the node. Importantly, once a node matches a template, children of that node are not checked for any match templates. This behavior implements a "most-general-template" match criterion.

The SLAX processor only applies a single match template to a given node. Therefore, even if there are multiple match templates that match a given node, the processor only executes one of the templates. (At this point, you might be tempted to wonder about the precedence; however, our advice is to simply avoid the situation where precedence matters.)

Because all match templates are checked against all nodes (until a match is found for a node), you have slightly more flexibility in writing the XPath expressions that define the match templates. Due to this behavior, the match template's XPath expression typically only needs to match the righthand side of a node's path.

Consider the interface matched by the XPath expression `configuration/interfaces/interface[name="ge-1/0/0"]`. You could use any of the following match template definitions to match the same node:

- `match configuration/interfaces/interface[name="ge-1/0/0"]`
- `match interfaces/interface[name="ge-1/0/0"]`
- `match interface[name="ge-1/0/0"]`

However, you need to be aware of possible collateral damage from underspecifying an XPath expression. For example, the last match template in the previous listing also matches `[edit snmp interface ge-1/0/0]`, and possibly others.

On the other hand, there are times you can use this behavior to your advantage. For example, specifying `match interfaces/interface[name="ge-1/0/0"]` is helpful if you want to match any interface configuration in both the main logical system and also child logical systems.

Finally, keep in mind where we are: we are talking about match templates. Just as in Python and other languages, there are many ways to arrive at the same end. Match templates are just one way to operate on a specific node. You also have the option of merely matching on the `<configuration>` tag and then using conditionals, `for-each` loops, and other SLAX operations to operate on specific nodes.

There is a way to override the "most-general-template" match criterion discussed in this section. Specifying `apply-templates` *`XPath`* inside a more general template indicates the SLAX processor should try to apply additional match templates to any node matching the XPath expression. Alternatively, entering `apply-templates` without an XPath expression causes the SLAX processor to try to apply further match templates against all children of the current XML node.

Whether or not you specify an XPath expression, the `apply-templates` statement causes the SLAX processor to follow the normal match template process. The SLAX processor will begin with the selected nodes and descend to all the leaf nodes until it finds a matching template. And, once it finds a matching template, it will execute the matching template and cease further processing on that node.

For example, this syntax causes the SLAX processor to execute the contents of the `match interfaces` template and continue checking for other match templates that match the XML node's children. Therefore, the SLAX processor executes the `match interfaces` template against the `[edit interfaces]` hierarchy, and also executes the `match interfaces/interface` template against each `[edit interfaces interface` *`interface`*`]` hierarchy:

```
match interfaces {
    /* Do something. */
    apply-templates;
}
match interfaces/interface {
    /* Do something else. */
}
```

Defining and calling named templates

By contrast to match templates, named templates are quite easy to understand because they more easily map to concepts from other programming languages. You define named templates with a `template` statement; however, named templates are only executed when another template contains a `call` statement. The current XML node (the "dot" location) is inherited from the calling template.

Named Templates Versus Functions

SLAX has the concepts of both named templates and functions. While named templates may remind you of functions in other languages, the concepts of named templates and functions are distinct from each other in SLAX.

Named templates are written in the SLAX or XSLT language, and are called using the `call` statement. They can only be used in a context where you can use the `call` statement. For example, XPath expressions cannot contain `call` statements.

Functions are usually written in a compiled language (such as C) and appear in libraries. You can call functions in more contexts than named templates.

For example, because variable assignments take XPath expressions, you cannot call a template in the XPath expression. However, you can use a function call in the XPath expression:

```
var $some-variable = must-be-a-function(name);
```

If you want to call a template to produce a variable's value, you must instead create a code block to create the variable assignment and call the template inside the code block:

```
var $some-variable = {
    call some-template();
}
```

You include the output of templates in your document by using the `call` statement. If you want to call a function in a code block and insert the function's output in your document, you instead use the `expr` statement, like this:

```
<output> {
    expr jcs:printf("Template results:");
}
```

Some functions return nothing, but perform important actions. An example of a function that returns nothing is `jcs:syslog()`, which logs a message to syslog, but returns no value. In this case, you can still use the `expr` statement to call this function; however, because the function returns no value, it will not modify the output document. For example:

```
<output> {
    if ($something-bad-happened) {
        expr jcs:syslog("Something bad happened!");
    }
}
```

In the `jcs` namespace, Juniper provides a number of extension functions and some predefined templates. The documentation distinguishes between the templates and functions. Because you call templates and functions differently, it is important that you pay attention to this distinction.

The syntax to define a named template is similar to the syntax to define a method in Python. You use the `template` statement, provide a template name, and then provide a list of parameters. Like in Python, the parameters can optionally have default values.

Here is an example of a named template that produces a warning:

```
template emit-warning($message) {
    <xnm:warning> {
        call jcs:edit-path();
        <message> $message;
    }
}
```

This template is named `emit-warning()`. It takes a single parameter, `$message`, which must be provided at the time the template is called.

We can add a default value to the `$message` parameter using syntax similar to Python. In Example 5-5, we use the text `(none)` as the default value for the `$message` parameter.

Example 5-5. The emit-warning() template

```
template emit-warning($message="(none)") {
    <xnm:warning> {
        call jcs:edit-path();
        <message> $message;
    }
}
```

To call named templates, you use the `call` statement. Here is an example that calls the `emit-warning()` template with the message of `test`:

```
call emit-warning($message="test");
```

Alternatively, you can use the `with` statement to provide longer parameters, or parameters with complex syntax. Using the `with` statement, you can use curly braces to define logic that the SLAX processor uses to build the parameter values that are passed to a template.

Here is an extraordinarily simple example of the `with` statement:

```
call emit-warning {
    with $message = "test";
}
```

Here is an example of a more complex use of the `with` statement:

```
call do-something {
    with $xml-frag = {
        <root> {
            <leaf>;
        }
    }
    with $data = {
        call another-template();
    }
}
```

Template results

Templates return XML fragments. By default, the XML fragments are output at the point of the `call` or `apply-templates` statement. When one template calls another, the called template's output may become part of the calling template's return document.

In this example, the match template matches each interface in the main configuration. It then calls the `print-descr()` template. The output of the `print-descr()` template is placed right where the `call` statement appears. In other words, it forms part of the XML emitted by the `match configuration/interfaces/interface` template.

Similarly, the `print-descr()` template calls the `emit-warning()` template shown in Example 5-5. The output of the `emit-warning()` template is placed where the `call` statement appears. In other words, it forms part of the XML returned by the `print-descr()` template:

```
template print-descr() {
    call emit-warning {
        with $message = {
            expr "Interface " _ name _ ": ";
            if (description) {
                expr description;
            }
            else {
                expr "(no description)";
            }
        }
    }
}

match configuration/interfaces/interface {
    call print-descr();
}
```

After running this script, you will see a return document like this:

```
<xnm:warning>
    <edit-path>[edit interfaces interface ge-1/0/0]</edit-path>
    <message>Interface ge-1/0/0: interface 1</message>
</xnm:warning>
<xnm:warning>
    <edit-path>[edit interfaces interface ge-1/0/1]</edit-path>
    <message>Interface ge-1/0/1: interface 2</message>
</xnm:warning>
<xnm:warning>
    <edit-path>[edit interfaces interface lo0]</edit-path>
    <message>Interface lo0: (no description)</message>
</xnm:warning>
<xnm:warning>
    <edit-path>[edit interfaces interface fxp0]</edit-path>
    <message>Interface fxp0: (no description)</message>
</xnm:warning>
```

And, if you invoke this as a commit script, you'll see output like this:

```
[edit]
user@r0# commit check
[edit interfaces interface ge-1/0/0]
  warning: Interface ge-1/0/0: interface 1
[edit interfaces interface ge-1/0/1]
  warning: Interface ge-1/0/1: interface 2
[edit interfaces interface lo0]
  warning: Interface lo0: (no description)
[edit interfaces interface fxp0]
  warning: Interface fxp0: (no description)
configuration check succeeds
```

You can also use template results in other ways, such as assigning them to variables in your code. Take, for example, this reformulation of the preceding script. Here, the `print-descr()` template calls the `get-message()` template to create the `$message` argument to the `emit-warning()` template. Because the result of the `get-message()` template is placed right where the `call` statement appears, the result becomes the contents of the `$message` argument:

```
template get-message() {
    expr "Interface " _ name _ ": ";
    if (description) {
        expr description;
    }
    else {
        expr "(no description)";
    }
}

template print-descr() {
    call emit-warning {
```

```
            with $message = {
                call get-message();
            }
        }
    }

    match configuration/interfaces/interface {
        call print-descr();
    }
```

Flow Control

As you have seen in previous examples, SLAX offers normal flow control statements, such as `for` loops and `if/else` statements. Obviously, these statements are very useful in controlling the logic of a script.

for-each loops over XML nodes

You can loop over XML nodes that match an XPath expression using the `for-each` statement. The SLAX processor finds matching XML nodes and changes the current node (the "dot" location) to each matching node in turn. You can then perform actions on each matching node.

So, let's reformulate the repetitive interface description printing examples to use the `for-each` statement. Here, we match on the `<configuration>` node, and then use a `for-each` statement to loop through all interfaces and print their descriptions. This example uses the `emit-warning()` template we showed in Example 5-5:

```
    match configuration {
        for-each (interfaces/interface) {
            call emit-warning {
                with $message = {
                    expr "Interface " _ name _ ": " _ description;
                }
            }
        }
    }
```

When called as a commit script, this again produces the expected results:

```
    [edit]
    user@r0# commit check
    [edit interfaces interface ge-1/0/0]
      warning: Interface ge-1/0/0: interface 1
    [edit interfaces interface ge-1/0/1]
      warning: Interface ge-1/0/1: interface 2
    [edit interfaces interface lo0]
      warning: Interface lo0:
    [edit interfaces interface fxp0]
      warning: Interface fxp0:
    configuration check succeeds
```

for loops over number ranges

Sometimes, you want to loop over a range of numbers. For example, this code creates 10 units (logical interfaces) on the `ge-1/0/0` physical interface:

```
match configuration/interfaces/interface[name = "ge-1/0/0"] {
    call jcs:emit-change {
        with $content = {
            for $i (1 ... 10) {
                <unit> {
                    <name> $i;
                    <vlan-id> $i;
                    <family> {
                        <inet> {
                            <address> {
                                <name> "10.10." _ $i _ ".1/24";
                            }
                        }
                    }
                }
            }
        }
    }
}
```

After running this commit script, 10 units are added to the configuration:

```
[edit]
user@r0# commit
commit complete

[edit]
user@r0# show | compare rollback 1
[edit interfaces ge-1/0/0]
+    unit 1 {
+        vlan-id 1;
+        family inet {
+            address 10.10.1.1/24;
+        }
+    }
+    unit 2 {
+        vlan-id 2;
+        family inet {
+            address 10.10.2.1/24;
+        }
+    }
+    unit 3 {
+        vlan-id 3;
+        family inet {
+            address 10.10.3.1/24;
+        }
+    }
+    unit 4 {
```

```
+         vlan-id 4;
+         family inet {
+             address 10.10.4.1/24;
+         }
+     }
+     unit 5 {
+         vlan-id 5;
+         family inet {
+             address 10.10.5.1/24;
+         }
+     }
+     unit 6 {
+         vlan-id 6;
+         family inet {
+             address 10.10.6.1/24;
+         }
+     }
+     unit 7 {
+         vlan-id 7;
+         family inet {
+             address 10.10.7.1/24;
+         }
+     }
+     unit 8 {
+         vlan-id 8;
+         family inet {
+             address 10.10.8.1/24;
+         }
+     }
+     unit 9 {
+         vlan-id 9;
+         family inet {
+             address 10.10.9.1/24;
+         }
+     }
+     unit 10 {
+         vlan-id 10;
+         family inet {
+             address 10.10.10.1/24;
+         }
+     }
```

if/else statements

You can use `if/else` statements to control the flow of your program. The `if` statement's test conditions are XPath expressions (with added support for the `&&`, `||`, and `!` logical operators). Some XPath expressions (such as `starts-with()`) return Boolean values. Other XPath expressions are generally "true" if they match one or more nodes, and "false" if they match zero nodes.

Let's write a quick script to configure a description on any interface that does not already have a description. Here, we choose to use a match template that matches all interfaces, and then use an `if` statement to match the interfaces with no description. And, just to demonstrate the use of the `else` statement, we print a warning message if there already is a description:

```
match configuration/interfaces/interface {
    if (!description) {
        call jcs:emit-change {
            with $content = {
                <description> "Automatically configured description";
            }
        }
    }
    else {
        call emit-warning($message = "Already had a description");
    }
}
```

When executed, this script prints a warning for the interfaces that already had descriptions, and adds a description to any that need one:

```
[edit]
user@r0# commit
[edit interfaces interface ge-1/0/0]
  warning: Already had a description
[edit interfaces interface ge-1/0/1]
  warning: Already had a description
commit complete

[edit]
user@r0# show | compare rollback 1
[edit interfaces fxp0]
+   description "Automatically configured description";
[edit interfaces lo0]
+   description "Automatically configured description";
```

SLAX also supports the `else if` construction. You can string a list of conditionals together with `else if` statements. The list is optionally terminated with a single `else` statement. The software executes the first conditional that evaluates to true.

For example, this script takes different actions depending on the kind of interface it is evaluating:

```
match configuration/interfaces/interface {
    if (starts-with(name, "fe-") || starts-with(name, "ge-") ||
        starts-with(name, "xe-")) {
        /* Add VLAN tagging. */
        call jcs:emit-change {
            with $content = {
                <vlan-tagging>;
            }
```

```
            }
        }
        else if (name == "lo0") {
            /* Add MPLS. */
            call jcs:emit-change {
                with $content = {
                    <unit> {
                        <name> 0;
                        <family> {
                            <mpls>;
                        }
                    }
                }
            }
        }
        else if (name == "fxp0") {
            /* Warn if unit 0 does not have an IPv4 address. */
            if (!unit[name == "0"]/family/inet/address) {
                call emit-warning($message="No IPv4 address configured");
            }
        }
    }
```

When run as a commit script, it takes appropriate actions:

```
[edit]
user@r0# commit
commit complete

[edit]
user@r0# show | compare rollback 1
[edit interfaces ge-1/0/1]
+   vlan-tagging;
[edit interfaces lo0 unit 0]
+      family mpls;
```

Predefined Templates

Juniper provides access to several predefined templates you may find helpful.

jcs:emit-change()

This template creates changes to the Junos configuration. It has several options to cover a variety of situations.

It accepts the following arguments:

`$content`
: This argument is the XML representation of the configuration change. The configuration change is *relative* to the current node. For example, if the current node

is [edit protocols bgp], you could simply add a BGP group without specifying the <protocols> and <bgp> hierarchies.

This is the only required argument.

$tag
: This argument controls whether the change is a transient change or a permanent change. The default value is change, which indicates this is a permanent change. Alternatively, you can specify transient-change to make this a transient change.

$message
: This argument specifies a warning message the template displays to the user. By default, the template displays no warning message.

$dot
: This argument changes the current node for the purposes of this template. The $content argument is evaluated relative to the new current node. This argument also changes the [edit] path of any message displayed to the user.

  For example, assume the current node is configuration/protocols/bgp (corresponding to the [edit protocols bgp] configuration hierarchy), but you want to make a change to the [edit routing-options] hierarchy. You can specify a $dot argument of ../../routing-options. Including this argument causes the $content argument to be evaluated relative to the [edit routing-options] hierarchy.

  The $dot argument must point to a node that already exists. You cannot use the $dot argument to "wish" a node into existence. Instead, if you need to create a new node, you can use the $dot argument to choose a higher level of hierarchy that already exists and use the $content argument to create the new hierarchy you want to add under that higher level.

  By default, the value of the $dot argument is the current node at the time the template is called.

$name
: Some Juniper documentation lists the $name argument. However, you should not use this argument. It appears that the main purpose of the argument is to support recursive calls to the jcs:emit-change() template.

The jcs:emit-change() template is fairly easy to use. This example sets a description on an interface and warns a user about the action:

```
match configuration/interfaces/interface[not(description)] {
    call jcs:emit-change {
        with $message = "Setting default description";
        with $content = {
```

```
                <description> "Automatically configured description";
            }
        }
    }
```

When executed, the output looks like this:

```
[edit]
user@r0# commit
[edit interfaces interface fxp0]
  warning: Setting default description
commit complete

[edit]
user@r0# show | compare rollback 1
[edit interfaces fxp0]
+   description "Automatically configured description";
```

jcs:edit-path()

This template creates an appropriate `[edit]` path to a configuration hierarchy. The template is useful in creating warning and error messages.

However, rather than calling this template directly, we suggest you simply create appropriate templates to emit warning or error messages for you. For example, the `emit-warning()` template from Example 5-5 generates a suitable warning. The `emit-warning()` template calls the `jcs:edit-path()` template to display the current node.

Like the `jcs:emit-change()` template, this template accepts an optional `$dot` parameter, which points to an alternate node to use as the current location.

Commit Script Examples

Now that you have some background about basic commit script operations and SLAX, let's implement the examples from our introductory use cases. These examples demonstrate how to use commit scripts to meet specific configuration needs. You can use the same concepts to solve the configuration needs of your network.

Example: Custom Configuration Checks

Let's begin with the use case in "Custom Configuration Checks" on page 249. This use case checks the BGP configuration. We can distill the requirements to:

- Only three BGP groups are allowed: `internal`, `peers`, and `customers`.
- All BGP neighbors in the `peers` and `customers` groups must have both import and export policies applied.

- For BGP neighbors in the `peers` and `customers` groups, the `deny-all` policy must be the last policy in each import and export policy chain.

We can combine these three checks into fairly succinct logic. But let's start with the first requirement: only three BGP groups are allowed.

We could either create a match template for `configuration/protocols/bgp/group` or create a match template for `configuration` and use the `for-each` statement to loop over all BGP groups. The difference is somewhat stylistic. The logic within the `for-each` loop would be the same as the logic within a match template that matched on `configuration/protocols/bgp/group`. Here, we use a match template that matches on `configuration/protocols/bgp/group`.

Within the match template, we simply use an `if` statement to ensure the group has an appropriate name:

```
match configuration/protocols/bgp/group {
    if (name == "internal" || name == "peers" || name == "customers") {
        /* This is acceptable. */
    }
    else {
        /* This is NOT acceptable. */
    }
}
```

Now that we have the logic to detect an error, we need to define the action to take when this error occurs. Because we could end up with a variety of errors, let's write a named template to report errors. We want to let the user specify a message and an alternate node to use when emitting the `[edit]` path for the error message.

Also, just to demonstrate the concept, we send an error message to the user (aborting the commit) and also send a message to the device's syslog.

This template meets the requirements:

```
template emit-error($message, $dot=.) {
    /* Get the [edit] path. */
    var $path = {
        call jcs:edit-path($dot=$dot);
    }

    /* Emit the error. */
    <xnm:error> {
        expr $path;
        <message> $message;
    }

    /* Log the syslog message. */
    <syslog> {
        <message> jcs:printf("%s: %s", $path/edit-path, $message);
```

```
        }
    }
```

The code is fairly obvious, except for, perhaps, one important detail. The `jcs:edit-path()` template returns the `[edit]` path (e.g., `[edit protocols bgp]`) within an XML fragment suitable for using in the `<xnm:warning>` or `<xnm:error>` tags. This means the text of the `[edit]` path is contained in an `<edit-path>` element. This is the appropriate formatting for use within the `<xnm:error>` tag. However, when you want to use only the text of the `<edit-path>` tag in a syslog message, you must access the content of the `<edit-path>` tag. The `$path/edit-path` XPath expression returns the value of the matching node. It is used as one of the arguments in the `jcs:printf()` function call.

Now, we modify the match template to call the `emit-error()` template:

```
match configuration/protocols/bgp/group {
    if (name == "internal" || name == "peers" || name == "customers") {
        /* This is acceptable. */
    }
    else {
        call emit-error($message=jcs:printf("Group %s is not allowed", name));
    }
}
```

Let's test what we have so far and see how it works. When we have a valid configuration, it appears to work correctly:

```
[edit]
user@r0# show protocols bgp
group internal {
    neighbor 10.1.1.4 {
        peer-as 655532;
    }
}
group peers {
    neighbor 10.2.2.4 {
        peer-as 65533;
    }
}
group customers {
    neighbor 10.3.3.4 {
        peer-as 65534;
    }
}

[edit]
user@r0# commit check
configuration check succeeds
```

However, once we hit one of the error conditions, we see some strange errors:

```
[edit]
user@r0# rename protocols bgp group customers to group other

[edit]
user@r0# commit check
error: Invalid type
error: xmlXPathCompOpEval: parameter error
error: xmlXPathCompiledEval: 1 objects left on the stack.
error: runtime error: file /var/db/scripts/commit/test.slax line 23
element value-of
error: XPath evaluation returned no result.
error: Group other is not allowed
error: 6 errors reported by commit scripts
error: commit script failure
```

Notice the error messages point to line 23 of the script. Line 23 is the `jcs:printf()` call in the `emit-error()` template:

```
/* Log the syslog message. */
<syslog> {
    <message> jcs:printf("%s: %s", $path/edit-path, $message);
}
```

The problem is that the `$path` variable is a result tree fragment. As we noted in "XML Result Tree Fragments" on page 273, you can't just create a result tree fragment and then access its contents using an XPath expression. Instead, you must convert the result tree fragment to a node set using the := SLAX operator. (How did we know this was the cause of the error message? It was a good guess based on experience. And, now that you've read this book, you can make the same guess when you see similar errors in your own scripts.)

This simple change to the script helps a great deal:

```
/* Get the [edit] path. */
var $path := {
    call jcs:edit-path($dot=$dot);
}
```

With the change made, let's execute the script again:

```
[edit]
user@r0# commit check
error: Group other is not allowed
error: 1 error reported by commit scripts
error: commit script failure
```

This output seems odd. It does contain our error message, but where is our `[edit]` path? To troubleshoot further, look at the XML response:

```
[edit]
user@r0# commit check | display xml
```

```
<rpc-reply xmlns:junos="http://xml.juniper.net/junos/15.2D0/junos">
    <commit-results>
        <routing-engine junos:style="normal">
            <name>re0</name>
            <xnm:error xmlns:xnm="http://xml.juniper.net/xnm/1.1/xnm">
                [edit protocols bgp group other]
                <message>
                    Group other is not allowed
                </message>
            </xnm:error>
        </routing-engine>
        <xnm:error xmlns="http://xml.juniper.net/xnm/1.1/xnm"
                   xmlns:xnm="http://xml.juniper.net/xnm/1.1/xnm">
            <message>
                1 error reported by commit scripts
            </message>
        </xnm:error>
        <xnm:error xmlns="http://xml.juniper.net/xnm/1.1/xnm"
                   xmlns:xnm="http://xml.juniper.net/xnm/1.1/xnm">
            <message>
                commit script failure
            </message>
        </xnm:error>
    </commit-results>
    <cli>
        <banner>[edit]</banner>
    </cli>
</rpc-reply>
```

That output seems quite strange. The path (`[edit protocols bgp group other]`) appears in the `<xnm:error>` element, but it is not enclosed in `<edit-path>` tags, as expected. Looking at our code more closely, we see the problem. We used the `expr` statement:

```
/* Emit the error. */
<xnm:error> {
    expr $path;
    <message> $message;
}
```

The `expr` statement tells SLAX to insert the *value* of an expression. In this case, `$path` is an XML node set. Therefore, SLAX should insert the node set here, right? Not exactly. Instead, an `expr` statement causes SLAX to insert the CDATA elements (basically, the text values, but none of the tags) from an XML node set. That is why we saw the path in the XML output, but we didn't see the XML tags we expected.

Because we actually want to output a copy of the node tree here (including the XML tags, attributes, etc.), we can use the `copy-of` statement instead of the `expr` statement. (Recall that all variables in SLAX need to be used in some context. You can use variables as arguments to functions or templates, or with a statement to tell the SLAX processor how to use them. If you simply want to output a variable, the `expr` or `copy-of` statements usually will let you accomplish your task, with the slight difference demonstrated here.)

When we make the change from using the `expr` statement to using the `copy-of` statement, things work much better:

```
[edit]
user@r0# commit check
[edit protocols bgp group other]
  Group other is not allowed
error: 1 error reported by commit scripts
error: commit script failure
```

Here is our full script so far:

```
version 1.1;

ns junos = "http://xml.juniper.net/junos/*/junos";
ns xnm = "http://xml.juniper.net/xnm/1.1/xnm";
ns jcs = "http://xml.juniper.net/junos/commit-scripts/1.0";

import "../import/junos.xsl";

template emit-error($message, $dot=.) {
    /* Get the [edit] path. */
    var $path := {
        call jcs:edit-path($dot=$dot);
    }

    /* Emit the error. */
    <xnm:error> {
        copy-of $path;
        <message> $message;
    }

    /* Log the syslog message. */
    <syslog> {
        <message> jcs:printf("%s: %s", $path/edit-path, $message);
    }
}

match configuration/protocols/bgp/group {
    if (name == "internal" || name == "peers" || name == "customers") {
        /* This is acceptable. */
    }
    else {
        call emit-error($message=jcs:printf("Group %s is not allowed", name));
    }
}
```

Let's move on to the next requirement: all BGP neighbors in the `peers` and `customers` groups must have both import and export policies applied. This requirement is somewhat ambiguous. Does it require each neighbor have *its own* import and export policy applied to it at the neighbor level? Or does it merely require that each neighbor have *some* import and export policy applied, even if it is inherited from the group or global BGP configuration? In this case, we assume the latter interpretation: each neighbor must have *some* import and export policy applied, even if it is inherited from the group or global BGP configuration.

We'll integrate this check with our existing logic. First, split the `if` statement into two parts: one accepts the `peers` and `customers` groups, and another accepts the `internal` group. Next, add the per-neighbor check into the block that accepts the `peers` and `customers` groups:

```
match configuration/protocols/bgp/group {
    if (name == "internal") {
        /* This is acceptable. */
    }
    else if (name == "peers" || name == "customers") {
        /* This is acceptable. */
        for-each (neighbor) {
            /* Check each neighbor's policies. */
        }
    }
    else {
        call emit-error($message=jcs:printf("Group %s is not allowed", name));
    }
}
```

Now, how do we implement the policy check? Because the logic for checking import and export policies is the same, we write a template that our script can call twice: once for import policies and once for export policies. This template does the trick:

```
template check-neighbor-policies($type) {
    /*
     * Make sure the type of policy exists at either the
     * current (neighbor), parent (group), or parent's parent
     * (BGP global) level.
     */
    if (not(*[name() == $type] || ../*[name() == $type] ||
            ../../*[name() == $type])) {
        call emit-error($message=$type _ " policy required, but not defined");
    }
}
```

This template is called with a `$type` argument of either `import` or `export` (the names of the tags used for import and export policies, respectively). Recall that we will run this template with the current node set to a BGP neighbor. The logic looks for any child of the current node with a tag name equal to the `$type` argument, any child of the parent's node with a tag name equal to the `$type` argument, and any child of the grandparent's node with a tag name equal to the `$type` argument. If none of these nodes exist, there is no policy of that type applied to the neighbor. In that case, the script returns an error message. (The script includes the `$type` argument in the error message to explain which type of policy is missing.)

We add calls to the `check-neighbor-policies()` template from the neighbor loop. Once we do that, the script looks like this:

```
version 1.1;

ns junos = "http://xml.juniper.net/junos/*/junos";
ns xnm = "http://xml.juniper.net/xnm/1.1/xnm";
ns jcs = "http://xml.juniper.net/junos/commit-scripts/1.0";

import "../import/junos.xsl";

template emit-error($message, $dot=.) {
    /* Get the [edit] path. */
    var $path := {
        call jcs:edit-path($dot=$dot);
    }

    /* Emit the error. */
    <xnm:error> {
        copy-of $path;
        <message> $message;
    }

    /* Log the syslog message. */
    <syslog> {
        <message> jcs:printf("%s: %s", $path/edit-path, $message);
    }
}

template check-neighbor-policies($type) {
    /*
     * Make sure the type of policy exists at either the
     * current (neighbor), parent (group), or parent's parent
     * (BGP global) level.
     */
    if (not(*[name() == $type] || ../*[name() == $type] ||
            ../../*[name() == $type])) {
        call emit-error($message=$type _ " policy required, but not defined");
    }
}

match configuration/protocols/bgp/group {
    if (name == "internal") {
        /* This is acceptable. */
    }
```

```
        else if (name == "peers" || name == "customers") {
            /* This is acceptable. */
            for-each (neighbor) {
                /* Check each neighbor's policies. */
                call check-neighbor-policies($type="import");
                call check-neighbor-policies($type="export");
            }
        }
        else {
            call emit-error($message=jcs:printf("Group %s is not allowed", name));
        }
    }
```

When the script is run, you will immediately see that it reports the missing policies:

```
[edit]
user@r0# show protocols bgp
group internal {
    neighbor 10.1.1.4 {
        peer-as 655532;
    }
}
group peers {
    neighbor 10.2.2.4 {
        peer-as 65533;
    }
}
group customers {
    neighbor 10.3.3.4 {
        peer-as 65534;
    }
}

[edit]
user@r0# commit check
[edit protocols bgp group peers neighbor 10.2.2.4]
  import policy required, but not defined
[edit protocols bgp group peers neighbor 10.2.2.4]
  export policy required, but not defined
[edit protocols bgp group customers neighbor 10.3.3.4]
  import policy required, but not defined
[edit protocols bgp group customers neighbor 10.3.3.4]
  export policy required, but not defined
error: 4 errors reported by commit scripts
error: commit script failure
```

After defining export policies at the group level and import policies at the neighbor level, the configuration commits successfully:

```
[edit]
user@r0# show protocols bgp
group internal {
    neighbor 10.1.1.4 {
```

```
            peer-as 655532;
        }
    }
    group peers {
        export [ customer-routes deny-all ];
        neighbor 10.2.2.4 {
            import [ AS_65534_routes deny-all ];
            peer-as 65533;
        }
    }
    group customers {
        export [ customer-routes peer-routes transit-routes deny-all ];
        neighbor 10.3.3.4 {
            import AS_65535_routes;
            peer-as 65534;
        }
    }

[edit]
user@r0# commit check
configuration check succeeds
```

Finally, let's move on to the last requirement. This requirement specifies the `deny-all` policy must be the final policy in the policy chains for all peers in the `peers` and `customers` groups. In order to enforce this requirement, we need to first determine which policy applies to a peer: the one configured at the neighbor level, the one configured at the group level, or the one configured at the global BGP configuration level. Then, we need to select the last policy from the list.

At this point, it is helpful to ensure we understand the structure of the XML we are evaluating. Let's take a look at the way an example policy chain is represented in XML:

```
[edit]
user@r0# show protocols bgp group peers neighbor 10.2.2.4
import [ AS_65534_routes deny-all ];
peer-as 65533;

[edit]
user@r0# show protocols bgp group peers neighbor 10.2.2.4 | display xml
<rpc-reply xmlns:junos="http://xml.juniper.net/junos/15.2D0/junos">
    <configuration junos:changed-seconds="1443558469"
                   junos:changed-localtime="2015-09-29 13:27:49 PDT">
        <protocols>
            <bgp>
                <group>
                    <name>peers</name>
                    <neighbor>
                        <name>10.2.2.4</name>
                        <import>AS_65534_routes</import>
                        <import>deny-all</import>
```

```
                    <peer-as>65533</peer-as>
                </neighbor>
            </group>
        </bgp>
    </protocols>
</configuration>
<cli>
    <banner>[edit]</banner>
</cli>
</rpc-reply>
```

Note the way import policies are listed: each one is in an <import> node, and the nodes are listed in order. We can use the XPath `last()` function to select the last node.

We reformulate the `check-neighbor-policies()` template to handle these extra checks:

```
template check-neighbor-policies($type) {
    /*
     * For the type of policy, determine whether the policy
     * chain is at the current (neighbor), parent (group), or
     * parent's parent (BGP global) level.
     *
     * Then, determine the last policy in the policy chain at
     * that level.
     */
    var $last-policy = { ❶
        if (*[name() == $type]) {
            expr *[name() == $type][last()]; ❷
        }
        else if (../*[name() == $type]) {
            expr ../*[name() == $type][last()];
        }
        else { ❸
            expr ../../*[name() == $type][last()];
        }
    }
    if ($last-policy == "") { ❹
        call emit-error($message=$type _ " policy required, but not defined");
    }
    else if ($last-policy != "deny-all") { ❺
        call emit-error {
            with $message = {
                expr jcs:printf("%s policy error: last policy should be " _
                                "'deny-all', but found '%s' instead",
                                $type, $last-policy);
            }
        }
    }
}
```

❶ Here, we use one of the SLAX tricks of making the contents of a variable depend on a conditional. We have broken the previous conditional into three parts, which we use to determine the level of the hierarchy where the policy exists.

❷ Once we have determined which policy chain we will use, we select the set of nodes with matching names using `*[name() == $type]`. We then select the last node of that set using the `[last()]` selector.

❸ The `else` statement performs correctly here even if there is no policy chain at the global BGP level. At this point in the code, either there is a policy chain at the global BGP level or there is no matching policy chain for this neighbor. Either way, we can try to select the policy chain from the global BGP level. If there is no policy chain defined at the global level, the variable will end up being empty.

❹ Here, we check if the `$last-policy` variable is empty. If it is, the code raises an error indicating no import or export policy is applied to this peer.

❺ If the value of the `$last-policy` variable is not `deny-all`, the code raises an error explaining the problem.

Finally, we have our complete script:

```
version 1.1;

ns junos = "http://xml.juniper.net/junos/*/junos";
ns xnm = "http://xml.juniper.net/xnm/1.1/xnm";
ns jcs = "http://xml.juniper.net/junos/commit-scripts/1.0";

import "../import/junos.xsl";

template emit-error($message, $dot=.) {
    /* Get the [edit] path. */
    var $path := {
        call jcs:edit-path($dot=$dot);
    }

    /* Emit the error. */
    <xnm:error> {
        copy-of $path;
        <message> $message;
    }

    /* Log the syslog message. */
    <syslog> {
        <message> jcs:printf("%s: %s", $path/edit-path, $message);
    }
}
```

```
template check-neighbor-policies($type) {
    /*
     * For the type of policy, determine whether the policy
     * chain is at the current (neighbor), parent (group), or
     * parent's parent (BGP global) level.
     *
     * Then, determine the last policy in the policy chain at
     * that level.
     */
    var $last-policy = {
        if (*[name() == $type]) {
            expr *[name() == $type][last()];
        }
        else if (../*[name() == $type]) {
            expr ../*[name() == $type][last()];
        }
        else {
            expr ../../*[name() == $type][last()];
        }
    }
    if ($last-policy == "") {
        call emit-error($message=$type _ " policy required, but not defined");
    }
    else if ($last-policy != "deny-all") {
        call emit-error {
            with $message = {
                expr jcs:printf("%s policy error: last policy should be " _
                                "'deny-all', but found '%s' instead",
                                $type, $last-policy);
            }
        }
    }
}

match configuration/protocols/bgp/group {
    if (name == "internal") {
        /* This is acceptable. */
    }
    else if (name == "peers" || name == "customers") {
        /* This is acceptable. */
        for-each (neighbor) {
            /* Check each neighbor's policies. */
            call check-neighbor-policies($type="import");
            call check-neighbor-policies($type="export");
        }
    }
    else {
        call emit-error($message=jcs:printf("Group %s is not allowed", name));
    }
}
```

Now, test the script by disabling one of the import policies:

```
[edit protocols bgp]
user@r0# deactivate group customers neighbor 10.3.3.4 import

[edit protocols bgp]
user@r0# commit check
[edit protocols bgp group customers neighbor 10.3.3.4]
  import policy required, but not defined
error: 1 error reported by commit scripts
error: commit script failure
```

At this point, we breathe a sigh of relief, because the script seems to be working correctly. Thinking we are all done, we rollback to the previous configuration and commit it:

```
[edit protocols bgp]
user@r0# top

[edit]
user@r0# rollback
load complete

[edit]
user@r0# commit
[edit protocols bgp group customers neighbor 10.3.3.4]
  import policy error: last policy should be 'deny-all', but found
'AS_65535_routes' instead
error: 1 error reported by commit scripts
error: commit script failure
```

Uh-oh. Looking at the configuration, you see the error reported is exactly correct: this neighbor's import policy does not have the `deny-all` policy as the last policy in the import policy chain:

```
[edit]
user@r0# protocols bgp group customers neighbor 10.3.3.4
import AS_65535_routes;
peer-as 65534;
```

And that is a wonderful feeling. Your commit script may have just prevented its first major outage. Unfiltered BGP neighbors have been the source of serious Internet outages in the past. Your commit script just caught the fact that one of your BGP neighbors was not properly filtered.

Once you fix this configuration error and commit, you will have extra protection against a user accidentally leaving a peer unfiltered:

```
[edit protocols bgp]
user@r0# set group customers neighbor 10.3.3.4 import deny-all

[edit protocols bgp]
```

```
user@r0# commit
commit complete
```

Example: Automatically Fixing Mistakes

Next, let's revisit one of the examples we gave in "Automatically Fixing Mistakes" on page 250. In particular, we will write a commit script that ensures any interface listed in the `[edit protocols mpls]` hierarchy also has `family mpls` configured on the interface.

Let's begin by considering the algorithm. We could approach this one of two ways. On the one hand, we could examine all interfaces in the `[edit interfaces]` hierarchy that do not have `family mpls` configured and then consult the `[edit protocols mpls]` hierarchy to determine whether they should have it configured. On the other hand, we could examine the interfaces listed in the `[edit protocols mpls]` hierarchy and then check that all of those interfaces have `family mpls` configured in the `[edit interfaces]` hierarchy.

While either approach could work, the former approach seems easier. Let's look at the data structures to understand the challenge. Example 5-6 shows a partial configuration sample in both text and XML formats.

Example 5-6. Interface and MPLS configuration sample in text and XML formats

```
interfaces {
    ge-1/0/0 {
        unit 0 {
            family inet {
                address 10.1.1.4/24;
            }
            family mpls;
        }
    }
    ge-1/0/1 {
        unit 0 {
            family inet {
                address 10.2.2.4/24;
            }
        }
    }
    fxp0 {
        unit 0 {
            family inet {
                address 10.255.255.17/24;
            }
        }
    }
    lo0 {
        unit 0 {
```

```
            family mpls;
        }
    }
}
protocols {
    mpls {
        interface all;
        interface ge-1/0/0.0 {
            disable;
        }
    }
}
```

```
<configuration>
    <interfaces>
        <interface>
            <name>ge-1/0/0</name>
            <unit>
                <name>0</name>
                <family>
                    <inet>
                        <address>
                            <name>10.1.1.4/24</name>
                        </address>
                    </inet>
                    <mpls/>
                </family>
            </unit>
        </interface>
        <interface>
            <name>ge-1/0/1</name>
            <unit>
                <name>0</name>
                <family>
                    <inet>
                        <address>
                            <name>10.2.2.4/24</name>
                        </address>
                    </inet>
                </family>
            </unit>
        </interface>
        <interface>
            <name>fxp0</name>
            <unit>
                <name>0</name>
                <family>
                    <inet>
                        <address>
                            <name>10.255.255.17/24</name>
                        </address>
                    </inet>
                </family>
```

```
                </unit>
            </interface>
            <interface>
                <name>lo0</name>
                <unit>
                    <name>0</name>
                    <family>
                        <mpls/>
                    </family>
                </unit>
            </interface>
        </interfaces>
        <protocols>
        <mpls>
            <interface>
                <name>all</name>
            </interface>
            <interface>
                <name>ge-1/0/0.0</name>
                <disable/>
            </interface>
        </mpls>
        </protocols>
    </configuration>
```

Using the XPath expression `configuration/interfaces/interface/unit[not(family/mpls)]`, it is easy to get a list of logical interfaces (interface units) that do not have `family mpls` configured. On the other hand, it may be difficult to get a list of interfaces enabled under the `[edit protocols mpls]` hierarchy. If the user has enabled `interface all` in this hierarchy, then MPLS is enabled on all interfaces listed in the `[edit interfaces]` hierarchy, except those the user has specifically disabled in the `[edit protocols mpls]` hierarchy.

Given a single interface, it is fairly easy to assess whether that interface is enabled in the `[edit protocols mpls]` hierarchy. However, it is much harder to devise a loop through the interfaces that are enabled in the `[edit protocols mpls]` hierarchy.

For this reason, we recommend looping through the logical interfaces in the `[edit interfaces]` hierarchy that do not have `family mpls` enabled and then checking the `[edit protocols mpls]` hierarchy to see if those logical interfaces should have `family mpls` enabled.

Let's build the script now. The basic building blocks are the XPath to match the logical interfaces over which we want to loop, the XPath to determine whether a logical interface is enabled in the `[edit protocols mpls]` hierarchy, and the call to the `jcs:emit-change()` template to make the configuration change.

We start with the basic decision of which kind of template to use. As we discussed in "Example: Custom Configuration Checks" on page 288, we could either create a match template for `configuration/interfaces/interface/unit[not(family/mpls)]` or create a match template for `configuration` and use the `for-each` statement to loop over all the matching logical interfaces. Because we chose to use a match template for the specific items in the preceding section, we'll use a `for-each` loop in this section.

Let's start with the basic structure and then build on it:

```
version 1.1;

ns junos = "http://xml.juniper.net/junos/*/junos";
ns xnm = "http://xml.juniper.net/xnm/1.1/xnm";
ns jcs = "http://xml.juniper.net/junos/commit-scripts/1.0";

import "../import/junos.xsl";

match configuration {
    var $mpls = protocols/mpls;
    for-each (interfaces/interface/unit[not(family/mpls)]) {
        /* Insert logic here */
    }
}
```

You will notice that we saved the configuration hierarchy matched by the `protocols/mpls` XPath expression in the `$mpls` variable. Recall that a `for-each` loop changes the current node during each iteration to point to one of the elements matching the `for-each` loop's XPath expression. By saving the `[edit protocols mpls]` hierarchy to a variable before we enter the `for-each` loop, we are able to access data from it more easily later.

Now, we add the logic to detect whether matching logical interfaces are enabled in the `[edit protocols mpls]` hierarchy. The basic logic is that a logical interface is enabled if either `interface all` or the specific logical interface is listed, unless the specific logical interface is disabled. One small additional detail is that `interface all` may itself be disabled. The script must check for this condition and, if found, ensure the particular logical interface is present and not disabled.

We add this logic to our script:

```
version 1.1;

ns junos = "http://xml.juniper.net/junos/*/junos";
ns xnm = "http://xml.juniper.net/xnm/1.1/xnm";
ns jcs = "http://xml.juniper.net/junos/commit-scripts/1.0";

import "../import/junos.xsl";
```

```
match configuration {
    var $mpls = protocols/mpls;
    for-each (interfaces/interface/unit[not(family/mpls)]) {
        /* Calculate the IFL name. */
        var $intname = ../name _ "." _ name;

        /*
         * Determine if the interface is configured under
         * protocols/mpls. The interface is "configured" if:
         * 1. "interface all" is configured (and not disabled), or
         *    "interface $intname" is configured.
         * and
         * 2. "interface $intname" is not disabled.
         */
        if (($mpls/interface[name == "all" && not(disable)] ||
             $mpls/interface[name == $intname]) &&
            not($mpls/interface[name == $intname]/disable)) {

            /* Do configuration change here. */
        }
    }
}
```

Note that we calculated the logical interface name (*interface.unit*) using the interface's name (`../name`) and the unit's name (`name`). We use text splicing to insert a dot (`.`) between them and store the result in the `$intname` variable.

Now, all that is left is to add the logic to actually configure `family mpls` on the interface. We use the `jcs:emit-change()` template to perform that configuration. At the same time, we have the `jcs:emit-change()` template log a warning message to inform the user of the configuration change.

With these additions, our final script looks like this:

```
version 1.1;

ns junos = "http://xml.juniper.net/junos/*/junos";
ns xnm = "http://xml.juniper.net/xnm/1.1/xnm";
ns jcs = "http://xml.juniper.net/junos/commit-scripts/1.0";

import "../import/junos.xsl";

match configuration {
    var $mpls = protocols/mpls;
    for-each (interfaces/interface/unit[not(family/mpls)]) {
        /* Calculate the IFL name. */
        var $intname = ../name _ "." _ name;

        /*
         * Determine if the interface is configured under
         * protocols/mpls. The interface is "configured" if:
         * 1. "interface all" is configured (and not disabled), or
```

```
            *    "interface $intname" is configured.
            * and
            * 2. "interface $intname" is not disabled.
            */
            if (($mpls/interface[name == "all" && not(disable)] ||
                 $mpls/interface[name == $intname]) &&
                not($mpls/interface[name == $intname]/disable)) {

                /*
                 * This IFL is enabled under [edit protocols mpls],
                 * but does not appear to have "family mpls"
                 * configured on the IFL. Add it.
                 */
                call jcs:emit-change {
                    with $content = {
                        <family> {
                            <mpls>;
                        }
                    }
                    with $message = "Adding 'family mpls' to " _ $intname;
                }
            }
        }
    }
```

Now, let's try the script on the configuration shown in Example 5-6:

```
[edit]
user@r0# commit
[edit interfaces interface ge-1/0/1 unit 0]
  warning: Adding 'family mpls' to ge-1/0/1.0
[edit interfaces interface fxp0 unit 0]
  warning: Adding 'family mpls' to fxp0.0
commit complete

[edit]
user@r0# show | compare rollback 1
[edit interfaces ge-1/0/1 unit 0]
+      family mpls;
[edit interfaces fxp0 unit 0]
+      family mpls;
```

Next, let's delete `family mpls` from logical interface `ge-1/0/0.0`, but leave `ge-1/0/0.0` disabled in the `[edit protocols mpls]` hierarchy. Our script correctly ignores this interface:

```
[edit]
user@r0# delete interfaces ge-1/0/0 unit 0 family mpls

[edit]
user@r0# commit
commit complete
```

```
[edit]
user@r0# show | compare rollback 1
[edit interfaces ge-1/0/0 unit 0]
-      family mpls;
```

What if we remove the statement from the [edit protocols mpls] hierarchy that disables the ge-1/0/0.0 interface? Our script now tries to correct that interface:

```
[edit]
user@r0# delete protocols mpls interface ge-1/0/0

[edit]
user@r0# show | compare
[edit protocols mpls]
-    interface ge-1/0/0.0 {
-        disable;
-    }

[edit]
user@r0# show protocols mpls
interface all;

[edit]
user@r0# commit
[edit interfaces interface ge-1/0/0 unit 0]
  warning: Adding 'family mpls' to ge-1/0/0.0
commit complete

[edit]
user@r0# show | compare rollback 1
[edit interfaces ge-1/0/0 unit 0]
+      family mpls;
[edit protocols mpls]
-    interface ge-1/0/0.0 {
-        disable;
-    }
```

Those of you with eagle eyes may have noticed that the `[edit]` paths produced by the commit script were not quite correct in some cases. In particular, `[edit interfaces interface ge-1/0/0 unit 0]` is not quite right; rather, it should be `[edit interfaces ge-1/0/0 unit 0]`.

This occurs because of the mechanical way in which the `jcs:edit-path()` template converts the XML hierarchy into a path. It takes the tag name from each hierarchy level and inserts it into the `[edit]` path. In a very few cases, this is incorrect because the XML tag name does not appear in the `[edit]` path. The template does not currently have a way to detect this situation, leading it to make the wrong decision in these cases.

Even with this small bug, the path is still helpful and usable, as it still uniquely and clearly identifies the location in question.

Example: Dynamically Expanding Configuration

Finally, let's implement the example we gave in "Dynamically Expanding Configuration" on page 250. It is a complex example, so it may be worth rereading it. In summary, we want to read information from the configuration found in Example 5-2, apply it against the template found in Example 5-1, and expand it to the configuration found in Example 5-3.

One thing to consider is whether we want to make these changes transient or permanent. To make it easier to understand the implications of both, we show the change both ways. We start by making it a transient change.

We want to match on any interface IP address that has the `apply-macro bgp` configuration. To make this easier to understand, let's view the XML representation of the configuration in Example 5-2 (shown in Example 5-7).

Example 5-7. The XML representation of a sample configuration snippet that provides values for a commit script

```
<configuration>
    <interfaces>
        <interface>
            <name>ge-1/0/0</name>
            <unit>
                <name>0</name>
                <family>
                    <inet>
                        <address>
                            <name>192.168.1.1/30</name>
                            <apply-macro>
                                <name>bgp</name>
```

```
                                <data>
                                    <name>peer_as</name>
                                    <value>65534</value>
                                </data>
                                <data>
                                    <name>route_type</name>
                                    <value>full_routes</value>
                                </data>
                            </apply-macro>
                        </address>
                    </inet>
                </family>
            </unit>
        </interface>
    </interfaces>
</configuration>
```

To match on any interface IP address that has the apply-macro bgp configuration, we use the following XPath expression. This XPath expression finds an IPv4 <address> node that has an <apply-macro> node which itself has a <name> node with a value of bgp:

```
match configuration/interfaces/interface/unit/family/inet/address
                                    [apply-macro[name == "bgp"]] {
}
```

Next, we assign values from the <apply-macro> node to variables. Because we chose to match on the <address> node, we need to get the values from the <apply-macro> node. If we find one of the required values is missing, or empty, we return an error (using our old friend, the emit-error() template).

Don't forget that we also have one optional value: a prefix limit. We apply a default of 10,000 if this value is missing. To catch a malformed prefix-limit value, we convert it to a number and then check to make sure that the number is valid (its string representation is not NaN) and the number is within a sane range:

```
version 1.1;

ns junos = "http://xml.juniper.net/junos/*/junos";
ns xnm = "http://xml.juniper.net/xnm/1.1/xnm";
ns jcs = "http://xml.juniper.net/junos/commit-scripts/1.0";

import "../import/junos.xsl";

template emit-error($message, $dot=.) {
    /* Get the [edit] path. */
    var $path := {
        call jcs:edit-path($dot=$dot);
    }

    /* Emit the error. */
```

```
        <xnm:error> {
            copy-of $path;
            <message> $message;
        }

        /* Log the syslog message. */
        <syslog> {
            <message> jcs:printf("%s: %s", $path/edit-path, $message);
        }
    }

    match configuration/interfaces/interface/unit/family/inet/address
                                            [apply-macro[name=="bgp"]] {
        var $peer_as = apply-macro[name=="bgp"]/data[name="peer_as"]/value;
        var $route_type = apply-macro[name=="bgp"]/data[name="route_type"]/value;
        var $prefix_limit = {
            if (apply-macro[name=="bgp"]/data[name="prefix_limit"]) {
                number(apply-macro[name=="bgp"]/data[name="prefix_limit"]/value);
            }
            else {
                number("10000");
            }
        }

        if (not($peer_as) || string-length($peer_as) == 0) {
            call emit-error {
                with $dot = apply-macro[name=="bgp"];
                with $message = "Required 'peer_as' element is missing or " _
                                "empty";
            }
        }
        else if (not($route_type) || string-length($route_type) == 0) {
            call emit-error {
                with $dot = apply-macro[name=="bgp"];
                with $message = "Required 'route_type' element is missing or " _
                                "empty";
            }
        }
        else if (not($prefix_limit) || string($prefix_limit) == "NaN" ||
                 $prefix_limit < 1 || $prefix_limit > 10000000) {
            call emit-error {
                with $dot = apply-macro[name=="bgp"];
                with $message = "Optional 'prefix_limit' element appears to " _
                                "be malformed (expected a number between " _
                                "1 and 10000000";
            }
        }
    }
```

Now, we need to work out the last piece of information we need to fill in our configuration template: the peer's IP address. We assume this network follows a standard of always applying the lower IP address of a /30 network to the local device and the higher IP address to the peer.

To accomplish this task, we create a new named template that expects an IP address in the form of *w.x.y.z/nn*:

```
template get-remote-ip($local-address) {
    var $pattern = "([0-9]+\.[0-9]+\.[0-9]+\.)([0-9]+)/"; ❶
    var $ip-split = slax:regex($pattern, $local-address); ❷

    if (string($ip-split[1]) != "") { ❸
        expr jcs:printf("%s%d", $ip-split[2], number($ip-split[3]) + 1); ❹
    }
}
```

❶ This regular expression is used to parse the IP address. We really don't need to make a variable to hold this. The main reason we did that was just to make the script format better for the book.

The regular expression uses parentheses to create two groups. The first group holds the first three octets of the IP address and the trailing dot. The second group holds the final octet. These groupings are significant, because we will later be able to access the values that match each group.

The trailing slash is not part of any group. It ensures that the second grouping matches everything up to the slash.

❷ This line matches the regular expression (given in the first argument) against a string (given in the second argument). The result is a node set that you can evaluate with an array-like syntax.

Because of the XPath standard, the first node has an index of 1, rather than 0. In addition, the first node contains the entire matching string. Subsequent nodes contain, in order, the values that matched each group from the regular expression.

Given a `$local-address` argument of `192.168.1.1/30`, we expect the following values:

Variable	Value
`$ip-split[1]`	`192.168.1.1/`
`$ip-split[2]`	`192.168.1.`
`$ip-split[3]`	`1`

❸ This line checks whether a match occurred. If a match occurred, `string($ip-split[1])` should be a nonempty string. On the other hand, if no match occurred, `string($ip-split[1])` should evaluate to the empty string.

If no match occurred, the template will simply return nothing. The calling template can check for that condition and react accordingly.

❹ This line prints the value of the remote IP address. Because we assume that the lower IP address is always assigned to the local device, we calculate the remote address by merely adding one to the last octet of the local IP address.

We can test this function using one of our favorite tricks: the spurious warning or error. This trick is handy for debugging. You can use it to print out data to see what is occurring during the operation of your script. You can even print XML hierarchies (using the `copy-of` statement) and then view them using the `commit check | display xml` command.

Here, we add a simple diagnostic line to our main template to print out the remote IP address:

```
match configuration/interfaces/interface/unit/family/inet/address
                                        [apply-macro[name=="bgp"]] {
    var $peer_as = apply-macro[name=="bgp"]/data[name="peer_as"]/value;
    var $route_type = apply-macro[name=="bgp"]/data[name="route_type"]/value;
    var $prefix_limit = {
        if (apply-macro[name=="bgp"]/data[name="prefix_limit"]) {
            number(apply-macro[name=="bgp"]/data[name="prefix_limit"]/value);
        }
        else {
            number("10000");
        }
    }
    var $peer-ip = { ❶
        call get-remote-ip($local-address=name);
    }
    <xnm:error> {
        <message> "local address: " _ name _ "; remote ip: " _ $peer-ip; ❷
    }

    if (not($peer_as) || string-length($peer_as) == 0) {
        call emit-error {
            with $dot = apply-macro[name=="bgp"];
            with $message = "Required 'peer_as' element is missing or " _
                            "empty";
        }
    }
    else if (not($route_type) || string-length($route_type) == 0) {
        call emit-error {
            with $dot = apply-macro[name=="bgp"];
            with $message = "Required 'route_type' element is missing or " _
```

```
                                    "empty";
            }
        }
        else if (not($prefix_limit) || string($prefix_limit) == "NaN" ||
                 $prefix_limit < 1 || $prefix_limit > 10000000) {
            call emit-error {
                with $dot = apply-macro[name=="bgp"];
                with $message = "Optional 'prefix_limit' element appears to " _
                                "be malformed (expected a number between " _
                                "1 and 10000000";
            }
        }
    }
```

❶ Recall that this statement is executed in the context of an `<address>` node. And, as you can see in Example 5-7, the IP prefix is contained in the `<name>` node. Therefore, we pass the contents of the `<name>` node as the `$local-address` argument to the `get-remote-ip()` template. We store the results of the `get-remote-ip()` template in the `$peer-ip` variable.

❷ Here, we print a simple error message that shows the local IP prefix from the `<name>` node and the remote IP address we calculated.

When we run the script, we see that our `get-remote-ip()` template appears to be working correctly:

```
[edit]
user@r0# commit check
error: local address: 192.168.1.1/30; remote ip: 192.168.1.2
error: 1 error reported by commit scripts
error: commit script failure
```

Now that we know all the variables, we just need to emit the configuration change to implement the configuration template from Example 5-1. We create a new SLAX template named `emit-bgp-config()`:

```
template emit-bgp-config($peer-ip, $peer-as, $route-type, $prefix-limit) {
    <protocols> {
        <bgp> {
            <group> {
                <name> "customers";
                <neighbor> {
                    <name> $peer-ip;
                    <import> "filter-customer-generic";
                    <import> "prefix-size";
                    <import> "handle-communities";
                    <import> "as-" _ $peer-as;
                    <import> "deny-all";
                    <family> {
                        <inet> {
                            <unicast> {
```

```
                                <accepted-prefix-limit> {
                                    <maximum> $prefix-limit;
                                    <teardown> {
                                        <limit-threshold> "80";
                                        <idle-timeout> {
                                            <timeout> "10";
                                        }
                                    }
                                }
                            }
                        }
                        <inet6> {
                            <unicast> {
                                <accepted-prefix-limit> {
                                    <maximum> $prefix-limit;
                                    <teardown> {
                                        <limit-threshold> "80";
                                        <idle-timeout> {
                                            <timeout> "10";
                                        }
                                    }
                                }
                            }
                        }
                        <export> $route-type;
                        <export> "deny-all";
                        <peer-as> $peer-as;
                    }
                }
            }
        }
    }
}
```

You will notice that we have put the <name> element in the group hierarchy. As we explained in "Discovering the Unique Key Used to Identify Configuration Elements" on page 74, you must include the keys to differentiate between multiple elements that use the same tag. In this case, the <group> elements are distinguished by their <name> element.

We now modify the main match template to call the `emit-bgp-config()` template with the appropriate arguments:

```
var $top-level = ../../../../../..;
call jcs:emit-change {
    with $tag = "transient-change";
    with $dot = $top-level;
    with $content = {
        call emit-bgp-config {
            with $peer-ip = $peer-ip;
            with $peer-as = $peer-as;
            with $route-type = $route-type;
```

```
                with $prefix-limit = $prefix-limit;
            }
        }
    }
```

You will notice that we found the top level of the hierarchy using a relative XPath statement, which will be applied relative to the address node. This allows you to extend the same template to work equally well in a logical system as the main logical system. If you don't care about logical systems, another way to find the top of the hierarchy is with the XPath expression `/commit-script-input/configuration`.

To allow this transient change to occur, we must also configure Junos to permit transient changes:

```
[edit]
user@r0# set system scripts commit allow-transients
```

Finally, we check the new BGP configuration with the `display commit-scripts` pipe command:

```
[edit]
user@r0# show protocols bgp | display commit-scripts
error: load of commit script changes failed (transients)
```

Obviously, that doesn't look good! Now may be a good time to introduce you to troubleshooting steps for commit scripts. You can see the input and output of the commit script by activating traceoptions. In this case, let's start by just looking at the commit script's output:

```
[edit]
user@r0# set system scripts commit traceoptions flag output

[edit]
user@r0# set system scripts commit traceoptions file commit-script

[edit]
user@r0# show protocols bgp | display commit-scripts
error: load of commit script changes failed (transients)

[edit]
user@r0# run show log commit-script
Oct  1 05:48:45 cscript script processing begins
Oct  1 05:48:45 reading commit script configuration
Oct  1 05:48:45 testing commit script configuration
Oct  1 05:48:45 opening commit script '/var/db/scripts/commit/test.slax'
Oct  1 05:48:45 script file '/var/db/scripts/commit/test.slax': size = 5421 ;
md5 = fe39e3dcca9b4bef7c0646a922154bcb sha1 =
09303aedfe3fb07fa86728da39912604777c2264 sha-256 =
863a79ea08f6d4c56364dac18b0b647a96cdf63b4eade34a1c590318af5bd53a
Oct  1 05:48:45 reading commit script 'test.slax'
Oct  1 05:48:45 running commit script 'test.slax'
Oct  1 05:48:45 processing commit script 'test.slax'
```

```
Oct  1 05:48:45 results of 'test.slax'
Oct  1 05:48:45 begin dump
<commit-script-results>
    <transient-change>
        <protocols xmlns:junos="http://xml.juniper.net/junos/*/junos"
                   xmlns:xnm="http://xml.juniper.net/xnm/1.1/xnm"
                   xmlns:jcs="http://xml.juniper.net/junos/commit-scripts/1.0">
            <bgp>
                <group>
                    <name>customers</name>
                    <neighbor>
                        <name>192.168.1.2</name>
                        <import>filter-customer-generic</import>
                        <import>prefix-size</import>
                        <import>handle-communities</import>
                        <import>as-65534</import>
                        <import>deny-all</import>
                        <family>
                            <inet>
                                <unicast>
                                    <accepted-prefix-limit>
                                        <maximum>10000</maximum>
                                        <teardown>
                                            <limit-threshold>
                                                80
                                            </limit-threshold>
                                            <idle-timeout>
                                                <timeout>10</timeout>
                                            </idle-timeout>
                                        </teardown>
                                    </accepted-prefix-limit>
                                </unicast>
                            </inet>
                            <inet6>
                                <unicast>
                                    <accepted-prefix-limit>
                                        <maximum>10000</maximum>
                                        <teardown>
                                            <limit-threshold>
                                                80
                                            </limit-threshold>
                                            <idle-timeout>
                                                <timeout>10</timeout>
                                            </idle-timeout>
                                        </teardown>
                                    </accepted-prefix-limit>
                                </unicast>
                            </inet6>
                            <export>full_routes</export>
                            <export>deny-all</export>
                            <peer-as>65534</peer-as>
                        </family>
```

```
                    </neighbor>
                </group>
            </bgp>
        </protocols>
    </transient-change>
</commit-script-results>Oct  1 05:48:45 end dump
Oct  1 05:48:45 no errors from test.slax
Oct  1 05:48:45 saving commit script changes for script test.slax
Oct  1 05:48:45 summary of script test.slax: changes 0, transients 1
(allowed), syslog 0
Oct  1 05:48:45 cscript script processing ends
```

This output makes the problem obvious: we accidentally included the export policy chain and peer AS in the `<family>` hierarchy. Fixing the issue is as simple as moving the export policy chain and peer AS out of the `<family>` hierarchy. Once we make this change, we can view the new configuration both with and without the transient changes:

```
[edit]
user@r0# show protocols bgp group customers
type external;

[edit]
user@r0# show protocols bgp group customers | display commit-scripts
type external;
neighbor 192.168.1.2 {
    import [ filter-customer-generic prefix-size handle-communities as-65534
deny-all ]; ## 'as-65534' is not defined
    family inet {
        unicast {
            accepted-prefix-limit {
                maximum 10000;
                teardown 80 idle-timeout 10;
            }
        }
    }
    family inet6 {
        unicast {
            accepted-prefix-limit {
                maximum 10000;
                teardown 80 idle-timeout 10;
            }
        }
    }
    export [ full_routes deny-all ];
    peer-as 65534;
}
```

The good news is this output matches our configuration template! The bad news is that this highlights another thing we should consider. Note the comment on the import policy chain that policy as-65534 is not defined. This results in a commit failure:

```
[edit]
user@r0# commit check
[edit]
  'policy-options'
    Policy error: Policy as-65534 referenced but not defined
[edit protocols bgp group customers neighbor 192.168.1.2]
  'import'
    BGP: import list not applied
error: configuration check-out failed
```

Depending on the way this script will be used, you may actually want to fail the commit until the appropriate policy is configured. However, in other cases, you may want to insert an appropriate default policy.

Here, we decide to add an appropriate default policy that simply skips over the policy if it is not defined. This decision seems safe enough, given the fact that the next policy in the chain denies all routes. We also display a warning message if this occurs.

So, we modify our script by adding logic that implements this decision. We add a new template (`emit-default-policy()`) that emits the XML configuration for the new policy. If it is necessary to add the default policy, we call the **`emit-default-policy()`** template from the main match template and emit the change:

```
template emit-default-policy($peer-as) {
    <policy-options> {
        <policy-statement> {
            <name> "as-" _ $peer-as;
            <then> {
                <next> "policy";
            }
        }
    }
}
...output trimmed...
        if (! $top-level/policy-options/policy-statement[name ==
                                                        "as-" _ $peer-as]) {
            call jcs:emit-change {
                with $tag = "transient-change";
                with $dot = $top-level;
                with $content = {
                    call emit-default-policy($peer-as = $peer-as);
                }
                with $message = {
                    expr jcs:printf("Adding default '%s' policy",
                                    "as-" _ $peer-as);
                }
            }
```

```
        }
    ...output trimmed...
```

After making this change, the commit check succeeds:

```
[edit]
user@r0# commit check
[edit]
  warning: Adding default 'as-65534' policy
configuration check succeeds
```

We can also look at the new policy. However, you see that an attempt to view the specific policy with the command `show policy-options policy-statement as-65534 | display commit-scripts` fails to show the policy:

```
[edit]
user@r0# show policy-options policy-statement as-65534 | display commit-scripts

[edit]
user@r0#
```

This command fails to show the policy because the requested configuration node does not exist in the candidate configuration. Instead, you need to choose a higher-level node that does exist and use the `display commit-scripts` pipe command while displaying the configuration of that node.

In this case, the direct parent of the policy (`[edit policy-options]`) does exist in the candidate configuration, so we display that hierarchy using the `display commit-scripts` pipe command:

```
[edit]
user@r0# edit policy-options

[edit policy-options]
user@r0# show | display commit-scripts | find "policy-statement as-65534"
policy-statement as-65534 {
    then next policy;
}
...output trimmed...
```

Finally, the new configuration commits successfully:

```
[edit policy-options]
user@r0# commit
[edit]
  warning: Adding default 'as-65534' policy
commit complete
```

Example 5-8 shows the complete script.

Example 5-8. A SLAX script to expand BGP configuration using transient changes

```
version 1.1;

ns junos = "http://xml.juniper.net/junos/*/junos";
ns xnm = "http://xml.juniper.net/xnm/1.1/xnm";
ns jcs = "http://xml.juniper.net/junos/commit-scripts/1.0";

import "../import/junos.xsl";

template emit-error($message, $dot=.) {
    /* Get the [edit] path. */
    var $path := {
        call jcs:edit-path($dot=$dot);
    }

    /* Emit the error. */
    <xnm:error> {
        copy-of $path;
        <message> $message;
    }

    /* Log the syslog message. */
    <syslog> {
        <message> jcs:printf("%s: %s", $path/edit-path, $message);
    }
}


template get-remote-ip($local-address) {
    var $pattern = "([0-9]+\.[0-9]+\.[0-9]+\.)([0-9]+)/";
    var $ip-split = slax:regex($pattern, $local-address);

    if (string($ip-split[1]) != "") {
        expr jcs:printf("%s%d", $ip-split[2], number($ip-split[3]) + 1);
    }
}

template emit-bgp-config($peer-ip, $peer-as, $route-type, $prefix-limit) {
    <protocols> {
        <bgp> {
            <group> {
                <name> "customers";
                <neighbor> {
                    <name> $peer-ip;
                    <import> "filter-customer-generic";
                    <import> "prefix-size";
                    <import> "handle-communities";
                    <import> "as-" _ $peer-as;
                    <import> "deny-all";
                    <family> {
                        <inet> {
```

```
                                <unicast> {
                                    <accepted-prefix-limit> {
                                        <maximum> $prefix-limit;
                                        <teardown> {
                                            <limit-threshold> "80";
                                            <idle-timeout> {
                                                <timeout> "10";
                                            }
                                        }
                                    }
                                }
                            }
                            <inet6> {
                                <unicast> {
                                    <accepted-prefix-limit> {
                                        <maximum> $prefix-limit;
                                        <teardown> {
                                            <limit-threshold> "80";
                                            <idle-timeout> {
                                                <timeout> "10";
                                            }
                                        }
                                    }
                                }
                            }
                        }
                        <export> $route-type;
                        <export> "deny-all";
                        <peer-as> $peer-as;
                    }
                }
            }
        }
    }

template emit-default-policy($peer-as) {
    <policy-options> {
        <policy-statement> {
            <name> "as-" _ $peer-as;
            <then> {
                <next> "policy";
            }
        }
    }
}


match configuration/interfaces/interface/unit/family/inet/address
                                      [apply-macro[name == "bgp"]] {
    var $peer-as = apply-macro[name=="bgp"]/data[name="peer_as"]/value;
    var $route-type = apply-macro[name=="bgp"]/data[name="route_type"]/value;
    var $prefix-limit = {
```

```
        if (apply-macro[name=="bgp"]/data[name="prefix_limit"]) {
            number(apply-macro[name=="bgp"]/data[name="prefix_limit"]/value);
        }
        else {
            number("10000");
        }
    }
    var $peer-ip = {
        call get-remote-ip($local-address=name);
    }

    if (not($peer-as) || string-length($peer-as) == 0) {
        call emit-error {
            with $dot = apply-macro[name=="bgp"];
            with $message = "Required 'peer_as' element is missing or " _
                            "empty";
        }
    }
    else if (not($route-type) || string-length($route-type) == 0) {
        call emit-error {
            with $dot = apply-macro[name=="bgp"];
            with $message = "Required 'route_type' element is missing or " _
                            "empty";
        }
    }
    else if (not($prefix-limit) || string($prefix-limit) == "NaN" ||
             $prefix-limit < 1 || $prefix-limit > 10000000) {
        call emit-error {
            with $dot = apply-macro[name=="bgp"];
            with $message = "Optional 'prefix_limit' element appears to " _
                            "be malformed (expected a number between " _
                            "1 and 10000000";
        }
    }
    else {
        var $top-level = ../../../../../..;
        call jcs:emit-change {
            with $tag = "transient-change";
            with $dot = $top-level;
            with $content = {
                call emit-bgp-config {
                    with $peer-ip = $peer-ip;
                    with $peer-as = $peer-as;
                    with $route-type = $route-type;
                    with $prefix-limit = $prefix-limit;
                }
            }
        }
        if (! $top-level/policy-options/policy-statement[name ==
                                                      "as-" _ $peer-as]) {
            call jcs:emit-change {
                with $tag = "transient-change";
```

```
                with $dot = $top-level;
                with $content = {
                    call emit-default-policy($peer-as = $peer-as);
                }
                with $message = {
                    expr jcs:printf("Adding default '%s' policy",
                                    "as-" _ $peer-as);
                }
            }
        }
    }
}
```

One of the benefits of the current script design is that your configuration stays small. As we saw earlier when we viewed the new configuration with and without the transient changes, the BGP configuration in the candidate configuration is much smaller than the committed configuration.

However, not all users like this behavior. Some users prefer to see the full configuration appear in the static configuration database. In that case, we merely use the commit script to make initial provisioning easier and forgo some of the other benefits of using transient changes (as described in "Handling Transient Changes" on page 258).

In order to modify the commit script so it changes the candidate configuration, rather than using transient changes, we need to do two things. First, we need to change the `$tag` argument for each call to the `jcs:emit-change()` template. Instead of setting a value of `transient-change`, the value should now be `change`. (Or, because `change` is the default value for the `$tag` argument, we could instead remove the `$tag` argument altogether.) Second, as explained in "Handling Permanent Changes" on page 260, we must delete the `apply-macro bgp` configuration from the interface.

All of these changes occur in the main match template. We have called out the changes in the template:

```
match configuration/interfaces/interface/unit/family/inet/address
                                        [apply-macro[name == "bgp"]] {
    var $peer-as = apply-macro[name=="bgp"]/data[name="peer_as"]/value;
    var $route-type = apply-macro[name=="bgp"]/data[name="route_type"]/value;
    var $prefix-limit = {
        if (apply-macro[name=="bgp"]/data[name="prefix_limit"]) {
            number(apply-macro[name=="bgp"]/data[name="prefix_limit"]/value);
        }
        else {
            number("10000");
        }
    }
    var $peer-ip = {
        call get-remote-ip($local-address=name);
```

```
}

if (not($peer-as) || string-length($peer-as) == 0) {
    call emit-error {
        with $dot = apply-macro[name=="bgp"];
        with $message = "Required 'peer_as' element is missing or " _
                        "empty";
    }
}
else if (not($route-type) || string-length($route-type) == 0) {
    call emit-error {
        with $dot = apply-macro[name=="bgp"];
        with $message = "Required 'route_type' element is missing or " _
                        "empty";
    }
}
else if (not($prefix-limit) || string($prefix-limit) == "NaN" ||
         $prefix-limit < 1 || $prefix-limit > 10000000) {
    call emit-error {
        with $dot = apply-macro[name=="bgp"];
        with $message = "Optional 'prefix_limit' element appears to " _
                        "be malformed (expected a number between " _
                        "1 and 10000000";
    }
}
else {
    var $top-level = ../../../../../..;
    call jcs:emit-change { (1)
        with $content = {
            <apply-macro delete="delete"> {
                <name> "bgp";
            }
        }
    }
    call jcs:emit-change {
        with $tag = "change"; (2)
        with $dot = $top-level;
        with $content = {
            call emit-bgp-config {
                with $peer-ip = $peer-ip;
                with $peer-as = $peer-as;
                with $route-type = $route-type;
                with $prefix-limit = $prefix-limit;
            }
        }
    }
    if (! $top-level/policy-options/policy-statement[name ==
                                                  "as-" _ $peer-as]) {
        call jcs:emit-change {
            with $tag = "change"; (3)
            with $dot = $top-level;
            with $content = {
```

```
                    call emit-default-policy($peer-as = $peer-as);
                }
                with $message = {
                    expr jcs:printf("Adding default '%s' policy",
                                    "as-" _ $peer-as);
                }
            }
        }
    }
}
```

❶ We added another call to the `jcs:emit-change()` template. This one deletes the `<apply-macro>` node that is identified by a `<name>` element with the value `bgp`. The `delete="delete"` attribute on the `<apply-macro>` node tells Junos to delete that node.

Recall that changes are relative to the current location (unless we include the `$dot` argument, which we have not done here). That is why we only need to specify the `<apply-macro>` element (which is a child of the current node) without including any of the hierarchy above it.

❷ We changed the `$tag` argument from `transient-change` to `change`.

❸ We changed the `$tag` argument from `transient-change` to `change`.

After committing the configuration, you see the changes take effect, as expected:

```
[edit]
user@r0# commit
[edit]
  warning: Adding default 'as-65534' policy
commit complete

[edit]
user@r0# show | compare rollback 1
[edit interfaces ge-1/0/0 unit 0 family inet address 192.168.1.1/30]
-        apply-macro bgp {
-            peer_as 65534;
-            route_type full_routes;
-        }
[edit protocols bgp group customers]
+     neighbor 192.168.1.2 {
+         import [ filter-customer-generic prefix-size handle-communities
as-65534 deny-all ];
+         family inet {
+             unicast {
+                 accepted-prefix-limit {
+                     maximum 10000;
+                     teardown 80 idle-timeout 10;
+                 }
```

```
+             }
+         }
+         family inet6 {
+             unicast {
+                 accepted-prefix-limit {
+                     maximum 10000;
+                     teardown 80 idle-timeout 10;
+                 }
+             }
+         }
+         export [ full_routes deny-all ];
+         peer-as 65534;
+     }
[edit policy-options]
+   policy-statement as-65534 {
+       then next policy;
+   }
```

Chapter Summary

Commit scripts are very powerful tools for working with Junos configurations. Using commit scripts, you can enforce configuration standards, implement provisioning templates, and attempt to automatically correct errors.

Commit scripts receive a copy of the configuration, process it, and produce an appropriate output XML document. The output XML document directs Junos on how it should proceed with the commit operation. The script can make configuration changes, log messages, produce warnings, or abort the commit with an error.

Because commit scripts work on XML input and produce XML output, the Junos software uses XML transformations to process the XML data. The XML transformation is conducted by a script written in XSLT or SLAX. A SLAX script is functionally equivalent to an XSLT script, but the SLAX syntax may be easier to learn. Once mastered, the SLAX language provides powerful tools for parsing Junos configurations.

As we will see in the following chapters, you can also use SLAX or XSLT to write op and event scripts. Op and event scripts allow you to further customize the Junos software to fit the needs of your network.

CHAPTER 6

Op Scripts

Op and event scripts are powerful tools you can use to automate the operation of your router. Have you ever wished you had a way to script a CLI command on the router? Or that you could program your router to always run a particular CLI command when a particular event occurs? Op and event scripts can do these things and more.

In this chapter, we will focus on op scripts. However, much of this information will also help you work with event scripts, which we cover in Chapter 7.

Use Cases

Before diving into the way op scripts work, let's take a moment to look at the big picture: what can you do with op and event scripts? To give you an idea, let's look at some use cases.

Custom CLI Commands

Junos has a robust and useful CLI, with many, many commands to cover a variety of situations. Using the CLI, it is fairly easy to perform just about any action you desire. However, there are times when you could make things even easier if you were able to script command sequences.

Consider this example. Imagine your network has a monitoring system that reports when a BGP session goes down. Your standard response is to log in to the router, run `show interfaces terse` to find the interface that carries the session, and then run `show interfaces extensive` to look at the details for that interface.

You could simplify this process by simply being able to run a single command that automatically figures out which interface has the destination and then runs `show interfaces extensive` for that interface.

For example, this op script takes a remote IP address and runs `show interfaces extensive` for that interface:

```
user@r0> op show-interface ip 10.10.10.253
Physical interface: ge-1/0/7, Enabled, Physical link is Up
  Interface index: 148, SNMP ifIndex: 524, Generation: 151
  Link-level type: Ethernet, MTU: 1514, MRU: 1522, LAN-PHY mode,
  Speed: 1000mbps, BPDU Error: None, MAC-REWRITE Error: None,
  Loopback: Disabled, Source filtering: Disabled, Flow control: Enabled,
  Auto-negotiation: Enabled, Remote fault: Online
  Pad to minimum frame size: Disabled
  Device flags   : Present Running
  Interface flags: SNMP-Traps Internal: 0x4000
  Link flags     : None
  CoS queues     : 8 supported, 4 maximum usable queues
  Schedulers     : 0
  Hold-times     : Up 0 ms, Down 0 ms
...output trimmed...
```

Automatically Responding to Events

Of course, while automating CLI command sequences is useful, it is even better if we can have the router automatically respond to events. To extend our preceding example further, imagine your standard response to a down BGP session is:

1. Determine the interface over which the session should run. Determine whether it is down, has errors, or has high utilization.
2. Try to ping the remote side. If this fails, assume a connectivity problem. Try to reset the interface.
3. Get the reason the BGP session went down from the `show bgp neighbors` output and send it (along with this troubleshooting information) to an escalation engineer.

It is possible to write a script that performs all these steps and tell the router to execute that script anytime a BGP session goes down. If the BGP session stays down, it can then send a trap to an SNMP management station that includes the information gathered.

Customizing Your Device

In addition to the specific examples just shown, you have the general benefit of being able to customize your device to do what you want in the way you want, all without asking Juniper to schedule a feature change to the operating system.

For example, one of the authors of this book helped a customer with an event script to change the way the router responded to errors on aggregated interface bundles. This customer wanted to automatically deactivate member links when a certain number of errors were seen in a short enough time. We were able to satisfy the customer's desire using a fairly simple event script.

And we've even heard of larger requirements (such as "don't advertise any BGP routes for the first 10 minutes a router is up") that could be at least partially handled through some creative event scripts. (See "Use Cases" on page 605 for examples of use cases involving event scripts.)

In short, if you wish your device behaved differently, you may be able to use an op or event script to change its behavior.

Now, with that said, there are still limits to what an op or event script can do. They can access or modify current operational or configuration state using existing CLI or shell commands, they can process their arguments and the operational or configuration state they can access, and they can produce output using a custom format. However, they cannot add new routing protocols, modify the way daemons process information, or allow access to new kinds of information that you could not discern from existing CLI or shell commands. But even with their limitations, op and event scripts can be very powerful.

Overview of Op Script Operation

Op and event scripts share some similarities. In fact, their basic operation is so similar that we will treat them interchangeably when we begin talking about some of the core functionality, such as calling operational RPCs or changing the configuration. However, there are some differences between these scripts that arise from the way they are used.

Both op and event scripts also bear similarities to commit scripts. As we discussed in Chapter 5, commit scripts receive an XML input document, process it, and produce an XML output document. Because of the nature of this work (known as an *XML transformation*), commit scripts are written in XSLT or SLAX. Like commit scripts, op and event scripts receive an XML input document, process it, and produce an XML output document. And like commit scripts, op and event scripts are written in XSLT or SLAX.

Just as we suggested in Chapter 5, we suggest that you use SLAX to write your op and event scripts. You can see "Writing Commit Scripts in SLAX/XSLT" on page 261 for information on writing SLAX scripts.

One big difference between op and event scripts on the one hand and commit scripts on the other is the nature of the work they do in processing the XML input document. With commit scripts, the bulk of the processing may very well be examining the configuration that is contained in the XML input document. With op and event scripts, the bulk of the processing may involve operational or configuration state that the script accesses from the router. In fact, many op scripts may not even access any information from the input document. We will cover the method for accessing operational and configuration state in "Operational and Configuration State" on page 338.

A user runs op scripts using the `op` command. A user can run scripts that are in the `[edit system scripts op]` section of the configuration. Alternatively, a user can use the `op url` command to run any op script that the router can access from either a local or a remote location.

While op scripts are very useful, they run at the privilege level of the user who runs the `op` command. Scripts can perform just about any operation that the user has permission to perform. This can include changing the configuration, as well as disruptive things such as clearing BGP sessions or label-switched paths (LSPs). And the script does not have to display a message to the user telling the user it is performing these operations.

Therefore, just as you should be careful in running computer programs you obtain from untrusted sources, you should also be careful in running op scripts that you obtain from untrusted sources.

The execution of an op script goes through several phases:

1. CSCRIPT (the helper program that actually runs op scripts) reads the op script and looks for an `$arguments` global variable. If it finds this global variable, it passes the information back to the CLI for it to use in command completion and CLI help.

   Even if a user never types the ? key, the system will still go through this process as the user types the command. (On the other hand, this process will not occur if you run an op script through a means other than the CLI. For example, the system will not look for the `$arguments` global variable if you run an op script through a NETCONF session.)

2. Once you execute an op script, CSCRIPT loads the script and provides it with the following data:

   - The arguments the user provided
   - Arguments indicating the hostname, local time, product name, script name, and username of the user who executed the script

- An input document with an <op-script-input> root element

3. CSCRIPT runs the script and produces an output document. The output document should have a root element of <op-script-results>. (However, an interesting fact is that the name of the output document's root element is actually irrelevant, as long as it is not one of the few tags that have a special meaning to the script-parsing infrastructure. The tag is discarded by MGD as the response makes its way from CSCRIPT to the end user.)
4. MGD takes the output document it receives from CSCRIPT, replaces the top-level tag with the <rpc-reply> tag, and passes the response to the user.

Op Script Input Document

The only important part of the input document's contents is the <junos-context> element, which is also available in the $junos-context variable. (The variable is a pointer to the <junos-context> element from the input document. Therefore, the content is literally the same.)

You can see the contents of the input document by enabling traceoptions at the [edit system scripts op] hierarchy level and specifying the input flag. Here is a sample input document from a recent Junos version:

```
<?xml version="1.0"?>
<op-script-input xmlns:junos="http://xml.juniper.net/junos/*/junos">
  <junos-context>
    <hostname>r0</hostname>
    <product>mx240</product>
    <localtime>Fri Nov 13 11:02:27 2015</localtime>
    <localtime-iso>2015-11-13 11:02:27 PST</localtime-iso>
    <script-type>op</script-type>
    <pid>7786</pid>
    <tty>/dev/pts/0</tty>
    <chassis>others</chassis>
    <routing-engine-name>re0</routing-engine-name>
    <re-master/>
    <user-context>
      <user>user</user>
      <class-name>super-user</class-name>
      <uid>1001</uid>
      <login-name>user</login-name>
    </user-context>
    <op-context>
    </op-context>
  </junos-context>
</op-script-input>
```

Op Script Arguments

An op script can receive arguments from the user who executes the script. You declare an argument using the `param` statement. For example, this statement tells SLAX to accept an argument named `interface`:

```
param $interface;
```

You can also provide default values for these arguments. This statement tells SLAX to accept an argument named `interface`, but to use a default value of `fxp0` if the user does not provide this argument:

```
param $interface = "fxp0";
```

Some of the information from the input document is also available through automatic arguments. The following arguments are automatically available (without including `param` statements):

- `$hostname`
- `$localtime`
- `$localtime-iso`
- `$product`
- `$script`
- `$user`

These arguments (which are accessed just like variables) should have the same values as the corresponding elements in the `<junos-context>` element of the input document (as shown in the previous section). There is one argument that does not appear in the input document, though, and that is the `$script` argument. The `$script` argument contains the filename of the op script. It may or may not contain the path to the file. If it does not contain a path to the file, you can assume that the file is in the */var/db/scripts/op/* directory.

You should avoid defining your own arguments with the same names as the automatic arguments. The user will be unable to override the automatic values assigned to the arguments.

As mentioned in "Overview of Op Script Operation" on page 331, you can set the `$arguments` global variable to provide argument help for users. Users can include any argument—even if it is not listed in the `$arguments` global variable—when executing an op script. Therefore, you can create "hidden" arguments by including a `param` statement, but not listing the argument in the `$arguments` global variable.

The `$arguments` global variable contains a set of `<argument>` elements, each of which contains a `<name>` element and a `<description>` element. These values will be displayed to the user in the CLI help.

For example, consider this SLAX syntax:

```
var $arguments = {
    <argument> {
        <name> "ip";
        <description> "The remote IP address.";
    }
    <argument> {
        <name> "routing-instance";
        <description> "The routing instance (default: the default instance).";
    }
}
```

The preceding SLAX syntax will cause the CLI to render the following help:

```
user@r0> op example-script ?
Possible completions:
  <[Enter]>            Execute this command
  <name>               Argument name
  detail               Display detailed output
  invoke-debugger      Invoke script in debugger mode
  ip                   The remote IP address.
  routing-instance     The routing instance (default: the default instance).
  |                    Pipe through a command
```

The CLI will provide command completion for these arguments, just as it would for any other CLI command. Typing `op example-script rout<space>` will cause the CLI to expand the command line to `op example-script routing-instance`.

However, unlike with many other CLI commands, you can provide any argument you desire. The system will pass these to the op script. If the op script has a matching `param` statement, it can use the argument. Otherwise, the argument will be silently discarded.

Here, you see an example of a user entering an argument that is not in the help output:

```
user@r0> op example-script not-an-argument foo
```

The CLI does not complain when the user enters this command, and dutifully passes it along to the op script.

Op Script Document Processing

Similar to the way commit scripts process an input document to produce an output document, op scripts needs to process the input document and create an output document. However, op script input and output documents carry different information than commit script input and output documents. Unlike commit scripts, op scripts usually do not receive much information in the input document that tells them what they should do. Rather, they often care about arguments, or need only state information in order to produce an output document. And unlike a commit script output document, which sends directions to the router to control the process of committing a configuration, an op script output document contains XML output that the CLI will convert to text and display to the user. This process is illustrated in Figure 6-1.

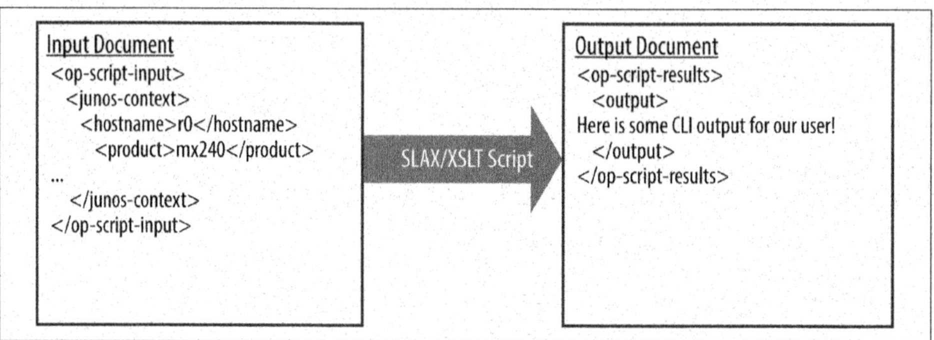

Figure 6-1. Sample op script XML documents

Even though a SLAX script normally does not need to process the input document, the input document still serves as the trigger to launch the SLAX script's processing. You still should have a match template to serve as the equivalent to a `main()` function for the script.

Example 6-1 can serve as a boilerplate SLAX op script.

Example 6-1. A SLAX boilerplate template for op scripts

```
version 1.1;

ns junos = "http://xml.juniper.net/junos/*/junos";
ns xnm = "http://xml.juniper.net/xnm/1.1/xnm";
ns jcs = "http://xml.juniper.net/junos/commit-scripts/1.0";

import "../import/junos.xsl";

match / {
    <op-script-results> {
        /* Your logic goes here... */
    }
}
```

This script imports a standard file with some helpful contents, defines a match template that will match the input document, and encloses your output within appropriate XML tags.

The contents of your script will likely be calls to access some sort of operational or configuration state. We will discuss the method for using those RPC calls in "Operational and Configuration State" on page 338.

Op Script Output Document

The output document is enclosed in a root element. The tag for the root element is generally ignored and blindly discarded (unless you happen to use one of a few tags with a reserved meaning), but we recommend using the `<op-script-results>` tag.

Within this outer tag, you can insert any XML data that the CLI knows how to interpret. A few common tags are:

`<output>`
: This should contain text to display to the user. The contents of the element are displayed on the CLI as plain text.

`<xnm:warning>`
: This should contain a `<message>` element with a warning message to display to the user. When printed on the CLI, `warning:` and a space will be prepended to the message.

`<xnm:error>`
: This should contain a `<message>` element with an error message to display to the user. When printed on the CLI, `error:` and a space will be prepended to the message.

In addition to these tags, the CLI can display the XML output of any other CLI command. You can use an RPC call to gather the XML output of one or more CLI commands and then include all, or some, of that XML data in your output document. The CLI will display it just as if it had received the data in response to the actual CLI command.

Of course, you also have the option of using your own XML schema for your output document. While the Junos CLI may not be able to display it to the user, you can program other applications that understand your XML schema to run an op script and read the XML data it produces.

Operational and Configuration State

You will usually want your op and event scripts to interact with your device's operational or configuration state. In op and event scripts, you can view the current operational and configuration states. You can also change those states.

Interacting with Operational State

You use RPCs to interact with a router's operational state. As we described in Chapter 2, you can use RPCs to do many things you can do in the CLI. We assume that you have read that chapter and already know how to discover both the correct RPC to use and the expected reply syntax.

Making a connection to the device

If you only want to run operational RPCs on the local device, there is no need to make a specific connection to the device's management system. Instead, you can automatically connect to it.

However, if you want to manage other systems, you can connect to them using the Junoscript or NETCONF protocols. That means that (at least in theory) you can manage any device that supports NETCONF, regardless of the vendor.

As you will see in later sections, there is a slightly different execution path when you have an explicit connection than there is when you are relying on the implicit connection to the local system. In addition, there are times when you really do need a connection to the local system (particularly, when you want to use the `jcs:load-configuration()` helper template.

You make an explicit connection to a management system using the `jcs:open()` function. The function returns a connection handle. If you call the function with no arguments, it will create a connection to the local system:

```
var $con = jcs:open();
```

If you want to connect to a remote Junos device, you can instead call a version with three or four arguments. Calling `jcs:open(`*`hostname`*`, `*`username`*`, `*`password`*`[, `*`routing-instance`*`])` will open a connection to the given hostname using the specified username and password. If a routing instance is specified, the device will source the SSH connection from the specified routing instance. For example, to connect to `r1` with the username `user` and the password `user123` over the default routing instance, you could use this call:

```
var $con = jcs:open("r1", "user", "user123");
```

If you want to connect to a remote system any other way, then you will want to specify session options. You can specify as few or as many as you want. The remaining options will be filled in by the default values:

`<username>`
: The username that should be used when connecting to the remote device via SSH. If this element is missing, the device uses the username of the user executing the script.

`<password>`
: The password that should be used when connecting to the remote device via SSH. If this element is missing, the device will prompt the user to enter a password when she runs the script.

`<port>`
: The port number used when connecting to the remote device. If this element is missing, the device will use port 22 when using the `junoscript` or `junos-netconf` methods, or port 830 when using the `netconf` method.

`<routing-instance>`
: The name of the routing instance that should be used as the source of the SSH connection. If this element is missing, the device sources the SSH connection from the default routing instance.

`<method>`
: The protocol that will be used for communication with the remote device. This element should contain one of three values: `junoscript`, `netconf`, or `junos-netconf`. The router uses SSH to transport all three of the protocols. The default is the `junoscript` method.

  If connecting to a Junos device, you should use the `junoscript` or `junos-netconf` protocols. If connecting to another vendor's device, you should use the `netconf` protocol.

For example, to connect to the Junos device `r1` with the username `user` and have the script prompt you for the password, you could use:

```
var $session-options := {
    <username> "user";
}
var $con = jcs:open("r1", $session-options);
```

Or, to open a NETCONF session to the Junos device `r1` using the username of the user running the script and prompting the user for the password, you could use:

```
var $session-options := {
    <method> "junos-netconf";
}
var $con = jcs:open("r1", $session-options);
```

Executing RPCs

You execute an operational RPC by forming the XML that specifies the RPC operation and then passing that as an argument to either the `jcs:execute()` or the `jcs:invoke()` function. When you use the `jcs:invoke()` function, the RPC is executed on the local device using an implicit connection to the local device. When you use the `jcs:execute()` function, the RPC is executed on a connection you have opened using the `jcs:open()` function.

The `jcs:invoke()` function creates a connection to the local RE, executes the RPC, and closes the connection. This means that the software creates a new, temporary connection to the management system for each `jcs:invoke()` function call. For this reason, if you will be executing more than one or two RPCs, it is a good idea to create a connection handle using the `jcs:open()` function and use the `jcs:execute()` function to execute RPCs over the connection you establish.

Both functions take the XML RPC as an argument. For example, to execute the RPC equivalent of the `show version brief` CLI command, you would form the XML like this:

```
var $rpc-query = {
    <get-software-information> {
        <brief>;
    }
}
```

To execute this RPC against the local system, you can call `jcs:invoke()`. To execute this against a connection handle, you can call `jcs:execute()`. Therefore, the two templates in the following code block do the same thing. The main difference between the templates is that it is easy to rewrite `sw-info-local-explicit()` to execute the same RPCs against a remote connection, while it would be harder to rewrite `sw-info-local-implicit()` to execute the RPCs against a remote connection:

```
var $rpc-query = {
    <get-software-information> {
        <brief>;
    }
```

```
}
template sw-info-local-explicit() {
    var $con = jcs:open();
    copy-of jcs:execute($con, $rpc-query);
    expr jcs:close($con);
}
template sw-info-local-implicit() {
    copy-of jcs:invoke($rpc-query);
}
```

Normally, you need to include the XML hierarchy for the RPC. However, there is a shortcut available if you want to execute an RPC with no options. In that case, you can just provide the RPC string as an option to the `jcs:invoke()` and `jcs:execute()` functions. For example, these two RPC calls are equivalent:

```
var $rpc-query = {
    <get-system-uptime-information>;
}
copy-of jcs:invoke($rpc-query);
copy-of jcs:invoke("get-system-uptime-information");
```

The `jcs:invoke()` and `jcs:execute()` functions return the XML output of the RPC call. You can assign this to a variable and then use XPath expressions to gather the desired information. Or, if you want to include the full XML output in your output document, you can use the `copy-of` statement to include the full XML output in the output document. If you return the full XML output to the user and the user runs the op script from a CLI session, the CLI will accept the XML output and display the output in the normal CLI format for that command.

For example, consider the *get-software-information* RPC. When you run the *get-software-information* RPC, it produces a return document with this information (although we've greatly trimmed it for purposes of this book):

```
<rpc-reply>
    <software-information>
        <host-name>r0</host-name>
        <product-model>mx240</product-model>
        <product-name>mx240</product-name>
        <junos-version>15.1R1.9</junos-version>
        ...output trimmed...
    </software-information>
</rpc-reply>
```

You can assign the RPC results to a variable like this:

```
var $results = jcs:execute($con, "get-software-information");
```

Once you assign the RPC results using this syntax, `$results` contains the XML reply results just shown, rooted at the `<software-information>` node. Therefore, to access the `<junos-version>` element, you would use the XPath expression `$results/junos-version`.

For example, this script shows the current Junos version:

```
version 1.1;

ns junos = "http://xml.juniper.net/junos/*/junos";
ns xnm = "http://xml.juniper.net/xnm/1.1/xnm";
ns jcs = "http://xml.juniper.net/junos/commit-scripts/1.0";

import "../import/junos.xsl";

match / {
    <op-script-results> {
        var $con = jcs:open();
        var $results = jcs:execute($con, "get-software-information");
        <output> "The Junos version is: " _ $results/junos-version;
        expr jcs:close($con);
    }
}
```

And when you run this script, you see the expected results:

```
user@r0> op url /tmp/version.slax
The Junos version is: 15.1R1.9
```

If you desire, you can instead pass the full XML output of the command to the user. If the user runs the op script from the CLI, the CLI will format the output normally.

For example, this script will run the *get-system-uptime-information* RPC (the equivalent of the `show system uptime` CLI command) and return the XML results to the user:

```
version 1.1;

ns junos = "http://xml.juniper.net/junos/*/junos";
ns xnm = "http://xml.juniper.net/xnm/1.1/xnm";
ns jcs = "http://xml.juniper.net/junos/commit-scripts/1.0";

import "../import/junos.xsl";

match / {
    <op-script-results> {
        var $con = jcs:open();
        copy-of jcs:execute($con, "get-system-uptime-information");
        expr jcs:close($con);
    }
}
```

The `copy-of` statement tells the SLAX processor to include a copy of the XML results in the output document. When you run this script on a Junos device, you see this output:

```
user@r0> op url /tmp/uptime.slax
Current time: 2015-11-17 17:03:19 PST
```

```
Time Source:  LOCAL CLOCK
System booted: 2015-11-17 02:27:35 PST (14:35:44 ago)
Protocols started: 2015-11-17 02:29:36 PST (14:33:43 ago)
Last configured: 2015-11-13 12:00:12 PST (4d 05:03 ago) by user
 5:03PM  up 14:36, 1 users, load averages: 0.15, 0.21, 0.18
```

The op script returned the XML output. (In fact, you can see this for yourself by adding the `display xml` pipe command to the preceding command.) However, the CLI rendered the XML output as normal.

You can also use this to your advantage by returning filtered XML output. We will show an example of this in "Example: Filtering CLI Output" on page 380.

In addition to viewing operational state using RPCs, you can also change operational state using appropriate RPCs. For example, this script will clear the BGP session specified by the `neighbor` parameter:

```
version 1.1;

ns junos = "http://xml.juniper.net/junos/*/junos";
ns xnm = "http://xml.juniper.net/xnm/1.1/xnm";
ns jcs = "http://xml.juniper.net/junos/commit-scripts/1.0";

import "../import/junos.xsl";

param $neighbor;

match / {
    <op-script-results> {
        var $con = jcs:open();

        var $rpc-query = {
            <clear-bgp-neighbor> {
                <neighbor> $neighbor;
            }
        }

        var $rpc-result = jcs:execute($con, $rpc-query);
        expr jcs:close($con);
    }
}
```

Closing your session

If you made a connection to a device using the `jcs:open()` function, you should close it using the `jcs:close(`*`handle`*`)` function. The following example will close a connection with the handle `$con`:

```
expr jcs:close($con);
```

Interacting with Configuration State

Just as you can interact with operational state using RPCs, Junos provides a method for you to interact with configuration state using RPCs. However, as we described in "Operational RPCs to View and Change the Configuration" on page 78, the process may be more complex than your normal RPC call.

Accessing configuration data

You can access the committed configuration using the *get-configuration* RPC. More information on this RPC is found in "Viewing the Configuration" on page 79.

There are two particular attributes to note. First, you will probably want to add the `database="committed"` attribute for this RPC. This will ensure you are viewing the committed, and not the candidate, configuration. Second, you *might* want to add the `inherit="inherit"` attribute. This will have the impact of expanding the configuration groups and `apply-path` statements, and placing those expanded configuration statements in the correct portion of the configuration. Without the `inherit="inherit"` attribute, configuration groups and `apply-path` statements will not be expanded in the configuration. Depending on your use case, it might be more appropriate to use or to not use the `inherit="inherit"` attribute.

For example, this script will return the XML representation of the committed `[edit interfaces]` configuration. If the user provides an `inheritance` argument, it will return the configuration with inheritance. This script is not very useful on its own, but it does provide a quick way to demonstrate a few aspects of accessing the configuration:

```
version 1.1;

ns junos = "http://xml.juniper.net/junos/*/junos";
ns xnm = "http://xml.juniper.net/xnm/1.1/xnm";
ns jcs = "http://xml.juniper.net/junos/commit-scripts/1.0";

import "../import/junos.xsl";

param $inheritance;

match / {
    <op-script-results> {
        var $con = jcs:open();

        var $rpc-query = {
            <get-configuration database="committed"> { ❶
                if ($inheritance) {
                    attribute "inherit" { ❷
                        expr "inherit";
                    }
```

```
                }
                <configuration> { ❸
                    <interfaces>;
                }
            }
        }

        copy-of jcs:execute($con, $rpc-query);
        expr jcs:close($con);
    }
}
```

❶ Because we always want to access the committed configuration, we place the `database="committed"` attribute in the `<get-configuration>` tag.

❷ When the user supplies the `inheritance` argument (with any nonempty value), we want to add the `inherit="inherit"` attribute. This syntax does that.

❸ This XML stanza limits the query to the contents of the `[edit interfaces]` hierarchy.

When we run the script, we see the expected data. Note especially the `<apply-groups>` element, which shows that the `int` group is applied to this section of the configuration. Also, note that the MPLS address family does not appear for any unit:

```
user@r0> op url /tmp/get-config.slax | display xml
<rpc-reply xmlns:junos="http://xml.juniper.net/junos/15.1R1/junos">
    <configuration junos:commit-seconds="1448051403"
                   junos:commit-localtime="2015-11-20 12:30:03 PST"
                   junos:commit-user="root">
        <interfaces>
            <apply-groups>
                int
            </apply-groups>
            <interface>
                <name>
                    ge-1/0/0
                </name>
                <vlan-tagging/>
                <unit>
                    <name>
                        0
                    </name>
                    <vlan-id>
                        60
                    </vlan-id>
                    <family>
                        <inet>
                            <address>
                                <name>
```

```
                                    192.168.2.1/24
                                </name>
                            </address>
                        </inet>
                        <inet6>
                        </inet6>
                    </family>
                </unit>
            </interface>
            <interface>
                <name>
                    ge-1/0/1
                </name>
                <unit>
                    <name>
                    0
                    </name>
                    <family>
                        <inet>
                            <address>
                                <name>
                                    10.2.3.4/24
                                </name>
                            </address>
                        </inet>
                    </family>
                </unit>
            </interface>
        </interfaces>
    </configuration>
    <cli>
    <banner></banner>
    </cli>
</rpc-reply>
```

When we rerun the script with the `inheritance` argument, note that the `<apply-groups>` element is no longer present. Because the contents of the group are shown in the configuration, it is no longer necessary to show the `<apply-groups>` element. Also, note that the MPLS address family now appears for all units:

```
user@r0> show configuration groups int
interfaces {
    <*> {
        unit <*> {
            family mpls;
        }
    }
}

user@r0> op url /tmp/get-config.slax inheritance true | display xml
<rpc-reply xmlns:junos="http://xml.juniper.net/junos/15.1R1/junos">
    <configuration junos:commit-seconds="1448051403"
```

```
            junos:commit-localtime="2015-11-20 12:30:03 PST"
            junos:commit-user="root">
<interfaces>
    <interface>
        <name>
            ge-1/0/0
        </name>
        <vlan-tagging/>
        <unit>
            <name>
                0
            </name>
            <vlan-id>
                60
            </vlan-id>
            <family>
                <inet>
                    <address>
                        <name>
                            192.168.2.1/24
                        </name>
                    </address>
                </inet>
                <inet6>
                </inet6>
                <mpls>
                </mpls>
            </family>
        </unit>
    </interface>
    <interface>
        <name>
            ge-1/0/1
        </name>
        <unit>
            <name>
            0
            </name>
            <family>
                <inet>
                    <address>
                        <name>
                            10.2.3.4/24
                        </name>
                    </address>
                </inet>
                <mpls>
                </mpls>
            </family>
        </unit>
    </interface>
</interfaces>
```

```
    </configuration>
    <cli>
    <banner></banner>
    </cli>
</rpc-reply>
```

Changing configuration data

Changing configuration data is a snap, thanks to the Juniper-supplied `jcs:load-configuration()` template that automates much of the work. The `jcs:load-configuration()` template locks the configuration, loads the configuration change, and commits it. The template only supports the exclusive configuration mode (see "Exclusive configuration mode" on page 17 for more information on this mode).

Let's take a look at the arguments you can pass to this template:

`$connection`
: This required argument provides the connection handle that the template should use to execute the configuration change. Note that this template does not support the use of the implicit connection to the local RE. Instead, to reconfigure the local router, you must use the `jcs:open()` function to open a connection and pass the resulting connection handle using this argument.

`$configuration`
: This argument specifies the configuration change that the template should make. The value of the argument is the XML content (enclosed in a `<configuration>` element) that the template should include as a child node inside the *load-configuration* RPC, as described in "Loading configuration changes" on page 83.

  You should include either the `$configuration` or the `$rollback` argument, but not both.

`$rollback`
: This argument specifies the rollback configuration that the script should try to load. The value of the argument is a number that corresponds to the number of commits that have occurred since the configuration was committed. (The current configuration is 0, the previously committed configuration is 1, the one before that is 2, etc.) This is the same number used to identify the rollback configurations in the CLI.

  You should include either the `$configuration` or the `$rollback` argument, but not both.

`$action`
: This optional argument specifies the way the system should load the configuration you provide. The value should be one of the values for the `action` attribute,

as described in “Loading configuration changes” on page 83. If you do not supply this argument, the default is to use the `merge` action.

`$commit-options`
: This optional argument controls the way the configuration should be committed. If provided, the contents of the argument should be enclosed in a `<commit-options>` element.

  The contents of the `<commit-options>` element may be one or more of the child elements you could include in the `<commit-configuration>` RPC call. (See “Choosing a commit style” on page 89 for a list of these elements.) The exceptions are that you may not include the `<confirmed/>` or `<confirm-timeout>` elements.

We will demonstrate the usage of the `jcs:load-configuration()` template using a simple script that resets the hostname on our device. The script opens a connection to the local system. It then loads the configuration change using that connection and specifying a log message of `test commit`. Then it closes the session.

Because we call the `jcs:load-configuration()` template directly in the body of the script, the results of the template will be added to our output document. The CLI knows how to interpret the results. Therefore, our script should produce output similar to what you would see if you typed `commit` in configuration mode in the CLI:

```
version 1.1;

ns junos = "http://xml.juniper.net/junos/*/junos";
ns xnm = "http://xml.juniper.net/xnm/1.1/xnm";
ns jcs = "http://xml.juniper.net/junos/commit-scripts/1.0";

import "../import/junos.xsl";

match / {
    <op-script-results> {
        var $con = jcs:open();
        call jcs:load-configuration {
            with $connection = $con;
            with $configuration = {
                <configuration> {
                    <system> {
                        <host-name> "r1";
                    }
                }
            }
            with $commit-options = {
                <commit-options> {
                    <log> "test commit";
                }
            }
```

```
        }
        expr jcs:close($con);
    }
}
```

When you execute this script, you should see output similar to the following:

```
user@r0> op url /tmp/config-change.slax
commit complete
```

And as these commands show, the change did take effect:

```
user@r0> show configuration | compare rollback 1
[edit system]
-   host-name r0;
+   host-name r1;

user@r0> show system commit
0   2015-11-20 16:55:26 PST by user via junoscript
    test commit
...output trimmed...

user@r1>
```

You may have noticed that the CLI prompt did not change until after the `show system commit` command completed. It is unclear why it takes the CLI so long to change the prompt, but these results are replicable. So, don't be surprised if you see similar results when you attempt to complete this example in your environment.

Op Script Input and Output

As we mentioned in "Op Script Output Document" on page 337, the primary way your script can return output is through the XML return document that it builds as it executes. As we demonstrated in "Executing RPCs" on page 340, you can include many XML elements in the output document. You can use the `<output>` element to display raw text to a user. You can also include XML output from CLI commands and allow the CLI to automatically format the output. Or, you can include errors or warnings.

And, as we discussed in "Op Script Arguments" on page 334, users can provide input to op scripts by providing arguments at the time they run the scripts. However, this method may not be desirable for all use cases.

There are several other options for handling input and output. We will review some of those in this section.

Formatting Output

You can use the options discussed in "Formatting text" on page 266 to format text. In particular, the `jcs:printf()` function can help you format your text output in the way you desire.

You can use the `jcs:printf()` (or `slax:printf()`) function[1] to format text regardless of how it will be used. You certainly can include the text in an `<output>` element in your return document. However, you can also use it to produce the arguments passed to other functions (such as the `jcs:output()` function).

Displaying Immediate Output

At times, it may be desirable to produce intermediate output to let your users know what is happening as the script executes. Consider, for example, a script that executes a large number of RPCs to determine information. It may be desirable to let the user know that the script is running and has not entered an error state. Likewise, if a script monitors information over a period of time, it might be wise to print a message advising users that the script will execute for some time.

You can send immediate output to a CLI session using the `jcs:output()` (or `slax:output()`) function. The `jcs:output()` function takes a text argument and immediately displays it to the CLI. The function will wrap the text argument in an `<output>` element, so there is no need for your script to do so. Instead, you just provide a text argument to the `jcs:output()` function and the function will send it to the CLI to display to the user.

This is perhaps best illustrated by a script. To obtain the full effect, you should run this script on your own Junos device:

```
version 1.1;

ns junos = "http://xml.juniper.net/junos/*/junos";
ns xnm = "http://xml.juniper.net/xnm/1.1/xnm";
ns jcs = "http://xml.juniper.net/junos/commit-scripts/1.0";

import "../import/junos.xsl";

match / {
    <op-script-output> {
        for $i (1 ... 3) {
            <output> jcs:printf("Waiting (<output> element %d)...", $i);
```

1 Several functions appear in both the `jcs` and `slax` namespace. The functions are exactly the same—the two function entries point to the same code. When introducing extension functions that exist in both namespaces, we will generally note this. However, when discussing them, we will generally refer to the function with the `jcs` namespace.

```
                expr jcs:output(jcs:printf("Waiting (jcs:output call %d)...", $i));
                expr jcs:sleep(1);
            }
        }
    }
```

When you execute this script, you see this output. In addition, you should see that the lines produced by `jcs:output()` calls are printed immediately, while the lines produced by `<output>` elements in the output document are printed at the end of the script's execution:

```
user@r0> op url /tmp/outputtest.slax
Waiting (jcs:output call 1)...
Waiting (jcs:output call 2)...
Waiting (jcs:output call 3)...
Waiting (<output> element 1)...
Waiting (<output> element 2)...
Waiting (<output> element 3)...
```

Normally, your script shouldn't need to return the contents of a CLI command immediately. However, if you do find the need to do so, you can have the RPC return text-formatted output by adding the `format="text"` XML attribute to the RPC. You can then pass the results of the RPC to the `jcs:output()` function.

For example, this sequence will get the text-formatted output of the *get-system-uptime-information* RPC (equivalent to the `show system uptime` CLI command) and return it to the user immediately:

```
var $rpc = <get-system-uptime-information format="text">;
expr jcs:output(jcs:invoke($rpc));
```

Obtaining User Input

You can obtain user input through runtime arguments. However, you may find it desirable to interactively obtain user input. This is particularly useful for secret strings (such as passwords) that you do not want exposed on the command line.

There are two functions you can use to interactively obtain input from a user. The functions behave the same way, except that one displays user input on the console, while the other one disables the display of user input.

Obtaining normal user input

The `jcs:get-input()` (or `slax:get-input()`) function obtains user input. The function takes a single argument, which is a text string that should be used as the prompt. Note that the CLI will use the *exact* text string as the prompt it displays to the user. Therefore, if you want a space or other delimiter (such as :, $, or >) to follow the prompt, you need to supply it.

The result of the `jcs:get-input()` function is a text string with the user's input.

This simple script demonstrates the concept. It prompts a user for input and then outputs it in the CLI session:

```
version 1.1;

ns junos = "http://xml.juniper.net/junos/*/junos";
ns xnm = "http://xml.juniper.net/xnm/1.1/xnm";
ns jcs = "http://xml.juniper.net/junos/commit-scripts/1.0";

import "../import/junos.xsl";

match / {
    <op-script-output> {
        var $userstring = jcs:get-input("Enter a string: ");
        <output> jcs:printf("The user string was: \"%s\".", $userstring);
    }
}
```

When you execute this script, you see that the CLI prompts the user using the *exact* prompt (including the trailing space) that the script provided. You see that the script receives the user input and outputs it to the user:

```
user@r0> op url /tmp/userinputtest.slax
Enter a string: abc
The user string was: "abc".

user@r0> op url /tmp/userinputtest.slax
Enter a string: foo bar baz
The user string was: "foo bar baz".
```

The `jcs:get-input()` function returns *exactly* what the user provided, including leading and trailing spaces. As usual when dealing with user input, your script must thoroughly validate the user input to ensure the format and value are what the script expects to receive.

If you want to accept user input through arguments and interactively prompt for missing arguments, you can modify your script to conditionally request user input. In this example, we modify the script so it accepts user input through a `string` argument. If the user does not supply a `string` argument, the script will prompt the user for the argument:

```
version 1.1;

ns junos = "http://xml.juniper.net/junos/*/junos";
ns xnm = "http://xml.juniper.net/xnm/1.1/xnm";
ns jcs = "http://xml.juniper.net/junos/commit-scripts/1.0";
```

```
import "../import/junos.xsl";

param $string;

match / {
    <op-script-output> {
        var $userstring = {
            if ($string) {
                expr $string;
            }
            else {
                expr jcs:get-input("Enter a string: ");
            }
        }
        <output> jcs:printf("The user string was: \"%s\".", $userstring);
    }
}
```

After the change, we see that the script accepts the user-supplied string either through an argument or interactively:

```
user@r0> op url /tmp/userinputtest.slax string foo
The user string was: "foo".

user@r0> op url /tmp/userinputtest.slax
Enter a string: foobar
The user string was: "foobar".
```

Obtaining secrets interactively

There are times you may want to obtain secrets (such as passwords) interactively from a user. Indeed, you often do *not* want to obtain secrets through CLI arguments. Commands entered through the CLI are not secure, as they may be logged. Instead, it is best to obtain secrets interactively.

You can use the `jcs:get-secret()` (or `slax:get-secret()`) function to interactively obtain user input. The `jcs:get-secret()` function behaves the same as the `jcs:get-input()` function, except that it will tell the CLI not to echo back the user's input to him as he types.

This simple script again demonstrates the concept. It prompts a user for input and then outputs it in the CLI session:

```
version 1.1;

ns junos = "http://xml.juniper.net/junos/*/junos";
ns xnm = "http://xml.juniper.net/xnm/1.1/xnm";
ns jcs = "http://xml.juniper.net/junos/commit-scripts/1.0";

import "../import/junos.xsl";
```

```
match / {
    <op-script-output> {
        var $userstring = jcs:get-secret("Enter a string: ");
        <output> jcs:printf("The user string was: \"%s\".", $userstring);
    }
}
```

When you execute this script, you again see that the CLI prompts the user using the exact prompt (including the trailing space) that the script provided. The script receives the user input and outputs it to the user:

```
user@r0> op url /tmp/usersecrettest.slax
Enter a string:
The user string was: "abc".

user@r0> op url /tmp/usersecrettest.slax
Enter a string:
The user string was: "foo bar baz".
```

Some Useful Tools for Op and Event Scripts

There are a few tools that may come in handy with op and event scripts. We will cover these briefly here, but more information is available in other documents that we reference.

Dampening Events

You may find that you want to limit the number of times a particular script can be called in a short time. You can accomplish this in two ways: through configuration, or through the `jcs:dampen()` function.

You can configure resource limits with the **`dampen`** statement at the `[edit system scripts op]` or `[edit event-options event-script]` hierarchy level. You can also configure the **`dampen`** statement for just particular scripts within their configuration sections.

Alternatively, you can use the `jcs:dampen()` (or `slax:dampen()`) function to control dampening within your script. The `jcs:dampen()` function gives you more fine-grained control over the dampening. It takes three positional arguments: *`class`*, an arbitrary user-supplied string value that uniquely identifies the class of events you wish to dampen; *`max-number`*, the maximum number of events that you want to allow within the specified time interval; and *`interval`*, the number of minutes in the past during which you want to check for these events.

When you call the `jcs:dampen()` function, the SLAX parser examines the history of calls to this function with the same user-supplied *`class`* string value. If the function was successfully called less than *`max_number`* of times (not including the current call) over the preceding *interval* number of minutes, then the jcs:dampen() function returns the Boolean value True and adds an entry for the current call to the history file. Otherwise, the jcs:dampen() function returns the Boolean value False and does not add an entry for the current call to the history file.

It is important to note that the string value that uniquely identifies the class of events you wish to dampen is shared across *all* scripts. This allows you to dampen events across scripts.

Also, it is important to note that the history file is regenerated with each call to jcs:dampen(). For each user-supplied *class* string value, the code flushes history entries that occurred more than *interval* minutes in the past. In practice, this means that you must use the same *interval* value for each call to jcs:dampen() function for a given *class*.

Let's consider an example of using the jcs:dampen() function. Imagine you only want to allow one automated commit per minute. To meet this requirement, you could use this code to control commits in each of your scripts:

```
if (jcs:dampen("commit", 1, 1)) {
    /* Do the commit. */
} else {
    /* Display an error to the user. */
}
```

Parsing Strings

You can use extension functions such as jcs:regex() (or slax:regex()), jcs:split() (or slax:split()), and jcs:parse-ip() to parse strings. These extension functions are described in Juniper's documentation (*http://www.juniper.net/documentation/en_US/junos15.1/topics/reference/general/junos-script-automation-junos-extension-functions.html*).

We provide an example of using the jcs:regex() function in "Example: Dynamically Expanding Configuration" on page 309. For an example of using the jcs:split() function, see "Example: Custom CLI Command" on page 369.

Generating SNMP Objects and Traps

You can use the Junos Utility Management Information Base (MIB) to store custom data for a Simple Network Management Protocol (SNMP) client to query. You can have your op, commit, or event scripts populate SNMP objects in this MIB that your network management system (NMS) will read. Your NMS can track this information and/or raise alerts for operators based on this information.

The use of the Junos Utility MIB is documented in Juniper's technical documents, available on their website (*http://www.juniper.net/techpubs*). We also recommend consulting *This Week: Mastering Junos Automation Programming* by Jeremy Schulman and Curtis Call (Juniper Networks Books).

You can also generate SNMP traps. You can cause the device to generate one of the standard Junos traps using the *request-snmp-spoof-trap* RPC. You can also use that same RPC to generate a `jnxEventTrap`, to which you can assign custom attribute/value pairs. Again, this allows you to have your op, commit, or event scripts feed information to your NMS through SNMP. However, in this case, the scripts will be pushing information to the NMS, rather than waiting for the NMS to poll for the information. You can program your NMS to take appropriate actions when it receives SNMP traps generated by your scripts.

We again recommend consulting *This Week: Mastering Junos Automation Programming* for more information on generating SNMP traps.

Debugging Op and Event Scripts

There are several methods you can use to debug your op and event scripts. These range from printing extra messages about the script's progress to invoking an interactive debugger.

Printing Progress Messages

You can print progress messages to the CLI using the `jcs:progress()` function. These messages only appear when a user runs the script using the `detail` flag. (And because the `detail` flag is currently only available with op scripts, this functionality only works for debugging op scripts.)

The operation of this command is nearly identical to the operation of the `jcs:output()` command. The biggest differences are that the output only appears on the CLI when a user runs a script using the `detail` flag, and the output is preceded by a timestamp.

This is perhaps best illustrated by a script. To obtain the full effect, you should run this script on your own Junos device:

```
version 1.1;

ns junos = "http://xml.juniper.net/junos/*/junos";
ns xnm = "http://xml.juniper.net/xnm/1.1/xnm";
ns jcs = "http://xml.juniper.net/junos/commit-scripts/1.0";

import "../import/junos.xsl";

match / {
    <op-script-output> {
        for $i (1 ... 3) {
```

```
                <output> jcs:printf("Waiting (<output> element %d)...", $i);
                expr jcs:progress(jcs:printf("Waiting (jcs:progress call %d)...",
                                 $i));
                expr jcs:sleep(1);
            }
        }
    }
```

When you execute this script, you'll see output similar to the following. In addition, you should observe that there is an approximately three-second pause prior to seeing any output when you run the op script without the `detail` flag. When you run the op script with the `detail` flag, you should observe that the lines produced by the `jcs:progress()` calls are printed immediately, preceded by a timestamp:

```
user@r0> op url /tmp/progresstest.slax
Waiting (<output> element 1)...
Waiting (<output> element 2)...
Waiting (<output> element 3)...

user@r0> op url /tmp/progresstest.slax detail
2015-11-24 07:21:10 PST: reading op script input details
2015-11-24 07:21:10 PST: testing op details
2015-11-24 07:21:10 PST: running op script '/var/tmp/.../progresstest.slax'
2015-11-24 07:21:10 PST: opening op script '/var/tmp/.../progresstest.slax'
2015-11-24 07:21:10 PST: reading op script '/var/tmp/.../progresstest.slax'
2015-11-24 07:21:10 PST: Waiting (jcs:progress call 1)...
2015-11-24 07:21:11 PST: Waiting (jcs:progress call 2)...
2015-11-24 07:21:12 PST: Waiting (jcs:progress call 3)...
2015-11-24 07:21:13 PST: inspecting op output '/var/tmp/.../progresstest.slax'
Waiting (<output> element 1)...
Waiting (<output> element 2)...
Waiting (<output> element 3)...
2015-11-24 07:21:13 PST: finished op script '/var/tmp/.../progresstest.slax'
```

In this way, you can use the `jcs:progress()` function to insert lightweight debugging statements that any user can activate at runtime using the `detail` flag.

Trace Messages

The traceoptions functionality provided by the script system is useful in understanding the operation of your script. The system defines several categories of trace messages you can choose to record, including the input document provided to the script, the output document generated by the script, important events during the script execution, and RPCs. You can use the trace output to understand the execution of your script.

In addition to the standard system-generated trace messages, you can record custom trace messages to a trace file using the `jcs:trace()` function. This method of recording trace debugging information is useful when the item running the op script may not be able to run it with the `detail` flag. In addition, this method is especially useful for event scripts, which are not designed to return output to an interactive session. Finally, the `jcs:trace()` function is also useful when you want to be able to see user-defined trace messages placed in the trace file together with system-generated trace messages so you can correlate the system-generated trace messages with events in your script.

To record a custom trace message, you use the `jcs:trace()` function. The syntax is the same as the syntax for the `jcs:progress()` function. However, the message will be sent to a tracefile if (and only if) you have configured traceoptions for the kind of automation script in which the `jcs:trace()` call appears. For example, if you are running an op script, you must enable traceoptions in the `[edit system scripts op traceoptions]` hierarchy.

Here, we will modify our previous example to use the `jcs:trace()` function instead of the `jcs:progress()` function:

```
version 1.1;

ns junos = "http://xml.juniper.net/junos/*/junos";
ns xnm = "http://xml.juniper.net/xnm/1.1/xnm";
ns jcs = "http://xml.juniper.net/junos/commit-scripts/1.0";

import "../import/junos.xsl";

match / {
    <op-script-output> {
        for $i (1 ... 3) {
            <output> jcs:printf("Waiting (<output> element %d)...", $i);
            expr jcs:trace(jcs:printf("Waiting (jcs:trace call %d)...", $i));
            expr jcs:sleep(1);
        }
    }
}
```

Junos does not generate trace messages for scripts run though the `op url` command. Therefore, in order to use traceoptions, we need to move the script to the */var/db/scripts/op* directory and add it to the configuration. We will also add the traceoptions configuration. We will select to view the input document, output document, and important events. (Regardless of which traceoptions flags you configure, CSCRIPT includes messages generated by the `jcs:trace()` function anytime you have configured a trace file.)

The complete configuration is shown here:

```
user@r0> show configuration system scripts op
traceoptions {
    file op-trace;
    flag events;
```

```
    flag input;
    flag output;
}
file tracetest.slax;
```

When we run the script, we see the output from the `<output>` elements:

```
user@r0> op tracetest
Waiting (<output> element 1)...
Waiting (<output> element 2)...
Waiting (<output> element 3)...
```

After running the script, the traceoptions log file we specified (*op-trace*) contains the trace output we requested:

```
user@r0> show log op-trace
Nov 24 08:09:13 complete script processing begins ❶
Nov 24 08:09:13 opening op script '/var/db/scripts/op/tracetest.slax'
Nov 24 08:09:13 reading op script 'tracetest.slax'
Nov 24 08:09:13 complete script processing ends
Nov 24 08:09:14 complete script processing begins
Nov 24 08:09:14 opening op script '/var/db/scripts/op/tracetest.slax'
Nov 24 08:09:14 reading op script 'tracetest.slax'
Nov 24 08:09:14 complete script processing ends
Nov 24 08:09:14 op script processing begins ❷
Nov 24 08:09:14 reading op script input details
Nov 24 08:09:14 testing op details
Nov 24 08:09:14 op script input ❸
Nov 24 08:09:14 begin dump
<?xml version="1.0"?>
<op-script-input xmlns:junos="http://xml.juniper.net/junos/*/junos">
<junos-context>
<hostname>r0</hostname>
<product>mx240</product>
<localtime>Tue Nov 24 08:09:14 2015</localtime>
<localtime-iso>2015-11-24 08:09:14 PST</localtime-iso>
<script-type>op</script-type>
<pid>6593</pid>
<tty>/dev/pts/0</tty>
<chassis>others</chassis>
<routing-engine-name>re0</routing-engine-name>
<re-master/>
<user-context>
<user>user</user>
<class-name>j-superuser</class-name>
<uid>1001</uid>
<login-name>user</login-name>
</user-context>
<op-context>
</op-context>
</junos-context>
</op-script-input>
Nov 24 08:09:14 end dump
```

```
Nov 24 08:09:14 running op script 'tracetest.slax'
Nov 24 08:09:14 opening op script '/var/db/scripts/op/tracetest.slax'
Nov 24 08:09:14 reading op script 'tracetest.slax'
Nov 24 08:09:14: Waiting (jcs:trace call 1)... ❹
Nov 24 08:09:15: Waiting (jcs:trace call 2)...
Nov 24 08:09:16: Waiting (jcs:trace call 3)...
Nov 24 08:09:17 op script output ❺
Nov 24 08:09:17 begin dump
<?xml version="1.0"?>
<op-script-results xmlns:junos="http://xml.juniper.net/junos/*/junos" xmlns:xnm=
"http://xml.juniper.net/xnm/1.1/xnm" xmlns:jcs="http://xml.juniper.net/junos/com
mit-scripts/1.0">
  <output>Waiting (&lt;output&gt; element 1)...</output>
  <output>Waiting (&lt;output&gt; element 2)...</output>
  <output>Waiting (&lt;output&gt; element 3)...</output>
</op-script-results>
Nov 24 08:09:17 end dump
Nov 24 08:09:17 inspecting op output 'tracetest.slax'
Nov 24 08:09:17 results of op script
Nov 24 08:09:17 begin dump
<output>Waiting (&lt;output&gt; element 1)...</output>Nov 24 08:09:17 end dump
Nov 24 08:09:17 results of op script
Nov 24 08:09:17 begin dump
<output>Waiting (&lt;output&gt; element 2)...</output>Nov 24 08:09:17 end dump
Nov 24 08:09:17 results of op script
Nov 24 08:09:17 begin dump
<output>Waiting (&lt;output&gt; element 3)...</output>Nov 24 08:09:17 end dump
Nov 24 08:09:17 finished op script 'tracetest.slax'
Nov 24 08:09:17 op script processing ends
```

❶ This line indicates that CSCRIPT has begun evaluating the script for the purpose of gathering the value of the `$arguments` variable to support the CLI question-mark help and command-completion operations. This mode is called the "complete" mode; hence, the line begins with `complete script processing`.

❷ This line indicates that CSCRIPT has begun running the script. This mode is called the "op" mode; hence, the line begins with `op script processing`. When the script is complete, we will see a line that says `op script processing ends`.

❸ This line marks the start of the input document tracing. The following lines display the XML input document that is passed to the script.

❹ These lines are the tracing lines the script generated with the `jcs:trace()` function call. Note that the tracing lines can be interspersed with other tracing information. For example, if we choose to trace RPCs and we call RPCs in between `jcs:trace()` function calls, all the tracing information should appear in the trace file in the order it was generated during script processing.

❺ This line marks the start of the output document tracing. The following lines display the XML output document that the script generates.

Syslog Messages

You can use the `jcs:syslog()` (or `slax:syslog()`) function to generate syslog messages. You can use these syslog messages to create a record of actions taken by the script, to inform users of notable conditions, or to debug your script. These messages are particularly useful for event scripts, which are meant to run without human interaction.

The `jcs:syslog()` function takes a minimum of two arguments, and can be prototyped like this:

```
syslog(priority, message[, message2[, message3[, ...]]]);
```

The *`priority`* argument is a text field that contains a facility and severity in the format *`facility.severity`*, where the *`facility`* and *`severity`* values are the normal facility and severity values used on a Junos router. The following arguments are concatenated to form the message that is sent to the syslog service. The function has no return value.

For example, this code will log the syslog message `This is a test message!` to the `user` facility with a severity of `debug`:

```
expr jcs:syslog("user.debug", "This ", "is ", "a ", "test message", "!");
```

The configuration under the `[edit system syslog]` hierarchy defines the way syslog events are handled by a Junos device. You should ensure that the `[edit system syslog]` configuration will correctly handle the messages your scripts generate.

The SLAX Debugger

The SLAX debugger can be useful in tracking down what is happening while your SLAX scripts execute. To use it, you invoke the op script using the `op invoke-debugger cli` *`script-name`* CLI command.

You can only invoke the SLAX debugger for op scripts that are configured under the `[edit system scripts op]` hierarchy.

To debug an event script using the SLAX debugger, you can provide a static input document in a global variable and change your XPath expressions to read values from there instead of the normal input document. You can then configure this modified script under the `[edit system scripts op]` hierarchy and use the SLAX debugger to monitor its execution.

When you invoke an op script in this way, your CLI session enters the debugger:

```
user@r0> op invoke-debugger cli testscript
sdb: The SLAX Debugger (version 0.17.1)
Type 'help' for help
(sdb)
```

The `help` command lists some of the available commands:

```
(sdb) help
List of commands:
  break [loc]      Add a breakpoint at [file:]line or template
  callflow [val]   Enable call flow tracing
  continue [loc]   Continue running the script
  delete [num]     Delete all (or one) breakpoints
  finish           Finish the current template
  help             Show this help message
  info             Showing info about the script being debugged
  list [loc]       List contents of the current script
  next             Execute the over instruction, stepping over calls
  over             Execute the current instruction hierarchy
  print <xpath>    Print the value of an XPath expression
  profile [val]    Turn profiler on or off
  reload           Reload the script contents
  run              Restart the script
  step             Execute the next instruction, stepping into calls
  verbose          Turn on verbose (-v) output logging
  where            Show the backtrace of template calls
  quit             Quit debugger
Command name abbreviations are allowed
```

The debugger works similarly to other debuggers you may have used. You can set breakpoints, where execution of the script will stop. You can use the `step` command to step through each instruction in a script. You can use the `next` command to step through the instructions in a template, without descending into other templates that the script calls. And you can use the `print` command to evaluate XPath expressions. Like with GDB, hitting the Return key without entering a command causes the SLAX debugger to repeat the last command you entered.

The debugger can help you track down problems with your scripts by letting you monitor their execution. As an example, take this simple script:

```
version 1.1;

ns junos = "http://xml.juniper.net/junos/*/junos";
ns xnm = "http://xml.juniper.net/xnm/1.1/xnm";
ns jcs = "http://xml.juniper.net/junos/commit-scripts/1.0";

import "../import/junos.xsl";

template get_version_info() {
    var $ver = jcs:invoke("get-software-information");
```

```
        copy-of $ver;
    }

    match / {
        <op-script-results> {
            var $version_info = {
                call get_version_info();
            }
            var $outstring = "The Junos version is: " _ $version_info/junos-version;
            <output> $outstring;
        }
    }
```

When we execute this script, we see that the script produces an error:

```
user@r0> op testscript
error: Invalid type
error: runtime error: file /var/db/scripts/op/testscript.slax line 19 element
       variable
error: Failed to evaluate the expression of variable 'outstring'.
```

The line number tells us that the error is generated on the line that assigns a value to the `$outstring` variable. But how did we get into this situation? Let's step through the script to find out:

```
user@r0> op invoke-debugger cli testscript
sdb: The SLAX Debugger (version 0.17.1)
Type 'help' for help
(sdb) step ❶
junos.xsl:31:         event-script-input/junos-context"/>
(sdb)
testscript.slax:14: match / {
(sdb)
testscript.slax:15:     <op-script-results> {
(sdb)
testscript.slax:16:         var $version_info = {
(sdb)
testscript.slax:17:     call get_version_info();
(sdb)
testscript.slax:9: template get_version_info() {
(sdb)
testscript.slax:10:     var $ver = jcs:invoke("get-software-information");
(sdb)
testscript.slax:11:     copy-of $ver;
(sdb) print $ver/junos-version ❷
[node-set] (1)
<junos-version>15.1R2.9</junos-version>
(sdb) step ❸
testscript.slax:19:         var $outstring = "The Junos version is: " _ ...
(sdb) print $version_info/junos-version ❹
error: Invalid type
(sdb) print $version_info ❺
[rtf] (1)
```

```
<software-information>
<host-name>r0</host-name>
<product-model>mx240</product-model>
<product-name>mx240</product-name>
<junos-version>15.1R2.9</junos-version>
<package-information>
<name>os-kernel</name>
<comment>JUNOS OS Kernel 32-bit  [20150917.314761_builder_stable_10]</comment>
</package-information>
<package-information>
<name>os-libs</name>
<comment>JUNOS OS libs [20150917.314761_builder_stable_10]</comment>
...output trimmed...
```

❶ We start by stepping through the code to the line that executes the RPC. (We hit the Return key to repeat that command on subsequent lines.) We also make sure that the SLAX compiler has completed executing the RPC call by stepping until the debugger displays the line *after* the RPC call.

❷ We print the Junos version here. This test proves that we received the Junos version string in the RPC response and that the version string is accessible using the expected XPath expression.

Also, note that the response tells us that this is a node set and that exactly one node matched our XPath expression.

❸ We step to the line that will form the `$outstring` variable. Recall that this is the line that generated the error when we tried to execute the op script. Therefore, we will check the value of the XPath expression used in this line.

❹ We test the XPath expression used to form the `$outstring` variable. When trying to display the XPath expression `$version_info/junos-version`, the SLAX debugger tells us that the expression is applied to an "invalid type" for the expression. So, we need to examine the `$version_info` variable.

❺ We print the value of the `$version_info` variable. We see the full value of the RPC response, but we also see the variable type. Note that the variable is of type `rtf`—the dreaded result tree fragment. (See "XML Result Tree Fragments" on page 273 for more details on why this produces an error in this context.)

Seeing that the problem is related to a result tree fragment, we update the portion of the code that assigns the `$version_info` variable to convert the result tree fragment to a node set:

```
var $version_info := {
    call get_version_info();
}
```

Once we make this change, we rerun the script. It doesn't return an error, but it doesn't exactly work as expected, either:

```
user@r0> op testscript
The Junos version is:
```

So, we launch the debugger again:

```
user@r0> op invoke-debugger cli testscript
sdb: The SLAX Debugger (version 0.17.1)
Type 'help' for help
(sdb) step ❶
junos.xsl:31:       event-script-input/junos-context"/>
(sdb)
testscript.slax:14: match / {
(sdb)
testscript.slax:15:     <op-script-results> {
(sdb)
testscript.slax:16:         var $version_info := {
(sdb)
testscript.slax:17:     call get_version_info();
(sdb)
testscript.slax:9: template get_version_info() {
(sdb)
testscript.slax:10:     var $ver = jcs:invoke("get-software-information");
(sdb)
testscript.slax:11:     copy-of $ver;
(sdb)
testscript.slax:16:         var $version_info := {
(sdb)
testscript.slax:19:         var $outstring = "The Junos version is: " _ $versi...
(sdb)
testscript.slax:20:         <output> $outstring;
(sdb) print $outstring ❷
[string] "The Junos version is: "
(sdb) print $version_info/junos-version ❸
[node-set] (0)
(sdb) print $version_info ❹
[node-set] (1) rtf-doc
<software-information>
<host-name>r1</host-name>
<product-model>mx240</product-model>
<product-name>mx240</product-name>
<junos-version>15.1R2.9</junos-version>
<package-information>
<name>os-kernel</name>
<comment>JUNOS OS Kernel 32-bit  [20150917.314761_builder_stable_10]</comment>
</package-information>
<package-information>
<name>os-libs</name>
<comment>JUNOS OS libs [20150917.314761_builder_stable_10]</comment>
...output trimmed...
</package-information>
```

```
</software-information>
(sdb) print $version_info/software-information/junos-version ❺
[node-set] (1)
<junos-version>15.1R2.9</junos-version>
```

❶ We start by stepping through the code until we are past the line that forms the `$outstring` variable.

❷ We print the `$outstring` variable. As we saw previously, the portion that is formed using the `$version_info/junos-version` XPath expression is blank. Note that the SLAX debugger tells us that this variable is of type `string`.

❸ We test the XPath expression used to form the `$outstring` variable. The SLAX debugger tells us that zero nodes matched the `$version_info/junos_version` XPath expression. This explains why our XPath expression evaluated to an empty string.

❹ We again print the value of the `$version_info` variable. We see that this is a node set, and that only one node matched our XPath expression. However, we also see a note that the matching node is an `rtf-doc`. In this case, our variable points to a container element that contains the `<software-information>` element. Even though the RPC response was rooted at the `<software-information>` element, the conversion to a result tree fragment and back to a node set added a new root element.

❺ We confirm the correct XPath expression to use by trying to print the value of the `$version_info/software-information/junos-version` XPath expression. We see that the result is a node set, that the query matches only one node, and that the result contains the Junos version string.

We modify our script to use the correct XPath expression:

```
var $outstring = "The Junos version is: " _
                 $version_info/software-information/junos-version;
```

When we run the modified script, we see the expected output:

```
user@r0> op testscript
The Junos version is: 15.1R2.9
```

Configuring Op Scripts

To truly use op scripts effectively, you need to configure the router to use them. True, it is possible to use the `op url` command to run op scripts you have not configured; however, some of their features require configuration. Plus, users can use the CLI help to determine which pre-configured op scripts are available for them to use.

You configure op scripts at the `[edit system scripts op]` hierarchy level. You configure each script using the `file` configuration statement, giving the name of a script located in the */var/db/scripts/op/* directory.

You can provide a number of options for each script. Some of the common ones are:

`allow-commands`
: You can use this statement to override normal user permissions. Normally, an op script runs with the same permissions that the executing user has. That means that an attempt to run an RPC in an op script will return an error unless the user has permission to run the equivalent command in the CLI.

  However, there may be times when you do not want to give a user unfettered freedom to run a certain CLI command, but you feel it is acceptable to let that user access the RPC when it is being executed by a trusted op script. In these cases, you can add the CLI command to the `allow-commands` statement under the script's configuration. The syntax for this command is the same as the syntax for the `allow-commands` statement in the `[edit system login class]` hierarchy.

`arguments`
: You can use this configuration hierarchy to manually configure the help text for the available arguments. Configuring the arguments here is an alternative to including the `$arguments` variable in your script.

`checksum`
: When you configure a checksum, the CSCRIPT utility will verify the script's checksum prior to executing the script. It will perform this check each time it executes the script. This ensures that the script has not been modified (either accidentally or purposefully) from the version you intended to add to the configuration.

`command`
: By default, the command to run a script is `op` *`filename`*, where *`filename`* is the filename of the script, without the suffix. (For example, *tesfile.slax* would be executed using the command `op testfile`.)

  This statement allows you to specify a different name to use with the `op` command. For example, you might want to use this command if your filename includes versioning information.

  Take this configuration:

```
system scripts op {
    file testfile1_3_2a.slax {
        command testfile;
```

```
        }
    }
```

To execute the script in the file at */var/db/scripts/op/testfile1_3_2a.slax*, you would use the CLI command `op testfile`.

`description`
: You use this statement to configure a description for the script. The description will appear in the CLI question-mark help.

`source`
: You use this statement to configure a URL that the router can access in order to load the latest version of a script. You can trigger a manual refresh of the op scripts when new versions become available. Note that the router must be able to access the URL in order for this feature to be useful.

There are also two other important pieces of configuration you might want to consider:

`set system scripts synchronize`
: You can use this statement to cause the master RE to synchronize configured scripts (op, commit, and event scripts) to the backup RE when a user initiates a synchronized commit. This statement helps to ensure that the two REs are fully synchronized and that your backup RE will be able to seamlessly take over all the functionality your master usually provides, if need be.

`set system scripts op no-allow-url`
: You can use this statement to disable the execution of unconfigured op scripts using the `op url` command. When this statement is present in your configuration, users will only be able to execute op scripts that are configured in the `[edit system scripts op]` hierarchy.

  In certain high-security environments, it may be desirable to prevent users from running op scripts other than those that an administrator has approved.

Examples

Now that we have covered the theory, let's get into some examples. We will review a couple of examples of how you can use op scripts to perform some of the tasks we've discussed in this chapter.

Example: Custom CLI Command

Here, we will implement the CLI command we discussed in "Custom CLI Commands" on page 329. Recall that the requirement is to accept a BGP peer's IP address as an argument, use that to determine the output interface, and display the output of `show interfaces extensive` for that interface.

To keep the problem small enough to be manageable in this book, we will limit this script to BGP peers that peer over directly connected interfaces and use their interface IPs as their peering addresses.

We start by considering the question of how we can determine the interface to which a peer is attached. We *could* parse the output of `show interfaces terse` and look for the most specific matching subnets. However, that might fail if the router has overlapping address space used in multiple routing instances. Also, we can't use the output of `show route`, as the routing table does not include `direct` routes for interfaces that are down. However, we *can* use the output of `show route forwarding-table`, as the forwarding table *does* include routes for interfaces that are down.

After some experimentation in the CLI, we find that the command `show route forwarding-table destination` *`remote_ip`* seems to show the directly attached interface, even if the interface is down:

```
user@r0> show route forwarding-table destination 10.23.21.17
Routing table: default.inet
Internet:
Destination        Type RtRef Next hop           Type Index    NhRef Netif
10.23.21.0/24      ifdn     0                    rslv     671      1 ge-1/0/5.0

Routing table: __juniper_services__.inet
Internet:
Destination        Type RtRef Next hop           Type Index    NhRef Netif
default            perm     0                    dscd     518      2

Routing table: __master.anon__.inet
Internet:
Destination        Type RtRef Next hop           Type Index    NhRef Netif
default            perm     0                    rjct     542      1

Routing table: __pfe_private__.inet
Internet:
Destination        Type RtRef Next hop           Type Index    NhRef Netif
default            perm     0                    dscd     527      2
```

There are two issues here. First, we don't need the extra information from the Junos software's private routing instances, so it would be nice to avoid processing the extraneous information. But, second, what will happen if the BGP neighbor is in a nondefault routing instance? Worse, what if the same IP address is used on multiple interfaces assigned to different routing instances? For these reasons, we decide to specifically limit the output to a single routing instance:

```
user@r0> show route forwarding-table destination 10.23.21.17 table default
Routing table: default.inet
Internet:
```

```
Destination        Type RtRef Next hop           Type Index    NhRef Netif
10.23.21.0/24      ifdn     0                    rslv      671      1 ge-1/0/5.0
```

After some more experimentation, we learn that the route could be of type `ifdn` (if the interface is down), `intf` (if the interface is up, but the router has no specific entry, such as an ARP entry, for the remote IP), or `dest` (if the router has a specific entry for the remote IP).

Two final pieces of information we need to gather are the RPC call and the expected XML response document. We use the `display xml rpc` and `display xml` pipe commands, respectively, to determine these pieces of information:

```
<rpc-reply xmlns:junos="http://xml.juniper.net/junos/15.1R2/junos">
    <rpc>
        <get-forwarding-table-information>
            <table>default</table>
            <destination>10.23.21.17</destination>
        </get-forwarding-table-information>
    </rpc>
    <cli>
        <banner></banner>
    </cli>
</rpc-reply>

<rpc-reply xmlns:junos="http://xml.juniper.net/junos/15.1R2/junos">
    <rpc>
    <forwarding-table-information
            xmlns="http://xml.juniper.net/junos/15.1R2/junos-rtinfo">
        <route-table>
            <table-name>default.inet</table-name>
            <address-family>Internet</address-family>
            <enabled-protocols></enabled-protocols>
            <rt-entry junos:style="brief">
                <rt-destination>10.23.21.0/24</rt-destination>
                <destination-type>ifdn</destination-type>
                <route-reference-count>0</route-reference-count>
                <nh>
                    <to></to>
                    <nh-type>rslv</nh-type>
                    <nh-index>671</nh-index>
                    <nh-reference-count>1</nh-reference-count>
                    <via>ge-1/0/5.0</via>
                </nh>
            </rt-entry>
        </route-table>
    </forwarding-table-information>
    <cli>
        <banner></banner>
    </cli>
</rpc-reply>
```

We now have what we need to begin writing our script. Let's start by getting the script to print the name of the interface that matches our query. We start with our boilerplate script, define our arguments, and add a template that seeks to find a matching interface:

```
version 1.1;

ns junos = "http://xml.juniper.net/junos/*/junos";
ns xnm = "http://xml.juniper.net/xnm/1.1/xnm";
ns jcs = "http://xml.juniper.net/junos/commit-scripts/1.0";

import "../import/junos.xsl";

param $ip; ❶
param $routing-instance = "default";

var $arguments = { ❷
    <argument> {
        <name> "ip";
        <description> "The remote IP address.";
    }
    <argument> {
        <name> "routing-instance";
        <description> "The routing instance (optional; defaults to the " _
                      "default routing instance).";
    }
}

match / {
    <op-script-results> { ❸
        /* Connect to mgd. */
        var $con = jcs:open();

        /* Find the interface. */
        var $interface = { ❹
            call find-intf($con=$con);
        }

        /* Print the interface. */
        <output> "Found: " _ $interface;

        /* Close the connection to mgd. */
        expr jcs:close($con);
    }
}

template find-intf($con) { ❺
    var $get-route-rpc = {
        <get-forwarding-table-information> {
            <table> $routing-instance;
            <destination> $ip;
        }
```

```
    }
    var $route-info = jcs:execute($con, $get-route-rpc);

    expr $route-info/route-table/rt-entry[destination-type = "dest" ||
        destination-type = "intf" || destination-type = "ifdn"]/nh/via;
}
```

❶ The `param` statements tell the SLAX processor to accept these user-supplied arguments. If the user does not supply the `routing-instance` argument, the SLAX processor will use the string `default` as the value of that argument.

❷ Here, we define the arguments that the CLI should display to the user when the user uses question-mark help. The CLI may also use these to support command completion.

❸ Recall that we need to enclose our output in a top-level tag, as shown in the boilerplate template (see Example 6-1).

❹ This section calls the `find-intf()` template and then returns an `<output>` element that contains the interface name.

❺ The `find-intf()` template runs the *get-forwarding-table-information* RPC and uses an XPath expression to return the name of the interface found in a route entry with a matching destination type. If no routes are found, or the route entries do not have a matching destination type, this will return an empty string.

When we run the script, we see it works as expected. It determines the correct interface for 10.23.21.17, and finds no interface for 10.23.20.17 (which is not attached to a local interface):

```
user@r0> op show-interface ip 10.23.21.17
Found: ge-1/0/5.0

user@r0> op show-interface ip 10.23.20.17
Found:
```

As this portion of our script is working, it is time to add some defensive measures to it. We'll check to ensure that the `ip` argument is provided and that the `jcs:open()` call succeeded.

In the `find-intf()` template, we should also add a check to ensure that the RPC succeeds without errors. If there are errors, we want to show those to users. However, this causes us to make a small design change. Junos returns errors in an XML hierarchy. To include those in our output document, we will need to return an XML hierarchy to our main match template. And if we are going to return XML errors in an XML hierarchy, we might as well return the interface in an XML hierarchy, too.

After implementing our changes, our script looks like this:

```
version 1.1;

ns junos = "http://xml.juniper.net/junos/*/junos";
ns xnm = "http://xml.juniper.net/xnm/1.1/xnm";
ns jcs = "http://xml.juniper.net/junos/commit-scripts/1.0";

import "../import/junos.xsl";

param $ip;
param $routing-instance = "default";

var $arguments = {
    <argument> {
        <name> "ip";
        <description> "The remote IP address.";
    }
    <argument> {
        <name> "routing-instance";
        <description> "The routing instance (optional; defaults to the " _
                      "default routing instance).";
    }
}

match / {
    <op-script-results> {
        /*
         * Check the arguments. The key requirement is that the "ip" argument
         * exist and be nonempty.
         */
        if (not($ip)) { ❶
            <xnm:error> {
                <message> "Missing required argument 'ip'.";
            }
        }
        else {
            /* Connect to mgd. */
            var $con = jcs:open();

            if (not($con)) { ❷
                <xnm:error> {
                    <message> "Unable to connect to local mgd.";
                }
            }
            else {
                /* Find the interface. */
                var $interface := { ❸
                    call find-intf($con=$con);
                }

                if ($interface//xnm:error) { ❹
```

```
                        copy-of $interface;
                    }
                    else if ($interface/interface = "") { ❺
                        <xnm:error> {
                            <message> "Unable to determine output interface for " _
                                $ip;
                        }
                    }
                    else {
                        /* Print the interface. */
                        <output> "Found: " _ $interface/interface; ❻
                    }

                    /* Close the connection to mgd. */
                    expr jcs:close($con);
                }
            }
        }
    }

template find-intf($con) {
    var $get-route-rpc = {
        <get-forwarding-table-information> {
            <table> $routing-instance;
            <destination> $ip;
        }
    }
    var $route-info = jcs:execute($con, $get-route-rpc);

    if ($route-info//xnm:error) { ❼
        <output> "Error determining interface IP address:";
        copy-of $route-info;
    }
    else {
        <interface> { ❽
            expr $route-info/route-table/rt-entry[destination-type = "dest" ||
                destination-type = "intf" || destination-type = "ifdn"]/nh/via;
        }
    }
}
```

❶ Before doing anything else, the script checks that the user has provided a value for the `ip` argument. If the user has not provided a value, the script returns an error.

❷ We check that the `$con` variable has a nonempty value.

❸ Note that we've changed this from the `=` operator to the `:=` operator. Because we expect the `find-intf()` template to return a block of XML and we want to be able to access values within that XML block, we need to convert this from a result tree fragment to a node set.

❹ This XPath expression tests for any `<xnm:error>` element (at any depth) within the XML hierarchy stored in the `$interface` variable. If the test is true, the script simply returns a copy of the XML block stored in the `$interface` variable.

❺ This statement tests to see if the `$interface/interface` element evaluates to an empty string. This will occur either if the `$interface/interface` element is empty or if it does not exist. If the `$interface/interface` element evaluates to an empty string, the script will return an error message stating that it could not determine the output interface.

❻ Because the `$interface` variable is now an XML hierarchy, this statement is changed to print the value of the `$interface/interface` XPath expression.

❼ This XPath expression tests for any `<xnm:error>` element (at any depth) within the XML hierarchy returned by the RPC. If the test is true, the template will return an `<output>` element and a copy of the RPC's XML output.

❽ If the RPC did not produce an error, the template will return an interface as it did previously. However, it will now enclose the interface in an `<interface>` element.

What happens when we run the script to test the new code? We see that it returns an error when the user fails to specify an IP address, returns the error produced by the RPC when the user specifies an invalid IP address, returns an error when the user specifies an IP address that is not attached to an interface, and returns the associated interface when the user specifies an IP address directly connected to an interface:

```
user@r0> op show-interface
error: Missing required argument 'ip'.

user@r0> op show-interface ip a.b.c.d/aa
Error determining interface IP address:
error: a.b.c.d: invalid prefix specifier

user@r0> op show-interface ip 10.23.20.17
error: Unable to determine output interface for 10.23.20.17

user@r0> op show-interface ip 10.23.21.17
Found: ge-1/0/5.0
```

Now, we need to modify the script to show the output of `show interfaces extensive`. There are two things involved in this change. First, we must translate the logical interface (e.g., `ge-1/0/5.0`) into a physical interface (e.g., `ge-1/0/5`). Second, we need to invoke the *get-interface-information* RPC to get the XML output for `show interfaces extensive`.

We modify the script as shown here:

```
version 1.1;

ns junos = "http://xml.juniper.net/junos/*/junos";
ns xnm = "http://xml.juniper.net/xnm/1.1/xnm";
ns jcs = "http://xml.juniper.net/junos/commit-scripts/1.0";

import "../import/junos.xsl";

param $ip;
param $routing-instance = "default";

var $arguments = {
    <argument> {
        <name> "ip";
        <description> "The remote IP address.";
    }
    <argument> {
        <name> "routing-instance";
        <description> "The routing instance (optional; defaults to the " _
                      "default routing instance).";
    }
}

match / {
    <op-script-results> {
        /*
         * Check the arguments. The key requirement is that the "ip" argument
         * exist and be nonempty.
         */
        if (not($ip)) {
            <xnm:error> {
                <message> "Missing required argument 'ip'.";
            }
        }
        else {
            /* Connect to mgd. */
            var $con = jcs:open();

            if (not($con)) {
                <xnm:error> {
                    <message> "Unable to connect to local mgd.";
                }
            }
            else {
                /* Find the interface. */
                var $interface := {
                    call find-intf($con=$con);
```

```
                }

                if ($interface//xnm:error) {
                    copy-of $interface;
                }
                else if ($interface/interface = "") {
                    <xnm:error> {
                        <message> "Unable to determine output interface for " _
                            $ip;
                    }
                }
                else {
                    var $get-interface-info-rpc = {
                        <get-interface-information> {
                            <extensive>;
                            <interface-name> $interface/interface;
                        }
                    }
                    copy-of jcs:execute($con, $get-interface-info-rpc); ❶
                }

                /* Close the connection to mgd. */
                expr jcs:close($con);
            }
        }
    }
}

template find-intf($con) {
    var $get-route-rpc = {
        <get-forwarding-table-information> {
            <table> $routing-instance;
            <destination> $ip;
        }
    }
    var $route-info = jcs:execute($con, $get-route-rpc);

    if ($route-info//xnm:error) {
        <output> "Error determining interface IP address:";
        copy-of $route-info;
    }
    else {
        var $ifl = $route-info/route-table/rt-entry[destination-type = "dest" ||
            destination-type = "intf" || destination-type = "ifdn"]/nh/via;

        var $if-split = jcs:split("(\\.)", $ifl); ❷
        <interface> $if-split[1];
    }
}
```

❶ If the script is able to determine the interface to which an IP address is attached, it will call the *get-interface-information* RPC and request extensive-level information about the interface. It will send a copy of that information to the CLI for the CLI to display. The end result is the same as the user typing `show interfaces extensive` *`interface`* in her CLI session.

❷ This block of code converts the logical interface (e.g., `ge-1/0/5.0`) into a physical interface (e.g., `ge-1/0/5`).

This template now assigns the route's next-hop interface to the `$ifl` variable. This line uses the `jcs:split()` function to split the result into multiple elements, using a dot (`.`) as a delimiter. Because the dot has a special meaning as a wildcard character in a regular expression, we need to escape it with a backslash. And because the backslash has a special meaning to SLAX, we need to escape the backslash. In the end, the code shown in the script will split the contents of the `$ifl` variable into groupings, using a literal dot as a delimiter. The next line returns the first grouping inside an `<interface>` element.

When we run the script, we see it works as expected. It still returns an error when it is unable to determine the interface to which an IP address is attached, and it now returns the output of `show interfaces extensive` when it is able to determine the interface to which an IP address is attached:

```
user@r0> op show-interface ip 10.23.20.17
error: Unable to determine output interface for 10.23.20.17

user@r0> op show-interface ip 10.23.21.17
Physical interface: ge-1/0/5, Enabled, Physical link is Down
  Interface index: 146, SNMP ifIndex: 522, Generation: 149
  Link-level type: Ethernet, MTU: 1514, MRU: 1522, LAN-PHY mode,
  Speed: 1000mbps, BPDU Error: None, MAC-REWRITE Error: None,
  Loopback: Disabled, Source filtering: Disabled, Flow control: Enabled,
  Auto-negotiation: Enabled, Remote fault: Online
  Pad to minimum frame size: Disabled
  Device flags   : Present Running Down
  Interface flags: Hardware-Down SNMP-Traps Internal: 0x4000
  Link flags     : None
  CoS queues     : 8 supported, 4 maximum usable queues
  Schedulers     : 0
  Hold-times     : Up 0 ms, Down 0 ms
  Damping        : half-life: 0 sec, max-suppress: 0 sec, reuse: 0, suppress: 0,
 state: unsuppressed
  Current address: 3c:8a:b0:cd:a2:9a, Hardware address: 3c:8a:b0:cd:a2:9a
  Last flapped   : 2015-11-23 09:57:05 PST (07:00:16 ago)
  Statistics last cleared: Never
  Traffic statistics:
   Input  bytes  :                    0                    0 bps
   Output bytes  :                    0                    0 bps
   Input  packets:                    0                    0 pps
   Output packets:                    0                    0 pps
...output trimmed...
```

Exercise

This script could still use at least one small refinement. If an IP address is in a logical system, you can find it by changing the value you put in the `<table>` element in the *get-forwarding-table-information* RPC. If you want to query a logical system, the table argument should be in the form *`logical-system/routing-instance`*. For example, the default routing instance in the `foo` logical system can be referenced as `foo/default`, and the `bar` routing instance in the `foo` logical system can be referenced as `foo/bar`. However, the `bar` routing instance in the main logical system is referenced simply as `bar`.

Try to modify the script to accept a logical system argument. The script should search the default logical system when the user does not supply the *`logical-system`* argument, and when the user does supply the *`logical-system`* argument it should search the logical system the user supplied.

Hint: Remember that you can put `if` statements inside variable assignments.

Example: Filtering CLI Output

One of the ways you can use op scripts is to produce custom CLI output. In this example, we will tackle a seemingly simple problem, which should illustrate the method you can use to solve similar CLI customization requirements.

Assume that you want to run the command `show interfaces terse` and show only interfaces with IPv6 addresses. Because the address may be printed on a separate line from the interface, you cannot reliably use the `match` command to conduct this filtering:

```
user@r0> show interfaces terse | match inet6
                                       inet6
                                       inet6    fdff:aabb:1133::1/64
                                       inet6
                                       inet6
                                       inet6    fdff:aabb:dca1::1/64
                                       inet6
                                       inet6
                                       inet6
                                       inet6    fe80::200:ff:fe00:4/64
                                       inet6    fe80::200:1ff:fe00:4/64
                                       inet6    abcd::10:255:106:103
```

However, you can easily use an op script to produce such filtered output. Let's begin by examining the XML produced by the equivalent RPC (Example 6-2).

Example 6-2. The XML results of the get-interface-information RPC (with the terse option)

```
<rpc-reply>
 <interface-information
     xmlns="http://xml.juniper.net/junos/15.1R1/junos-interface"
     junos:style="terse">
  <physical-interface>
   <name>ge-1/0/7</name>
   <admin-status>up</admin-status>
   <oper-status>up</oper-status>
   <logical-interface>
    <name>ge-1/0/7.0</name>
    <admin-status>up</admin-status>
    <oper-status>up</oper-status>
    <filter-information>
    </filter-information>
    <address-family>
     <address-family-name>inet</address-family-name>
     <interface-address>
      <ifa-local junos:emit="emit">10.10.10.254/24</ifa-local>
     </interface-address>
    </address-family>
    <address-family>
     <address-family-name>inet6</address-family-name>
     <interface-address>
      <ifa-local junos:emit="emit">fdff:aabb:1133::1/64</ifa-local>
     </interface-address>
     <interface-address>
      <ifa-local junos:emit="emit">fe80::3e8a:b0ff:fecd:a29c/64</ifa-local>
     </interface-address>
    </address-family>
    <address-family>
     <address-family-name>multiservice</address-family-name>
    </address-family>
   </logical-interface>
  </physical-interface>
 </interface-information>
</rpc-reply>
```

We now can filter this to show only the information we want to see by using appropriate XPath expressions.

We start with this simple script, which will include the full XML output for all interfaces that have IPv6 addresses:

```
version 1.1;

ns junos = "http://xml.juniper.net/junos/*/junos";
ns xnm = "http://xml.juniper.net/xnm/1.1/xnm";
ns jcs = "http://xml.juniper.net/junos/commit-scripts/1.0";
```

```
import "../import/junos.xsl";

match / {
    <op-script-results> { ❶
        var $con = jcs:open();
        var $rpc-query = {
            <get-interface-information> {
                <terse>;
            }
        }
        var $results = jcs:execute($con, $rpc-query); ❷
        expr jcs:close($con);

        <interface-information> { ❸
            for-each ($results/physical-interface[logical-interface/
                      address-family[address-family-name="inet6"]]) { ❹
                copy-of .; ❺
            }
        }
    }
}
```

❶ Recall that we need to enclose our output in a top-level tag, as shown in the boilerplate template (see Example 6-1).

❷ Here, we execute the *get-interface-information* RPC with the `terse` option and store the results in the variable `$results`.

❸ Here, we provide the outer `<interface-information>` tag. Recall that the output in Example 6-2 showed that all the interface information was enclosed in an `<interface-information>` element. Therefore, we need to have the script do the same when it outputs the interface information. The easiest way to do that is to manually hardcode the tag.

❹ This XPath expression matches any `<physical-interface>` element that has a logical interface with an IPv6 address. Because it matches the `<physical-interface>` element, the current node (the "dot" location) will move to each matching `<physical-interface>` element in turn as the SLAX processor executes the loop.

❺ This statement copies the entire `<physical-interface>` element (including the `<physical-interface>` tags and attributes) to the output document. This should make the output document contain all the information for each physical interface that has a logical interface with an IPv6 address.

However, when we run this script, we see that something hasn't quite worked correctly:

```
user@r0> op url /tmp/show-int-filtered.slax

user@r0>
```

To try to figure out what is happening, let's rerun the command with the `display xml` pipe command:

```
user@r0> op url /tmp/show-int-filtered.slax | display xml
<rpc-reply xmlns:junos="http://xml.juniper.net/junos/15.1R1/junos">
  <interface-information>
    <physical-interface
      xmlns="http://xml.juniper.net/junos/15.1R1/junos-interface">
      <name>
        pfe-1/0/0
      </name>
      <admin-status>
        up
      </admin-status>
      <oper-status>
        up
      </oper-status>
      <logical-interface>
        <name>
          pfe-1/0/0.16383
        </name>
        <admin-status>
          up
        </admin-status>
        <oper-status>
          up
        </oper-status>
...output trimmed...
```

At this point, you may really be wondering what's going on. To try to figure it out, let's look again at the sample XML output we gathered from our router using `show interfaces terse | display xml`, as shown in Example 6-2. When we compare the XML output from Example 6-2 with the XML output our script produced, there is one obvious difference: the XML attributes of the `<interface-information>` element. It turns out that the attributes are important for some of these elements!

To solve this correctly, we should copy both the namespace elements and the attributes. To do that, we need to break out some SLAX judo. We modify our script as shown here:

```
version 1.1;

ns junos = "http://xml.juniper.net/junos/*/junos";
ns xnm = "http://xml.juniper.net/xnm/1.1/xnm";
```

```
ns jcs = "http://xml.juniper.net/junos/commit-scripts/1.0";

import "../import/junos.xsl";

match / {
    <op-script-results> {
        var $con = jcs:open();
        var $rpc-query = {
            <get-interface-information> {
                <terse>;
            }
        }
        var $results = jcs:execute($con, $rpc-query);
        expr jcs:close($con);

        for-each ($results) { ❶
            copy-node { ❷
                for-each (@*) { ❸
                    attribute name(.) {
                        expr .;
                    }
                }
                for-each (physical-interface[logical-interface/
                          address-family[address-family-name="inet6"]]) {
                    copy-of .; ❹
                }
            }
        }
    }
}
```

❶ This statement will loop over the single root element of the `$results` variable. In this case, the main point of the statement is to change the current node (the "dot" location) to the `<interface-information>` element, which is the root element in the `$results` variable.

Because we changed the current node, we also adjust the later XPath expression to be relative to the new current node, rather than being absolute paths anchored at the `$results` variable. It is not absolutely necessary to make this change, but it makes the script look a little cleaner.

❷ The `copy-node` statement makes a "shallow" copy of the current node. It creates a new element with the same tag and namespace attributes as the current node. However, it does not copy any other attributes or any child nodes.

❸ This block of code copies the non-namespace XML attributes from the original `<interface-information>` element to the copy we are building.

The `for-each` statement matches each attribute in the current node (which is still the original `<interface-information>` element). Each invocation of the loop changes the current node to that attribute.

The contents of the loop use the **`attribute`** statement to add an attribute with the same name and value as each attribute that appeared in the original `<interface-information>` element.

❹ Unlike the `copy-node` statement, the `copy-of` statement makes a "deep" copy of the current node (including namespace, attributes, and child nodes). Also unlike the `copy-node` statement, the `copy-of` statement both allows and requires an XPath expression to choose the node that the SLAX processor should copy.

Once we make these changes, we try rerunning the script and find that it produces the `<interface-information>` tag with the expected namespace identifier and attributes:

```
user@r0> op url /tmp/show-int-filtered.slax | display xml
<rpc-reply xmlns:junos="http://xml.juniper.net/junos/15.1R1/junos">
  <interface-information
      xmlns="http://xml.juniper.net/junos/15.1R1/junos-interface"
      junos:style="terse">
    <physical-interface>
      <name>
        pfe-1/0/0
      </name>
      <admin-status>
        up
      </admin-status>
      <oper-status>
        up
      </oper-status>
        <logical-interface>
          <name>
            pfe-1/0/0.16383
          </name>
          <admin-status>
            up
          </admin-status>
          <oper-status>
            up
          </oper-status>
...output trimmed...
```

Even better, it produces the expected CLI output:

```
user@r0> op url /tmp/show-int-filtered.slax
Interface               Admin Link Proto    Local                 Remote
pfe-1/0/0               up    up
pfe-1/0/0.16383         up    up   inet
                                   inet6
```

```
ge-1/0/7                up   up
ge-1/0/7.0              up   up   inet     10.10.10.254/24
                                  inet6    fdff:aabb:1133::1/64
                                           fe80::3e8a:b0ff:fecd:a29c/64
                                  multiservice
pfe-1/1/0               up   up
pfe-1/1/0.16383         up   up   inet
                                  inet6
pfe-1/2/0               up   up
pfe-1/2/0.16383         up   up   inet
                                  inet6
ge-1/2/2                up   down
ge-1/2/2.0              up   down inet     10.3.2.1/30
                                  inet6    fdff:aabb:dca1::1/64
                                           fe80::3e8a:b0ff:fecd:a3e1/64
                                  multiservice
pfe-1/3/0               up   up
pfe-1/3/0.16383         up   up   inet
                                  inet6
...output trimmed...
```

Now that our output is printing correctly, we can move on to further logic refinements. Some physical interfaces may have multiple logical interfaces. And it may be the case that only some of those logical interfaces use IPv6. So, let's limit the script's logic so it skips printing information about logical interfaces unless they have IPv6 configured.

We implement the change by adding a new template to handle each physical interface:

```
version 1.1;

ns junos = "http://xml.juniper.net/junos/*/junos";
ns xnm = "http://xml.juniper.net/xnm/1.1/xnm";
ns jcs = "http://xml.juniper.net/junos/commit-scripts/1.0";

import "../import/junos.xsl";

template handle-physical-intf($family) {
    copy-node { ❶
        for-each (@*) {
            attribute name(.) {
                expr .;
            }
        }
        for-each (*[name() != "logical-interface"]) { ❷
            copy-of .;
        }
        for-each (logical-interface[address-family[
                  address-family-name=$family]]) { ❸
            copy-of .;
        }
```

```
        }
    }

    match / {
        <op-script-results> {
            var $con = jcs:open();
            var $rpc-query = {
                <get-interface-information> {
                    <terse>;
                }
            }
            var $results = jcs:execute($con, $rpc-query);
            expr jcs:close($con);

            for-each ($results) {
                copy-node {
                    for-each (@*) {
                        attribute name(.) {
                            expr .;
                        }
                    }
                    for-each (physical-interface[logical-interface/
                              address-family[address-family-name="inet6"]]) {
                        call handle-physical-intf($family="inet6"); ❹
                    }
                }
            }
        }
    }
```

❶ Having learned our lesson about the importance of attributes, we use the `copy-node` and `attribute` statements to copy the namespace identifiers and attributes for each `<physical-interface>` element.

❷ This loop makes copies of the `<name>`, `<admin-state>`, and `<oper-status>` elements, including the tags, attributes (if any), and namespace identifiers (if any). In addition, the loop will include copies of any additional information, other than logical interfaces, that is included at the physical interface level. Writing the script this way provides some measure of future-proofing against additions to the XML schema.

❸ This XPath expression matches any `<logical-interface>` element with the IPv6 address family. The `copy-of` statement places a "deep" copy of the matching `<logical-interface>` elements in the output document.

❹ We have replaced the `copy-of .;` statement that used to be here with a call to the `handle-physical-intf()` template. The `handle-physical-intf()` template will output the <physical-interface> element and the appropriate <logical-interface> child elements.

When we run the script, we see that it is still working:

```
user@r0> op url /tmp/show-int-filtered.slax
Interface               Admin Link Proto    Local                 Remote
pfe-1/0/0               up    up
pfe-1/0/0.16383         up    up   inet
                                   inet6
ge-1/0/7                up    up
ge-1/0/7.0              up    up   inet     10.10.10.254/24
                                   inet6    fdff:aabb:1133::1/64
                                            fe80::3e8a:b0ff:fecd:a29c/64
                                   multiservice
pfe-1/1/0               up    up
pfe-1/1/0.16383         up    up   inet
                                   inet6
pfe-1/2/0               up    up
pfe-1/2/0.16383         up    up   inet
                                   inet6
ge-1/2/2                up    down
ge-1/2/2.0              up    down inet     10.3.2.1/30
                                   inet6    fdff:aabb:dca1::1/64
                                            fe80::3e8a:b0ff:fecd:a3e1/64
                                   multiservice
pfe-1/3/0               up    up
pfe-1/3/0.16383         up    up   inet
                                   inet6
...output trimmed...
```

Now, let's take this a step further and trim out all the address lines for other address families. To accomplish this goal, we need to filter the <address-family> elements that we include in each <logical-interface> element.

We implement the change by adding a new template to handle each logical interface:

```
version 1.1;

ns junos = "http://xml.juniper.net/junos/*/junos";
ns xnm = "http://xml.juniper.net/xnm/1.1/xnm";
ns jcs = "http://xml.juniper.net/junos/commit-scripts/1.0";

import "../import/junos.xsl";

template handle-logical-intf($family) {
    copy-node { ❶
        for-each (@*) {
            attribute name(.) {
                expr .;
            }
        }
```

```
        for-each (*[name() != "address-family"]) { ❷
            copy-of .;
        }
        for-each (address-family[address-family-name=$family]) { ❸
            copy-of .;
        }
    }
}

template handle-physical-intf($family) {
    copy-node {
        for-each (@*) {
            attribute name(.) {
                expr .;
            }
        }
        for-each (*[name() != "logical-interface"]) {
            copy-of .;
        }
        for-each (logical-interface[address-family[
                    address-family-name=$family]]) {
            call handle-logical-intf($family=$family); ❹
        }
    }
}

match / {
    <op-script-results> {
        var $con = jcs:open();
        var $rpc-query = {
            <get-interface-information> {
                <terse>;
            }
        }
        var $results = jcs:execute($con, $rpc-query);
        expr jcs:close($con);

        for-each ($results) {
            copy-node {
                for-each (@*) {
                    attribute name(.) {
                        expr .;
                    }
                }
                for-each (physical-interface[logical-interface/
                            address-family[address-family-name="inet6"]]) {
                    call handle-physical-intf($family="inet6");
                }
            }
        }
    }
}
```

❶ In the handle-logical-intf() template, we again use the copy-node and attribute statements to copy the namespace identifiers and attributes for each <logical-interface> element.

❷ This loop makes copies of the <name>, <admin-state>, and <oper-status> elements, including the tags, attributes (if any), and namespace identifiers (if any). If any additional elements other than <address-family> elements are present, the template will also copy those elements into the output document.

❸ This XPath expression matches any <address-family> element with the IPv6 address family. The copy-of statement will copy the matching <address-family> elements into the output document.

❹ We have replaced the copy-of .; statement that used to be here with a call to the handle-logical-intf() template. The handle-logical-intf() template will output the <logical-interface> element and the appropriate child elements.

When we run the script, we see that it is still working and is now filtering to match just the address family we desired:

```
user@r0> op url /tmp/show-int-filtered.slax
Interface               Admin Link Proto    Local                  Remote
pfe-1/0/0               up    up
pfe-1/0/0.16383         up    up   inet6
ge-1/0/7                up    up
ge-1/0/7.0              up    up   inet6    fdff:aabb:1133::1/64
                                            fe80::3e8a:b0ff:fecd:a29c/64
pfe-1/1/0               up    up
pfe-1/1/0.16383         up    up   inet6
pfe-1/2/0               up    up
pfe-1/2/0.16383         up    up   inet6
ge-1/2/2                up    down
ge-1/2/2.0              up    down inet6    fdff:aabb:dca1::1/64
                                            fe80::3e8a:b0ff:fecd:a3e1/64
pfe-1/3/0               up    up
pfe-1/3/0.16383         up    up   inet6
pfe-2/0/0               up    up
pfe-2/0/0.16383         up    up   inet6
pfe-2/2/0               up    up
pfe-2/2/0.16383         up    up   inet6
em0                     up    up
em0.0                   up    up   inet6    fe80::200:ff:fe00:4/64
                                            fec0::a:0:0:4/64
em1                     up    up
em1.0                   up    up   inet6    fe80::200:1ff:fe00:4/64
                                            fec0::a:0:0:4/64
lo0                     up    up
```

```
lo0.0                   up    up   inet6    abcd::10:255:106:103-->
                                            fe80::2a0:a50f:fc7e:9bc5-->
```

But what if you want to perform the same service for another address family? Let's update our script to change the family from a hardcoded value to a user-supplied argument:

```
version 1.1;

ns junos = "http://xml.juniper.net/junos/*/junos";
ns xnm = "http://xml.juniper.net/xnm/1.1/xnm";
ns jcs = "http://xml.juniper.net/junos/commit-scripts/1.0";

import "../import/junos.xsl";

var $arguments = { ❶
    <argument> {
        <name> "family";
        <description> "The address family to match.";
    }
}

param $family; ❷

template handle-logical-intf($family) {
    copy-node {
        for-each (@*) {
            attribute name(.) {
                expr .;
            }
        }
        for-each (*[name() != "address-family"]) {
            copy-of .;
        }
        for-each (address-family[address-family-name=$family]) {
            copy-of .;
        }
    }
}

template handle-physical-intf($family) {
    copy-node {
        for-each (@*) {
            attribute name(.) {
                expr .;
            }
        }
        for-each (*[name() != "logical-interface"]) {
            copy-of .;
        }
        for-each (logical-interface[address-family[
                  address-family-name=$family]]) {
```

```
            call handle-logical-intf($family=$family);
        }
    }
}

match / {
    <op-script-results> {
        var $con = jcs:open();
        var $rpc-query = {
            <get-interface-information> {
                <terse>;
            }
        }
        var $results = jcs:execute($con, $rpc-query);
        expr jcs:close($con);

        if ($family) { ❸
            for-each ($results) {
                copy-node {
                    for-each (@*) {
                        attribute name(.) {
                            expr .;
                        }
                    }
                    for-each (physical-interface[logical-interface/
                              address-family[address-family-name=$family]]) {
                        call handle-physical-intf($family=$family); ❹
                    }
                }
            }
        } else {
            copy-of $results; ❺
        }
    }
}
```

❶ The `$arguments` variable defines the argument. This allows the CLI to provide appropriate help to the user. This is not strictly required to allow the script to function, but it is good practice to include all user-visible arguments for the benefit of your users.

❷ The `param` statement tells the SLAX processor to expect to receive an argument named `family`.

❸ We have added a test to determine whether the user provided the `family` argument. If the user did provide the `family` argument, the script proceeds to the logic that we had previously defined and filters the results to only show information for that address family.

❹ On these two lines, we have replaced the hardcoded `inet6` with the parameter `$family`. The remaining templates already used a parameter to determine the address family on which they should filter. Therefore, the other templates do not require changes.

You might be wondering about the fact that the global `$family` parameter and the template `$family` parameter share the same name. A template parameter takes precedence over a global parameter of the same name. Therefore, if we left the template `$family` parameter hardcoded to `inet6`, we would see that the script continued to return interfaces with IPv6 addresses, regardless of the address family we specified in the global `$family` parameter.

❺ If the user did not supply the `family` argument, the script just outputs a copy of the interface information without conducting any filtering.

When we run this script, we can see that the question-mark help is working as expected:

```
user@r0> op url /tmp/show-int-filtered.slax ?
Possible completions:
  <[Enter]>             Execute this command
  <name>                Argument name
  detail                Display detailed output
  family                The address family to match.
...output trimmed...
```

We also see that it correctly produces unfiltered input when no argument is provided:

```
user@r0> op url /tmp/show-int-filtered.slax
Interface               Admin Link Proto    Local                 Remote
ge-1/0/0                up    up
lc-1/0/0                up    up
lc-1/0/0.32769          up    up   vpls
pfe-1/0/0               up    up
pfe-1/0/0.16383         up    up   inet
inet6
pfh-1/0/0               up    up
pfh-1/0/0.16383         up    up   inet
pfh-1/0/0.16384         up    up   inet
ge-1/0/1                up    up
ge-1/0/2                up    down
ge-1/0/3                up    down
ge-1/0/4                up    down
ge-1/0/5                up    down
ge-1/0/6                up    up
ge-1/0/7                up    up
ge-1/0/7.0              up    up   inet     10.10.10.254/24
                                   inet6    fdff:aabb:1133::1/64
                                            fe80::3e8a:b0ff:fecd:a29c/64

multiservice
```

```
ge-1/0/8                up    down
ge-1/0/9                up    down
...output trimmed...
```

Finally, we see that it correctly produces filtered output when the user supplies a `family` argument:

```
user@r0> op url /tmp/show-int-filtered.slax family inet
Interface               Admin Link Proto    Local                 Remote
pfe-1/0/0               up    up
pfe-1/0/0.16383         up    up   inet
pfh-1/0/0               up    up
pfh-1/0/0.16383         up    up   inet
pfh-1/0/0.16384         up    up   inet
ge-1/0/7                up    up
ge-1/0/7.0              up    up   inet     10.10.10.254/24
pfe-1/1/0               up    up
pfe-1/1/0.16383         up    up   inet
pfe-1/2/0               up    up
pfe-1/2/0.16383         up    up   inet
ge-1/2/2                up    down
ge-1/2/2.0              up    down inet     10.3.2.1/30
pfe-1/3/0               up    up
pfe-1/3/0.16383         up    up   inet
pfe-2/0/0               up    up
pfe-2/0/0.16383         up    up   inet
pfh-2/0/0               up    up
pfh-2/0/0.16383         up    up   inet
pfh-2/0/0.16384         up    up   inet
pfe-2/2/0               up    up
pfe-2/2/0.16383         up    up   inet
em0                     up    up
em0.0                   up    up   inet     10.0.0.4/8
                                            128.0.0.1/2
                                            128.0.0.4/2
em1                     up    up
em1.0                   up    up   inet     10.0.0.4/8
                                            128.0.0.1/2
                                            128.0.0.4/2
fxp0                    up    up
fxp0.0                  up    up   inet     10.92.250.9/23
jsrv                    up    up
jsrv.1                  up    up   inet     128.0.0.127/2
lo0                     up    up
lo0.0                   up    up   inet     10.255.106.103      --> 0/0
                                            127.0.0.1           --> 0/0
lo0.16384               up    up   inet     127.0.0.1           --> 0/0
lo0.16385               up    up   inet

user@r0> op url /tmp/show-int-filtered.slax family inet6
Interface               Admin Link Proto    Local                 Remote
pfe-1/0/0               up    up
pfe-1/0/0.16383         up    up   inet6
```

```
ge-1/0/7                up    up
ge-1/0/7.0              up    up   inet6    fdff:aabb:1133::1/64
                                            fe80::3e8a:b0ff:fecd:a29c/64
pfe-1/1/0               up    up
pfe-1/1/0.16383         up    up   inet6
pfe-1/2/0               up    up
pfe-1/2/0.16383         up    up   inet6
ge-1/2/2                up    down
ge-1/2/2.0              up    down inet6    fdff:aabb:dca1::1/64
                                            fe80::3e8a:b0ff:fecd:a3e1/64
pfe-1/3/0               up    up
pfe-1/3/0.16383         up    up   inet6
pfe-2/0/0               up    up
pfe-2/0/0.16383         up    up   inet6
pfe-2/2/0               up    up
pfe-2/2/0.16383         up    up   inet6
em0                     up    up
em0.0                   up    up   inet6    fe80::200:ff:fe00:4/64
                                            fec0::a:0:0:4/64
em1                     up    up
em1.0                   up    up   inet6    fe80::200:1ff:fe00:4/64
                                            fec0::a:0:0:4/64
lo0                     up    up
lo0.0                   up    up   inet6    abcd::10:255:106:103-->
                                            fe80::2a0:a50f:fc7e:9bc5-->
```

Chapter Summary

As you have seen, op scripts can be a powerful way to customize the Junos software to behave the way you want it to behave. You can create custom CLI commands or customize the behavior of existing CLI commands.

You should now have the tools you need to begin writing your own op scripts. To practice your skills, try to think of a series of CLI commands that you frequently run together and write an op script that runs the commands for you and displays the output. Or perhaps you can find a CLI command whose output you would like to customize and implement your own custom view of the information from that command. Whatever script you decide to try, the `op url` command makes it easy to try out your new script on a few Junos devices without modifying the configuration to include the script.

In the next chapter, we will cover event scripts and event policies. Event scripts and policies are another way you can customize the Junos software to behave the way you want it to behave in your network.

CHAPTER 7

Event Scripts and Event Policies

In Chapter 6, we discussed the way you can use op and event scripts to customize your Junos device. As we noted in that chapter, there are many similarities between op and event scripts. However, there are also some considerations unique to event scripts. In this chapter, we will build on the material we covered in Chapter 6 as we discuss the ways you can use event scripts to customize your Junos device.

In addition, we will consider event policies. The system uses event policies to decide when to execute event scripts. In fact, it is possible to carry out some automatic event responses directly in an event policy without executing an event script.

Because this chapter builds on the information found in Chapter 6, it may be helpful to review that chapter if you have not already done so. In particular, you should review "Operational and Configuration State" on page 338, "Some Useful Tools for Op and Event Scripts" on page 355, and "Debugging Op and Event Scripts" on page 357.

Overview of Event Script Operation

As we mentioned in "Overview of Op Script Operation" on page 331, op and event scripts share some similarities with each other and with commit scripts. Recall that all three of these scripts work on XML documents: they receive an XML input document, process it, and produce an XML output document. Because of the nature of this work (an XML transformation), these scripts are written in XSLT or SLAX. We suggest that you use SLAX for writing these scripts.

While the operation of event scripts shares many similarities with the operation of op scripts, there are some differences. Therefore, let's begin with an overview of event script operation.

The system uses event policies to determine when it should respond to events on the device. In this context, an "event" is usually equivalent to a syslog message. The event policies can be configured directly in the `[edit event-options]` hierarchy, or they can be imported from an event script.

Event policies can take many actions. One action is to run an event script. Event scripts are stored in the */var/db/scripts/event* directory and are configured in the `[edit event-options event-scripts]` hierarchy.

Op scripts and event scripts are *very* similar. The main differences are:

- Event scripts receive details of events in the input document.
- Event scripts are not intended to be run interactively.
- Event scripts are not intended to produce output.

However, there is nothing to prevent you from using an op script in an event policy. In fact, you may very well want to run an op script in response to an event.

The execution of an event script goes through several phases:

1. When an event script configuration change is committed, or any time the `request system scripts event-scripts reload` CLI command is executed, the software rereads the event scripts and looks for event policies defined in the event scripts in an `$event-definition` global variable.
2. When EVENTD (the event processing daemon) finds that one or more events have satisfied the conditions in an event policy, it executes the actions in the `then` part of the event policy. If one of the actions is the execution of an event script, EVENTD uses CSCRIPT to run the event script.
3. Once the system executes an event script, CSCRIPT loads the script and provides it with the following data:
   - The arguments the user provided in the event policy configuration
   - The hostname, local time, product name, script name, and username of the user who executed the script
   - An input document with an `<event-script-input>` root element.
4. CSCRIPT runs the script and produces an output document. The output document should have a root element of `<event-script-results>`. (However, like with op script output documents, the actual top-level tag is discarded during processing. So, any tag is acceptable, as long as it is not one of the few that have a special meaning to the script-parsing infrastructure. Neither `<op-script-results>` nor `<event-script-results>` has a special meaning, so you can liter-

ally use the same script as both an op and an event script and have them work acceptably.)

5. The system takes the output document it receives from CSCRIPT, replaces the top-level tag with the `<event-script-results>` tag, and records the output document in the destination configured in the event policy. If no destination is configured, the output is discarded.

As of this writing, the Junos software does not specifically support handling output from event scripts. (The software will let you commit a configuration that saves event script output and it will actually save the output, but it will only save it in XML format, and even this is not officially supported.) So, for example, you cannot write an event script to output diagnostics on a regular basis and save the script's output for further analysis.

On the other hand, the Junos software does support handling output from op scripts. When you run an op script from an event policy, the software will let you save the op script's output and choose whether to save it in XML or text format.

Event Script Input Document

An event script receives an input document that contains information about the event (or events) that triggered the script, as well as a similar `<junos-context>` element to that received by op scripts. Like with op scripts, the `<junos-context>` element is also available in the `$junos-context` variable.

However, it is often the case that the really useful information in an event script's input document is the event information. An event script receives information about the events that caused EVENTD to run the event script. There is always a trigger event (which is the final event that caused the event policy conditions to be satisfied), but there may also be correlated events that were necessary prerequisites to satisfying the event policy conditions. The script receives information about both kinds of events. In short, the script should receive information about every event that was necessary to satisfy the event policy conditions. (We will discuss trigger events and correlated events in "Event Policies" on page 403.)

You can see the contents of the input document by enabling traceoptions at the `[edit event-options event-script]` hierarchy level and specifying the `input` flag. Example 7-1 shows a sample input document.

Example 7-1. A sample event script input document

```
<?xml version="1.0"?>
<event-script-input xmlns:junos="http://xml.juniper.net/junos/*/junos">
  <trigger-event>
    <id>LACPD_TIMEOUT</id>
    <type>syslog</type>
    <generation-time junos:seconds="1448477797">
      2015-11-25 10:56:37 PST
    </generation-time>
    <process>
      <name>lacpd</name>
      <pid>14597</pid>
    </process>
    <hostname>r0</hostname>
    <message>
      ge-5/0/6: lacp current while timer expired current Receive State:
      CURRENT
    </message>
    <facility>user</facility>
    <severity>notice</severity>
    <attribute-list>
      <attribute>
        <name>error-message</name>
        <value>ge-5/0/6</value>
      </attribute>
    </attribute-list>
  </trigger-event>
  <received-events>
    <received-event>
      <id>UI_COMMIT</id>
      <type>syslog</type>
      <generation-time junos:seconds="1448477767">
        2015-11-25 10:56:07 PST
      </generation-time>
      <process>
        <name>mgd</name>
        <pid>14623</pid>
      </process>
      <hostname>r0</hostname>
      <message>
        UI_COMMIT: User 'user' requested 'commit' operation (comment: none)
      </message>
      <facility>interact</facility>
      <severity>notice</severity>
      <attribute-list>
        <attribute>
          <name>username</name>
          <value>user</value>
        </attribute>
        <attribute>
          <name>command</name>
```

```
          <value>commit</value>
        </attribute>
        <attribute>
          <name>message</name>
          <value>none</value>
        </attribute>
      </attribute-list>
    </received-event>
  </received-events>
  <remote-execution-details>
    <remote-execution-detail>
      <remote-hostname>r1</remote-hostname>
      <username>user</username>
      <passphrase>password</passphrase>
    </remote-execution-detail>
  </remote-execution-details>
  <junos-context>
    <hostname>r0</hostname>
    <product>mx240</product>
    <localtime>Wed Nov 25 10:56:37 2015</localtime>
    <localtime-iso>2015-11-25 10:56:37 PST</localtime-iso>
    <script-type>event</script-type>
    <pid>14598</pid>
    <chassis>others</chassis>
    <routing-engine-name>re0</routing-engine-name>
    <re-master/>
    <user-context>
      <user>root</user>
      <class-name>super-user</class-name>
      <uid>0</uid>
    </user-context>
  </junos-context>
</event-script-input>
```

The `<trigger-event>` element contains a description of the event that satisfied the event policy, triggering EVENTD to launch the event script. The `<received-events>` element contains one or more `<received-event>` elements. Each `<received-event>` element contains a description of a single event that was a necessary prerequisite to satisfying the event policy. (If there were no prerequisite events necessary to satisfy the event policy, the `<received-events>` element will not be present in the input document.) Within each event, you see that there is an event ID, a log message, and one or more attribute/value pairs. We will discuss the significance of these in more detail in "Event Policies" on page 403.

However, even now, you should be able to see how it is useful to be able to see information about the events that triggered EVENTD to run the event script. And, you should be able to see how the error message was formed from the attribute/value pairs in the event description. Receiving this information in a structured format allows your script to easily access details of the event. Your event script can use this information to make intelligent decisions about the actions it should take in response to events.

The input document may also contain a `<remote-execution-details>` element with login information for remote hosts. This information is populated from the configuration. See "Configuring Event Scripts" on page 429 for more information about this element.

Finally, the input document contains a `<junos-context>` element with information similar to the `<junos-context>` element provided to op scripts. (In fact, the main differences should arise from the way the script is run: event scripts normally do not have an associated terminal or login user.)

Event Script Arguments

Like an op script, an event script can receive arguments. In this case, the arguments need to be included in the event policy definition.

Because an event script is not meant to be run interactively, there is no need for the global `$arguments` variable. In all other respects (including the automatic arguments), event script arguments operate in the same way as op script arguments. See "Op Script Arguments" on page 334 for more information on arguments.

Event Script Document Processing

Similar to the way commit scripts process an input document to produce an output document, event scripts needs to process the input document and create an output document.

This can serve as a boilerplate SLAX event script:

```
version 1.1;

ns junos = "http://xml.juniper.net/junos/*/junos";
ns xnm = "http://xml.juniper.net/xnm/1.1/xnm";
ns jcs = "http://xml.juniper.net/junos/commit-scripts/1.0";

import "../import/junos.xsl";

match / {
    <event-script-results> {
        /* Your logic goes here... */
    }
}
```

This script imports a standard file with some helpful contents, defines a match template that will match the input document, and encloses your output within appropriate XML tags.

You have a few interesting options with event scripts, which you may want to consider. First, if the same event script is called in slightly different contexts, you can use specific match templates for the different situations. In this case, you would likely write XPath expressions that match on children of the `<event-script-input>` element. For example, `event-script-input[trigger-event/id == "LACPD_TIMEOUT" && received-events/received-event[id == "UI_COMMIT"]]` would match the input document shown in Example 7-1. Second, if you intend to use the same script as an op or event script, depending on how it is called, you can match on `<event-script-input>` in the event script case or `<op-script-input>` in the op script case.

Event Script Output Document

The output document is enclosed in a root element. The tag for the root element is generally ignored and blindly discarded (unless you happen to use one of a few tags with a reserved meaning), but we recommend using the `<event-script-results>` tag.

Event scripts are not expected to return any data within the output document. However, if they do, the Junos software currently allows you to save the XML output. (But see the note in "Overview of Event Script Operation" on page 397.)

Event Policies

Event policies tell the Junos device how it should respond to events it observes. In this context, an "event" almost always corresponds to a syslog message. So, if a daemon generates a syslog message (even a debug-level message that you usually ignore) in response to an event, you can generally write an event policy to automate the router's response to it. Event policies are a powerful way to automate your router's response to events.

Event Discovery

Before we can really talk about event policies, we need to talk about the events that form the basis of event policies. Specifically, what are events, and where can you get information about events?

Most syslog messages have been converted to the event infrastructure. As you saw in Example 7-1, these events have attribute/value pairs that describe them. These attribute/value pairs are also used to build a message which is sent to the syslog system.

You can see information about events in several ways. One way is using the `help syslog` command. You can get a filtered list of events by typing `help syslog | match` *`match_string`*. By replacing *`match_string`* with a value you want to search, you can find a list of all events that contain the *match_string* in their ID or brief description. For example, `help syslog | match BGP` will display all events with "BGP" in either their ID or their brief description.

Once you have decided on an event, you can obtain more information by looking at its help text. For example, let's look at the help text for the `UI_COMMIT` event, which we encountered in Example 7-1:

```
user@r0> help syslog UI_COMMIT
Name:          UI_COMMIT
Message:       User '<username>' requested '<command>' operation (comment:
               <message>)
Help:          User requested commit of candidate configuration
Description:   The indicated user requested the indicated type of commit
               operation on the candidate configuration and added the indicated
               comment. The 'commit' operation applies to the local Routing
               Engine and the 'commit synchronize' operation to both Routing
               Engines.
Type:          Event: This message reports an event, not an error
Severity:      notice
Facility:      ANY
```

Of particular note is the `Message` field. The portions of the message field that appear in angle brackets (`<username>`, `<command>`, and `<message>`) are event attributes. When a daemon creates this event, it will send these attributes to EVENTD. When the message is sent to a syslog server, the Junos software replaces the attributes in the message with their values. However, you can access the attribute/value pairs and use them in both event policies and event scripts.

Looking back at Example 7-1, you can see that the `UI_COMMIT` message included the `username`, `command`, and `message` attributes.

Some log messages do not use the events infrastructure. Instead, the source originates them as unstructured syslog messages. EVENTD converts these to generic events based on the source. The generic event has a single attribute (named `message`) that contains the syslog message.

You can read about the generic event IDs by searching the Junos documentation (*http://www.juniper.net/techpubs/en_US/release-independent/junos/information-products/pathway-pages/junos/product*) for "Using nonstandard system log messages to trigger event policies."

Another way to see these attribute/value pairs is to configure the `structured-data` statement for a syslog file in the `[edit system syslog]` hierarchy, which causes the software to produce messages in the structured data format specified by RFC 5424 (*https://tools.ietf.org/html/rfc5424*). When you do this, you can see the attribute/value pairs listed in the syslog file. For example, here is the way a sample UI_COMMIT message appears when structured-data is configured for a syslog file:

```
<189>1 2015-11-25T14:09:18.618-08:00 r0 mgd 14623 UI_COMMIT [junos@2636.1.1.1
.2.21 username="user" command="commit" message="none"] User 'user' requested
'commit' operation (comment: none)
```

Defining Event Policy Match Criteria

You configure event policies under the [edit event-options] hierarchy. The simplest policy just matches on an event and then takes an action.

For example, this policy is named on_commit. It matches all UI_COMMIT events. When a UI_COMMIT event occurs, it will run the *commit.slax* event script:

```
event-options {
    policy on_commit {
        events ui_commit;
        then {
            event-script commit.slax;
        }
    }
}
```

In every event policy, the policy will only match when an event listed in the events statement occurs. You can list more than one event in the events statement. In this case, the policy will match when any one of the events listed in the statement occurs. (In other words, there is a logical "or" relationship between the events in the events statement.) The event that satisfies the event policy criteria is called the "trigger" event. The trigger event is always listed in the events statement.

Correlating events

We can refine these match criteria by correlating events. When one of the events listed in the events statement occurs, the software checks to see if the correlating events have occurred within the time frame we configure. If so, the event policy criteria will be satisfied and the software will take the actions specified in the then statement.

You specify correlating events using within statements. Each within statement takes as an argument the maximum number of seconds that may elapse between the correlating events and the trigger event. The software will only correlate correlating events with a trigger event if both occur within the given number of seconds.

The `within` statements are always backward-looking. When an event occurs which is listed in the `events` statement of an event policy, the software checks the history of recent events to see if the events in the `within` statement occurred within the *previous* number of seconds specified by the policy.

Therefore, an event will not match an event policy if the event is listed in the `events` statement and the events that satisfy the `within` statement occur just after it.

You can specify multiple events in a single `within` statement. The `within` statement is satisfied if *any* of the events specified in it occur. (In other words, there is a logical "or" relationship between the events in a single `within` statement.)

You can also specify multiple `within` statements, provided each specifies a different time period to check. In order for an event policy to be triggered, *all* conditions within the event policy must be satisfied, including each `within` statement. (In other words, there is a logical "and" relationship between multiple `within` statements.)

If you want an event policy to correlate with two different events within the same time period, vary the time periods by a second in order to create two different `within` statements. For example, specifying `within 60` *`event1`* and `within 61` *`event2`* will cause the policy to match only if both *`event1`* and *`event2`* occurred within the approximately 60 seconds prior to the time the trigger event occurs.

For example, this policy will trigger if a BGP peer changes state in the 120 seconds after a commit occurs:

```
event-options {
    policy after_commit {
        events rpd_bgp_neighbor_state_changed;
        within 120 events ui_commit;
        then {
            event-script commit.slax;
        }
    }
}
```

This policy will trigger if two commits occur within a 120-second period:

```
event-options {
    policy two_commits {
        events ui_commit;
        within 120 events ui_commit;
        then {
            event-script commit.slax;
```

```
        }
    }
}
```

You can also add the not statement to change a within statement from a positive correlation to a negative correlation. For the within statement to be true, none of the events listed in the not statement can have occurred in the given time period.

For example, this policy will trigger if a BGP peer changes state, *unless* the event occurs within 120 seconds of a commit occurring:

```
event-options {
    policy after_commit {
        events rpd_bgp_neighbor_state_changed;
        within 120 not events ui_commit;
        then {
            event-script bgp-state.slax;
        }
    }
}
```

Matching on event counts

You can also add a number of events that must occur for a within statement to match. You can use the trigger statement to specify that the policy only matches after a number of events, on a certain number of events, or until a certain number of events. (These correlate to greater than, equals, and less than comparisons, respectively.)

For example, this policy will match the third and subsequent LACPD_TIMEOUT events occurring within 30 seconds of a UI_COMMIT event:

```
event-options {
    policy lacp {
        events lacpd_timeout;
        within 30 {
            trigger after 2;
            events ui_commit;
        }
        then {
            event-script lacp.slax;
        }
    }
}
```

Note that you may end up with trigger statements and correlating events in the same within statement. However, the two are unrelated. The trigger event (in this case, LACPD_TIMEOUT) must occur the number of times indicated by the trigger statement. In addition, the correlating event (in this case, UI_COMMIT) must have occurred *at least once* within the indicated time period.

If there are multiple events in the `events` statement, the `trigger` statement is compared to the total number of all events listed in the `events` statement that have occurred within the specified time period. And, just to complicate things a bit further, if the event policy contains an `attributes-match` statement, the software only counts events listed in the `events` statement if they also match any relevant comparisons that use the `matches` operator. If there are no relevant comparisons that use the `matches` operator, the event is counted. (We discuss the `attributes-match` statement and `matches` operator in the next section.)

Comparing attribute values

You can also further refine event matches by comparing the values of the attributes included with the events. You can compare these attribute values to fixed values or to the attribute values from other events. A policy's conditions will only be satisfied if the trigger event matches all the attribute value match criteria and EVENTD finds enough events that satisfy the attribute value match criteria to satisfy all the `within` criteria.

You can reference attribute values in one of three ways:

`event.attribute`
: This selects the value of the *`attribute`* from the *`event`*. The *`event`* must be listed as a trigger event or correlated event.

`{$$.`*`attribute`*`}`
: This selects the value of the *`attribute`* from the trigger event. In some cases, the trigger event ID is also used as a correlating event ID (such as when you want to match on multiple events within a short time). In these cases, you can use this syntax to ensure the value from the trigger event is used for the match.

`{$`*`event.attribute`*`}`
: This selects the value of the *`attribute`* from the most recent event with the event ID *`event`*.

  In most cases, this syntax is equivalent to the *`event.attribute`* syntax. However, it does differ in one case: if you are using a `matches` comparison and the same event appears as both a trigger event and a correlating event, this syntax will only select an attribute from the correlating event. In this case, you can use the `$$.`*`attribute`* syntax to select an attribute from the trigger event.

You can use three comparison operators:

`equals`
: Both the left and right side of the comparison must reference event attributes. One of the event attributes must come from the trigger event and the other event

attribute must come from a correlating event. The comparison is true if the value of the two event attributes exactly match.

`starts-with`
: Both the left and right side of the comparison must reference event attributes. One of the event attributes must come from the trigger event and the other event attribute must come from a correlating event. The comparison is true if the value of the event attribute on the left starts with the value of the event attribute on the right.

`matches`
: The left side of the comparison must reference an event attribute. The event attribute can come from either the trigger event or a correlating event. The right side of the comparison is a regular expression. The comparison is true if the value of the event attribute on the left matches the regular expression on the right. This is the only one of the three comparison operators that is considered when determining whether to count an event towards satisfying a `trigger` statement.

You list the attribute value match conditions in an `attributes-match` statement.

For example, this policy is triggered when a BGP session goes down within 120 seconds of a commit. When a BGP session changes state, RPD emits a `RPD_BGP_NEIGHBOR_STATE_CHANGED` event. If an established BGP session goes down, the `RPD_BGP_NEIGHBOR_STATE_CHANGED` event should have an `old-state` attribute with a value of `Established`:

```
event-options {
    policy bgp {
        events rpd_bgp_neighbor_state_changed;
        within 120 events ui_commit;
        attributes-match {
            "{$$.old-state}" matches Established;
        }
        then {
            event-script bgp-state.slax;
        }
    }
}
```

This policy will match an `RPD_OSPF_NBRDOWN` event that arrives within 5 seconds after an `SNMP_TRAP_LINK_DOWN` event for the same interface. However, we must use a `starts-with` match because the `RPD_OSPF_NBRDOWN` event's `interface-name` attribute includes a logical interface (e.g., `ge-1/0/0.0`) and the `SNMP_TRAP_LINK_DOWN` event's `interface-name` attribute includes a physical interface (e.g., `ge-1/0/0`. Because the `SNMP_TRAP_LINK_DOWN` event's `interface-name` attribute includes a subset of the logical interface found in the `RPD_OSPF_NBRDOWN` event's `interface-name` attribute, we place the RPD_OSPF_NBRDOWN event on the left side of the match condition and place the SNMP_TRAP_LINK_DOWN event on the right side. Because this comparison isn't precise (ge-1/0/1 is a subset of ge-1/0/10.0), you should verify the comparison in the referenced event script:

```
event-options {
    policy ospf_link_down {
        events rpd_ospf_nbrdown;
        within 5 events snmp_trap_link_down;
        attributes-match {
            rpd_ospf_nbrdown.interface-name starts-with snmp_trap_link_down.
interface-name;
        }
        then {
            event-script bgp-state.slax;
        }
    }
}
```

This policy will match two commits by the same user within 90 seconds of each other. Because the software always requires that one of the two events used in a comparison be the trigger event and the other event be a correlating event, the software will compare the username attribute from the trigger event ($$) with the username attribute from the UI_COMMIT correlating event:

```
event-options {
    policy multi_commits {
        events ui_commit;
        within 120 events ui_commit;
        attributes-match {
            "{$$.username}" equals ui_commit.username;
        }
        then {
            event-script commit.slax;
        }
    }
}
```

Creating events on a schedule

You can have the router run event scripts on a schedule (achieving cron-like functionality) by creating events. You can create an event with an arbitrary event ID (including custom event IDs that are not otherwise defined by the Junos software) on a schedule. The events will not contain any attributes, but they will nonetheless be created. Therefore, you can use these events in event policies. If you use a generated event as the trigger event in an event policy, the event policy will be evaluated every time the event fires. Assuming the other conditions in the event policy are satisfied, then the Junos software will execute the actions defined in the event policy. You can also use generated events as correlated events (in a within clause). If used in a within clause, EVENTD will check to ensure the events occurred (or did not occur, if the `not` statement is used) within the specified time period before the trigger event.

You can use any string for your event ID. The event ID is case-insensitive. However, the Junos software will internally convert the letters in the event ID to uppercase.

You can configure events to occur every *n* seconds using the `time-interval` *n* statement. When you commit the configuration with the new (or changed) event, the Junos software creates the event immediately. After that, it creates the event every *n* seconds.

You can configure events to occur at a specific time every day using the `time-of-day` statement. The Junos software will create the event at the given time within the next 24 hours. After that, it will treat this like a recurring event scheduled to occur at a 24-hour interval.

For either form of generated event, the actual time at which it occurs can drift slightly over time. This may be due to the amount of time it takes to process the event, or due to a delay between the time when the event is scheduled to occur and the time when the software has free CPU cycles to create it. You can add the `no-drift` statement to have the software spend extra CPU cycles to correct the drift each time the event is created and rescheduled.

If the Junos software believes the configuration for a particular event has changed (which can occur due to changes to the configuration of a particular event, but also due to events such as `load override` or `rollback` operations), the Junos software will reset the events. For `time-interval` *n* events, it will create a new event at the time of commit and then schedule the event to occur every *n* seconds after that. For `time-of-day` events, it will reschedule the next event to occur at the next occurrence of the given time. In other words, changing a generated event configured using the `time-interval` *n* statement will change the time of day when the event occurs and will cause the software to create the event immediately (even if a full time interval has not passed since the last time the event was created). On the other hand, changing a generated event configured using the `time-of-day` statement will merely reset the event to run the next time that time of day arrives, which has an impact much like resetting the drift.

For example, this configuration defines a `DAILY` event, which occurs at 06:00:00 UTC and every 24 hours after that. This configuration also defines `HOURLY` and `WEEKLY` events, which will occur when the configuration is committed and every 60 minutes and every 7 days, respectively, thereafter. The policy uses the `no-drift` flag on the `HOURLY` event. Because of the `no-drift` flag, the software will create each `HOURLY` event exactly one hour after it created the previous `HOURLY` event. However, because the `DAILY` and `WEEKLY` events do not have the `no-drift` flag, the software will create each `DAILY` and `WEEKLY` event 24 hours and one week, respectively, after it finished the processing associated with creating the previous event:

```
event-options {
    generate-event {
        daily time-of-day "06:00:00 +0000";
        hourly time-interval 3600 no-drift;
        weekly time-interval 604800;
    }
}
```

Defining Event Policy Actions

You define the actions that an event policy should take within a `then` statement. Over recent years, Juniper has added a number of options to event policies. So, you can conduct common activities directly within an event policy without needing to use event scripts. However, event (or op) scripts give you more power for customization.

Regardless of the order in which you configure the event policy actions within a single policy's `then` clause, the software executes the actions found within a policy's `then` clause in this order:

1. `ignore`
2. `priority-override`
3. `upload`
4. `execute-commands`
5. `event-script`
6. `raise-trap`
7. `change-configuration`

The policy actions for each policy are conducted serially. The `ignore` action terminates further processing; however, the other actions do not. In the case of the `event-script` action (which can run either op or event scripts, despite the name), the router runs and, if requested, uploads the output of each event script prior to running the next op or event script.

Modifying default behavior

You can use an event policy to modify the default behavior of an event. You can choose to suppress an event, change its priority, or translate it to an SNMP trap.

Suppressing events. If you configure the `ignore` action, the trigger event is simply suppressed. EVENTD will cease further processing of that event. It will not even create a syslog message for the event. The suppression is immediate: EVENTD will not even check the trigger event against event policies that appear after the policy that suppresses the event.

For example, this policy chain will cause EVENTD to run the *commit1.slax* script when it sees a `UI_COMMIT` event. However, EVENTD will not run the *commit2.slax* script, nor will it create a syslog message for the `UI_COMMIT` event:

```
event-options {
    policy before_ignore_ui_commit {
        events ui_commit;
        then {
            event-script commit1.slax;
        }
    }
    policy ignore_ui_commit {
        events ui_commit;
        then {
            ignore;
        }
    }
    policy after_ignore_ui_commit {
        events ui_commit;
        then {
            event-script commit2.slax;
        }
    }
}
```

You can use the `insert` CLI command to reorder policies.

Changing event priorities. You use the `priority-override` statement to override the facility and/or severity associated with an event. For example, the `RPD_BGP_NEIGHBOR_STATE_CHANGED` event usually has a facility of `daemon` and a severity of `warning`. This policy will change the severity to `error` if the event records a neighbor going down (transitioning from the `Established` state to another state):

```
event-options {
    policy bgp {
        events rpd_bgp_neighbor_state_changed;
        attributes-match {
            "{$$.old-state}" matches Established;
        }
        then {
            priority-override {
                severity error;
```

```
            }
        }
    }
}
```

After configuring this policy, we also configure the `explicit-priority` statement for one of our log files. The `explicit-priority` statement causes Junos to include the facility and severity in syslog messages. When we manually clear a BGP neighbor, we see that the log message for the neighbor going down has a severity of `3` (corresponding to the `error` level), while the log message for the neighbor coming back up has a severity of `4` (corresponding to the default `warning` level). Because the event policy did not override the facility, both messages use the `daemon` facility:

```
Nov 27 09:41:57  r0 rpd[17699]: %DAEMON-3-RPD_BGP_NEIGHBOR_STATE_CHANGED: BGP
peer 10.10.10.2 (External AS 131074) changed state from Established to Idle
(event Stop) (instance master)
Nov 27 09:42:29  r0 rpd[17699]: %DAEMON-4-RPD_BGP_NEIGHBOR_STATE_CHANGED: BGP
peer 10.10.10.2 (External AS 131074) changed state from OpenConfirm to Establ
ished (eventRecvKeepAlive) (instance master)
```

Raising an SNMP trap. You use the `raise-trap` configuration statement to generate a `jnxSyslogTrap` SNMP trap. The SNMP trap is sent to all SNMP trap destinations, regardless of the categories the destinations are configured to receive. The `jnxSyslogTrap` SNMP trap includes the syslog message and the attribute/value pairs associated with the event.

For example, this configuration causes Junos to generate a `jnxSyslogTrap` SNMP trap whenever a BGP peering session goes down (transitions from the `Established` state to another state):

```
event-options {
    policy bgp {
        events rpd_bgp_neighbor_state_changed;
        attributes-match {
            "{$$.old-state}" matches Established;
        }
        then {
            raise-trap;
        }
    }
}
```

Executing commands

You can configure an event policy to have the Junos software run operational-mode or configuration-mode commands, optionally saving the output of those commands to a local or remote destination. Because the ability to save files to a local or remote destination uses a similar configuration to uploading files, we will cover this functionality in "Uploading files" on page 416.

Running operational-mode commands. You can configure an event policy to have the Junos software run operational-mode commands by including the `execute-commands` statement. You can include multiple commands and the Junos software will execute them in the order in which they appear in the policy configuration.

The commands cannot use attribute values from the events to form arguments for the commands; therefore, you can only use this method to run operational-mode commands when you can accurately predict all the arguments to the commands. If you need to use different arguments based on the attribute values from the events, you should use an op or event script to run the commands.

If you need to enter a quote in your command, you can escape the quote with a backslash. (The sample event policy configuration in "Event Policy Loops" on page 421 shows an example of backslash escaping in the context of a configuration command.)

You can save the output from these commands. We discuss that in "Uploading files" on page 416. Otherwise, the syntax and options are fairly straightforward and well documented in the CLI help.

Running configuration-mode commands. You can configure an event policy to have the Junos software run configuration-mode commands by including the `change-configuration` statement. You can include multiple commands and the Junos software will execute them in the order in which they appear in the policy configuration. The commands should be entered as you would enter them at the top level of the configuration (the `[edit]` level), including the necessary commands such as `set`, `delete`, `deactivate`, etc. You do not need to include the `commit` command. The Junos software will configure and commit the changes using the exclusive configuration mode.

If you include `retry` parameters in the `change-configuration` statement and EVENTD is unable to obtain the configuration lock on its first attempt, it will retry the specified additional number of times to obtain the configuration lock. If EVENTD is able to obtain the configuration lock but encounters an error at a later point in the process, it will not retry the configuration change additional times.

On success, EVENTD creates an `EVENTD_CONFIG_CHANGE_SUCCESS` event. On failure, EVENTD creates an `EVENTD_CONFIG_CHANGE_FAILED` event that includes a reason for the failure.

The commands cannot use attribute values from the events to form arguments for the commands; therefore, you can only use this method to commit configuration changes when you can accurately predict all the arguments to the configuration changes. If you need to use different arguments based on the attribute values from the events, you should use an op or event script to accomplish the configuration change.

If you need to enter a quote in your configuration command, you can escape the quote with a backslash. The event policy configuration in "Event Policy Loops" on page 421 shows an example of escaping a configuration command that contains quotes.

Otherwise, the syntax and options are fairly straightforward and well documented in the CLI help.

Uploading files

You can configure the software to copy a file to a local or remote destination (without running any other commands). Alternatively, you can configure the software to save the output of an op script or operational-mode commands and upload the output to a local or remote destination. Because all of these capabilities use the common `destinations` hierarchy, we cover these options together.

Defining a destination. Before configuring the Junos software to automatically copy a file to a local or remote destination, you must define the destination at the `[edit event-options destination]` hierarchy level.

Each destination is configured as an ordered list of URLs. The software will attempt to upload the data to each URL in the list in turn, until the upload succeeds. Once the upload to one of the locations succeeds, the software will not attempt to upload the data to any of the subsequent URLs. So, you can think of the list of URLs as containing a primary URL and, optionally, one or more backup URLs.

For remote destinations, the URL is in the form of *`protocol`*`://`*`username`*`@`*`host`*`[:`*`port`*`]//`*`path`*. The Junos software supports these values for the *`protocol`* component of the URL:

- `scp`: SCP
- `ftp`: active FTP
- `pasvftp`: passive FTP

The *`host`* component may be a hostname, an IPv4 address, or an IPv6 address. If the *`host`* element is an IPv6 address, it should be enclosed in square brackets (e.g., `[fc08::1]`).

The *`port`* component is optional. If provided, it tells the software to use a nondefault port to contact the host.

You configure an associated `password` element for each URL. The software will attempt to authenticate with the host given in the URL using the username from the URL and the password from the `password` configuration element associated with the URL.

The password is stored in the `password` configuration element using a reversible encryption method. For security purposes, you should assume that it can easily be decrypted. Therefore, you should be careful to only use credentials for accounts that have low permission levels.

When you enter a URL using the SCP protocol, the software may attempt to connect to the remote host. It does this solely to give you the option of evaluating and saving the host key. You must save the host key prior to uploading the file; otherwise, the SCP program may not trust the remote host, causing it to reject the connection for security reasons. If the software is unable to immediately connect to the remote host, you will see an error message; however, the software will still save the URL you entered.

If you fail to add the key at this time, you can use one of the options in the `[edit security ssh-known-hosts]` hierarchy to add the key. Alternatively, you can try deleting and re-entering the URL configuration at a later time to have the software automatically save the key.

As an alternative to specifying a URL to save the data in a remote location, you can also have the software save the data in a local file. To do this, you can simply specify a local directory (e.g., */var/tmp/uploads*) instead of the URL.

When storing the file, the destination filename takes the format *`hostname_YYYYMMDD_HHMMSS_filename`*. In this case, the *`hostname`* is the name of the Junos device that is uploading the file, *`YYYYMMDD`* and *`HHMMSS`* are date and time stamps for the time the data was queued for transfer, and *`filename`* is the base filename for the data that the software is storing.

By default, the software only tries to upload each file once. However, you can configure the software to retry multiple times by specifying a `retry-count` when you configure it to upload the specific data file.

Saving output from commands or scripts. You can have the software save output from commands or scripts by including the following statements in the `then execute-commands` or `then event-script` configuration stanza:

`destination`
: The `destination` statement defines the destination to which the software should save the command output. The argument should be a destination listed in the `[edit event-options destinations]` hierarchy.

`output-filename`
: The `output-filename` statement defines the base filename the software will use when storing the data in the destination.

`output-format`
: The `output-format` statement defines the format in which the software will save the command output. The choices are `xml` and `text`.

For example, this configuration will save the output of the `show interfaces terse` command any time a BGP peering session goes down:

```
event-options {
    policy bgp {
        events rpd_bgp_neighbor_state_changed;
        attributes-match {
            "{$$.old-state}" matches Established;
        }
        then {
            execute-commands {
                commands {
                    "show interfaces terse";
                }
                output-filename show-int-terse;
                destination oss-systems {
                    retry-count 3 retry-interval 30;
                }
                output-format text;
                }
            }
        }
    }
    destinations {
        oss-systems {
            archive-sites {
                "scp://log@h0/var/uploads" password "$9$QDYEz/tu0IcrvBIwgJDmP";
            }
        }
    }
}
```

When a BGP peering session goes down, the Junos software will run the `show` interfaces `terse` command, save the output in text format, and transfer it to the remote system. If the software is unable to transfer this on the first attempt, it will retry three additional times, pausing 30 seconds between each attempt. When the software transfers the file, the base filename will be `show-int-terse`. Therefore, if the router named `r0` runs this command on December 1, 2016 at 11:12:13, the output will be saved on the host `h0` in the file */var/uploads/r0_20161201_111213_show-int-terse*.

Again, because of the sequential way in which the system executes event policies and event policy actions, there may be a delay between the time of the event and the time the software executes the commands. The actual time the software runs the commands will be apparent from the timestamp included in the filename.

Saving a copy of a file. You can have the software save a copy of a local file by including the `upload` statement in an event policy's actions.

For example, this configuration will save a copy of the */var/log/messages* file any time a BGP peering session goes down:

```
event-options {
    policy bgp {
        events rpd_bgp_neighbor_state_changed;
        attributes-match {
            "{$$.old-state}" matches Established;
        }
        then {
            upload filename /var/log/messages destination oss-systems {
                retry-count 3 retry-interval 30;
            }
        }
    }
    destinations {
        oss-systems {
            archive-sites {
                "scp://log@h0/var/uploads" password "$9$QDYEz/tu0IcrvBIwgJDmP";
            }
        }
    }
}
```

When a BGP peering session goes down, the Junos software will transfer the local */var/log/messages* file to the host `h0`. The software uses the base filename of the file you are copying to form the remote filename. Therefore, if the router named `r0` runs this event policy on December 1, 2016 at 11:12:13, the output will be saved on the host `h0` in the file */var/uploads/r0_20161201_111213_messages*.

Because of the sequential way in which the system executes event policies and event policy actions, there may be a delay between the time of the event and the time the software tries to copy the file. The actual time the software first queues the file for copying will be apparent from the timestamp included in the filename.

However, the contents of the file will be the contents of the file as of the *actual time the file is uploaded*. In the case of a transfer that the software retries several times, there may be a significant delay between the file's timestamp and the time the file is uploaded.

Running an op or event script

You can configure the software to run an op or event script in an event policy. Regardless of whether you want to run an op or event script, you use the `event-script` policy action. If a matching script is defined in the `[edit event-options event-script]` hierarchy, then the software will run that script as an event script. Otherwise, the software will look for a matching script in the `[edit system scripts op]` hierarchy. If a matching script is found in that hierarchy, the software will run that script as an op script. (To understand the significance of running an op script instead of an event script, review the differences noted in "Overview of Event Script Operation" on page 397.)

By default, op or event scripts executed as part of an event policy are run as the root user. You can configure the software to execute these scripts as a different user by including the `user-name` configuration statement. For example, this event policy will cause the Junos software to run the *commit.slax* event or op script when a `UI_COMMIT` event occurs. It will execute the script with the username `user`:

```
event-options {
    policy on_commit {
        events ui_commit;
        then {
            event-script commit.slax {
                user-name user;
            }
        }
    }
}
```

You can pass arguments to op or event scripts. You can form the arguments using static values. You can also use the variables described in "Comparing attribute values" on page 408. By forming arguments from these variables, you may make it easier to obtain the information you want. Also, this provides a way for you to feed information about events to op scripts (which do not receive event information in their input documents).

For example, this event policy configuration will cause the Junos software to run the *commit.slax* event or op script when a `UI_COMMIT` event occurs. The software will run the script with a `committed-by` argument that contains the value of the trigger event's `username` attribute:

```
event-options {
    policy on_commit {
        events ui_commit;
        then {
            event-script commit.slax {
                arguments {
                    committed-by "{$$.username}";
```

```
                    }
                }
            }
        }
    }
```

You can configure more than one event script in the same event policy. In this case, EVENTD will run the scripts sequentially.

Event Policy Loops

Event policies do not contain built-in logic that prevents them from triggering other event policies with their actions. For example, consider an event policy named `policy-a` that is triggered by the `UI_COMMIT` event. If an event triggers another policy named `policy-b` that contains a `change-configuration` statement, the software will attempt to commit those configuration changes. That commit will create a `UI_COMMIT` event, which will itself trigger the `policy-a` event policy. There is nothing in the event policy infrastructure to prevent this policy interaction.

Normally, this behavior is actually a feature. When it can cause issues is if it creates a policy loop, where policies are continually taking actions that trigger other policies. This can quickly cause a problem.

To demonstrate this on your own Junos device, try committing the following policy. The policy is triggered by any `UI_COMMIT` event and will cause the software to attempt to annotate the `[edit system]` stanza with the comment "demonstrate a loop":

```
event-options {
    policy on_commit {
        events ui_commit;
        then {
            change-configuration {
                commands {
                    "annotate system \"demonstrate a loop\"";
                }
                commit-options {
                    log "committed by the on_commit policy";
                }
            }
        }
    }
}
```

When you commit this policy, nothing noticeable will happen. On the first commit, the `UI_COMMIT` event occurs prior to the time the system has parsed and installed the new event policy. However, when you commit the configuration a second time using the `commit and-quit` command, you will trigger an infinite loop of commits. You can see this by monitoring a log file that receives the `UI_COMMIT` messages, or by viewing the output of the `show system commit` CLI command. For example, here is the result of that CLI command on one of our test systems:

```
user@r0> show system commit
0   2015-11-27 13:05:02 PST by root via junoscript
    committed by the on_commit policy
1   2015-11-27 13:05:01 PST by user via cli
2   2015-11-27 13:05:00 PST by root via junoscript
    committed by the on_commit policy
3   2015-11-27 13:04:59 PST by root via junoscript
    committed by the on_commit policy
4   2015-11-27 13:04:59 PST by root via junoscript
    committed by the on_commit policy
5   2015-11-27 13:04:58 PST by root via junoscript
    committed by the on_commit policy
6   2015-11-27 13:04:58 PST by root via junoscript
    committed by the on_commit policy
7   2015-11-27 13:04:57 PST by root via junoscript
    committed by the on_commit policy
8   2015-11-27 13:04:56 PST by root via junoscript
    committed by the on_commit policy
9   2015-11-27 13:04:55 PST by root via junoscript
    committed by the on_commit policy
10  2015-11-27 13:04:55 PST by root via junoscript
    committed by the on_commit policy
11  2015-11-27 13:04:54 PST by root via junoscript
    committed by the on_commit policy
12  2015-11-27 13:04:54 PST by root via junoscript
    committed by the on_commit policy
13  2015-11-27 13:04:53 PST by root via junoscript
    committed by the on_commit policy
14  2015-11-27 13:04:52 PST by root via junoscript
    committed by the on_commit policy
15  2015-11-27 13:04:52 PST by root via junoscript
    committed by the on_commit policy
16  2015-11-27 13:04:51 PST by root via junoscript
    committed by the on_commit policy
17  2015-11-27 13:04:50 PST by user via cli
...output trimmed...
```

To end an event policy loop (including the loop in our example), enter configuration mode, enter `deactivate event-options`, and commit the configuration change.

Not all event loops are this obvious. Some may involve complex interactions of multiple policies, and some may only appear in very unusual situations. However, when they occur, event policy loops can consume your system's resources in an infinite loop of actions. Therefore, you want to take care to avoid them.

Embedding Event Policies in Event Scripts

Thus far, we have conducted all of the event policy configuration in the main Junos configuration. It is also possible to embed event policy configuration in an event script.

You embed event policies in an event script by putting the XML representation of the event policy configuration in a global variable named `$event-definition`. The process that reads this variable is lightweight and only supports static data within the `$event-definition` variable. If you try to read from variables or parameters to build the global `$event-definition` variable, it will not work.

On commit, EVENTD first processes the committed configuration. It then reads the Junos configuration snippets from the `$event-definition` variables in all event scripts listed in the configuration and inserts them into a temporary configuration database that only EVENTD uses. Then it reads the `[event-options destinations]`, `[event-options policy]`, and `[event-options generate-event]` hierarchies from this temporary database.

The implication of the way that event script policies are merged with the policies from the main configuration is that policies loaded from event scripts always appear after the statically configured policies.

Additionally, by default, the event script files that contain the policies are processed in alphabetical order. The policies from each event script are added in the order in which they appear in each file. (To modify this default ordering, you can include in the `$event-definition` variable the XML syntax to reorder policies. You can reorder event policies within the set of policies loaded from event scripts. However, you cannot insert an event policy loaded from an event script before a statically configured policy.) Also, when combining the event policy configuration from the various script files, the system uses the normal rules to merge configuration from multiple sources. Therefore, if two event scripts define two different policies with the same policy name, the system will try to merge these into a single policy with that name. This may not produce the desired result.

By default, EVENTD only re-reads the event script policies when a user commits a configuration change that EVENTD uses. If you update the content of an event script, you can have EVENTD re-read the policies using the `request system scripts event-scripts reload` operational-mode CLI command.

You can also see the configuration dynamically loaded from event scripts using the `show event-options event-scripts policies` command. However, this CLI command has some caveats:

- To build the output for the CLI command, the system re-reads all event scripts at the time the command is run. Therefore, the command output displays what the configuration *would be* if the event policies were loaded from all event scripts at that exact moment. However, there is no guarantee that the command output matches the policies that are *currently* loaded by EVENTD.
- When displaying the output for the CLI command, the system displays all the `[edit event-options]` configuration it read from the event scripts. However, when actually loading the configuration data from the event scripts, EVENTD only processes the three hierarchies mentioned earlier in this section.

Event Policy Ordering

Like routing policies and firewall filters, Junos does evaluate event policies in order. However, unlike routing policies and firewall filters, event policies usually do not contain logic that impacts later event policies. The main exception to this rule is event policies that use the `ignore` action to suppress an event. (We discussed the `ignore` action in "Suppressing events" on page 412.) Because event policies are processed serially, event policies that use the `ignore` action to suppress an event can prevent the software from considerng later policies that would otherwise match the event.

Another consideration with regard to ordering is the behavior of the EVENTD process when faced with too many concurrent event policies to execute. By default, the software forks a new process or thread to execute each event policy's actions; however, there is a limit to the number of concurrent event policies that EVENTD will execute. Once you pass that limit, EVENTD refuses to execute the actions from additional policies until it has completed executing the actions from one of the current event policies. If this occurs, EVENTD logs a syslog message indicating which policy it skipped executing. EVENTD does *not* queue the execution for a later time; rather, it simply skips executing the policy.

The reason the order of event policies matters is that, at least in situations with no more than a moderate event load, it seems logical that event policies that are listed earlier in the configuration are more likely to be executed than event policies listed later in the configuration. However, under very heavy load, all policies are probably equally likely to be ignored.

You can control the number of concurrent event policies that EVENTD will execute using the `[edit event-options max-policies]` configuration setting. As of this writing, the default value is 15, and the supported range is 1 to 20.

Given all these caveats, you may ask why someone would define their event policies within event scripts. The usual use case is to ensure that an event policy that calls an event script is distributed with the script. Configuring event policies this way also lets you keep a single data source (the script) instead of two data sources (the script and the event policy in the Junos configuration). If you prefer this method and can manage your event policies such that you avoid the pitfalls to this approach, it is a perfectly valid approach and may be well suited for your environment.

Example of embedding an event policy in an event script

The easiest way to embed an event policy in an event script is to create the configuration in the Junos CLI and then copy the relevant XML to the script. Here, we will create a configuration that does the following:

- Generate a `DAILY` event every day at 04:00 UTC.
- When the `DAILY` event occurs:
  - — Save the output of `show chassis hardware extensive`
  - — Run the *daily.slax* event script.

To meet these requirements, we create this configuration in the Junos CLI:

```
[edit event-options]
user@r0# show
generate-event {
    daily time-of-day "04:00:00 +0000" no-drift;
}
policy daily {
    events daily;
    then {
        execute-commands {
            commands {
                "show chassis hardware extensive";
            }
            output-filename inventory;
            destination hardware;
            output-format text;
        }
        event-script daily.slax;
    }
}
destinations {
    hardware {
        archive-sites {
            "ftp://ftp@inventory.example.com/junos" password "$9$hB4ylMxNbw2a";
        }
    }
}
```

We now use the display xml pipe command to display the XML representation of this hierarchy:

```
[edit event-options]
user@r0# show | display xml | no-more
<rpc-reply xmlns:junos="http://xml.juniper.net/junos/15.1R2/junos">
    <configuration junos:changed-seconds="1448998871"
                   junos:changed-localtime="2015-12-01 19:41:11 UTC">
        <event-options>
            <generate-event>
                <name>daily</name>
                <time-of-day>04:00:00 +0000</time-of-day>
                <no-drift/>
            </generate-event>
            <policy>
                <name>daily</name>
                <events>daily</events>
                <then>
                    <execute-commands>
                        <commands>
                            <name>show chassis hardware extensive</name>
                        </commands>
                        <output-filename>inventory</output-filename>
                        <destination>
                            <name>hardware</name>
                        </destination>
                        <output-format>text</output-format>
                    </execute-commands>
                    <event-script>
                        <name>daily.slax</name>
                    </event-script>
                </then>
            </policy>
            <destinations>
                <name>hardware</name>
                <archive-sites>
                    <name>ftp://ftp@inventory.example.com/junos</name>
                    <password>$9$hB4ylMxNbw2a</password>
                </archive-sites>
            </destinations>
        </event-options>
    </configuration>
    <cli>
        <banner>[edit event-options]</banner>
    </cli>
</rpc-reply>
```

Next, we place this content, reformatted in SLAX format, in our event script:

```
version 1.1;

ns junos = "http://xml.juniper.net/junos/*/junos";
ns xnm = "http://xml.juniper.net/xnm/1.1/xnm";
```

```
ns jcs = "http://xml.juniper.net/junos/commit-scripts/1.0";

import "../import/junos.xsl";

var $event-definition = {
    <event-options> {
        <generate-event> {
            <name> "daily";
            <time-of-day> "04:00:00 +0000";
            <no-drift>;
        }
        <policy> {
            <name> "daily";
            <events> "daily";
            <then> {
                <execute-commands> {
                    <commands> {
                        <name> "show chassis hardware extensive";
                    }
                    <output-filename> "inventory";
                    <destination> {
                        <name> "hardware";
                    }
                    <output-format> "text";
                }
                <event-script> {
                    <name> "daily.slax";
                }
            }
        }
        <destinations> {
            <name> "hardware";
            <archive-sites> {
                <name> "ftp://ftp@inventory.example.com/junos";
                <password> "$9$hB4ylMxNbw2a";
            }
        }
    }
}

match / {
<event-script-results>;
}
```

Finally, we rollback our temporary changes and configure the event script:

```
[edit event-options]
user@r0# top

[edit]
user@r0# rollback

[edit]
```

```
user@r0# set event-options event-script file daily.slax

[edit]
user@r0# show event-options

[edit]
user@r0# commit and-quit
commit complete
Exiting configuration mode
```

Now, we can see that our event policy is inherited from the event script:

```
user@r0> show event-options event-scripts policies
## Last changed: 2015-12-01 20:01:03 UTC
event-options {
    generate-event {
        daily time-of-day "04:00:00 +0000" no-drift;
    }
    policy daily {
        events daily;
        then {
            execute-commands {
                commands {
                    "show chassis hardware extensive";
                }
                output-filename inventory;
                destination hardware;
                output-format text;
            }
            event-script daily.slax;
        }
    }
    destinations {
        hardware {
            archive-sites {
                "ftp://ftp@inventory.example.com/junos" password "...;
            }
        }
    }
}
```

Testing Event Policies

The best way to test event policies is to trigger the events in a lab testbed and ensure that the event policies behave as expected. However, there may be times when this is not possible, either due to resource constraints or because it is difficult to replicate the conditions. In this case, you can log a test event using the *logger* program from the shell.

The command takes the form `logger -e` *`EVENT_ID`* `[-a` *`attribute=value`* `[-a` *`attribute=value`* `[-a ... ]]` *`message`*. You specify the *`EVENT_ID`* using the `-e` argument. You can specify one or more attribute/value pairs using -a arguments. You then specify the syslog message after the arguments.

For example, this command will create a UI_COMMIT event with a username attribute of user, a command attribute of commit, and a message attribute of none. It will also log a syslog message using the normal format of the UI_COMMIT event (although this is probably only important if your event script uses the actual value of the syslog message in its processing):

```
% logger -e UI_COMMIT -a username=user -a command=commit -a message=none \
"User 'user' requested 'commit' operation (comment: none)"
```

You can verify that this created the expected event by viewing the output of a log file that uses the structured-data format for logging. (See "Event Discovery" on page 403 for more information on the structured-data format.) If you view the event generated from our sample command in a log file that uses the structured-data format for logging, you'll see an event like this:

```
<13>1 2015-11-27T13:34:50.188-08:00 r0 logger - UI_COMMIT [junos@2636.1.1.1.2.21
username="user" command="commit" message="none"] User 'user' requested 'commit'
operation (comment: none)
```

Configuring Event Scripts

You configure event scripts in the [edit event-options event-script] hierarchy. You configure each script using the file configuration statement, giving the name of a script located in the */var/db/scripts/event/* directory.

Like with op scripts, there are several options you can provide when configuring event scripts. Some of these are:

checksum
: When you configure a checksum, the CSCRIPT utility will verify the script's checksum prior to executing the script. It will perform this check each time it executes the script.

remote-execution
: You can use this hierarchy to provide the script with one or more hostnames with an associated username and password. The script will receive this information in the <remote-execution-details> element of the input document. The script can use this information to form arguments to the jcs:open() function call. The sole purpose of providing information in the remote-execution configuration is to provide information to the script. It does not change the way the script calls the jcs:open() function.

  When you enter the remote-execution configuration statement, the system will check to see if it has an SSH key for the host. If not, it will try to contact the remote host to gather an SSH key. This process ensures that the event script will be able to establish a secure connection to the remote host. If the software is unable to immediately connect to the remote host, you will see an error message; however, the software will still save the information you entered.

If you fail to add the key at this time, you can use one of the options in the `[edit security ssh-known-hosts]` hierarchy to add the key. Alternatively, you can try deleting and re-entering the `remote-execution` configuration at a later time to have the software automatically save the key.

Note that the use of the `remote-execution` configuration statement is completely optional. You can choose to provide the remote host details to your script in another way. However, if you do provide remote host details to your script another way, you should still ensure that the device has the SSH host key. One way to do that is to use one of the options in the `[edit security ssh-known-hosts]` hierarchy to add the key to the Junos configuration.

`source`
: You use this statement to configure a URL that the router can access in order to load the latest version of a script. You can trigger a manual refresh of the event scripts when new versions become available. Note that the router must be able to access the URL in order for this feature to be useful.

And, as we discussed in "Configuring Op Scripts" on page 367, you can use the `set system scripts synchronize` configuration statement to have the master RE synchronize configured scripts (op, commit, and event scripts) to the backup RE when a user initiates a synchronized commit. This ensures that the backup RE will have the same event configuration and the same event scripts in case it needs to take over from the master. (Of course, this also means that all your event scripts will run on both REs, which is something to consider carefully when writing your scripts. In your event scripts, you can check for the existence of the `$junos-context/re-master` node to determine whether a given script is being executed on the master RE. Once you have determined that, you can have your script take actions appropriate for the RE on which it is running.)

Example: Responding to a Flapping Link

Now that we have covered the theory, let's consider an example. We will look at the way you can use an event script to modify the way a Junos device works.

Imagine you want to modify the way the router responds when a member link in an aggregated Ethernet (AE) bundle is flapping. Rather than suffering periodic traffic loss due to an unreliable link, you want the Junos device to disable the link.

It seems like a reasonable feature request to implement this behavior, and you are welcome to ask Juniper to implement something like it. However, you can also implement this behavior yourself using an event script.

Let's use these specific requirements to implement an event script:

- If a member link in an AE bundle goes down at least two times in 30 seconds, disable it.
- You should be able to mark specified interfaces that the script can autodisable. Only those interfaces should be disabled by the script.
- It is acceptable for the script to disable all interfaces in a bundle if all are flapping. You have decided that you would rather disable all interfaces in the bundle than have an unreliable bundle.

We start our consideration of these requirements with the actual event ID that shows the link has been disabled. You observed that you were seeing the `LACPD_TIMEOUT` message when your links were flapping. So, we start by writing our event policy to handle this event.

The Event

Let's examine the `help syslog` output for this event:

```
user@r0> help syslog LACPD_TIMEOUT
Name:          LACPD_TIMEOUT
Message:       <error-message>: lacp current while timer expired current
               Receive State: CURRENT
Help:          lacp timer expired
Description:   The Link Aggregation Control Protocol process (lacpd)
               experienced timeout hence Receive State will change from Current
               to Expired/Defaulted.
Type:          Event: This message reports an event, not an error
Severity:      notice
Facility:      LOG_DAEMON
```

In this case, the help output does not immediately make it clear what the value of the `error-message` attribute represents. It really helps to see an actual `LACPD_TIMEOUT` message:

```
May 21 03:45:10  r0 lacpd[1588]: LACPD_TIMEOUT: ge-5/0/1: lacp current while
timer expired current Receive State: CURRENT
```

Looking at the message, you see that the `error-message` attribute contains the name of the physical interface for which the `LACPD_TIMEOUT` event was created. We can use this information to retrieve the interface name from the event's attributes.

The Event Policy

We use the following event policy to meet the requirements:

```
event-options {
    policy lacp {
        events lacpd_timeout; ❶
        within 30 { ❷
            trigger after 1;
            events lacpd_timeout;
        }
        attributes-match {
            "{$$.error-message}" equals lacpd_timeout.error-message; ❸
        }
        then {
            event-script lacp.slax; ❹
        }
    }
}
```

❶ This statement sets the trigger event to be a `LACPD_TIMEOUT` event. EVENTD will only evaluate the remainder of this event policy when it receives a `LACPD_TIMEOUT` event.

❷ The event policy will only execute on the second (or subsequent) `LACPD_TIMEOUT` event within 30 seconds. In addition, this specifies the `LACPD_TIMEOUT` event as a correlating event. This allows us to enforce `attributes-match` conditions between the two `LACPD_TIMEOUT` events in the 30-second period (the trigger event and one other `LACPD_TIMEOUT` event, which will be the correlating event).

❸ In order for the policy to be satisfied, the `error-message` attribute (recall that this is the physical interface) of the trigger event must match the `error-message` attribute of one of the other `LACPD_TIMEOUT` events received in the 30-second period. If none of the other `LACPD_TIMEOUT` events received in the 30-second period satisfy the `attributes-match` condition, then none of the `LACPD_TIMEOUT` events can serve as correlating events. This means the `within 30` clause will not be satisfied, and the event policy will not be satisfied.

❹ If the conditions of the policy are satisfied, EVENTD will use CSCRIPT to run the *lacp.slax* event script.

The Event Script

We start the event script with some basic infrastructure:

```
version 1.1;

ns junos = "http://xml.juniper.net/junos/*/junos";
ns xnm = "http://xml.juniper.net/xnm/1.1/xnm";
ns jcs = "http://xml.juniper.net/junos/commit-scripts/1.0";

import "../import/junos.xsl";

var $self = "lacp.slax"; ❶
var $logprefix = $self _ ": ";
var $debug = false();

match / {
    <event-script-results> {
        var $event_id = event-script-input/trigger-event/id; ❷
        var $interface = event-script-input/trigger-event/attribute-list/
            attribute[name == "error-message"]/value;

        if ($event_id && $event_id != "LACPD_TIMEOUT") { ❸
            expr jcs:syslog("user.info", $logprefix,
                            "called for unexpected event ", $event_id);
        }
        else if (not($event_id) || not($interface)) { ❹
            expr jcs:syslog("user.info", $logprefix,
                            "called with unexpected input document ",
                            "(unable to find expected elements)");
        }
        else { ❺
            if ($debug) { ❻
                expr jcs:syslog("user.debug", $logprefix, "found: ",
                                "$event_id=", $event_id,
                                ", $interface=", $interface);
            }

            call check_disable_interface($interface); ❼
        }
    }
}
```

❶ We begin by setting up a few global variables. `$self` is the name of the script. We could have retrieved this from the `$script` argument; however, statically coding this allows us to use a stable name even if we incorporate a variation (such as a version number) in the script name.

We also set up a `$logprefix` variable, which we will use in our log messages. While this seems simple, it is something we will use repetitively.

Finally, we set up the `$debug` variable with a Boolean false value (produced by the `false()` function). We use this variable to control whether we log extra debugging information. You can enable the extra debugging messages by assigning the variable a Boolean true value (produced by the `true()` function).

❷ In our main match template, we begin by extracting two important pieces of information from the input document: the event ID (which we assign to the `$event_id` variable) and the interface (which we assign to the `$interface` variable). Recall that the interface is found in the event's `error-message` attribute, so our XPath expression extracts the value for this attribute.

If either piece of information is missing, the XPath expression will match no nodes, leaving us with an empty variable.

❸ The logic moves to a set of tests meant to detect error conditions. This first check ensures that the script was not called for any event other than the `LACPD_TIMEOUT` event. If it was, the script logs an error message to syslog and exits without taking further action.

❹ This next check catches the case where the script could not determine the event ID or the interface from the input document. This should not occur; however, if it does, we do not want the script to proceed further with what may be incomplete or inaccurate information. Instead, if the script could not determine the event ID or the interface from the input document, the script logs an error message to syslog and exits without taking further action.

❺ If the basic sanity checks passed, the script's processing moves to this `else` statement, which calls the main logic of the script.

❻ If extra debugging is enabled, the script will log a debugging message to syslog giving the event ID and interface from the input document.

❼ The script now calls the `check_disable_interface()` template to carry out the remainder of the script's logic.

Next, let's move to examining the `check_disable_interface()` template:

```
/*
 * Check to see if the interface should be disabled. If so, do it.
 */
template check_disable_interface($interface) {
    var $get_conf_rpc = { ❶
        <get-configuration database="committed" inherit="inherit"> {
            <configuration> {
                <interfaces> {
                    <interface> {
```

```
                        <name> $interface;
                    }
                }
            }
        }
    }

    var $config = jcs:invoke($get_conf_rpc); ❷
    var $disable_val = $config/interfaces/interface[name = $interface]/
        apply-macro[name = $self]/data[name = "auto-disable"]/value; ❸

    var $pattern = "^(([Tt][Rr][Uu][Ee])|([Yy][Ee][Ss]))$";
    var $match_result = jcs:regex($pattern, $disable_val); ❹
    if (string-length($match_result[1]) > 0) {
        call disable_interface($interface); ❺
    }
    else if ($debug) {
        expr jcs:syslog("user.debug", $logprefix,
                        "ignoring event for interface ",
                        $interface, " due to apply-macro ", $self,
                        " configuration"); ❻
    }
}
```

❶ The `$get_conf_rpc` variable holds the RPC to retrieve the configuration for the physical interface whose name is stored in the `$interface` variable. Note that the RPC requests the post-inheritance committed configuration.

❷ This line calls the RPC and stores the result in the `$config` variable.

❸ This line looks for an `apply-macro` statement with the name of the script (as stored in the `$self` variable). Within that stanza, it looks for an attribute/value pair named `auto-disable`.

For example, for the interface `ge-5/0/1`, it looks for a configuration like this:

```
interfaces {
    ge-5/0/1 {
        apply-macro lacp.slax {
            auto-disable yes;
        }
    }
}
```

Automation scripts can use the `apply-macro` statement to store or retrieve information they use in their execution. For more information on the `apply-macro` syntax, see "Passing information to commit scripts" on page 256.

❹ This call to the `jcs:regex()` function checks to see whether the value of the `apply-macro` statement matches the pattern shown in `$pattern`. The pattern matches the strings "true" and "yes" in a case-insensitive way. The result of the regex comparison is stored in an array in the `$match_result` variable. The portion of the `apply-macro` statement's value that matches the regex is stored in the first array member. If the value matched the regular expression, the first array member will have a nonzero string length. If the value did not match the regular expression (either because the `apply-macro` statement did not exist, or because the value was something other than "true" or "yes"), then the first array member will have a string length of zero.

❺ This branch is true if the `apply-macro` statement's value matched our regular expression. That means that the user does want the script to attempt to automatically disable the interface. The script calls the `disable_interface()` template to accomplish that.

❻ If the user did not configure the `apply-macro` statement for the interface to give the script permission to disable it, the script will log a message if the `$debug` variable is true.

Finally, let's move on to examine the `disable_interface()` template. Recall that the script will call this template to disable the interface if the interface has met all our criteria thus far:

```
/*
 * Disable the interface
 */
template disable_interface($interface) {
    var $config-results := { ❶
        var $con = jcs:open();
        if (not($con)) { ❷
            <xnm:error> {
                <message> "Unable to connect to local mgd.";
            }
        }
        else { ❸
            call jcs:load-configuration {
                with $connection = $con;
                with $configuration = {
                    <configuration> {
                        <interfaces> {
                            <interface> {
                                <name> $interface;
                                <disable>;
                            }
                        }
                    }
```

```
                }
                with $commit-options = {
                    <commit-options> {
                        <log> "interace " _ $interface _
                              " disabled by event-script (" _ $self _
                              ") due to LACP flaps";
                    }
                }
            }
            expr jcs:close($con);
        }
    }

    if ($config-results//xnm:error) { ❹
        expr jcs:syslog("user.error", $logprefix,
                        "error making configuration change for interface ",
                        $interface, ": ", $config-results//xnm:error/message);
    }
    else { ❺
        expr jcs:syslog("user.info", $logprefix, "interface ", $interface,
                        " disabled by ", $self, " due to LACP flaps - ",
                        "please enable it manually once the link is stable");
    }
}
```

❶ The bulk of the template's logic is contained within an assignment to the `$config-results` variable. Because we will be storing XML fragments within the variable, we use the `:=` operator to convert the result tree fragment to a node set.

Organizing our logic this way allows us to conduct a single check for the success of the operation at the end of our logic. By checking for any `<xnm:error>` elements, we can determine whether there was a failure, regardless of the particular portion of the logic that failed.

❷ If the connection to the local system failed, the code creates an `<xnm:error>` element with a `<message>` element that explains the reason the script was unable to disable the interface. This `<xnm:error>` element will be placed directly in the `$config-results` variable.

❸ If it was able to connect to the local system, the script calls the `jcs:load-configuration()` template to disable the interface in question. The script has the `jcs:load-configuration()` template commit the configuration change with a log message that records the reason for this configuration change.

The `call` statement places the results of the template directly in the `$config-results` variable.

❹ After completing the logic to change the configuration, the `disable_interface()` template checks the `$config-results` variable for the presence of any `<xnm:error>` elements. If it finds any, it determines that the configuration change failed and logs a syslog message with the contents of the `<message>` element from one of the `<xnm:error>` elements.

❺ If the `disable_interface()` template did not find any `<xnm:error>` elements in the `$config-results` variable, it determines that the change succeeded and it logs a syslog message indicating the change it made.

The Results

Let's look at the event script in practice. We will use the logger utility to generate messages for several interfaces and see the reaction of the router.

As a reminder, we use this command to generate the log messages, replacing the interface as appropriate:

```
% logger -e LACPD_TIMEOUT -a error-message=ge-5/0/6 \
"ge-5/0/6: lacp current while timer expired current Receive State: CURRENT"
```

We will use three interfaces, configured as follows:

```
interfaces {
    ge-2/0/7 {
        gigether-options {
            802.3ad ae0;
        }
    }
    ge-3/0/8 {
        apply-macro lacp.slax {
            auto-disable true;
        }
        gigether-options {
            802.3ad ae0;
        }
    }
    ge-5/0/6 {
        apply-macro lacp.slax {
            auto-disable true;
        }
        gigether-options {
            802.3ad ae0;
        }
    }
}
```

We also will make one change to the script. We will enable the debugging feature by setting the `$debug` variable to `true()`.

We now generate several events for these interfaces and look at the results in the log file. As you can see, the six LACPD_TIMEOUT events generated only two invocations of the event script:

```
Dec  1 17:49:55  r0 logger: LACPD_TIMEOUT: ge-5/0/6: lacp current while timer
expired current Receive State: CURRENT ❶
Dec  1 17:50:11  r0 logger: LACPD_TIMEOUT: ge-2/0/7: lacp current while timer
expired current Receive State: CURRENT ❷
Dec  1 17:50:25  r0 logger: LACPD_TIMEOUT: ge-3/0/8: lacp current while timer
expired current Receive State: CURRENT ❸
Dec  1 17:50:27  r0 logger: LACPD_TIMEOUT: ge-5/0/6: lacp current while timer
expired current Receive State: CURRENT ❹
Dec  1 17:50:28  r0 logger: LACPD_TIMEOUT: ge-2/0/7: lacp current while timer
expired current Receive State: CURRENT ❺
Dec  1 17:50:28  r0 cscript.crypto: lacp.slax: found: $event_id=LACPD_TIMEOUT,
$interface=ge-2/0/7
Dec  1 17:50:29  r0 cscript.crypto: lacp.slax: ignoring event for interface g
e-2/0/7 due to apply-macro lacp.slax configuration
Dec  1 17:50:50  r0 logger: LACPD_TIMEOUT: ge-5/0/6: lacp current while timer
expired current Receive State: CURRENT ❻
Dec  1 17:50:50  r0 cscript.crypto: lacp.slax: found: $event_id=LACPD_TIMEOUT,
$interface=ge-5/0/6
Dec  1 17:50:51  r0 cscript.crypto: lacp.slax: interface ge-5/0/6 disabled by
lacp.slax due to LACP flaps - please enable it manually once the link is stable
```

❶ Because no other LACPD_TIMEOUT event occurred for interface ge-5/0/6 in the preceding 30 seconds, EVENTD did not run the event script in response to this event.

❷ Because no other LACPD_TIMEOUT event occurred for interface ge-2/0/7 in the preceding 30 seconds, EVENTD did not run the event script in response to this event.

❸ Because no other LACPD_TIMEOUT event occurred for interface ge-3/0/8 in the preceding 30 seconds, EVENTD did not run the event script in response to this event.

❹ This event occurred 32 seconds after the preceding LACPD_TIMEOUT event for interface ge-5/0/6. Because no other LACPD_TIMEOUT event occurred for interface ge-5/0/6 in the preceding 30 seconds, EVENTD did not run the event script in response to this event.

❺ This event occurred 17 seconds after the preceding LACPD_TIMEOUT event for interface ge-2/0/7. Therefore, this event matched the event criteria for the event policy, and EVENTD ran the event script in response to this event. However, you see that the script chose not to disable the interface because the interface does not have the `apply-macro lacp.slax` configuration indicating that the script should try to disable the interface.

❻ This event occurred 23 seconds after the preceding `LACPD_TIMEOUT` event for interface `ge-5/0/6`. Therefore, this event matched the event criteria for the event policy, and EVENTD ran the event script in response to this event. In addition, because the interface does have the `apply-macro lacp.slax` configuration indicating that the script should try to disable the interface, the event script disabled the interface.

We can confirm the script made the change by using the CLI to examine the commit logs and the configuration change:

```
user@r0> show system commit
0    2015-12-01 17:50:51 PST by root via junoscript
     interace ge-5/0/6 disabled by event-script (lacp.slax) due to LACP flaps
1    2015-12-01 17:49:19 PST by user via cli
2    2015-12-01 17:46:33 PST by user via cli
...output trimmed...

user@r0> show configuration | compare rollback 1
[edit interfaces ge-5/0/6]
+    disable;
```

Chapter Summary

Event scripts and policies are powerful tools that enable you to customize the way the Junos software responds to events. Using event scripts and policies, you can automate basic troubleshooting, change the way your device responds to abnormal network events (such as a flapping link), or perform periodic tasks—and you need to worry neither about polling for information to determine when an event has occurred nor about losing connectivity between your automation station and the Junos device. Instead, the event-processing engine receives all events and processes the event policy locally.

With the addition of commit scripts, op scripts, and event scripts, your automation toolbox now contains tools that let you perform complex automation on your network device once it is already connected to the network. In the next chapter, we will cover some automation tools that help you with the initial provisioning of your Junos devices.

CHAPTER 8

Initial Provisioning

Your personal toolbox now contains several tools for automating Junos devices: some that run off-box and remotely control a set of Junos devices and some that run directly on a Junos device. This chapter introduces two new tools that integrate with, and extend, the tools you've already learned. These tools, Zero Touch Provisioning (ZTP) and Netconify, focus on initial provisioning of the Junos device.

You can't provision customer-facing services on a network until each participating network device is provisioned with a core set of services and protocols. This core set of services enables administrative access to the network device. In addition, initial provisioning may include one or more routing protocols to dynamically exchange routing information within the network. At a minimum, initial provisioning typically includes configuring the parameters required to administer the device over an IP network. Along with some network-specific configuration parameters, you will usually need to configure:

- A root password
- A hostname
- A management interface IP address
- A default route
- DNS name servers
- System management protocols (SSH, NETCONF, REST, etc.)

Either ZTP or Netconify can be used to speed the deployment of this initial configuration on hundreds of devices. In addition, ZTP and Netconify can be combined with some of the tools we've already explored, or integrated with the Ansible framework covered in Chapter 10, to automate the deployment of thousands of Juniper devices.

ZTP

Zero Touch Provisioning allows the automated installation of a Junos image and configuration file on a Junos device. This occurs by simply connecting the physical cabling and powering on a Junos device that is in the factory default state. ZTP uses DHCP with vendor-specific options to communicate the Junos image file and configuration file to be loaded on the device. The Junos device then requests these image and configuration files from the specified file server via the HTTP, FTP, or TFTP protocols. This process is illustrated in Figure 8-1.

ZTP is currently supported on EX and QFX model devices. However, support for additional platforms is likely in the future. Check Juniper's Feature Explorer page (*https://pathfinder.juniper.net/feature-explorer/search.html#q=Zero+Touch+Provisioning*) to confirm whether your device model and factory default Junos software version support ZTP.

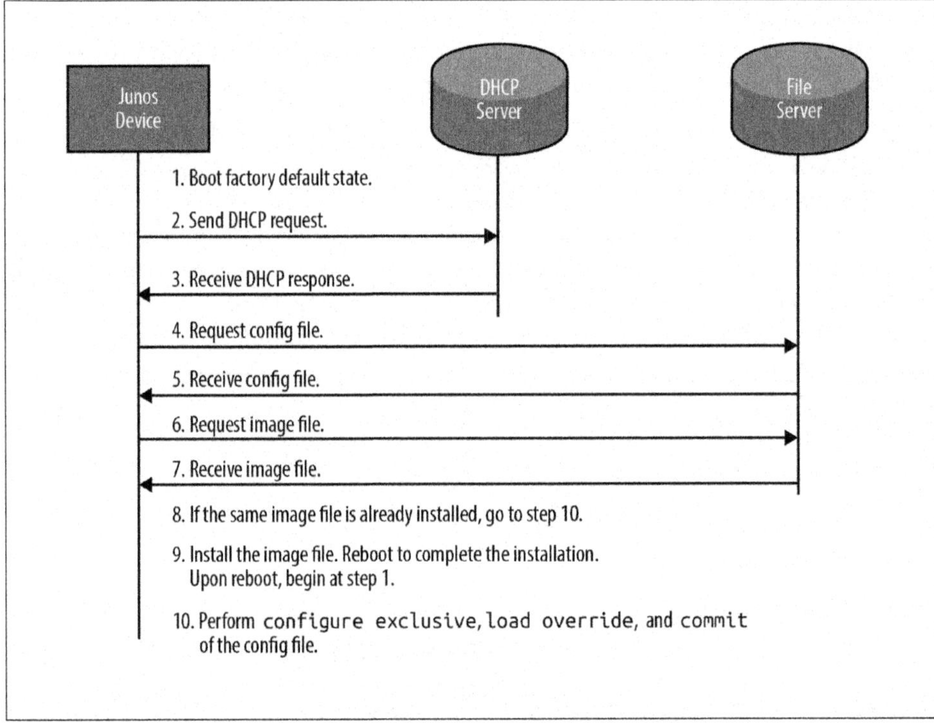

Figure 8-1. An overview of the Zero Touch Provisioning process

Let's investigate each of these 10 steps in more detail:

1. The ZTP process begins when a ZTP-capable device is booted in its factory default state. The device is shipped in this state, but it can also be returned to this state at any time by issuing the CLI command `request system zeroize`. If you were to view the factory default configuration of a ZTP-capable device, you would see that it has the DHCP client feature enabled on one or more interfaces and that the `auto-image-upgrade` configuration statement is enabled at the `[edit chassis]` level of the configuration. Here is an example from the factory default configuration of an EX2200-C:

   ```
   {master:0}
   root> show configuration chassis
   auto-image-upgrade;

   {master:0}
   root> show configuration interfaces me0
   unit 0 {
       family inet {
           dhcp {
               vendor-id Juniper-ex2200-c-12p-2g;
           }
       }
   }
   ```

2. The Junos device sends a DHCP request on all interfaces configured as DHCP clients.

   The exact interfaces configured as DHCP clients is platform-specific, but they generally include the device's management interface and may include additional interfaces. You can check the specific behavior of a Junos device by viewing the factory default interface configuration.

   This output from an EX2200-C confirms that the DHCP client is configured on the `me0.0` management interface and the `vlan.0` logical interface:

   ```
   root> show configuration interfaces | display set | match dhcp
   set interfaces me0 unit 0 family inet dhcp vendor-id Juniper-ex2200-c...
   set interfaces vlan unit 0 family inet dhcp vendor-id Juniper-ex2200-...
   ```

3. The DHCP server returns a DHCP response. The information contained in this response is used to assign the device an IP address, subnet mask, and router. In addition, the DHCP response includes vendor-specific DHCP attributes which specify the image file and configuration file to be installed by the ZTP process. Table 8-1 details the mandatory and optional DHCP attributes that may be specified in the DHCP response. If the hostname, syslog servers, or NTP servers are

specified in the response's DHCP attributes, a Junos configuration snippet is produced with the corresponding parameters. The configuration snippet is merged with the device's factory default configuration and committed.

4. The DHCP response is used to determine the protocol, server IP address, and pathname from which to retrieve the configuration file. If the DHCP response specified a configuration file, the Junos device requests the configuration file using the specified protocol. Only the TFTP, FTP, and HTTP protocols are currently supported.
5. The file server delivers the requested configuration file to the Junos device.

The configuration file must be in text (curly brace) format. XML and set configuration formats are not supported by ZTP. In addition, the configuration file must include a root password at the `[edit system root-authentication]` configuration hierarchy level.

6. The DHCP response is used to determine the pathname to retrieve the image file. If the DHCP response specified an image file, the Junos device requests the image file using the specified protocol and server IP address.
7. The file server delivers the requested image file to the Junos device.
8. The Junos device checks the content of the downloaded image and determines if the exact same version of Junos is already running on the device. If the same version is already running, the image installation is skipped, the image is deleted, and the process continues with step 10. If the images are different, the process continues with step 9.

The requested image file is always downloaded to the Junos device, even if the same Junos version is already running on the device. The download is necessary because the version of the new image is determined by inspecting the actual content of the image file rather than being derived from the image's filename. While this process may seem inefficient, it works correctly even if the image file has been renamed.

It is possible to use ZTP to *downgrade* the Junos version of a device. However, if the target version of Junos does not support ZTP, the configuration portion of the Zero Touch Provisioning process will not be performed. This will leave the device with the correct target version of Junos, but a factory default configuration.

9. A `request system software add` command is executed to install the new Junos image. The device is rebooted to complete the software installation, and the process begins again at step 1 with the newly installed Junos software version.
10. The Junos device concatenates the configuration snippet produced from the DHCP response with the configuration file downloaded from the file server. The resulting configuration is loaded onto the device using the equivalent of the `configure exclusive`, `load override`, and `commit` commands.

ZTP is a little different from some of the other tools in our automation toolbox. Rather than writing a Python or SLAX script to implement the automation, ZTP requires the configuration of a DHCP server and a corresponding file server. In addition, configuring a DHCP server with the correct parameters is very specific to the particular DHCP server implementation in use. Therefore, let's begin by analyzing the DHCP attributes that the DHCP server should return to a ZTP-capable Junos device. These attributes are detailed in Table 8-1. In addition to these ZTP-specific attributes, the DHCP server should also assign the standard IP address, subnet mask, and router parameters necessary to provide the Junos device with IP-level connectivity to the file server.

Table 8-1. DHCP attributes used by the Junos Zero Touch Provisioning process

ZTP parameter	DHCP option	Mandatory or optional?	Description
File server IP address	Option 150 (preferred) or option 66	Mandatory	The IP address of the file server. Used to fetch the image and configuration files. One of option 150 or option 66 must be specified. If both options are specified, option 150 takes precedence.
File transfer protocol	Option 43, suboption 03	Optional	The protocol used to communicate with the file server. The default protocol is TFTP. If this option is specified, it must have a value of `http`, `ftp`, or `tftp`.
Image file path	Option 43, suboption 00 (preferred) or option 43, suboption 04	Optional	The full path to the Junos image file on the file server. If both suboption 00 and suboption 04 are specified, suboption 00 is preferred. While the image file path is not mandatory, either the image file path or the configuration file path must be specified.
Configuration file path	Option 43, suboption 01 (preferred) or the boot filename field from the DHCP header	Optional	The full path to the configuration file on the file server. The configuration file should be in text (curly brace) format. If both option 43, suboption 01 and the boot filename DHCP header are specified, option 43, suboption 01 is preferred. While the configuration file path is not mandatory, either the image file path or the configuration file path must be specified.

<table>
<thead>
<tr><th>ZTP parameter</th><th>DHCP option</th><th>Mandatory or optional?</th><th>Description</th></tr>
</thead>
<tbody>
<tr><td>Syslog servers</td><td>Option 7</td><td>Optional</td><td>An array of IP addresses specifying syslog server(s) used by the Junos device. If specified, the following configuration snippet is appended to the Junos device's configuration file:
<pre>
system {
    syslog {
        host ip-address {
            any any;
        }
    }
}
</pre>
This configuration snippet is repeated for each syslog server listed in the DHCP option 7 array.</td></tr>
<tr><td>NTP servers</td><td>Option 42</td><td>Optional</td><td>An array of IP addresses specifying NTP server(s) used by the Junos device. If specified, the following configuration snippet is appended to the Junos device's configuration file:
<pre>
system {
    ntp {
        server ip-address;
    }
}
</pre>
This configuration snippet is repeated for each NTP server listed in the DHCP option 42 array.</td></tr>
<tr><td>Hostname</td><td>Option 12</td><td>Optional</td><td>A string to be used as the device's hostname. If specified, the following configuration snippet is appended to the Junos device's configuration file:
<pre>
system {
    host-name hostname;
}
</pre></td></tr>
</tbody>
</table>

The following example demonstrates using ZTP to install a new Junos image and configuration file on a Juniper EX2200-C switch. The example topology is shown in Figure 8-2.

In this topology, the `me0.0` management interface of the EX2200-C switch is attached to the `ge-0/0/10.0` interface of the `fw0` SRX device. The SRX firewall also acts as the DHCP server. It uses the Junos DHCP local server feature to deliver the DHCP response required by ZTP. An HTTP file server is configured to serve the image and configuration files. This server has an IP address of `10.210.58.38` and is connected to the `vlan.100` interface of `fw0`. The file server is configured to serve the new Junos image file from the URL `http://10.210.58.38/images/jinstall-ex-2200-14.1X53-D25.2-domestic-signed.tgz` and the new configuration file from the URL `http://10.210.58.38/configs/s0.config`.

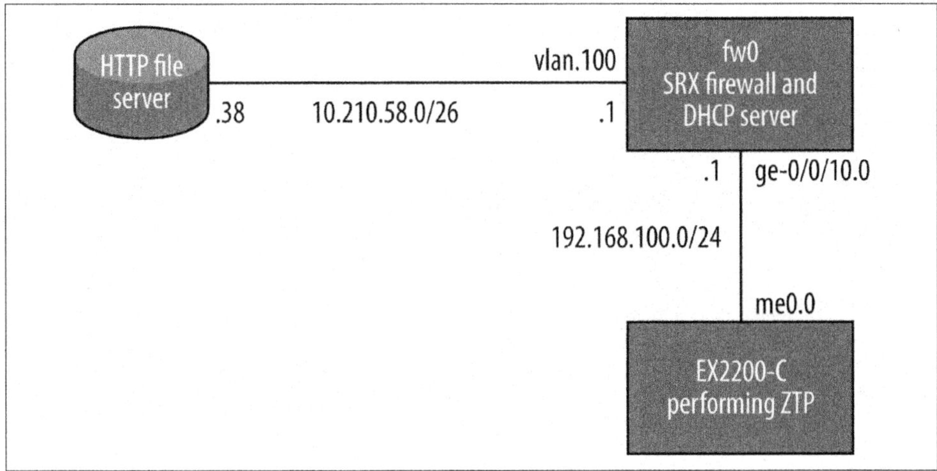

Figure 8-2. An example ZTP topology

The relevant configuration of the `fw0` SRX device is:

```
user@fw0> show configuration interfaces vlan
unit 100 {
    family inet {
        address 10.210.58.1/26;
    }
}

user@fw0> show configuration interfaces ge-0/0/10
unit 0 {
    family inet {
        address 192.168.100.1/24;
    }
}

user@fw0> show configuration system services dhcp-local-server
group ZTP_group {
    interface ge-0/0/10.0;
}

user@fw0> show configuration access
address-assignment {
    pool ZTP_pool {
        family inet {
            network 192.168.100.0/24;
            range ZTP_range {
                low 192.168.100.2;
                high 192.168.100.254;
            }
            dhcp-attributes {
                maximum-lease-time 3600;
```

```
                router {
                    192.168.100.1;
                }
                /* File server IP address */
                option 150 ip-address 10.210.58.38;
                /* Syslog server */
                option 7 array ip-address 10.210.58.38;
                /* NTP server */
                option 42 array ip-address 10.210.58.38;
                /* Suboption 00 - Image file path -
                      /images/jinstall-ex-2200-14.1X53-D25.2-domestic-signed.tgz
                   Suboption 01 - Configuration file path -
                      /configs/s0.config
                   Suboption 03 - File transfer protocol - http */
                option 43 hex-string 003a2f696d616765732f6a696e7374616c6c2d65782
d323230302d31342e315835332d4432352e322d646f6d65737469632d7369676e65642e74677a011
22f636f6e666967732f73302e636f6e666967030468747470;
                /* hostname */
                option 12 string s0;
            }
        }
    }
}
```

Compare the DHCP attribute configuration of `fw0` against Table 8-1. Notice that the `fw0` configuration includes all of the mandatory and optional DHCP attributes supported by ZTP.

As detailed in Table 8-1, several ZTP-specific parameters are encoded in DHCP option 43. This DHCP attribute specifies vendor-specific options. DHCP option 43 is encoded as a set of suboptions in type, length, value (TLV) format. Each suboption is composed of a one-byte type field, a one-byte length field, and a value field of variable length. The interpretation of these suboptions is vendor-defined.

The Junos DHCP local server implementation requires the entire set of option 43 TLVs to be encoded as a single value. The example `fw0` configuration adds annotations to assist you in the interpretation of the option 43 hex string value. If you want to use the Junos DHCP local server with ZTP, you may want to download and execute the simple *encode_ztp_option43.sh* shell script from GitHub (*https://github.com/AutomatingJunosAdministration/examples*). This shell script prompts for each ZTP option 43 suboption and outputs the resulting TLVs as a hex string suitable for pasting into the Junos configuration.

As mentioned in the chapter introduction, the goal of initial provisioning is to load a minimal configuration that allows further administration of the Junos device over an

IP network. ZTP is typically used to load and commit this minimal Junos configuration. Once a minimal configuration has been committed, further automation can be accomplished using other tools from our automation toolbox. In the following example, we assume PyEZ will be used to further configure the EX2200-C via NETCONF over SSH. Therefore, the minimal configuration includes the NETCONF-over-SSH service. In our example, the configuration file at `http://10.210.58.38/configs/s0.config` contains the following content:

```
system {
    host-name s0;
    domain-name example.com;
    backup-router 192.168.100.1;
    root-authentication {
        encrypted-password "$1$Lr4wV85J$donAf2XF8t4JXlEVDUYiC.";
    }
    name-server {
        10.210.58.6;
    }
    login {
        user user {
            uid 2000;
            class super-user;
            authentication {
                encrypted-password "$1$ak.4auXS$f5znOvmpVHuTwNugHoSBa/";
            }
        }
    }
    services {
        ssh;
        netconf {
            ssh;
        }
    }
    syslog {
        user * {
            any emergency;
        }
        file messages {
            any notice;
            authorization info;
        }
        file interactive-commands {
            interactive-commands any;
        }
    }
}
interfaces {
    me0 {
        unit 0 {
            family inet {
                address 192.168.100.2/24;
```

```
                }
            }
        }
    }
    routing-options {
        static {
            route 0.0.0.0/0 next-hop 192.168.100.1;
        }
    }
```

This configuration applies a unique hostname, management IP address, and default route. In addition, a root password is configured, SSH and NETCONF-over-SSH services are enabled, and a user account with superuser privileges is added.

The ZTP process is initiated by simply powering on the Juniper EX2200-C switch in its factory default state. After the switch boots, the factory default configuration automatically initiates the ZTP process. Afterward, you may want to review the operation of ZTP by viewing the following log files:

/var/log/dhcp_logfile
: Logs the details of DHCP client operation. Details the DHCP attributes received in the DHCP response message.

/var/log/image_load_log
: Logs the details of the auto-image upgrade progress, including fetching the image and configuration files.

/var/log/op-script.log
: Logs the details of loading and committing the new configuration.

If necessary, these log files can also be used after the fact to troubleshoot a failed ZTP installation. The following outputs are taken from these three log files and demonstrate a successful ZTP image and configuration installation on the EX2200-C switch. These logs are a small subset of the complete logs recorded by ZTP:

```
Jun 25 18:07:15 option `dhcp-message-type' code 53 extracted from buffer
Jun 25 18:07:15 option `dhcp-lease-time' code 51 extracted from buffer
Jun 25 18:07:15 option `subnet-mask' code 1 extracted from buffer
Jun 25 18:07:15 option `server-identifier' code 54 extracted from buffer
Jun 25 18:07:15 option `router' code 3 extracted from buffer
Jun 25 18:07:15 option `domain-name' code 15 extracted from buffer
Jun 25 18:07:15 option `name-server' code 6 extracted from buffer
Jun 25 18:07:15 option `vendor-encap-options' code 43 extracted from buffer
Jun 25 18:07:15 option `tftp-server-ip' code 150 extracted from buffer
Jun 25 18:07:15 option `log-servers' code 7 extracted from buffer
Jun 25 18:07:15 option `ntp-servers' code 42 extracted from buffer
Jun 25 18:07:15 looking for overloaded options
Jun 25 18:07:15 AIU: Fetched TFTP server ip 10.210.58.38 from server ip optio...
Jun 25 18:07:15 AIU: Parsing vendor options
Jun 25 18:07:15 AIU: DHCP vendor option total length = 86
```

```
Jun 25 18:07:15 AIU Vendor options: subcode= 0, optlen= 58, offset= 0
Jun 25 18:07:15 AIU: Extracting Image Filename, vendor sub option= 0 offset= 0
Jun 25 18:07:15 AIU: Image Filename is /images/jinstall-ex-2200-14.1X53-D25.2...
Jun 25 18:07:15 AIU Vendor options: subcode= 1, optlen= 18, offset= 60
Jun 25 18:07:15 AIU: Extracting Config Filename, vendor sub option= 1 offset= 60
Jun 25 18:07:15 AIU: Config Filename is /configs/s0.config
Jun 25 18:07:15 AIU Vendor options: subcode= 3, optlen= 4, offset= 80
Jun 25 18:07:15 AIU: Extracting Transfer Mode, vendor sub option= 3 offset= 80
Jun 25 18:07:15 AIU: Transfer Mode is http
Jun 25 18:07:15 AIU: DHCP Vendor options parse ret = 16 : 'DHCPD Vendor optio...
Jun 25 18:07:15 DHCPD_OPTION_LOG_SERVER: DHCP Log Server Option [ 10.210.58.38 ]
Jun 25 18:07:15 DHCPD_OPTION_NTP_SERVER: DHCP NTP Server Option [ 10.210.58.38 ]

ALERT:Auto-image upgrade will start. This can terminate config CLI sess
ion(s). Modified configuration will be lost. To stop Auto-image, in CLI do the
following: 'edit; delete chassis auto-image-upgrade; commit'.

Jun 25 18:07:23 AIU: spawn : /bin/sh /usr/sbin/image_load -G 10.210.58.38 -I me0
 -O install_reboot -D /var/tmp
 -C /configs/s0.config
 -F /images/jinstall-ex-2200-14.1X53-D25.2-domestic-signed.tgz -T http
[Thu Jun 25 18:07:43 UTC 2015] fetch http://10.210.58.38//configs/s0.config
[Thu Jun 25 18:07:43 UTC 2015] s0.config
[Thu Jun 25 18:07:43 UTC 2015] File fetch done.
[Thu Jun 25 18:07:44 UTC 2015] fetch http://10.210.58.38//images/jinstall-ex-...
[Thu Jun 25 18:08:40 UTC 2015] jinstall-ex-2200-14.1X53-D25.2-domestic-signed...
[Thu Jun 25 18:08:40 UTC 2015] File fetch done.
Auto-image upgrade starts now

WARNING!!! On successful installation, system will reboot automatically

[Thu Jun 25 18:09:37 UTC 2015] request system software add
 /var/tmp/jinstall-ex-2200-14.1X53-D25.2-domestic-signed.tgz no-validate force
[Thu Jun 25 18:18:47 UTC 2015] Image installation is done

[Thu Jun 25 18:19:14 UTC 2015] After reboot, see /var/log/op-script.log and
 /var/log/event-script.log for status of config commit.

*** FINAL System shutdown message from root@ ***

System going down IMMEDIATELY
```

While this simple example demonstrates the correct operation of ZTP on a single switch, a typical real-world ZTP setup is slightly more complicated. A typical ZTP setup supports the simultaneous installation of unique configuration files on multiple Junos devices. This is possible by using a DHCP server implementation and configuration that returns:

- A unique IP address for each Junos device performing ZTP. Each Juniper chassis is labeled with its unique MAC address. This unique MAC address is also present in the DHCP request and can be used to map a device to its assigned IP address.

- A unique configuration filename for each Junos device performing ZTP.
- An appropriate image filename for each device. The image file must be appropriate to for Junos device's model which can be determined by the `vendor-id` field present in the DHCP request.

A typical ZTP setup is often combined with additional automation which generates the minimal configurations delivered by the file server. One such system is the Jinja2 templating language used by PyEZ. "Configuration Templates" on page 220 covered using Jinja2 with PyEZ, but Jinja2 can also be used independently. Later, in Chapter 10, we will also see how Jinja2 can be used with the Ansible framework to generate Junos configuration files.

The major drawback of ZTP is simply that it is not currently supported on all Juniper devices and Junos software versions. SRX devices, for example, do not currently support ZTP. They do support a similar autoinstallation (*https://pathfinder.juniper.net/feature-explorer/search.html#q=autoinstallation*) feature that allows a configuration file to be automatically downloaded and committed. However, autoinstallation does not support automated Junos software upgrades. An alternative tool for initial provisioning of a Junos device is the Netconify program, covered in the next section.

Netconify

The Netconify (*https://github.com/Juniper/py-junos-netconify*) library and command-line utility allows basic administration of a Junos device over a serial console connection. It is designed primarily to perform the initial provisioning process. Once this initial provisioning has been completed, further administration of the device can occur over an IP network. Netconify is written in Python and requires Python 2.6 or 2.7. The Python Package Index (PyPI) system should also be installed on the target. PyPI (*https://pypi.python.org/pypi*) is the typical method for installing Netconify. To install Netconify and its prerequisite Python libraries using PyPI, simply execute the command `pip install junos-netconify` at a root shell prompt on your automation host. This command installs the latest stable release of Netconify. Assuming Git is installed, you can also use `pip install git+https://github.com/Juniper/py-junos-netconify.git` to install the latest development version of Netconify directly from GitHub.

The `netconify` command-line utility is actually a wrapper around a Python Netconify library that can be used by other Python scripts. In fact, this library is used as a console driver for the Junos Ansible modules covered in Chapter 10.

Unlike ZTP, Netconify works with all Juniper device models and Junos software versions. It simply requires a serial console connection to the Junos device.[1] The serial console connection can be a direct connection to a serial port device on the automation host running the Netconify utility, or it can be a Telnet connection to a specific TCP port on a terminal server. By default, `netconify` connects to the serial console using the `/dev/ttyUSB0` device.

In its simplest form, the `netconify` command can be invoked with the `--file` command-line argument to perform a `load override` and commit a configuration file on a Junos device in its factory default state. By default, `netconify` performs a `load override` of the configuration file specified by the `--file` argument.

Just like with ZTP, the initial configuration file loaded by Netconify must be in text (curly brace) format. XML and set formats are not supported. In addition, the configuration file must include a root password at the `[edit system root-authentication]` configuration hierarchy level.

Here is an example that loads the *s0.config* configuration file on the `s0` switch:

```
user@h0$ netconify --file s0.config
TTY:login:connecting to TTY:/dev/ttyUSB0 ...
TTY:login:logging in ...
TTY:login:starting NETCONF
conf:loading into device ...
conf:commit ... please be patient
conf:commit completed.
TTY:logout:logging out ...
user@h0$ ssh s0
Warning: Permanently added the ECDSA host key for IP address '192.168.100.2'...
Password:
--- JUNOS 14.1X53-D25.2 built 2015-04-01 01:56:52 UTC
{master:0}
user@s0> exit

Connection to s0 closed.
user@h0$
```

The preceding example demonstrates that, after applying the *s0.config* initial configuration, the switch is now reachable on its `192.168.100.2` address via SSH.

1 Technically, Netconify has an additional requirement. As the name implies, Netconify uses NETCONF (over the serial console connection) to perform its work. Using NETCONF obviously means the Junos software version must support NETCONF. Because all currently supported Junos software versions include NETCONF support, you can safely ignore this detail.

Of course, Netconify also supports several command-line arguments to control its behavior. Table 8-2 details some of these arguments and their default values.

Table 8-2. Netconify command-line arguments

Argument	Description	Default value
`--port`	The serial port device attached to the console of the Junos device.	*/dev/ttyUSB0*
`--baud`	The serial port baud rate.	`9600`
`--telnet`	The hostname (or IP address) and TCP port number used to reach the serial console of the Junos device. The hostname and TCP port number are separated by a comma (*`hostname,port`*).	None
`--user`	The username used to log in to the Junos device.	`root`
`--passwd`	The password used to log in to the Junos device.	An empty string
`-k`	Prompt the user for the password of the Junos device.	Do not prompt for password
`--timeout`	The TTY connection timeout.	0.5 seconds
`--attempts`	The number of times to attempt logging in to the Junos device.	10
`--merge`	Perform a `load merge` of the `--file` configuration file rather than a `load override`.	Perform a `load override`

In addition to loading and committing a configuration with the `--file` argument, Netconify supports several additional actions which are often performed over a device's serial console. These actions are specified as command-line arguments and are detailed in Table 8-3.

Table 8-3. Netconify actions

Argument	Description
`--file`	Load and commit the device configuration. The `--merge` argument may be used with `--file` to perform a `load merge` operation rather than the default `load override`.
`--qfx-node`	Set a QFX model device into "node" mode.
`--qfx-switch`	Set a QFX model device into "switch" mode.
`--zeroize`	Run the `request system zeroize` command to restore the device to its factory default state.
`--shutdown`	Perform a shutdown, reboot, or power off of the device. The default action is to shut down the device. A reboot is specified with `--shutdown reboot`. A power off is specified with `--shutdown poweroff`.

Argument	Description
`--facts`	Gather facts about the device and save the results into the files *hostname-facts.json* and *hostname-inventory.xml* in the directory *savedir*. By default, *savedir* is the current working directory, but that location can be overridden by also specifying the `--savedir` *savedir* command-line argument. Alternatively, you can specify the `--no-save` command-line argument to prevent the resulting facts from being saved.
`--srx_cluster`	This argument requires a *cluster-id* value. It configures an SRX Series device in cluster mode with a cluster ID of *cluster-id*.
`--srx_cluster_disable`	Disable cluster mode on an SRX Series device and reboot.

Here's an example of using Netconify to gather facts about the `s0` switch whose serial console is connected to a terminal server on TCP port 8003 of `10.210.58.4`. The resulting *s0-facts.json* and *s0-inventory.xml* files are stored in the */var/tmp/* directory of the automation host:

```
user@h0$ netconify --telnet 10.210.58.4,8003 --facts --user user \
> --passwd user123 --savedir /var/tmp/ s0
TTY:login:connecting to TTY:10.210.58.4:8003 ...
TTY:login:logging in ...
TTY:login:starting NETCONF
facts:retrieving device facts...
facts:saving: /var/tmp/s0-facts.json
inventory:saving: /var/tmp/s0-inventory.xml
TTY:logout:logging out ...
user@h0$ more /var/tmp/s0-facts.json
{"model": "EX2200-C-12P-2G, POE+", "version": "14.1X53-D25.2", "serialnumber": "
GR0214378719", "hostname": "s0"}
user@h0$
```

The contents of the JSON facts file produced by Netconify are *not* the same as the facts produced by PyEZ (see Chapter 4). The Netconify facts include only the `model`, `version`, `serialnumber`, and `hostname` keys. While limited, these keys are typically sufficient to automate the generation of device-specific initial configuration files with a templating tool like Jinja2.

Chapter Summary

ZTP and Netconify are both helpful tools for performing the initial provisioning of Junos devices. While ZTP is limited to specific Junos platforms and software versions, it is more scalable and supports upgrading the Junos software installed on the device. You can combine ZTP with a full-featured DHCP server, Jinja2 templates, and Ansible for a complete automation solution.

Netconify is a simple yet powerful tool that solves the specific problem of initial device configuration. Resist the temptation to use the tool for other purposes. For example, loading a complete large device configuration over a 9600-baud serial console connection would be very time-consuming. Instead, combine Netconify with other automation tools, such as PyEZ, Jinja2, and Ansible, to create a complete automation solution.

CHAPTER 9
Puppet

In the previous chapter, we looked at two tools, ZTP and Netconify, which are focused on the initial provisioning of a Junos device. However, neither of these tools is appropriate for the provisioning of new customer-facing network services. This chapter introduces Puppet, the first of two tools that can be used to automate the provisioning of new customer-facing network services quickly, efficiently, and predictably even as the network scales to thousands of devices and millions of users. The other tool, Ansible, is covered in Chapter 10.

Puppet and Ansible are IT frameworks born out of the DevOps approach to software development and IT operations. Puppet is based on Ruby, while Ansible is based on Python. These tools began by focusing on automating aspects of the computing infrastructure, while the network infrastructure lagged behind using manual provisioning processes; however, it has recently become possible to use these tools to automate network provisioning. By building on the PyEZ framework and the NETCONF Ruby gem, Juniper has now created modules for these IT frameworks that extend the DevOps approach to network provisioning.

Puppet is an IT framework developed by Puppet Labs (*https://puppetlabs.com*) and comes in two flavors: Puppet Enterprise and Open Source Puppet.[1] Puppet allows an operator to automate the management of a set of *nodes* that make up the IT infrastructure. The operator defines the desired state of the IT infrastructure using a simple declarative language. The Puppet software then ensures that each node is updated to, and remains at, the desired state. If your organization has a DevOps team that already uses Puppet to manage servers, you may find it especially useful to delegate

1 Open Source Puppet is a subset of Puppet Enterprise. Puppet Enterprise includes Open Source Puppet and adds additional capabilities. This architecture allows Junos devices to work with either flavor of Puppet.

the provisioning of Ethernet ports, Link Aggregation Groups (LAGs), and VLANs to the DevOps team using Puppet.

Puppet Architecture

Before we dive into the specifics of managing Junos devices with Puppet, it is helpful to understand the overall Puppet architecture. Figure 9-1 illustrates this architecture.

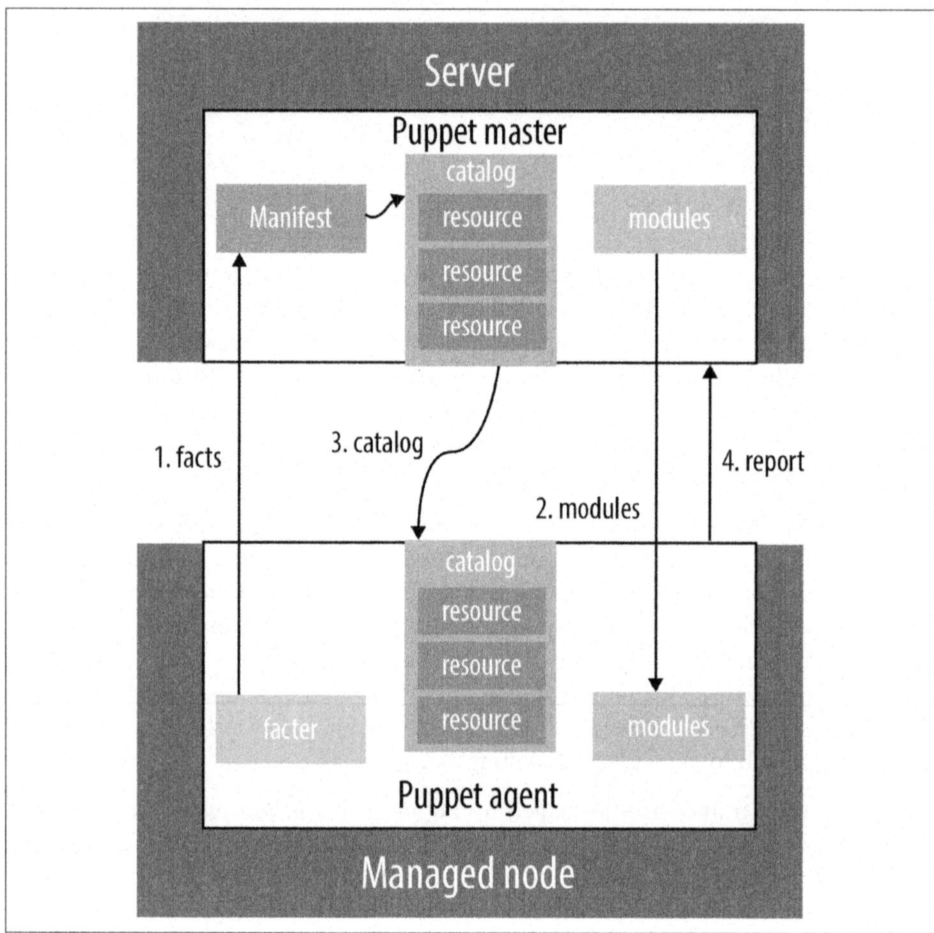

Figure 9-1. The Puppet architecture

Puppet is usually deployed in a client/server model where each managed node periodically queries a server for its state information. The client software running on the managed node is called the *Puppet agent*, and the software running on the server is the *Puppet master*. While Figure 9-1 only illustrates the process for a single node, every managed node in the IT infrastructure queries the shared Puppet master using this same process.

The Puppet agent connects to the Puppet master over an HTTPS connection on a Puppet-specific port (TCP port 8140 by default), and each of the four steps (which make up a Puppet run) illustrated in Figure 9-1 happens over this HTTPS connection. The steps of a Puppet run include:

1. The *facter* component on the Puppet agent gathers a set of information about the managed node, and sends these facts to the Puppet master.
2. Puppet modules are synced from the Puppet master to the Puppet agent. A Puppet module is a collection of classes, resources, files, and templates, organized around a particular purpose. Puppet modules can be installed on the central Puppet master and synced to each Puppet agent as needed. This synchronization occurs as part of the Puppet run and ensures each managed node has the correct version of each module.
3. The Puppet master executes a manifest, which compiles a node-specific catalog. The manifest is a set of instructions, or code, written in the Puppet language. It may contain conditional logic, function calls, and references to variables (including the fact variables from step 1). A catalog is a collection of resource types and a description of the relationships between those resources. A resource type is Puppet's unit of configuration and represents a state that is managed by Puppet. It's a generic description of *what* state should be configured on a node, but not *how* to configure that state. The resulting catalog, compiled by the Puppet master, is sent to the Puppet agent.
4. The Puppet agent translates each resource type in the catalog into specific actions on the managed nodes. This translation is accomplished using resource providers. A resource provider is code from a module that implements a given resource type on a particular kind of system. In other words, the resource type is the *what* and the resource provider is the *how*. In the final step, the agent sends the master a report detailing each step of the Puppet run.

Each Puppet run is initiated by the Puppet agent on the managed node (an architecture sometimes referred to as a *pull model*.) This pull can happen manually by executing the `puppet agent` command from the command line, but usually happens automatically by running the Puppet agent at regularly scheduled intervals.

One important property of the Puppet software is that Puppet configurations are idempotent. That property means a Puppet configuration may safely be applied to a node multiple times. Puppet only makes changes to the node if the node's system state does not match the configured state described in the node's catalog. During each Puppet run the state of each resource is checked and modified as needed. This property allows Puppet not only to configure a node to a desired state, but also to ensure that the node remains in the desired state.

Components for Junos Devices

Now that you understand the overall Puppet architecture, let's look more closely at the specifics of managing a Junos device with Puppet. Figure 9-2 illustrates the primary components required.

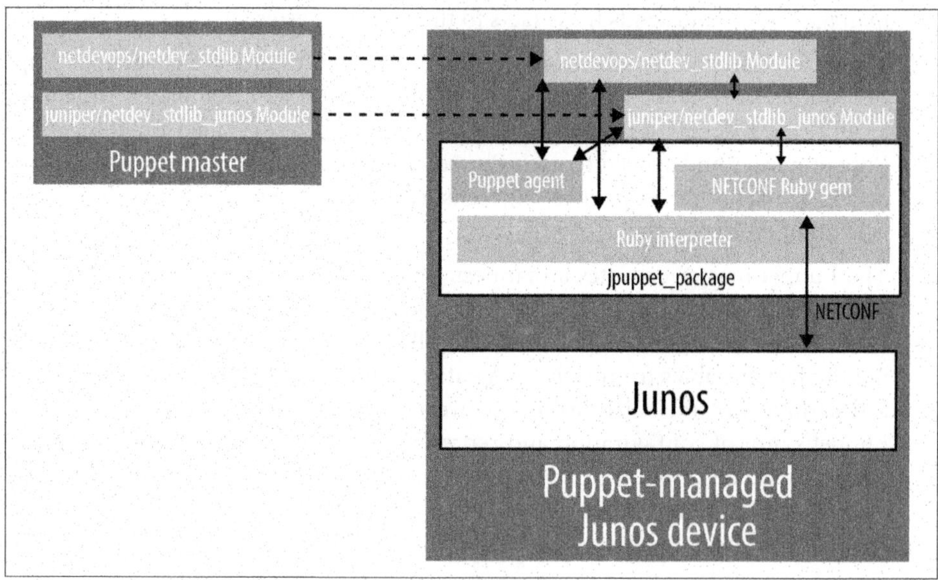

Figure 9-2. A Junos device managed with Puppet

Like all nodes managed by Puppet, the Junos device must be running the Puppet agent software. Because Puppet is written in Ruby, a Ruby interpreter must also be present on the Junos device. The Puppet agent and Ruby interpreter, along with other required Ruby gems, are published in an optional `jpuppet` software package that may be downloaded and installed on a compatible Junos device.

In addition to the `jpuppet` package, two Puppet modules are required to manage a Junos device. The first module, `netdevops/netdev_stdlib`, defines vendor-independent resource types that abstract physical network interfaces, VLANs, Layer 2 network interfaces, and LAGs. The second module, `juniper/netdev_stdlib_junos`, is a Junos-specific resource provider for these resource types. It translates the vendor-independent resource types into Junos-specific configuration and commands over NETCONF. The `juniper/netdev_stdlib_junos` module communicates with the local Junos device using the NETCONF Ruby gem, which is included in the `jpuppet` package. These modules are installed on the Puppet master and, like other Puppet modules, copied to the Junos device on demand as part of each Puppet run.

Installation and Configuration

This section covers the specific installation tasks required for Puppet to manage a Junos device. These tasks include steps that must be performed on both the Puppet master and the Junos device. You must have a functioning Puppet master installed before proceeding to the Junos device installation. Because installing and configuring a Puppet master is very specific to the server's operating system, it is not covered in this book. If your environment doesn't already have a functional Puppet master, refer to PuppetLabs' "Installing Puppet Guide" (*https://docs.puppetlabs.com/guides/install_puppet/pre_install.html*) for information on installing and configuring the Puppet master.

Puppet Master

The first step in configuring an already functional Puppet master to manage Junos devices is to install the NETCONF Ruby gem and its prerequisite Ruby gems on the Puppet master. This task is accomplished by simply running the command `gem install netconf` as the root user:

```
user@h0$ sudo gem install netconf
Building native extensions.  This could take a while...
Successfully installed nokogiri-1.6.7.rc3
Fetching: net-ssh-3.0.1.rc1.gem (100%)
Successfully installed net-ssh-3.0.1.rc1
Fetching: net-scp-1.2.1.gem (100%)
Successfully installed net-scp-1.2.1
Fetching: netconf-0.3.1.gem (100%)
Successfully installed netconf-0.3.1
Parsing documentation for net-scp-1.2.1
Installing ri documentation for net-scp-1.2.1
Parsing documentation for net-ssh-3.0.1.rc1
Installing ri documentation for net-ssh-3.0.1.rc1
Parsing documentation for netconf-0.3.1
Installing ri documentation for netconf-0.3.1
Parsing documentation for nokogiri-1.6.7.rc3
Installing ri documentation for nokogiri-1.6.7.rc3
Done installing documentation for net-scp, net-ssh, netconf, nokogiri after 7 ...
4 gems installed
```

One of the NETCONF gem's prerequisites is the Nokogiri gem used for parsing XML in Ruby. As part of its installation, the Nokogiri gem insists on downloading and compiling the latest version of the `libxml2` C library from source code, even if your system already has a functional `libxml2` library installed. This requirement means that your Puppet master must have all of the necessary tools installed to compile `libxml2`. These include a C compiler, a *make* program, the Ruby header files (usually found in a `ruby-dev` package), and a `zlib` compression library including header files (usually found in a `zlib-dev` package). If the Puppet master is missing any of these necessary tools, the `gem install netconf` command may fail with an error message similar to the one shown here:

```
user@h0$ sudo gem install netconf
Building native extensions.  This could take a while...
ERROR:  Error installing netconf:
ERROR: Failed to build gem native extension.
```

In this case, closely examine the lines following this error message to determine the missing tool. Install the tool, and rerun the `gem install netconf` command.

The second step in preparing the Puppet master is to install the `juniper/netdev_stdlib_junos` Puppet module. This step also causes the prerequisite `netdevops/netdev_stdlib` Puppet module to be installed. Install the latest version of these two Puppet modules by executing the command `puppet module install juniper-netdev_stdlib_junos` as the root user:

```
user@h0$ sudo puppet module install juniper-netdev_stdlib_junos
Notice: Preparing to install into /etc/puppet/modules ...
Notice: Downloading from https://forgeapi.puppetlabs.com ...
Notice: Installing -- do not interrupt ...
/etc/puppet/modules
└┬ juniper-netdev_stdlib_junos (v2.0.0)
  └── netdevops-netdev_stdlib (v1.0.0)
```

Next, edit the Puppet configuration file (usually found in */etc/puppet/puppet.conf*) on the Puppet master to include `pluginsync = true` in the `[main]` section of the configuration. This setting ensures modules are synced between the Puppet master and

Puppet agents. Here is a complete example configuration file from a working Puppet master configured on the `h0.example.com` server using directory environments:[2]

```
[main]
logdir=/var/log/puppet
vardir=/var/lib/puppet
ssldir=/var/lib/puppet/ssl
rundir=/var/run/puppet
factpath=$vardir/lib/facter
prerun_command=/etc/puppet/etckeeper-commit-pre
postrun_command=/etc/puppet/etckeeper-commit-post
dns_alt_names = puppet,puppet.example.com,h0,h0.example.com
pluginsync = true

[master]
# These are needed when the puppetmaster is run by Passenger
# and can safely be removed if WEBrick is used.
ssl_client_header = SSL_CLIENT_S_DN
ssl_client_verify_header = SSL_CLIENT_VERIFY
environmentpath = $confdir/environments
```

The final step required on the Puppet master is to restart the Puppet master process to ensure it is using the updated configuration file. Again, the exact method of restarting the Puppet master is environment-specific. Consult PuppetLabs' documentation (*https://docs.puppetlabs.com*) for more details.

Junos Device

As discussed in "Components for Junos Devices" on page 460, Puppet for Junos requires the `jpuppet` package to be installed on the Junos device. The `jpuppet` package *must* be compatible with the specific hardware model of your Juniper device, the specific Junos version running on your device, and the Puppet software version running on the Puppet master. Consult the `jpuppet` release notes found with the Puppet for Junos documentation (*http://www.juniper.net/techpubs/en_US/release-independent/junos-puppet/information-products/pathway-pages/index.html*) to determine whether your particular Juniper device and Junos software version are supported and, if so, identify the specific `jpuppet` package required. The Puppet for Junos documentation also includes links to download the required `jpuppet` package.

2 A Puppet environment is a grouping of Puppet agent nodes. A Puppet master can serve each environment using a different set of manifests. Puppet 3.x versions support two ways of configuring environments: directory environments and configuration file environments. In Puppet 4.x, configuration file environments have been deprecated. Therefore, the examples in this book use directory environments. For more detail on Puppet environments see "About Environments" (*http://docs.puppetlabs.com/puppet/3.8/reference/environments.html*) on the Puppet Labs website.

Some platforms, including the QFX5100, QFX10002, and OCX1100, support a *Junos with Enhanced Automation* software image. Junos with Enhanced Automation is a single software image that includes both the Junos package and a compatible `jpuppet` package. If your Juniper device has a Junos with Enhanced Automation software image installed, you *do not* need to download and install a separate `jpuppet` package. However, you *do* still need to follow most of the remaining configuration steps in this section to properly configure Puppet. Unless noted, all of the following configuration steps are also required for Junos with Enhanced Automation images.

The `jpuppet` package is a Junos extension package that cannot be installed or executed without explicit configuration. Therefore, the first step in configuring a Junos device to be managed by Puppet is to add and commit this configuration snippet at the `[edit system extensions]` configuration hierarchy level:

```
{master:0}[edit system extensions]
user@s0# show
providers {
    juniper {
        license-type juniper deployment-scope commercial;
    }
}

{master:0}[edit system extensions]
user@s0# commit and-quit
configuration check succeeds
commit complete
Exiting configuration mode

{master:0}
user@s0>
```

This configuration snippet may not be required for some Junos with Enhanced Automation software images. However, there are some Junos with Enhanced Automation software images that *do* require this configuration to be present. For this reason, it is highly recommended that you explicitly add this configuration snippet even if your device is running a Junos with Enhanced Automation software image. If you are upgrading from a traditional Junos image to a Junos with Enhanced Automation software image, add this configuration *before* the upgrade.

The next step is to place the appropriate jpuppet package on the local device, or a remote file server, and install the package with the request system software add command. This example demonstrates loading the jpuppet-3.6.1_1.junos.i386.tgz package on a QFX5100 running Junos release 14.1X53-D27.3. The show version | match puppet command is used to verify the package installation:

```
{master:0}
user@s0> request system software add /var/tmp/jpuppet-3.6.1_1.junos.i386.tgz
NOTICE: Validating configuration against jpuppet-3.6.1_1.junos.i386.tgz.
NOTICE: Use the 'no-validate' option to skip this if desired.
WARNING: validate not currently implemented  for qfx5100-48s-6q.
WARNING: Please install package with 'no-validate' option.
+junos-package.xml validates
3.6.1_1.junos.i386: not found
Verified jpuppet-3.6.1_1.junos.i386 signed by juniper-cdbu-commercial-1
juniper
Available space: 448630 require: 7460
Mounted jpuppet package on /dev/md12...
Verified manifest signed by juniper-cdbu-commercial-1
Saving package file in /var/sw/pkg/jpuppet-3.6.1_1.junos.i386.tgz ...
Saving state for rollback ...

{master:0}
user@s0> show version | match puppet
Puppet on Junos [3.6.1_1.junos.i386]

{master:0}
user@s0>
```

Because Junos with Enhanced Automation already includes the jpuppet package, this step is not necessary on devices running Junos with Enhanced Automation. Again, the presence of the jpuppet package can be confirmed with the show version command:

```
user@s0> show version | match "puppet|automation"
Puppet on Junos [2.7.19_1.junos.i386]
Junos for Automation Enhancement
```

It is best practice to create a dedicated user account to run the Puppet agent. This account may have any username, but common practice is to use the puppet username. Because the Puppet agent must be executed from the Unix command line, this account must be configured with the hidden shell csh configuration statement. This configuration statement sets the user's default shell to Unix *csh* rather than the normal Junos CLI. In addition, the account must be configured with sufficient privileges to perform any functions that will be managed by Puppet. At a minimum, this means the account should have configure, control, and view-configuration permissions. For some Puppet operations, the puppet account will be modifying system files. In this case, it is required to give this account all permissions by assigning it to the predefined super-user class. An example Puppet user configuration is shown here:

```
{master:0}[edit system login]
user@s0# set user puppet class super-user

{master:0}[edit system login]
user@s0# set user puppet shell csh

{master:0}[edit system login]
user@s0# commit and-quit
configuration check succeeds
commit complete
Exiting configuration mode

{master:0}
user@s0>
```

This example does not assign a password to the puppet user. A user cannot directly log into a Junos account that does not have a password configured (unless permitted to do so by RADIUS or TACACS+). While you may choose to assign a password to your puppet account, this passwordless configuration provides an additional layer of security by ensuring that a remote user cannot directly log into the Puppet account. If you follow this recommendation, access the puppet user by first logging into a root shell and then executing the command su - puppet (the hyphen is important; it ensures the puppet user's environment is properly set up by simulating a full login):

```
root@s0:RE:0% su - puppet
% id
uid=2002(puppet) gid=20 groups=20, 0(wheel), 10(field)
% pwd
/var/home/puppet
%
```

In this example, the id and pwd commands were used to confirm the current user and working directory.

The jpuppet package installs the Puppet programs in the */opt/sdk/juniper/bin* directory, and the Puppet agent will not run correctly unless this directory is included in the Puppet user's path. To ensure it is included in the path, log into the newly created puppet account and create a *.cshrc* file in the user's home directory:

```
root@s0:RE:0% su - puppet
% echo 'setenv PATH ${PATH}:/opt/sdk/juniper/bin' >> ~/.cshrc
```

```
% cat ~/.cshrc
setenv PATH ${PATH}:/opt/sdk/juniper/bin
%
```

The content of the file is confirmed with the `cat ~/.cshrc` command. Now, in order for this new path to take effect, you must exit the `puppet` user account and then log back into the account:

```
% exit
logout
root@s0:RE:0% su - puppet
% echo $PATH
/bin:/usr/bin:/sbin:/usr/sbin:/opt/sbin:/opt/bin:/opt/sdk/juniper/bin
% facter
ldapname is deprecated and will be removed in a future version
architecture => qfx5100-48s-6q
domain => example.com
facterversion => 2.0.1
fqdn => s0.example.com
hardwareisa => i386
hardwaremodel => qfx5100-48s-6q
hostname => s0
id => puppet
...output trimmed...
```

The `echo $PATH` command verifies the */opt/sdk/juniper/bin* directory is included in the path, and the `facter` command, which is included in the `jpuppet` package, confirms the Puppet software has been successfully installed.

The final step in preparing a Junos device to be managed by Puppet is to create a minimal Puppet configuration file on the device. This file is named *puppet.conf* and is located in a *.puppet* subdirectory of the Puppet user's home directory. Because the *~/.puppet* directory does not exist by default, create it by executing the command `mkdir ~/.puppet` as the Puppet user. Once the directory has been created, edit the *~/.puppet/puppet.conf* file and ensure it has the following content:

```
[main]
    pluginsync = true

[agent]
    server = h0.example.com
    daemonize = false
```

The value of the `server` parameter should be set to the hostname of the Puppet master. In the example, the Puppet master resides on the host `h0.example.com`. The Puppet master's hostname must resolve to an IP address (using either DNS or a static host mapping), and the Puppet master must be reachable on TCP port 8140.

The `pluginsync = true` line ensures that the content of modules on the Puppet master are synced to the Puppet agent, and the `daemonize = false` line prevents the

Puppet agent from executing in the background. On the Junos platform, it is best practice to run the Puppet agent periodically rather than having the agent constantly running as a daemon. "Managing the Puppet Agent with the cron Resource" on page 484 details the process for automatically executing the Puppet agent on the Junos device from a cron entry.

Creating a Minimal Manifest

Once the agent node (the Junos device, in this case) has been properly configured, the next step in managing any node with Puppet is to create a manifest file (or set of manifest files) on the Puppet master. As mentioned in "Puppet Architecture" on page 458, a Puppet manifest is a set of instructions written in the Puppet language. Manifests may contain node definitions, resource type declarations, conditional logic, function calls, and references to variables. When executed, a manifest produces a node-specific catalog.

The location of Puppet manifest files depends on the configuration of the Puppet master. Puppet starts compiling with either a single manifest file or a directory of manifests that get treated like a single file. This starting point is called the *main manifest* or *site manifest*. Determine the manifest your Puppet master expects by executing the command `puppet config print manifest --section master` as the root user. The example output here is taken from a Puppet master configured to use directory environments:

```
user@h0$ sudo puppet config print manifest --section master
/etc/puppet/environments/production/manifests
```

If the command `puppet config print manifest --section master` produces the output `no_manifest`, this may indicate the manifest directory your Puppet master expects to use does not exist. Check your setup to ensure that the manifest directory exists.

If the main manifest is a directory, Puppet will parse every **.pp* file in the directory. The files are parsed in alphabetical order, and the result is executed as if all the content was in a single file. This behavior means that variables defined in one file can be referenced in a later file, or a class defined in a file can be imported in a later file. Separating your manifests into multiple files within a directory is recommended and is the configuration used in this chapter. This separation allows each file to perform a discrete purpose. Naming each manifest file according to its purpose further allows a Puppet administrator to quickly understand the directory's structure and the function of each manifest file. The example uses the filename format *XX_purpose.pp*, where *XX* is a two-digit integer that ensures the manifest files are parsed in the desired order.

Begin by defining a minimal manifest in the file */etc/puppet/environments/production/manifests/90_example.com_nodes.pp*. Initially, this manifest file simply has an empty node definition for the `s0.example.com` Junos switch:

```
node 's0.example.com' {
}
```

Puppet uses certificates to authenticate between the Puppet master and Puppet agents. Each node is identified by the common name (CN) value in its certificate, and it is this value that is used in the node definition in the manifest file. The Puppet agent running on Junos generates a certificate with the CN value set to the device's fully qualified domain name (FQDN). The FQDN is based on the `[edit system host-name]` and `[edit system domain-name]` configuration. Ensure these values are properly configured on each Junos device managed by Puppet.

Later examples will build on this minimal node definition. Additional manifest files will be added, and the content of this node definition will be augmented with additional information. However, this minimal manifest is sufficient to begin managing the Junos device with Puppet.

Executing the Puppet Agent for the First Time

Now that the Puppet master has been configured, the Junos device has been configured, and the minimal manifest has been prepared on the Puppet master, it's time to execute the Puppet agent on the Junos device. The first time the Puppet agent is executed, it generates an SSL certificate request for the Certificate Authority (CA). In installations with a single Puppet master, the CA is typically the same server as the Puppet master. Before a Puppet run is allowed to continue, the Puppet agent must receive its signed certificate from the CA.

Begin by confirming that there are no outstanding certificate signing requests by executing the command `puppet cert list` as the root user on the CA (the CA resides on the Puppet master in this example):

```
user@h0$ sudo puppet cert list
user@h0$
```

The empty output confirms that there are no outstanding certificate signing requests at this time.

Ensure you are logged in to the Junos device as the Puppet user, then invoke the Puppet agent for the first time by executing the command `puppet agent --test --waitforcert 5` as the Puppet user. The `--test` option is a synonym for several options that are useful when executing the Puppet agent interactively. The

`--waitforcert 5` option causes the Puppet agent to check every 5 seconds to see if it has received the signed certificate:

```
% puppet agent --test --waitforcert 5
Info: Creating a new SSL key for s0.example.com
Info: Caching certificate for ca
Info: csr_attributes file loading from /var/home/puppet/.puppet/csr_attributes...
Info: Creating a new SSL certificate request for s0.example.com
Info: Certificate Request fingerprint (SHA256): D5:90:CD:D3:91:E2:F9:DB:94:EC:
 E6:87:1C:EE:8D:C3:4C:E2:83:09:B5:B0:3F:6B:67:92:3D:F8:6C:CE:E5:97
Info: Caching certificate for ca
Notice: Did not receive certificate
Notice: Did not receive certificate
...output trimmed...
```

Once the certificate signing request has been sent, the `Notice: Did not receive certificate` line will be output every 5 seconds until the signed certificate is received.

At this time, leave the `puppet agent` command running on the Junos device and log in to the CA (Puppet master). Confirm the certificate signing request has been received by executing the command `puppet cert list` as the root user. Before proceeding, compare the certificate signature displayed by the Puppet agent with the signature displayed by the `puppet cert list` command. Ensure this is the same certificate you expected:

```
user@h0$ sudo puppet cert list
  "s0.example.com" (SHA256) D5:90:CD:D3:91:E2:F9:DB:94:EC:
     E6:87:1C:EE:8D:C3:4C:E2:83:09:B5:B0:3F:6B:67:92:3D:F8:6C:CE:E5:97
```

For the Puppet agent to continue execution, the certificate must be signed by executing the command `puppet cert sign` *`common-name`* as the root user on the CA:

```
user@h0$ sudo puppet cert sign s0.example.com
Notice: Signed certificate request for s0.example.com
Notice: Removing file Puppet::SSL::CertificateRequest s0.example.com at
    '/var/lib/puppet/ssl/ca/requests/s0.example.com.pem'
```

As mentioned earlier, the *`common-name`* is the fully qualified domain name configured on the Junos device.

Once the Junos device receives the signed certificate, the Puppet run will proceed:

```
...output trimmed...
Notice: Did not receive certificate
Notice: Did not receive certificate
Info: Caching certificate for s0.example.com
Info: Caching certificate_revocation_list for ca
Info: Retrieving pluginfacts
Info: Retrieving plugin
Notice: /File[/var/home/puppet/.puppet/var/lib/puppet]/ensure: created
Notice: /File[/var/home/puppet/.puppet/var/lib/puppet/provider]/ensure: created
```

```
Notice: /File[/var/home/puppet/.puppet/var/lib/puppet/provider/netdev_group]/...
Notice: /File[/var/home/puppet/.puppet/var/lib/puppet/provider/netdev_lag]/en...
Notice: /File[/var/home/puppet/.puppet/var/lib/puppet/provider/netdev_l2_inte...
Notice: /File[/var/home/puppet/.puppet/var/lib/puppet/provider/netdev_l2_inte...
...output trimmed...
Notice: /File[/var/home/puppet/.puppet/var/lib/puppet/provider/junos/junos_vl...
ldapname is deprecated and will be removed in a future version
Info: Caching catalog for s0.example.com
Info: Applying configuration version '1443480397'
Info: Creating state file /var/home/puppet/.puppet/var/state/state.yaml
Notice: Finished catalog run in 0.09 seconds
%
```

During this initial Puppet run, Puppet modules are downloaded to the Junos device. On subsequent Puppet runs, only Puppet modules that have been added or changed will be downloaded to the device. From now on, interactive Puppet runs can be initiated by simply executing `puppet agent --test` as the Junos device's Puppet user. In "Managing the Puppet Agent with the cron Resource" on page 484, a recipe will be provided that initiates Puppet runs on a user-defined interval.

The Puppet Language

While the `h0.example.com` Puppet master is now managing the `s0.example.com` node, no resource types have been defined in the manifest. Without resource types, Puppet has no state to configure on the Puppet-managed Junos device. The next step is to augment the minimal manifest file with some useful resource types. Note that this section introduces the basics of the Puppet language used to write manifests. The following two sections will build on this knowledge to create sample manifests for managing Junos devices. This section is not a reference manual. It only covers the highlights of the Puppet language. Refer to the Puppet Labs documentation (*http://docs.puppetlabs.com*) for the full language reference.

Basic Resource Syntax

Puppet's basic unit of configuration is the resource. Manifest files exist to define a set of resources for each node, so it makes sense to begin our exploration of the Puppet language syntax with the basic syntax for declaring a resource. Each resource declaration consists of a type, a title, and set of attribute/value pairs:

```
# A resource declaration ❶
resource_type ❷ { resource_title: ❸
  attribute1 => value1, ❹
  attribute2 => value2,
  attributeN => valueN,
}
```

❶ While it has nothing to do with resource declarations, this is a good place to sneak in Puppet comment syntax. Puppet supports shell-style comments that begin with a hash symbol (#) and continue to the end of the line. While less frequently used, Puppet also supports C-style comments, which may span multiple lines:

```
/*
  This is a C-style comment.
*/
```

❷ The *`resource_type`* must be specified in lowercase. It indicates the kind of resource being declared. This type is the name of one of Puppet's built-in resource types or a resource type specified in a Puppet module. Each resource declaration is surrounded by curly braces ({}). The opening curly brace appears after the *`resource_type`*. The closing curly brace signifies the end of the resource declaration.

❸ The *`resource_title`* is an identifying string. It must be unique per resource type. Some resource types allow any unique value to be used as the *`resource_title`*. Other resource types use the *`resource_title`* as the default value of a key attribute. For example, the core `file` resource type uses the *`resource_title`* to specify the path of the file to be managed. A colon always separates the *`resource_title`* from its attribute/value pairs.

It's possible to configure multiple resources of type *`resource_type`* by simply specifying a list (using the format `[` *`resource_title1, resource_title2`* `]`) for the resource's title.

❹ Attributes describe the desired state of the resource. Each resource type defines its own set of supported attributes and its own meanings for those attributes. A resource type may specify an attribute as either mandatory or optional. Attributes can also be referred to as parameters.

Attributes and values are separated by the => string. Each specified attribute must have a value. Each attribute defines its own set of acceptable data types and acceptable values. A comma (`,`) separates each attribute/value pair. While the comma is optional after the final attribute/value pair, it is best practice to always include it in case additional attribute/value pairs are added to the resource at a later time.

Many resource types define an `ensure` attribute, which accepts values of `present` and `absent`. Depending on the resource type, the `ensure` attribute may also accept some resource-specific values.

Variables

Variable names are prefixed with a dollar sign (`$`) and values are assigned to a variable with the equals (`=`) operator. The string `/tmp/puppet_run.log` is assigned to a variable with the name `junos_run_log` using the statement:

```
$junos_run_log = '/tmp/puppet_run.log'
```

It's worth noting that the term "variable" is somewhat of a misnomer in the Puppet language. Similar to variables in XSLT, Puppet variables are immutable. Once they have been assigned an initial value their value cannot be changed, and they cannot be assigned a new value.[3]

The previous example assigned a scalar value to `$junos_run_log`. Alternatively, a Puppet variable can be assigned an array value using the syntax:

```
$customer_interface = [ 'et-0/0/1', 'et-0/0/5', 'et-0/0/7' ]
```

A hash value can be assigned using the syntax:

```
$port_to_vlan = { 'et-0/0/1' => 'accounting',
                  'et-0/0/5' => 'software',
                  'et-0/0/7' => 'sales' }
```

A variable can be referenced any place where a value of the variable's data type would be accepted. Puppet will replace the variable reference with its value. Puppet also has several built-in variables that can be referenced in a manifest. In general, any fact displayed by executing `facter -p` on a Junos device can be referenced in a manifest by simply preceding the fact's name with a `$`. For example, `facter` returns this information about the Junos device's operating system:

```
% facter -p | grep operatingsystem
operatingsystem => JUNOS
operatingsystemrelease => 14.1X53-D27.3
```

These facts can be referenced in a Puppet manifest file using the variables `$operatingsystem` and `$operatingsystemrelease`, respectively.

---

3 It is possible to create a local variable with the same name as a variable in another scope. While having two variables with the same name but different scopes provides some of the functionality of a mutable variable, they are still technically two immutable variables which happen to have the same name. Further coverage of variable scoping in the Puppet language is outside the scope (pun intended) of this book. Refer to the Puppet Labs documentation for additional information.

Strings

Next, let's look at strings in the Puppet language, and how variable references are used within strings. The Puppet language uses both single quotes, `'like this'`, and double quotes, `"like this"`, to delineate strings. In addition, the quotation marks may be omitted completely for contiguous strings `like_this`. (Contiguous strings contain only letters, digits, hyphens, and underscores.)

It's important to note that double-quoted strings allow variable interpolation while single-quoted strings do not. Assuming the previous assignment `$this = 'foo'`, the string `"$this bar"` will evaluate to `foo bar` while the string `'$this bar'` will evaluate to the literal `$this bar`. Similar to Bourne shell variables, you can reference variable names within `${}` to disambiguate them within a double-quoted string. As an example, the string `"$thisbar"` evaluates to the value of the variable `$thisbar`, while the string `"${this}bar"` evaluates to `foobar`.

Classes

In the Puppet language, a class is simply a named container for a block of Puppet code. A class is first defined in a manifest using this basic format:

```
class class_name {
  <Puppet code>
  ...
}
```

The Puppet code within a class is *not* executed at the time it is defined. Instead, the execution is deferred until the class is later "declared" within the manifest. There are multiple ways to execute the class's code (which Puppet calls "declaring" the class) in a Puppet manifest. The simplest method is the `include class_name` statement. This statement simply inserts and executes the Puppet code from the *`class_name`* definition at the point of the `include` statement. Class declarations may occur at the top level of a manifest file, within a node definition, or within the definition of another class (nested classes.) Regardless of how many times a class is declared, the resources within a class are only added to a node's catalog one time and the class's code is only executed once.

Conditional Statements

Like other programming languages, the Puppet language provides statements to execute different branches of code based on the evaluation of Boolean conditions. The two most common conditional statements are `if` and `case`. The `if` statement has the syntax:

```
if boolean_condition1 {
  <Puppet code block 1>
```

```
    ...
}
elsif boolean_condition2 {
  <Puppet code block 2>
  ...
}
else {
  <Puppet code block 3>
  ...
}
```

Puppet's `if` statement behaves much like an if statement in any other language. First, *boolean_condition1* is evaluated. If *boolean_condition1* evaluates to true, then *<Puppet code block 1>* is executed. Otherwise, *boolean_condition2* is evaluated. If *boolean_condition2* is true, then *<Puppet code block 2>* is executed. If neither *boolean_condition1* nor *boolean_condition2* is true, then *<Puppet code block 3>* is executed. The result is that, at most, one of the code blocks is executed. Both the `elsif` and the `else` clauses are optional.

Like the `if` statement, the `case` statement chooses one of several blocks of code to execute. The `case` statement takes a control expression and a list of case values. Each case value is followed by a colon and a corresponding code block. The `case` statement executes the first code block where the corresponding case value matches the control expression. The case statement has the syntax:

```
case control_expression {
  case_value1: {
    <Puppet code block 1>
    ...
  }
  case_value2,case_value3 : {
    <Puppet code block 2>
    ...
  }
  default: {
    <Puppet code block N>
    ...
  }
}
```

A case value may be a scalar value or a regular expression. Rather than a single value, a case may also have a comma-separated list of case values, as shown by the *case_value2,case_value3* line in the syntax listing. If a list of case values is specified, the corresponding code block is executed if *any* of the case values in the list matches the control expression. The `default` keyword is similar to the `else` clause in an `if` statement. Its code block is executed only if no match has occurred. Like the `else` clause, the `default` block is optional.

Node Definitions

In "Creating a Minimal Manifest" on page 468, we created a minimal manifest for the `s0.example.com` node before running the Puppet agent for the first time. That manifest contained a simple node definition with no content. The formal syntax for the `node` statement, used to define a node, is:

```
node node_name {
  <Puppet code block>
  ...
}
```

The node definition matches a node, or set of nodes, by name. As in our minimal example in "Creating a Minimal Manifest" on page 468, the *`node_name`* portion of the syntax may simply be a quoted string with a node's exact name,[4] such as `'s0.example.com'` in our previous example. Alternatively, the *`node_name`* portion of the syntax can be a comma-separated list of exact node names, a regular expression, or the keyword `default`. A node definition with the `default` keyword is invoked only when no other matching node definition is found. Multiple node definitions containing the same node name are not allowed. While it is possible to create regular expressions that match an overlapping set of nodes, this should also be avoided. (Puppet behavior is undefined in this case.)

When the manifest is compiled, a given node will get the content of *only one* node definition. If multiple node definitions might match a given node, the order of preference is:

1. The node definition with the node's exact name
2. A node definition with a regex that matches the node's name
3. The `default` node definition

Manifest Organization

Now that you've seen some of the key building blocks of the Puppet language, let's investigate how those building blocks fit together. Remember, the primary purpose of manifest files, and the Puppet language, is to produce a per-node catalog. In turn, catalogs are simply collections of resources that describe the desired state of the node.

Because resources describe state, rather than a set of steps to perform, the order in which they appear in a manifest file does not matter. There is also no guarantee that Puppet will apply resources to the node in any specific order. However, some resour-

4 Remember a node's name is based on the CN of its certificate. The CN is usually the same as the node's FQDN.

ces are dependent upon other resources. In this case, Puppet will apply the prerequisite resources first and only apply the dependent resources if all prerequisites succeed.

The dependency relationships between resources are defined using *metaparameters*. Metaparameters are specified using a resource's attributes. All resources support these optional metaparameters: `before`, `require`, and `subscribe`. Metaparameters define dependency (and therefore order) relationships between resources rather than the state of a resource itself.

While the order in which resource declarations are independent of the order in which they appear in the manifest file is unimportant, parsing of the Puppet language *does* depend upon ordering. A manifest file is compiled from top to bottom.[5] Like in many languages, variables must be set before they can be referenced. Likewise, classes must be defined with the `class` statement before they are declared (executed) with a statement such as `include`.

Using Core Resource Types

Puppet provides a few core resource types, which are normally included with the Puppet agent. The Junos Puppet agent implementation does *not* support all of the core resource types, but it does support three important core types: `file`, `cron`, and `notify`. This section introduces these core resource types and applies concepts learned about the Puppet language from the previous section. The resulting examples will be helpful in managing any Junos device with Puppet.

Managing ~/.cshrc with the file Resource

The `file` resource allows Puppet to manage the existence, ownership, permissions, and content of any file or directory on the node's filesystem. It can be used to maintain the contents of the Puppet user's *.cshrc* file.

Begin by defining the `$id` variable in a *00_common_vars.pp* manifest file in the appropriate manifest directory of the Puppet master (on the `h0.example.com` Puppet server, the manifests are located in */etc/puppet/environments/production/manifests*):

```
$junos_home_dir = "/var/home/$id"
```

The `$id` variable is one of the fact variables provided by Puppet. It is set to the username of the user executing the Puppet agent. In this variable assignment, the `$id`

5 As discussed in "Creating a Minimal Manifest" on page 468, a directory of manifest files is executed as if all the content were in a single file. The **.pp* files within the directory are parsed in alphabetical order.

variable is interpolated within a string to set `$junos_home_dir` to the correct value regardless of the Puppet account username on the Junos device.

Next, create a *10_junos_puppet_user_cshrc.pp* manifest file in the same directory, with the following contents. This manifest file demonstrates both the `file` and `notify` core resource types. In addition, it uses a `class` to group these resources together:

```
class junos_puppet_user_cshrc { ❶
  $puppet_path = '/opt/sdk/juniper/bin' ❷
  notify { 'cshrc': ❸
    message => "Maintaining .cshrc on $hostname" ❹
  }
  file { "$junos_home_dir/.cshrc": ❺
    ensure => file, ❻
    owner => $id, ❼
    mode => 0644, ❽
    content => "setenv PATH \${PATH}:$puppet_path\n", ❾
  }
}
```

❶ The `class` statement is used to define a class with the name `junos_puppet_user_cshrc`. The code within this class is not executed as part of this definition. Instead, the execution is deferred until the class is later declared with an `include` statement.

❷ The variable `$puppet_path` is assigned the string `/opt/sdk/juniper/bin`. Because this string does not require variable interpolation, it is enclosed in single quotes. Variables assigned inside a class are local to the class. This means the `$puppet_path` cannot be referenced outside the `junos_puppet_user_cshrc` class.

❸ The `notify` resource logs a message during the Puppet run. The message is logged locally on the managed node and is also included in the report that is sent to the Puppet master.

❹ The `message` parameter defines the message to be logged. As shown in this example, the value of the `message` parameter can reference variables, which are interpolated to their corresponding values during the Puppet run. If no `message` parameter is present, the title of the `notify` resource becomes the log message.

❺ The `file` resource defines a file or directory managed by Puppet. The title of the resource specifies the path of the file to be managed. The title may reference variables, as demonstrated in this example.

❻ The `ensure` parameter of the `file` resource accepts five possible values: `present`, `absent`, `file`, `directory`, and `link`. The `present` value ensures the file exists, but doesn't check if it's a regular file, directory, or link. If the file doesn't exist, `present` will create a regular file. The `file`, `directory`, and `link` values check for existence, but also ensure the file is of the specified type. The `absent` value ensures the file does *not* exist by removing it if necessary. The example ensures *~/.cshrc* is a regular file.

❼ If present, the `owner` parameter specifies the owner of the file. In the example, the owner is the username of the Puppet user.

❽ The `mode` parameter specifies the permissions set on the file.

❾ The `content` parameter allows the content of the file to be specified as a string. Line breaks must be explicitly specified in this value. Like other strings, double-quoted strings support variable interpolation. The `source` parameter is an alternative to the `content` parameter. The `source` parameter copies a file specified by a URI. The special `puppet://` URI can be used to copy files from the Puppet master.

The `junos_puppet_user_cshrc` class has been defined, but it must be declared before the code within the class is executed. Create a new *80_all_nodes.pp* manifest file with the following content. Because the content of this *~/.cshrc* file is specific to managed nodes running Junos, the example uses a `case` statement that only includes the `junos_puppet_user_cshrc` class on Junos devices:

```
case $operatingsystem { ❶
  'JUNOS': { ❷
      include junos_puppet_user_cshrc ❸
  }
  default: { ❹
      fail('Unknown operating system!') ❺
  }
}
```

❶ The Puppet fact variable `$operatingsystem` is used as the control expression for the `case` statement.

❷ All Junos devices set the `operatingsystem` fact to `JUNOS`. View this by executing the command `facter -p | grep operatingsystem` as the Puppet user on the Junos device. The string `JUNOS` is used as the value for the `case` statement.

❸ The `include` statement declares the `junos_puppet_user_cshrc` class. It's essentially as if the code from the class is pasted into this location of the manifest.

❹ The special value `default` defines a case that is executed if no other case values match.

❺ Invoke the core function `fail()` to interrupt compilation with a Puppet parse error. The function's argument is logged as an error message. Puppet provides an assortment of functions that may be helpful in your own manifests.

In our example, only Junos nodes are being managed. If your installation is managing nodes running other operating systems, add additional values to this `case` statement or change the `default` case to use the `info()` function.

All of the pieces are now in place to have Puppet manage the *~/.cshrc* file on all Junos devices. Test your work by executing the command `puppet agent --test` from the Junos device as the Puppet user:

```
% puppet agent --test
Info: Retrieving pluginfacts
Info: Retrieving plugin
ldapname is deprecated and will be removed in a future version
Info: Caching catalog for s0.example.com
Info: Applying configuration version '1443926426'
Notice: Maintaining .cshrc on s0
Notice: /Stage[main]/Junos_puppet_user_cshrc/Notify[cshrc]/message: defined
  'message' as 'Maintaining .cshrc on s0'
Notice: Finished catalog run in 0.10 seconds
%
```

The output of the Puppet run includes the `Maintaining .cshrc on s0` message from the `notify` resource. However, it doesn't say anything about modifying the *~/.cshrc* file itself. That's because the content specified in the `file` resource's `content` parameter exactly matched the already existing content of the *~/.cshrc* file. Remember, this file was created manually before the first Puppet run. This demonstrates the idempotent nature of Puppet configurations. If the node already complies with the state specified in its catalog, no changes are applied.

In order to see Puppet in action, edit the *~/.cshrc* file on the Junos device by adding a comment to the file as shown here:

```
# My extra comment.
setenv PATH ${PATH}:/opt/sdk/juniper/bin
```

Now, rerun the Puppet agent:

```
% puppet agent --test
Info: Retrieving pluginfacts
Info: Retrieving plugin
ldapname is deprecated and will be removed in a future version
```

```
Info: Caching catalog for s0.example.com
Info: Applying configuration version '1443927560'
Notice: Maintaining .cshrc on s0
Notice: /Stage[main]/Junos_puppet_user_cshrc/Notify[cshrc]/message: defined
  'message' as 'Maintaining .cshrc on s0'
Notice: /Stage[main]/Junos_puppet_user_cshrc/File
  [/var/home/puppet/.cshrc]/content:
--- /var/home/puppet/.cshrc Sat Oct  3 19:59:39 2015
+++ /tmp/puppet-file20151003-19740-3x9i7z-0 Sat Oct  3 20:00:26 2015
@@ -1,2 +1 @@
-# My extra comment.
 setenv PATH ${PATH}:/opt/sdk/juniper/bin

Info: /Stage[main]/Junos_puppet_user_cshrc/File[/var/home/puppet/.cshrc]:
  Filebucketed /var/home/puppet/.cshrc to puppet with
  sum 4b1584c57f955dbff6c07af326783756
Notice: /Stage[main]/Junos_puppet_user_cshrc/File[/var/home/puppet/.cshrc]
  /content: content changed '{md5}4b1584c57f955dbff6c07af326783756' to
 '{md5}820e0d127d758177416d6fff2c472970'
Notice: Finished catalog run in 0.35 seconds
%
```

In this output, the file is changed by Puppet. In fact, a diff-style output shows the extra comment has been removed. Indeed, if we check the file, this change is confirmed:

```
% cat ~/.cshrc
setenv PATH ${PATH}:/opt/sdk/juniper/bin
%
```

The next section shows a slightly more complex use of the `file` resource.

Managing puppet.conf with an ERB Template

In addition to specifying the exact content of a file resource to a string, or using the `source` parameter, it is possible to generate the file's content using a template. Puppet supports ERB templates using the `template()` core function. ERB templates are very similar in functionality to the Jinja2 templates covered in "Configuration Templates" on page 220. However, they use a completely different syntax, which embeds Ruby code within the file. This section uses an ERB template to manage the content of the *~/.puppet/puppet.conf* file on a Junos node. This example only provides a very simple introduction to ERB templates. For details on the full capabilities and syntax of ERB templates, refer to the Puppet Labs ERB documentation (*https://docs.puppetlabs.com/puppet/latest/reference/lang_template_erb.html*).

Begin by appending two new variables to the existing content of the *00_common_vars.pp* manifest file. The lines to be added to the manifest are:

```
$junos_puppet_dir = "$junos_home_dir/.puppet"
$junos_template_dir = '/etc/puppet/files/junos_templates'
```

Now, create a new *12_junos_puppet_user_puppet_conf.pp* manifest file. This file defines a new `junos_puppet_user_puppet_conf` class that uses the `notify` and `file` core resource types. The contents are:

```
class junos_puppet_user_puppet_conf {
  notify { 'puppet.conf':
    message => "Maintaining puppet.conf on $hostname"
  }
  file { "$junos_puppet_dir": ❶
    ensure => directory, ❷
    owner => $id,
    mode => 0755,
  }
  file { "$junos_puppet_dir/puppet.conf": ❸
    ensure => file,
    owner => $id,
    mode => 0644,
    content => template("$junos_template_dir/puppet_agent_conf.erb") ❹
  }
}
```

❶ This `file` resource ensures that the *~/.puppet* directory is present and has the correct owner and permissions. It is very similar to the `file` resource used to manage the *~/.cshrc* file, but doesn't require a `content` parameter.

❷ In this case, the `ensure` parameter is set to a value of `directory`. If the *~/.puppet* path exists but is a regular file or link, it will be replaced with a directory.

❸ Another file resource manages the *~/.puppet/puppet.conf* file. Because this path is within the *~/.puppet* path, Puppet automatically makes this resource dependent upon the *~/.puppet* file resource.

❹ The `template()` function is used to generate a string from an ERB template. In this example, the argument to the `template()` function is an absolute path to a template file on the Puppet master (*/etc/puppet/files/junos_templates/puppet_agent_conf.erb*). Alternatively, the argument to the `template` function can be a shortened path of the form *<module_name>/<template_file>*. If this shortened form is used, the template file is loaded from *<modulepath>/<module_name>/templates/<template_file>*. In this case, the value of *<modulepath>* is the set of directories on the Puppet master where modules are installed. Use the command `sudo puppet config print modulepath --section master` to determine the module path on your Puppet master:

```
user@h0$ sudo puppet config print modulepath --section master
/etc/puppet/environments/production/modules:/etc/puppet/modules:
  /usr/share/puppet/modules
```

The content of the ERB template is:

```
user@h0$ cat /etc/puppet/files/junos_templates/puppet_agent_conf.erb
# Source: /etc/puppet/files/junos_templates/puppet_agent_conf.erb
[main]
    pluginsync = true

[agent]
    <%# @servername gets the $servername fact %>
    server = <%= @servername %>
    daemonize = false
```

Most of this content is returned unmodified by the `template()` function. The only content that gets expanded by the `template()` function appears within the `<% ...content... %>` syntax. The text `<%= @servername %>` evaluates to the value of the `$servername` variable. The text within `<%# ...content... %>` is an ERB comment. It appears *only* in the template, *not* in the string returned by the `template()` function. Contrast this with the template line that begins with `# Source`. While that line happens to be a comment in a Puppet configuration file, it has *no special meaning* within a template file. It is treated as literal text just like any other portion of the template file that's not within the `<% ...content... %>` syntax. While this template only demonstrates a simple fact variable substitution, ERB templates support more advanced capabilities, such as loops, conditionals, and user-defined variables, including hashes.

Before executing the Puppet agent, include the `junos_puppet_user_puppet_conf` class for all Junos devices by modifying the *80_all_nodes.pp* manifest file. The complete content of this file is now:

```
case $operatingsystem {
  'JUNOS': {
      include junos_puppet_user_cshrc
      include junos_puppet_user_puppet_conf
  }
  default: {
      fail('Unknown operating system!')
  }
}
```

Test the ERB template by executing the `puppet agent --test` command:

```
% puppet agent --test
Info: Retrieving pluginfacts
Info: Retrieving plugin
ldapname is deprecated and will be removed in a future version
Info: Caching catalog for s0.example.com
Info: Applying configuration version '1443928430'
Notice: Maintaining puppet.conf on s0
Notice: /Stage[main]/Junos_puppet_user_puppet_conf/Notify[puppet.conf]/message:
  defined 'message' as 'Maintaining puppet.conf on s0'
```

```
Notice: Maintaining .cshrc on s0
Notice: /Stage[main]/Junos_puppet_user_cshrc/Notify[cshrc]/message:
  defined 'message' as 'Maintaining .cshrc on s0'
Notice: /Stage[main]/Junos_puppet_user_puppet_conf/
  File[/var/home/puppet/.puppet/puppet.conf]/content:
--- /var/home/puppet/.puppet/puppet.conf Mon Sep 28 15:19:13 2015
+++ /tmp/puppet-file20151003-19787-h7l0a3-0 Sat Oct  3 20:14:56 2015
@@ -1,6 +1,8 @@
+# Source: /etc/puppet/files/junos_templates/puppet_agent_conf.erb
 [main]
     pluginsync = true

 [agent]
     server = h0.example.com
     daemonize = false

Info: /Stage[main]/Junos_puppet_user_puppet_conf/
  File[/var/home/puppet/.puppet/puppet.conf]:
  Filebucketed /var/home/puppet/.puppet/puppet.conf to puppet with
  sum 2b73100678b169f3bafb9210d28b0011
Notice: /Stage[main]/Junos_puppet_user_puppet_conf/
  File[/var/home/puppet/.puppet/puppet.conf]/content: content changed
  '{md5}2b73100678b169f3bafb9210d28b0011' to
  '{md5}2b780b8be905736009df8e0ddf4ad56d'
Notice: Finished catalog run in 0.35 seconds
%
```

The output shows the *~/.puppet/puppet.conf* file was modified on the Junos device. However, the only modification was the first comment line, which didn't previously exist in the manually created file.

Managing the Puppet Agent with the cron Resource

The last core resource type covered in this section is the `cron` resource. As you might have guessed, it manages a cron job (a command executed at a regular frequency). The `cron` resource is extremely useful in controlling the execution of Puppet itself. The `cron` resource is used to execute the Puppet agent at a regular interval without manual intervention from a user.

Begin by appending three new variables (and a comment) to the *00_common_vars.pp* manifest file. The lines to be added to the manifest are:

```
$junos_puppet_dir = "$junos_home_dir/.puppet"

# Frequency, in minutes, to execute the puppet agent.
# Must be between 1 and 60.
$junos_puppet_run_frequency = '5'

$junos_run_log = '/tmp/puppet_run.log'
```

The `$junos_puppet_run_frequency` variable has been set to 5. In a production environment, Puppet nodes typically pull their catalog from the Puppet master less frequently. Five minutes is convenient for example purposes, but 30 minutes is more appropriate for a production deployment.

Like the previous examples, the `cron` resource is declared within a class definition. Create a new *14_junos_puppet_run_cron.pp* manifest file with the following content:

```
class junos_puppet_run_cron {
  notify { 'puppet_cron':
    message => "Maintaining Puppet cron entry on $hostname"
  }
  cron { puppetrun: ❶
      ensure => present, ❷
      environment => "PATH=${path}", ❸
      command => "puppet agent -v -o --no-daemonize > $junos_run_log 2>&1", ❹
      user => "$id", ❺
      minute => "*/$junos_puppet_run_frequency", ❻
  }
}
```

❶ Like other resources, `cron` requires a title. The `puppetrun` title is only used in Puppet reports and within comments that Puppet adds to the crontab entry.

❷ The `cron` resource only accepts two values for the `ensure` parameter. A value of `present` ensures the crontab entry exists. A value of `absent` ensures the crontab entry *does not* exist.

❸ The `environment` parameter specifies environment variable settings that apply to the command. In this case, the `$PATH` environment variable must be set. The `${path}` syntax is an alternate way to reference the `$path` Puppet fact variable. It distinguishes variable names within a longer string.

❹ The `command` parameter specifies the exact command to be executed at the Junos device shell. The `-o` and `--no-daemonize` parameters execute the `puppet agent` command one time in the foreground. The `-v` parameter specifies verbose output, and the remainder of the command string redirects both standard output and standard error to the */tmp/puppet_run.log* file on the Junos device.

❺ The `user` parameter specifies the user who owns the cron job.

❻ The `minute` parameter specifies the minute of the hour when the cron job runs. The `*/`*`num`* syntax executes the command every *`num`* minutes.

Again, use an `include` statement to declare the new class for all Junos devices. This statement is added to the *80_all_nodes.pp* manifest file. The complete content of the file is now:

```
case $operatingsystem {
  'JUNOS': {
      include junos_puppet_user_cshrc
      include junos_puppet_user_puppet_conf
      include junos_puppet_run_cron
  }
  default: {
      fail('Unknown operating system!')
  }
}
```

Test your work by executing the `puppet agent --test` command:

```
% puppet agent --test
Info: Retrieving pluginfacts
Info: Retrieving plugin
ldapname is deprecated and will be removed in a future version
Info: Caching catalog for s0.example.com
Info: Applying configuration version '1443989708'
Notice: Maintaining Puppet cron entry on s0
Notice: /Stage[main]/Junos_puppet_run_cron/Notify[puppet_cron]/message:
  defined 'message' as 'Maintaining Puppet cron entry on s0'
Notice: Maintaining puppet.conf on s0
Notice: /Stage[main]/Junos_puppet_user_puppet_conf/Notify[puppet.conf]/message:
  defined 'message' as 'Maintaining puppet.conf on s0'
Notice: Maintaining .cshrc on s0
Notice: /Stage[main]/Junos_puppet_user_cshrc/Notify[cshrc]/message:
  defined 'message' as 'Maintaining .cshrc on s0'
Notice: /Stage[main]/Junos_puppet_run_cron/Cron[puppetrun]/ensure: created
Notice: Finished catalog run in 0.21 seconds
%
```

In this case, the `notice` resource is helpful because the output does not include any other indication the `cron` resource was added. However, executing the `crontab -l` command at the Puppet user's shell confirms the cron job has been added:

```
% crontab -l
# HEADER: This file was autogenerated at Sun Oct 04 13:16:13 -0700 2015 by pup...
# HEADER: While it can still be managed manually, it is definitely not recomme...
# HEADER: Note particularly that the comments starting with 'Puppet Name' should
# HEADER: not be deleted, as doing so could cause duplicate cron jobs.
# Puppet Name: puppetrun
PATH=/bin:/usr/bin:/sbin:/usr/sbin:/opt/sbin:/opt/bin:/opt/sdk/juniper/bin
*/5 * * * * puppet agent -v -o --no-daemonize > /tmp/puppet_run.log 2>&1
%
```

The Puppet agent is now executed at regular five-minute intervals. The */tmp/puppet_run.log* file is created upon the first execution of the cron job. You can monitor the activity of each Puppet run with the `tail -F /tmp/puppet_run.log` command:

```
% tail -F /tmp/puppet_run.log
Info: Retrieving plugin
ldapname is deprecated and will be removed in a future version
Info: Caching catalog for s0.example.com
Info: Applying configuration version '1443988750'
Notice: Maintaining puppet.conf on s0
Notice: /Stage[main]/Junos_puppet_user_puppet_conf/Notify[puppet.conf]/message:
  defined 'message' as 'Maintaining puppet.conf on s0'
Notice: Maintaining .cshrc on s0
Notice: /Stage[main]/Junos_puppet_user_cshrc/Notify[cshrc]/message:
  defined 'message' as 'Maintaining .cshrc on s0'
Notice: /Stage[main]/Junos_puppet_run_cron/Cron[puppetrun]/ensure: removed
Notice: Finished catalog run in 0.18 seconds
^C
%
```

Type Control-C to interrupt the `tail` command and return to the shell prompt.

Before continuing on to the next section, temporarily disable the cron job. This change prevents the Puppet agent from running while you continue to edit the manifest files by adding resources from the `netdev` module. Disabling the cron job is easy. Simply change the `ensure` parameter of the `puppetrun cron` resource to a value of `absent`. The full content of the *14_junos_puppet_run_cron.pp* manifest file is now:

```
class junos_puppet_run_cron {
  notify { 'puppet_cron':
    message => "Maintaining Puppet cron entry on $hostname"
  }
  cron { puppetrun:
      ensure => absent,
      environment => "PATH=${path}",
      command => "puppet agent -v -o --no-daemonize > $junos_run_log 2>&1",
      user => "$id",
      minute => "*/$junos_puppet_run_frequency",
  }
}
```

The cron job will be removed the next time the Puppet agent runs. You may wait until the next (and final) cron job runs, or you can manually execute the Puppet agent with the `puppet agent --test` command:

```
% puppet agent --test
Info: Retrieving pluginfacts
Info: Retrieving plugin
ldapname is deprecated and will be removed in a future version
Info: Caching catalog for s0.example.com
Info: Applying configuration version '1443990154'
Notice: Maintaining Puppet cron entry on s0
Notice: /Stage[main]/Junos_puppet_run_cron/Notify[puppet_cron]/message:
```

```
  defined 'message' as 'Maintaining Puppet cron entry on s0'
Notice: Maintaining puppet.conf on s0
Notice: /Stage[main]/Junos_puppet_user_puppet_conf/Notify[puppet.conf]/message:
  defined 'message' as 'Maintaining puppet.conf on s0'
Notice: Maintaining .cshrc on s0
Notice: /Stage[main]/Junos_puppet_user_cshrc/Notify[cshrc]/message:
  defined 'message' as 'Maintaining .cshrc on s0'
Notice: /Stage[main]/Junos_puppet_run_cron/Cron[puppetrun]/ensure: removed
Notice: Finished catalog run in 0.18 seconds
%
```

The `crontab -l` command confirms the crontab entry has been removed. The comments in the crontab indicate Puppet is still managing the crontab:

```
% crontab -l
# HEADER: This file was autogenerated at Sun Oct 04 13:23:39 -0700 2015 by pup...
# HEADER: While it can still be managed manually, it is definitely not recomme...
# HEADER: Note particularly that the comments starting with 'Puppet Name' should
# HEADER: not be deleted, as doing so could cause duplicate cron jobs.

%
```

The cron job has now been disabled. Future changes to the manifest are only applied during a Puppet run. While you can set `ensure => present` on the `puppetrun` resource, this change will *not* take effect automatically. You must manually execute the Puppet agent one more time to update the resource and re-enable the cron job.

Using the netdev Resource Types

While Puppet's core resource types are helpful, the real value of Puppet comes in managing the network resources of a Junos device. The generic network resource types are published in the `netdevops/netdev_stdlib` module, and the corresponding resource providers for Junos are published in `juniper/netdev_stdlib_junos`. This section looks at each of these `netdev` resource types in more detail.

The netdev_device Resource

The `netdev_device` resource models the management connection to the agent node running Junos. Like all resource declarations, it requires a unique title. However, it does not require any parameters. All other `netdev` resources are dependent upon the `netdev_device` resource; you must declare the `netdev_device` resource in order to use any other `netdev` resources.

The *80_all_nodes.pp* manifest file already contains a case that executes on all Junos devices. This is a logical and convenient place to declare the `netdev_device` resource. The complete content of the *80_all_nodes.pp* manifest file is now:

```
case $operatingsystem {
  'JUNOS': {
      netdev_device { $hostname: }
      include junos_puppet_user_cshrc
      include junos_puppet_user_puppet_conf
      include junos_puppet_run_cron
  }
  default: {
      fail('Unknown operating system!')
  }
}
```

The title of the `netdev_device` resource is set to the `$hostname` fact variable. While this title can be any user-defined identifier, it is convenient and recommended to simply set the title to the node name stored in the `$hostname` variable.

The netdev_vlan Resource

The `netdev_vlan` resource models the configuration of a VLAN on a Junos device. Create a new *70_junos_switch_uplinks.pp* manifest file with the following content:

```
class junos_switch_uplinks {
  if $junos_personality == 'JUNOS_switch' {
    netdev_vlan { 'net_mgmt': vlan_id => 99, description => 'Net Management' }
  }
}
```

The `netdev_vlan` line in the preceding output uses a compressed, one-line syntax to declare the resource. Whitespace is optional in Puppet manifest files; therefore, this syntax is exactly equivalent to the multiline syntax used for previous resource declarations.

This configuration declares a single `net_mgmt` VLAN on any node where the `$junos_personality` fact variable has a value of `JUNOS_switch`. The title of the `netdev_vlan` resource (`net_mgmt`, in this case) is used as the VLAN name in the Junos configuration. The `vlan_id` parameter sets the VLAN ID to 99, and the `description` parameter configures a friendly name for the VLAN. The `netdev_vlan` resource also supports the standard `ensure` parameter with values of `present` or `absent`. If necessary, the `present` value creates the VLAN configuration on the switch and the `absent` value deletes the configuration. The `active` parameter controls whether the VLAN configuration is active or not. It takes a value of `true` or `false`. The default values are `ensure => present` and `active => true`.

Declare the `junos_switch_uplinks` class for all Junos devices by adding an `include junos_switch_uplinks` line to the *80_all_nodes.pp* manifest file. The full content of the *80_all_nodes.pp* manifest file is now:

```
case $operatingsystem {
  'JUNOS': {
      netdev_device { $hostname: }
      include junos_puppet_user_cshrc
      include junos_puppet_user_puppet_conf
      include junos_puppet_run_cron
      include junos_switch_uplinks
  }
  default: {
      fail('Unknown operating system!')
  }
}
```

Finally, execute the Puppet agent to verify the manifest changes and apply the `net_mgmt` VLAN to the Junos switch:

```
% puppet agent --test
Info: Retrieving pluginfacts
Info: Retrieving plugin
ldapname is deprecated and will be removed in a future version
Info: Caching catalog for s0.example.com
Info: Applying configuration version '1444061705'
Notice: Maintaining Puppet cron entry on s0
Notice: /Stage[main]/Junos_puppet_run_cron/Notify[puppet_cron]/message:
  defined 'message' as 'Maintaining Puppet cron entry on s0'
Notice: Maintaining puppet.conf on s0
Notice: /Stage[main]/Junos_puppet_user_puppet_conf/Notify[puppet.conf]/message:
  defined 'message' as 'Maintaining puppet.conf on s0'
Notice: Maintaining .cshrc on s0
Notice: /Stage[main]/Junos_puppet_user_cshrc/Notify[cshrc]/message:
  defined 'message' as 'Maintaining .cshrc on s0'
Notice: /Stage[main]/Junos_switch_uplinks/Netdev_vlan[net_mgmt]/ensure: created
Info: JUNOS: Committing 1 changes.
Notice: JUNOS:

[edit]
+  vlans {
+      net_mgmt {
+          description "Net Management";
+          vlan-id 99;
+      }
+  }

kill: 23824: No such process
kill: 23828: No such process
Notice: JUNOS: OK: COMMIT success!
Notice: Finished catalog run in 3.88 seconds
%
```

The output from the Puppet run shows the new configuration that was added to the `s0.example.com` node in the form of a diff. Checking the configuration on the switch confirms the VLAN configuration is present and active:

```
{master:0}
user@s0> show configuration vlans
net_mgmt {
    description "Net Management";
    vlan-id 99;
}
```

The current example configures the `net_mgmt` VLAN on all Junos switches managed by Puppet. If you want additional VLANs to be present on all switches, declare additional `netdev_vlan` resources inside the `junos_switch_uplinks` class. What if you only want to configure VLANs on one switch? You can declare node-specific `netdev_vlan` resources within a `node` statement. Modify the empty `node` statement in the *90_example.com_nodes.pp* manifest file as follows:

```
node 's0.example.com' {

  $customer_vlans = {
    'accounting' => { vlan_id => 100, description => 'Accounting Department' },
    'hardware'   => { vlan_id => 101, description => 'Hardware Engineering' },
    'software'   => { vlan_id => 102, description => 'Software Development' },
  }

  create_resources( netdev_vlan, $customer_vlans )
}
```

This manifest file demonstrates Puppet's `create_resources()` function. It defines a `$customer_vlans` hash, which is keyed on VLAN names. Each VLAN's value is another hash, which is keyed on the parameters to the `netdev_vlan` resource. The `create_resources()` function is then used to create multiple `netdev_vlan` resources with a single statement. The first argument to `create_resources` is the name of the resource to create. The second argument is a hash variable. The outer key of the hash is used as the title for each `netdev_vlan` resource, and the inner keys are used as parameters to each `netdev_vlan` resource.

Performing a Puppet run creates the new VLANs on the `s0.example.com` node:

```
% puppet agent --test
Info: Retrieving pluginfacts
Info: Retrieving plugin
ldapname is deprecated and will be removed in a future version
Info: Caching catalog for s0.example.com
Info: Applying configuration version '1444062994'
Notice: Maintaining Puppet cron entry on s0
Notice: /Stage[main]/Junos_puppet_run_cron/Notify[puppet_cron]/message:
  defined 'message' as 'Maintaining Puppet cron entry on s0'
Notice: Maintaining puppet.conf on s0
```

```
Notice: /Stage[main]/Junos_puppet_user_puppet_conf/Notify[puppet.conf]/message:
  defined 'message' as 'Maintaining puppet.conf on s0'
Notice: /Stage[main]/Main/Node[s0.example.com]/
  Netdev_vlan[accounting]/ensure: created
Notice: /Stage[main]/Main/Node[s0.example.com]/
  Netdev_vlan[software]/ensure: created
Notice: Maintaining .cshrc on s0
Notice: /Stage[main]/Junos_puppet_user_cshrc/Notify[cshrc]/message:
 defined 'message' as 'Maintaining .cshrc on s0'
Notice: /Stage[main]/Main/Node[s0.example.com]/
  Netdev_vlan[hardware]/ensure: created
Info: JUNOS: Committing 3 changes.
Notice: JUNOS:

[edit vlans]
+   accounting {
+       description "Accounting Department";
+       vlan-id 100;
+   }
+   hardware {
+       description "Hardware Engineering";
+       vlan-id 101;
+   }
+   software {
+       description "Software Development";
+       vlan-id 102;
+   }

kill: 24278: No such process
Notice: JUNOS: OK: COMMIT success!
Notice: Finished catalog run in 4.00 seconds
%
```

In addition, the net_mgmt VLAN is maintained:

```
{master:0}
user@s0> show configuration vlans
accounting {
    description "Accounting Department";
    vlan-id 100;
}
hardware {
    description "Hardware Engineering";
    vlan-id 101;
}
net_mgmt {
    description "Net Management";
    vlan-id 99;
}
software {
    description "Software Development";
    vlan-id 102;
}
```

The netdev_interface Resource

The `netdev_interface` resource models a physical interface on a network device. The title of each `netdev_interface` is the interface to be managed. The `speed`, `duplex`, and `mtu` parameters allow Puppet to manage common physical interface properties. In addition, the `description` parameter controls a user-defined description string.

Additional content added to the *70_junos_switch_uplinks.pp* manifest file demonstrates the `netdev_interface` resource. The full content of the *70_junos_switch_uplinks.pp* manifest file is as follows. This Puppet code configures different physical interfaces to act as the switch's uplink interface depending upon the switch's hardware model. In addition to demonstrating the `netdev_interface` resource, it also demonstrates some additional capabilities of the Puppet language:

```
class junos_switch_uplinks {
  if $junos_personality == 'JUNOS_switch' {
    netdev_vlan { 'net_mgmt': vlan_id => 99, description => 'Net Management' }
    Netdev_interface { ❶
      ensure => present,
      active => true,
      admin => up,
    }
    if $hardwaremodel =~ /^qfx5100-48s-6q$/ ❷ {
      notify { 'Uplinks':
        message => "Hardware: $hardwaremodel Uplinks: et-0/0/[50-53]"
      }
      netdev_interface { ❸
        'et-0/0/50':
          description => 'Uplink 0 Member 0',
        ;
        'et-0/0/51':
          description => 'Uplink 0 Member 1',
        ;
        'et-0/0/52':
          description => 'Uplink 1 Member 0',
        ;
        'et-0/0/53':
          description => 'Uplink 1 Member 1',
        ;
      }
    }
    elsif $hardwaremodel =~ /^qfx5100/ ❹ {
      notify { 'Uplinks':
        message => "Hardware: $hardwaremodel Uplinks: et-0/0/[0-3]"
      }
      netdev_interface { 'et-0/0/0': ❺
        description => 'Uplink 0 Member 0',
      }
      netdev_interface { 'et-0/0/1':
```

```
      description => 'Uplink 0 Member 1',
    }
    netdev_interface { 'et-0/0/2':
      description => 'Uplink 1 Member 0',
    }
    netdev_interface { 'et-0/0/3':
      description => 'Uplink 1 Member 1',
    }
  }
  else {
    fail("Unrecognized Junos switch model $hardwaremodel")
  }
}
}
```

❶ This line sets a resource default for the `netdev_interface` resource. A resource default looks similar to a normal resource declaration, but begins with a capitalized resource name. In addition, resource defaults omit the title and trailing colon. In other words, only parameter value pairs appear within the curly braces. A resource declaration for the specified type that omits any of these parameters will inherent the parameter's value from the resource default. In this case, default values are set for the `ensure`, `active`, and `admin` parameters of any `netdev_interface` resource declarations. The `admin` parameter controls whether or not the interface is administratively enabled.

❷ This `if` block uses a regular expression to match the `qfx5100-48s-6q` hardware model.

❸ This line begins a `netdev_interface` resource declaration. This declaration uses an alternative syntax that specifies multiple `netdev_interface` resources within a single set of curly braces. Each resource has its own title, followed by a colon and a set of parameter/value pairs. Each resource ends with a semicolon. Each of these `netdev_interface` resources will inherit the `ensure`, `active`, and `admin` parameters from the `Netdev_interface` resource default.

❹ This `elsif` block uses a regular expression to match any hardware models that begin with the string `qfx5100`.

❺ This statement begins a set of four separate `netdev_interface` resource declarations. Each of these `netdev_interface` resources will also inherit the `ensure`, `active`, and `admin` parameters from the `Netdev_interface` resource default.

Before the Puppet run, the `s0.example.com` switch has only a management interface configuration present:

```
{master:0}
user@s0> show configuration interfaces
em0 {
    unit 0 {
        family inet {
            address 10.92.250.71/23;
        }
    }
}

{master:0}
user@s0>
```

A Puppet run is initiated to apply the new `netdev_interface` resources:

```
% puppet agent --test
Info: Retrieving pluginfacts
Info: Retrieving plugin
ldapname is deprecated and will be removed in a future version
Info: Caching catalog for s0.example.com
Info: Applying configuration version '1444075168'
Notice: Maintaining Puppet cron entry on s0
Notice: /Stage[main]/Junos_puppet_run_cron/Notify[puppet_cron]/message:
  defined 'message' as 'Maintaining Puppet cron entry on s0'
Notice: Maintaining puppet.conf on s0
Notice: /Stage[main]/Junos_puppet_user_puppet_conf/Notify[puppet.conf]/message:
  defined 'message' as 'Maintaining puppet.conf on s0'
Notice: /Stage[main]/Junos_switch_uplinks/Netdev_interface[et-0/0/51]/ensure:
  created
Notice: /Stage[main]/Junos_switch_uplinks/Netdev_interface[et-0/0/53]/ensure:
  created
Notice: /Stage[main]/Junos_switch_uplinks/Netdev_interface[et-0/0/52]/ensure:
  created
Notice: Maintaining .cshrc on s0
Notice: /Stage[main]/Junos_puppet_user_cshrc/Notify[cshrc]/message:
  defined 'message' as 'Maintaining .cshrc on s0'
Notice: Hardware: qfx5100-48s-6q Uplinks: et-0/0/[50-53]
Notice: /Stage[main]/Junos_switch_uplinks/Notify[Uplinks]/message:
  defined 'message' as 'Hardware: qfx5100-48s-6q Uplinks: et-0/0/[50-53]'
Notice: /Stage[main]/Junos_switch_uplinks/Netdev_interface[et-0/0/50]/ensure:
  created
Info: JUNOS: Committing 4 changes.
Notice: JUNOS:

[edit]
+  interfaces {
+      et-0/0/50 {
+          description "Uplink 0 Member 0";
+      }
+      et-0/0/51 {
```

```
+           description "Uplink 0 Member 1";
+       }
+       et-0/0/52 {
+           description "Uplink 1 Member 0";
+       }
+       et-0/0/53 {
+           description "Uplink 1 Member 1";
+       }
+   }

kill: 24916: No such process
Notice: JUNOS: OK: COMMIT success!
Notice: Finished catalog run in 4.19 seconds
%
```

The `show configuration interfaces` CLI command now shows the additional interface configuration created by Puppet:

```
{master:0}
user@s0> show configuration interfaces
et-0/0/50 {
    description "Uplink 0 Member 0";
}
et-0/0/51 {
    description "Uplink 0 Member 1";
}
et-0/0/52 {
    description "Uplink 1 Member 0";
}
et-0/0/53 {
    description "Uplink 1 Member 1";
}
em0 {
    unit 0 {
        family inet {
            address 10.92.250.71/23;
        }
    }
}

{master:0}
user@s0>
```

The netdev_l2_interface Resource

Of course, a physical interface configuration is of limited value without a corresponding Layer 2 network configuration. That's the purpose of the `netdev_l2_inteface` resource type. The `netdev_l2_interface` resource supports the same `ensure`, `active`, and `description` parameters supported by the `netdev_interface` resource. In addition, it supports `vlan_tagging`, `untagged_vlan`, and `tagged_vlans` parameters to control VLAN configuration on the Layer 2 network interface.

Edit the *90_example.com_nodes.pp* manifest file to define a set of new Layer 2 customer ports on the switch. In addition, configure the `ae0` and `ae1` interfaces (defined in the next section) with VLAN trunking and a native VLAN. The full content of the *90_example.com_nodes.pp* manifest file is:

```
node 's0.example.com' {

  $customer_vlans = {
    'accounting' => { vlan_id => 100, description => 'Accounting Department' },
    'hardware'   => { vlan_id => 101, description => 'Hardware Engineering' },
    'software'   => { vlan_id => 102, description => 'Software Development' },
  }

  $customer_ports = {
    'et-0/0/0' => { untagged_vlan => 'accounting' },
    'et-0/0/1' => { untagged_vlan => 'software' },
    'et-0/0/2' => { untagged_vlan => 'hardware' },
  }

  create_resources( netdev_vlan, $customer_vlans )

  create_resources( netdev_l2_interface, $customer_ports )

  netdev_l2_interface { [ 'ae0','ae1' ]:
    untagged_vlan => 'net_mgmt',
    tagged_vlans => keys( $customer_vlans ),
  }
}
```

The customer ports are configured from a `$customer_ports` hash using the `create_resources()` function. The `ae0` and `ae1` interfaces are specified in a single `netdev_l2_interface` resource declaration by specifying a list of interfaces as the title.

The `ae0` and `ae1` interfaces have an untagged, or native, VLAN of `net_mgmt`. All customer VLANs are configured as tagged VLANs on these interfaces. The `keys` function produces a list of VLANs from the keys of the `$customer_vlans` hash.

The keys() function is not part of the base Puppet installation. Instead, it's found in a puppetlabs/stdlib module that provides several useful Puppet functions. Install the puppetlabs/stdlib module by executing the command puppet module install puppetlabs/stdlib as the root user on the Puppet master:

```
user@h0$ sudo puppet module install puppetlabs/stdlib
Notice: Preparing to install into /etc/puppet/modules ...
Notice: Downloading from https://forgeapi.puppetlabs.c...
Notice: Installing -- do not interrupt ...
/etc/puppet/modules
└── puppetlabs-stdlib (v4.9.0)
user@h0$
```

In addition, add netdev_l2_interface resources to the *70_junos_switch_uplinks.pp* manifest file to ensure that the switch uplinks do *not* have a Layer 2 network configuration. In the next section, these switch uplinks will be configured as part of a Link Aggregation Group:

```
class junos_switch_uplinks {
  if $junos_personality == 'JUNOS_switch' {
    # ... Existing Puppet code ...
    if $hardwaremodel =~ /^qfx5100-48s-6q$/ {
      # ... Existing Puppet code ...
      netdev_l2_interface { [ 'et-0/0/50','et-0/0/51','et-0/0/52','et-0/0/53' ]:
        ensure => absent,
      }
    }
    elsif $hardwaremodel =~ /^qfx5100/ {
      # ... Existing Puppet code ...
      netdev_l2_interface { [ 'et-0/0/0','et-0/0/1','et-0/0/2','et-0/0/3' ]:
        ensure => absent,
      }
    }
    # ... Existing Puppet code ...
  }
}
```

Physical interfaces can only be added to a LAG if they do not have a Layer 2 network configuration, and these resources use ensure => absent to enforce this configuration constraint.

Execute another Puppet run to update the s0.example.com device with the netdev_l2_interface resources:

```
% puppet agent --test
Info: Retrieving pluginfacts
Info: Retrieving plugin
... notices from the puppetlabs-stdlib module files ...
Info: Caching catalog for s0.example.com
Info: Applying configuration version '1444080194'
```

```
Notice: Maintaining Puppet cron entry on s0
Notice: /Stage[main]/Junos_puppet_run_cron/Notify[puppet_cron]/message:
  defined 'message' as 'Maintaining Puppet cron entry on s0'
Notice: Maintaining puppet.conf on s0
Notice: /Stage[main]/Junos_puppet_user_puppet_conf/Notify[puppet.conf]/message:
  defined 'message' as 'Maintaining puppet.conf on s0'
Notice: /Stage[main]/Main/Node[s0.example.com]/
  Netdev_l2_interface[et-0/0/1]/ensure: created
Notice: Maintaining .cshrc on s0
Notice: /Stage[main]/Junos_puppet_user_cshrc/Notify[cshrc]/message:
  defined 'message' as 'Maintaining .cshrc on s0'
Notice: /Stage[main]/Main/Node[s0.example.com]/
  Netdev_l2_interface[et-0/0/0]/ensure: created
Notice: Hardware: qfx5100-48s-6q Uplinks: et-0/0/[50-53]
Notice: /Stage[main]/Junos_switch_uplinks/Notify[Uplinks]/message:
  defined 'message' as 'Hardware: qfx5100-48s-6q Uplinks: et-0/0/[50-53]'
Notice: /Stage[main]/Main/Node[s0.example.com]/
  Netdev_l2_interface[et-0/0/2]/ensure: created
Notice: /Stage[main]/Main/Node[s0.example.com]/
  Netdev_l2_interface[ae0]/ensure: created
Notice: /Stage[main]/Main/Node[s0.example.com]/
  Netdev_l2_interface[ae1]/ensure: created
Info: JUNOS: Committing 5 changes.
Notice: JUNOS:

[edit interfaces]
+   et-0/0/0 {
+       unit 0 {
+           description "Puppet created netdev_l2_interface: et-0/0/0";
+           family ethernet-switching {
+               interface-mode access;
+               vlan {
+                   members accounting;
+               }
+           }
+       }
+   }
+   et-0/0/1 {
+       unit 0 {
+           description "Puppet created netdev_l2_interface: et-0/0/1";
+           family ethernet-switching {
+               interface-mode access;
+               vlan {
+                   members software;
+               }
+           }
+       }
+   }
+   et-0/0/2 {
+       unit 0 {
+           description "Puppet created netdev_l2_interface: et-0/0/2";
+           family ethernet-switching {
```

```
+                 interface-mode access;
+                 vlan {
+                     members hardware;
+                 }
+             }
+         }
+     }
+     ae0 {
+         native-vlan-id 99;
+         unit 0 {
+             description "Puppet created netdev_l2_interface: ae0";
+             family ethernet-switching {
+                 interface-mode trunk;
+                 vlan {
+                     members [ accounting hardware software ];
+                 }
+             }
+         }
+     }
+     ae1 {
+         native-vlan-id 99;
+         unit 0 {
+             description "Puppet created netdev_l2_interface: ae1";
+             family ethernet-switching {
+                 interface-mode trunk;
+                 vlan {
+                     members [ accounting hardware software ];
+                 }
+             }
+         }
+     }

kill: 25460: No such process
kill: 25464: No such process
Notice: JUNOS: OK: COMMIT success!
Notice: Finished catalog run in 4.40 seconds
%
```

The netdev_lag Resource

The last resource type currently supported by the `netdevops/netdev_stdlib` module is the `netdev_lag` resource. This resource models a Link Aggregation Group. Junos refers to LAGs as aggregated Ethernet bundles (or ae interfaces). The `netdev_lag` resource has a mandatory `links` parameter, which specifies a list of physical interfaces that make up the LAG. It also supports an optional `lacp` parameter, which controls the state of the LACP protocol on the LAG. Acceptable values for the `lacp` parameter are `disabled` (the default), `active`, and `passive`. The optional `minimum_links` parameter specifies the number of member interfaces that must be in the up state for the LAG to be in the up state. Finally, the `netdev_lag` resource also supports the common `ensure` and `active` parameters.

Edit the *70_junos_switch_uplinks.pp* manifest file to add `netdev_lag` resources for the switch uplinks:

```
class junos_switch_uplinks {
  if $junos_personality == 'JUNOS_switch' {
    # ... Existing Puppet code ...
    Netdev_lag {
      ensure => present,
      active => true,
      lacp => active,
      minimum_links => '1',
    }
    if $hardwaremodel =~ /^qfx5100-48s-6q$/ {
      # ... Existing Puppet code ...
      netdev_lag {
        'ae0':
          links => [ 'et-0/0/50','et-0/0/51' ],
        ;
        'ae1':
          links => [ 'et-0/0/52','et-0/0/53' ],
        ;
      }
    }
    elsif $hardwaremodel =~ /^qfx5100/ {
      # ... Existing Puppet code ...
      netdev_lag { 'ae0':
        links => [ 'et-0/0/0','et-0/0/1' ],
      }
      netdev_lag { 'ae1':
        links => [ 'et-0/0/2','et-0/0/3' ],
      }
    }
    # ... Existing Puppet code ...
  }
}
```

The `Netdev_lag` resource defaults defines a set of default parameters for the netdev_`lag` resource. The `ae0` and `ae1` `netdev_lag` resources are defined with different member links depending on the switch model.

Initiate a Puppet run to apply these new resources to the `s0.example.com` switch:

```
% puppet agent --test
Info: Retrieving pluginfacts
Info: Retrieving plugin
... notices from the puppetlabs-stdlib module files ...
Info: Caching catalog for s0.example.com
Info: Applying configuration version '1444086985'
Notice: Maintaining Puppet cron entry on s0
```

```
Notice: /Stage[main]/Junos_puppet_run_cron/Notify[puppet_cron]/message:
  defined 'message' as 'Maintaining Puppet cron entry on s0'
Notice: Maintaining puppet.conf on s0
Notice: /Stage[main]/Junos_puppet_user_puppet_conf/Notify[puppet.conf]/message:
  defined 'message' as 'Maintaining puppet.conf on s0'
Notice: /Stage[main]/Junos_switch_uplinks/Netdev_lag[ae0]/lacp:
  lacp changed 'disabled' to 'active'
Notice: /Stage[main]/Junos_switch_uplinks/Netdev_lag[ae0]/minimum_links:
  minimum_links changed '0' to '1'
Notice: /Stage[main]/Junos_switch_uplinks/Netdev_lag[ae0]/links:
  links changed [] to 'et-0/0/50 et-0/0/51'
Notice: /Stage[main]/Junos_switch_uplinks/Netdev_lag[ae1]/lacp:
  lacp changed 'disabled' to 'active'
Notice: /Stage[main]/Junos_switch_uplinks/Netdev_lag[ae1]/minimum_links:
  minimum_links changed '0' to '1'
Notice: /Stage[main]/Junos_switch_uplinks/Netdev_lag[ae1]/links:
  links changed [] to 'et-0/0/52 et-0/0/53'
Notice: Maintaining .cshrc on s0
Notice: /Stage[main]/Junos_puppet_user_cshrc/Notify[cshrc]/message:
  defined 'message' as 'Maintaining .cshrc on s0'
Notice: Hardware: qfx5100-48s-6q Uplinks: et-0/0/[50-53]
Notice: /Stage[main]/Junos_switch_uplinks/Notify[Uplinks]/message:
  defined 'message' as 'Hardware: qfx5100-48s-6q Uplinks: et-0/0/[50-53]'
Info: JUNOS: Committing 2 changes.
Notice: JUNOS:

[edit interfaces et-0/0/50]
+    ether-options {
+        802.3ad ae0;
+    }
[edit interfaces et-0/0/51]
+    ether-options {
+        802.3ad ae0;
+    }
[edit interfaces et-0/0/52]
+    ether-options {
+        802.3ad ae1;
+    }
[edit interfaces et-0/0/53]
+    ether-options {
+        802.3ad ae1;
+    }
[edit interfaces ae0]
+    apply-macro "netdev_lag[:links]" {
+        et-0/0/50;
+        et-0/0/51;
+    }
[edit interfaces ae0]
+    aggregated-ether-options {
+        minimum-links 1;
+        lacp {
+            active;
```

```
+        }
+    }
[edit interfaces ae1]
+    apply-macro "netdev_lag[:links]" {
+        et-0/0/52;
+        et-0/0/53;
+    }
[edit interfaces ae1]
+    aggregated-ether-options {
+        minimum-links 1;
+        lacp {
+            active;
+        }
+    }

kill: 26148: No such process
kill: 26152: No such process
Notice: JUNOS: OK: COMMIT success!
Notice: Finished catalog run in 4.68 seconds
%
```

The Junos resource provider for the netdev_lag resource type uses apply-macro Junos configuration statements to track the links that are members of the LAG. Do not modify these apply-macro statements.

While these netdev_lag and netdev_l2_interface resources maintain the appropriate Junos configuration at the [edit interfaces] level of the Junos configuration hierarchy, they do not ensure that the appropriate aggregated Ethernet devices have been created at the [edit chassis] hierarchy level. However, the configuration to create aggregated Ethernet interfaces can still be managed by Puppet using the netdev_stdlib_junos::apply_group resource covered in the next section.

The netdev_stdlib_junos::apply_group Resource

There are both strengths and weaknesses to the netdevops/netdev_stdlib Puppet module. One *strength* is that the netdev resource types defined by this module are vendor-independent. One *weakness* is that the netdev resource types defined by this module are vendor-independent. It's a strength that any networking vendor can publish a corresponding netdev provider module to implement the netdev resource types. This allows a Puppet administrator to declare these resources in a Puppet manifest file independent of the network equipment type where the resources will be configured. However, this strength is also a weakness. Consensus must be achieved before new netdev resource types can be added to the module, and new resources must be limited to the lowest common denominator of features between multiple networking vendors.

On the other hand, the netdev_stdlib_junos::apply_group resource type takes the opposite approach. This resource type's strength is that it provides full access to all Junos device configuration capabilities. Its weakness is that because of this capability, it's specific to Juniper Networks devices. The netdev_stdlib_junos::apply_group resource type allows the content of any Junos configuration group to be managed by Puppet. Because any Junos configuration statements can be configured and applied using a configuration group, this provides full access to all Junos configuration capabilities.

The netdev_stdlib_junos::apply_group resource requires that an ERB template be specified with the mandatory template_path parameter. The corresponding ERB template must produce a Junos configuration snippet in either text (curly brace), set, or XML format. The format of the configuration snippet is determined by the name of the template file. Text (curly brace) format must be specified in a template named **.text.erb*, set format must be specified in a template named **.set.erb*, and XML format must be specified in a template named **.xml.erb*.

The netdev_stdlib_junos::apply_group resource also supports the common ensure parameter for controlling if the configuration group is present (the default) or absent. The active parameter controls if the configuration group is applied to the configuration. A value of active => true is the default and means the configuration group is applied, and is therefore an active part of the configuration. A value of active => false means the configuration group is not applied, and therefore not active.

Let's look at two examples of using this resource. The first example creates an apply-group to configure the aggregated Ethernet devices required[6] by the netdev_lag resource. Begin by creating a new *60_junos_ae_device_config.pp* manifest file with the following content:

```
class ae_device_config {
    netdev_stdlib_junos::apply_group { 'ae_device':
        template_path => "$junos_template_dir/ae_device_config.xml.erb",
    }
}
```

The resource title (ae_device) is also used as the name of the configuration group in the Junos configuration. The default values of ensure => present and active => true are in effect.

6 Technically, this configuration is no longer required on some newer Junos software versions on certain hardware platforms. However, it is still required on some hardware platforms and on older Junos software versions. Because all Junos software versions and hardware platforms still permit this configuration, the examples will work even if they are not technically required on your particular hardware platform and Junos software version.

Because the resource title (ae_device, in this case) of the netdev_stdlib_junos::apply_group resource is used as the name of the configuration group in the Junos configuration, you must ensure the resource title does not conflict with any existing configuration groups in your Junos device's configuration.

The template_path value matches **.xml.erb*, so the template must produce a configuration in XML format. Create the */etc/puppet/files/junos_templates/ae_device_config.xml.erb* template file with the following content:

```
<chassis>
    <aggregated-devices>
        <ethernet>
            <device-count><%= @ae_count %></device-count>
        </ethernet>
    </aggregated-devices>
</chassis>
```

This template configures $ae_count aggregated Ethernet devices. Now, set the $ae_count variable and declare the ae_device_config class by adding the following content to the *70_junos_switch_uplinks.pp* manifest file:

```
class junos_switch_uplinks {
  if $junos_personality == 'JUNOS_switch' {
    # ... Existing Puppet code ...
    $ae_count = 2
    include ae_device_config
    if $hardwaremodel =~ /^qfx5100-48s-6q$/ {
      # ... Existing Puppet code ...
    }
    elsif $hardwaremodel =~ /^qfx5100/ {
      # ... Existing Puppet code ...
    }
    # ... Existing Puppet code ...
  }
}
```

The following example creates a second apply-group template with the Junos configuration required to run the Puppet agent. Create a new *16_puppet_junos_config.pp* manifest file with the following content:

```
class puppet_junos_config {
    netdev_stdlib_junos::apply_group{ 'puppet':
        ensure => present,
        active => true,
        template_path => "$junos_template_dir/puppet_junos_config.text.erb",
    }
}
```

The matching ERB template produces a configuration snippet in text format. The content of */etc/puppet/files/junos_templates/puppet_junos_config.text.erb* is:

```
system {
    extensions {
        providers {
            juniper {
                license-type juniper deployment-scope commercial;
            }
        }
    }
    login {
        user <%= @id %> {
            class super-user;
            shell csh;
        }
    }
}
```

This resource does not guarantee that the configuration required to run the Puppet agent is always present. If a user manually deletes this Puppet-managed configuration group, the Puppet agent cannot run to reapply the group. In this case, you'll need to manually reapply the group. However, because this configuration is stored in a configuration group, it *may* be less susceptible to user error than configuration applied directly at the `[edit system]` configuration hierarchy level. Having the required configuration *both* in a configuration group *and* at the `[edit system]` configuration hierarchy level provides a belt-and-suspenders approach that may be even *less* susceptible to user error.

Now, declare the `puppet_junos_config` class in the *80_all_nodes.pp* manifest file:

```
case $operatingsystem {
  'JUNOS': {
    # ... Existing Puppet code ...
    include puppet_junos_config
  }
  # ... Existing Puppet code ...
}
```

Execute the Puppet agent to apply the new resources:

```
% puppet agent --test
Info: Retrieving pluginfacts
Info: Retrieving plugin
... notices from the puppetlabs-stdlib module files ...
Info: Caching catalog for s0.example.com
Info: Applying configuration version '1444139418'
Notice: /Stage[main]/Ae_device_config/Netdev_stdlib_junos::Apply_group
  [ae_device]/File[/var/tmp/ae_device]/ensure: created
```

```
Info: /Stage[main]/Ae_device_config/Netdev_stdlib_junos::Apply_group [ae_device]
  /File[/var/tmp/ae_device]: Scheduling refresh of Netdev_group[ae_device]
Notice: Maintaining Puppet cron entry on s0
Notice: /Stage[main]/Junos_puppet_run_cron/Notify[puppet_cron]/message:
  defined 'message' as 'Maintaining Puppet cron entry on s0'
Notice: Maintaining puppet.conf on s0
Notice: /Stage[main]/Junos_puppet_user_puppet_conf/Notify[puppet.conf]/message:
  defined 'message' as 'Maintaining puppet.conf on s0'
Notice: /Stage[main]/Ae_device_config/Netdev_stdlib_junos::Apply_group
  [ae_device]/Netdev_group[ae_device]/ensure: created
Error: /Stage[main]/Ae_device_config/Netdev_stdlib_junos::Apply_group[ae_device]
  /Netdev_group[ae_device]: Failed to call refresh: Document already has a root
  node
Error: /Stage[main]/Ae_device_config/Netdev_stdlib_junos::Apply_group[ae_device]
  /Netdev_group[ae_device]: Document already has a root node
Notice: Maintaining .cshrc on s0
Notice: /Stage[main]/Junos_puppet_user_cshrc/Notify[cshrc]/message:
  defined 'message' as 'Maintaining .cshrc on s0'
Notice: Hardware: qfx5100-48s-6q Uplinks: et-0/0/[50-53]
Notice: /Stage[main]/Junos_switch_uplinks/Notify[Uplinks]/message:
  defined 'message' as 'Hardware: qfx5100-48s-6q Uplinks: et-0/0/[50-53]'
Notice: /Stage[main]/Puppet_junos_config/Netdev_stdlib_junos::Apply_group[puppet]
  /File[/var/tmp/puppet]/ensure: created
Info: /Stage[main]/Puppet_junos_config/Netdev_stdlib_junos::Apply_group[puppet]
  /File[/var/tmp/puppet]: Scheduling refresh of Netdev_group[puppet]
Notice: /Stage[main]/Puppet_junos_config/Netdev_stdlib_junos::Apply_group[puppet]
  /Netdev_group[puppet]/ensure: created
Notice: /Stage[main]/Puppet_junos_config/Netdev_stdlib_junos::Apply_group[puppet]
  /Netdev_group[puppet]: Triggered 'refresh' from 1 events
Info: JUNOS: Committing 6 changes.
Notice: JUNOS:

[edit groups]
   member0 { ... }
+  ae_device {
+      chassis {
+          aggregated-devices {
+              ethernet {
+                  device-count 2;
+              }
+          }
+      }
+  }
+  puppet {
+      system {
+          login {
+              user puppet {
+                  class super-user;
+                  shell csh;
+              }
+          }
+          extensions {
```

```
+             providers {
+                 juniper {
+                     license-type juniper deployment-scope commercial;
+                 }
+             }
+         }
+     }
+ }
[edit]
+ apply-groups [ ae_device puppet ];

kill: 27718: No such process
kill: 27722: No such process
Notice: JUNOS: OK: COMMIT success!
Notice: Finished catalog run in 5.36 seconds
%
```

Once you're satisfied with your Puppet configuration, you may want to re enable scheduled execution of the Puppet agent by setting `ensure => present` on the `cron` resource in the *14_junos_puppet_run_cron.pp* manifest file. Don't forget to manually execute `puppet agent --test` one more time to apply this change.

The `netdev_stdlib_junos::apply_group` resource concludes the set of resource types available for managing Junos devices. You should now have a fully working set of example Puppet manifest files that can be extended to manage the Junos devices in your network. As with other chapters, the full set of example Puppet manifest files presented in this chapter are available on GitHub (*https://github.com/AutomatingJunosAdministration/examples*).

Chapter Summary

Puppet is a powerful and flexible IT framework. However, as is often the case with power and flexibility, it can have a relatively steep learning curve. If your organization has a DevOps team that already uses Puppet to manage servers, you may find it especially useful to also use Puppet with your Junos network. Currently, there are two significant disadvantages to managing Junos devices with Puppet. The first disadvantage is the limited platform and Junos version support, and the second disadvantage is the limited number of vendor-independent resource types. If your organization does not already have Puppet or Ansible deployed, we recommend that you investigate both before deciding which tool best meets your organization's requirements.

CHAPTER 10
Ansible

This chapter describes Ansible, another IT automation framework. While the end goal of both Puppet and Ansible is similar, Ansible takes a different approach to achieving this end goal. Whereas Puppet requires agent software to be installed on the managed node, Ansible uses an "agentless" architecture that does not require any Ansible-specific software to be installed on the managed node. Next, Puppet typically utilizes a "pull" model where managed nodes periodically fetch the latest state information from a server, but Ansible typically uses a "push" model where this state information is sent from the server to the managed nodes on demand. Finally, Puppet is written in Ruby while Ansible is written in Python.

Like Puppet, Ansible was originally focused more on automating aspects of the computing infrastructure, but now supports automating the network infrastructure as well. Juniper Networks publishes a collection of Ansible for Junos modules that simplify the execution of specific operational and configuration tasks on Junos devices. Before we look at these Ansible for Junos modules, let's explore the overall architecture of Ansible in more detail.

Architecture and Communication

Like Puppet, Ansible comes in two flavors. The base version of Ansible is sometimes referred to as "Ansible Core." Ansible Core is both free and open source. On the other hand, Ansible Tower is a commercial application. Ansible Tower includes Ansible Core and adds a visual dashboard, role-based access control, job scheduling, and graphical inventory management. Because Ansible Tower is a superset of Ansible Core, either flavor of Ansible can manage Junos devices. In this chapter, we will use the free and open source Ansible Core flavor, and simply refer to it as "Ansible."

Ansible itself is written in Python, but extensive Python knowledge is not required to use Ansible. Instead, Ansible automation jobs are expressed in YAML syntax. Because Ansible uses YAML extensively, now is a good time to review the general YAML syntax covered in "YAML at a Glance" on page 201. Make sure you understand both the primary and alternative YAML syntax for specifying lists and associative arrays (dictionaries).

In addition, Ansible uses the Jinja2 templating language introduced in "Configuration Templates" on page 220. While describing PyEZ configuration templates, we introduced the Jinja2 `{{ variable_name }}` variable expression syntax. Jinja2 templates evaluate a variable expression by substituting the variable's value. Jinja2 variable expressions (along with additional Jinja2 features) are used extensively in Ansible.

Now that you understand the two flavors of Ansible, and some of the technologies used by Ansible, let's investigate how Ansible communicates with managed nodes.

Typical Communication

Ansible uses a client/server architecture. The Ansible control machine, or server, is a Linux or BSD[1] that runs the Ansible software to manage one or more nodes. As mentioned in the chapter introduction, Ansible typically uses a "push" model where automation jobs are pushed to a managed node by the Ansible control machine. The managed node then executes the automation job and returns the result to the Ansible control machine. This communication is illustrated in Figure 10-1.

"Ansible orchestration engine" is a term used to describe the multiple components that make up the Ansible software running on the control machine. However, there is no Ansible "daemon" constantly running on the control machine. The Ansible software runs only when a user invokes Ansible to perform an automation task on a set of managed nodes.

Ansible's basic unit of automation is an "Ansible module." In Ansible parlance, a module is a small program that models a specific resource on a managed node. When executed, a module ensures the resource is in a specific state.

1 While Ansible can be used to manage Windows hosts, the Ansible control machine must be a Linux or BSD host. Windows, including Cygwin, is not supported as the Ansible control machine.

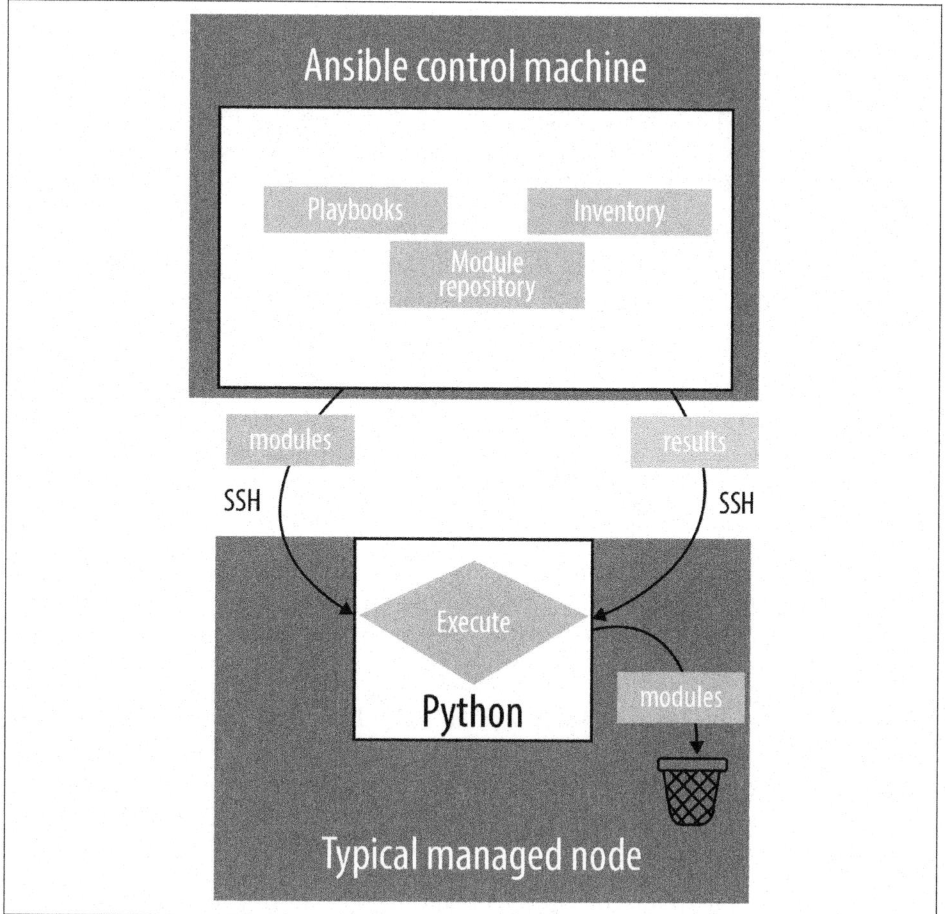

Figure 10-1. Typical Ansible communication

An Ansible module typically comes from one of four sources. The different module types are:

Core modules
: Maintained by the core Ansible team, and guaranteed to be included with the Ansible software itself.

Extras modules
: Currently shipped with Ansible, but might be shipped separately in the future. Most extras modules are maintained by the Ansible community. Popular extras modules may be promoted to core modules over time.

Galaxy modules
: Developed by the Ansible community, and published on the Ansible Galaxy website (*https://galaxy.ansible.com*). The Ansible Galaxy website provides a forum for freely sharing, finding, and reusing Ansible content. Modules published on the Ansible Galaxy website are maintained by their respective authors. The Juniper-provided Ansible for Junos modules currently fall into this category.

User-developed modules
: Written and maintained by you, the Ansible user. Ansible provides well-documented APIs and examples for developing your own modules to meet specific automation goals.

As illustrated in Figure 10-1, an SSH session is initiated from the control machine to the managed node, and Ansible modules are copied to the managed node over this SSH session. The module is then executed on the managed node itself. Results are returned to the control machine, in JSON format, over the SSH connection. Once executed, the Ansible module is deleted from the managed node.

This communication mechanism requires that Ansible managed nodes run an SSH server and accept SSH connections from the Ansible control machine. It is best practice to set up SSH keys between the control machine and each managed node, but passwords are also supported.

While Ansible modules are typically written in Python, they can be written in any language that provides file I/O and can output results to standard out. The only catch is that the managed node must have the ability to execute the Ansible module. Because most Ansible modules are written in Python, this effectively makes Python a requirement for each managed node.

This communication architecture means that only SSH and Python are required on the managed nodes. No Ansible-specific software needs to be installed, and because Ansible modules are removed after execution, there's no Ansible-specific software to be maintained or upgraded on the managed node.

While Figure 10-1 illustrates the communication with a single managed node, Ansible is obviously not limited to communicating with just one node. In fact, Ansible concurrently communicates with multiple managed nodes. This concurrent communication allows modules to execute in parallel on each managed node and minimizes the time each automation task takes to run.

Finally, Figure 10-1 illustrates the *typical* communication between an Ansible control machine and a managed node. However, this communication mechanism is not the *only* communication mechanism Ansible supports. For example, a mode called "ansible-pull" inverts this design and has managed nodes "phone home" via a scheduled `git checkout` to pull configuration directives from a central repository.

Some Ansible modules are also designed to execute locally on the Ansible control machine. This design is common among Ansible's cloud provisioning APIs. These APIs support creating, managing, and destroying virtual machines (VMs) on various cloud providers. Because these modules are actually creating the (virtual) machines to be managed, it is impossible for them to execute on a managed node that does not yet exist.

Communicating with Junos Managed Nodes

The Ansible for Junos modules also use the atypical (at least for Ansible) communication mechanism where modules are executed locally on the Ansible control machine. The Junos-specific communication mechanism is illustrated in Figure 10-2.

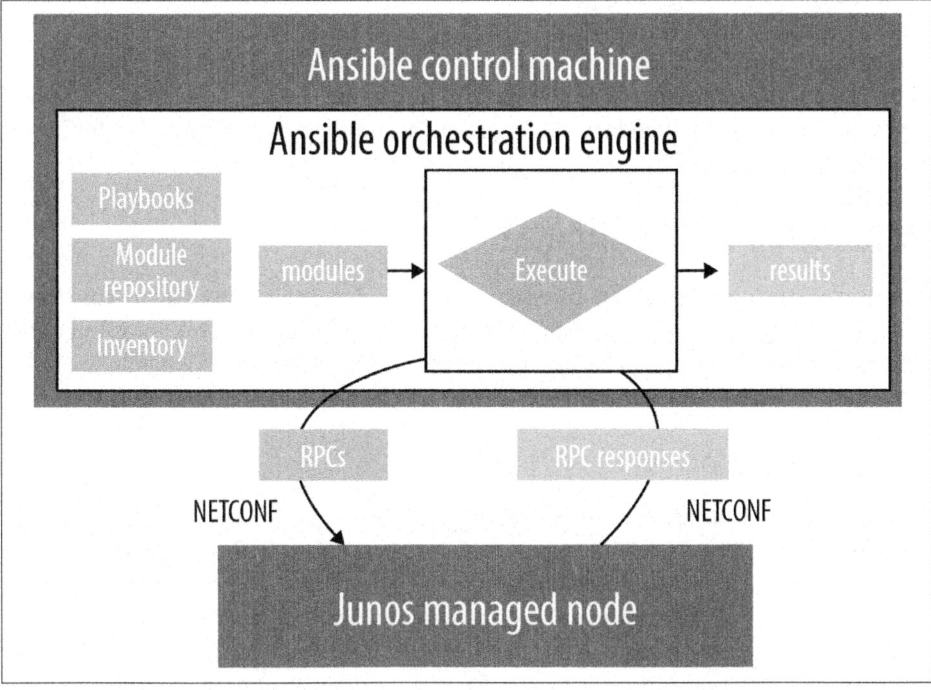

Figure 10-2. Junos Ansible communication

As the module executes locally on the Ansible control machine, it establishes a NETCONF session to the Junos device. XML RPCs are sent over this NETCONF session and XML responses are returned over this NETCONF session. The module then processes the response and returns the JSON-formatted results the Ansible orchestration engine expects from an Ansible module.

Some Juniper-provided Ansible modules can establish this NETCONF session over either an SSH connection or a console connection to the Junos device. When using a

NETCONF-over-SSH session, the Ansible module uses the PyEZ framework (covered in Chapter 4); when using a NETCONF-over-console session, the Ansible module uses the Netconify library (covered in Chapter 8).[2]

There are several important implications to the communication mechanism used between Ansible and Junos. First, Junos devices only need to have NETCONF support; they do not require Python on the Junos device. This requirement allows Ansible to manage all Juniper hardware models and all currently supported Junos software releases. Second, because the Ansible for Junos modules rely on PyEZ and Netconify, those software packages are prerequisites that must be installed on the Ansible control machine. Third, many core Ansible modules are designed to run directly on the managed node, and therefore cannot be used to automate Junos devices. Finally, when using the typical communication mechanism, the Ansible orchestration engine, not the module, handles authentication and establishes the SSH connection to the managed device. However, when using the Ansible for Junos modules, the module establishes the NETCONF connection. Connection and authentication parameters must therefore be passed as arguments to each Ansible for Junos module.

Installation and Configuration

Before you can use Ansible to automate Junos devices, you must have a functional Ansible control machine. This section details the installation and configuration of the Ansible control machine, including the Ansible Core software and Ansible for Junos modules.

Installing Ansible

Because Ansible is written in Python, it requires that Python 2.6 or 2.7 is installed on the control machine.[3] Ansible Core and its dependent Python libraries can be installed with the specific package manager of your Ansible control machine or with PyPI (*https://pypi.python.org/pypi*). In this chapter, we will demonstrate installation with PyPI because it applies equally to all control machine distributions and operating systems. Reference the Ansible installation documentation (*http://docs.ansible.com/ansible/intro_installation.html*) for instructions on installing Ansible directly from source or using the native package manager on various Linux and BSD distributions.

2 Because the NETCONF-over-console session is extremely slow, it should only be used to automate initial provisioning tasks such as installing a minimal configuration, zeroizing the device, or forming an SRX cluster. For this reason, some Ansible for Junos modules work *only* with a NETCONF-over-SSH session.

3 Ansible does not currently support Python 3.x.

Once Python and PyPI are installed,[4] simply execute `pip install ansible` as the root user to install the latest stable version of Ansible Core on the Ansible control machine:[5]

```
user@h0$ sudo pip install ansible
Downloading/unpacking ansible
  Downloading ansible-1.9.4.tar.gz (937kB): 937kB downloaded
  Running setup.py (path:/tmp/pip-build-STxkcN/ansible/setup.py) egg_info ...
... output trimmed ...
Successfully installed ansible paramiko jinja2 PyYAML pycrypto ecdsa
Cleaning up...
user@h0$ ansible --version
ansible 1.9.4
  configured module search path = None
user@h0$
```

You can also use the command `pip install git+https://github.com/ansible/ansible.git`[6] to install the latest development version of Ansible directly from the GitHub repository:

```
user@h0$ sudo pip install git+https://github.com/ansible/ansible.git
Downloading/unpacking git+https://github.com/ansible/ansible.git
  Cloning https://github.com/ansible/ansible.git to /tmp/pip-tAXVuI-build
  Running setup.py (path:/tmp/pip-tAXVuI-build/setup.py) egg_info for package ...
... output trimmed ...
    Successfully installed paramiko jinja2 PyYAML pycrypto ansible ecdsa Marku ...
Cleaning up...
user@h0$ ansible --version
ansible 2.0.0
  config file =
  configured module search path = Default w/o overrides
user@h0$
```

As of this writing, Ansible 2.0 is nearing initial release. In fact, the preceding output of the latest development version from the GitHub repository actually displays a version string of `2.0.0`. Ansible 2.0 represents some significant new features and design changes to Ansible. The examples in this chapter are based on version 1.9.4. We recommend you check the Ansible documentation (*http://docs.ansible.com/*) for additional details on version 2.0.

4 Using PyPI to install Ansible also requires that a C compiler and Python header files be installed.

5 The Ansible for Junos modules require Ansible 1.6 or later. The examples in this chapter use Ansible 1.9.4. While the Ansible for Junos modules work on Ansible 1.6 and later, some Ansible Core features demonstrated in the examples may not work on releases earlier than 1.9.4.

6 In addition to the Ansible software requirements, installing from the GitHub repository requires that *git* be installed on the Ansible control machine.

Installing the Juniper.junos Role

The Ansible for Junos modules are packaged as an Ansible role named `Juniper.junos`. Before you can manage Junos devices with Ansible, this `Juniper.junos` role must be installed on the Ansible control machine.

"Roles" on page 548 discusses roles in more detail. For now, it's sufficient to know that a role can be used to package a set of Ansible modules into a single *.tar.gz* file, which is installed in a single directory on the Ansible control machine.

Install the `Juniper.junos` Ansible role by simply executing the command `ansible-galaxy install Juniper.junos` as the root user:

```
user@h0$ sudo ansible-galaxy install Juniper.junos
[sudo] password for user:
- downloading role 'junos', owned by Juniper
- downloading role from https://github.com/Juniper/ansible-junos-stdlib/archi ...
- extracting Juniper.junos to /etc/ansible/roles/Juniper.junos
- Juniper.junos was installed successfully
user@h0$
```

The Ansible for Junos modules are now installed, but they will not work until the prerequisite PyEZ and Netconify libraries are installed. Ensure both are installed on the Ansible control machine at this time. Refer to "Installation" on page 164 for instructions on installing PyEZ and "Netconify" on page 452 for instructions on installing Netconify.

The Ansible Configuration File

Once Ansible, PyEZ, Netconify, and the Ansible for Junos modules are installed, you can begin configuring Ansible for your automation needs. Certain Ansible behavior is controlled by a configuration file. While most Ansible default settings are reasonable, you may want to override a few default values. Throughout this chapter, we will call out various configuration settings you might want to override in order to ease the management of Junos devices. The full list of available configuration settings is available in the Ansible documentation (*http://docs.ansible.com/*).

Ansible configuration files use the INI file format to specify a set of key/value pairs. The format is as follows:

```
[section1]
key1=value1
key2=value2
[section2]
key3=value3
key4=value4
```

An INI file organizes keys into sections; section names are enclosed in square brackets, and each key/value pair appears on a line separated by an equals sign. Most of the commonly used Ansible settings appear in a section named `[defaults]`.

Ansible searches for a configuration file in the following locations, in this order:

1. The file path specified by the user's `ANSIBLE_CONFIG` environment variable.
2. The current directory (*./ansible.cfg.*)
3. The user's home directory (*~/.ansible.cfg.*)
4. The */etc/ansible* directory (*/etc/ansible/ansible.cfg*).

Ansible does not merge values from multiple configuration files; it takes all configuration settings from the first configuration found. By default, no configuration file is present, and Ansible's default settings are used.

Begin by creating an */etc/ansible/ansible.cfg* file with the following content:

```
[defaults]
log_path=~/.ansible/log/ansible.log
forks=50
```

By default, Ansible logs a minimal amount of information about each execution to syslog. Setting the `log_path` key overrides this behavior. The `log_path` key specifies the location where Ansible logs detailed information about each execution. This key is extremely helpful when debugging a new Ansible automation job.

Ensure the user running Ansible has write permissions on the specified log file.

As described in "Typical Communication" on page 510, an Ansible automation task is executed concurrently on a set of managed nodes. The `forks` configuration key controls the maximum number of parallel processes spawned by the Ansible control machine. The default value of `forks` is `5`. This setting is *very* conservative. It means Ansible executes a task in parallel on a maximum of five hosts at a time. Increasing this setting allows an automation task to be run against a large number of hosts in a shorter amount of total time. The trade-off is increased network and CPU load on the Ansible control machine. A value of `50` is usually a good start, but you should really set `forks` to the maximum value that can be handled by your Ansible control machine.

Junos Authentication and Authorization

As described in "Communicating with Junos Managed Nodes" on page 513, the Ansible for Junos modules run locally on the Ansible control machine and communicate with the Junos managed device using NETCONF. All of the Ansible for Junos modules support NETCONF-over-SSH sessions using the PyEZ library. When using a NETCONF-over-SSH session, the modules require the same connectivity that a PyEZ script requires. Specifically, the following conditions must be met:

- The Ansible control machine must have IP connectivity to the Junos managed device.
- The Junos managed device must have the NETCONF-over-SSH service configured by specifying the `ssh` keyword at the `[edit system services netconf]` configuration hierarchy level.
- The Junos managed device must have a login account with sufficient authorization to run the underlying operational and configuration commands used by the Ansible for Junos modules.
- The Ansible control machine must have the necessary credentials (username and password/SSH key and passphrase) to log in to the account on the Junos managed device.

Refer back to "Device Connectivity" on page 165 for more detail on making a NETCONF-over-SSH connection using PyEZ. When using Ansible to manage a Junos device, the most convenient way to access the device is to configure SSH keys. "Authentication and Authorization" on page 170 details the steps required to configure a Junos device to use SSH keys.

While a NETCONF-over-SSH session is the preferred method for managing a Junos device, this access requires that an initial configuration be applied to the Junos device. Some of the Ansible for Junos modules also support a NETCONF-over-console session specifically so Ansible can deploy this initial configuration. The NETCONF-over-console session utilizes the Netconify library (covered in "Netconify" on page 452). In order for Ansible to establish a NETCONF-over-console session, the following conditions must be met:

- The console of the Junos managed device must be attached to a terminal server.
- The terminal server must support Telnet connections, on a specific IP address and TCP port number, to reach this Junos device's console.
- The Ansible control machine must have IP connectivity to the terminal server.
- The terminal server must not require any additional authentication or authorization to access the console connection.

- The Junos managed device must have a login account with sufficient authorization to run the underlying operational and configuration commands used by the Ansible for Junos modules.
- The Ansible control machine must have the necessary credentials (username and password) to log in to the account on the Junos managed device.

Again, it is important to understand that each Ansible for Junos module establishes its own NETCONF session with the Junos managed device. Unlike most modules, the Ansible for Junos modules require the necessary connection and authentication parameters to be passed as arguments to each module. Table 10-1 details the common connection and authentication arguments supported by Ansible for Junos modules. "Tasks and Modules" on page 528 will explain the syntax for passing arguments to modules and "Example Playbooks" on page 567 will demonstrate using these arguments with the Ansible for Junos modules.

Table 10-1. Connection and authentication arguments of Ansible for Junos modules

Argument	Description	Default value
`host`	A hostname, domain name, or IPv4 or IPv6 address on which the Junos device is running the NETCONF-over-SSH service. If a host name or domain name is used, it must resolve to an IPv4 or IPv6 address. It is best practice to set this argument to the value `{{ inventory_hostname }}`.	None (Must be specified by the caller.)
`port`	The TCP port on which the NETCONF-over-SSH service is reachable.	`830`

`user`	The username used to log in to the Junos device. Module execution is controlled by the authorization configuration of this user account on the Junos device.	The value of the `$USER` environment variable for the account running Ansible. This is useful if the usernames on the control machine and the Junos device are the same. At the Python interactive shell, you can confirm the value of the `$USER` environment variable with:
		`>>> import os`
		`>>> print(os.environ['USER'])`
		`user`

`passwd`	The password used to authenticate the user on the Junos device. If SSH keys are being used, this value is used as the passphrase to unlock the SSH private key. Otherwise, this value is used for password authentication.	None (A password is not needed for an SSH key with an empty passphrase.)

Argument	Description	Default value
`console`	This argument specifies a NETCONF-over-console session should be established. It is only accepted by a subset of the Ansible for Junos modules. The argument value must be in the format `--telnet=`*`terminal_server_hostname_or_ip, tcp_port_of_console`*	None (NETCONF-over-SSH connections are used.)

Creating Ansible Playbooks

Ansible automation jobs are written in the YAML language with a simple Ansible-specific structure called a "playbook." A user executes an Ansible playbook against a set of managed hosts, which are listed in an inventory file. Therefore, the first step in creating an automation job in Ansible is to create an Ansible inventory file that lists all hosts managed by Ansible.

Inventory

The inventory file defines hosts and groups using a format similar to the INI format used for an Ansible configuration file. Ultimately, playbooks are executed against *hosts* listed in the Ansible inventory file. However, the real power of Ansible comes from running playbooks against *groups* (groups expand to lists of hosts.) Each group is named, and a playbook can use the group names to define the target hosts.

By default, Ansible uses the */etc/ansible/hosts* inventory file. While you can list your hosts in this file, we recommend creating one or more inventory files in the same directory where you create your Ansible playbooks. This scheme allows a playbook to be explicitly run against different sets of hosts and provides a safeguard to prevent accidentally running a playbook against more hosts than intended.

Creating an empty */etc/ansible/hosts* file helps ensure playbooks are run against the correct set of managed hosts:

```
user@h0$ sudo touch /etc/ansible/hosts
```

Now, if a user forgets to specify the inventory file for a playbook run, the playbook executes against the empty */etc/ansible/hosts* inventory file and, therefore, performs no action.

Begin by creating a *~/playbooks/* directory for this chapter's example playbooks. Within this directory, create an inventory file named *prod.inv*. This file organizes the "production" Junos devices in the example network into several groups based on both geography and the device's role in the network. The *prod.inv* file has the following content:

```
h0

[junos-core-site1] ❶
core1.site1
core2.site1

[junos-edge-site1]
edge[1:3].site1 ❷

[junos-core-site2]
core1.site2

[junos-edge-site2] ❸

[junos-site1:children] ❹
junos-core-site1
junos-edge-site1

[junos-site2:children]
junos-core-site2
junos-edge-site2

[junos-core:children] ❺
junos-core-site1
junos-core-site2

[junos-edge:children]
junos-edge-site1
junos-edge-site2

[junos-all:children] ❻
junos-site1
junos-site2
```

❶ A section in the INI file specifies a group. This line specifies a group named `junos-core-site1`. This group is used to identify Junos core routers in `site1`. The `junos-core-site1` group consists of two devices (or hosts), `core1.site1` and `core2.site1`.

❷ A range specifies multiple hosts on a single line using the `[`*x*`:`*y*`]` syntax. The line `edge[1:3].site1` is equivalent to explicitly listing the hosts `edge1.site1`, `edge2.site1`, and `edge3.site1`. Ranges are inclusive. Alphabetic ranges can also be specified.

❸ Specifying a group with no members is acceptable.

❹ Groups can be nested. The group `junos-site1` consists of two member groups: `junos-core-site1` and `junos-edge-site1`. The `[`*group-name*`:children]` syntax indicates each member is another group rather than a host. A group cannot list a nonexistent group as a member. However, as we've seen, a group can have no members.

❺ Hosts can be members of multiple groups. For example, the host `core1.site1` is a member of the groups `junos-core-site1`, `junos-site1`, `junos-core`, and `junos-all`.

❻ Every host listed in the inventory file is also a member of the implicit group `all`. At first glance, this seems to make the `junos-all` group redundant. However, the separate `junos-all` group allows non-Junos hosts to be added to an inventory file in the future while still allowing Junos-specific playbooks to be executed against all Junos devices. An inventory file can also begin with a list of hosts that are not part of a group. These hosts are members of the implicit `all` group, and they are also members of the implicit `ungrouped` group.[7] The `h0` host on the first line of the inventory file represents the Ansible control machine itself, and is an example of a host that is only a member of the implicit `all` and `ungrouped` groups.

The Ansible control machine must resolve hostnames from the inventory file to corresponding IP addresses. DNS or an */etc/hosts* file can be used for this purpose. It is best practice to omit the domain name from the hostnames in the inventory file. For example, the fully qualified domain name of a device is `core1.site1.example.com`, but only `core1.site1` is used in the inventory file.

In general, groups are the targets of playbooks. If you need to run an automation task against a set of devices, then you should probably define a group that consists of the target devices. The *prod.inv* example inventory file allows devices to be targeted based on their physical location or their logical role in the network (or a combination of both). The `junos-all` group allows a playbook to be run against all Junos devices. The `junos-site1` and `junos-site2` groups allow a playbook to target all Junos devices in a particular physical location, and the `junos-core` and `junos-edge` groups allow a playbook to be run against all Junos devices that have a particular role in the network. Finally, the `junos-core-site1`, `junos-core-site2`, `junos-edge-site1`, and `junos-edge-site2` groups allow a playbook to target Junos devices based on both their physical location and their logical role in the network.

It's also common to execute an Ansible playbook against all Junos devices of a certain platform or model. Model- and platform-based groups could be created in the inven-

7 Yes, the "`ungrouped` group" is an oxymoron.

tory file, but it's easier to create such groups dynamically. "Gathering Junos Facts and Dynamic Groups" on page 573 provides an example of creating these groups dynamically, and "Initial Configuration" on page 587 uses these dynamic groups to control the content of an initial configuration file.

In addition to the *prod.inv* file, a corresponding *lab.inv* file organizes a small "lab" network into a similar set of groups:

```
h0

[junos-core-lab]
core1.lab

[junos-edge-lab]
edge[1:3].lab

[junos-lab:children]
junos-core-lab
junos-edge-lab

[junos-core:children]
junos-core-lab

[junos-edge:children]
junos-edge-lab

[junos-all:children]
junos-lab
```

Separating the production and lab networks into two different inventory files allows playbooks to be developed and tested against the lab network. Once the playbook has been tested, it can then be executed against the production network. Details for executing a playbook with a specific inventory file are provided in "Execution" on page 531.

In addition to static inventory files, Ansible provides other methods of dynamically generating inventory for Ansible managed hosts. There is even an API for developing your own inventory plugin. Ansible for Junos modules work with any inventory source; however, detailed coverage of dynamic inventory sources is outside the scope of the book. Consult the Ansible documentation for additional information on inventory plugins.

Playbooks and Plays

An Ansible playbook defines a set of automation steps to be performed. A playbook can be organized into plays, tasks, and handlers. This playbook organization is illustrated in Figure 10-3.

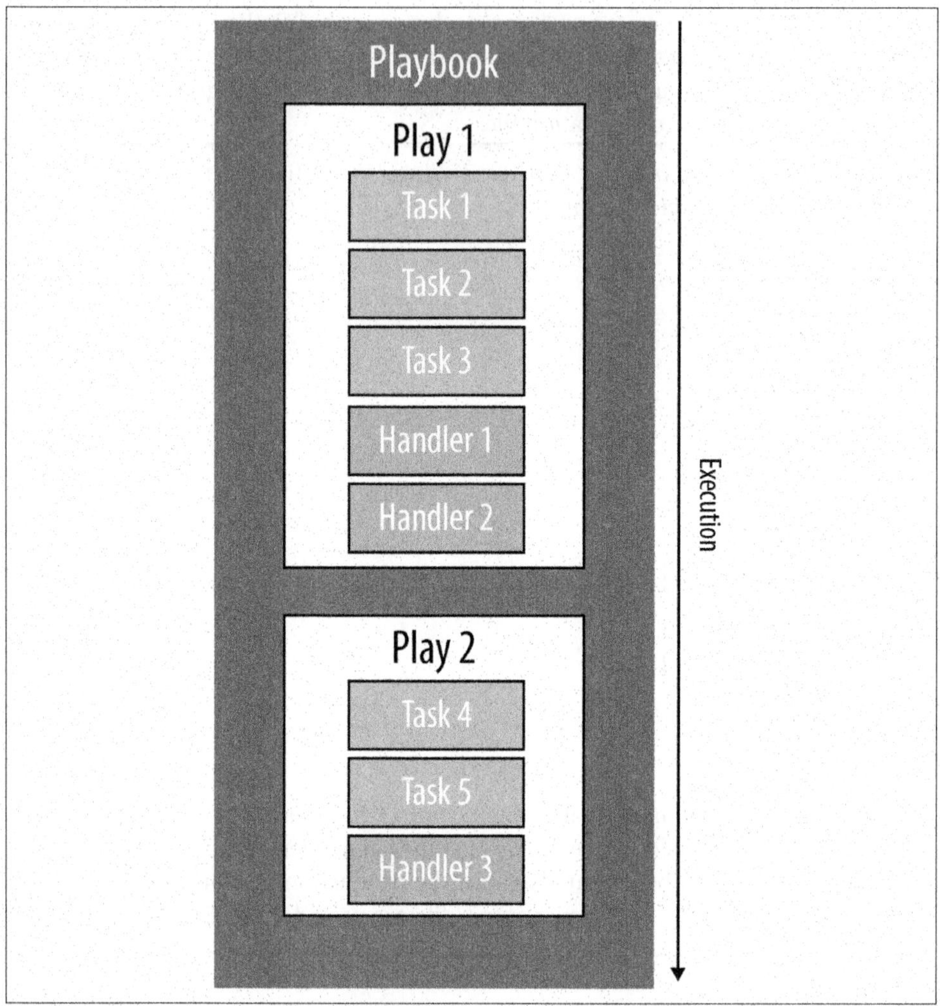

Figure 10-3. Ansible playbook organization

Each playbook contains one or more plays. In turn, a play executes one or more tasks. Once all tasks have run, a play may execute zero or more handlers. We discuss the details of tasks (and modules) in "Tasks and Modules" on page 528, and cover the details of handlers in "Handlers" on page 529.

Everything in a playbook is sequentially ordered with strict dependencies. The plays, tasks, and handlers are executed in the order they appear in a playbook. Each task executes on all hosts in parallel (up to the maximum specified by the `forks` configuration setting). Once the task finishes executing on all hosts, the next task begins. This process continues until all tasks (and handlers) in the playbook have been executed.

Playbooks are based on the YAML file format and are designed to be human readable. The playbook syntax is designed to represent a "configuration" or a "process" rather than being a full-blown scripting language. The general format of a playbook is shown in Example 10-1. This example demonstrates the playbook organization illustrated in Figure 10-3, but it doesn't actually do anything productive. It simply executes the command `/bin/true` (which always succeeds, but performs no action) on the Ansible control host.

Example 10-1. An example Ansible playbook file (~/playbooks/example.pb.yaml)

```
---
- name: Play 1
  hosts: junos-core-site1
  connection: local
  gather_facts: no
  tasks:
    - name: Task 1
      command: /bin/true
      notify:
        - Handler 2
        - Handler 1
    - name: Task 2
      command: /bin/true
    - name: Task 3
      command: /bin/true
      notify: Handler 2
  handlers:
    - name: Handler 1
      command: /bin/true
    - name: Handler 2
      command: /bin/true

- name: Play 2
  hosts: junos-core-site1
  connection: local
  gather_facts: no
  tasks:
    - name: Task 4
      command: /bin/true
    - name: Task 5
      command: /bin/true
  handlers:
    - name: Handler 3
      command: /bin/true
```

Like all YAML documents, a playbook file begins with three hyphens (`---`) on the first line. At the top level of the YAML hierarchy, a playbook is a list of plays. The list members are identified by the dash (`-`) in the first column of the YAML file. In the example, `Play 1` is the first member of the YAML list, and `Play 2` is the second member of the list.

A YAML associative array (dictionary) specifies the components that make up an Ansible play. Remember, a YAML associative array is specified as a set of colon-separated key/value pairs. Each key/value pair appears on a separate line with common indentation. Example 10-1 demonstrates some of the keys that may be specified for a play. These keys include:

`name`
: A user-defined friendly description of the play. This key is optional but highly recommended. The name of the play is included in the output when the play is executed and is helpful when debugging a playbook.

`hosts`
: The host or group that is the target of the play. This value defines the default (and largest) set of hosts that are targeted by the play. When the playbook is executed, the target hosts may be further limited to only a subset of this `hosts` value. In the example, the `hosts` key is set to the group `junos-core-site1`, which expands to the devices `core1.site1` and `core2.site1`.

`connection`
: The method used to connect to the target hosts. The default connection value is `smart`. The value `smart` makes an SSH connection to the target host, as detailed in "Typical Communication" on page 510. It first attempts to use OpenSSH to establish this SSH session. If the version of OpenSSH installed on the control host does not support the `ControlPersist` feature, then `smart` resorts to using the Python Paramiko SSH library to establish the SSH session. As explained in "Communicating with Junos Managed Nodes" on page 513, the Ansible for Junos modules *do not support* the default SSH communication method. When managing a Junos device, you *must* set `connection` to `local` as shown in Example 10-1. The `local` setting runs all tasks and handlers in the play locally on the Ansible control host.

If you are using Ansible primarily to manage Junos devices, you may choose to set `transport = local` in the `[defaults]` section of your Ansible configuration file. This configuration file setting changes the default connection method to `local` (the default method can still be overridden by specifying `connection: smart` in an individual play). The example playbooks in "Example Playbooks" on page 567 demonstrate a third, recommended way to configure Junos devices to use a `local` connection. In "Inventory, Variables, and Ansible Configuration Settings" on page 567, a group variable of `ansible_connection: local` is set for the `junos-all` group. This method ensures all Junos devices default to a `local` connection while non-Junos devices continue to default to a `smart` connection.

`gather_facts`
: Whether or not to gather host-specific "fact" variables from the play's target hosts. By default, Ansible implicitly executes the core `setup` module to discover information about a system and assigns that information to variables. Normally, tasks and handlers can use these variable to determine host-specific actions. When managing Junos devices, however, the `setup` module is executed locally on the Ansible control host. This means facts are gathered about the control host rather than the target Junos device. Because information about the control host is seldom relevant to managing the target Junos device, this fact-gathering step is not needed. Specifying `gather_facts: no`, as shown in Example 10-1, avoids fact gathering and speeds the execution of the play.

The Ansible for Junos modules provide an equivalent `junos_get_facts` module that gathers information about the target Junos device. "junos_get_facts" on page 557 provides details on this module. "Example Playbooks" on page 567 demonstrates using these facts to control the behavior of subsequent plays.

If you are using Ansible primarily to manage Junos devices, you may choose to set `gathering = explicit` in the `[defaults]` section of your Ansible configuration file. This configuration file setting disables the default fact gathering (fact gathering can still be explicitly enabled by specifying `gather_facts: yes` in an individual play).

`tasks`
: A list of the tasks executed by the play. The content of this list is covered in the next section.

`handlers`
: A list of the handlers that may be executed by the play. The content of this list is covered in "Handlers" on page 529.

These are only a subset of the keys that may be specified for a play, but they cover the most common settings used when managing Junos devices. Subsequent sections of this chapter introduce additional settings specific to play execution, variables, and roles. You may also consult the Ansible documentation (*http://docs.ansible.com*) for less frequently used settings.

Tasks and Modules

As explained in the preceding section, a play specifies a list of tasks to be executed on a set of target hosts. The task list is defined in the play's `tasks` key, and each task in the list is executed in order, one at a time, against the target hosts specified by the play's `hosts` key.

Each task invokes a single module with a specific set of parameters (or arguments.) The Example 10-1 demonstrates several simple tasks that all invoke Ansible's core `command` module with a parameter of `/bin/true`. Each module defines its own set of mandatory and optional parameters which control the module's execution. The `command` module has one mandatory argument: the name of the command to be executed.[8] Like plays, tasks are specified using a YAML associative array. The simplest format of a task is:

```
- name: A friendly name for the task
  module_name: arg1=value1 arg2=value2
```

This key is simply a user-defined description of the task. The `name` key is optional, but highly recommended. The task's name is printed in the output when the playbook is executed, and can aid in debugging the playbook.

The *`module_name`* key is the name of the module to invoke. In Example 10-1, all of the tasks invoke the `command` module. The value of the *`module_name`* key is a string. The string specifies the module's arguments as a set of space-separated key/value pairs.[9] Alternatively, the module's arguments may be specified as an associative array, rather than a string. A simple task specified in this format is:

---

8 The `command` module also accepts several optional parameters. For details, reference the `command` module documentation (*http://docs.ansible.com/ansible/command_module.html*).

9 At first glance, the value of the `command` key in each of the Example 10-1 tasks does not appear to be a set of "space-separated key/value pairs." The `command` module does support optional named arguments, but it requires a single unnamed argument. This unnamed argument specifies the command to invoke (`/bin/true` in the example.)

```
- name: A friendly name for the task
  module_name:
    arg1: value1
    arg2: value2
```

Specifying the arguments as an associative array generally results in easier-to-read playbooks. This method of specifying arguments is recommended, and it's the format used throughout the rest of this chapter. As an example, a simple task that calls the `junos_get_facts` module is written as:

```
- name: Gather Facts from a Junos Device
  junos_get_facts:
    host: "{{ inventory_hostname }}"
    user: user
    passwd: user123
```

Tasks do support other keys in addition to the `name` and *`module_name`* keys introduced in this section. Some of those keys are introduced in subsequent sections, and you may refer to the complete Ansible documentation for further details.

Similar to Puppet modules, Ansible modules strive to be idempotent. However, not every Ansible module is idempotent. Some modules perform specific actions, rather than describing the state of a resource. One example is the `junos_shutdown` module, which shuts down or reboots a Junos device. When using these types of modules, you must carefully construct and execute your plays to avoid problems. Handlers and conditionals are two tools that control the execution of tasks. We cover handlers in the next section, and discuss conditionals in "Conditionals" on page 552.

Handlers

Handlers are simply a special kind of task. Like a regular task, a handler executes an Ansible module with a set of arguments. Any module that can be executed from a task can also be executed from a handler. Handlers are special because of how they are executed, not because of their content.

Handlers are triggered by tasks, and execute after all of the tasks in the play's `tasks` section have executed. A task triggers a handler by specifying the `notify` key. This syntax is demonstrated by `Task 1` and `Task 3` in Example 10-1.

The value of the task's `notify` key must exactly match the value of a handler's `name` key. The value may be the name of a single handler, as shown in `Task 3` in Example 10-1, or it may be a list of handler names, as shown in `Task 1`.

Handlers are executed in the order they appear in the play's `handlers` list. They are *not* executed in the order they are notified. A handler is only executed if it is notified by at least one task. In addition, if multiple tasks notify the same handler, the handler is still only executed once (per target host).

Refer back to Example 10-1. The output from executing this example playbook is:

```
PLAY [Play 1] ******************************************************************

TASK: [Task 1] *****************************************************************
changed: [core2.site1]
changed: [core1.site1]

TASK: [Task 2] *****************************************************************
changed: [core1.site1]
changed: [core2.site1]

TASK: [Task 3] *****************************************************************
changed: [core2.site1]
changed: [core1.site1]

NOTIFIED: [Handler 1] **********************************************************
changed: [core1.site1]
changed: [core2.site1]

NOTIFIED: [Handler 2] **********************************************************
changed: [core2.site1]
changed: [core1.site1]

PLAY [Play 2] ******************************************************************

TASK: [Task 4] *****************************************************************
changed: [core2.site1]
changed: [core1.site1]

TASK: [Task 5] *****************************************************************
changed: [core1.site1]
changed: [core2.site1]

PLAY RECAP *********************************************************************
core1.site1                : ok=7    changed=7    unreachable=0    failed=0
core2.site1                : ok=7    changed=7    unreachable=0    failed=0
```

This output demonstrates several important points about handlers:

- All of the tasks and handlers from `Play 1` are executed before any of the tasks or handlers from `Play 2` are executed.
- Each task and handler is executed on all of the target hosts before execution of the next task or handler begins.
- Plays are executed in the order they appear in the playbook.
- Tasks are executed in the order they appear within the play.
- Handlers are executed in the order they appear within the play. Specifically, `Handler 1` is executed before `Handler 2`, even though `Task 1` notifies `Handler 2` before `Handler 1`.

- Handlers are executed only once. Both `Task 1` and `Task 3` notify `Handler 2`. However, `Handler 2` is still only executed once.
- Handlers are only executed if they are notified by at least one task. `Handler 3` is not executed because none of the tasks in `Play 2` notify it.

There is one more important handler behavior that should be mentioned. A task only notifies the handlers in its `notify` key when the module returns the `changed` attribute. The next section discusses this concept in more detail.

Handlers are a useful tool when creating idempotent plays. For example, a play may create a Junos configuration file from a Jinja2 template. By using a handler to load and commit the configuration, the play can ensure the newly generated configuration file is only installed and committed on the Junos device when the configuration file has actually changed.

Execution

Now that we've seen the organization and components of a playbook, let's look at how to execute an Ansible automation job. Ansible provides two methods for executing automation jobs: a simple ad hoc method and a more sophisticated playbook method.

The simple ad hoc method is invoked with the command `ansible` and executes a single Ansible task. The general format of the `ansible` command is:

```
ansible target_host -m module_name
```

The *`target_host`* must be a host or group listed in the inventory file. Here's a simple example that executes the `debug` module on `localhost` (the local Ansible control machine):

```
user@h0$ ansible localhost -m debug
localhost | success >> {
    "msg": "Hello world!"
}
```

Make sure `localhost` is listed in */etc/ansible/hosts* (the default inventory file) before executing the preceding example.

It's also possible to specify a nondefault inventory file using the `-i` command-line argument. In addition, module arguments can be passed using the `-a` command-line argument. The following output invokes the `debug` module to print the group memberships of each host in the `junos-core` group:

```
user@h0$ ansible junos-core -i ~/playbooks/prod.inv -m debug -a "var=group_names"
core1.site1 | success >> {
    "var": {
        "group_names": [
            "junos-all",
            "junos-core",
            "junos-core-site1",
            "junos-site1"
        ]
    }
}

core2.site1 | success >> {
    "var": {
        "group_names": [
            "junos-all",
            "junos-core",
            "junos-core-site1",
            "junos-site1"
        ]
    }
}

core1.site2 | success >> {
    "var": {
        "group_names": [
            "junos-all",
            "junos-core",
            "junos-core-site2",
            "junos-site2"
        ]
    }
}
```

In the preceding output, the `-i` command-line argument reads the inventory from the nondefault *~/playbooks/prod.inv* inventory file, and the `-a` argument passes the string `var=group_names` as an argument to the `debug` module. This argument string causes the `debug` module to print the value of the `group_names` variable rather than its default `"Hello world!"` message.

While this ad hoc task execution is an easy way to print group membership, it's not the best way to execute an Ansible for Junos module. As an example, executing the `junos_get_facts` module against the `core1.site1` router requires specifying several arguments to the `ansible` command:

```
user@h0$ ansible core1.site1 -i ~/playbooks/prod.inv -c local \
> -M /etc/ansible/roles/Juniper.junos/library -m junos_get_facts \
> -a "host=core1.site1 user=user passwd=user123"
core1.site1 | success >> {
    "changed": false,
    "facts": {
        "HOME": "/var/home/user",
        "RE0": {
            "last_reboot_reason": "Router rebooted after a normal shutdown.",
            "mastership_state": "master",
            "model": "RE-VMX",
            "status": "OK",
            "up_time": "27 days, 33 minutes, 28 seconds"
        },
        ... output trimmed ...
    }
}
```

These extra arguments are required to specify the `local` connection method, the path to the Ansible for Junos modules, and the module arguments required to connect to the Junos device, respectively. When executing any Ansible for Junos module, it's usually easier to create a simple playbook file and invoke the playbook using the `ansible-playbook` command. The following example demonstrates the execution of the `junos_get_facts` module against the `core1.site1` router using a simple playbook:

```
user@h0$ cat facts.pb.yaml
---
- name: Get facts from core1.site1 Junos router
  hosts: core1.site1
  connection: local
  gather_facts: no
  roles:
    - Juniper.junos
  tasks:
    - name: Get Junos Facts
      junos_get_facts:
        host: "{{ inventory_hostname }}"
        user: user
        passwd: user123
user@h0$ ansible-playbook -i prod.inv facts.pb.yaml

PLAY [Get facts from core1.site1 Junos router] ********************************

TASK: [Get Junos Facts] *******************************************************
ok: [core1.site1]

PLAY RECAP ********************************************************************
core1.site1                : ok=1    changed=0    unreachable=0    failed=0
```

The `ansible-playbook` command requires an argument specifying the playbook name. In the previous example, the `facts.pb.yaml` playbook is executed. Just like the `ansible` command, `ansible-playbook` uses the `-i` option to specify a nondefault inventory file. The additional information (previously specified with command-line arguments to `ansible`) is now included in the *facts.pb.yaml* playbook file.

Executing the command `ansible-playbook --help` gives a summary of the available command-line arguments. The `-l` (or `--limit`) option is useful to limit the hosts targeted by a play to only a subset of the hosts specified by the play's `hosts` key. The `--list-hosts` option is also useful. This option prints a list of the hosts targeted by each play in the playbook, but does not actually execute the playbook.

Now that we've demonstrated how to execute a playbook, let's look at the results of executing a playbook. When Ansible executes a playbook, a summary of each play, task, and handler is included in the output. The output also indicates the results of executing each task on each target host.

There are three possible return values for a task: `ok`, `unreachable`, and `failed`. The `ok` status means the task executed successfully, while the `failed` status indicates the task failed due to an error. The `unreachable` status indicates Ansible was unable to connect to the target host.

Because the Ansible for Junos modules use the `local` connection method, it is very uncommon for these modules to return an `unreachable` status. Instead, a `failed` status is returned when the Ansible for Junos module is unable to establish a NETCONF session to the target Junos device.

If a task executes successfully (the return status is `ok`), it may also return the `changed` attribute. Modules use the `changed` attribute to implement idempotency. A `changed` attribute value of `true` indicates the module made a change to the state of the target host, while a `changed` attribute value of `false` (or missing) indicates the module did not change the state of the target host. As mentioned in "Handlers" on page 529, handlers are only notified if the task sets the `changed` attribute in its return value.

It's also important to understand how the return status of each task affects a playbook's execution. If a task (including a handler) fails (return status of `unreachable` or `failed`) on a target host, then no further tasks are executed on the target host. While this behavior is usually reasonable, it is sometimes desirable to ignore a task failure and continue executing subsequent tasks on the target host. This alternate behavior is accomplished by adding the `ignore_errors: True` key to the task.

A failed task can also leave the target host in an unexpected state. If a task notifies a handler, but then a subsequent task fails, the handler is never executed. If a play depends on the handler's execution, even when tasks have failed, add the `force_handlers: True` key to the play or globally set `force_handlers = True` in the Ansible configuration file.

The following example displays the output from executing a playbook similar[10] to Example 10-1. It illustrates the return statuses of several tasks and how they affect the play's execution:

```
user@h0$ ansible-playbook -i prod.inv example-10-1-modified.pb.yaml

PLAY [Play 1] *****************************************************************

TASK: [Task 1] ****************************************************************
changed: [core2.site1]
changed: [core1.site1]

TASK: [Task 2] ****************************************************************
changed: [core2.site1]
changed: [core1.site1]

TASK: [Task 3] ****************************************************************
changed: [core1.site1]
changed: [core2.site1]

NOTIFIED: [Handler 1] *********************************************************
changed: [core1.site1]
failed: [core2.site1] => ... output trimmed ...

NOTIFIED: [Handler 2] *********************************************************
changed: [core1.site1]

PLAY [Play 2] *****************************************************************

TASK: [Task 4] ****************************************************************
ok: [core1.site1]

TASK: [Task 5] ****************************************************************
changed: [core1.site1]

PLAY RECAP ********************************************************************
           to retry, use: --limit @/home/user/example.pb.yaml.retry

core1.site1                : ok=7    changed=6    unreachable=0     failed=0
core2.site1                : ok=3    changed=3    unreachable=0     failed=1
```

10 `Handler 1` was modified to demonstrate a failure for the `core2.site1` device and `Task 4` was modified to not set the changed attribute.

The PLAY RECAP section at the end of the output summarizes the task (including handlers) statuses for each target host. Seven tasks were executed against the core1.site1 device, and all of those tasks succeeded (return status of ok). Of those seven tasks, all but one set the changed attribute. The status of each task is detailed in each TASK section of the output. Notice the output of Task 4 for the core1.site1 target device shows a state of ok rather than changed.

The output for Handler 1 shows a state of failed for the core2.site1 target device. This failure is also reported in the PLAY RECAP section. After the failure of Handler 1, no further tasks or handlers are executed on the core2.site1 target device. This fact is apparent both in the play's output and in the core2.site1 line of the PLAY RECAP section, which shows three tasks returned ok (all three of those tasks also set the changed attribute) and one task returned failed.

By default, Ansible creates a *.retry* file when a playbook fails for one or more target hosts. This file contains a list of the target hosts for which it failed. A playbook can quickly be executed against only these previously failed hosts by specifying the `--limit @path_to_retry_file` argument to the ansible-playbook command. The first line of the PLAY RECAP section includes a reminder of this syntax.

By default, Ansible creates *.retry* files directly in the user's home directory. This behavior tends to litter your home directory with lots of files. We recommend avoiding this clutter by setting the retry_files_save_path configuration variable to a dedicated directory. The following output appends the retry_files_save_path setting to the previous content of our Ansible configuration file (*/etc/ansible/ansible.cfg*):

```
[defaults]
log_path=~/.ansible/log/ansible.log
forks=50
retry_files_save_path = ~/.ansible/retry
```

Now, *.retry* files will be saved to *~/.ansible/retry/<playbook_name>.retry*.

There are two additional command-line arguments to ansible-playbook that are helpful when debugging a playbook. The first option, --syntax-check, simply checks the syntax of a playbook without actually executing the playbook. The second option, --step, allows you to step through the execution of a playbook one task at a time:

```
user@h0$ ansible-playbook -i prod.inv --step example-10-1-modified.pb.yaml

PLAY [Play 1] ********************************************************************
Perform task: Task 1 (y/n/c): y

Perform task: Task 1 (y/n/c):  *************************************************
```

```
changed: [core1.site1]
changed: [core2.site1]
Perform task: Task 2 (y/n/c):
... output trimmed ...
```

Variables

The real power of Ansible begins to shine through when tasks and handlers use variables. Variables allow tasks and handlers to be written in a generic way yet still produce host-specific content or perform host-specific behavior.

Before we look at how variables are assigned, let's begin with how variables are referenced in Ansible playbooks. We've already seen an example of referencing an Ansible variable in the *facts.pb.yaml* file in the previous section. This simple playbook is repeated here for your convenience:

```
---
- name: Get facts from core1.site1 Junos router
  hosts: core1.site1
  connection: local
  gather_facts: no
  roles:
    - Juniper.junos
  tasks:
    - name: Get Junos Facts
      junos_get_facts:
        host: "{{ inventory_hostname }}"
        user: user
        passwd: user123
```

This playbook sets the value of the `host` argument to the `junos_get_facts` module to the value of the variable `inventory_hostname`. The `{{ inventory_hostname }}` syntax may look familiar from "Configuration Templates" on page 220. In fact, it is the same syntax. Just like PyEZ uses Jinja2 templates for configuration files, Ansible uses Jinja2 syntax in its playbook files. Anywhere `{{ variable_name }}` appears within a playbook, the value of *`variable_name`* is substituted.

Notice the double quotes around `{{ inventory_hostname }}` in the preceding output. Surrounding a Jinja2 expression with double quotes prevents YAML from interpreting the expression as a YAML associative array. The double quotes are only *required* when a YAML string value starts with a `{`. However, if a playbook value includes a Jinja2 expression, we strongly recommend always surrounding the value with double quotes.

Because Ansible variable references are really just Jinja2 expressions, you can also use Jinja2 filters (*http://jinja.pocoo.org/docs/dev/templates/#builtin-filters*) within the expression. The `default()` filter is demonstrated in this modified *facts2.pb.yaml* playbook:

```
---
- name: Get facts from core1.site1 Junos router
  hosts: core1.site1
  connection: local
  gather_facts: no
  roles:
    - Juniper.junos
  tasks:
    - name: Get Junos Facts
      junos_get_facts:
        host: "{{ inventory_hostname }}"
        user: "{{ netconf_user | default('root') }}"
        passwd: user123
```

This modified playbook sets the module's `user` argument to the value of the variable `netconf_user`. If `netconf_user` is undefined, the module's `user` argument is set to the value `root`.

Ansible variables are not limited to simple scalar values. They may also contain dictionaries or lists. They can also be arbitrarily nested to create more complex data structures. Dictionaries may be accessed using a bracket notation:

```
{{ var_name["key1"]["key2"] }}
```

Alternatively, dictionaries may be accessed using a dot notation (as long as *`key1`* and *`key2`* don't collide with any Python dictionary attributes or methods):

```
{{ var_name.key1.key2 }}
```

As you might expect, lists can be accessed using a zero-based integer index with the notation:

```
{{ var_name[index] }}
```

Now that we've seen how to access the value of a variable in an Ansible playbook, let's look at how variables are assigned. Ansible provides several different ways to assign values to variables. While these different options offer power and flexibility, they also introduce some complexity.

First, some variables are built into Ansible. Ansible automatically assigns values for these "magic" variables. We've already seen one of these built-in variables, `inventory_hostname`, in previous examples. Here's a list of some of Ansible's most useful built-in variables:

`inventory_hostname`
: The name (from the inventory file) of the current target host. This built-in variable is frequently used as the mandatory host argument to the Ansible for Junos modules.

`group_names`
: A list of all groups of which the current target host is a member.

`groups`
: A list of all groups in the current inventory file. The value of each group in the `groups` list is a list of all hosts that are a member of the group.

`inventory_file`
: The filename of the current inventory file.

`inventory_dir`
: The pathname of the directory containing the current inventory file.

`hostvars`
: A dictionary that allows access to another host's variables. The *`var_name`* variable on the *`host_name`* host is accessed using the format `hostvars['`*`host_name`*`']['`*`var_name`*`']`.

Next, *inventory variables* describe a class of variables that have host-specific or group-specific values. Inventory variables can be further divided into host variables and group variables.

Ansible provides multiple methods for assigning values to inventory variables. One method is to assign the variable in the inventory file itself by defining a `[`*`host_or_group_name`*`:vars]` section. For example, the `mgmt_ip` host variable for the `core1.site1` and `core2.site1` hosts is set using this syntax:

```
[junos-core-site1]
core1.site1
core2.site1

[core1.site1:vars]
mgmt_ip=10.102.167.104

[core2.site1:vars]
mgmt_ip=10.102.163.92
```

Likewise, this syntax sets the `netconf_user` group variable for the `junos-all` group:

```
[junos-all:children]
junos-site1
junos-site2

[junos-all:vars]
netconf_user=user
```

While Ansible supports setting variables directly in the inventory file, the preferred method for setting host and group variables is to create separate files specifically for storing host and group variables. This is done by creating subdirectories with the special names *host_vars* and *group_vars* in the directory that contains the inventory file. The files within these directories are named after the specific host or group. Each file then contains a YAML document that assigns variables and values.

Here's an example which uses the preferred method to set the same `mgmt_ip` host variable and `netconf_user` group variable as the previous example:

```
user@h0$ cat prod.inv
h0

[junos-core-site1]
core1.site1
core2.site1

... output trimmed ...

[junos-all:children]
junos-site1
junos-site2
user@h0$ cat host_vars/core1.site1
---
mgmt_ip: 10.102.167.104
user@h0$ cat host_vars/core2.site1
---
mgmt_ip: 10.102.163.92
user@h0$ cat group_vars/junos-all
---
netconf_user: user
user@h0$
```

The preceding output only showed a single host variable and a single group variable, but what happens when variables are defined for more than one group? The answer is a host inherits group variables from *all* groups of which it is a member. Assume the following group variable is added to the preceding example:

```
user@h0$ cat group_vars/junos-site1
---
dns_resolvers:
  - 8.8.8.8
  - 8.8.4.4
```

Because `core1.site1` is a member of both the `junos-all` and `junos-site1` groups, it inherits both the `netconf_user` and `dns_resolvers`[11] group variables, as shown in this simple playbook output (the playbook simply contains tasks to print each variable using the `debug` module):

```
user@h0$ ansible-playbook -i prod.inv vars.pb.yaml
```

11 The `dns_resolvers` variable is an example of a variable with a list value.

```
PLAY [Get facts from core1.site1 Junos router] ********************************

TASK: [Print NETCONF User] ****************************************************
ok: [core1.site1] => {
    "var": {
        "netconf_user": "user"
    }
}

TASK: [Print DNS Resolvers] ***************************************************
ok: [core1.site1] => {
    "var": {
        "dns_resolvers": [
            "8.8.8.8",
            "8.8.4.4"
        ]
    }
}

PLAY RECAP ********************************************************************
core1.site1                : ok=2    changed=0    unreachable=0    failed=0
```

In addition to inventory variables, Ansible supports setting variables within a play. Variables are set within a play by adding the `vars` key to the play, as shown in this example playbook:

```
---
- name: Get facts from core1.site1 Junos router
  hosts: core1.site1
  connection: local
  gather_facts: no
  roles:
    - Juniper.junos
  vars:
    default_user: root
    default_port: 830
  tasks:
    - name: Get Junos Facts
      junos_get_facts:
        host: "{{ inventory_hostname }}"
        user: "{{ netconf_user | default(default_user) }}"
        port: "{{ default_port }}"
        passwd: user123
```

The value of the `vars` key is an associative array keyed with each variable's name. In the preceding output, two variables are defined: `default_user` and `default_port`. The `default_user` variable is referenced within a `default()` filter in the task's `user` argument. The `default_port` variable is referenced in the task's `port` argument.

It's best to use play variables to hold "constant" or "default" values used within the play. This practice makes it easier to share and reuse plays. However, it is possible to use play variables and still keep sensitive or site-specific variables separate from the playbook itself. This separation is accomplished by using the `vars_files` key in the play definition, as shown in this example:

```
user@h0$ cat facts3.pb.yaml
---
- name: Get facts from core1.site1 Junos router
  hosts: core1.site1
  connection: local
  gather_facts: no
  roles:
    - Juniper.junos
  vars:
    default_port: 830
    default_user: user
  vars_files:
    - private_vars.yaml
  tasks:
    - name: Get Junos Facts
      junos_get_facts:
        host: "{{ inventory_hostname }}"
        user: "{{ netconf_user | default(default_user) }}"
        port: "{{ default_port }}"
        passwd: "{{ netconf_password | default(default_password) }}"
user@h0$ cat private_vars.yaml
---
default_password: user123
user@h0$
```

Another useful tool is the `vars_prompt` key, which allows a play to prompt the user for a variable's value. This example prompts the user for both the `netconf_user` and `netconf_password` variables:

```
user@h0$ cat facts4.pb.yaml
---
- name: Get facts from core1.site1 Junos router
  hosts: core1.site1
  connection: local
  gather_facts: no
  roles:
    - Juniper.junos
  vars_prompt:
    - name: netconf_user
      prompt: Username
      private: no
    - name: netconf_password
      prompt: Password
      private: yes
  vars:
    default_port: 830
  tasks:
    - name: Get Junos Facts
```

```
        junos_get_facts:
          host: "{{ inventory_hostname }}"
          user: "{{ netconf_user }}"
          port: "{{ default_port }}"
          passwd: "{{ netconf_password }}"
user@h0$ ansible-playbook -i prod.inv facts4.pb.yaml
Username: user
Password:

PLAY [Get facts from core1.site1 Junos router] ********************************

TASK: [Get Junos Facts] *******************************************************
ok: [core1.site1]

PLAY RECAP ********************************************************************
core1.site1                : ok=1    changed=0    unreachable=0    failed=0

user@h0$
```

As shown in the preceding output, the `vars_prompt` key takes a list of dictionaries. Each dictionary includes the `name`, `prompt`, and `private` keys. The `name` key defines the name of the variable being set. The `prompt` key defines the prompt string provided to the user, and the `private` key defines whether or not the user's input should be echoed to the screen.

Ansible also allows the result of a task to be assigned to a variable. This assignment is accomplished by adding the key `register:` *`var_name`* to the task's dictionary, as shown in this updated example:

```
user@h0$ cat facts5.pb.yaml
---
- name: Get facts from core1.site1 Junos router
  hosts: core1.site1
  connection: local
  gather_facts: no
  roles:
    - Juniper.junos
  vars_prompt:
    - name: netconf_user
      prompt: Username
      private: no
    - name: netconf_password
      prompt: Password
      private: yes
  vars:
    default_port: 830
  tasks:
    - name: Get Junos Facts
      junos_get_facts:
        host: "{{ inventory_hostname }}"
        user: "{{ netconf_user }}"
```

```
        port: "{{ default_port }}"
        passwd: "{{ netconf_password }}"
      register: junos_facts_result
    - name: Print Junos Facts Result
      debug:
        var: junos_facts_result
    - name: Print Junos HOME Dir
      debug:
        var: junos_facts_result.facts.HOME
user@h0$ ansible-playbook -i prod.inv facts5.pb.yaml
Username: user
Password:

PLAY [Get facts from core1.site1 Junos router] ********************************

TASK: [Get Junos Facts] *******************************************************
ok: [core1.site1]

TASK: [Print Junos Facts Result] **********************************************
ok: [core1.site1] => {
    "var": {
        "junos_facts_result": {
            "changed": false,
            "facts": {
                "HOME": "/var/home/user",
                "RE0": {
                    "last_reboot_reason": "Router rebooted after a normal sh...",
                    "mastership_state": "master",
                    "model": "RE-VMX",
                    "status": "OK",
                    "up_time": "2 days, 2 hours, 21 minutes, 6 seconds"
                },
                ... output trimmed ...
            },
            "invocation": {
                "module_args": "",
                "module_complex_args": {
                    "host": "core1.site1",
                    "passwd": "user123",
                    "port": "830",
                    "user": "user"
                },
                "module_name": "junos_get_facts"
            }
        }
    }
}

TASK: [Print Junos HOME Dir] **************************************************
ok: [core1.site1] => {
    "var": {
        "junos_facts_result.facts.HOME": "/var/home/user"
```

```
    }
}

PLAY RECAP ********************************************************************
core1.site1                : ok=3    changed=0    unreachable=0    failed=0

user@h0$
```

In the preceding output, the key `register: junos_facts_result` is added to the `Get Junos Facts` task. This key creates the variable `junos_facts_result` and assigns it the value returned by the `junos_get_facts` module. This variable may be accessed by any subsequent tasks in the playbook.

In the preceding example, a new `Print Junos Facts Result` task is added which uses the `debug` module to print the value of the `junos_facts_result` variable. The output shows the `junos_get_facts` module returns the information gathered from the Junos device within the `facts` dictionary key. Values within this dictionary are accessed by specifying the full path of dictionary keys. For example, the `Print Junos HOME Dir` task accesses the `HOME` fact with the variable `junos_facts_result.facts.HOME`.

Remember, Ansible performs "fact gathering" by default. This fact gathering is accomplished by executing the Ansible Core module `setup`. The `setup` module automatically assigns variables using a method similar to the `register` key. However, the `setup` module doesn't require any specific configuration to register these discovered variables. All of the `setup` module's variable names begin with the string `ansible_`. We don't cover these variables in detail because they are rarely used when managing Junos devices. Execute the command `ansible localhost -c local -m setup` if you are interested in seeing an example of these discovered variables.

The last method we'll cover for setting a variable's value is using the `-e` argument to the `ansible-playbook` command. The `-e` argument takes a space-separated list of *`variable=value`* pairs. This example executes the *facts6.pb.yaml* playbook, and overrides the `default_port` value using the `-e` argument:

```
user@h0$ cat facts6.pb.yaml
---
- name: Get facts from core1.site1 Junos router
  hosts: core1.site1
  connection: local
  gather_facts: no
  roles:
    - Juniper.junos
  vars_prompt:
    - name: netconf_user
```

```
        prompt: Username
        private: no
      - name: netconf_password
        prompt: Password
        private: yes
  vars:
    default_port: 830
  tasks:
    - name: Get Junos Facts
      junos_get_facts:
        host: "{{ inventory_hostname }}"
        user: "{{ netconf_user }}"
        port: "{{ default_port }}"
        passwd: "{{ netconf_password }}"
      register: junos_facts_result
    - name: Print Junos Facts Result
      debug:
        var: junos_facts_result
    - name: Print Junos HOME Dir
      debug:
        var: junos_facts_result.facts.HOME
    - name: Print value of default_port
      debug:
        var: default_port
user@h0$ ansible-playbook -i prod.inv facts6.pb.yaml -e "default_port=22"
Username: user
Password:

PLAY [Get facts from core1.site1 Junos router] *******************************

TASK: [Get Junos Facts] ******************************************************
ok: [core1.site1]

TASK: [Print Junos Facts Result] *********************************************
ok: [core1.site1] => {
    "var": {
        "junos_facts_result": {
            ... output trimmed ...
            }
        }
    }
}

TASK: [Print Junos HOME Dir] *************************************************
... output trimmed ...

TASK: [Print value of default_port] ******************************************
ok: [core1.site1] => {
    "var": {
        "default_port": "22"
    }
}
```

```
PLAY RECAP ********************************************************************
core1.site1                : ok=4    changed=0    unreachable=0    failed=0

user@h0$
```

The output of the `Print value of default_port` task in the preceding output shows the `default_port` variable was indeed set by the command line's `-e` argument.

The `-e` command line example also demonstrates another important topic: variable precedence. If the same variable name is set in multiple locations, the variable's value gets overwritten in a certain order. Here's the general precedence of variables (from least preferred to most preferred):

Role defaults
: Role default variables are covered in "Roles" on page 548

Inventory group variables
: Variables defined in the *group_vars* subdirectory.

Inventory host variables
: Variables defined in the *host_vars* subdirectory

Discovered variables
: Variables assigned by the `setup` module

Play and task variables
: Variables set in the play (using the `vars`, `vars_prompt`, or `vars_files` keys) or variables set in the task (using the `register` key)

Command-line variables
: Variables specified with the `-e` command line option to the `ansible-playbook` command

While it's useful to understand Ansible's variable precedence, avoid the temptation of depending on this behavior. It's best to assign a given variable in only one location. This follows the path of "least surprise" and eases the pain of debugging.

It is especially important to avoid assigning the same group variable in multiple overlapping groups. In the preceding example, the variable `dns_resolvers` was assigned in the *group_vars/junos-site1* file. Problems will occur if `dns_resolvers` is also assigned in the *group_vars/junos-all* file. Because some hosts are members of both the `junos-site1` and `junos-all` groups, the value of `dns_resolvers` is unpredictable for those target hosts. On the other hand, because the memberships of the `junos-site1` and `junos-site2` groups do not overlap, it is acceptable (and encouraged) to assign `dns_resolvers` in both the *group_vars/junos-site1* and *group_vars/junos-site2* files.

Roles

Ansible roles are simply a way of organizing plays into smaller reusable units. As soon as a play grows beyond the very simple examples we've seen so far, roles become an essential tool. In fact, roles should be considered "best practice" for any production Ansible deployment. The examples in "Example Playbooks" on page 567 demonstrate this best practice by creating roles for common tasks shared between multiple playbooks.

Roles contain all of the same components that are found in a play: variables, tasks, and handlers. In addition, roles can define default variables, pull in other dependent roles, and embed modules within themselves. Rather than including all the components in a single file, as playbooks do, roles consist of multiple files organized into a well-known directory structure. When a role is referenced, Ansible automatically loads and executes the files in this directory structure.

Let's begin by examining the well-known directory structure of roles:

```
playbook.yaml
roles/
   role1/
     tasks/
     handlers/
     vars/
     defaults/
     meta/
     files/
     templates/
   role2/
     tasks/
```

```
handlers/
vars/
defaults/
meta/
files/
templates/
```

As shown in this example, roles are typically stored within a *roles* subdirectory. This *roles* subdirectory is relative to the directory where playbook files are stored. Ansible first searches for a role in the playbook's *roles* subdirectory and then in the */etc/ansible/roles* directory. If a role is not found in either of these locations, Ansible searches the colon-separated list of paths specified by the optional `roles_path` configuration setting.

Within a given *roles* directory, each subdirectory defines a named role. Within each named role directory, there are a common set of subdirectories:

tasks
: The *tasks/main.yaml* file contains a list of tasks which are automatically added to the play. If other YAML files exist in the *tasks* directory, they may be referenced from a task using an `include` key. The full path to these additional task files is not required.

handlers
: The *handlers/main.yaml* file contains a list of handlers which are automatically added to the play.

vars
: The *vars/main.yaml* file contains a dictionary of variables which are automatically added to the play. For purposes of precedence, these variables are considered play variables.

defaults
: The *defaults/main.yaml* file contains a dictionary of variables which are automatically added to the play. Variables assigned in this file are role default variables and have the lowest precedence. They can be overridden by any other variables, including inventory variables.

meta
: The *meta/main.yaml* file contains a list of role dependencies. The list of dependencies must appear under a `dependencies` dictionary key within this YAML file. Role dependencies are executed before the role that includes them, and are recursive. By default, dependent roles are only executed once. If another role lists the same dependency, the dependent role is not executed again.

library

Role-specific modules may be placed in this directory. Modules in this directory are defined, but not executed, when the role is referenced. Just as we saw with playbook files, a module is only executed when it is referenced from a task with a specific set of arguments.

files

The `copy` module can reference source files in this directory without having to include the files' paths. Because the Ansible for Junos modules require a `local` connection, the `copy` module cannot be used to copy files to a Junos target host. Therefore, the `copy` module and *files* directory are rarely used when managing Junos devices.

templates

The core Ansible `template` module can reference template files in this directory without having to include their paths. Unlike the `copy` module, the core Ansible `template` module is extremely useful when managing Junos devices. The `template` module allows Junos configuration files to be built from Jinja2 templates and then installed by the `junos_install_config` module. This strategy is demonstrated in "Example Playbooks" on page 567.

A role is not required to include all of these directories. If a given role subdirectory is missing (or doesn't have a *main.yaml* file), that component is simply skipped.

Roles are referenced from a play's `roles` key. The value of the `roles` key is a YAML list of role names. Roles are invoked in the order they appear in the list. In fact, previous examples have already demonstrated this `roles` attribute. Consider this partial playbook file repeated from previous examples:

```
---
- name: Get facts from core1.site1 Junos router
  hosts: core1.site1
  connection: local
  gather_facts: no
  roles:
    - Juniper.junos
  vars_prompt:
    ... output trimmed ...
  vars:
    default_port: 830
  tasks:
    - name: Get Junos Facts
    ... output trimmed ...
```

In the preceding output, the value of the `roles` key is a single-item list. The list references the `Juniper.junos` role. You may remember from "Installing the Juniper.junos Role" on page 516 that the `Juniper.junos` role was installed from the Ansible Galaxy. By default, roles installed from the Ansible Galaxy are installed in */etc/ansible/roles*. The `Juniper.junos` role doesn't include any variables, tasks, or handlers, but it does embed all of the Ansible for Junos modules in its *library* directory:

```
user@h0$ ls -1 /etc/ansible/roles/Juniper.junos/library/
__init__.py
junos_commit
junos_get_config
junos_get_facts
junos_install_config
junos_install_os
junos_rollback
junos_shutdown
junos_srx_cluster
junos_zeroize
```

Because the Ansible for Junos modules are part of the `Juniper.junos` role, this role must be included with the `roles` key before any Ansible for Junos modules are called from a task.

In "Example Playbooks" on page 567, we will demonstrate more complicated roles that include variables, tasks, and handlers. We will also use the *meta/main.yaml* file to declare these new roles as dependent upon the `Juniper.junos` role.

Before we move on to look at conditionals, let's revisit the order in which a play's tasks are executed. We discussed the basics of how plays are executed in "Tasks and Modules" on page 528 and "Handlers" on page 529. Now that you've learned about roles, we can provide more details. Each play can include multiple keys. The tasks specified in the values of each of these keys are executed in the order the keys are listed in this example:

```
---
- name: Play 1
  hosts: junos-all

  pre_tasks:
  roles:
  tasks:
  post_tasks:
```

As shown in the preceding output, any tasks listed under the play's `pre_tasks` key are executed first. Any handlers notified by the `pre_tasks` tasks are executed next. The tasks of each role are then executed in the order specified by the `roles` list value. Handlers notified by any of the `roles` tasks are then executed in the order they were notified. After all roles are executed, any tasks specified in the `tasks` key are executed in order. Any handlers notified by any of these tasks are then executed in the order they were notified. Next, any tasks listed in the `post_tasks` key are executed in order. Finally, any handlers notified by any of these `post_tasks` tasks are executed in the order they were notified.

Conditionals

Each task can optionally include a `when` key. The value of the `when` key is a Jinja2 expression without the curly braces. The task is only executed if this Jinja2 expression evaluates to true. This Jinja2 expression can evaluate the value of a variable. It can contain Jinja2 filters, and it can also include logical operators and groupings.

Here's an example of a simple playbook that contains several conditional tasks:

```
user@h0$ cat conditional_example.pb.yaml
---
- name: Example Play With Conditional Tasks
  hosts: junos-core-site1
  connection: local
  gather_facts: no
  tasks:
    - name: Execute Some Command
      command: /bin/true
      register: result
      when: inventory_hostname == "core1.site1"
    - name: Print success
      debug:
          msg: "Some command succeeded."
      when: result|success
    - name: Print failure
      debug:
          msg: "Some command failed."
      when: result|failed
    - name: Print skipped
      debug:
          msg: "Some command was skipped."
      when: result|skipped
    - name: Print changed
      debug:
          msg: "Some command changed something."
      when: result|changed
```

The `Execute Some Command` task contains the key `when: inventory_hostname == "core1.site1"`. This task is only executed against the `core1.site1` target host because that is the only host for which the Jinja2 expression evaluates to true. For other target hosts, the task is simply skipped.

The remaining tasks use the Ansible-specific Jinja2 filters of `success`, `failed`, `skipped`, and `changed` to test the result variable registered by the `Execute Some Command` task. Here's the output from running the preceding playbook:

```
user@h0$ ansible-playbook -i prod.inv conditional_example.pb.yaml

PLAY [Example Play With Conditional Tasks] ************************************
```

```
TASK: [Execute Some Command] **************************************************
skipping: [core2.site1]
changed: [core1.site1]

TASK: [Print success] *********************************************************
ok: [core1.site1] => {
    "msg": "Some command succeeded."
}
ok: [core2.site1] => {
    "msg": "Some command succeeded."
}

TASK: [Print failure] *********************************************************
skipping: [core1.site1]
skipping: [core2.site1]

TASK: [Print skipped] *********************************************************
skipping: [core1.site1]
ok: [core2.site1] => {
    "msg": "Some command was skipped."
}

TASK: [Print changed] *********************************************************
ok: [core1.site1] => {
    "msg": "Some command changed something."
}
skipping: [core2.site1]

PLAY RECAP ********************************************************************
core1.site1                : ok=3    changed=1    unreachable=0    failed=0
core2.site1                : ok=2    changed=0    unreachable=0    failed=0

user@h0$
```

Notice the `Execute Some Command` task is executed for `core1.site1` and skipped for `core2.site1`. The `Print success` task is executed for both the `core1.site1` and `core2.site2` target hosts because both the changed and skipped results are a form of success. The `Print failure` task is skipped for both target hosts because the `Execute Some Command` task did not fail for either target host. Finally, the `Print skipped` task is executed for `core2.site1` and the `Print changed` task is executed for `core1.site1`.

Loops

In addition to the `when` conditional statement, Ansible provides several statements for repeating a task multiple times. Each of these statements is defined with a task-specific key beginning with the string `with_`. The simplest key is `with_items`, which loops over a list as shown in this example:

```
user@h0$ cat loop_example.pb.yaml
---
- name: Example Play With A Loop
  hosts: core1.site1
  connection: local
  gather_facts: no
  tasks:
    - name: Generating individual user configs
      template:
        src: "/tmp/templates/user.conf.j2"
        dest: "/tmp/configs/users/{{ item }}.conf"
      with_items:
        - jonathan
        - stacy
```

When this simple playbook is executed, the `Generating individual user configs` task is executed once for each item in the `with_items` list. During each iteration, the special variable `item` is set to the current list item. This behavior allows the `item` variable to be referenced within the task's argument values. The preceding playbook generates a small configuration fragment from a Jinja2 template. The generated configuration fragment is written to a user-specific file by referencing the `item` variable within the `template` module's `dest` argument. When this playbook is executed, the output shows two iterations of the `Generating individual user configs` task:

```
user@h0$ ansible-playbook -i prod.inv loop_example.pb.yaml

PLAY [Example Play With A Loop] ************************************************

TASK: [Generating individual user configs] *************************************
changed: [core1.site1] => (item=jonathan)
changed: [core1.site1] => (item=stacy)

PLAY RECAP *********************************************************************
core1.site1                : ok=1    changed=1    unreachable=0    failed=0
```

The first iteration displays `(item=jonathan)` in the output and the second iteration displays `(item=stacy)`. However, the `PLAY RECAP` section counts this execution as a single task rather than counting each iteration of the task.

While `with_items` iterates over a simple list, Ansible provides other keys for more advanced loops. For example, the `with_dict` key iterates over a dictionary and the `with_file` key iterates over the contents of a list of files. There's even a `with_random_choice` key to randomly select a single item from a list. Reference the Loops documentation (*http://docs.ansible.com/ansible/playbooks_loops.html*) for a more detailed description of the available keys.

Vaults

Before we look at the available Ansible for Junos modules, let's look at one final Ansible tool: vaults. Ansible can store sensitive information in encrypted files, called vaults, rather than the normal plain-text variable, playbook, and role files. The `ansible-vault` command is used to create, edit, encrypt, and decrypt these vault files.

Let's demonstrate a vault by encrypting the common usernames and passwords configured in our example network. Because these usernames and passwords are common to all Junos devices in the network, we will create group variables in the *group_vars/junos-all* file. Initially, the unencrypted file has this content:

```
user@h0$ cat group_vars/junos-all
---
jaccess:
  netconf_user: user
  netconf_password: user123
  root_password: root123
```

We can encrypt this file by executing the command `ansible-vault encrypt group_vars/junos-all`:

```
user@h0$ ansible-vault encrypt group_vars/junos-all
Vault password:
Confirm Vault password:
Encryption successful
```

Ansible prompts for a vault password. This password is required to unlock the encrypted file.

Here, you can see the file is now encrypted:

```
user@h0$ cat group_vars/junos-all
$ANSIBLE_VAULT;1.1;AES256
33643235646432326535626666663032653239363838643166363030373735393364333762313133
306337303464376135663363633034333137653939393633300a356434343134323264626136616637
35306566373461663934323839393766386331323134323133636638363664616230663365333637
6165376463323963310a373533353139366430323064316332383139353762336632303564373839
65333737376630323931616163393266333330653063633232623532363561393639346630666430
64663931336361333366343339333438663332356332313935343237663762343538663739616436
66626334363439303266373837303237666336623863636164666665323836316231643536653664
64663231326537333361323366313436303439326233366134653030343762343165663366666630
3132
user@h0$
```

The command `ansible-vault view group_vars/junos-all` prompts for the vault password and then displays the decrypted file:

```
user@h0$ ansible-vault view group_vars/junos-all
Vault password:
---
```

```
jaccess:
  netconf_user: user
  netconf_password: user123
  root_password: root123
```

Attempting to execute a playbook now requires the user to specify the `--ask-vault-pass` option to the `ansible-playbook` command:

```
user@h0$ ansible-playbook -i prod.inv vault_example.pb.yaml
ERROR: A vault password must be specified to decrypt /home/user/playbooks/...
user@h0$ ansible-playbook -i prod.inv --ask-vault-pass vault_example.pb.yaml
Vault password:

PLAY [Get facts from core1.site1 Junos router] *******************************

TASK: [Get Junos Facts] *****************************************************
ok: [core1.site1]

PLAY RECAP ******************************************************************
core1.site1                : ok=1    changed=0    unreachable=0    failed=0
```

By specifying `ask_vault_pass=True` in the Ansible configuration file, you avoid having to specify the `--ask-vault-pass` option every time the `ansible-playbook` command is executed.

If a playbook references multiple vault files, they *must* all have the same vault password.

We've now covered the basics of using vaults to encrypt sensitive configuration data. In "junos_get_facts" on page 557, we'll provide a more detailed example with best practices for using vaults.

Ansible for Junos Modules

Now that you have the foundation for using Ansible to manage Junos devices, this section provides more detail on each of the Ansible for Junos modules. There are modules for:

- Gathering facts (model, OS version, serial number, etc.) about a device
- Returning a device to factory default state
- Forming or breaking a cluster between two Junos SRX devices
- Shutting down or rebooting a Junos device
- Loading and committing a Junos configuration in text (curly brace), set, or XML format
- Upgrading the Junos version on a device

- Downloading the configuration of a Junos device
- Rolling back the configuration of a Junos device
- Confirming a previous configuration commit issued with the confirm option

Each of the Ansible for Junos modules supports the `host`, `port`, `user`, and `passwd` arguments listed in Table 10-1. Some of the modules also support the `console` argument for connecting to the console of the device using the Netconify library.

If the `log_path` setting is specified in the Ansible configuration file, then Ansible logs detailed messages about each task's execution. These detailed messages include each argument and value specified for the task. This behavior means that the plain-text value of the `passwd` argument for each Ansible for Junos module gets logged as shown in this example log message:

```
2015-12-08 13:24:52,996 p=1914 u=user |  /usr/local/bin/
        ansible core1.site1
  -i /home/user/playbooks/prod.inv -m junos_get_facts
    -a host=core1-site1
  connection=local user=user password=user123
  -M /etc/ansible/roles/Juniper.junos/library
```

Be aware of this behavior and ensure the log file is only readable by trusted users.

The remainder of this section provides specific information on each of the Ansible for Junos modules. In "Example Playbooks" on page 567, some of these modules are demonstrated in practical examples.

junos_get_facts

We've already demonstrated the `junos_get_facts` module in many of the previous examples in this chapter. This module gathers device-specific information from the Junos device. The response from the `junos_get_facts` module is a dictionary that contains the key `facts`. The `facts` key is also a dictionary, and each individual fact is a key within `facts`. The `junos_get_facts` module does accept the `console` argument and supports NETCONF-over-console sessions. However, as of release 1.2.0, the facts returned when using the console connection are only a subset of the facts returned for NETCONF-over-SSH sessions. When operating over a NETCONF-over-SSH session, the `junos_get_facts` module returns the same facts returned by the PyEZ `facts_refresh()` method. When operating over a console connection, the `junos_get_facts` module returns the same facts returned by the `netconify --facts` command.

The `junos_get_facts` module accepts two other arguments, in addition to the standard connection arguments:

`savedir`
: The path to the directory on the local Ansible control machine where device fact files will be stored. When connecting over the console, the default value of `savedir` is the current working directory. When connecting over NETCONF, device fact files are not stored unless the `savedir` argument is specified. Files are stored in the format *savedir/`device_name`-facts.json*.

`logfile`
: The path to a log file on the local Ansible control machine. A log of the interaction with the Junos device is stored in this file for debugging purposes. The `logfile` option is only used when the `console` argument is also specified. The default value of the `logfile` argument is `None`, which means no logging occurs (even if the `console` argument is specified).

The return value of this module always has the `changed` attribute set to a value of `False`.

junos_zeroize

The `junos_zeroize` module reverts a Junos device to its factory default state by removing all data files from the routing engine. This operation includes the removal of configurations, logs, keys, and any user-created files. This module is equivalent to the `request system zeroize` CLI command or the *request-system-zeroize* RPC. The `junos_zeroize` module does accept the `console` argument. It supports both NETCONF-over-console and NETCONF-over-SSH sessions.

The `junos_zeroize` module accepts two other arguments, in addition to the standard connection arguments:

`zeroize`
: A safety mechanism to confirm the user really does intend to zeroize the device. This argument must be specified and the value must be set to the string `'zeroize'`. If this argument is not present and set to a value of `'zeroize'`, the module will return a status of `failed`.

`logfile`
: The path to a log file on the local Ansible control machine. A log of the interaction with the Junos device is stored in this file for debugging purposes. Unlike with the `junos_get_facts` module, the `logfile` option is used for both NETCONF-over-console and NETCONF-over-SSH sessions. The default value of the `logfile` argument is `None`, which means no logging occurs.

The return value of this module sets the `changed` attribute to a value of `True` if the `request system zeroize` command was successfully initiated.

This module returns immediately after the `request system zeroize` command is initiated. It does *not* wait for the command to complete. The zeroize operation may take 15 minutes or more to complete and may involve rebooting the Junos device one or more times. Ansible playbooks that include other tasks after a `junos_zeroize` task must account for this fact. In addition, because the device is returned to a factory-default state, any subsequent tasks must be performed via the console.

junos_srx_cluster

The `junos_srx_cluster` module creates or reverts a chassis cluster on an SRX-Series device by setting the device to cluster mode or standalone mode, respectively. When creating an SRX cluster, the target Junos devices must be capable of forming an SRX cluster. As part of this prerequisite, the pair of SRX-Series devices must have the proper cabling installed to interconnect the chassis members. When creating a cluster, this module is equivalent to the `set chassis cluster cluster-id` *`cluster_id`* `node` *`node_id`* `reboot` CLI command. When reverting an existing cluster, this module is equivalent to the `set chassis cluster disable reboot` CLI command. The `junos_srx_cluster` module does accept the `console` argument. It supports both NETCONF-over-console and NETCONF-over-SSH sessions.

The `junos_srx_cluster` module also accepts the following arguments (in addition to the standard connection arguments):

`cluster_enable`
: This Boolean argument is mandatory and must be set to a `true`/`false` (or `yes`/`no`) value. If `cluster_enable` is `true` a cluster is created and both the `cluster_id` and `node` arguments must also be specified. If `cluster_enable` is `false`, the cluster is disabled.

`cluster_id`
: This argument must be specified when `cluster_enable` is `true`. The value must be an integer between 0 and 255 that uniquely identifies this SRX cluster within the Layer 2 network.

`node`
: This argument must be specified when `cluster_enable` is `true`. This argument identifies the node within the cluster and must be set to a unique value (either `0` or `1`) for each node within the cluster.

`logfile`
: This argument specifies the path to a log file on the local Ansible control machine. A log of the interaction with the Junos device is stored in this file for debugging purposes. The `logfile` option is used for both NETCONF-over-console and NETCONF-over-SSH sessions. The default value of the `logfile` argument is `None`, which means no logging occurs.

The return value of this module sets the `changed` attribute to a value of `True` and the `reboot` attribute to a value of `True` when disabling a cluster (the equivalent of the `set chassis cluster disable reboot` command). Currently, it does *not* set the `changed` or `reboot` attributes when enabling a cluster (the equivalent of the `set chassis cluster cluster-id` *`cluster_id`* `node` *`node_id`* `reboot` CLI command).

This module returns immediately after the `cluster` command is initiated. It does *not* wait for the command to complete. The cluster operation may take 15 minutes or more to complete and involves rebooting the Junos device. Ansible playbooks that include other tasks after a `junos_srx_cluster` task must account for this fact.

junos_shutdown

The `junos_shutdown` module gracefully powers off or reboots a Junos device. This module does *not* accept the `console` argument. It only supports NETCONF-over-SSH sessions.

The `junos_shutdown` module accepts two arguments in addition to the standard connection arguments:

`shutdown`
: This mandatory argument is a safety mechanism to confirm the user really does intend to power off or reboot the device. The value must be set to the string `'shutdown'`. If this argument is present and not set to a value of `'shutdown'`, the module will return a status of `failed`.

`reboot`
: If this optional Boolean argument is `true`, then the device is rebooted rather than powered off. The default value is `false`.

The return value of this module sets the `changed` attribute to a value of `True` if the power off or reboot operation is successfully initiated.

This module returns immediately after the operation is initiated. It does *not* wait for the command to complete. Of course, no further operations are possible if the device is powered off. If the device is rebooted, Ansible playbooks that include other tasks after a `junos_shutdown` task must account for the time required to reboot the device to a reachable state.

junos_install_os

The `junos_install_os` module installs a Junos software package on one or more of the target device's routing engines. This module is equivalent to performing the `request system software add` CLI command or the *request-package-add* RPC.

The `junos_install_os` module does *not* accept the `console` argument. It only supports NETCONF-over-SSH sessions. The module does accept several other arguments, in addition to the standard connection arguments:

`package`
: The file path, on the local Ansible control machine, of the Junos software package to install. This package is SCP'd to the */var/tmp/* directory of the target Junos device. If the `no_copy` argument is `true`, the copy is skipped and the `package` argument refers to a file path on the target Junos device.

`version`
: The desired Junos version string. If the current Junos version reported by the `show version` CLI command matches the value of this argument, the installation is skipped and no action is performed. If the `version` argument is not specified, the module attempts to determine the desired version from the value of the `package` argument.

Because Junos installation package names vary widely, the module may be unable to determine the desired version from the package name. In this case, the software package is always installed (even if the device was already running the desired software version). To avoid this situation, we recommend always specifying the `version` argument.

`no_copy`
: An optional Boolean argument that specifies whether or not to skip the copy of the package from the local control machine to the target Junos device. If `no_copy` is `true`, the copy is skipped. If `no_copy` is `false`, the default, the package is SCP'd from the Ansible control machine to the target Junos device.

`reboot`
: An optional Boolean argument that indicates whether the device will be rebooted after the software installation completes. The default value is `true` (reboot).

`reboot_pause`
: An optional integer argument that specifies the number of seconds to wait after the reboot is initiated before the module returns. The default value is 10 seconds.

`logfile`
: The path to a log file on the local Ansible control machine. A log of the interaction with the Junos device is stored in this file for debugging purposes. The default value of the `logfile` argument is `None`, which means no logging occurs.

If the current Junos version matches the desired version, specified by the module's `version` argument, no action is performed and the `changed` attribute is set to `False`. If the current Junos version does *not* match the desired version, the `changed` attribute is set to `True`.

This module supports running in Ansible's "check mode." When run in check mode, the module returns a `changed` attribute value of `True` or `False` but does not actually perform the software installation.

This module does not return until the `request system software add` command completes. If the `reboot` argument is `true`, the module initiates a reboot and then waits `reboot_pause` more seconds before returning.

junos_get_config

This module retrieves the current configuration of a Junos device and saves it to a file on the Ansible control machine.

The module does *not* accept the `console` argument. It only supports NETCONF-over-SSH sessions. The `junos_get_config` module does accept several arguments in addition to the standard connection arguments:

`dest`
: The file path, on the local Ansible control machine, where the configuration is saved. This argument must be specified.

`format`
: The format in which the configuration file is saved. Choices are `text` (aka curly brace format) and `xml`. The default value is `text`.

`options`
: Additional options to be passed as attributes to the *get-configuration* RPC. The value of the `options` argument is a dictionary of key/value pairs. For more information on the available options, refer back to "Viewing the Configuration" on page 79.

`filter`
: A simplified XPath expression consisting of XML tag names separated by slashes (`/`) that filters the configuration output to only the subset that matches the XPath expression. The filter is relative to the `<configuration>` XML hierarchy. By default, no filter is specified and the entire configuration is returned.

`logfile`
: The path to a log file on the local Ansible control machine. A log of the interaction with the Junos device is stored in this file for debugging purposes. The default value of the `logfile` argument is `None`, which means no logging occurs.

This module does not set the `changed` attribute in its response.

junos_install_config

This module loads and commits a configuration, or configuration snippet, on a Junos device. It attempts to perform an exclusive lock on the configuration database and will fail if it is unable to obtain the lock. Depending on the arguments passed, the module performs the equivalent of a `load merge` (the default), a `load override`, or a `load replace`. The configuration file may be specified in either XML, text (curly brace), or set format.

The `junos_install_config` module does accept the `console` argument, but there are a couple of restrictions when the module uses a NETCONF-over-console session. The first restriction is that the configuration file must be specified in the text (curly brace) format when loaded over the console connection. The other restriction is simply a practical one. Because the console of a Junos device operates at 9600 bps, you must restrict configurations loaded over the console connection to the minimum size necessary. We recommend using the console connection only to load a minimal initial configuration that configures the NETCONF-over-SSH service and allows additional configuration to be performed via a NETCONF-over-SSH connection.

The `junos_install_config` module also accepts several other arguments (in addition to the standard connection arguments):

`file`
: The file path, on the local Ansible control machine, of the configuration file to be loaded and committed. If the configuration file is in text (curly brace) format, the filename must end with the *.conf* extension. If the configuration file is in XML

format, the filename must end with the *.xml* extension, and if the configuration file is in set format, the filename must end with the *.set* extension. This argument must be specified.

`overwrite`
: An optional Boolean argument that specifies if a `load override` should be performed. If `overwrite` is `true`, a `load override` is performed. If `overwrite` is `false`, a `load merge` or `load replace` is performed. The default value is `false`.

`replace`
: An optional Boolean argument that specifies if a `load replace` should be performed. If `replace` is `true`, a `load replace` is performed. If `replace` is `false`, a `load merge` or `load override` is performed. The default value is `false`. This value is not supported for NETCONF-over-console sessions.

`diffs_file`
: The file path, on the local Ansible control machine, where configuration differences are saved. This value is not supported for NETCONF-over-console sessions.

`savedir`
: The file path, on the local Ansible control machine, where device fact and inventory files are stored. This argument is only used when the `console` argument is also specified and the module is using a NETCONF-over-console connection. If the `savedir` argument is not specified, device fact and inventory files are saved in the current working directory.

`timeout`
: The NETCONF RPC timeout (in seconds) for the commit operation. The default value is 30 seconds. This argument is useful when the Junos device has a large configuration that might take more than 30 seconds to commit. It is not supported for NETCONF-over-console sessions.

`comment`
: An optional string argument passed as a comment to the commit operation. The default value is no comment. This argument is not supported for NETCONF-over-console sessions.

`confirm`
: An optional integer argument specifying that a second commit operation must be confirmed within `confirm` minutes or the newly committed configuration will be rolled back. Use the `junos_commit` module to perform the second commit operation. This argument is not supported for NETCONF-over-console sessions.

`logfile`
: The path to a log file on the local Ansible control machine. A log of the interaction with the Junos device is stored in this file for debugging purposes. The default value of the `logfile` argument is `None`, which means no logging occurs.

This module sets the `changed` attribute to `True` if the commit was successful.

junos_rollback

This module loads and commits a previous (rollback) configuration on a Junos device. It attempts to perform an exclusive lock on the configuration database and will fail if it is unable to obtain the lock.

The `junos_rollback` module does *not* accept the `console` argument. It only supports NETCONF-over-SSH sessions. The `junos_rollback` module does accept several other arguments (in addition to the standard connection arguments):

`rollback`
: The rollback ID value. This value is an integer between 0 and 49 which determines how many previous commits should be rolled back. This argument is mandatory.

`diffs_file`
: The file path, on the local Ansible control machine, where configuration differences are saved. This value is not supported for NETCONF-over-console sessions.

`timeout`
: The NETCONF RPC timeout (in seconds) for the commit operation. The default value is 30 seconds. This argument is useful when the Junos device has a large configuration that might take more than 30 seconds to commit. It is not supported for NETCONF-over-console sessions.

`comment`
: An optional string argument passed as a comment to the commit operation. The default value is no comment. This argument is not supported for NETCONF-over-console sessions.

`confirm`
: An optional integer argument specifying that a second commit operation must be confirmed within `confirm` minutes or the newly committed configuration will be rolled back. Use the `junos_commit` module to perform the second commit operation. This argument is not supported for NETCONF-over-console sessions.

`logfile`
: The path to a log file on the local Ansible control machine. A log of the interaction with the Junos device is stored in this file for debugging purposes. The default value of the `logfile` argument is `None`, which means no logging occurs.

This module sets the `changed` attribute to `True` if the commit was successful.

junos_commit

This module performs a commit operation on a Junos device without modifying the configuration. This is really only useful to confirm a previous commit operation that was performed by the `junos_install_config` or `junos_rollback` modules with the `confirm` argument specified. This module attempts to perform an exclusive lock on the configuration database and will fail if it is unable to obtain the lock.

The `junos_commit` module does *not* accept the `console` argument. It only supports NETCONF-over-SSH sessions. The `junos_commit` module does accept several other arguments, in addition to the standard connection arguments:

`timeout`
: The NETCONF RPC timeout (in seconds) for the commit operation. The default value is 30 seconds. This argument is useful when the Junos device has a large configuration that might take more than 30 seconds to commit.

`comment`
: An optional string argument passed as a comment to the commit operation. The default value is no comment.

`confirm`
: An optional integer argument specifying that a second commit operation must be performed within `confirm` minutes or the newly committed configuration will be rolled back. This argument rarely makes sense for the `junos_commit` module, because `junos_commit` is typically used only to confirm a previous commit, and there are typically no configuration changes that have been committed.

`logfile`
: The path to a log file on the local Ansible control machine. A log of the interaction with the Junos device is stored in this file for debugging purposes. The default value of the `logfile` argument is `None`, which means no logging occurs.

This module sets the `changed` attribute to `True` if the commit was successful.

Example Playbooks

Now that you understand the workings of both the Ansible for Junos modules and Ansible Core, let's put the two pieces together into some example playbooks for managing Junos devices. Like all examples, the playbooks in this section may not exactly match your network's requirements. However, they provide some useful building blocks that may be applied when managing any network of Junos devices.

Inventory, Variables, and Ansible Configuration Settings

Let's begin by looking at the inventory files, variable organization, and Ansible configuration settings used in these examples. With the exception of the Ansible configuration settings, all of these files reside within a single *~/playbooks/* directory. As we've suggested before, all of these files are best stored in a revision control system that can track differences between revisions, log who made each change, and record why the changes were made.

First, the inventory is organized into two files: *prod.inv* and *lab.inv*. The *prod.inv* file contains devices in the "production" network, while *lab.inv* contains test devices in the "lab" network. Both files are organized into the same set of groups. The groups divide devices based on their physical location (site) and their role in the network (core or edge). There is also a very important group named `junos-all`. All Junos devices are a member of this `junos-all` group. This membership allows settings that are common to all Junos devices to be set in a single group variable file[12] while still allowing Ansible to manage other non-Junos devices. The contents of the *prod.inv* and *lab.inv* files are exactly the same as previously shown in "Inventory" on page 520. Refer back to that section for details.

Next, three inventory variables are used in the examples. The values of each of three inventory variables are actually dictionaries with multiple keys. Using only three dictionaries minimizes the potential for conflict with other Ansible variables that may be defined and allows similar inventory variables to be grouped together. The three top-level inventory variables are:

`jaccess`
: A dictionary containing the parameters necessary to access a Junos device. In the examples, the values in this dictionary are used both to log in to the Junos device and to build the device's initial configuration. The keys in this dictionary include:

12 Technically there are two group variable files, as the examples use vaults. That distinction will be covered soon.

`console_ts`
: The hostname or IP address of the terminal server attached to the console of this Junos device

`console_port`
: The TCP port number that directly connects to the console of this Junos device

`netconf_user`
: The username used to access the device when connecting using a NETCONF-over-SSH session

`netconf_password`
: The password of the `jaccess.netconf_user` account

`ssh_key_file`
: The path, on the local Ansible control machine, to the SSH public key file that permits access to the `jaccess.netconf_user` account

`root_password`
: The password of the root user account

`jcfg`
: A dictionary containing the parameters necessary to configure a Junos device. Some of these parameters are used to build the device's initial configuration, while other parameters are used to build protocol-specific device configurations. The keys in this dictionary include:

`mgmt_ip`
: The IPv4 address (in CIDR notation) of the Junos device's management interface

`mgmt_gw`
: The IPv4 address of a gateway on the Junos device's management network that routes traffic to management addresses outside the local management subnet

`mgmt_int`
: The name of the physical interface (`fxp0`, `me0`, `em0`, etc.) used as the Junos device's management interface

`domain`
: The DNS domain name of the Junos device

`timezone`
: The time zone of the Junos device

`dns_resolvers`
: A list of DNS resolvers (name servers) used by the Junos device

`ntp_servers`
: A list of NTP servers used by the Junos device

`ospf`
: A dictionary containing OSPF-specific configuration parameters used in the example in "Core OSPF Configuration" on page 597

`jvault`
: A dictionary containing the sensitive parameters used to access or configure a Junos device. Keys within this dictionary are only set within an Ansible vault file, and are only used to set the value of other inventory variables. We'll see how this works when we examine the contents of some example inventory variable files.

In the example environment, some values are unique to each host (e.g., `jcfg.mgmt_ip`), other values are unique to each site (e.g., `jcfg.timezone`), still other values are unique to the device platform or model (e.g., `jcfg.mgmt_int`), and yet other values are common among all Junos devices in the example network (e.g., `jcfg.domain`.)

The examples organize inventory variables based on their uniqueness. Host-specific values are stored in host variables that are set in files named *~/playbooks/host_vars/<hostname>*, as shown in this example output for `core1.site1`:

```
user@h0$ pwd
/home/user/playbooks
user@h0$ cat host_vars/core1.site1
---
jaccess:
  console_ts: ts1.site1
  console_port: 17490

jcfg:
  mgmt_ip: 10.102.167.104/19
  mgmt_gw: 10.102.191.254
```

Site-specific values are stored in group variables that are set in files named *~/playbooks/group_vars/junos-<site>*, as shown in this example output for `site1`:

```
user@h0$ pwd
/home/user/playbooks
user@h0$ cat group_vars/junos-site1
---
jcfg:
  timezone: America/Denver
  dns_resolvers:
    - 8.8.8.8
    - 8.8.4.4
```

```
ntp_servers:
  - 128.138.141.172
```

Values common to all Junos devices (at least in our example network) are stored in group variables that are set in a *directory* named *~/playbooks/group_vars/junos-all*. Because some of these values are sensitive (e.g., `jaccess.netconf_password`) and other values are not (e.g., `jcfg.domain`), they are broken into two files: *~/playbooks/group_vars/junos-all/vars* and *~/playbooks/group_vars/junos-all/vault*. As you might guess from the name, the *~/playbooks/group_vars/junos-all/vault* file is an Ansible vault. Its contents are encrypted, as shown in this output, which displays both the encrypted and unencrypted contents of the file:

```
user@h0$ pwd
/home/user/playbooks
user@h0$ cat group_vars/junos-all/vault
$ANSIBLE_VAULT;1.1;AES256
33313366663839353462303065666261616230353233646337353164303666663835363763383435
38626137303564326538303665366431663466363135363 60a646334346430633630316663666330
36626166636539366631333238666438323333616137333831613364316534366137306333656530
303931336132656231 0a316630326138303235336230386164356632393066386165306361613134
37346631386233373630663838313738623163663832323463613065366163333632643434376137
32356338336637623434633264316266373238396332373532646161353333623630396166613063
31666339616662633933646261646666653639343032373537306634303736303962616537343664
636435646133653337 34
user@h0$ ansible-vault view group_vars/junos-all/vault
Vault password:
---
jvault:
  netconf_password: "user123"
  root_password: "root123"
```

Notice only values that are keys within the `jvault` dictionary are stored in the Ansible vault file.

The Ansible vault files used in these examples have a vault password of `user123`.

In addition, the values from the `jvault` dictionary are only referenced within the unencrypted *~/playbooks/group_vars/junos-all/vars* file, as shown in this output:

```
user@h0$ pwd
/home/user/playbooks
user@h0$ cat group_vars/junos-all/vars
---
ansible_connection: local
jaccess:
  ssh_key_file: "~/.ssh/id_dsa.pub"
```

```
    netconf_user: user
    netconf_password: "{{ jvault.netconf_password }}"
    root_password: "{{ jvault.root_password }}"
  jcfg:
    domain: example.com
```

While this variable naming and organization is only a convention, it does provide benefit. The convention only uses values from *vault* files in the corresponding *vars* files. This allows the use of search tools, such as `grep`, to quickly discover where a variable is set. Also, the convention only sets keys of the `jvault` dictionary in Ansible vaults. Finally, it provides a quick visual indicator that a variable is set in a vault.

There are three important points about the *~/playbooks/group_vars/junos-all/vars* and *~/playbooks/group_vars/junos-all/vault* files shown in the preceding outputs:

- The examples only use an Ansible vault for the `junos-all` group. However, this same convention may be followed for other group variables, or host variables. Just remember to use the same vault password for all vaults.
- The *vault* and *vars* files in the preceding outputs illustrate a feature that hasn't been previously discussed. Rather than placing a group's variables in a *file* named *group_vars/<group_name>*, it is possible to create a *directory* named *group_vars/<group_name>* and place multiple variable files within the directory. Ansible reads variables from all files within the directory. The preceding examples used the filenames *vars* and *vault*, but any filenames are allowed, and any number of files are allowed within the *group_vars/<group_name>* directory. There's also nothing special about the fact that the file named *vault* is an Ansible vault. Any variable, playbook, or role file may be an Ansible vault, and there's nothing special about the name of the file. We simply chose the filename *vault* as a convenient indicator that the file is an Ansible vault. Finally, just like it's possible to specify group variables in multiple files within a *group_vars/<group_name>* directory, it is also possible to specify host variables in multiple files within a *host_vars/<host_name>* directory.
- The `ansible_connection` variable in the *~/playbooks/group_vars/junos-all/vars* file is very important. Setting this Ansible-defined variable to a value of `local` in the `junos-all` group's variable file avoids having to set `connection: local` in each play that targets a Junos device. Setting this variable for the `junos-all` group, instead of setting `transport = local` globally in the Ansible configuration file, ensures all Junos devices default to a `local` connection while non-Junos devices continue to default to a `smart` connection.

Values that are common to a Junos platform or device model are stored in group variables that are set in files named *~/playbooks/group_vars/junos-plattform-<platform_name>* or *~/playbooks/group_vars/junos-model-<model_name>*, as shown in this example for MX platforms:

```
user@h0$ pwd
/home/user/playbooks
user@h0$ cat group_vars/junos-platform-MX
---
jcfg:
  mgmt_int: fxp0
```

The astute reader may have noticed that there are no `junos-platform-`*`platform_name`* or `junos-model-`*`model_name`* groups defined in the inventory files. These groups do not appear in the inventory files because they are *dynamic* groups. The members of these groups are automatically discovered and set by the `login_facts_and_dynamic_groups` role, covered in the next section.

As you modify these examples for your network environment, it is very important not to set the same variable in multiple groups that have overlapping membership. For example, setting `jcfg.domain` to different values in the `junos-all` group and the `junos-site1` group is problematic because some devices are members of both the `junos-all` group and the `junos-site1` group. For these devices, it is indeterminate whether the value of `jcfg.domain` will be set from the `junos-all` group or the `junos-site1` group. However, it is acceptable to set the same variable to different values in nonoverlapping groups, as the examples do by setting the `jcfg.timezone` variable in both the `junos-site1` and `junos-site2` groups.

It is also acceptable to override a group variable with a host variable. For example, if the `jaccess.netconf_user` is usually common to all devices in the network, its value can be set in the `junos-all` group variables. However, this value can still be overridden for a specific device with a nonstandard user by setting the same `jaccess.netconf_user` variable as a host variable in the *~/playbooks/host_vars/<hostname>* file.

The final step before we dive into the specific example playbooks is verifying the settings used in the Ansible configuration. Here are the contents of */etc/ansible/ansible.cfg* used with the examples:

```
[defaults]
log_path=~/.ansible/log/ansible.log ❶
forks=50 ❷
retry_files_save_path = ~/.ansible/retry ❸
hash_behaviour=merge ❹
gathering = explicit ❺
ask_vault_pass=True ❻
```

❶ The `log_path` key specifies the location where Ansible logs detailed information about each execution. This key is extremely helpful when debugging a new Ansible automation job.

❷ The `forks` key controls the maximum number of parallel processes spawned by the Ansible control machine. The default value of `forks` is `5`. This default value is *very* conservative and should probably be increased. A value of `50` is usually a good start, but you should really set `forks` to the maximum value that doesn't overload your Ansible control machine.

❸ By default, Ansible creates *.retry* files directly in the user's home directory. This behavior tends to litter your home directory with lots of files. We recommend avoiding this clutter by setting the `retry_files_save_path` configuration variable to a dedicated directory.

❹ By default, Ansible overwrites the value of any variable that is set in multiple locations using the precedence order described in "Variables" on page 537. By setting `hash_behaviour=merge`, this behavior is changed for dictionary variables. If the same dictionary variable is set in multiple locations, but each location sets different keys within the dictionary, this setting merges the values into a single dictionary. This setting is *critical* to the examples that set keys to the `jaccess`, `jcfg`, and `jvault` dictionary keys in multiple locations.

❺ As we've seen, Ansible automatically gathers facts for each target host in a play by automatically executing the core `setup` module. When using the Ansible for Junos modules, these facts are unnecessary and slow execution of the playbook. Previous examples have overridden the default behavior by adding `gather_facts: no` to each example play. Setting `gathering = explicit` in the Ansible configuration file reverses this behavior. With this setting, facts are *not* gathered by default, but an individual play may still override this behavior by setting `gather_facts: yes`.

❻ When Ansible vaults are in use, each execution of the `ansible-playbook` command must include the `--ask-vault-pass` command-line option. Setting `ask_vault_pass=True` in the Ansible configuration file avoids this requirement by making the `--ask-vault-pass` command-line option the default behavior.

Gathering Junos Facts and Dynamic Groups

Our first example gathers facts from Junos devices in the network by executing the `junos_get_facts` module. Based on these facts, it also creates dynamic groups of the format `junos-platform-`*`platform_name`* and `junos-model-`*`model_name`*. In turn, these dynamic groups set group variable values which are specific to a platform or model and may be referenced in later tasks.

Because the devices in the example network may be in an unknown state, this example attempts to log in to the device using the following steps:

1. Attempt to make a TCP connection to `jaccess.netconf_port` (or default port 830) of the target Junos device. If this connection fails, skip to step 5.
2. Attempt a NETCONF-over-SSH connection using the `jaccess.netconf_user` without a password (assumes an SSH key with an empty passphrase is configured).
3. Attempt a NETCONF-over-SSH connection using `jaccess.netconf_user` and `jaccess.netconf_password`.
4. Attempt a NETCONF-over-SSH connection using `root` and `jaccess.root_password`.
5. Attempt a console connection using `root` and no password (a factory default configuration).
6. Attempt a console connection using `root` and `jaccess.root_password`.
7. Attempt a console connection using `jaccess.netconf_user` and `jaccess.netconf_password`.

These steps are followed until a successful login occurs. Once a successful login occurs, the credentials used are stored in a new `jlogin` dictionary variable for use by later tasks and the remaining steps in this process are skipped.

This example is used by all of the remaining examples to discover the correct login credentials and set the correct dynamic group memberships, so the bulk of this example is contained within a reusable role named `login_facts_and_dynamic_groups`.

An example playbook file is also created to demonstrate the role by printing the login credentials for each device and the membership of each group, including the dynamic groups. Let's begin exploring this example by investigating the contents of this playbook file:

```
user@h0$ pwd
/home/user/playbooks ❶
user@h0$ cat print_login_creds_and_group_members.yaml ❷
---
- name: Gather login info and facts. Create groups ❸
  hosts: junos-all ❹
  roles:
    - login_facts_and_dynamic_groups ❺
  tasks:
  - name: Print jlogin
```

```
    debug:
      var=jlogin ❻

- name: Print groups
  hosts: h0 ❼
  tasks:
  - name: Print groups
    debug:
      var=groups ❽
```

❶ All files in this example are contained in the *~/playbooks/* directory.

❷ An example playbook is found in the file named *print_login_creds_and_group_members.yaml*.

❸ There are two plays in this playbook. The first play gathers the login information, gathers the facts, and creates the dynamic groups.

❹ This play is written to work with all Junos devices in the example network. Therefore, the `hosts` value for the play is the group `junos-all`. When the playbook is executed, the target hosts can always be limited to a smaller subset of the `junos-all` group by specifying the `--limit` command-line parameter to the `ansible-playbook` command.

❺ The bulk of the work for this playbook is done within the `login_facts_and_dynamic_groups` role. This playbook simply calls the role in its `roles` list.

❻ The `login_facts_and_dynamic_groups` role sets the `jlogin` dictionary to the successful login credentials that were discovered for each target device. This task simply prints those `jlogin` credentials for debugging purposes.

❼ A second play targets only the `h0` device (the local Ansible control machine). The tasks listed in this play will be run only once, against this device.

❽ The built-in `groups` variable lists all groups in the inventory (including dynamic groups). The value of each group in the `groups` list is a list of all hosts that are members of that group. This task prints this group membership for debugging purposes.

Running this playbook produces the following results:

```
user@h0$ ansible-playbook -i prod.inv print_login_creds_and_group_members.yaml
Vault password:

PLAY [Gather login info and facts. Create groups] *****************************
```

```
... output trimmed ...

TASK: [Print jlogin] **********************************************************
ok: [core1.site1] => {
    "var": {
        "jlogin": {
            "console": "",
            "passwd": "",
            "user": "user"
        }
    }
}
... output trimmed ...

PLAY [Print groups] ***********************************************************

TASK: [Print groups] **********************************************************
ok: [h0] => {
    "var": {
        "groups": {
            "all": [
                "h0",
                "core1.site1",
                "core2.site1",
                "core1.site2",
                "edge1.site1",
                "edge2.site1",
                "edge3.site1"
            ],
            "junos-all": [
                "core1.site1",
                "core2.site1",
                "edge1.site1",
                "edge2.site1",
                "edge3.site1",
                "core1.site2"
            ],
            ... output trimmed ...
            "junos-model-MX960": [
                "core1.site1",
                "core2.site1",
                "edge1.site1",
                "edge2.site1",
                "edge3.site1",
                "core1.site2"
            ],
            "junos-platform-MX": [
                "core1.site1",
                "core2.site1",
                "edge1.site1",
                "edge2.site1",
                "edge3.site1",
```

```
                "core1.site2"
            ],
            ... output trimmed ...
            "junos-version-15.1R2.9": [
                "core1.site1",
                "core2.site1",
                "edge1.site1",
                "edge2.site1",
                "edge3.site1",
                "core1.site2"
            ],
            "ungrouped": [
                "h0"
            ]
        }
    }
}

PLAY RECAP *********************************************************************
core1.site1                : ok=8    changed=3    unreachable=0    failed=0
core1.site2                : ok=8    changed=3    unreachable=0    failed=0
core2.site1                : ok=8    changed=3    unreachable=0    failed=0
edge1.site1                : ok=8    changed=3    unreachable=0    failed=0
edge2.site1                : ok=8    changed=3    unreachable=0    failed=0
edge3.site1                : ok=8    changed=3    unreachable=0    failed=0
h0                         : ok=1    changed=0    unreachable=0    failed=0

user@h0$
```

The `jlogin` output for `core1.site` shows the `user` key is set to `user` and the `password` and `console` keys have empty values. This output shows `core1.site` matched step 2 (NETCONF connection using `jaccess.netconf_user` with SSH key and empty passphrase) in the login algorithm. The trimmed output for the remaining target hosts shows similar information.

The second play shows the dynamic group membership of the `junos-model-MX960`, `junos-platform-MX`, and `junos-version-15.1R2.9` groups.

Now, let's look at the details of the `login_facts_and_dynamic_groups` role by examining the following output:

```
user@h0$ pwd
/home/user/playbooks ❶

user@h0$ ls roles/login_facts_and_dynamic_groups/
files  meta  tasks ❷

user@h0$ cat roles/login_facts_and_dynamic_groups/meta/main.yaml
---
dependencies:
  - { role: Juniper.junos } ❸
```

❶ Again, the role is contained within the *~/playbooks/* directory.

❷ The *roles/<role_name>* directory uses the roles' directory structure detailed in "Roles" on page 548.

❸ The *roles/login_facts_and_dynamic_groups/meta/main.yaml* file contains role dependencies. Listing the `Juniper.junos` role in this file avoids having to include the `Juniper.junos` role in each play that uses an Ansible for Junos module.

The real meat of the `login_facts_and_dynamic_groups` role is found in the role's tasks. The *roles/login_facts_and_dynamic_groups/tasks/main.yaml* file is executed first. Let's explore the contents of this task file:

```
user@h0$ cat roles/login_facts_and_dynamic_groups/tasks/main.yaml
---
- name: Resetting jlogin and jfacts ❶
  set_fact:
    jlogin: false
    jfacts: false

- name: Checking NETCONF connectivity ❷
  wait_for:
    host: "{{ inventory_hostname }}"
    port: "{{ jaccess.netconf_port | default(830) }}"
    timeout: 3
  register: netconf
  ignore_errors: True

- include: netconf_facts.yaml ❸
  vars:
    user: "{{ jaccess.netconf_user }}"

- include: netconf_facts.yaml
  vars:
    user: "{{ jaccess.netconf_user }}"
    passwd: "{{ jaccess.netconf_password }}"

- include: netconf_facts.yaml
  vars:
    user: "root"
    passwd: "{{ jaccess.root_password }}"

- include: console_facts.yaml ❹
  vars:
    user: "root"
    pause: 0

- include: console_facts.yaml
  vars:
    user: "root"
```

```
      passwd: "{{ jaccess.root_password }}"
      pause: 15

  - include: console_facts.yaml
    vars:
      user: "{{ jaccess.netconf_user }}"
      passwd: "{{ jaccess.netconf_password }}"
      pause: 15

  - fail: ❺
      msg: "Unable to successfully log in."
    when: not jfacts

  - name: Creating junos-version-* groups ❻
    group_by:
      key="junos-version-{{ jfacts.version }}"

  - name: Creating junos-model-* groups
    group_by:
      key="junos-model-{{ jfacts.model }}"

  - name: Creating junos-platform-* groups ❼
    group_by:
      key="junos-platform-{{ jfacts.model | regex_replace('\-|\d.*$','') }}"
```

❶ The core `set_fact` module sets variables (aka facts) to specific values within a play's execution. This task sets both the `jlogin` and `jfacts` variables to the value `false`. Resetting these variables avoids any potential conflicts from previous executions of this role within the same playbook. If the configuration of the Junos target devices has changed since the previous execution of this role, initializing these values avoids stale values appearing in the `jlogin` or `jfacts` dictionaries.

❷ The core `wait_for` module attempts to make a TCP connection to a specific TCP `port` on a specific `host`. In this case, it's the NETCONF port on the target Junos device. If the TCP connection succeeds within `timeout`, the task succeeds. Otherwise, the task fails. The `ignore_errors: True` line prevents the task from registering a failure even if the NETCONF port is unreachable. Instead, the status of the task is registered in the `netconf` variable, for use in later tasks. This task represents step 1 of the login algorithm presented earlier.

❸ The `include` statement is a way to include a file, which contains a list of tasks, from within a task list. In this case, the *netconf_facts.yaml* task file is included. This file is relative to the role's task directory: *roles/login_facts_and_dynamic_groups/tasks/*. An `include` statement also allows variables to be set for the included tasks. In essence, this syntax is similar to a parameterized function call. The *netconf_facts.yaml* task file is included multiple times, but with different variables set for each `include` statement. These `include` statements represent steps 2 through 4 of the login algorithm presented earlier.

❹ This `include` statement, and the two following it, execute tasks from the *console_facts.yaml* task file. We'll cover the contents of this file in detail later. For now, it's sufficient to understand that these `include` statements represent steps 5 through 7 of the login algorithm presented earlier.

❺ If a successful login was found during the previous tasks, the `jfacts` variable will have been populated with the device's facts. If the `jfacts` variable is still false, this indicates no successful login has been found. The core `fail` module generates a failure, which stops execution of the play for the target host, and logs a message.

❻ The core `group_by` module creates a dynamic group and places the target host in the group. This particular task creates the dynamic group `junos-version-`*`version_number`* by using the value of the `jfacts.version` variable. The following task creates the dynamic group `junos-model-`*`model`* by using the value of the `jfacts.model` variable.

❼ This task creates the dynamic group `junos-platform-`*`platform`* by using the value of the `jfacts.model` variable. The `regex_replace` Jinja2 filter removes any characters after the first hyphen (`-`) or digit (`0-9`) from the value of `jfacts.model`.

The *main.yaml* task file included the *netconf_facts.yaml* task file. Let's investigate the contents of the that task file:

```
user@h0$ cat roles/login_facts_and_dynamic_groups/tasks/netconf_facts.yaml
---
- name: Facts via NETCONF
  junos_get_facts:
    host: "{{ inventory_hostname }}" ❶
    port: "{{ jaccess.netconf_port | default(omit) }}" ❷
    user: "{{ user | default(omit) }}" ❸
    passwd: "{{ passwd | default(omit) }}" ❹
    savedir: "{{ role_path }}/files" ❺
  register: j ❻
  ignore_errors: True ❼
  when: (not jfacts) and
        netconf|success ❽

- include: set_jlogin_and_jfacts.yaml ❾
  vars:
    user_var: "{{ user | default('') }}"
    passwd_var: "{{ passwd | default('') }}"
```

❶ The `Facts via NETCONF` task calls the `junos_get_facts` module. As for all Ansible for Junos modules, the connection-related arguments must be specified for the module. The `host` argument is set to the `inventory_hostname` variable (a built-in variable whose value is automatically set to the current target host).

❷ The `port` argument is set to the value of `jaccess.netconf_port`, if defined. If `jaccess.netconf_port` is undefined, the `port` argument is omitted. This is accomplished using the `default` Jinja2 filter with a special value of `omit`.

❸ The `user` argument is set to the value of the `user` variable. This variable is set in the calling `include` statement. If the `user` variable is undefined, the `user` argument is omitted.

❹ The `passwd` argument is set to the value of the `passwd` variable. This variable is set in the calling `include` statement. Again, if the `passwd` variable is undefined, the `passwd` argument is omitted.

❺ The JSON and XML fact files generated by the `junos_get_facts` module are saved in the role's *files* subdirectory. The value of the `savedir` argument is derived using the value of the `role_path` variable. The built-in `role_path` variable contains the directory path of the current role.

❻ The result of executing the `junos_get_facts` module is stored in the temporary variable `j` using the `register` attribute.

❼ Setting `ignore_errors: True` ignores any task failures. (Some task failures are expected when probing for the correct login values.)

❽ This task is only executed when `jfacts` is false (indicating a successful login has not yet occurred) and `netconf` is successful (indicating a TCP connection to the NETCONF port succeeded).

❾ Another task file, *set_jlogin_and_jfacts.yaml*, is included. Again, the `include` syntax is similar to a function call. This allows the tasks defined in the *set_jlogin_and_jfacts.yaml* file to be reused in other places. The `user` and `passwd` values are passed in the variables `user_var` and `passwd_var`, respectively. If either value is undefined, an empty string is passed.

The *set_jlogin_and_jfacts.yaml* task file, included from the *netconf_facts.yaml* task file, has the following contents:

```
user@h0$ cat \
> roles/login_facts_and_dynamic_groups/tasks/set_jlogin_and_jfacts.yaml
---
```

```
- set_fact:
    jlogin: ❶
      user: "{{ user_var | default('') }}"
      passwd: "{{ passwd_var | default('') }}"
      console: "{{ console_var | default('') }}"
    jfacts: "{{ j.facts }}" ❷
  when: j.facts is defined ❸
```

❶ This line sets the value of the `jlogin.user`, `jlogin.passwd`, and `jlogin.console` variables using the values of the `user_var`, `passwd_var`, and `console_var` variables, respectively. These values contain the successful login parameters.

❷ The `facts` key of the `j` variable contains the facts returned by the `junos_get_facts` module. This line sets the value of the `jfacts` variable to these facts.

❸ This task is only run when `j.facts` is defined. The presence of the `facts` key in the value of the `j` variable indicates a successful login.

The *main.yaml* task file also included the *console_facts.yaml* task file, which implements steps 5 through 7 of the login algorithm. While this file is similar to the *netconf_facts.yaml* file we've already examined, there are some differences. Let's investigate the contents of the *console_facts.yaml* task file:

```
user@h0$ cat roles/login_facts_and_dynamic_groups/tasks/console_facts.yaml
---
- name: Pausing {{ pause }} seconds to let second login prompt recover... ❶
  command: /bin/sleep {{ pause }} ❷
  when: pause is defined and pause and
        (not jfacts) and
        netconf|failed ❸

- name: Facts via console
  junos_get_facts:
    host: "{{ inventory_hostname }}"
    console: "--telnet={{ jaccess.console_ts }},{{ jaccess.console_port }}" ❹
    user: "{{ user | default(omit) }}"
    passwd: "{{ passwd | default(omit) }}"
    savedir: "{{ role_path }}/files"
  register: j
  ignore_errors: True
  when: (not jfacts) and
        netconf|failed ❺

- include: set_jlogin_and_jfacts.yaml ❻
  vars:
    user_var: "{{ user | default('') }}"
    passwd_var: "{{ passwd | default('') }}"
    console_var: "--telnet={{ jaccess.console_ts }},{{ jaccess.console_port }}"
```

❶ This task includes the value of the pause variable in the task name. The pause variable is set by the including task file.

❷ The core command module is used to invoke the sleep command. This task sleeps for pause seconds to allow the Junos device to recover from any previous failed console login attempts. The first time this task file is included, pause is set to the value of 0 because no previous logins have been attempted on the console. On subsequent includes, pause is set to 15.

❸ This task is only executed when pause is set to a nonzero value, the NETCONF port is unreachable (netconf|failed), and the jfacts variable is false (indicating a login attempt has not yet succeeded).

❹ The junos_get_facts module is invoked with arguments similar to those found in the *netconf_facts.yaml* file. However, the console argument is now included. The value of the console argument is a string derived from the jacess.console_ts and jaccess.console_port values.

❺ Again, this task is only executed when the NETCONF port is unreachable (netconf|failed) and the jfacts variable is false (indicating a login attempt has not yet succeeded).

❻ This task file also includes the *set_jlogin_and_jfacts.yaml* task file rather than duplicating the file's contents. In addition to passing the user_var and password_var variables, this task passes the console connection string as console_var.

Now that we've seen the complete content of the login_facts_and_dynamic_groups role, we're ready to look at other playbooks that utilize this role.

Zeroize

The next example playbook returns a set of Junos devices back to a factory default state. This playbook utilizes the login_facts_and_dynamic_groups role created in the previous example and also creates a new zeroize role. Let's begin exploring this example by investigating the contents of the *zeroize.pb.yaml* playbook file:

```
user@h0$ pwd
/home/user/playbooks
user@h0$ cat zeroize.pb.yaml
---
- name: Zeroize Junos Devices ❶
  hosts: junos-all ❷
  roles:
  - login_facts_and_dynamic_groups ❸
```

```
    - zeroize ❹
  - name: Check the login ❺
    hosts: junos-all
    pre_tasks:
      - name: Waiting {{ wait_time | default(15) }} min. for zeroize to complete
        pause:
          minutes: "{{ wait_time | default(15) }}" ❻
    roles:
    - login_facts_and_dynamic_groups ❼
    tasks:
      - fail:
          msg: "Not in factory default state, or not reachable on console"
        when: (jlogin is undefined) or
              (jlogin.user is undefined) or (jlogin.user != "root") or
              (jlogin.console is undefined) or (not jlogin.console) or
              ((jlogin.passwd is defined) and (jlogin.passwd)) ❽
```

❶ The first play in the playbook returns the target devices to the factory default state.

❷ This play targets the `junos-all` group. Remember, it's always possible to limit execution to a subset of target hosts with the `--limit` command-line option to the `ansible-playbook` command.

❸ The `login_facts_and_dynamic_groups` role is invoked to discover the login credentials and create dynamic groups.

❹ The `zeroize` role is invoked to return the target devices to the factory default state.

❺ The second play in the playbook tries to confirm whether the target devices are in the factory default state.

❻ Execution is paused for `wait_time` (or the default 15) minutes (using the core `pause` module) to wait for the `request system zeroize` Junos command to complete. The `wait_time` value is not set in the playbook, but may be set with the `-e` command-line option to the `ansible-playbook` command.

❼ The `login_facts_and_dynamic_groups` role is invoked again to discover the new login credentials.

❽ If the target device is in a factory-default state, none of the conditions specified in the `when` clause will be true. If any of these conditions are true, the `fail()` method is invoked.

Let's take a closer look at the zeroize role invoked by the preceding playbook:

```
user@h0$ pwd
/home/user/playbooks

user@h0$ ls roles/zeroize/
files  meta  tasks  vars ❶

user@h0$ cat roles/zeroize/meta/main.yaml
---
dependencies:
  - { role: Juniper.junos } ❷

user@h0$ cat roles/zeroize/vars/main.yaml
---
log_dir: "{{ role_path }}/files/{{ inventory_hostname }}" ❸

user@h0$ cat roles/zeroize/tasks/main.yaml
---
- name: Make sure log dir exists ❹
  file:
    path: "{{ log_dir }}"
    state: directory

- name: Zeroize
  junos_zeroize:
    host: "{{ inventory_hostname }}"
    port: "{{ jlogin.port | default(omit,true) }}" ❺
    user: "{{ jlogin.user | default(omit,true) }}" ❻
    passwd: "{{ jlogin.passwd | default(omit,true) }}" ❼
    console: "{{ jlogin.console | default(omit,true) }}" ❽
    zeroize: 'zeroize' ❾
    logfile: "{{ log_dir }}/changes.log" ❿
```

❶ Again, the role is found in the *roles/zeroize/* subdirectory and follows the standard directory layout for a role.

❷ The `Juniper.junos` role is included as a dependency. This avoids the need to invoke the `Juniper.junos` role within the play definition.

❸ The `log_dir` variable is set to a value of `{{ role_path }}/files/{{ inventory_hostname }}`.

❹ The task file consists of two tasks. The first task calls the core `file` module to ensure the `log_dir` path exists and is a directory.

❺ The `jlogin` value has previously been set by the `login_facts_and_dynamic_groups` role. If the `jlogin.port` value is defined and not false, this value is passed as the `port` argument to the `junos_zeroize` module. Otherwise, the `port` argument to the `junos_zeroize` module is omitted.

❻ If the `jlogin.user` value is defined and not false, the `jlogin.user` value is passed as the `user` argument to the `junos_zeroize` module. Otherwise, the `user` argument to the `junos_zeroize` module is omitted.

❼ If the `jlogin.passwd` value is defined and not false, the `jlogin.passwd` value is passed as the `passwd` argument to the `junos_zeroize` module. Otherwise, the `passwd` argument to the `junos_zeroize` module is omitted.

❽ If the `jlogin.console` value is defined and not false, the `jlogin.console` value is passed as the `console` argument to the `junos_zeroize` module. Otherwise, the `console` argument to the `junos_zeroize` module is omitted. Thanks to the `login_facts_and_dynamic_groups` role, these `host`, `port`, `user`, `passwd`, and (optionally) `console` values can now be used with any Ansible for Junos modules.

❾ The `zerioize` attribute must be hardcoded to a value of `'zeroize'` as a safety mechanism.

❿ The `logfile` attribute is set to the *changes.log* file in the *log_dir* directory.

This output summarizes the result of invoking the *zeroize.pb.yaml* playbook for the `edge3.lab` device:

```
user@h0$ ansible-playbook -i lab.inv --limit edge3.lab zeroize.pb.yaml
Vault password:

PLAY [Zeroize Junos Devices] ****************************************************

TASK: [login_facts_and_dynamic_groups | Resetting jlogin and jfacts] **********
ok: [edge3.lab]

TASK: [login_facts_and_dynamic_groups | Checking NETCONF connectivity] ********
ok: [edge3.lab]

... output trimmed ...

TASK: [zeroize | Make sure log dir exists] ************************************
ok: [edge3.lab]

TASK: [zeroize | Zeroize] *****************************************************
changed: [edge3.lab]

PLAY [Check the login] ********************************************************
```

```
TASK: [Waiting 15 min. for zeroize to complete] ******************************
(^C-c = continue early, ^C-a = abort)
[edge3.lab]
Pausing for 900 seconds
ok: [edge3.lab]

TASK: [login_facts_and_dynamic_groups | Resetting jlogin and jfacts] **********
ok: [edge3.lab]

TASK: [login_facts_and_dynamic_groups | Checking NETCONF connectivity] ********
failed: [edge3.lab] => {"elapsed": 6, "failed": true}
msg: Timeout when waiting for edge3.lab:830
...ignoring

TASK: [login_facts_and_dynamic_groups | Facts via NETCONF] *******************
skipping: [edge3.lab]

... output trimmed ...

TASK: [fail ] ****************************************************************
skipping: [edge3.lab]

PLAY RECAP *******************************************************************
edge3.lab                  : ok=17   changed=4    unreachable=0    failed=0
```

The play executes successfully, indicating the `edge3.lab` device has been returned to a factory-default state.

Initial Configuration

The next example builds an initial Junos configuration from a Jinja2 template and installs the configuration on a target Junos device. The Jinja2 template uses the `jaccess` and `jcfg` dictionaries to build this initial configuration. The generated initial configuration is then installed only if the target Junos device is in the factory-default state, or if the initial configuration has changed.

As in the previous examples, let's begin by looking at the playbook:

```
user@h0$ pwd
/home/user/playbooks

user@h0$ cat initial_config.pb.yaml
---
- name: Generate initial config ❶
  hosts: junos-all
  roles:
  - login_facts_and_dynamic_groups ❷
  - role: generate_hash ❸
    user: 'root'
    pw: "{{ jaccess.root_password }}"
  - role: generate_hash ❹
```

```
      user: "{{ jaccess.netconf_user }}"
      pw: "{{ jaccess.netconf_password }}"
    - generate_initial_config ❺
  - name: Check the login
    hosts: junos-all
    pre_tasks:
    - name: Wait {{ netconf_timeout | default(60) }} sec for NETCONF reachability
      wait_for:
        host: "{{ inventory_hostname }}"
        port: "{{ jaccess.netconf_port | default(830) }}"
        timeout: "{{ netconf_timeout | default(60) }}" ❻
    roles:
    - login_facts_and_dynamic_groups ❼
    tasks:
      - fail:
          msg: "Unable to login via NETCONF"
        when: ((jlogin.console is defined) and
                jlogin.console) or
               (jlogin.user is undefined) or
               (not jlogin.user) ❽
```

❶ The first play in this playbook generates the initial configuration and installs it on the target Junos device.

❷ The `login_facts_and_dynamic_groups` role is invoked to discover the login credentials and create dynamic groups.

❸ A new `generate_hash` role is invoked with `user` and `pw` arguments for the `root` user.

❹ The `generate_hash` role is invoked again with `user` and `pw` arguments for the `jaccess.netconf_user` account.

❺ A new `generate_initial_config` role is invoked to generate, and install, the initial configuration.

❻ The `wait_for` module is invoked to check if the NETCONF-over-SSH service is now reachable. The 60-second default timeout is intended to give the Junos device time to activate the initial configuration. An alternate `netconf_timeout` value may be specified with the `-e` command-line option to the `ansible-playbook` command.

❼ The `login_facts_and_dynamic_groups` role is invoked again to update the `jlogin` variable.

❽ If any of the when clause conditions are true, the target Junos device is not reachable via NETCONF. There must have been a problem deploying the initial configuration. The `fail` module is invoked to report the error.

Now, let's investigate the `generate_hash` role called from the playbook. This role takes a username and plain-text password and creates the MD5 crypt string Junos uses in the `encrypted-password` field of a configuration. MD5 crypt strings are in the format `$1$`*`salt`*`$`*`encrypted_password`*. The *`salt`* value is used as part of the input to the MD5 algorithm. If the MD5 crypt string *has not* been previously generated for this user, a random salt value should be chosen. If the MD5 crypt string *has* been previously generated for this user, the previous salt value should be used. This ensures the generated MD5 crypt string will remain the same as long as the unencrypted password has not changed. Because the generated configuration will only be deployed if it has changed, ensuring the MD5 crypt string does not change unnecessarily is crucial to maintaining idempotency for this role (and its calling playbook). Here is the content of the role:

```
user@h0$ pwd
/home/user/playbooks

user@h0$ ls roles/generate_hash/
files  tasks

user@h0$ cat roles/generate_hash/tasks/main.yaml
---
- name: Set hash_dir fact
  set_fact:
    hash_dir: "{{ role_path }}/files/{{ inventory_hostname }}" ❶

- name: Make sure hash dir exists
  file:
    path: "{{ hash_dir }}"
    state: directory ❷

- name: Create/touch the hash file
  file:
    path: "{{ hash_dir}}/{{ user }}_hash"
    state: touch ❸

- name: Read hash file into the jhash fact
  set_fact:
    jhash: "{{ lookup('file', hash_dir + '/' + user + '_hash') }}" ❹

- name: Write new hash file
  copy:
    content: "{{ pw |password_hash('md5') }}" ❺
    dest: "{{ hash_dir }}/{{ user }}_hash" ❻
  register: new_hash_file ❼
  when: jhash is undefined or jhash == "" ❽
```

```
- name: Rewrite hash file
  copy:
    content: "{{ pw |password_hash('md5',
               jhash |regex_replace('^\\$1\\$(.*)\\$.*$', '\\\\1')) }}" ❾
    dest: "{{ hash_dir }}/{{ user }}_hash" ❿
  when: new_hash_file.skipped is defined and new_hash_file.skipped ⓫
```

❶ Within the *roles/generate_hash/files/* directory, a unique subdirectory is created for each target host. This task simply saves this directory path as the value of the `hash_dir` variable.

❷ This task simply ensures the *hash_dir* directory exists and is a directory. The *hash_dir* directory is used to store the generated MD5 crypt string for each user. Saving the previously generated MD5 crypt string for each user allows the randomly generated salt value from the initial invocation to be reused by later invocations.

❸ Within the *hash_dir* directory, a file of the format *<username>_hash* is created for each user. This task makes sure the file exists by using the core `file` module with a `state` of `touch`. If the file already exists, it will be unmodified by this task. If the file does not already exist, it will be created by this task.

❹ This task reads the content of the *roles/generate_hash/files/<username>_hash* file into the new variable `jhash` using the `lookup()` function.

❺ The core `copy` module is used to "copy" the contents of a variable to a file. The value of the `content` argument is set to the result of passing the `pw` variable to the `password_hash` filter. The `password_hash` filter produces crypt strings for multiple algorithms. In this case, the `md5` algorithm is specified. Because no salt argument was supplied to the `password_hash` filter, a new random salt will be used.

❻ The core `copy` module writes the generated MD5 crypt string (from the `content` argument) to the *roles/generate_hash/files/<username>_hash* file.

❼ The result of this `Write new hash file` task is saved in the variable `new_hash_file` (which is used in the `when` clause of the following `Rewrite hash file` task).

❽ This `Write new hash file` task is only executed if the variable `jhash` is undefined or empty. This situation only occurs if no hash has previously been generated for the user on the target host. In this case, a new hash (with a random salt) is created by this task. However, if `jhash` is nonempty, this task is skipped and the next `Rewrite hash file` task is executed.

❾ This line is similar to the `content` line of previous `copy` task, but in this case a salt value is passed to the `password_hash` filter. The salt value is obtained by taking the current MD5 crypt string (the value of `jhash`) and passing it through the `regex_replace` filter. The complicated regular expression retrieves the salt from the current MD5 crypt string. The salt value is between the second and third dollar signs (`$`) in the MD5 crypt string's `$1$salt$encrypted_password` format.

❿ The core `copy` module writes the generated MD5 crypt string (from the `content` argument) to the *roles/generate_hash/files/<userame>_hash* file.

⓫ This `Rewrite hash file` task is only executed when the previous `Write new hash file` task has been skipped (`new_hash_file.skipped` is true). This situation occurs because an MD5 crypt string already exists for the user on the target host. In this case, the MD5 crypt string is recalculated with the existing salt value and the unencrypted password value stored in `pw`. If the value of `pw` has not changed, the resulting MD5 crypt string will also be the same.

Now let's look at the second role called from the *initial_config.pb.yaml* playbook. The `generate_initial_config` role has the following content:

```
user@h0$ pwd
/home/user/playbooks

user@h0$ ls roles/generate_initial_config/
files  handlers  meta  tasks  templates  vars

user@h0$ cat roles/generate_initial_config/meta/main.yaml
---
dependencies:
  - { role: Juniper.junos }

user@h0$ cat roles/generate_initial_config/vars/main.yaml
---
root_hash: "{{ lookup('file', hash_dir + '/' + 'root_hash') }}" ❶
netconf_user_hash:
  "{{ lookup('file', hash_dir + '/' + jaccess.netconf_user + '_hash') }}" ❷
ssh_key: "{{ lookup('file', jaccess.ssh_key_file) }}" ❸
files_dir: "{{ role_path }}/files/{{ inventory_hostname }}" ❹
```

❶ The value of the `root_hash` variable is set to the contents of the file *roles/generate_hash/files/root_hash*. This file contains the root user's password as an MD5 crypt string. It was previously generated when the playbook invoked the `generate_hash` role with `user: 'root'` and `pw: "{{ jaccess.root_password }}"`.

❷ The value of the `netconf_user_hash` variable is set to the contents of the file *roles/generate_hash/files/<netconf_user>_hash*. This file contains the NETCONF user's password as an MD5 crypt string. It was previously generated when the playbook invoked the `generate_hash` role with `user: "{{ jaccess.netconf_user }}"` and `pw: "{{ jaccess.netconf_password }}"`.

❸ The value of the `ssh_key` variable is set to the contents of the SSH key file. The path to the SSH key file is stored in the `jaccess.ssh_key_file` variable.

❹ The value of the `files_dir` variable is set to *roles/generate_initial_config/files/<hostname>*.

The tasks for the `generate_initial_config` role are:

```
user@h0$ cat roles/generate_initial_config/tasks/main.yaml
---
- name: Make sure files dir exists
  file:
    path: "{{ files_dir }}"
    state: directory ❶

- name: Make sure log dir exists
  file:
    path: "{{ files_dir }}/log"
    state: directory ❷

- name: Building initial configuration
  template:
    src: initial.conf.j2 ❸
    dest: "{{ files_dir }}/initial.conf" ❹
  notify: Install initial config ❺

- name: Currently in factory default mode ❻
  command: /bin/true ❼
  notify: Install initial config ❽
  when: ((jlogin.user is defined) and (jlogin.user == "root")) and
        ((jlogin.passwd is not defined) or (not jlogin.passwd)) and
        ((jlogin.console is defined) and (jlogin.console) ❾
```

❶ This task ensures *roles/generate_initial_config/files/<hostname>* exists and is a directory.

❷ This task ensures *roles/generate_initial_config/files/<hostname>/log* exists and is a directory.

❸ This task performs the primary function of the role (and the playbook). It uses the core `template` module to generate the Junos initial configuration file from a Jinja2 template named *initial.conf.j2*.

❹ The file generated from the template is saved in *roles/generate_initial_config/files/<hostname>/initial.conf*.

❺ If the newly generated Junos configuration has changed, this `notify` line will notify the `Install initial config` handler.

❻ This task checks to see if the target device is in a factory-default state. If so, it notifies the `Install initial config` handler. Notifying the handler in this case ensures that the initial config is installed on the target device even if it has not changed.

❼ When the `command` module executes the `/bin/true` command it performs no action, but it always sets the `changed` attribute. This command ensures the handler is always notified if the task is executed.

❽ This `notify` line will notify the `Install initial config` handler.

❾ The conditions in this `when` clause will only be true if the device is in a factory-default state. Therefore, this task notifies the `Install initial config` handler only when the target device is in the factory-default state.

Now let's take a look at the *initial.conf.j2* template.[13] The preceding task file uses this template to generate the initial Junos configuration:

```
user@h0$ cat roles/generate_initial_config/templates/initial.conf.j2
system {
    host-name {{ inventory_hostname }}; ❶
    domain-name {{ jcfg.domain }}; ❷
    backup-router {{ jcfg.mgmt_gw }}; ❸
    time-zone {{ jcfg.timezone }}; ❹
    root-authentication {
        encrypted-password "{{ root_hash }}"; ❺
    }
    name-server {
    {% for name_server in jcfg.dns_resolvers %}
        {{ name_server }};
    {% endfor %} ❻
    }
    login {
        user {{ jaccess.netconf_user }} { ❼
            class super-user;
            authentication {
```

13 This template uses text (curly brace) format because text format is the only format supported by the `junos_install_config` module when using a NETCONF-over-console connection. In other words, the initial configuration must always be in text format.

```
                    encrypted-password "{{ netconf_user_hash }}"; ❽
                    ssh-dsa "{{ ssh_key }}"; ❾
                }
            }
        }
        services {
            ssh;
            netconf {
                ssh; ❿
            }
        }
        syslog {
            user * {
                any emergency;
            }
            file messages {
                any notice;
                authorization info;
            }
            file interactive-commands {
                interactive-commands any;
            }
        }
        ntp {
            boot-server {{ jcfg.ntp_servers[0] }}; ⓫
        {% for ntp_server in jcfg.ntp_servers %}
            server {{ ntp_server }};
        {% endfor %} ⓬
        }
    }
    interfaces {
        {{ jcfg.mgmt_int }} { ⓭
            unit 0 {
                family inet {
                    address {{ jcfg.mgmt_ip }}; ⓮
                }
            }
        }
    }
    routing-options {
        static {
            route 0.0.0.0/0 next-hop {{ jcfg.mgmt_gw }}; ⓯
        }
    }
```

❶ The device's `host-name` is taken from the built-in `inventory_hostname` variable.

❷ The `domain-name` comes from the `jcfg.domain` variable. This variable is set in *group_vars/junos-all/vars*.

❸ The `backup-router` is set to the value of the `jcfg.mgmt_gw` variable. This variable is set in *host_vars/<hostname>*.

❹ The `time-zone` is taken from `jcfg.timezone`, which is set in *group_vars/<site>*.

❺ The `encrypted-password` for the root user comes from the role's `root_hash` variable.

❻ This `for` loop iterates over the list of DNS resolvers in the `jcfg.dns_resolvers` variable. Each iteration through the loop sets the `name_server` variable. The `jcfg.dns_resolvers` variable is set in *group_vars/<site>*.

❼ The username is taken from `jaccess.netconf_user`, which is set in *group_vars/junos-all/vars*.

❽ The `encrypted-password` for the user comes from the role's `netconf_user_hash` variable.

❾ The `ssh-dsa` key value is set from the role's `ssh_key` variable.

❿ The NETCONF-over-SSH service is enabled to allow future access from Ansible using NETCONF over SSH.

⓫ The `boot-server` is set from the first NTP server in the `jcfg.ntp_servers` list.

⓬ This `for` loop iterates over the list of NTP servers in the `jcfg.ntp_servers` variable. Each iteration through the loop sets the `ntp_server` variable. The `jcfg.ntp_servers` variable is set in *group_vars/<site>*.

⓭ The name of the management interface comes from the `jcfg.mgmt_int`, which is set in the *group_vars/junos-platform-<platform>* file. This setting shows the power of setting a variable based on the dynamic groups that are created by the `login_facts_and_dynamic_groups` role.

⓮ The management IP address is set to the value of the `jcfg.mgmt_ip` variable. This variable is set in *host_vars/<hostname>*.

⓯ The `next-hop` of the default route is set to the value of the `jcfg.mgmt_gw` variable. This variable is set in *host_vars/<hostname>*.

Finally, the `generate_initial_config` role's handler performs the commit. The handler's content is:

```
user@h0$ cat roles/generate_initial_config/handlers/main.yaml
---
- name: Install initial config
  junos_install_config:
    host: "{{ inventory_hostname }}"
    port: "{{ jlogin.port | default(omit,true) }}"
    user: "{{ jlogin.user | default(omit,true) }}"
    passwd: "{{ jlogin.passwd | default(omit,true) }}"
    console: "{{ jlogin.console | default(omit,true) }}" ❶
    file: "{{ files_dir }}/initial.conf" ❷
    overwrite: yes ❸
    logfile: "{{ files_dir }}/log/changes.log"
```

❶ The standard `jlogin` values, set by the `login_facts_and_dynamic_groups` role, are used for the connection parameters to the `junos_install_config` module.

❷ The `file` argument is set to the value of the configuration file generated from the Jinja2 template, *roles/generate_initial_config/files/<hostname>/initial.conf*. This filename must have the *.conf* extension to signal the `junos_install_config` module that the configuration is in text (curly brace) format.

❸ The `overwrite: yes` line instructs the module to perform a `load override` command rather than the default `load merge` command.

When the *initial_config.pb.yaml* playbook is executed against the `edge3.lab` device, the following output is generated:

```
user@h0$ ansible-playbook -i lab.inv --limit edge3.lab initial_config.pb.yaml
Vault password:

PLAY [Generate initial config] ************************************************

TASK: [login_facts_and_dynamic_groups | Resetting jlogin and jfacts] **********
... output trimmed ...

TASK: [generate_hash | Set hash_dir fact] *************************************
ok: [edge3.lab]

TASK: [generate_hash | Make sure hash dir exists] *****************************
ok: [edge3.lab]

TASK: [generate_hash | Create/touch the hash file] ****************************
changed: [edge3.lab]

TASK: [generate_hash | Read hash file into the jhash fact] ********************
ok: [edge3.lab]

TASK: [generate_hash | Write new hash file] ***********************************
skipping: [edge3.lab]
```

```
TASK: [generate_hash | Rewrite hash file] **************************************
ok: [edge3.lab]

... output trimmed ...

TASK: [generate_initial_config | Make sure files dir exists] *******************
ok: [edge3.lab]

TASK: [generate_initial_config | Make sure log dir exists] *********************
ok: [edge3.lab]

TASK: [generate_initial_config | Building initial configuration] ***************
ok: [edge3.lab]

TASK: [generate_initial_config | Currently in factory default mode] ************
changed: [edge3.lab]

NOTIFIED: [generate_initial_config | Install initial config] *******************
changed: [edge3.lab]

PLAY [Check the login] *********************************************************

TASK: [Wait 60 sec for NETCONF reachability] ***********************************
ok: [edge3.lab]

... output trimmed ...

PLAY RECAP *********************************************************************
edge3.lab                  : ok=30   changed=7    unreachable=0    failed=0
```

The output shows the initial configuration has been successfully deployed to `edge3.lab`.

Core OSPF Configuration

The final example demonstrates configuring the core network's Open Shortest Path First (OSPF) protocol using Ansible. This playbook uses information from the `jcfg.ospf` inventory variable to build the necessary configuration snippet. It configures OSPF on the loopback interface and places interfaces in areas. This example is a relatively simple case of performing configuration with Ansible. However, this general concept could be extended to generate detailed real-world configurations for any portion of a Junos configuration file.

Let's begin by looking at the `jcfg.ospf` variable for the `edge3.lab` device:

```
user@h0$ cat host_vars/edge3.lab
---
jaccess:
  console_ts: ts4.lab
  console_port: 23
```

```
jcfg:
  mgmt_ip: 10.92.228.82/23
  mgmt_gw: 10.92.229.254
  ospf: ❶
    areas: ❷
      - 0.0.0.0: ❸
        - xe-0/0/1.0
        - xe-0/0/2.0
      - 0.0.0.42:
        - xe-2/0/1.0
        - xe-2/0/2.0
```

❶ An `ospf` key is specified within the `jcfg` dictionary. The value of this key is also a dictionary.

❷ The `areas` key within the `ospf` dictionary contains a list of OSPF areas.

❸ Each area contains a list of interfaces that are members of the area.

The playbook file is very short:

```
user@h0$ cat core_ospf_config.pb.yaml
---
- name: Generate and apply core OSPF config ❶
  hosts: junos-all
  roles:
  - login_facts_and_dynamic_groups ❷
  - generate_core_ospf_config ❸
```

❶ The playbook contains a single play, `Generate and apply core OSPF config`.

❷ The play begins by invoking the `login_facts_and_dynamic_groups` role to gather login credentials and create dynamic groups.

❸ The `generate_core_ospf_config` role performs most of the playbook's work.

The `generate_core_ospf_config` role includes this familiar content:

```
user@h0$ pwd
/home/user/playbooks

user@h0$ ls roles/generate_core_ospf_config/
files  handlers  meta  tasks  templates  vars

user@h0$ cat roles/generate_core_ospf_config/vars/main.yaml
---
files_dir: "{{ role_path }}/files/{{ inventory_hostname }}" ❶

user@h0$ cat roles/generate_core_ospf_config/meta/main.yaml
---
```

```
dependencies:
  - { role: Juniper.junos }
```

❶ The value of the `files_dir` variable is set to *roles/generate_core_ospf_config/files/<hostname>*.

Here are the contents of the role's task file:

```
user@h0$ cat roles/generate_core_ospf_config/tasks/main.yaml
---
- name: Check for NETCONF login
  fail:
    msg: "Ensure NETCONF login is configured before configuring core OSPF."
  when: (jlogin.console is defined) and
        jlogin.console ❶

- name: Make sure files dir exists
  file:
    path: "{{ files_dir }}"
    state: directory ❷

- name: Make sure log dir exists
  file:
    path: "{{ files_dir }}/log"
    state: directory ❸

- name: Building core OSPF configuration
  template:
    src: core_ospf_config.j2 ❹
    dest: "{{ files_dir }}/core_ospf_config.xml" ❺
  notify: Install core OSPF config ❻
```

❶ The example network's convention is to configure OSPF only if the router is reachable via NETCONF over SSH. This task causes the playbook to fail if the target host is using a NETCONF-over-console connection (indicating NETCONF over SSH failed).

❷ This task uses the core `file` module to ensure *roles/generate_core_ospf_config/files/<hostname>* exists and is a directory.

❸ This task ensures the *log* subdirectory exists within *roles/generate_core_ospf_config/files/<hostname>*.

❹ This task uses the core `template` module to generate a Junos configuration snippet from the *core_ospf_config.j2* template. This template is found in the *roles/generate_core_ospf_config/templates/* directory.

❺ The template's output is written to the file *roles/generate_core_ospf_config/files/<hostname>/core_ospf_config.xml*. The *.xml* filename extension informs the `junos_install_config` module the configuration is in XML format.

❻ The `Install core OSPF config` handler is notified if the generated *core_ospf_config.xml* file has changed.

The Jinja2 template that drives the OSPF configuration has the following content:

```
user@h0$ cat roles/generate_core_ospf_config/templates/core_ospf_config.j2
<configuration>
        <protocols>
            <ospf replace="replace"> ❶
                {% if jcfg.ospf is defined %} ❷
                    <traffic-engineering/>
                    <area>
                        <name>0.0.0.0</name>
                        <interface>
                            <name>lo0.0</name> ❸
                            <passive>
                            </passive>
                        </interface>
                    </area>
                    {% for area_list in jcfg.ospf.areas %} ❹
                        {% for area, ints in  area_list.iteritems()%} ❺
                            <area>
                                <name>{{ area }}</name> ❻
                                {% for int in ints %} ❼
                                    <interface>
                                        <name>{{ int }}</name> ❽
                                    </interface>
                                {% endfor %}
                            </area>
                        {% endfor %}
                    {% endfor %}
                {% endif %}
            </ospf>
        </protocols>
</configuration>
```

❶ The `replace="replace"` XML attribute (which must be paired with the `replace: true` argument to the `junos_install_config` module) causes this configuration snippet to replace any content currently configured at the `[edit protocols ospf]` configuration hierarchy level.

❷ The content of the `if` block is included only if the `jcfg.ospf` inventory variable is defined for this target host. This configuration deploys an empty OSPF configuration block (which ensures OSPF is not configured) for any target host that doesn't specify `jcfg.ospf` in its host variables.

❸ The example network's configuration standard is to always configure the `lo0.0` interface as a member of the `0.0.0.0` backbone area. The `passive` keyword is also included.

❹ This outer `for` loop iterates over each area in the `jcfg.ospf.areas` list.

❺ This inner `for` loop iterates over each key in the current `area_list` dictionary and retrieves the key (`area`) and value (`ints`).

❻ The value of the `area` variable is the area's number.

❼ This `for` loop iterates over each `int` in the `ints` list.

❽ The current interface, held in the `int` variable, is emitted inside `<name>` tags.

When the generated configuration changes, the `Install core OSPF config` handler is notified. Let's look at that handler's content:

```
user@h0$ cat roles/generate_core_ospf_config/handlers/main.yaml
---
- name: Install core OSPF config
  junos_install_config:
    host: "{{ inventory_hostname }}"
    port: "{{ jlogin.port | default(omit,true) }}"
    user: "{{ jlogin.user | default(omit,true) }}"
    passwd: "{{ jlogin.passwd | default(omit,true) }}"
    timeout: "{{ jaccess.commit_timeout | default(omit,true) }}" ❶
    replace: true ❷
    file: "{{ files_dir }}/core_ospf_config.xml" ❸
    logfile: "{{ files_dir }}/log/changes.log"
```

❶ An optional `jacess.commit_timeout` inventory variable allows the commit timeout to be extended if the configuration is large or the commit operation takes longer than the 30-second default timeout.

❷ The `replace: true` argument causes the equivalent of a `load replace` operation rather than the default `load merge` operation. This must be combined with the `replace="replace"` XML attributes found in the configuration template.

❸ The `junos_install_config` module loads and commits the configuration fragment found in the *roles/generate_core_ospf_config/files/<hostname>/core_ospf_config.xml* file. This is configuration generated by the template.

When the playbook is invoked on the edge3.lab device, the following output is produced:

```
user@h0$ ansible-playbook -i lab.inv --limit edge3.lab core_ospf_config.pb.yaml
Vault password:

PLAY [Generate and apply core OSPF config] ************************************

TASK: [login_facts_and_dynamic_groups | Resetting jlogin and jfacts] **********
... output trimmed ...

TASK: [generate_core_ospf_config | Check for NETCONF login] *******************
skipping: [edge3.lab]

TASK: [generate_core_ospf_config | Make sure files dir exists] ****************
changed: [edge3.lab]

TASK: [generate_core_ospf_config | Make sure log dir exists] ******************
changed: [edge3.lab]

TASK: [generate_core_ospf_config | Building core OSPF configuration] **********
changed: [edge3.lab]

NOTIFIED: [generate_core_ospf_config | Install core OSPF config] **************
changed: [edge3.lab]

PLAY RECAP ********************************************************************
edge3.lab                  : ok=11   changed=7    unreachable=0    failed=0
```

Notice the changed result for the Building core OSPF configuration task and the execution of the Install core OSPF config handler. This indicates the configuration was successfully generated and deployed to the router. This result is confirmed via the CLI on the edge3.lab router:

```
user@edge3.lab> show configuration protocols
ospf {
    traffic-engineering;
    area 0.0.0.0 {
        interface lo0.0 {
            passive;
        }
        interface xe-0/0/1.0;
        interface xe-0/0/2.0;
    }
    area 0.0.0.42 {
        interface xe-2/0/1.0;
        interface xe-2/0/2.0;
    }
```

This example could easily be extended to support OSPF metrics for each interface or configure additional OSPF parameters. Alternatively, it may be used as a blueprint for deploying any Junos configuration snippet with Ansible.

You should now have a fully working set of example Ansible playbooks that can be modified and extended to manage the Junos devices in your network. As with other chapters, the full set of example Ansible files presented in this chapter are available on GitHub (*https://github.com/AutomatingJunosAdministration/examples*).

Chapter Summary

As you've seen in this chapter, Ansible is a powerful tool for managing Junos devices. It extends the power of PyEZ inside a framework that makes it easy to manage and maintain a network with thousands of Junos devices. Currently, the Ansible for Junos integration provides more capability than the Puppet integration we covered in Chapter 9. However, there are also some limitations to Ansible.

First, each task that calls an Ansible for Junos module requires the establishment of a new NETCONF session. You can speed this connection establishment by only using console connections when absolutely necessary, and by using SSH keys with the NETCONF-over-SSH sessions.

Next, Ansible configurations can grow to become somewhat complex. There are multiple files for inventory, variables, playbooks, and roles. Like with any critical system, it's a good idea to keep all of these files under a revision control system such as Git. You may also want to couple revision control with a review and testing process to ensure any changes to the Ansible configurations are thoroughly verified before applying them to a production network.

Finally, Ansible isn't very good at pulling data from the Junos device and manipulating it. There's currently no mechanism to invoke a generic RPC like PyEZ. Even if the Ansible for Junos modules did support a generic RPC mechanism, Ansible doesn't provide easy tools for gathering and manipulating the data. In those cases, we recommend using PyEZ directly.

In reality, however, it's not an either-or situation. Because Ansible provides the ability to execute arbitrary commands using the core `command` module, you can always write your own PyEZ or RESTful API script and invoke that script from Ansible. The next chapter covers some best practices for Junos automation and provides additional ideas on how you can combine the new tools in your automation toolbox to create powerful systems for automating your Juniper network.

CHAPTER 11

Putting Automation into Practice

Throughout this book, you've learned lots of techniques for carrying out automation. But just as you wouldn't use a screwdriver to drive a nail into a board, you need to make sure you use the correct tool for each automation task. Moreover, you need to make sure that you use the tools correctly.

This chapter provides examples of which tools to use to automate various tasks. It also discusses best practices for using your automation tools safely.

Use Cases

Here are some ways you might want to use automation to ease the management of your Junos devices. These use cases are derived from a combination of our experience automating and managing networks, and requests we have seen from Junos users.

The use cases are presented in a scenario/solution format. The scenario describes the goal of the automation, while the solution gives a high-level overview of the way (or ways) recommended to implement the automation.

The use cases are roughly divided into two categories: configuration and operation. However, the categories are necessarily imprecise, as much automation involves configuration and is used in the operation of a network.

Configuration Use Cases

These use cases cover automation scenarios that are primarily focused on the initial configuration of a device, or on the ongoing management of a device's configuration.

Automate initial deployment

Scenario. You want to perform new out of box (NOOB) configuration on a large number of Junos devices.

Solutions. As discussed in Chapter 8, there are two primary tools for initial provisioning: Zero Touch Provisioning (ZTP) and Netconify. ZTP tends to be a faster method, but it's only supported on limited Junos platforms. Netconify is supported on all Junos platforms, but requires a console connection (usually via a terminal server) to each device.

We recommend combining either ZTP or Netconify with additional automation tools to simplify the initial provisioning process. ZTP might be combined with Puppet to generate the proper DHCP configuration file for the network's DHCP server, or Netconify might be combined with Ansible to perform initial provisioning via the console, as demonstrated in "Initial Configuration" on page 587.

You may also wish to integrate the initial process with other systems. For example, an inventory system might provide the serial numbers and MAC addresses of new systems that must be provisioned, and an address management database might allocate the appropriate management IP addresses. In addition to receiving information from external systems, the initial automation tool might update external systems with information about the newly provisioned Junos device. For example, the automation tool might update DNS, Ansible inventory files, and your customer provisioning database with information about the new device.

As recommended earlier in the book, you should attempt to minimize the size of the initial configuration. Configure just the interfaces and services required so the device can be managed by the rest of your automation infrastructure. Typically, this means configuring basic authentication, the NETCONF-over-SSH service, and IP reachability to the device's management interface.

Configure BGP "overload" on bootup

Scenario. You want to configure your router so that your BGP peers will not advertise routes until the router has been up for 10 minutes. (The behavior of not advertising routes may be called "overload" behavior because it mimics similar behavior with the same name found in the ISIS routing protocol.)

Solutions. This is a somewhat complicated scenario. It requires three things:

Requirement #1
: The committed configuration (which is loaded on bootup) must not advertise routes.

Requirement #2
: The automation system must detect that the device has been booted for 10 minutes.

Requirement #3
: After the device has been booted for 10 minutes, the automation system must commit a configuration change that causes it to advertise routes.

Requirement #1 by itself may seem difficult to achieve. It requires that the committed configuration be such that the device will advertise routes just before it reboots, but (without a configuration change) will *not* advertise routes just after it reboots. The most obvious solution to this is to use a commit script.

A commit script that makes transient changes can dynamically modify the configuration in different ways at different times. To meet requirement #1, you can write a commit script that checks the uptime. If the system uptime is less than 10 minutes, it emits transient configuration changes that reject all routes. If the system uptime is more than 10 minutes, it accepts the routes as normal.

Once you have such a commit script, then any commit will satisfy requirement #3. Therefore, requirements #2 and #3 can be reduced to: conduct a commit once the system has been up for 10 minutes. There are many ways to do this. Perhaps the most obvious is to use an event policy.

The event policy can match on a user-created once-a-minute event that occurs within 13 minutes of the `RPD_START` event. (Running this for 13 minutes provides an opportunity to retry the action if the event policy's actions encounter an error during the first attempt.) The event policy can run an event script. The event script can check the system uptime and the time the configuration was last committed. If the system uptime is more than 10 minutes, and the configuration was last committed before the system had been up for 10 minutes, the script can commit the configuration.

Note that the check will need to take into account the time the commit script last checked the uptime, which may have been earlier than the time the system will report it was last configured. The system will report that it was last configured at the time the commit process concluded, while the commit script will check the uptime when it is called sometime during the commit process. For very large configurations, there may be a substantial difference between these two times. The commit script can record the time it last checked the uptime in an `apply-macro` statement in the configuration.

In addition to an event script, you could use just about any off-box automation program to trigger a commit externally. The off-box automation program will need to notice that the system was rebooted (e.g., by monitoring SNMP messages) and use one of the off-box automation processes (e.g., PyEZ) to trigger a commit.

Enforce configuration compliance

Scenario. You want to ensure the configuration on your router matches the standards you use for the configuration of your network.

Solutions. In general, this is a great use of a commit script. A commit script executes when a user tries to commit the configuration. If the user's change does not comply with your network's configuration standards, the commit script can reject the changes.

See "Example: Custom Configuration Checks" on page 288 for a more detailed example.

Generate eBGP prefix filters

Scenario. You want to filter routes accepted from external BGP peers based on an automatically generated prefix filter in order to prevent malicious or accidental injection of incorrect routing information into your network.

Solutions. The first step in creating this tool is to determine the source of acceptable BGP prefixes for a given origin autonomous system (AS). One potential source of information is the Internet Routing Registry (IRR) (*http://www.irr.net*), which is a loose collection of routing policy databases using the Routing Policy Specification Language (RPSL) (*http://www.irr.net/docs/rpsl.html*). You may choose to query an existing IRR database, deploy your own public or private IRR database, or store the list of acceptable prefixes in a proprietary database.

Regardless of the exact database and access method, the list of acceptable prefixes for each origin AS comes from an external source. Querying an external data store is best handled by an off-box tool like PyEZ. PyEZ allows the use of standard Python tools to query and manipulate external data. In addition, PyEZ offers an easy API for both querying the operational state and modifying the configuration of a Junos device.

Once you've determined the source of acceptable BGP prefixes, you must determine the method for accessing this data store. If you are querying an IRR database, you might choose to have your PyEZ script invoke an existing command-line utility such as the IRRToolSet (*http://irrtoolset.isc.org/*) to perform *whois* queries of the IRR database. Another option is to perform RESTful API queries to one of the IRR databases, such as the European Regional Internet Registry (Réseaux IP Européens or RIPE) IRR database.[1] Alternatively, you might choose to use a Python client database library to query an internal proprietary database.

1 See the RIPE WHOIS REST API documentation (*https://github.com/RIPE-NCC/whois/wiki/WHOIS-REST-API*) for details on performing RESTful API queries of the RIPE IRR database.

The next step is to determine which origin autonomous systems should be announced by a particular eBGP peer. The PyEZ script can use the *get-bgp-neighbor-information* operational RPC to determine existing eBGP peers and neighboring ASs. If the neighboring AS provides transit for other autonomous systems, you might choose to store that information in the router's configuration using an `apply-macro` statement. The value of the `appy-macro` statement might be a list of origin ASs, the name of an RPSL `aut-num` object, or the name of an RPSL `as-set` object. The external data store can then be queried to return a list of acceptable prefixes for the given origin AS(s).

PyEZ configuration templates might be used to generate a configuration snippet from the list of acceptable prefixes. The configuration statement might include a `prefix-list` at the `[edit policy-options]` configuration hierarchy level as well as an appropriate `import` statement for the eBGP neighbor configuration. Once the new configuration has been loaded and committed, the PyEZ script might choose to perform *get-route-information* operational RPCs to generate a report of accepted and rejected prefixes for each BGP neighbor.

You might also choose to invoke this PyEZ script using Ansible's core `command` module. Invoking Ansible in this way doesn't use the Ansible for Junos modules, but it does take advantage of Ansible's inventory system and management of multiple parallel processes for each target host.

As with all automation tools, appropriate error checking is critical with this tool. It is important that the tool distinguish between an empty response from the external prefix data store and an error querying the external data store. One of the authors has personal experience cleaning up the mess caused by a similar tool with poor error handling. In that case, the tool deployed a "deny all" prefix filter to hundreds of eBGP peers due to an unhandled error condition when querying the prefix data store. While automation tools may help reduce the frequency of "fat finger" misconfigurations, the network impact of a poorly written, or poorly tested, automation tool may be much more significant.

Deploy configuration templates

Scenario. Your network uses a template for deploying new customer connections. You want to simplify the provisioning process and increase accuracy by automating the creation of the configuration from those templates. You would like to only require users to enter the variables for the template and then automatically create the configuration using those variables.

Solutions. Depending on the exact parameters, there are a large number of possible solutions. For example, you can do this on a Junos device by using a commit script to expand the parameters into a full configuration. You can do this one time, when the customer is initially configured, or you can store the parameters in the configuration and have the commit script dynamically generate the configuration from the template with each commit. In this latter case, you can make changes to the configuration template that will immediately be applied to all customers. We discuss these two methods for using commit scripts in "Changing the Configuration" on page 258, and we show examples of both methods in "Example: Dynamically Expanding Configuration" on page 309.

Using a commit script allows users to provision new customer connections in the Junos CLI. Those that are familiar with the Junos CLI might find this to be a benefit. Additionally, this ensures that the Junos configuration remains the single "source of truth" about the way a network is configured. On the other hand, you might want to manage your configuration templates and provisioning data in a central location and use a central system to configure the Junos device.

If you want to conduct provisioning from a central system, you can use either PyEZ or Ansible to deploy the configuration. Your Python script can use the template and parameters to deploy a fully expanded configuration, or it can work in conjunction with a commit script, deploying the parameters to the device and allowing the commit script to expand the configuration as part of the commit process.

Whichever process you choose to use, there are sufficient mechanisms to allow you to automate the creation of a configuration from templates.

Trigger configuration change from host state

Scenario. You want to configure the network to support a newly deployed service on a set of data center servers.

Solutions. The scenario demonstrates the synergy that can be gained from using a single orchestration system, such as Puppet or Ansible, to manage both the servers and network devices in your infrastructure. When a new service is deployed on a set of servers, the network can be automatically provisioned to permit the service.

A new Puppet manifest or Ansible role might be invoked that assigns VLANs, deploys security policies, and configures Class of Service (CoS) on the Junos device to which the server is attached. This system might be further integrated with a Puppet resource or Ansible module running on the server. The server might use an LLDP client that dynamically discovers the connected Junos device and port and reports the information via the Puppet resource or Ansible module.

Operational Use Cases

These next use cases cover automation scenarios that are primarily focused on the operation of a Junos device.

Detect and fix configuration errors

Scenario. You want to ensure the configuration on your router matches the standards you use for the configuration of your network. If you find an obvious error, you want to try to automatically fix it.

Solutions. This is really a variation on the scenario described in "Enforce configuration compliance" on page 608. Accordingly, the solution is similar.

Again, this is a great use of a commit script. A commit script executes when a user tries to commit the configuration. If the user's change does not comply with your network's configuration standards, the commit script can reject the changes. Or, instead, you can have the commit script try to fix obvious errors.

See "Example: Automatically Fixing Mistakes" on page 302 for a more detailed example.

Detect toxic commits

Scenario. You want to have the router automatically detect when a commit might be toxic and attempt to revert that commit. The way you determine if a commit is toxic is by checking if at least two BGP peering sessions go down after the commit and do not recover within three minutes.

Solutions. The premise of this scenario is fundamentally sound: an errant commit could cause BGP peering sessions to go down. Any BGP session might go down because of a firewall filter error, for example. Or, IBGP sessions might go down because of reachability problems over the network backbone.

An event policy and event script can meet the requirements of this scenario. The event policy should match on two `RPD_BGP_NEIGHBOR_STATE_CHANGED` events (with an `old-state` attribute of `Established`) occurring within three minutes of a `UI_COMMIT_PROGRESS` event with a `message` attribute of `notifying daemons of new configuration`. The script would then need to sleep until the three-minute timer completes, after which it can evaluate the BGP neighbor check.

However, this method needs careful evaluation. For example, you need to write the script to correctly handle multiple commits in a short time frame. In this circumstance, it needs to correctly determine which rollback configuration to load, or if it should automatically rollback at all. Also, it needs to exempt peer state changes due to a BGP peer being removed from the configuration. Finally, you may need to choose a different event (or `message` attribute for the `UI_COMMIT_PROGRESS` event) depending on your exact requirements. For example, if you want to look for peer state changes that occur after the start of the commit process, you could match on the `UI_COMMIT` event. (However the `UI_COMMIT` event is also generated for `commit check` operations as well as failed commits. Therefore, some slightly different logic would be required to validate the state prior to deciding that a commit produced a problem.)

In addition, you could easily extend this logic to other parameters that a router can monitor (such as RPM probe success, MPLS LSP state, etc.). You could even create an event script that tries to ping test hosts or examines route counts after every commit and uses those results to validate the success of the commit.

Therefore, in principle, it is possible to fulfill the requirements of this scenario using an event script. However, proper care must be taken to ensure that the script does not rollback legitimate commits.

Execute a "cron" job

Scenario. You want to execute a command on a Junos device every four hours.

Solutions. There are two basic ways you can do this. First, you can create an actual entry in the crontab. (See "Managing the Puppet Agent with the cron Resource" on page 484 for an example of how to do this with Puppet.) The crontab entry can directly run shell commands, or it can invoke CLI commands using the */usr/libexec/invoke-commands* shell script.

Second, you can generate an event every four hours. You can write an event policy to match this event and have it execute the command. The event policy can directly execute CLI commands, or it can invoke shell commands using the `request routing-engine execute` CLI command.

Gather inventories on a recurring basis

Scenario. You want to take a nightly inventory of the hardware and software installed on each of your devices.

Solutions. Fundamentally, it appears that the requirement is to run `show chassis hardware detail` and `show version detail` (or the RPC equivalents of those commands) and store the output. You can use many solutions to run those commands.

For example, you can use an event script to run the commands every night and upload the output to a central server, or you can use the REST API or PyEZ to run the commands from a remote automation system.

Other factors might influence the exact way you implement the solution. For example, if you need to archive the output for retrospective inspection, the event script solution may be the best. On the other hand, if you have no requirement to archive the raw output and, instead, you process the results in real time and use a Python script to add the information to a database, then it probably makes more sense to use something like PyEZ.

Migrate a port between devices

Scenario. You want to move all configuration associated with a specific network port from its current device to a new device.

Solutions. This is a common scenario when upgrading equipment in a network. A customer connection is provisioned on port X of current device A and needs to be moved to port Y of new device B. While it might be feasible to manually move the configuration of a handful of customer ports, this strategy is totally unacceptable for migrating 50,000 customer ports.

Because this scenario requires the automation tool to interact with both the current and the new device, it's best handled by an off-box tool like PyEZ. The PyEZ script needs four pieces of information for each port to be migrated: current device, current port, new device, and new port. This information might be provided by the user as command-line arguments, or read from an external data store (SQL database, YAML file, Excel spreadsheet, etc.).

The PyEZ `get_config()` device method might be used, along with operational RPCs, to retrieve the current configuration and current state of both the interface and any associated features (routing protocols, static routes, CoS, firewall filters, etc.). The corresponding configuration for the new port can then be generated. Using `replace` or `delete` attributes, the current configuration can then be deleted from the current device. Finally, the newly generated configuration can be loaded and committed on the new device.

In this scenario, it is wise for the automation tool to take a lock on the configuration of *both* the old and the new device before reading the current configuration, deleting the current configuration, or committing the new configuration. These three steps must happen as an atomic operation on both devices to ensure that the migration succeeds. Locking the database on both devices first avoids the situation where the configuration on the current device is read and deleted, but the configuration fails to deploy to the new device because another user has the database locked. Worse yet is the potential for other users to make conflicting configuration changes to either the current or the new device during the port migration process. Locking the configuration database on both devices prior to reading or modifying either configuration avoids these situations.

Deploy a root password vault

Scenario. Your network normally uses RADIUS or TACACS+ to authenticate Junos users. Root passwords are configured statically on each device and are only needed in emergency situations when the device is unable to reach an authentication server. You want to automate the generation and deployment of random unique root passwords to each device and store those passwords in a "vault" which is opened only in an emergency.

Solutions. Because this tool updates every Junos device in the network, an offline tool such as PyEZ and/or Ansible is a good choice. Combining a PyEZ script with Ansible's core `command` module allows you to take advantage of Ansible's inventory system and management of multiple parallel processes for each target host.

This system should minimize the exposure of the randomly generated root passwords. This is done by only storing the unencrypted form of the passwords in RAM while the automation tool runs. Junos stores encrypted passwords as either MD5 (the default), SHA256, or SHA512 crypt strings. The algorithm in use is indicated by the first three characters of the encrypted string: `$1$` indicates MD5, `$5$` indicates SHA256, and `$6$` indicates SHA512.

The Ansible `generate_hash` role from "Initial Configuration" on page 587 demonstrated using the Ansible `password_hash` filter to generate a Junos configuration snippet that includes the encrypted, rather than unencrypted, password. Following this recipe ensures that the configuration that is loaded and committed on the target Junos device never contains the unencrypted form of the password.

The next step is securing these randomly generated passwords in a "vault." For this requirement, you can utilize Python libraries that integrate with public key cryptography systems such as GNU Privacy Guard (GPG). By encrypting the list of randomly generated root passwords for each device with a user's public key, you ensure that only the intended recipient can open the vault.

The tool can encrypt the emergency password list separately for each public key in a list of trusted users. You can even take this a step further. If the emergency password list is encrypted with `user1`'s public key and the result is then encrypted again with `user2`'s public key, you've now created a "vault" that can only be opened by both users working together. No one user can access the emergency passwords without the knowledge of another user. When the list of trusted users changes, simply rerun the tool to generate and deploy a new set of emergency passwords known only to the new list of trusted users.

Best Practices

As even the few preceding examples showed, automation tools are very powerful and can be used to perform tasks quickly and efficiently. However, with that power comes responsibility. Automation tools make it easy to do the *wrong* thing many times very quickly. It is important to use them safely to ensure that they are helpful and not harmful.

Certainly, you want to ensure your automation works well because you don't want to create problems you need to resolve. But, moreover, it is important that you minimize automation problems in order to convince your management that it is safe to use automation. Otherwise, they may be reluctant to let you automate some tasks that you find cumbersome or repetitive because they instinctively overestimate the risk and underestimate the benefit.

This section briefly covers some important best practices for automation. It certainly isn't an exhaustive list, and we don't try to repeat all the tips we've covered in the individual chapters. But these best practices should help remind you of some important concepts about safely using automation tools.

General Recommendations

Some best practices are relevant to specific tools, while others are of general relevance. We'll begin by discussing some of the best practices that are of general relevance. These are culled from our years of experience writing automation tools, and from the stories we've heard from others who have written or used automation.

The section covers a wide range of things, beginning with the deceptively simple question of what to automate, and moving through the process of designing, writing, and refining your automation tools.

What to automate

One of the things you need to determine is which tasks you should automate. Some things lend themselves more easily to automation than others, and automating some tasks provides a larger benefit than automating other tasks.

To determine what to automate, some questions to ask are:

Where do you spend your time?
: When you expend a significant amount of time on a given task (or group of tasks), it is a potential candidate for automation.

What tasks do you repeat frequently?
Any task that you repeat frequently is a candidate for automation. Conversely, any task that you repeat so *infrequently* that it is hard to remember is also a candidate for automation.

What tasks have been prone to human error in the past?
Because automation will perform a set of steps consistently every time, it *may* reduce human error. (Of course, no automation tool can prevent the user from providing erroneous information as input.) Because automation tools can provide consistency, tasks that have been prone to human error in the past are candidates for automation.

What tasks are too complicated to remember easily?
Automation tools can help with these tedious tasks, provided they can be reduced to an algorithm that an automation tool can follow. In these cases, the user merely provides the input that the automation tool needs to determine the steps it should take. After that, the automation tool can perform the task without requiring the user to remember or perform the complicated task.

What tasks take too long to perform manually?
Again, automation tools can help with these tasks, provided they can be reduced to an algorithm an automation tool can follow. In some cases, tasks that seem reasonable to perform manually on a small scale begin to take too long as your network grows. In those cases, you may need to add automation merely to enable your business to continue to grow.

What new services can be enabled with automation?
Some services are impractical or not cost effective to offer without automation. Even if the service doesn't require automation, automation may assist with the provisioning of a service. As you implement new services, it is worth considering automation from the start. Even if you choose to start by manually performing some parts of a service, considering automation from the start may enable you to design it in such a way that you can easily add automation later.

What troubleshooting practices can be reduced to a flow chart?
If you can condense some set of troubleshooting practices to an algorithm that an automation tool can follow, why not let the automation tool do that set of steps? Even if you can't condense *all* of the troubleshooting steps to an algorithm, condensing some of them is still helpful. A tool should be able to perform these steps more quickly and consistently. It also has the benefit of allowing senior troubleshooters to share their knowledge and best practices as they develop the algorithm, and enables more junior troubleshooters to gain the insight and experience of the more senior troubleshooters as they run the script. All of these

things lead to quicker network restoration. (And, hopefully, they keep your senior people from being woken overnight and burning out on mundane tasks.)

As you considered these questions, you might have been overwhelmed by the number of the things you could automate, or the scope of some of the automation tasks. However, it is important to start somewhere. Even automating small tasks (or a small portion of a large task) should yield benefit. You can add to the automation library over time, building on your initial work. Automating the small tasks may also free you from mundane tasks, giving you some additional time to work on automating larger tasks. As you start automating, you will also gain experience that is valuable in writing further automation tools.

Determining requirements

Before you write your automation tool, it is important to determine the requirements the automation tool must meet. Getting the requirements correct is critical and drives the success or failure of the project.

Some aspects of requirements gathering are obvious. For example, you must determine the expected inputs and outputs of the automation tool, and the actions the tool will perform and the algorithms it will use. However, other requirements or design considerations may be less obvious.

For example, some things to consider include:

What systems must the automation tool integrate with?
: An automation tool may need to use information from other systems as an input. It may need to update data on other systems as a form of output. In fact, there may even be other levels of integration (such as sending an SNMP trap to a monitoring system, or triggering another automation script to run).

  For example, an automation script may need to use information from a provisioning database to properly provision a client. As part of the provisioning, it may need to update the DNS server's database.

  As another example, an automation script may automatically update an inventory database any time it notices a hardware change.

  You need to consider the format of the information and the protocol you can use to interact with the information. Due to the potential complexity of this integration, it may be best to start with limited data transfers of some sort (whether manual user input or periodic data transfers) and then work toward full real-time integration.

What location is the "authoritative" source for a given piece of data?
: For any given piece of data, it is important that there be a single source of authoritative information. Any time information changes, it must be changed at

this authoritative source for the change to really have been completed. Having a single authoritative source means that everyone (and every automation tool) knows where they can reliably determine the current state and value of that data. Not having a single authoritative source allows the data to diverge in different places with no way to resolve these discrepancies. (And as much as you think that won't happen, experience indicates it almost certainly will!)

It is not necessary that the same system be the authoritative source for *all* information. However, it is necessary that you know which system is authoritative for each piece of information. For example, it is acceptable to have the router be the authoritative source of customer interface assignments, a provisioning system be the authoritative source of customer routing information, and a database be the authoritative source of DNS information. What is required is that you know which system holds the authoritative information for each of these functions.

It is easy to add complexity by having multiple authoritative sources for the same information. For example, you may want to be able to configure interfaces both in the provisioning system and on the router and have both incorporate updates from the other system. However, this amounts to a multimaster distributed database. It is *very* complicated to do this correctly: just look at Microsoft's Active Directory for an indication of how complicated this is. Even if it requires changing your business practices, it is best to avoid this added complexity by choosing a single source of authority for each piece of data.

What data structures provide the best organization of the required information?
Data and algorithms are intertwined. You must actually have access to the data that your algorithm requires. Moreover, the data structure you choose will make it easier or harder to conduct certain tasks, or may constrain your design choices.

With object-oriented languages, this becomes both easier and harder. The object can contain a method or function that acts on the data within the object. In some ways, this makes the relationship between data and algorithms more clear. However, this also may make things harder because the nature of objects makes it that much more important to choose the data structure (and object boundaries) correctly.

What considerations may impact your choice of tools?
There are two aspects to this analysis. First, you must determine which tools support the required actions on the devices you need to manage. This provides you with the set of tools from which you can choose. Second, from that available set, you need to choose the best tool for the specific task.

Relevant to this analysis, it is important to examine which tools the devices in your network support. Juniper is regularly adding new automation features to Junos and extending existing features to additional hardware platforms. However, you need to use the latest software to use the latest features. As part of this analysis, you must check the availability of tools for the software and hardware running in your network. And if you want to use the same tool to manage equipment from multiple vendors, this further constrains your choices.

Once you have determined which tools are available, you need to choose the best tool for the task you are trying to automate. Some relevant considerations may include:

- Whether the script should run on the device or on a separate management system
- The required speed and scale
- Which tools you already use
- The way you have solved similar automation tasks in the past
- Whether there are existing automation scripts that you can easily extend to encompass the new task
- Which systems you need to integrate with (and what requirements that will impose)

Don't forget that you can combine tools to form an automation solution. For example, you can use the RESTful API to invoke an op script, or have an Ansible task call a PyEZ script.

Maintainability

When done right, automation quickly becomes indispensable as users see its benefits and begin relying on it. Therefore, it is important to have a good support structure for maintaining the automation tools. More than one person should be able to maintain every tool. Even if you don't come from a software development background, you need to use best practices from the software development world, such as:

- Include verbose inline comments.
- Remove unused code.
- Use a revision control system for source code management.
- Use a bug tracking system.
- Thoroughly test your code (ideally, using automated testing).
- Define and follow a change management methodology for deploying new releases.
- Create and use reusable components (libraries, classes, methods, objects, etc.) for anything that is needed more than once.

It may seem daunting to undertake your first automation project, but it is important to start with something. After you've written a few, you will probably have learned enough that you will want to go back and revise your first automation projects. Don't be afraid to rewrite your code. In fact, you may want to rewrite your code often for various reasons, including the need to reorganize your code into separate components so it can be reused.

Handling exceptional conditions

It is tempting to concentrate only on making your automation tool work correctly under normal conditions. However, it is just as important to make sure that the automation tool responds appropriately when it encounters abnormal conditions. It is acceptable for the automation tool to fail to perform its normal tasks, but it still must appropriately handle the conditions it encounters.

For example, imagine an automation tool is deploying a new configuration, but it fails to retrieve some of the data it needs to build the configuration. It must detect this and avoid deploying an incorrect or incomplete configuration. Further, it must reverse any actions it has taken, such as unlocking databases it had locked and reverting changes it had made. It must leave the network in a known state (ideally, the state it was in before the automation script ran).

Some exception conditions may be temporary. In those cases, it may be appropriate to retry for some period of time. You need to consider the appropriate parameters for retrying an action. (For example, how often should it retry, and how many times should it retry?) The appropriate parameters vary based on the circumstances.

Avoiding script-induced failures

Network automation scripts are particularly susceptible to some problems, and you'll need to take care to avoid inducing these problems with your automation scripts. Common issues include:

Closed feedback loops

A closed feedback loop occurs when your output impacts your input. We saw a simple example of this in "Event Policy Loops" on page 421, where a commit triggered an event policy that itself triggered a commit. However, closed feedback loops are not always so obvious.

Automation tools that use the state of the network as input but also adjust the state of the network must take care to avoid triggering an infinite loop of further changes. (Note that multiple automation tools together can form a closed feedback loop when they interact as a system.)

Oscillation

Oscillation can occur when an automation tool attempts to adjust network state, but does so in a way that creates a series of regular adjustments changing between the same set of states. This is particularly common when attempting to adjust traffic levels in the network.

For example, consider an automation tool that sees a high level of traffic on interface A, so it moves some of the traffic to interface B. It then sees a high level of traffic on interface B, so it moves some of the traffic to interface C. It then sees a high level of traffic on interface C, so it moves some of the traffic back to interface A. This cycle continues until overall traffic levels drop.

To reduce the possibility of oscillation, your automation tool should detect it and modify its behavior. For example, it may need to reduce the frequency with which it makes adjustments, or it may need to change the way it makes adjustments. In our example, the automation tool may need to begin moving traffic to multiple interfaces and also reduce the frequency with which it runs.

Cascading failures

Cascading failures occur when an automation script attempts to remediate a failure in the network by removing redundant components from service even when that action does not resolve the problem. If allowed to continue, this can cause the system to remove all redundant components from service.

For example, imagine that someone makes an MTU change that causes all full-size packets from a monitoring station to be dropped when carried over any of your core MPLS LSPs. If the monitoring station then takes all the LSPs out of service due to this failure, it will leave you with no remaining LSPs.

One way to prevent this is to place limits on the number of components that the automation script can remove from service before it will stop attempting automatic remediation.

Scaling

While writing automation tools, it is important to consider scaling. Even if you initially think that an automation tool will have low scale requirements, it is good to make design decisions that will allow you to increase scale in the future if that is required.

When considering scale, there are multiple dimensions. For example, one scaling dimension is the number of devices on which the tool will need to operate. Another dimension is the rate at which the automation tool will be executed. Other dimensions are the number of operations the tool conducts, the size of the data the script is handling, and the load the script will place on any device. Further, the automation tool will impact the overall scaling of your network devices. For example, the automation tool will contribute to the overall commit rate and RPC execution rate on your Junos devices. And further still, the automation tool will impact the overall scaling and performance of the host on which you execute the tool. Note that these are only a few examples of scale dimensions.

You must also consider multidimensional scaling: how will all of the automation tools running in your actual network impact your network's performance when their activity is combined with the normal activity of the network (e.g., manual commits)?

In evaluating scaling concerns, it is important to have a realistic view of the actual scale that is required in order to avoid adding unnecessary complexity through over-engineering. Also, because it is difficult to accurately predict the way code will perform (especially when placed in the context of a real-world network), it is important to verify the actual supported scale through real-world testing. When your testing shows there is a scaling problem (or that the performance is unacceptable), you need to conduct further testing to isolate the piece of code that is actually inducing the problem. Using actual testing will ensure that you spend your time optimizing the sections of code that will improve scale without unnecessarily optimizing sections of code that won't.

It is not necessary to focus on scaling considerations for the "first draft" of your code. In fact, it can be useful to write proof-of-concept code that simply proves that something can be done and provides a framework for the activities of an automation tool. However, you should not be afraid to rewrite the code as you move it from being a "draft" to being a final automation tool that is ready for production use on a network.

It is difficult to write a complete list of suggestions of ways to increase scale, because the ways you can increase scale are dependent on the environment, the language, and overall circumstances in which the automaton tool is run. However, here are some things to consider:

- Pool commits to reduce the number of commit operations.
- Operate on multiple devices in parallel to reduce total execution time.
- Scrutinize locks to ensure they are held only when truly necessary.
- Use Python generators instead of building and working on lists.
- Add jitter to distribute the load from periodic operations.

The preceding suggestions add complexity even as they improve scale. This is fairly typical for scaling improvements: they often involve trade-offs, one of which is typically increased complexity. Therefore, you should ensure that these improvements are actually necessary before you implement them. And you should thoroughly test all of your changes to ensure that they are functionally correct and have the expected impact.

Network standardization and automation

One aspect of creating automation tools is evaluating your network standards and processes. In some cases, the best way to automate something will include making changes to those standards and/or processes. (An example of this is the requirement mentioned in "Determining requirements" on page 617 to have a single authoritative data source for each piece of data. Doing this makes your automation tools *much* less complex. Another example is forcing all users to use `configure private` to edit the configuration, as mentioned in "Choosing a database" on page 82.)

In general, it is easier to automate things that are standardized because it limits the number of variations you need to consider. In turn, standardization reduces risk by forcing users to follow well-tested processes and configuration templates. Standardization may also reduce troubleshooting time by allowing operators to quickly identify abnormal conditions.

Of course, the trade-off with network standardization is reduced flexibility. Therefore, you will need to provide a process for handling situations that don't follow the standard. You need to make sure that your automation will still work even in the face of a nonstandard situation. The tool does not necessarily need to support acting on nonstandard configurations, but it must not break them.

Security

When writing your automation tools (as with all software), it is important to think about security. Everyone wants to be able to trust their users, but it is important to enforce proper controls to ensure that users do not exceed their authorization level. (And, even if you do trust your users, you should still set each user's authorization level to the lowest level necessary for her to successfully accomplish her job. Setting user authorization levels this way limits the amount of damage an attacker can accomplish if he compromises that user's account.)

You should conduct boundary condition testing. For example, if the valid range for an argument is `1–65535` (inclusive), you should test with values of `0`, `1`, `65535`, and `65536`.

You also need to thoroughly validate input from users before using this information. User input is anything that originates with a user and has not been properly sanitized. For example, you can safely trust provisioning system data that has been previously sanitized; however, you cannot trust provisioning system data that is raw, unvalidated user input. You should always thoroughly validate user input; however, this becomes much more critical as your user base increases. For example, an automation tool (such as a looking glass) that is open to any user of the public Internet must *take extreme care to* validate user input.

Validating user input includes both positive and negative checks: you must ensure that the user input meets the expected criteria for the field and also ensure that the user input does not violate any restrictions you have in place. An example of a positive check is ensuring that an integer argument contains an integer value. An example of a negative check is ensuring that an argument's value will not overflow an internal buffer.

Among the defensive checks you should consider are:

Ensure the value will fit in the internal storage
: The value should fit in the internal storage. For strings, this means that the value must fit in the internal buffer allocated for the string. For an integer, the value should be within the range supported by the internal variable that holds the value.

Ensure the value does not contain attempts at shell injection, XML injection, or any other form of injection
: Injection attacks occur when a user provides crafted data that contains unexpected instructions that will produce a different result. For example, consider this Python code that produces XML:

```
def do_xml(name, val):
    print """\
<item>
    <name>%s</name>
    <val>%s</val>
</item>""" % (name, val)
```

If your automation tool passes the user-supplied value directly to the do_xml() method, it is possible for the user to create different XML than you were expecting. For example, consider the user-supplied string test</val></item><item><name>execute-as</name><val>root, stored in the variable opt.ip_address. When the automation tool runs do_xml("ip_address", opt.ip_address), it produces the following XML output:

```
<item>
  <name>ip_address</name>
  <val>test</val>
</item>
<item>
  <name>execute-as</name>
  <val>root</val>
</item>
```

Similar things can happen with strings that are used as arguments to shell commands, Junos CLI commands, database queries, and other contexts. It is important to prevent these injections. You can do so either by rejecting input that contains characters with special meaning within the context in which they will be used or by escaping those special characters so they will lose their special meaning and be treated as normal data.

Even a space character can have special meaning. For example, the Junos CLI interprets the space as the separation between arguments. Therefore, if a user-supplied argument is passed to the Junos CLI, a user could conduct an injection attack simply by including a space character.

For example, this Python code escapes the user-supplied value (but not the trusted, script-supplied name) prior to using it:

```
from xml.sax.saxutils import escape

def do_xml(name, val):
    print """\
<item>
    <name>%s</name>
    <val>%s</val>
</item>""" % (name, escape(val))
```

Now, if the same user-supplied string `test</val></item><item><name>execute-as</name><val>root` is stored in the variable `opt.ip_address` and the automation tool runs `do_xml("ip_address", opt.ip_address)`, it produces the following XML output:

```
<item>
  <name>ip_address</name>
  <val>test&lt;/val&gt;&lt;/item&gt;&lt;item&gt;&lt;name&gt;execute-
as&lt;/name&gt;&lt;val&gt;root</val>
</item>
```

A line break was added to the escaped user-supplied string in the preceding output. This line break is *not* part of the string itself, but was added to make the string fit within the margins of this book.

Another thing to consider is rate limiting user-initiated execution. For example, consider a service (such as a looking glass) that allows any user of the public Internet to execute an automation tool that will in turn invoke RPCs on network devices. If this service does not include a rate-limiting function, it will allow any user of the Internet to invoke an unlimited number of RPCs against your network devices, potentially resulting in a denial-of-service attack against a device in your network.

Miscellaneous

It is important to filter data at the best location. Sometimes, it is best to filter the data as close to the source as possible. (For example, you might run the command `show interfaces ge-1/0/0` instead of the command `show interfaces`.) Filtering as close to the source as possible reduces the amount of data that must be processed by all the functions (and devices) in the path between the source and destination. In other cases, it is best to filter the data at the location that can do so most efficiently, or that has the most processing power or resources.

Also, it is important to consider the ways your tool might be used. For example, a tool that might disrupt management connectivity to a device should either run on the device itself or use a console connection.

Tool-Specific Recommendations

Now that we've looked at some general best practices, this section explores specific best practices for each of the tools we've covered in this book. Again, these recommendations are far from an exhaustive list. However, they will serve as a useful guide as you begin applying the examples in this book to your own network.

RESTful API

When using the RESTful API, we recommend the following practices:

Configure only HTTPS access to the RESTful API
: When querying production network devices, HTTPS access ensures authentication credentials are never passed in clear text.

Disable the RESTful API explorer
: While convenient to prototype RESTful API queries in a test environment, the API explorer should be disabled in production deployments.

Limit access to the RESTful API
: As with any service, you should limit access to the service using firewall filters and the service-specific configuration (covered in "Additional RESTful API Service Configuration" on page 157).

Perform small, short-duration queries
: Due to fixed timeouts, the RESTful API is not the best tool for queries that might contain very large responses or require a long time to generate a response.

Use the jxmlease library with Python scripts
: If you're querying the RESTful API from a Python script, the jxmlease library offers a powerful and easy-to-use mechanism for translating XML responses into native Python data structures. When querying Junos devices, we believe the com-

bination of XML and jxmlease is actually easier than the JSON parsing often associated with RESTful APIs.

PyEZ

When using PyEZ, we recommend the following best practices:

Create custom tables and views for common operational queries
: While the PyEZ RPC mechanism discussed in "RPC Execution" on page 175 is useful for infrequent RPC queries, the table and view mechanism eases the process of mapping an RPC response to a native Python data structure. If you're going to perform the same query in multiple places in your code, it's worth taking the time to use a table and view. Further, while PyEZ includes some prepackaged tables and views, they only cover a small set of operational commands. You can create your own table and view as shown in "Creating New Operational Tables and Views" on page 200.

Use the jxmlease library
: For less frequent RPC queries, or when building a small configuration block, the jxmlease library is an excellent tool for mapping between XML and native Python data structures. It is easier to use than the lxml library, and often quicker than writing a table and view.

Use configuration templates
: The integration with the Jinja2 templating engine, described in "Configuration Templates" on page 220, provides an easy yet powerful mechanism for performing configuration changes with PyEZ.

Use `delete` *attributes to delete configuration*
: As described in "Loading Configuration Changes" on page 218, the PyEZ `load()` method performs a `load replace` operation by default. This operation can also be used to delete a section of Junos configuration. If you add a `delete="delete"` attribute to an empty node in an XML configuration, or a `delete:` tag to an empty hierarchy in a text configuration, the corresponding section of the configuration is deleted. Here's an example of deleting the entire OSPFv2 configuration hierarchy using XML:

```
<configuration>
    <protocols>
        <ospf delete="delete">
        </ospf>
    </protocols>
</configuration>
```

Alternatively, this text configuration also deletes the OSPFv2 configuration hierarchy:

```
protocols {
    delete: ospf;
}
```

Participate in the PyEZ community
: The PyEZ Google Group (*https://groups.google.com/forum/#!forum/junos-python-ez*) is a great forum for sharing your new PyEZ knowledge, keeping up with the latest PyEZ features, and getting help when you're stuck.

Op, commit, and event scripts

When writing op, commit, or event scripts, we recommend the following practices:

Write your scripts in SLAX
: Unless you're already experienced at XSLT, SLAX is generally easier to understand. This makes it easier to both write and maintain SLAX scripts.

Include script versions in filenames
: Including a version string in the filename makes it easy to rollback to a previous version of a script and provides traceability about which version of a script is deployed at any given time.

Choose the appropriate configuration change type
: Commit scripts may make transient or permanent changes to the Junos configuration. "Changing the Configuration" on page 258 explained the differences between the two types. Review the considerations for each type and make the appropriate choice for your particular use case.

Understand script interaction
: Consider the way multiple scripts interact with each other, and with users performing manual Junos commands. Ensure these interactions don't lead to potentially negative situations such as loops, oscillation, or cascading failures (see "Avoiding script-induced failures" on page 620).

You should also ensure your commit scripts strike the correct balance between rigidity and flexibility. At 9 a.m. on Monday morning, it seems like a really great idea to enforce rigid commit checks to ensure that a provisioning employee cannot commit unusual changes that might break the network. On the other hand, when you are trying to troubleshoot the network at 3 a.m. and you are unable to commit a temporary change due to these same rigid commit checks, you might feel differently. Striking the correct balance between rigidly enforcing checks and providing sufficient flexibility to fix problems is a difficult judgment call.

Along those same lines, ensure that users (or, at least, *some* users) have a way to work around problems caused by a malfunctioning commit script. (This may be as simple as providing a way to rollback to the previous version of the commit script.)

Initial provisioning

When performing initial provisioning, we recommend that you:

Use ZTP when supported
: If your Junos device and software image support ZTP, we recommend using it rather than Netconify. ZTP supports both initial configuration and upgrading the Junos image, while Netconify only supports initial configuration. In addition, ZTP is typically faster.

Beware of console log messages
: Log messages on the console of a Junos device will confuse Netconify and cause it to fail. Because console log messages may be intermittent, this may cause unpredictable results when running Netconify. Be aware of this potential. You may want to wrap calls to the `netconify` command in a Python or shell script that retries failed commands.

Combine ZTP and Netconify with other tools
: Consider using Puppet, Ansible, or Python with Jinja2 templating to generate the initial Junos configuration file that is installed by ZTP or Netconify. These templating tools may also be used to generate configuration snippets for the DHCP server and file server used in a complete ZTP solution.

Puppet

We have the following recommendations when using Puppet:

Jitter the times Puppet agents contact the Puppet master
: When configuring the Puppet agent to execute periodically (either using the method described in "Managing the Puppet Agent with the cron Resource" on page 484 or "Execute a "cron" job" on page 612), ensure that all Puppet managed nodes do not attempt to contact the Puppet master server at the same time. In other words, if you want the Puppet agent on your Junos devices to run every 15 minutes, do not configure every node in the network to contact the Puppet master at exactly 0, 15, 30, and 45 minutes past the hour. Instead, configure the nodes to contact the Puppet master at different times in order to distribute the load on the Puppet master more evenly.

Use directories of manifest files
: As demonstrated in the examples in Chapter 9, split your manifests into multiple files using the directory organization scheme. Several smaller, well-named, manifest files are easier to maintain than one large manifest file.

Use the `netdev_stdlib_junos::apply_group` *resource to manage additional Junos configuration*
: As demonstrated in "The netdev_stdlib_junos::apply_group Resource" on page 503, Puppet is no longer limited to configuring VLANs and switch ports. Using the `netdev_stdlib_junos::apply_group` resource, Puppet can be used to manage any configuration on a Junos device.

Use the Junos with Enhanced Automation software image, when available
: Using this image avoids the extra step of having to install a separate, compatible `jpuppet` package on each Junos device.

Ansible

When using Ansible, we recommend that you:

Use roles
: Roles are the primary mechanism for organizing Ansible plays into reusable components. The examples in "Example Playbooks" on page 567 demonstrated how the same role can be used in multiple playbooks.

Use dynamic groups
: By creating dynamic groups of Junos devices based on platform, model, and Junos software version, you avoid manually maintaining certain values. Instead, the values of group variables can be assigned from these dynamic groups. An example of this method is found in "Initial Configuration" on page 587, which determined the name of the Junos device's management interface using a dynamic group.

Use the core `template` *and* `assemble` *modules*
: The `template` module allows Junos configurations to be dynamically generated from Jinja2 templates. The `assemble` module allows multiple configuration snippet files to be combined into a single file, which can then be loaded by the `junos_install_config` module.

Use the `replace` *argument to the* `junos_install_config` *module*
: If you combine the `replace` module argument with the `replace="replace"` attributes (described in "PyEZ" on page 627) in your configuration snippets, Ansible can be used to replace portions of the Junos configuration. You can also use the `delete="delete"` attribute in your XML configuration snippets to have Ansible delete portions of the configuration.

Participate in the Ansible for Junos community
: You are also encouraged to share questions and answers about managing Junos devices with Ansible on the PyEZ Google Group (*https://groups.google.com/forum/#!forum/junos-python-ez*).

Wrap-Up

In this book, we have described several tools you can use to stock your "automation toolbox." These tools are useful, and it is important to know how to use them. But just as knowing how to use a hammer does not make you a master carpenter, knowing how to use automation tools does not make you a master at network automation. True mastery of the craft takes practice.

We hope you have already begun to practice using these automation tools as you have been reading the book. We encourage you to continue using them. Even if you start with small projects, you will build skills and experience that will help you tackle bigger and bigger challenges.

When done right, automation allows you to do more with less—and any tool that allows you to do more with less quickly becomes indispensable to network operation. We trust that soon you will be writing tools that are indispensable to the operation of your network!

Glossary

Ansible
A framework for automating the configuration and management of systems.

Application programming interface (API)
A specification that defines how a program can interact with a library or system. In the context of this book, the Junos management API defines the way automation tools run RPCs to view and change the configuration, as well as gather or change operational state.

See Remote procedure call (RPC)

eXtensible Markup Language (XML)
A markup language for encoding complex structured data and metadata.

JavaScript Object Notation (JSON)
A lightweight data encoding format for transmitting structured data.

Jinja2
A language that supports the creation of documents from a template.

Junoscript
The protocol that the Junos CLI uses to communicate with MGD. It is a precursor to the standards-based NETCONF and it shares many similarities with NETCONF.

jxmlease
A Python module for converting XML documents to native Python data structures, and vice versa.

lxml
A Python module for parsing and building XML documents. The lxml module provides similar, but more advanced, functionality to the `ElementTree` module.

metadata
Data that provides additional information about other data.

MGD
The Junos management daemon. This is the daemon to which NETCONF and Junoscript clients connect. As described in "Management System Internals" on page 6, MGD manages much of the flow of operational and configuration data inside the system.

See Junoscript

See Network Configuration Protocol (NETCONF)

Netconify
A Python module (also executable as a command-line utility) to interact with a network device using NETCONF by communicating over the console port.

Network Configuration Protocol (NETCONF)
A protocol that defines a programmatic way to interact with a networking device's management system.

Puppet
A utility for automatically deploying and maintaining configuration on systems.

PyEZ
A Python package that provides classes and methods to manage Junos devices using NETCONF.

See Network Configuration Protocol (NETCONF)

PyEZ table
A class that executes a Junos RPC and parses the RPC response into separate items. The user builds each table class by writing a YAML file and parsing it with a PyEZ method.

See PyEZ view

PyEZ view
A class that maps PyEZ table items to a native Python data structure. The user builds each view class by writing a YAML file and parsing it with a PyEZ method.

See PyEZ table

Python
An object-oriented scripting language that is popular for network automation tasks.

Remote procedure call (RPC)
In the context of this book, an XML fragment that directs the Junos software to conduct an operation for the user, such as viewing or changing the configuration, or viewing or changing operational state.

Representational State Transfer (REST)
A set of architectural constraints for building scalable web services. Web services that provide APIs based on the REST architecture style are referred to as RESTful APIs.

schema
A document that describes the expected structure of an XML document.

SLAX
A programming language for implementing XML transformations. The SLAX parser converts SLAX syntax to XSLT syntax so the XSLT parser can conduct the XML transformation.

See XML transformations

See XSLT

XML transformations
The process of taking an XML input document and transforming it into a different XML output document. See "XML Transformations" on page 254 for an explanation and example.

XSLT
A programming language for implementing XML transformations.

See SLAX

See XML transformations

YAML Ain't Markup Language (YAML)
A language-independent data serialization format that is easily parsed by humans, designed for data structures or configuration files that are often hand-edited. Despite the humorous recursive acronym, you may think of this as a markup language.

YANG
As the specification (*https://tools.ietf.org/html/rfc6020*) says, "YANG is a data modeling language used to model configuration and state data manipulated by the Network Configuration Protocol (NETCONF), NETCONF remote procedure calls, and NETCONF notifications."

Juniper provides a method for a user to export YANG data models for Junos. YANG is also the basis for efforts in the industry to standardize on common data models. (For example, the OpenConfig Group (*http://www.openconfig.net*) is one such effort.)

See Network Configuration Protocol (NETCONF)

Zero-Touch Provisioning (ZTP)
A feature of the Junos software that helps ease initial device configuration. It allows you to automate the installation of a Junos software package and deployment of an initial configuration by sending appropriate attributes in a DHCP reply.

Index

A

D

E

F

G

H

I

J

K

L

M

N

O

P

R

T

U

V

W

X

Y

Z

About the Authors

Jonathan Looney (JNCIE-SP #254, JNCIE-ER #2, CCIE Routing & Switching #7797 [Emeritus]) is a senior testing engineer with Juniper Networks. He has managed and automated large enterprise, ISP network, ASP/MSP, and data center networks. He has also written tools to automate testing and debugging. He has written training courses for Juniper Networks and also taught an information security course at Syracuse University for several semesters. At Juniper, he currently focuses on testing the Junos kernel and UI features, and conducts product security testing. Jonathan lives in upstate New York with his wife, two children, and a lot of snow.

Stacy Smith is a senior testing engineer with Juniper Networks. He has over 20 years of experience developing network automation for enterprise and service provider networks, as well as automating internal testing of new Junos features at Juniper Networks. His experience with Junos dates back to version 3.1 with one of the first customers to deploy Juniper's first product, the M40 router. His roles at Juniper Networks have included writing training courseware, testing new routing protocol features, developing internal testing tools, and, most recently, testing the Junos kernel. He holds a BS in computer science from the United States Air Force Academy and is certified with Juniper Networks as JNCIE-SP #4. Stacy lives in Colorado with his wife, two sons, and a new Great Dane puppy.

About the Lead Technical Reviewers

Phil Shafer is a Distinguished Engineer at Juniper Networks, where he's been for over 18 years. His work includes the Junos UI and API architecture and many of the features of the Junos CLI, as well as the standardization work of these technologies in the IETF (NETCONF and YANG). His goal continues to be making Junos customizable, flexible, and powerful while containing complexity and making life simpler and easier for users.

Diogo Montagner is a member of Juniper's Advanced Services who has been working in the field with many SP customers around the globe, helping them to design, deploy, improve and operate large-scale IPv4/IPv6, MPLS, and broadband networks. Diogo holds a BS in computer science, an MBA in project management, and several certifications, including JNCIE-SP (1050) and PMP. He is also the author of *Day One: Using JSNAP to Automate Network Verifications* (Juniper Books).

Colophon

The animal on the cover of *Automating Junos Adminstration* is a purple-tailed wood hoopoe (*Irrisor viridis*).

This species is an inhabitant of most of sub-Saharan Africa and dwells in open woodland, savannah, or thornbrush. Because they are sensitive to cool night-time temperatures they are mostly non migratory.

The purple-tailed wood hoopoe has a long, straight bill as well as a long, wedge-shaped tail and measures about 14 1/2 inches in total length. Distinguished by a metallic gloss on its plumage, the breast and abdomen are green while the crown, nape, and wings are steel blue. The tail is purplish with violet reflections and the tail feathers have white chevron tips. Males and females look alike, and the young birds resemble the adults but have a more fluffy plumage.

These birds are cavity nesters, choosing sites in weak, partially rotten wood (which leaves them poorly protected from mammalian predators). The female sits closely on her eggs and is fed by her mate. Wood hoopoes are not defenseless, though; they can produce a powerful and disagreeable odor when threatened.

Wood hoopoes are experts at climbing tree trunks and feed on arthropods, especially insects, which they find by probing with their bills in crevices in bark. They are very shy and wary, and their movements are active and erratic. They spend most of their time in trees and seldom descend to the ground. They cluster in small, noisy groups and defend their territory with wing-fanning and tail-swaying displays.

Many of the animals on O'Reilly covers are endangered; all of them are important to the world. To learn more about how you can help, go to *animals.oreilly.com*.

The cover image is from *Lydekker's Royal Natural History*. The cover fonts are URW Typewriter and Guardian Sans. The text font is Adobe Minion Pro; the heading font is Adobe Myriad Condensed; and the code font is Dalton Maag's Ubuntu Mono.